Handbook of Neurofeedback: Dynamics and Clinical Applications

Handbook of Neurofeedback: Dynamics and Clinical Applications

Editor: Felix Nielsen

AMERICAN
MEDICAL PUBLISHERS
www.americanmedicalpublishers.com

AMERICAN
MEDICAL PUBLISHERS
www.americanmedicalpublishers.com

Cataloging-in-Publication Data

Handbook of neurofeedback : dynamics and clinical applications / edited by Felix Nielsen.
p. cm.
Includes bibliographical references and index.
ISBN 979-8-88740-151-5
1. Biofeedback training. 2. Neurology. 3. Nervous system--Diseases. I. Nielsen, Felix.
RC489.B53 H36 2023
615.851--dc23

American Medical Publishers,
41 Flatbush Avenue,
1st Floor, New York,
NY 11217, USA

ISBN 979-8-88740-151-5 (Hardback)

Contents

Preface

Neurofeedback refers to a type of biofeedback that uses brain waves to teach self-control of brain activities and then provides a feedback signal. Brainwave activity is recorded through electrodes, and feedback on brain functioning is delivered. Neurofeedback rewards healthy brainwave activity over unhealthy activity, which results in decreasing undesirable behavior and symptoms. Audio and video feedback is typically provided using neurofeedback. Negative or positive feedback is generated for desirable or undesirable brain actions. Neurofeedback has been used in various conditions, including attention disorders such as insomnia, dyslexia, and ADHD, drug addiction, epilepsy, learning impairments, and mental health problems like PTSD, depression and anxiety. It can also be utilized to develop mental performance as a whole, increase normal functioning and for restoring focus and serenity to an exhausted mind. There are other applications of neurofeedback, which includes enhancement of athletic and musical performance, and pain management. This book is compiled in such a manner, that it will provide in-depth knowledge about the dynamics and clinical applications of neurofeedback. Different approaches, evaluations, and advanced studies on this topic have been included in it. This book will serve as a reference to a broad spectrum of readers.

After months of intensive research and writing, this book is the end result of all who devoted their time and efforts in the initiation and progress of this book. It will surely be a source of reference in enhancing the required knowledge of the new developments in the area. During the course of developing this book, certain measures such as accuracy, authenticity and research focused analytical studies were given preference in order to produce a comprehensive book in the area of study.

This book would not have been possible without the efforts of the authors and the publisher. I extend my sincere thanks to them. Secondly, I express my gratitude to my family and well-wishers. And most importantly, I thank my students for constantly expressing their willingness and curiosity in enhancing their knowledge in the field, which encourages me to take up further research projects for the advancement of the area.

Editor

1

Source-based neurofeedback methods using EEG recordings: training altered brain activity in a functional brain source derived from blind source separation

David J. White[1]*, Marco Congedo[2] and Joseph Ciorciari[3]

[1] Centre for Human Psychopharmacology, School of Health Sciences, Swinburne University of Technology, Hawthorn, VIC, Australia
[2] Grenoble Images Parole Signal Automatique (Gipsa-lab), CNRS and Grenoble University, Grenoble, France
[3] Brain and Psychological Sciences Research Centre, School of Health Sciences, Swinburne University of Technology, Hawthorn, VIC, Australia

***Correspondence:**
David J. White, Centre for Human Psychopharmacology, School of Health Sciences, Swinburne University of Technology, Mail H24, PO Box 218, Hawthorn, VIC 3122, Australia
e-mail: dawhite@swin.edu.au

A developing literature explores the use of neurofeedback in the treatment of a range of clinical conditions, particularly ADHD and epilepsy, whilst neurofeedback also provides an experimental tool for studying the functional significance of endogenous brain activity. A critical component of any neurofeedback method is the underlying physiological signal which forms the basis for the feedback. While the past decade has seen the emergence of fMRI-based protocols training spatially confined BOLD activity, traditional neurofeedback has utilized a small number of electrode sites on the scalp. As scalp EEG at a given electrode site reflects a linear mixture of activity from multiple brain sources and artifacts, efforts to successfully acquire some level of control over the signal may be confounded by these extraneous sources. Further, in the event of successful training, these traditional neurofeedback methods are likely influencing multiple brain regions and processes. The present work describes the use of source-based signal processing methods in EEG neurofeedback. The feasibility and potential utility of such methods were explored in an experiment training increased theta oscillatory activity in a source derived from Blind Source Separation (BSS) of EEG data obtained during completion of a complex cognitive task (spatial navigation). Learned increases in theta activity were observed in two of the four participants to complete 20 sessions of neurofeedback targeting this individually defined functional brain source. Source-based EEG neurofeedback methods using BSS may offer important advantages over traditional neurofeedback, by targeting the desired physiological signal in a more functionally and spatially specific manner. Having provided preliminary evidence of the feasibility of these methods, future work may study a range of clinically and experimentally relevant brain processes where individual brain sources may be targeted by source-based EEG neurofeedback.

Keywords: neurofeedback, EEG, blind source separation, BSS, theta

INTRODUCTION

The activity-dependent nature of neuroplasticity in the brain has highlighted the potential for manipulations of brain activity in enhancing our understanding of brain processes, but also treating clinical conditions (Cramer et al., 2011). A number of methods exist which apply external stimulation or manipulations to alter brain activity, these include pharmacological interventions, electrical stimulation methods (e.g., deep brain stimulation, transcranial direct current and alternating current stimulation) and Transcranial Magnetic Stimulation (TMS). Unlike these external stimulus driven methods, neurofeedback offers a non-invasive technique capable of manipulating endogenous brain activity. A developing literature supports the use of neurofeedback in the treatment of a range of clinical conditions, particularly ADHD (Arns et al., 2013, 2014) and epilepsy (Sterman and Egner, 2006; Tan et al., 2009). In addition, experimental neurofeedback enables the study of brain activity as the independent variable, providing a powerful method for studying the functional significance of endogenous brain activity (Weiskopf, 2012).

Traditional EEG neurofeedback methods typically utilize a small number of active electrodes on the scalp. Scalp EEG at a given electrode site reflects a linear mixture of activity of multiple brain sources and artifacts, with skull and other tissue having a spatial smearing effect (Congedo et al., 2008). With this in mind, sources optimally aligned and in closer proximity to the scalp electrode represent a greater proportion of the observed activity, but far from the entirety of the observed signal. Thus, traditional neurofeedback methods training single electrode sites are likely influencing multiple brain regions and processes. It is therefore not surprising that training methods using a single scalp site influence large scale EEG dynamics beyond the training frequency and site (for example, Egner et al., 2004). Additionally, as the observed signal reflects multiple brain processes, it has also been suggested that this may impede the ability to acquire control over the feedback signal. This point was highlighted by Philippens and Vanwersch (2010), who demonstrated learned sensory-motor rhythm (SMR) enhancement in four sessions of neurofeedback in non-human primates using intracranial recordings. These authors stressed the ability to acquire control in such a short training period may have partially been a result of the increased spatial resolution, and reduced influence of EMG artifact. Given these limitations of traditional EEG neurofeedback methods, a number of more spatially and functionally specific neurofeedback techniques have been explored. The major development in this area is fMRI-based neurofeedback (Yoo and Jolesz, 2002; Weiskopf et al., 2003, 2004), but also includes spatially specific MEG-based neurofeedback (Florin et al., 2014).

In light of these emerging neurofeedback methods, efforts to develop methods which maximize the functional and spatial specificity of EEG-based neurofeedback techniques remain pertinent given the comparative availability and affordability of such technology, and the capacity to directly target endogenous electrophysiological activity (cf. fMRI methods based on the BOLD response). While source-based EEG neurofeedback using source localization methods has been demonstrated (Congedo et al., 2004), offering potential for an improved spatial precision of a training region, these methods remain limited by the susceptibility of source localization methods to artifacts, the inability to isolate neighboring but functionally separate sources, and the spatial precision offered. Perhaps for these reasons, the capacity for learned regulation using these methods has been inconsistently shown (Maurizio et al., 2014). Blind Source Separation (BSS) is a group of processing techniques which seek to identify source activity from a mixed signal. These methods have been employed in a variety of fields including speech processing (Jang et al., 2002), face recognition (Yuen and Lai, 2002), wireless communication (Van Der Veen et al., 1997), radar applications (Fiori, 2003), and with a range of biomedical signals (James and Hesse, 2005). The blind nature of these methods has facilitated such widespread applicability, where no knowledge of the source activity or mixing process is required. Given the properties of scalp EEG, viewed as an instantaneous linear mixture of multiple brain sources and artifacts as a result of volume conduction, BSS was identified as a method suited to EEG signal processing (Makeig et al., 1996), and has subsequently seen widespread use in EEG research both in the identification and removal of artifacts (Vigário, 1997; Delorme et al., 2007; Romero et al., 2008), and the exploration of functionally and spatially distinct brain sources (Makeig et al., 2004; Onton et al., 2005, 2006; Congedo et al., 2008; Kopřivová et al., 2011). It has recently been proposed that BSS methods may have important advantages in multi-channel neurofeedback beyond those methods based on source localization. Specifically, BSS-based neurofeedback may address the limitations of previous source-based neurofeedback methods by offering enhanced spatial and functional specificity of the training substrate, while being less susceptible to artifacts and noise, and being computationally inexpensive (Congedo and Joffe, 2007; Grandchamp and Delorme, 2009).

Neurofeedback based on sources derived from signal processing methods such as BSS may be ideally suited to isolating a spatially and functionally distinct source, which may be less susceptible to common artifacts, representing significant advantages over traditional methods. Further, given the prominence of BSS-based signal processing methods in the field of cognitive neuroscience, particularly with EEG, demonstrating the "trainability" of functional sources derived from these methods with neurofeedback may open future investigations to study the functional significance of identified sources via trained perturbation of this activity. To this end, the present investigation explores the capacity to learn enhanced activity on a BSS-derived source derived from functional brain activity during completion of a complex cognitive task.

MATERIALS AND METHODS

PARTICIPANTS AND EXPERIMENTAL DESIGN

Four healthy right-handed adult volunteers aged 24–38 years old participated in the study (1 female). Written informed consent was obtained from all participants, with all procedures carried out in accordance with the Swinburne University Human Research Ethics Committee. Participants underwent 20 sessions of neurofeedback over the course of 7 weeks. In addition, three assessment sessions were completed across the course of the neurofeedback period, one at baseline, one after 10 sessions, and a final assessment after the 20 sessions. Beyond the data from the baseline assessment session used to isolate individual sources for neurofeedback, these assessment sessions will not be further discussed in the present report.

BSS-BASED NEUROFEEDBACK

The linear BSS problem can be defined as:

$$x(t) = As(t)$$

where $x(t)$ is the observed data and $s(t)$ the underlying source signals, A is a time-invariant mixing matrix. Following matrix algebra, estimated source activity is thus given by:

$$\hat{s}(t) = Bx(t)$$

where B, known as the separating or demixing matrix, is the pseudo-inverse of A. In this way, reconstructed source activity is given by multiplying the separating matrix by the observed data. This BSS model assumes that observed signals are an instantaneous linear mixture of underlying sources (Cardoso, 1998). These methods typically seek the separating and mixing matrices through cancellation of second order or higher order statistics, seeking maximally independent sources.

When applied to EEG data, $x(t)$ above is an n (electrodes) by t (time points) matrix of observed scalp EEG, the mixing matrix (A) describes the relative weights with which each source projects to the scalp, and the separating matrix (B) obtains the estimated brain source activity, in the form of arbitrarily scaled reconstructed source time-series, when multiplied by the observed EEG. It follows that the estimated activity, or time-series, of a single source of interest ($\hat{s}_i(t)$) is obtained by:

$$\hat{s}_i(t) = B_i x(t)$$

that is, by multiplying the observed scalp data by the vector of weights (B_i) from the separating matrix which corresponds to the source of interest. The separating matrix can thus be conceived as a spatial filter, used to estimate source activity. In the context of real-time BSS-neurofeedback, online multiplication of scalp EEG by the vector of the separating matrix corresponding to the target training source will obtain the source time-series. The major issue with such an approach is identifying and obtaining a stable estimate of the spatial filter for the training source. The method adopted in order to achieve this in the present experiment was to base the training on a robust task-related source identified in a group BSS analysis, from which the most closely related individual source was sought.

Determining individual neurofeedback sources

The functional brain source selected for neurofeedback training was based on a previously reported BSS-derived source including medial-temporal lobe (MTL) and parietal lobe regions in which spatial memory performance was associated with source theta oscillatory activity (White et al., 2012). As part of this study, EEG data during completion of a spatial navigation task was analyzed using a BSS method known as Approximate Joint Diagonalization of Cospectral matrices (AJDC; Congedo et al., 2008). Using this method, a source was identified which demonstrated significantly increased theta oscillatory activity during navigation. Within a sample of 25 healthy adults, greater theta power within this source, localized to MTL and parietal regions using sLORETA (Pascual-Marqui, 2002), was associated with better task performance.

As part of the neurofeedback protocol, each participant required individually determined weights corresponding to the BSS component showing the strongest correlation with the group MTL—parietal theta source identified in White et al. (2012) during completion of this same task. Using identical EEG acquisition and pre-processing routines as that used in White et al. (2012), individual participants' EEG data during spatial navigation was decomposed using the identical BSS method (AJDC using the same parameters previously reported, using ICoN software, Version 3.1[1]). Source time-series derived from the individual BSS decomposition were then correlated with the group MTL/parietal theta source time-series described in White et al. (2012), with the individual source showing the strongest correlation selected as the feedback source (for all four participants, $r \geq \pm 0.550$). The weights corresponding to this component in the separating matrix were extracted for use as a spatial filter for neurofeedback, using a subset of electrodes which did not compromise the source signal (39–42 electrodes were retained for neurofeedback sessions, from the original 62). Peak theta for the feedback training band was determined as peak power within the 4–8 Hz band via Fast-Fourier Transform of individual source activity during completion of the navigation task.

Neurofeedback protocol

All participants underwent 20 neurofeedback sessions across 7 weeks. Each neurofeedback session involved a resting eyes open baseline, then five blocks of training each lasting 4 min. As this study represented a preliminary investigation exploring the feasibility of BSS-based training, no control neurofeedback group was included. Instead, a series of trials were conducted at a follow-up session upon completion of the 20 sessions in which participants were asked to increase or decrease the feedback signal. As the focus of this experiment was the feasibility of learned regulation of BSS-derived source activity, these trials were included to probe for evidence of learned volitional regulation of the target signal. SynAmps[2] amplifiers and Acquire 4.3 software were used to acquire the EEG data as part of the neurofeedback sessions (Neuroscan Inc., Abbotsford, VIC, Australia). Data acquisition for neurofeedback sessions employed a band-pass filter from 1–50 Hz, with a linked mastoid reference. This was done to ensure consistency with the reference used in the off-line analysis of the previous experiment. A second computer running the Open-ViBE software platform (Renard et al., 2010) provided the on-line processing and feedback required by the neurofeedback paradigm. The set-up made use of the built-in client/server operations available in Scan Acquire 4.3 software; whereby the acquisition system acted as the server which sent acquired data on to the client system (Open-ViBE) via a Local Area Network. An acquisition driver written in C++ facilitated this process within the Open-ViBE platform.

A "Scenario" was developed for each participant within the Open-ViBE software which applied a processing chain to generate the feedback signal, before providing visual feedback to the participant with minimal delay. The Scenario for each participant applied the individually defined spatial filter to the incoming EEG data, generated a ratio of peak theta ($p\theta$ = peak $\pm$ 0.5 Hz) to total theta ($tot\theta$ = 4–8 Hz) for the source time-series, then provided visual feedback. In order to obtain on-line band-power estimates for $p\theta$ and $tot\theta$ the time-series was first band-pass filtered in the designated frequency range (Butterworth filter, 0.5 dB band-pass ripple), then segmented into 1 s epochs with a 250 ms moving window, the data were then squared and an average calculated for each 1 s epoch. Finally, each estimate was log transformed ($\ln(x + 1)$) to minimize deviations from normality (Kiebel et al., 2005). The feedback signal was simply the ratio of these log transformed band-power estimates for peak and total theta ($p\theta/tot\theta$). Electro-oculogram (EOG) artifact remains an important consideration when dealing with theta-band activity. This motivated the use of a ratio, as opposed to absolute power. Eye blink and movement artifact is generally maximal in the delta range, decreasing in a steep and monotonous manner with increasing frequency (Gasser et al., 1985; Hagemann and Naumann, 2001). We reasoned that in using the ratio of peak theta activity relative to total theta, the potential confounding influence EOG artifact would be minimized. For example, it is highly unlikely that EOG artifact would manifest itself as

[1] http://sites.google.com/site/marcocongedo/software/icon

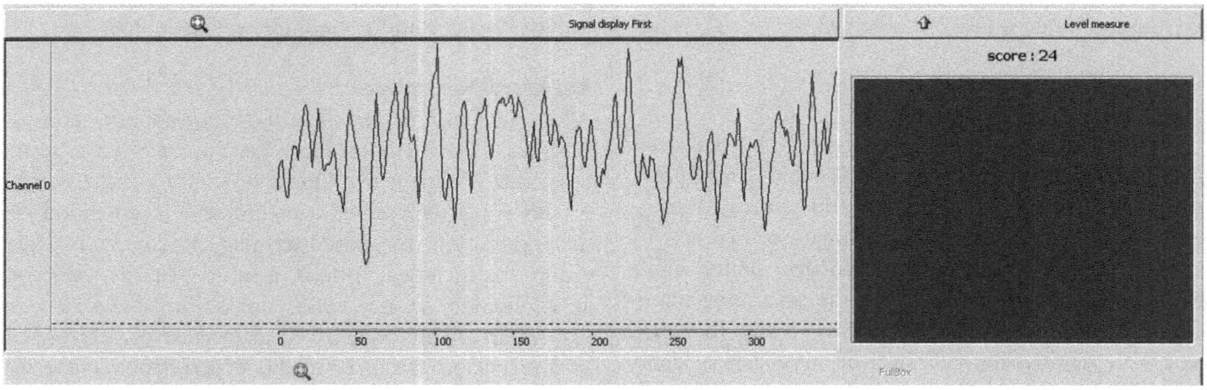

FIGURE 1 | Feedback viewed by participants during neurofeedback sessions. Line graph (left) showed continuous feedback as to the $p\theta/tot\theta$ ratio level, box and score (right) provided a discrete reward when ratio exceeded a predefined threshold.

a frequency-specific power increase coinciding with peak theta activity, and much more likely that the presence of EOG artifact would result in broadband theta power increases, largest at the low end of the bandwidth, resulting in little change or a drop in the $p\theta/tot\theta$ ratio.

The feedback received by the participant contained both continuous and discrete elements (see **Figure 1**). A scrolling line graph showing the exact ratio level formed the continuous feedback, whilst a reward box flashed blue and registered a point each time the ratio exceeded a predefined threshold. The continuous feedback has the advantage of being easy to interpret for the participant (Weiskopf et al., 2004), whilst the threshold score and blue flash provided a discrete reward, which utilizes the common conception of neurofeedback learning by means of operant conditioning. The importance of discrete feedback in neurofeedback protocol design has recently been emphasized (Sherlin et al., 2011). This threshold was determined by calculating a percentile during the baseline recording of the first neurofeedback session, where 6–12 discrete rewards would be received per minute at baseline levels.

Assessment of neurofeedback learning

The capacity to regulate the feedback signal, in the form of neurofeedback learning, forms the primary outcome for this feasibility study. A number of methods have been adopted for operationalizing and quantifying relative success at neurofeedback learning, yet there is little agreement on the most appropriate method (Dempster and Vernon, 2009). In order to demonstrate learned control over the feedback signal, evidence that changes occur beyond baseline levels appears a minimum requirement. In order to first assess this, non-learners were identified with an initial paired samples t-test, contrasting mean source $p\theta/tot\theta$ ratio scores at all 20 feedback sessions for each participant with the corresponding baseline. Only those to demonstrate significantly elevated source $p\theta/tot\theta$ ratio during feedback when contrasted with corresponding baseline were analyzed for evidence of neurofeedback learning. Learning within and across sessions involve desired changes emerging over the course of training, and thus can be plotted as a learning curve. In each of these cases, the presence of learning is demonstrated by the desired increase or decrease in the signal of interest across sessions or over blocks of time within sessions. Within and across sessions learning was assessed by ordinary least squares regression, with the time within training as the predictor (session number for across sessions, and minute from beginning of feedback for within sessions; both 1–20). For both learning analyses, data was normalized with respect to the mean and standard deviation of source $p\theta/tot\theta$ ratio during a baseline period. For within sessions learning, mean data was extracted for each minute of neurofeedback at each session, and normalized to the corresponding baseline data for that session. Across sessions learning analysis used the mean source $p\theta/tot\theta$ ratio for each session normalized to the baseline period at the first neurofeedback session.

Clearest demonstrations of volitional self-regulation use a series of trials in which the participant is instructed to produce the desired change in signal, contrasted with trials where the opposite change or no change are desired. Neurofeedback for Slow Cortical Potentials (SCP; for a review see Birbaumer, 1999) lends itself to this type of analysis, and self-regulation of positive and negative shifts have been demonstrated in this way (e.g., Schneider et al., 1992). Volitional self-regulation has also been demonstrated with the use of specifically conceived experimental design following LORETA neurofeedback training for enhanced low beta activity in the anterior cingulate gyrus (Congedo et al., 2004). As part of the present exploration, participants completed a follow-up session upon completion of the 20 neurofeedback sessions in which they were asked to increase or decrease the feedback signal in eight randomized blocks of 3-min each (total of four "up" and four "down" trials). A randomization t-test (Edgington, 1987) comparing the mean $p\theta/tot\theta$ ratio feedback signal obtained in each up trial vs. the mean of each down trial exploits the design of the trials, providing an appropriate assessment of volitional self-regulation of the feedback signal post-training.

A designated exploration of the relationship between ocular artifact and the feedback signal was undertaken offline, using data from the first neurofeedback session for each participant. Power in the delta range (1–3 Hz), averaged across frontal electrode sites, formed a surrogate measure of EOG artifact. For each participant, power estimates were calculated in the same way as those used to derive the source peak theta to total theta ratio, with an additional parallel processing stream calculating frontal delta power. The relationship between the two signals was then assessed by correlating the power estimates for the two signals for the first session in each neurofeedback participant.

Assessing the impact of neurofeedback training on navigation performance

Owing to the exploratory nature of the current experiment, the sample size limited the scope for a full exploration of the impact of the neurofeedback intervention, instead focussing on the feasibility of such a protocol. While this prevented the use of traditional statistical analysis of group differences in outcome measures across the intervention period, we briefly describe the trends in behavioral performance on the navigation task from which the neurofeedback source was derived across the neurofeedback training period contrasted with an age and gender matched no-treatment control group. Three assessment points were completed across 7 weeks for both neurofeedback and control participants (pre-treatment baseline, week 4, week 7 (post-treatment)). The difference in these trends, in the form of the gradient of the slope estimated by Ordinary Least Squares from all navigation performance observations for each group, was then contrasted between neurofeedback and control group using a small sample t-test for parallelism (Kleinbaum and Kupper, 1978).

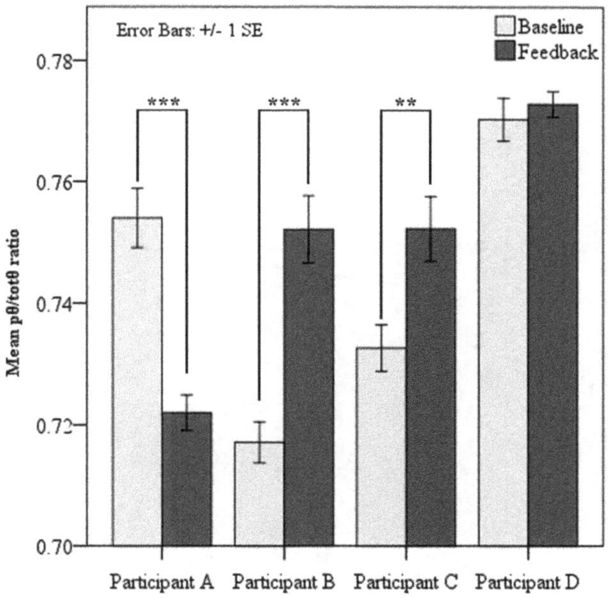

FIGURE 2 | Mean $p\theta/tot\theta$ ratio for feedback source at resting baseline and during feedback for each participant. Paired t-tests showed significantly increased $p\theta/tot\theta$ ratio during feedback when compared to baseline for Participants B and C. Participant A showed significantly lower $p\theta/tot\theta$ ratio during feedback (*** = $p < 0.001$, ** = $p < 0.01$).

RESULTS

EXCEEDING RESTING LEVELS

Paired samples t-tests revealed two of the four participants demonstrated significantly elevated source $p\theta/tot\theta$ during neurofeedback sessions, when contrasted with baseline at each session (see **Figure 2** below). Analysis of learning trends was pursued for these two participants only. Surprisingly, one participant showed a significant reduction in the feedback ratio during feedback sessions compared to baseline, while one showed slight non-significant increases from baseline to feedback.

NEUROFEEDBACK LEARNING WITHIN AND ACROSS SESSIONS

Both participants to show elevated source $p\theta/tot\theta$ during neurofeedback sessions demonstrated evidence of neurofeedback learning. **Figure 3** summarizes the results of linear regression analyses probing neurofeedback learning within and across sessions for these two participants. This learning emerged across sessions for Participant B, but within sessions for Participant C. Participant B appeared to demonstrate a sharp within sessions learning trend in the first half of each session, before significantly dropping away.

VOLITIONAL CONTROL OF SOURCE $p\theta/tot\theta$ RATIO

Results of the follow-up session exploring volitional control of the feedback signal corroborated findings of the neurofeedback learning analyses. **Figure 4** shows Participants B and C again demonstrated significantly greater $p\theta/tot\theta$ source activity during the "up" trials than the "down" trials (Participant B: $t = 4.19$, $p = 0.0143$; Participant C: $t = 2.75$, $p = 0.0143$). In addition, the findings from these trials suggested Participant D obtained some level of volitional control over the signal that did not translate into neurofeedback learning during the training period (Participant D: $t = 2.15$, $p = 0.0429$).

OCULAR ARTIFACT

The selection of a ratio feedback signal ($p\theta/tot\theta$) was motivated by a desire to minimize the influence of artifacts in neurofeedback sessions. However, the potential influence of ocular artifact was explored offline, correlating delta power estimates at frontal electrode sites with the feedback signal during neurofeedback. Results of this analysis suggested minimal relationship between the source feedback ratio and frontal delta power for each participant (Participant A: $r = 0.004$; Participant B: $r = -0.002$; Participant C: $r = 0.115$; Participant D: $r = 0.043$). As the maximum value, observed in Participant C corresponds to approximately 1% of variance explained, it appears unlikely that any participant experienced the capacity to achieve the desired signal increases through increasing the presence of ocular artifact.

NAVIGATION PERFORMANCE

Trends in behavioral performance on the navigation task assessed across the training period showed evidence of improvement in both neurofeedback and control groups. The two groups showed large baseline differences in performance, and evidence of practice effects across repeated assessments, but the trend across the training period did not significantly differ between

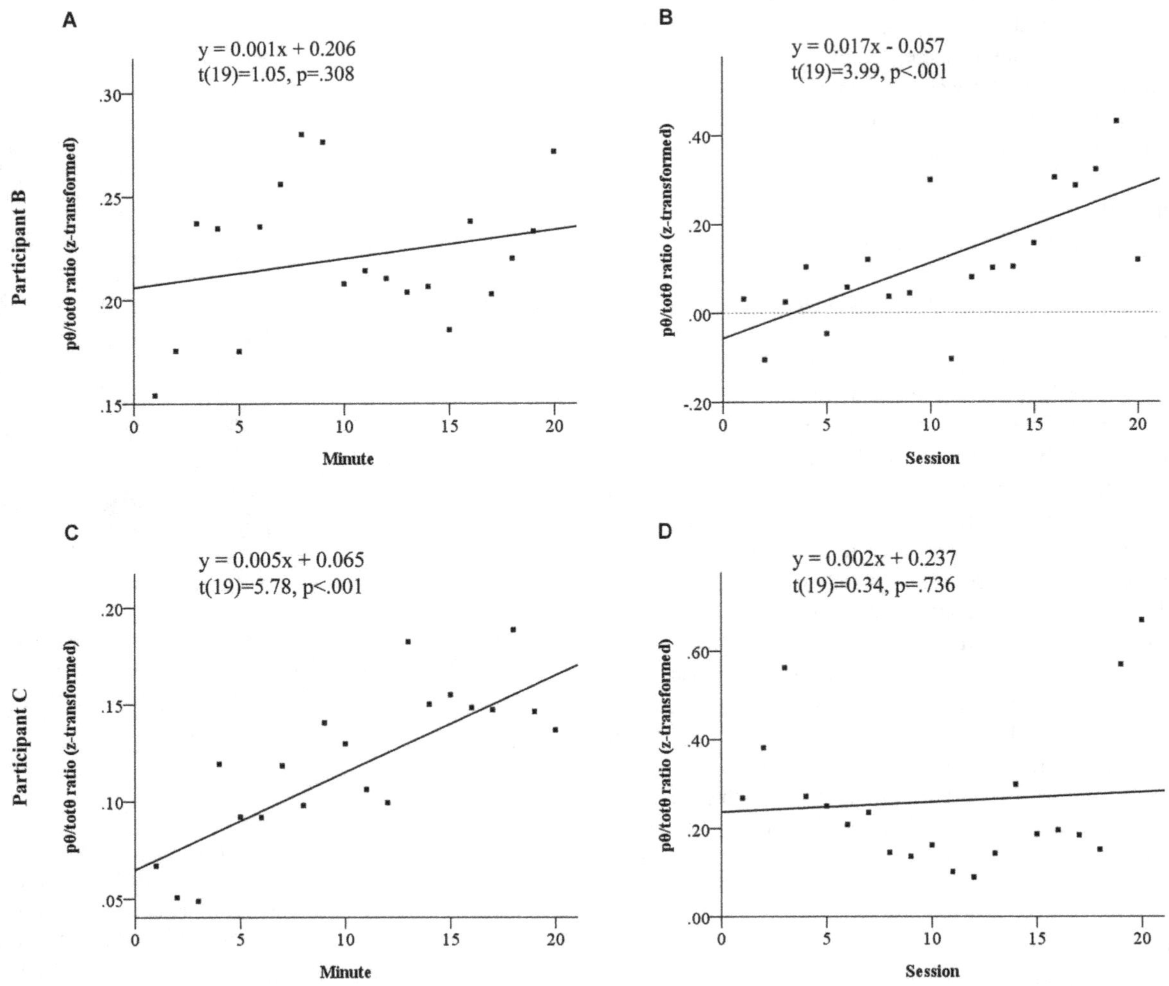

FIGURE 3 | Learning trends in normalized ***pθ/totθ*** **ratio for feedback source both within and across sessions for Participant B, see panels (A) and (B) and Participant C, see panels (C) and (D).** Participant B did not show a significant linear increase within sessions **(A)**, however showed significant across sessions learning **(B)**. Participant C showed significant within sessions learning **(C)**, but no linear increases across sessions.

the groups ($t_{(20)} = -0.27$, $p > 0.05$). These trends, in the form of the gradient of the slope estimated by Ordinary Least Squares (β), are plotted for performance on the navigation task in **Figure 5**.

DISCUSSION

The current study described the implementation of a neurofeedback paradigm using spatial filtering of scalp EEG to obtain ongoing activity of a BSS component derived from functional brain activity. The study aimed to explore the feasibility of training enhanced theta using this BSS-based neurofeedback. Results showed evidence of learned augmentation of source peak theta activity in 50% of the neurofeedback sample, providing preliminary evidence in support of the feasibility of BSS-based neurofeedback. Beyond this evidence of neurofeedback learning trends, the study also demonstrated volitional control of the feedback signal upon completion of the neurofeedback training period in three of the neurofeedback participants. No differences in behavioral performance were observed for the neurofeedback group on the navigation task from which the training source was derived, when compared to an age and gender matched no-treatment control group. Thus, the findings of this study suggest learned regulation of oscillatory activity derived from a BSS component represents a plausible line of inquiry for future research.

NON-LEARNERS AND STUDY LIMITATIONS

In the present study, two participants failed to show evidence of learned control over peak theta activity beyond baseline levels. An important consideration in analyzing neurofeedback learning is that not all those exposed to training will gain significant control over the feedback signal. Previous explorations of neurofeedback learners and non-learners suggest that as much as half of those participating in neurofeedback training may not demonstrate significant learning (Weber et al., 2011). In line with this, 50% of the present sample belongs to this non-learner group, while 25%

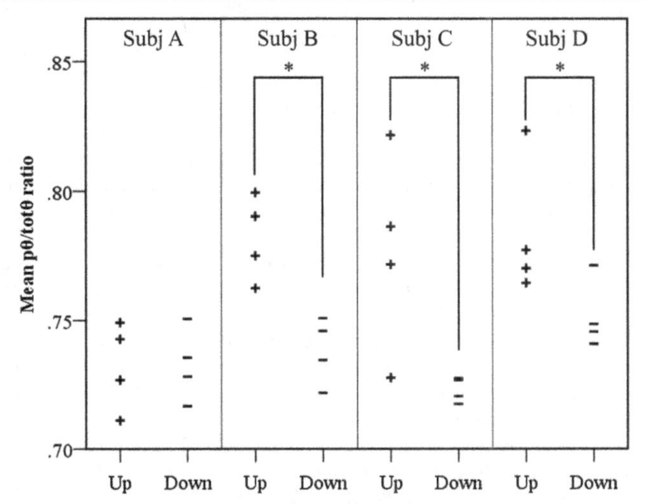

FIGURE 4 | Results of volitional control trials conducted after neurofeedback training. For each participant, the mean source $p\theta/tot\theta$ ratio for each trial is shown. A significantly elevated ratio was observed in up trials, contrasted with down trials using a randomization *t*-test, for three of the four participants, where * = $p < 0.05$.

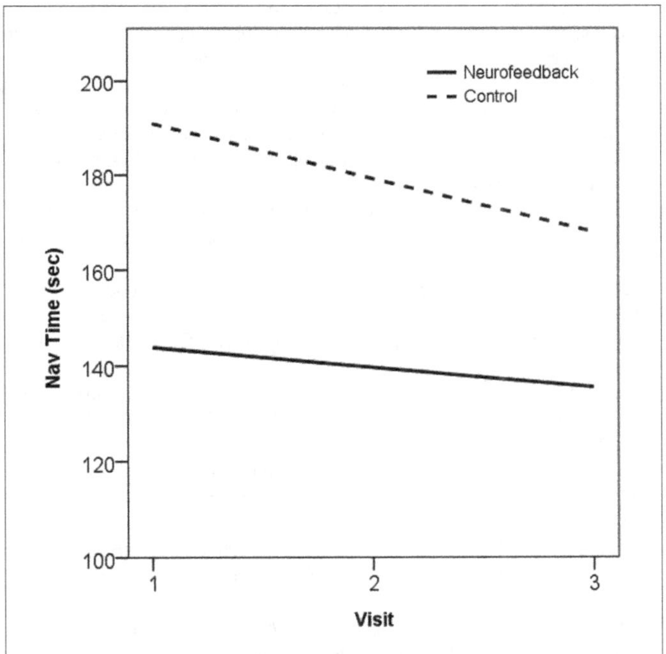

FIGURE 5 | Plot of trend in navigation performance across the training period, as the OLS line of best fit, in neurofeedback and no-treatment control groups. 1 = Baseline, 2 = Mid-training (week 4), 3 = Post-training (week 7).

showed no evidence of volitional control of the feedback signal upon completion of the training. This aspect of neurofeedback training is relatively unexplored, and the characteristics and predictors of learners and non-learners is an area requiring further empirical exploration.

One possible explanation for the difficulty in training source peak theta activity in these non-learners is that the source contained a spectral profile which included a low alpha component. The low alpha band shows basic attentional correlates and desynchronizes in response to task demands (for a review, see Klimesch, 1999). Individually determined peak theta for the two non-learners was slightly higher than in the other two participants. As the training frequency for these participants was adjacent to the low alpha band, spectral power associated with alpha activity may have leaked into peak theta estimates. Indeed, the functional source on which the feedback was based showed a clear alpha peak in the original group data around 10–11 Hz during a resting baseline (see White et al., 2012). Thus, a reduction in low alpha activity during training could have confounded efforts to increase peak theta activity for these non-learners during neurofeedback trials, as the increased attention associated with the training periods would be reasonably expected to reduce low alpha activity. Whilst the BSS-derived training source is argued to be functionally and spatially specific, this does not preclude spectral activity across multiple frequencies. Thus, the lack of learning in these participants may have been a result of contamination of the desired peak theta signal from the adjacent low alpha band. This may be particularly relevant for Participant A, who showed significant reductions in the feedback signal during feedback when contrasted with baseline. The findings of the present study further emphasize the need to account for fluctuations in a number of frequency bands beyond the training band in neurofeedback research.

As this study represents a preliminary investigation into BSS-based neurofeedback, interpretation of findings remain limited by the design implemented and small sample size. Neurofeedback research is increasingly utilizing experimental designs which incorporate control conditions to allow for stronger evidence of efficacy and specificity, but also the feasibility of learning. In examining efficacy and specificity of clinical and experimental neurofeedback protocols, the use of non-contingent feedback, variable feedback contingencies (e.g., Hoedlmoser et al., 2008), or alternate target bands for neurofeedback control groups have been used to minimize concerns to do with comparable therapist contact, placebo effects, and other non-specific effects of training. Having provided this preliminary evidence of the feasibility of training a BSS-based source, future work may further explore the validity and potential applications of neurofeedback training using controlled designs which can target sources identified from functional or resting state brain processes.

APPLICATIONS OF BSS-BASED NEUROFEEDBACK

Developing neurofeedback methods are increasingly refining the spatial and functional specificity with which the training neural substrate can be targeted. Using a BSS-derived source as the feedback source offers advantages in this respect, and the findings of the present study support the feasibility of such methods. Thus, future applications of BSS-based neurofeedback are only limited by the extent to which a stable estimate of the target source can be obtained. As BSS-derived sources can be identified from functional or resting activity, future research can extend the present work by applying neurofeedback protocols based on BSS components based on manipulating functional activity such as that described herein, or training problematic BSS components identified in clinical applications. The potential for clinical applications of BSS-based neurofeedback has recently been explored by Kopřivová et al. (2013), who tested neurofeedback training of a medial frontal EEG source identified as showing abnormally elevated low-frequency activity in Obsessive-Compulsive Disorder patients compared to healthy controls. This BSS-based neurofeedback training was associated with greater clinical improvement than a sham feedback control group and non-significant trends towards a shift in the trained frequency band, however, clinical improvement was not associated with EEG changes. In demonstrating the capacity for regulation of a task-derived BSS source, this study supports the use of BSS-derived sources in neurofeedback applications, as task-related decompositions such as that used to derive the feedback source herein can be considered stable enough to target outside the context of the specific task from which they were based. As such, experimental BSS-based neurofeedback may train functionally and spatially isolated brain sources, facilitating the study of these sources as the independent variable, in turn providing a powerful method for studying the functional significance of functionally and spatially isolated endogenous brain processes. Using BSS-based neurofeedback may enhance the success of neurofeedback protocols, reducing the influence of artifacts, and providing optimal conditions for training of the target activity.

CONCLUSIONS

The research described herein builds upon the increasing use of BSS methods in the study of brain function. Adopting BSS methods across a range of methods for recording brain activity, including fMRI and EEG, has offered novel insights into brain function (eg. Greicius et al., 2004; Onton et al., 2005). These findings provide preliminary evidence of the feasibility of source-based neurofeedback training derived from BSS, future work may explore further validation and potential applications of BSS-based neurofeedback training, targeting sources identified from functional or resting state brain processes.

ACKNOWLEDGMENTS

This work was partially supported by a research grant from the Barbara Dicker Brain Sciences Foundation.

REFERENCES

Arns, M., Conners, C. K., and Kraemer, H. C. (2013). A decade of EEG Theta/Beta Ratio Research in ADHD: a meta-analysis. *J. Atten. Disord.* 17, 374–383. doi: 10.1177/1087054712460087

Arns, M., Heinrich, H., and Strehl, U. (2014). Evaluation of neurofeedback in ADHD: the long and winding road. *Biol. Psychol.* 95, 108–115. doi: 10.1016/j.biopsycho.2013.11.013

Birbaumer, N. (1999). Slow cortical potentials: plasticity, operant control and behavioral effects. *Neuroscientist* 5, 74–78. doi: 10.1177/107385849900500211

Cardoso, J. F. (1998). Blind signal separation: statistical principles. *Proc. IEEE* 86, 2009–2025. doi: 10.1109/5.720250

Congedo, M., Gouy-Pailler, C., and Jutten, C. (2008). On the blind source separation of human electroencephalogram by approximate joint diagonalization of second order statistics. *Clin. Neurophysiol.* 119, 2677–2686. doi: 10.1016/j.clinph.2008.09.007

Congedo, M., and Joffe, D. (2007). "Multi-channel spatial filters for neurofeedback," in *Neurofeedback: Dynamics and Clinical Applications*, ed J. Evans (New York: Haworth Press), 85–108.

Congedo, M., Lubar, J. F., and Joffe, D. (2004). Low-resolution electromagnetic tomography neurofeedback. *IEEE Trans. Neural Syst. Rehabil. Eng.* 12, 387–397. doi: 10.1109/tnsre.2004.840492

Cramer, S. C., Sur, M., Dobkin, B. H., O'brien, C., Sanger, T. D., Trojanowski, J. Q., et al. (2011). Harnessing neuroplasticity for clinical applications. *Brain* 134, 1591–1609. doi: 10.1093/brain/awr039

Delorme, A., Sejnowski, T., and Makeig, S. (2007). Enhanced detection of artifacts in EEG data using higher-order statistics and independent component analysis. *Neuroimage* 34, 1443–1449. doi: 10.1016/j.neuroimage.2006.11.004

Dempster, T., and Vernon, D. (2009). Identifying indices of learning for alpha neurofeedback training. *Appl. Psychophysiol. Biofeedback* 34, 309–318. doi: 10.1007/s10484-009-9112-3

Edgington, E. S. (1987). *Randomization Tests.* New York: Marcel Dekker.

Egner, T., Zech, T. F., and Gruzelier, J. H. (2004). The effects of neurofeedback training on the spectral topography of the electroencephalogram. *Clin. Neurophysiol.* 115, 2452–2460. doi: 10.1016/j.clinph.2004.05.033

Fiori, S. (2003). Overview of independent component analysis technique with an application to synthetic aperture radar (SAR) imagery processing. *Neural Netw.* 16, 453–467. doi: 10.1016/s0893-6080(03)00016-9

Florin, E., Bock, E., and Baillet, S. (2014). Targeted reinforcement of neural oscillatory activity with real-time neuroimaging feedback. *Neuroimage* 88, 54–60. doi: 10.1016/j.neuroimage.2013.10.028

Gasser, T., Sroka, L., and Möcks, J. (1985). The transfer of EOG activity into the EEG for eyes open and closed. *Electroencephalogr. Clin. Neurophysiol.* 61, 181–193. doi: 10.1016/0013-4694(85)91058-2

Grandchamp, R., and Delorme, A. (2009). "NeuroTRIP: a framework for bridging between open source software. Application to training a brain machine interface," in *5th International Conference on Signal Image Technology and Internet Based Systems*, eds K. Yetongnon, R. Chbeir and A. Dipanda (Washington, DC: IEEE Computer Society Inc.), 451–457.

Greicius, M. D., Srivastava, G., Reiss, A. L., and Menon, V. (2004). Default-mode network activity distinguishes Alzheimer's disease from healthy aging: evidence from functional MRI. *Proc. Natl. Acad. Sci. U S A* 101, 4637–4642. doi: 10.1073/pnas.0308627101

Hagemann, D., and Naumann, E. (2001). The effects of ocular artifacts on (lateralized) broadband power in the EEG. *Clin. Neurophysiol.* 112, 215–231. doi: 10.1016/s1388-2457(00)00541-1

Hoedlmoser, K., Pecherstorfer, T., Gruber, G., Anderer, P., Doppelmayr, M., Klimesch, W., et al. (2008). Instrumental conditioning of human sensorimotor rhythm (12–15 Hz) and its impact on sleep as well as declarative learning. *Sleep* 31, 1401–1408.

James, C. J., and Hesse, C. W. (2005). Independent component analysis for biomedical signals. *Physiol. Meas.* 26, R15–R39. doi: 10.1088/0967-3334/26/1/r02

Jang, G.-J., Lee, T.-W., and Oh, Y.-H. (2002). Learning statistically efficient features for speaker recognition. *Neurocomputing* 49, 329–348. doi: 10.1016/s0925-2312(02)00527-1

Kiebel, S. J., Tallon-Baudry, C., and Friston, K. J. (2005). Parametric analysis of oscillatory activity as measured with EEG/MEG. *Hum. Brain Mapp.* 26, 170–177. doi: 10.1002/hbm.20153

Kleinbaum, D. G., and Kupper, L. L. (1978). *Applied Regression Analysis and Other Multivariable Methods.* Belmont, California: Wadsworth Publishing Company.

Klimesch, W. (1999). EEG alpha and theta oscillations reflect cognitive and memory performance: a review and analysis. *Brain Res. Brain Res. Rev.* 29, 169–195. doi: 10.1016/s0165-0173(98)00056-3

Kopřivová, J., Congedo, M., Horáček, J., Praško, J., Raszka, M., Brunovský, M., et al. (2011). EEG source analysis in obsessive-compulsive disorder. *Clin. Neurophysiol.* 122, 1735–1743. doi: 10.1016/j.clinph.2011.01.051

Kopřivová, J., Congedo, M., Raszka, M., Praško, J., Brunovský, M., and Horáček, J. (2013). Prediction of treatment response and the effect of independent component neurofeedback in obsessive-compulsive disorder: a randomized, sham-controlled, double-blind study. *Neuropsychobiology* 67, 210–223. doi: 10.1159/000347087

Makeig, S., Bell, A. J., Jung, T.-P., and Sejnowski, T. J. (1996). "Independent component analysis of electroencephaolgraphic data," in *Advances in Neural Information Processing Systems*, eds D. Touretzky, M. Mozer and M. E. Hasselmo (Cambridge, MA: MIT Press), 145–151.

Makeig, S., Debener, S., Onton, J., and Delorme, A. (2004). Mining event-related brain dynamics. *Trends Cogn. Sci.* 8, 204–210. doi: 10.1016/j.tics.2004.03.008

Maurizio, S., Liechti, M. D., Heinrich, H., Jäncke, L., Steinhausen, H. C., Walitza, S., et al. (2014). Comparing tomographic EEG neurofeedback and EMG biofeedback in children with attention-deficit/hyperactivity disorder. *Biol. Psychol.* 95, 31–44. doi: 10.1016/j.biopsycho.2013.10.008

Onton, J., Delorme, A., and Makeig, S. (2005). Frontal midline EEG dynamics during working memory. *Neuroimage* 27, 341–356. doi: 10.1016/j.neuroimage.2005.04.014

Onton, J., Westerfield, M., Townsend, J., and Makeig, S. (2006). Imaging human EEG dynamics using independent component analysis. *Neurosci. Biobehav. Rev.* 30, 808–822. doi: 10.1016/j.neubiorev.2006.06.007

Pascual-Marqui, R. D. (2002). Standardized low-resolution brain electromagnetic tomography (sLORETA): technical details. *Methods Find. Exp. Clin. Pharmacol.* 24(Suppl D), 5–12.

Philippens, I., and Vanwersch, R. (2010). Neurofeedback training on sensorimotor rhythm in marmoset monkeys. *Neuroreport* 21, 328–332. doi: 10.1097/WNR.0b013e3283360ba8

Renard, Y., Lotte, F., Gibert, G., Congedo, M., Maby, E., Delannoy, V., et al. (2010). OpenViBE: an open-source software platform to design, test and use brain-computer interfaces in real and virtual environments. *Presence Teleoper. Virtual Env.* 19, 35–53. doi: 10.1162/pres.19.1.35

Romero, S., Mañanas, M. A., and Barbanoj, M. J. (2008). A comparative study of automatic techniques for ocular artifact reduction in spontaneous EEG signals based on clinical target variables: a simulation case. *Comput. Biol. Med.* 38, 348–360. doi: 10.1016/j.compbiomed.2007.12.001

Schneider, F., Rocktroh, B., Heimann, H., Lutzenberger, W., Mattes, R., Elbert, T., et al. (1992). Self-regulation of slow cortical potential in psychiatric patients: Schizophrenia. *Biofeedback Self Regul.* 17, 277–292. doi: 10.1007/bf01000051

Sherlin, L. H., Arns, M., Lubar, J. F., Heinrich, H., Kerson, C., Strehl, U., et al. (2011). Neurofeedback and basic learning theory: implications for research and practice. *J. Neurother.* 15, 292–304. doi: 10.1080/10874208.2011.623089

Sterman, M. B., and Egner, T. (2006). Foundation and practice of neurofeedback for the treatment of epilepsy. *Appl. Psychophysiol. Biofeedback* 31, 21–35. doi: 10.1007/s10484-006-9002-x

Tan, G., Thornby, J., Hammond, D. C., Strehl, U., Canady, B., Arnemann, K., et al. (2009). Meta-analysis of EEG biofeedback in treating epilepsy. *Clin. EEG Neurosci.* 40, 173–179. doi: 10.1177/155005940904000310

Van Der Veen, A. J., Talwar, S., and Paulraj, A. (1997). A subspace approach to blind space-time signal processing for wireless communication systems. *IEEE Trans. Signal Process.* 45, 173–190. doi: 10.1109/78.552215

Vigário, R. N. (1997). Extraction of ocular artefacts from EEG using independent component analysis. *Electroencephalogr. Clin. Neurophysiol.* 103, 395–404. doi: 10.1016/s0013-4694(97)00042-8

Weber, E., Köberl, A., Frank, S., and Doppelmayr, M. (2011). Predicting successful learning of SMR neurofeedback in healthy participants: methodological considerations. *Appl. Psychophysiol. Biofeedback* 36, 37–45. doi: 10.1007/s10484-010-9142-x

Weiskopf, N. (2012). Real-time fMRI and its application to neurofeedback. *Neuroimage* 62, 682–692. doi: 10.1016/j.neuroimage.2011.10.009

Weiskopf, N., Scharnowski, F., Veit, R., Goebel, R., Birbaumer, N., and Mathiak, K. (2004). Self-regulation of local brain activity using real-time functional magnetic resonance imaging (fMRI). *J. Physiol. Paris* 98, 357–373. doi: 10.1016/j.jphysparis.2005.09.019

Weiskopf, N., Veit, R., Erb, M., Mathiak, K., Grodd, W., Goebel, R., et al. (2003). Physiological self-regulation of regional brain activity using real-time functional magnetic resonance imaging (fMRI): methodology and exemplary data. *Neuroimage* 19, 577–586. doi: 10.1016/s1053-8119(03)00145-9

White, D. J., Congedo, M., Ciorciari, J., and Silberstein, R. B. (2012). Brain oscillatory activity during spatial navigation: theta and gamma activity link medial temporal and parietal regions. *J. Cogn. Neurosci.* 24, 686–697. doi: 10.1162/jocn_a_00098

Yoo, S. S., and Jolesz, F. A. (2002). Functional MRI for neurofeedback: feasibility study on a hand motor task. *Neuroreport* 13, 1377–1381. doi: 10.1097/00001756-200208070-00005

Yuen, P. C., and Lai, J. H. (2002). Face representation using independent component analysis. *Pattern Recognit.* 35, 1247–1257. doi: 10.1016/s0031-3203(01)00101-7

2

Insula and inferior frontal triangularis activations distinguish between conditioned brain responses using emotional sounds for basic BCI communication

Linda van der Heiden[1,2‡], Giulia Liberati[2,3,4*‡], Ranganatha Sitaram[2,5,6], Sunjung Kim[2], Piotr Jaśkowski[1†], Antonino Raffone[3,7], Marta Olivetti Belardinelli[3,7], Niels Birbaumer[2,8] and Ralf Veit[2]

[1] *Department of Cognitive Psychology, University of Finance and Management, Pawia, Warsaw, Poland*
[2] *Institute of Medical Psychology and Behavioral Neurobiology, Eberhard Karls-University, Tübingen, Germany*
[3] *Interuniversity Centre for Research on Cognitive Processing in Natural and Artificial Systems (ECONA), Rome, Italy*
[4] *Institute of Neuroscience, Université Catholique de Louvain, Brussels, Louvain-la-Neuve, Belgium*
[5] *Department of Biomedical Engineering, University of Florida, Gainesville, FL, USA*
[6] *Biomedical Engineering, Sri Chitra Tirunal Institute of Medical Sciences and Technology, Trivandrum, India*
[7] *Department of Psychology, University "Sapienza" of Rome, Rome, Italy*
[8] *Ospedale San Camillo—IRCCS, Istituto di Ricovero e Cura a Carattere Scientifico, Venezia Lido, Italy*

Correspondence:
Giulia Liberati, Institute of Neuroscience, Université catholique de Louvain, Avenue Mounier 53 bte B1.53.02 à 1200 Woluwe-Saint-Lambert, Claude Bernard, Etage 02, Local 0826, Site Bruxelles Woluwe, Brussels, Louvain-la-Neuve, Belgium
e-mail: giulia.liberati@uclouvainb.be

In order to enable communication through a brain-computer interface (BCI), it is necessary to discriminate between distinct brain responses. As a first step, we probed the possibility to discriminate between affirmative ("yes") and negative ("no") responses using a semantic classical conditioning paradigm, within an fMRI setting. Subjects were presented with congruent and incongruent word-pairs as conditioned stimuli (CS), respectively eliciting affirmative and negative responses. Incongruent word-pairs were associated to an unpleasant unconditioned stimulus (scream, US1) and congruent word-pairs were associated to a pleasant unconditioned stimulus (baby-laughter, US2), in order to elicit emotional conditioned responses (CR). The aim was to discriminate between affirmative and negative responses, enabled by their association with the positive and negative affective stimuli. In the late acquisition phase, when the US were not present anymore, there was a strong significant differential activation for incongruent and congruent word-pairs in a cluster comprising the left insula and the inferior frontal triangularis. This association was not found in the habituation phase. These results suggest that the difference in affirmative and negative brain responses was established as an effect of conditioning, allowing to further investigate the possibility of using this paradigm for a binary choice BCI.

Keywords: classical conditioning, emotions, fMRI, Insula, inferior frontal triangularis, BCI

INTRODUCTION

The possibility to produce two differentiable conditioned responses, corresponding to "affirmative" and "negative" thinking, could be exploited for basic yes/no communication through a brain-computer interface (BCI). This would allow individuals who are not able to use standard communication pathways (e.g., because of severe motor disability or expressive deficits) to convey information on their basic needs. BCIs are traditionally based on operant conditioning (Wolpaw et al., 2002), which may however be problematic for some users, such as completely locked-in state individuals (Birbaumer, 2006) or persons with dementia (Liberati et al., 2012a).

In the present study, we investigated the possibility to use classical conditioning to discriminate between different brain responses. The advantages of such paradigm shift is that, since classical conditioning does not require users to perform cognitively challenging tasks, it could be used for communicating with cognitively impaired patients (e.g., with dementia Liberati et al., 2012a,b).

Differential classical conditioning has been well studied and described over the last century. The basic principle of this learning mechanism is that a conditioned stimulus (CS+) is paired with an unconditioned stimulus (US), while another CS remains unpaired (CS−). The pairing of CS with US results in a conditioned response (CR; Pavlov, 1927) reflecting a new learned stimulus-response association. Many variations of this procedure have been applied, using different CS modalities and pleasant/appetitive or unpleasant/aversive US. Semantic classical conditioning refers to the conditioning of responses to meaningful words or sentences, irrespective of the specific letters or sounds that constitute the words (Razran, 1939, 1961). The repeated association of words or sentences with a significant US, such as a painful stimulus, produces a CR, i.e., measured at the level of cortical evoked responses (Montoya et al., 1996). Recently, semantic conditioning experiments have been performed while electroencephalographic (EEG) potentials were measured (De Massari et al., 2012; Furdea et al., 2012; Ruf et al., 2013) using two different aversive auditory US or a single aversive electrical shock US. Up to now, semantic conditioning has not been investigated using functional magnetic resonance imaging (fMRI).

In the present fMRI study, we introduced a semantic double conditioning paradigm to condition two different responses, an affirmative and a negative one, in view of developing a BCI to allow basic yes/no communication. For this purpose, an innovative approach was tested in which congruent and incongruent word-pairs, eliciting respectively affirmative and negative thinking, were associated with two different emotional sounds, a pleasant and an unpleasant one.

Our aim was to assess whether it is possible to discriminate between the congruent and incongruent word-pairs, using a semantic conditioning protocol to condition two distinct brain responses at the same time, by associating two emotional stimuli to word-pairs presented aurally. We hypothesized that, after classical conditioning, the semantic stimuli would elicit differentially conditioned responses in emotion-related brain areas. More specifically, we expected that word-pairs associated with unpleasant emotional stimuli would elicit a negative emotional response (e.g., associated with ACC, insula and amygdala activation) (Büchel et al., 1998, 1999) and word-pairs associated with pleasant emotional stimuli a positive emotional response (e.g., associated with amygdala, hippocampus and prefrontal cortex activation) (Ito et al., 2005; Costa et al., 2010). In other words, we addressed two challenges, namely double semantic auditory conditioning using emotional sounds and—through this approach—the elicitation of distinctive brain responses, to enable basic yes/no BCI communication.

MATERIALS AND METHODS

PARTICIPANTS

Ten right-handed, native German speaking, healthy individuals (5 males, 5 females), ranging in age from 21 to 28 (mean age = 25.3, $SD = 1.77$ years), participated in this study. All participants gave written informed consent prior to participation in the fMRI experiment. The study was approved by the Ethics Committee of the Medical Faculty of the University of Tübingen and was performed in compliance with the Code of Ethics of the World Medical Association (Declaration of Helsinki).

STIMULI

The stimuli consisted of 300 German word-pairs, read aloud by a native German speaker, recorded using a SpeedLink USB microphone and QuickTime Player 7 program for Macintosh.

Each word-pair included a superordinate category (e.g., "animals") and a subordinate object (e.g., "dog"). Half of the word-pairs were congruent (e.g., "Obst-Apfel," "Fruit-Apple"), half incongruent (e.g., "Obst-Hund," "Fruit-Dog"). Congruence was given by the belonging of the object to the category. The categories that were used were Animals, Countries, Fruit, Furniture, Sports, Clothing, Instruments, Drinks, Crockery, and Jobs. The word-pairs were short (1.5 s) and simple, so that they did not represent a cognitive challenge. Word-pairs were chosen, instead of questions or sentences, as they could be more easily standardized in length, and could be also understandable by individuals with some degree of cognitive deficit. In fact, different studies have shown that even in presence of cognitive impairment, basic semantic information that may not be explicitly accessible could be relatively intact at the implicit level (Nebes, 1994; Laisney et al., 2011).

The brain responses associated to the congruent and incongruent word-pairs (associated respectively to "yes" and "no" thinking) constituted the conditioned stimuli (CS). The unconditioned stimuli (US) were two standardized emotional sounds drawn from the International Affective Digitized Sounds (IADS, Bradley and Lang, 1999; Stevenson and James, 2008): a pleasant emotional stimulus (a baby-laughter) and an unpleasant emotional stimulus (a scream). The duration of each US was also 1.5 s. To ascertain that all stimuli had the same precise length, their duration was adjusted using the software program Audacity 1.3.14 Beta for Mac OS X. As our final aim was communication, congruent word-pairs (eliciting affirmative thinking) where always associated with the pleasant emotional stimulus, and incongruent word-pairs (eliciting negative thinking) were always associated with the unpleasant emotional stimulus, in order to maximize the strength of the rewarding/aversive effects.

Stimuli presentation in the fMRI scanner was performed with a software interface developed in Matlab v. 6.5 (Mathworks, Inc., Sherbon, MA). Participants heard all auditory stimuli through MRI-compatible headphones with efficient gradient noise suppression (up to 45 dB) and a filter system with more than 90 dB RF-suppression (MR confon System, Leibniz-Institute for Neurobiology at Magdeburg, Germany).

EXPERIMENTAL PARADIGM

The paradigm consisted of a single session divided into six blocks (**Table 1**). In the first block, defined as habituation phase, 25 incongruent word-pairs (CS1), 25 congruent word-pairs (CS2), 25 unpleasant emotional stimuli (scream, US1) and 25 pleasant

Table 1 | Summary of the protocol.

Block	Phase	CS1 + US1	CS1	CS2 + US2	CS2	US1	CS2
1	Habituation		25		25	25	25
2	Early acquisition	25		25			
3		25		25			
4	Late acquisition	10	15	10	15		
5		5	20	5	20		
6	Extinction		25		25		

The classical conditioning procedure comprised six blocks: one habituation block (Wolpaw et al., 2002), two early acquisition blocks (Birbaumer, 2006; Liberati et al., 2012a), two late acquisition blocks (Pavlov, 1927; Liberati et al., 2012b), and one extinction block (Razran, 1939). In the habituation, incongruent word-pairs (CS1), congruent word-pairs (CS2), the scream (US1) and the laughter (US2) were all presented individually (25 times each). In the early acquisition, CS1 was always paired with US1 (25 times) and CS2 was always paired with US2 (25 times). In the late acquisition, the number of CS paired with US progressively decreased. In the extinction, only CS1 (25 times) and CS2 (25 times) were presented, without US.

emotional stimuli (laughter, US2) were presented to the subject in a pseudo-random order, so that the same stimulus was never presented consecutively more than three times. The inter-stimulus interval (ISI) was also randomized to optimize design efficiency, and could last for 6, 7.5, or 9 s. The habituation phase served to evaluate the activations relative to each type of stimulus individually, before their association in the conditioning process. In the second and third blocks, which were structured identically and constituted the early acquisition phase, 25 incongruent word-pairs (CS1) and 25 congruent word-pairs (CS2) were presented in a pseudo-random order, such that the same condition (congruent or incongruent) was never presented consecutively more than three times. Each word-pair was immediately followed by an US: scream (US1) after incongruent word-pairs and laughter (US2) after congruent word-pairs. Also in the fourth and fifth block (late acquisition phase), 25 CS1 and 25 CS2 were presented in a pseudo-random order. In the fourth block, only 10 CS1 and 10 CS2 were paired (40% of the word-pairs were followed by the appropriate US) with US1 and US2, respectively. In the fifth block, only 5 CS1 and 5 CS2 were paired (20%). In the sixth and final block (extinction block), none of the 50 word-pairs, also presented in a pseudo-random order, were followed by an US. The gradual diminution of the percentage of word-pairs followed by emotional stimulation served to verify whether the conditioning had taken place, meaning that congruent and incongruent word-pairs could be discriminated thanks to their association to the emotional sounds, even when the emotional sounds were not present anymore.

BEHAVIORAL MEASURES

Participants were instructed to use the Self-Assessment Manikin (SAM, Bradley and Lang, 1994) to rate the valence (pleasantness/unpleasantness) and the arousal related to the two emotional US (scream and laughter), both at the end of the first block and at the end of the fifth block, to allow for the comparison of the two stimuli and to assess whether the subjects habituated to them throughout the measurement. The SAM comprises two 9–point scales, ranging from "pleasant" to "unpleasant" and from "not arousing at all" to "very arousing," respectively.

fMRI DATA ACQUISITION

The experiment was performed using a Siemens AG (Erlangen, Germany) 3T Trio MRI scanner. Functional T2*-weighted images were acquired with a standard 12-channels head coil, in transversal orientation ($TR = 1.5$ s, $TE = 30$ ms, flip angle $= 70°$, matrix 64×64, voxel size $= 3.3 \times 3.3 \times 5.0\,mm^3$, 16 slices, 1 mm gap, bandwidth $= 1.954$ kHz/pixel) covering the whole brain. Moreover, a high-resolution T1-weighted anatomical scan of the whole brain was acquired from each participant (MPRAGE, matrix size $= 256 \times 256$, 160 slices, 1 mmisotropic voxels, $TR = 2300$ ms., $TE = 3.93$ ms., $TI = 1100$ ms, flip angle $\alpha = 8°$). The first 10 volumes of every block were discarded to permit T1 equilibrium.

fMRI DATA ANALYSIS

Data were analyzed using Statistical Parametric Mapping (SPM8, Wellcome Department of Imaging Neuroscience, London, UK) run on Matlab R2008b (Mathworks, Inc., Sherborn, MA, USA). Images of each subject were realigned and unwarped to correct for head movement, and were normalized to a standard Echo-Planar Imaging (EPI) template in Montreal Neurological Institute (MNI) space. Spatial smoothing was applied using a Gaussian kernel with full width at half-maximum of 9 mm. Prior to statistical analyses data were high-pass filtered (cutoff 128 s) and low-pass filtered (AR, Wolpaw et al., 2002).

Statistical analysis was carried out using the general linear model (GLM) with the canonical hemodynamic response function (HRF) as a basis set. In a first level analysis, regressors were defined to discriminate between paired and unpaired word-pairs separately for each block, condition and conditioning phase. The regressors were CS1 paired, CS2 paired, CS1 unpaired, CS2 unpaired, US1 and US2. The six movement regressors for each block were included as confounds in the design matrix to capture residual movement-related variance. The following contrasts were defined on the first level: US1 vs. US2, and unpaired CS1 compared to CS2 in the habituation phase CS1 paired, CS2 paired in the early acquisition phase and CS1 unpaired vs. CS2 unpaired, in the late acquisition phase as well as during extinction. Moreover contrasts were defined combining paired and unpaired word-pairs in the early and late acquisition. In a second level analysis, corresponding contrast images of all subjects were used to assess the main effects of conditioning. A paired t-test, performed by including the individual contrast images for US1 and US2 during habituation, was computed in order to detect significantly activated brain regions related to these emotional unconditioned stimuli during habituation. A paired t-tests was also performed to detect differences in brain regions involved in the laughter vs. scream and congruent vs. incongruent word-pairs in the extinction phases. To investigate the difference in brain regions for congruent and incongruent word-pairs, we performed a 2 x 2 full-factorial model with the factors Phase (early acquisition and late acquisition) and Condition (congruent and incongruent). Moreover, two different models were computed to observe activations in the early acquisition and late acquisition individually, to evaluate the progression of the conditioning process. For all group statistics a cluster-level threshold of $p < 0.05$ corrected for the Family Wise Error rate (FWER) of the whole brain was used.

RESULTS

BEHAVIORAL DATA

SAM ratings

A two-sample t-test indicated that participants rated the scream as significantly more unpleasant [block 1: $t_{(20)} = 10.62$, block 5: $t_{(20)} = 3.09$, $p < 0.01$] and more arousing [block 1: $t_{(20)} = 5.87$, block 5: $t_{(20)} = 2.66$, $p < 0.02$] than the laughter, both at the beginning and at the end of the measurement. The arousal associated to the scream was significantly less at the end of block 5 compared to block 1 [$t_{(20)} = 2.96$, $p < 0.01$], although no significant difference was found for the laughter (p = 0.3). The valence associated to the scream and laughter did not change significantly during the experiment ($p = 0.2$ in both cases).

NEUROIMAGING DATA

In the habituation phase (**Table 2**), significant differential activations were only found for the scream vs. laughter (US1>US2) contrast, in the left middle cingulate gyrus (MCG), in the right inferior frontal triangularis (IFT), and in the superior frontal gyrus (SFG). No difference was found for the reverse contrast (US2>US1), nor for the incongruent vs. congruent (CS1>CS2) and congruent vs. incongruent (CS2>CS1) contrasts.

In the acquisition phase (**Table 3**), significant differential activation for the incongruent vs. congruent contrast (CS1>CS2) was found in the left IFT, adjacent to the insula (**Figure 1**). Differential activation in the left insula was found for the incongruent vs. congruent (CS1>CS2) contrast in the early acquisition, as well as in the late acquisition, for the word-pairs that were no more followed by emotional stimuli (**Figure 2**).

In the extinction phase (**Table 4**), the only differential activation was found for the congruent vs. incongruent contrast (CS2>CS1) in the anterior cingulate cortex (ACC).

Finally, paired *t-tests* were computed to directly compare the incongruent vs. congruent contrast pairs in the habituation and in the extinction, as well as in the habituation and in the acquisition, not showing significant differences for corrected *p*-values.

DISCUSSION

The present study assessed the possibility to apply classical conditioning to two different responses (affirmative and negative) using positive and negative emotional US, in order to discriminate them. This was the first attempt to use such a protocol with fMRI. Our main hypothesis was that the effect of classical conditioning would have emerged as a differential activation for the incongruent and congruent word-pairs in emotion related areas. In fact, our results showed an effect of the aversive semantic classical conditioning, as demonstrated by the differential activation of the insula, known to be related to emotion processing (Phillips et al., 1998; Phan et al., 2002; Radua et al., 2010; Sitaram et al., 2011), and of a region adjacent to the insula, the IFT, for the incongruent vs. congruent word-pairs during acquisition. This is supported by the observation that there was no significant difference in the activation of the insula between the word-pairs in the habituation phase. The differential activation of the insula and of the IFT could be interpreted as a conditioned brain response for the incongruent word-pairs associated to the unpleasant sound. The IFT, corresponding to the BA 45 area, belongs to the inferior frontal articulatory network and is involved in phonological and semantic processing of language (McDermott et al., 2003; Amunts et al., 2004; Gold et al., 2005). More specifically, several studies have associated this area to verbal fluency (Abrahams et al., 2003) lexical search (Fiebach et al., 2002; Heim et al., 2005), and semantic memory retrieval (Rugg et al., 1999; Düzel et al., 2001). Most interestingly for our aim of developing a communication system, this region was also associated with the process of internal word generation (Friedman et al., 1998; Tremblay and Gracco, 2006). We may therefore speculate that IFT activation for the incongruent vs. congruent contrast could be related to the difference in the patterns of activation within this region pertaining "yes" and "no" responses. Hence, we propose that a multivariate pattern classifier that can discriminate between fMRI spatio-temporal patterns can be trained to decode "yes" and "no" answers for the purpose of communication.

To be able to use the present paradigm for communication, it is necessary to be able to discriminate incongruent and congruent responses also in the extinction phase. The fact that the conditioned response was evident in the late acquisition phase (when the word-pairs were not followed by emotional stimuli anymore),

Table 2 | Habituation.

Contrast	Region (Brodmann's Area)		*t*-value	MNI coordinate		
				x	*y*	*z*
Scream > Laughter	Middle cingulate gyrus (BA 24)	L	6.03	−18	−19	43
	Inferior frontal triangularis	R	5.56	54	20	4
	Superior frontal gyrus	R	5.25	24	47	19
	Superior frontal gyrus (BA 9)	R	5.25	15	53	40
Laughter > Scream	No differential activations					
Incongruent > Congruent without US	No differential activations					
Congruent > Incongruent without US	No differential activations					

P < 0.05 FWE corrected on cluster level; R, Right; L, Left.

Table 3 | Acquisition.

Contrast	Region		*t*-value	MNI coordinate		
				x	*y*	*z*
ACQUISITION						
Congruent > Incongruent	No differential activations					
Incongruent > Congruent	Inferior frontal triangularis	L	4.57	−45	26	13
EARLY ACQUISITION						
Congruent > Incongruent	No differential activations					
Incongruent > Congruent	Insula	L	4.80	−36	17	−14
LATE ACQUISITION						
Congruent > Incongruent	No differential activations					
Incongruent > Congruent	Insula	L	7.77	−30	23	−5

P < 0.05 FWE corrected on cluster level; R, Right; L, Left.

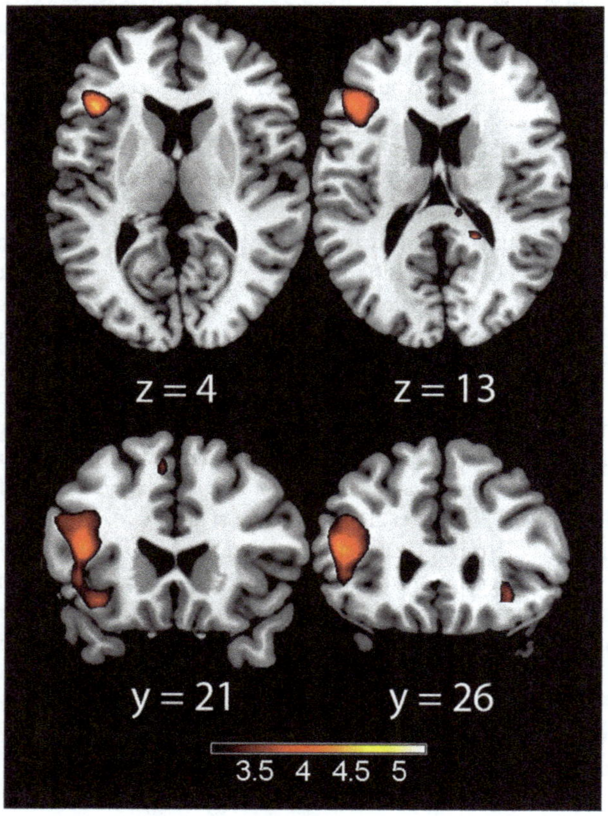

FIGURE 1 | Acquisition phase trials (early and late acquisition combined) for the incongruent > congruent contrast. Showing left insula (left) and left inferior frontal gyrus pars triangularis (right) on axial **(top)** and coronal **(bottom)** slices, Color map represents *t*-values.

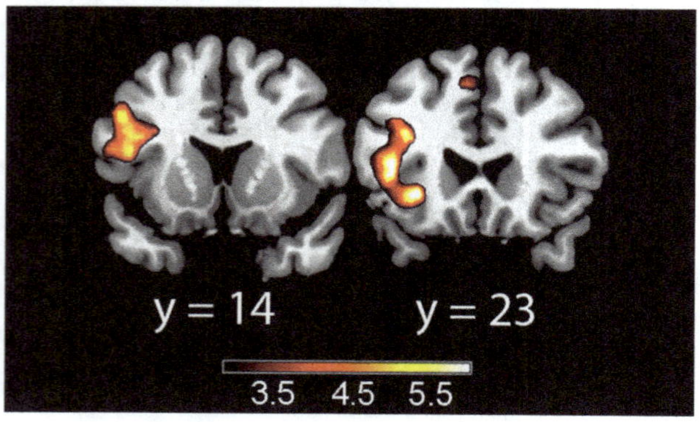

FIGURE 2 | Late acquisition phase unpaired trials for the incongruent > congruent contrast. Showing left inferior frontal gyrus pars triangularis (left) and left insula (right). Color map represents *t*-values.

Table 4 | Extinction.

Contrast	Region		*t*-value	MNI coordinate		
				x	*y*	*z*
Congruent > Incongruent without US	Anterior cingulate cortex	R	8.49	6	50	10
Incongruent > Congruent without US	No sign. Differential activations					

P < 0.05 FWE cluster < 0.05; R, Right; L, Left.

but not in the extinction phase, may indicate that the extinction was rapid, suggesting the need of increasing the number of trials during the acquisition phase and modifying the reinforcement schedule to establish sustained CR's. The number of acquisition trials was limited in this study, because the conditioning process took place in the fMRI scanner and we wanted to avoid tiring participants. In fact, once ascertained that the conditioning effect is visible in the acquisition phase, the first blocks of the protocol could be performed outside the scanner, and only the unpaired word-pairs would be subject to fMRI. After successful learning, the CR could be renewed faster and subsequently used for communication.

The comparisons between extinction and habituation, and between acquisition and habituation, concerning the incongruent vs. congruent contrast, are certainly important to evaluate the effect of conditioning. Although the present paradigm did not show significant differentiation for these phases, for binary communication aims, the decisive factor is the differentiation between two responses (i.e., "yes" and "no" answers). In fact, we could show that in the late acquisition phase, for the trials in which the word-pairs were not followed my emotional stimuli, there was a significant difference between incongruent and congruent word-pairs. Such differential activation could not be found in the habituation phase.

One possibility for the lack of strong differential activation for the congruent vs. incongruent word-pairs is that the appetitive US (baby-laugh) may have not been pleasant enough, although this explanation could be ruled out by considering the subjects' SAM ratings. It is possible that the presence of two distinct emotional US is confounding, so that the activations that would usually emerge with single conditioning are not elicited in double conditioning, in agreement with Lachnit (1991) and with Watt and Honey (1997). Another possible explanation for our results could be that appetitive conditioning is weaker compared to aversive conditioning, leading to weaker activations.

The lack of an independent parameter of the conditioning process, such as skin conductance response (SCR), startle response or contingency ratings, makes it difficult to judge whether the association between CS and US was identified, especially investigating a double conditioning. Nevertheless, the activations we found during acquisition, especially in the latest stage, suggests a conditioning effect for the incongruent word-pairs.

Improvements for this study comprise the reversed CS-US combination and the usage of different emotional US. To judge whether the conditioning of both CS was successful, the reversed CS-US combination should be tested, associating the congruent word-pairs with the scream and the incongruent word-pairs with the laughter, to investigate whether this results in similar CRs. Concerning a different US, Metereau et al. (Metereau and Dreher, 2012) found that both appetitive and aversive reinforcers activate the ACC, anterior insula and striatum, suggesting that the usage of appetitive and aversive US could activate the same areas, which may not be ideal for discriminating between the two conditioned responses. In our study the MCG, IFT, and SFG were activated more for the scream compared to the laughter, indicating a differentiable brain pattern but future studies should take possible overlap into consideration. It is well known that US intensity is a critical factor in effective classical conditioning. A more intense US improves learning and results in increased conditioned responses. Our suggestion for a different US would be to replace the laughter with an auditory stimulus eliciting disgust. Sitaram et al. (2011) showed that "disgust" and "sad" imagery are differentiable, indicating the possibility to classify the CRs and enable further investigation of double conditioning. Another possibility for the positive emotional US would be to use other appetitive US, such as smell or taste, depending on the individual salience of the stimuli.

The possibility to classify differential activations would be a first step in the direction of developing clinical applications, so that emotional stimuli may become tools for the conditioning of desirable behavior or brain responses. The demonstration that the response to congruent and incongruent word-pairs are differentiable (in the insula and in the IFT), at least until the late acquisition phase, introduces the possibility of applying such a paradigm for practical purposes, such as a binary BCI, which could allow basic "yes/no" communication with patients suffering from cognitive impairment.

Another aspect that should be considered when applying this classical conditioning protocol for basic communication is subject variability. Some individuals may be more easily conditioned, while others may require a higher number of trials in which word-pairs are associated to emotional stimuli. This introduces the need of developing an "adapted acquisition" protocol, based on the subjective ease of conditioning. For instance, if specialized pulse sequences become more sensitive to amygdala activation while enabling real-time fMRI for pattern classification, or if other biomarkers of acquisition are identified, it would be possible to obtain extra information about the conditioning process, both to improve the paradigm in the future, and to adapt it to different individuals.

CONCLUSION

This study represents a first step into a new direction of double conditioning of brain responses. The insula activations for unpaired word-pairs during the late acquisition suggest that conditioning took place for the incongruent word-pairs. The importance of the insula and neighboring inferior frontal gyrus pars triangularis throughout the association process is shown by the continuous differential activation during the different phases of conditioning. The possibility of using classical conditioning with emotional US opens the door to investigating more variations on double conditioning with different US or testing the usability for clinical applications.

The application we aimed at is a BCI for communication. If the negative and affirmative response can be classified from the BOLD response, this possibility could become reality (i.e., allowing to discriminate between affirmative and negative thinking). This application would be most beneficial for completely locked-in and cognitively impaired patients.

ACKNOWLEDGMENTS

This work was supported by the European Commission 7th Framework Programme (FP7) Marie Curie Initial Training Networks: ITN-LAN [PITN-GA-2008-214570], and by the Badenwürttemberg-Singapore Life Sciences Grant. We are grateful to Adelheid Kumpf and Dr. Daniele De Massari for helping in the preparation of the stimuli, Dr. Andrea Caria, Mohit Rana and Dr. Sangkyung Lee for their support in data acquisition, and Dr. Tamara Matuz, Dr. Carolin Ruf and Dr. Adrian Furdea for fruitful discussions.

REFERENCES

Abrahams, S., Goldstein, L. H., Simmons, A., Brammer, M. J., Williams, S. C., Giampietro, V. P., et al. (2003). Functional magnetic resonance imaging of verbal fluency and confrontation naming using compressed image acquisition to permit overt responses. *Hum. Brain Mapp.* 20, 29–40. doi: 10.1002/hbm.10126

Amunts, K., Weiss, P. H., Mohlberg, H., Pieperhoff, P., Eickhoff, S., Gurd, J. M., et al. (2004). Analysis of neural mechanisms underlying verbal fluency in cytoarchitectonically defined stereotaxic space—the roles of Brodmann areas 44 and 45. *Neuroimage* 22, 42–56. doi: 10.1016/j.neuroimage.2003.12.031

Birbaumer, N. (2006). Breaking the silence: brain-computer interfaces (BCI) for communication and motor control. *Psychophysiology* 43, 517–532. doi: 10.1111/j.1469-8986.2006.00456.x

Bradley, M. M., and Lang, P. J. (1994). Measuring emotion: the self-assessment manikin and the semantic differential. *J. Behav. Ther. Exp. Psychiatry* 25, 49–59.

Bradley, M. M., and Lang, P. J. (1999). *International Affective Digitized Sounds (IADS): Stimuli, Instruction Manual and Affective Ratings.* Gainesville, FL: University of Florida.

Büchel, C., Dolan, R. J., Armony, J. L., and Friston, K. J. (1999). Amygdala-hippocampal involvement in human aversive trace conditioning revealed through event-related functional magnetic resonance imaging. *J. Neurosci* 19, 10869–10876.

Büchel, C., Morris, J., Dolan, R. J., and Friston, K. J. (1998). Brain systems mediating aversive conditioning: an event-related fmri study. *Neuron* 20, 947–957.

Costa, V. D., Lang, P. J., Sabatinelli, D., Versace, F., and Bradley, M. M. (2010). Emotional imagery: assessing pleasure and arousal in the brain's reward circuitry. *Hum. Brain Mapp.* 31, 1446–1457. doi: 10.1002/hbm.20948

De Massari, D., Matuz, T., Furdea, A., Ruf, C. A., Halder, S., and Birbaumer, N. (2012). Brain-computer interface and semantic classical conditioning of communication in paralysis. *Biol. Psychol.* 92, 267–274. doi: 10.1016/j.biopsycho.2012.10.015

Düzel, E., Picton, T. W., Cabeza, R., Yonelinas, A. P., Scheich, H., Heinze, H. J., et al. (2001). Comparative electrophysiological and hemodynamic measures of neural activation during memory-retrieval. *Hum. Brain Mapp.* 13, 104–123. doi: 10.1002/hbm.1028

Fiebach, C. J., Friederici, A. D., Müller, K., and Von Cramon, D. Y. (2002). FMRI evidence for dual routes to the mental lexicon in visual word recognition. *J. Cogn. Neurosci.* 14, 11–23. doi: 10.1162/089892902317205285

Friedman, L., Kenny, J. T., Wise, A. L., Wu, D., Stuve, T. A., Miller, D. A., et al. (1998). Brain activation during silent word generation evaluated with functional MRI. *Brain Lang.* 64, 231–256.

Furdea, A., Ruf, C. A., Halder, S., De Massari, D., Bogdan, M., Rosenstiel, W., et al. (2012). A new (semantic) reflexive brain-computer interface: in search for a suitable classifier. *J. Neurosci. Methods* 203, 233–240. doi: 10.1016/j.jneumeth.2011.09.013

Gold, B. T., Balota, D. A., Kirchhoff, B. A., and Buckner, R. L. (2005). Common and dissociable activation patterns associated with controlled semantic and phonological processing: evidence from FMRI adaptation. *Cereb. Cortex* 15, 1438–1450. doi: 10.1093/cercor/bhi024

Heim, S., Alter, K., Ischebeck, A. K., Amunts, K., Eickhoff, S. B., Mohlberg, H., et al. (2005). The role of the left brodmann's areas 44 and 45 in reading words and pseudowords. *Brain Res. Cogn. Brain Res.* 25, 982–993. doi: 10.1016/j.cogbrainres.2005.09.022

Ito, R., Everitt, B. J., and Robbins, T. W. (2005). The hippocampus and appetitive pavlovian conditioning: effects of excitotoxic hippocampal lesions on conditioned locomotor activity and autoshaping. *Hippocampus* 15, 713–721. doi: 10.1002/hipo.20094

Lachnit, H. (1991). Simultaneous classical conditioning of two effector systems. *Integr. Physiol. Behav. Sci.* 26, 45–50. doi: 10.1007/BF02690978

Laisney, M., Giffard, B., Belliard, S., de la Sayette, V., Desgranges, B., and Eustache, F. (2011). When the zebra loses its stripes: semantic priming in early alzheimer's disease and semantic dementia. *Cortex* 47, 35–46. doi: 10.1016/j.cortex.2009.11.001

Liberati, G., Dalboni da Rocha, J. L., van der Heiden, L., Raffone, A., Birbaumer, N., Olivetti Belardinelli, M., et al. (2012a). Toward a brain-computer interface for alzheimer's disease patients by combining classical conditioning and brain state classification. *J. Alzheimer's Dis.* 29, 1–10. doi: 10.3233/JAD-2012-112129

Liberati, G., Veit, R., Dalboni da Rocha, J., Kim, S., Lulé, D., von Arnim, C., et al. (2012b). Combining classical conditioning and brain-state classification for the development of a brain-computer interface (BCI) for alzheimer's patients. *Alzheimer's Dementia* 8, P515. doi: 10.1016/j.jalz.2012.05.1397

McDermott, K. B., Petersen, S. E., Watson, J. M., and Ojemann, J. G. (2003). A procedure for identifying regions preferentially activated by attention to semantic and phonological relations using functional magnetic resonance imaging. *Neuropsychologia* 41, 293–303. doi: 10.1016/S0028-3932(02)00162-8

Metereau, E., and Dreher, J. C. (2012). Cerebral correlates of salient prediction error for different rewards and punishments. *Cereb. Cortex* 23, 477–487. doi: 10.1093/cercor/bhs037

Montoya, P., Larbig, W., Pulvermüller, F., Flor, H., and Birbaumer, N. (1996). Cortical correlates of semantic classical conditioning. *Psychophysiology* 33, 644–649.

Nebes, R. D. (1994). Contextual facilitation of lexical processing in alzheimer's disease: intralexical priming or sentence-level priming? *J. Clin. Exp. Neuropsychol.* 16, 489–497.

Pavlov, I. P. (1927). *Conditioned Reflexes* (Trans. By G. V. Anrep). London: Oxford University Press.

Phan, K. L., Wager, T., Taylor, S. F., and Liberzon, I. (2002). Functional neuroanatomy of emotion: a meta-analysis of emotion activation studies in PET and fmri. *Neuroimage* 16, 331–348. doi: 10.1006/nimg.2002.1087

Phillips, M. L., Young, A. W., Scott, S. K., Calder, A. J., Andrew, C., Giampietro, V., et al. (1998). Neural responses to facial and vocal expressions of fear and disgust. *Proc. Biol. Sci.* 265, 1809–1817.

Radua, J., Phillips, M. L., Russell, T., Lawrence, N., Marshall, N., Kalidindi, S., et al. (2010). Neural response to specific components of fearful faces in healthy and schizophrenic adults. *Neuroimage* 49, 939–946. doi: 10.1016/j.neuroimage.2009.08.030

Razran, G. (1939). A quantitative study of meaning by a conditioned salivary technique (semantic conditioning). *Science* 90, 89–90.

Razran, G. (1961). The observable unconscious and the inferable conscious in current soviet psychophysiology: interoceptive conditioning, semantic conditioning, and the orienting reflex. *Psychol. Rev.* 68, 1–147.

Ruf, C. A., De Massari, D., Furdea, A., Matuz, T., Fioravanti, C., van der Heiden, L., et al. (2013). Semantic classical conditioning and brain-computer interface control: encoding of affirmative and negative thinking. *Front. Neurosci.*7:23. doi: 10.3389/fnins.2013.00023

Rugg, M. D., Fletcher, P. C., Chua, P. M., and Dolan, R. J. (1999). The role of the prefrontal cortex in recognition memory and memory for source: an fmri study. *Neuroimage* 10, 520–529. doi: 10.1006/nimg.1999.0488

Sitaram, R., Lee, S., Ruiz, S., Rana, M., Veit, R., and Birbaumer, N. (2011). Real-time support vector classification and feedback of multiple emotional brain states. *Neuroimage* 56, 753–765. doi: 10.1016/j.neuroimage.2010.08.007

Stevenson, R. A., and James, T. W. (2008). Affective auditory stimuli: characterization of the international affective digitized sounds (IADS) by discrete emotional categories. *Behav. Res. Methods* 40, 315–321. doi: 10.3758/BRM.40.1.315

Tremblay, P., and Gracco, V. L. (2006). Contribution of the frontal lobe to externally and internally specified verbal responses: FMRI evidence. *Neuroimage* 33, 947–957. doi: 10.1016/j.neuroimage.2006.07.041

Watt, A., and Honey, R. C. (1997). Combining css associated with the same or different uss. *Q. J. Exp. Psychol. B.* 50, 350–367.

Wolpaw, J. R., Birbaumer, N., McFarland, D. J., Pfurtscheller, G., and Vaughan, T. M. (2002). Brain-computer interfaces for communication and control. *Clin. Neurophysiol.* 113, 767–791. doi: 10.1016/S1388-2457(02)00057-3

3

FRIEND Engine Framework: a real time neurofeedback client-server system for neuroimaging studies

Rodrigo Basilio[1], Griselda J. Garrido[1], João R. Sato[1,2], Sebastian Hoefle[1], Bruno R. P. Melo[1], Fabricio A. Pamplona[1], Roland Zahn[3] and Jorge Moll[1]*

[1] *Cognitive and Behavioral Neuroscience Unit and Neuroinformatics Workgroup, D'Or Institute for Research and Education, Rio de Janeiro, Brazil*
[2] *Center of Mathematics, Computation and Cognition, Universidade Federal do ABC, Santo André, Brazil*
[3] *Department of Psychological Medicine, Institute of Psychiatry, King's College, London, UK*

***Correspondence:**
Jorge Moll, Cognitive and Behavioral Neuroscience Unit and Neuroinformatics Workgroup, D'Or Institute for Research and Education, Diniz Cordeiro 30, Rio de Janeiro, 22281-100, Brazil
e-mail: jorge.moll@idor.org

In this methods article, we present a new implementation of a recently reported FSL-integrated neurofeedback tool, the standalone version of "Functional Real-time Interactive Endogenous Neuromodulation and Decoding" (FRIEND). We will refer to this new implementation as the FRIEND Engine Framework. The framework comprises a client-server cross-platform solution for real time fMRI and fMRI/EEG neurofeedback studies, enabling flexible customization or integration of graphical interfaces, devices, and data processing. This implementation allows a fast setup of novel plug-ins and frontends, which can be shared with the user community at large. The FRIEND Engine Framework is freely distributed for non-commercial, research purposes.

Keywords: brain computer interface (BCI), real-time fMRI, FSL, neurofeedback, EEG

INTRODUCTION

There is a growing push toward the use of real-time fMRI (rt-fMRI) neurofeedback in experimental and clinical investigation, with solid prospects for therapeutic applications (Sulzer et al., 2013; Stoeckel et al., 2014) through the development of brain computer interface (BCI) software integrated with commonly available devices such as fMRI scanners and EEG devices. Successful scientific exploration and application of rt-fMRI neurofeedback will be facilitated by the existence of freely available, user-friendly, and flexible software implementations. To this end, a few research groups have recently contributed with the development of computational tools, each with their own strengths and limitations (LaConte et al., 2007; Zotev et al., 2011; Sorger et al., 2012; Rana et al., 2013; Sato et al., 2013).

Nevertheless, because of the computational and technical complexities that are intrinsic to the emerging field of rt-fMRI neurofeedback and the diversity of approaches, there are still few available options for investigators in the area. More importantly, a number of features that could facilitate and encourage advanced users and developers to build on currently available platforms are still lacking. Here, we introduce a new framework that unleashes users to create frontends and customize pipelines for their own studies using the programming language and platform they are most familiar with, flexibly connecting them to a core processing engine. To attain this goal, we have revamped our recently reported rt-fMRI neurofeedback standalone software, "Functional Real-time Interactive Endogenous Modulation and Decoding system" (FRIEND) (Sato et al., 2013), as described below.

FRIEND ENGINE FRAMEWORK

The original FRIEND neurofeedback tool comprises three processing pipelines (**Figure 1**): (1) the brain decoding-based feedback using support-vector machines (SVM); (2) the single region-of-interest (ROI) based blood-oxygen level dependent (BOLD) feedback; and (3) functional connectivity feedback based on a sliding window of correlations between ROIs. These pipelines were developed and implemented across time, on the basis of research needs in our lab, including the techniques needed to support these pipelines. As such, the first version of FRIEND included only the SVM pipeline for brain decoding-based neurofeedback for emotion modulation, using the libSVM library (Chang and Lin, 2011) and was recently employed in a study of emotional enhancement (Moll et al., 2014). For the purpose of a new research line on motor control physiology and rehabilitation, an ROI activation pipeline for FRIEND was implemented, allowing the flexible creation of anatomically or functionally defined ROIs. Anatomical ROIs are created by selecting predefined areas from a variety of Montreal Neurological Institute (MNI) templates, which are automatically transformed into the subject space. Functionally-defined ROIs can also be created after running an fMRI functional localizer, and then selecting and thresholding a functional cluster for subsequent neurofeedback runs. The third pipeline, focusing on sliding window-based correlations between two brain regions as a guide for neurofeedback information, was developed to enable an ongoing clinical proof-of-concept study on remitted major depression, based on the findings of a recent study (Green et al., 2012).

The provision of the ideal feedback to the participant is crucial for the success of any neurofeedback study. In this vein,

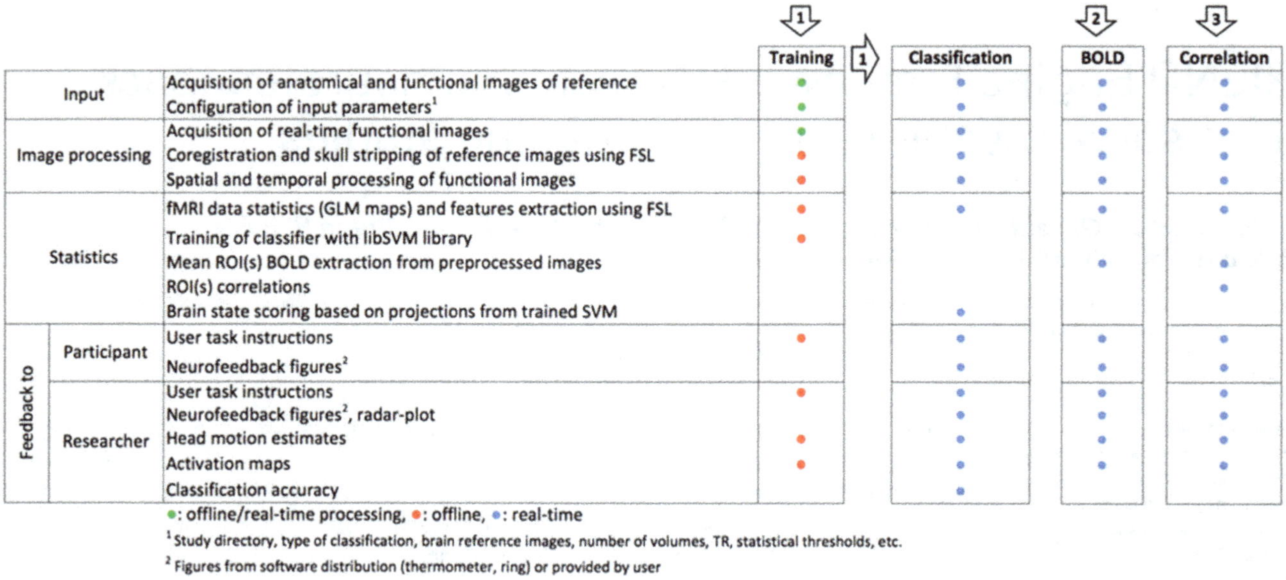

FIGURE 1 | Flowchart of three FRIEND processing neurofeedback pipelines. (1) Support Vector Machine-based neurofeedback, using projected values onto a discriminative hyperplane; (2) BOLD level real-time display from a set of pre-specified ROIs; (3) Real-time functional connectivity neurofeedback based on the correlation between the signals from different ROIs (Sato et al., 2013).

interoperability with other applications such as well-established stimulus presentation tools, including virtual reality ones, and response devices with the neurofeedback interface would be highly desirable (Renaud et al., 2011; Weiskopf, 2012). In the original implementation of FRIEND (Sato et al., 2013), a few standard strategies were implemented, based on a simple visual feedback interface (e.g., rings changing in shape or a thermometer). In that original implementation, the visual feedback could be modified by simply replacing the bitmap figures. However, this initial approach neither allows for a more sophisticated control of stimuli as specialized stimulus presentation softwares do (e.g., http://www.neurobs.com/), nor does it offer the possibility of immersive game-like experience, which could be more engaging for participants of neurofeedback studies.

In order to allow users to use their own stimulus feedback strategies and to develop additional processing strategies (e.g., Matlab® pipelines), we have broken the standalone version of FRIEND into smaller parts, encapsulating the complex calculations involving rt-fMRI neurofeedback processing in one unit and the graphic user interface in another. We expect that this approach will enable researchers with average to advanced programming skills to efficiently implement customized graphical interfaces and data processing functionalities, which can be shared with other users via NITRC (http://www.nitrc.org/projects/friend) and GitHub (https://github.com/InstitutoDOr/FriendENGINE). Toward this aim, FRIEND was restructured based on the well-established object oriented programming paradigm (Stroustrup, 1988), facilitating modification and implementation of new functionalities.

In FRIEND Engine, basic processes that are common to any neurofeedback pipeline such as anatomical segmentation, motion correction of functional images and gaussian smoothing (**Figure 1**)—largely based on FSL code (http://fsl.fmrib.ox.ac.uk/fsl/fslwiki/)—are encapsulated in a single unit, called FRIEND Engine (**Figure 2**), the first part of the FRIEND Engine framework. The engine determines the main processing pipeline and defines time points in this pipeline to execute functionalities not implemented in the engine. These functionalities are geared to attain the goal of the study (e.g., classification of brain states, ROI percent signal change and correlation between two ROIs in the previously presented pipelines) and coded separately in independent units, called plug-ins (**Figure 2**) here, the second component of the framework. By definition, a plug-in is an extension of the engine and must therefore be implemented in the same language and be executed on the same platform for compatibility. As such, the engine provides the basic workings whereas the plug-ins implement the specific functionalities necessary for estimation of feedback parameters on the basis of data analysis. The engine does not know and does not need to know how a specific plug-in handles the information. The plug-in library just needs to expose the necessary functions for the engine to work properly. The coordinator of the engine and the neurofeedback processing is the frontend (**Figure 2**), the third part of the FRIEND Engine framework. As the name intuitively implies, it is the graphical interface for the neurofeedback loop, essentially the *interface* of a BCI. It provides feedback information (e.g., BOLD activation level) to the participant, relevant information to the operator (e.g., motion correction parameters), and handles the necessary steps to synchronize the presentation of the feedback with the scanner acquisition. Ideally, the construction of the frontend should not demand learning new and complex technical skills. The optimal solution is allowing users to customize their applications using the programming language and platform of their choice. A TCP/IP network communication protocol is therefore defined to bridge

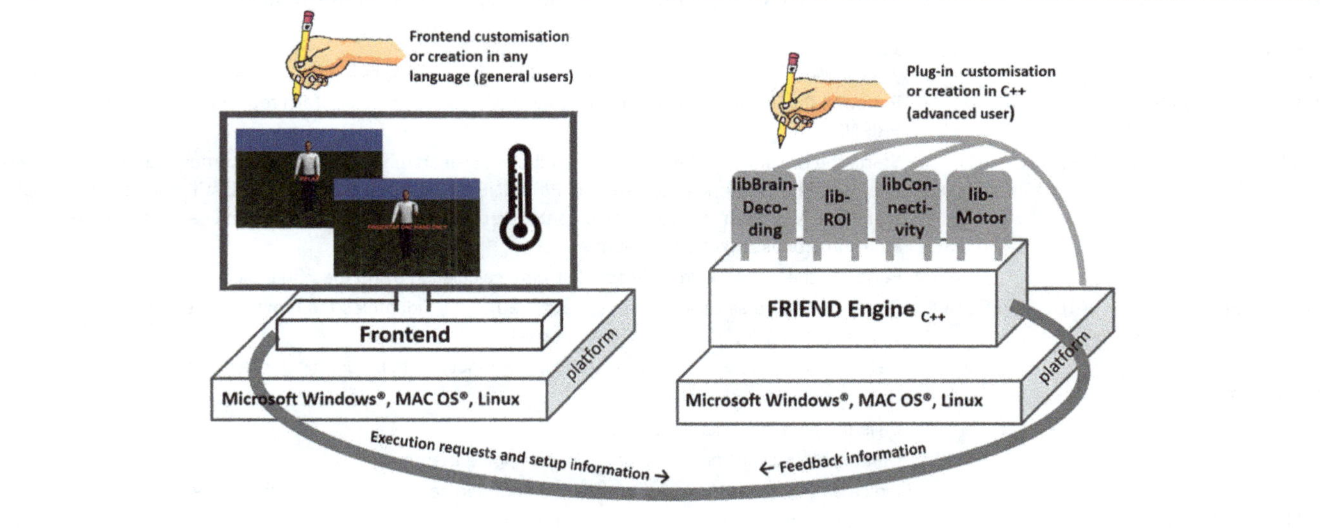

FIGURE 2 | The FRIEND Engine framework comprises three major components. The FRIEND Engine core and plug-ins, written in C++ and operating on the same platform, and the frontend that can be written in any language with sockets support. The TCP/IP communication protocol allows the frontend to be executed on a different computer platform from the FRIEND Engine. Users may customize or write their own frontends. Advanced users can also write their own plug-ins and processing pipelines.

the frontend and the engine. In this configuration, the engine listens to a port for incoming messages (requests) from the frontend, allowing the engine and frontend to operate on different platforms.

The first step of a neurofeedback study in the FRIEND Engine framework is the same as for the standalone version of FRIEND: the configuration of the specific parameters for the study, such as the input directory and the number of volumes in the acquisition run. This configuration should be provided by the frontend application, which gets the input from the operator of the study and passes it to FRIEND Engine. By default, FRIEND Engine reads the study_params.txt configuration file located in the same directory of the engine's executable file. The study_params.txt file is exactly the same as for the standalone version of FRIEND. The frontend can pass a whole configuration file by the TCP/IP network communication protocol to the engine by way of the command "READCONFIG," as explained in the following section. The next important and vital command the frontend must pass on, is the plug-in configuration, which comprises the plug-in library filename and the name of the functions that the engine should call at predefined time points, like the name of the function that calculates the feedback information for a volume. These two messages prepare the engine to properly handle the experiment. The next message the frontend should send is "PREPROC," which executes the same steps executed in the standalone version of FRIEND after the first configuration window.

Next, the frontend needs to send a message indicating that the engine should start processing the acquisition run. There are four options, "PIPELINE," "NBPIPELINE," "FEEDBACK," "NBFEEDBACK" (**Table 1**), explained in the following section. This is equivalent to clicking the "TRAIN" or "FEEDBACK" button in the standalone version of FRIEND. At specific points of the processing, such as the calculation of the feedback, the engine executes the proper plug-in function, previously assigned to the plug-in configuration phase. There is no direct communication between the frontend and the plug-in components.

During the acquisition run, the frontend sends "TEST" messages (**Table 1**), querying for neurofeedback information for each volume of the acquisition scan. The engine executes the configured feedback function of the plug-in to get the feedback information and returns it to the frontend. The frontend must interpret this value and properly display that information to the participant of the experiment. **Figure 3** depicts this message exchange between the frontend and the engine in the avatar finger tapping virtual scenario. It includes a new command, "NEWSESSION" (**Table 1**), which indicates that the engine should create a new session to work with the frontend. That message is only needed in asynchronous communications as explained in Section TCP/IP Communication Protocol. To illustrate this, excerpts of programming code from a Matlab® frontend and the libROI plug-in are provided in the Supplementary Material. FRIEND Engine expects the volume files in exactly the same way as standalone FRIEND does. This implies that the list of computers that can run the engine is restricted to the list of computers that can receive the volume files from the fMRI scanner (or EEG device) in real-time acquisition.

FRIEND Engine runs on Microsoft Windows® (XP or later), Apple Macintosh (OSX 10.8 and above) and Linux (Debian, CentOS 6.4). A mid/high end workstation is required (e.g., PC: quad-core i7, 8 GB RAM or higher, Macintosh: quad-core Intel Core i5, 8 GB RAM or higher). In the original standalone version of FRIEND, FSL (Jenkinson et al., 2012) toolbox commands were encapsulated in a dynamic link Microsoft Windows® library. In FRIEND Engine, this interrelationship was changed: for non-Microsoft Windows® systems, FSL toolbox installation is a pre-requisite and FSL executables are called using system calls to the operational system. This simplifies FSL upgrades, as they can be executed independently from the engine code. In Microsoft

Table 1 | List of commands expected by FRIEND Engine during the TCP/IP communication protocol with the frontend.

Command	Action
PREPROC/NBPREPROC	Performs the initial preprocessing (co-registration, skull stripping, MNI registration, etc.) steps of FRIEND
PIPELINE/NBPIPELINE/NBFEEDBACK	Starts the processing of each volume in the acquisition run as soon as it becomes available in the input directory. The difference between the PIPELINE/NBPIPELINE and NBFEEDBACK commands, is that NBFEEDBACK automatically calculates the feedback values and stores them in a session workspace after the processing of each volume
GLM/NBGLM	Performs the General Linear Model (fsl_glm) calculation using the FSL toolbox
FEATURESELECTION/NBFEATURESELECTION	Performs feature selection (see Sato et al., 2013), i.e., identifies the most representative subset of voxels for the calculation of the feedback value
PLUG-IN	Defines the library and the associated plug-in functions to be used in further calls
TRAIN/NBTRAIN	Calls the train function plug-in
TEST	Calls the plug-in feedback function
NEWSESSION	Creates a new session (workspace) in the engine memory
ENDSESSION	Indicates that the engine can terminate an opened session and closes the related thread
SESSION/GRAPHPARS	Queries for the motion parameters of a given volume
SESSION/TEST	Returns the feedback information of a volume, previously stored in the session workspace
SESSION/PREPROC, SESSION/FEEDBACK	Queries if a command, e.g. PREPROC or FEEDBACK has ended
READCONFIG	Sends an entire configuration file associated with the frontend neurofeedback study to set the parameters of the experiment

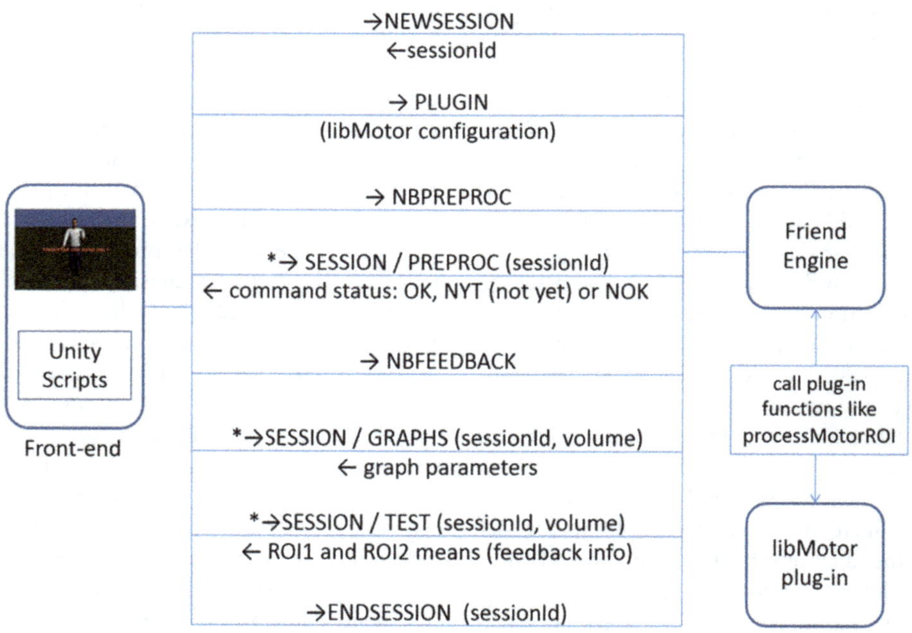

FIGURE 3 | TCP/IP network communication protocol between the frontend and the FRIEND Engine (avatar finger tapping virtual scenario). The steps marked with asterisk (*) are called as many times as needed. The first message sent is "NEWSESSION," which indicates that the engine should create a new session to work with the frontend. That message is only needed in asynchronous communications as explained in Section TCP/IP Communication Protocol.

Windows® FRIEND Engine version, our modified source code of the FSL toolbox functionality is embedded within the executable of FRIEND Engine. This embedding process transforms each needed FSL command in a function statically linked to the software. For this reason, no additional installation of the FSL software is necessary.

TCP/IP COMMUNICATION PROTOCOL

Table 1 lists the commands expected by the engine in the TCP/IP communication protocol. There are two types of connections: synchronous (blocked) and asynchronous (non-blocked [NB]) connections. In synchronous connections, the frontend needs to wait until command completion to receive the acknowledge response from the engine. Asynchronous connections need to be established when the frontend is not supposed to freeze the execution to wait for the acknowledge response, as in virtual reality scenario frontends. This situation happens when a time-consuming command needs to be executed, like "PREPROC" or "TRAIN." In this case, regular queries for command termination need to be issued until the expected response is obtained. To appropriately handle asynchronous connections, a multithread approach with at least two threads is adamant: one, the main thread, that performs all the raw real time processing; and the other, the response thread, which responds to queries of various types of information related to the main thread processing. The two threads can respond properly to the frontend by a shared access to the same session. To make these two threads inter-operate, the notion of session is introduced. A session is an independent location in the memory of the computer running the engine, capable of storing all the information that is required to be sent back to the frontend, such as neurofeedback information and motion-corrected volume parameters. It is a role of the frontend to present this information to the participant in a user-friendly manner. The Matlab® frontend provided with the software distribution has some built-in capabilities to display feedback and motion parameters.

PLUG-IN LIBRARY

A plug-in file is a dynamic library file (a .so file on the Linux system, a .dylib file on the Mac OSX system and a .dll file in Microsoft Windows®) that implements specific functions called internally by FRIEND Engine at specific times during the pipeline. This is a major advantage of the FRIEND Engine, because, when in need of additional features, users can focus on writing just the necessary functionality for their specific research needs. This allows customization of the neurofeedback tool, using encapsulated codes that run additional functionalities from external libraries, leaving the engine code intact. This characteristic favors usability and code maintenance, because errors in a plug-in library are also encapsulated in that library and do not affect other plug-ins. This framework makes it easier to setup pilot experiments and to explore new hypotheses.

Plug-in functions and parameters

The plug-in library must implement all the computational processes required to calculate the feedback responses. A small subset of variables needs to be defined to be used as parameters of the plug-in functions (**Table 2**).

The engine defines six functions (**Table 3**) that are called at predefined time points during the pipeline execution. Not all of those six functions must be implemented in a plug-in library, just the ones necessary to properly calculate the feedback information. We recommend advanced users to code those functions in C++ because that minimizes compatibility errors during the execution of the plug-in functions by the engine.

AVAILABLE PLUG-INS

The FRIEND Engine distribution comes with four plug-ins: one for the SVM pipeline (libBrainDecoding), using the libSVM library (Chang and Lin, 2011); one for the ROI pipeline (libROI), used in the Matlab® and the first game frontend examples (presented in the following sections); one for the functional connectivity between two ROIs (libConnectivity) and one (libMotor) that extracts ROI information from two ROIs located in the motor cortex area (left and right), used in the avatar finger tapping virtual scenario.

Table 2 | List of parameters used within plug-in functions.

Parameter	Definition
studyParams	Object that stores information from the study_params.txt file, which encloses all the information used by the processing pipeline to correctly identify the files, directories and expected number of data volumes
userData	Pointer referencing an area of memory created by the engine to be used by the plug-in for temporary calculations. The reason behind this approach is that subsequent calls to the same plug-in from different frontends would overwrite internal data structures if they were created within the plug-in library
classNum	Number of the class, i.e., the condition attributed to the scan during classification
volumeIndex	Number of the current processed scan
volumeFileName	The filename of the volume in the file system
Projection	Feedback value calculated
Index	Number of current scan

libROI plug-in functions and feedback value

Table 4 lists functions implemented in the libROI plug-in. The feedback value calculated by the processROI function (**Table 4**) is given by the equation:

$$\frac{\overline{ROI}_{curr\_vol} - \frac{1}{B}\sum_{k=1}^{B}\overline{ROI}_k}{\frac{1}{B}\sum_{k=1}^{B}\overline{ROI}_k} \tag{1}$$

where $\overline{ROI}_{curr\_vol}$ is the mean of the ROI on the current volume, B is the number of volumes in the previous baseline condition and $\overline{ROI}_k$ is the mean of the kth volume.

A code snippet of this function can be found in the Supplementary Material. The feedback function within the libMotor plug-in is similar to the one on libROI, except for the fact that two feedback values are calculated, one for each existing ROI.

libBrainDecoding plug-in functions and feedback value

Table 5 lists functions implemented in the libBrainDecoding plug-in. In trainSVM function, the voxels of an fMRI scan are first organized (by concatenation) in an input vector x. In this training phase, the vector is labeled according to the

Table 3 | List of functions a plug-in can define.

Function	Definition	Parameters (Table 2)
Train	Executed when the frontend issues the TRAIN command (**Table 1**). Normally, this function is used to analyze a complete data set (e.g. a training run). This function is generally more time consuming, and is therefore not a "real-time" operation. It is normally called at the end of the acquisition of a training run (e.g., for a multi voxel pattern analysis [MVPA] classification approach) or a functional localizer (e.g., for an ROI-based BOLD signal or functional connectivity study). This function builds a model that can be used on subsequent runs	studyParams userData
Test	Executed when the engine needs to calculate the feedback value for a given volume. There are two predefined values that the engine returns to the frontend: information about the condition of the processed image volume indicating, for example, a specific type of image volume classification in a MVPA study, and the feedback information value. The interpretation of these two variables is left to the frontend, which must implement how this information will be conveyed to the participant (e.g., a thermometer level, changes in a visual or auditory feedback)	studyParams userData classnum projection index
Initialization	Called after the engine reads information from the study configuration file (see Sato et al., 2013). All the memory data structure used by the plug-in must be initialized here. A pointer reference for this data structure has to be returned in the function argument. This reference will be used in further plug-in function calls issued by the FRIEND Engine	studyParams userData
Finalization	Called right before ending the processing of a session. All the memory data structures allocated in the Initialization function must be destroyed here	studyParams userData
Volume	Called before the processing of a volume	studyParams volumeIndex volumeFilename userData
PostProc	Called after the pre-processing of each volume	studyParams volumeIndex volumeFilename userData

Table 4 | Functions implemented in the libROI plug-in.

Plug-in	LibROI
initializeROIProcessing	Initialization function that creates the data structures necessary for processing ROIs. It also transforms the user-defined MNI ROI mask into subject space
processROI	Feedback function that calculates the percent signal change of a ROI in the current volume compared to the mean activation of a baseline block
finalizeROIProcessing	Finalization function that destroys all data structures created in the initialization function

Table 5 | Functions implemented in the libBrainDecoding plug-in.

Plug-in	LibROI
trainSVM	Function that uses the libSVM library to train the SVM model
testSVM	Function that calculates the feedback value of a scan based on its projected values on an SVM hyperplane
initSVM	Initialization function that creates the data structures required for SVM training and testing
finalSVM	Finalization function that deletes all temporary data structures created by initSVM

corresponding experimental condition (LaConte, 2011; Sitaram et al., 2011). This initial data is used to train the classifier (currently, a two-class SVM classifier is implemented) to discriminate between the experimental conditions of interest. The output of this function is the trained SVM model (i.e., the hyperplane coefficients). The trained SVM is then used in the subsequent brain decoding sessions (testing sessions), during which participants engage in the same tasks and conditions of interest.

In testSVM function, the projected value of a new observation is used to define the neurofeedback information (Sato et al., 2008). The projected value of a new image volume on the SVM discriminating hyperplane is given by $(x^T w + b)$, where w is a vector containing the hyperplane coefficients and b is a constant. The boundary between conditions is represented by the value of zero. This value obtained by projecting the new observation in the SVM discriminating hyperplane is then used to choose the feedback figure to be shown to the participant. Further information can be found in Sato et al. (2013).

Table 6 | Functions implemented in the libConnectivity plug-in.

Plug-in	LibROI
buildROIs	Training function responsible for building a mask containing two ROIs used to calculate the associated correlations
calculateFeedback	Feedback function that calculates the sliding window correlations based on the two ROIs calculated in buildROIs function
initializeFunctionalConnectivity	Initialization function that creates the necessary data structures
finalizeFunctionalConnectivity	Finalization function that destroys all data structures created by initializeFunctionalConnectivity function

libConnectivity plug-in functions and feedback value

Table 6 lists functions implemented in the libConnectivity plug-in. The buildROIs function transforms a mask with two MNI ROIs into the subject space. A subset of voxels from a GLM analysis of the localizer run is then selected by applying the preceding masks and selecting a user-defined percentage of these voxels. These two voxel populations are employed as new ROIs for the sliding window correlation calculation.

The calculateFeedback function calculates the Pearson correlation coefficient between two ROIs, where $ROI1$ and $ROI2$ are vectors containing the means of the ROIs on the last L scans:

$$\rho(ROI1, ROI2) = \frac{\sum_{i=1}^{L}(ROI1_i - \overline{ROI1})(ROI2_i - \overline{ROI2})}{\sqrt{\sum_{i=1}^{L}(ROI1_i - \overline{ROI1})^2}\sqrt{\sum_{i=1}^{L}(ROI2_i - \overline{ROI2})^2}} \quad (2)$$

Where L is the size of the sliding window, i.e., the last L scans acquired.

FRONTEND EXAMPLES

In all the "game" examples provided with the distribution, there is, in the engine directory, a pre-configured study_params.txt file that is read by default by the engine; all the volume files are already placed in the input directory referenced by the study_params.txt file. To read the volume files in a real-time online setup, users need to configure the arrival of images in the input directory in the same way as for the standalone version of FRIEND. Triggers from the scanner can be used to keep track of the time, e.g., the onset of a given experimental condition. It is the frontend that handles the syncing of the experimental paradigm with the scanner.

MATLAB® FRONTEND

Figure 4 is a screenshot of a frontend designed with the Matlab® GUIDE tool. Matlab® is a largely used language in the scientific community so it is important to provide a functional example of the Matlab® FRIEND Engine connection. GUIDE helps users to build graphical user interfaces for their applications in Matlab®.

This frontend application shows the activation of a ROI in the motor cortex during a finger-tapping task. It presents the feedback in the shape of a thermometer-like dynamic bar graph. This example uses the libROI plug-in. In this example and the first Unity example below, only one ROI located in the left motor cortex is used.

UNITY FRONTENDS

The frontends based on the Unity game engine (http://unity3d.com/) employ virtual reality scenarios. These scenarios are composed of objects, like rocks, trees and scripts. The scripts in Unity play an important role in how the virtual scenarios behave, such as the interactions between objects, and how, where and when avatars interact with the environment. This aspect is especially relevant for the interrelationship between Unity and FRIEND Engine. Scripts coordinate how the information returned by the engine will impact on the current state of the virtual scenario. The complexity of this coordination increases exponentially with the number of objects and avatars in the scene. Unity currently offers three options of scripting languages: C#, JavaScript and Boo. All game examples showed here were written in C# language. The initial learning curve of Unity for construction of scenarios and writing the scripts is quite demanding, but this pays off because of the great variety of high quality scenarios that can be produced in a short time. The Unity assets store also helps, because users can find a lot of interesting and complex materials, like characters, objects, and animations. The Unity game engine was employed here given its cross-platform availability (Microsoft Windows®, Linux and Mac OSX, web player, IOS and Android) and ease of use, but other tools, such as Unreal Development Kit (UDK, https://www.unrealengine.com/products/udk) and Cry Engine SDK (http://www.cryengine.com/), could also be potentially implemented as frontends.

Medieval virtual scenario frontend

Figure 5 is a screenshot of a frontend made in Unity. This frontend is a medieval virtual reality scenario in which the avatar, i.e., the participant, hovers over a path and stops in predetermined locations, blocked by a massive rock. Using the same finger tapping neurofeedback procedure exemplified in the Matlab® frontend (alternating rest and finger tapping blocks), and the same libROI plug-in, the feedback information to the participant is now given in a different way. As the participant moves across the scenario and stops right before the rock, he/she needs to perform the finger tapping task as instructed (as quickly as possible). If the percentage BOLD signal change returned by the engine reaches a predefined threshold, the rock levitates, thus unblocking the path so that the journey continues. If the threshold is not reached, the player stays at the same location until the next try, i.e., the next activation block. This scenario was constructed using objects from the iTween path editor and the Big Environment pack, available in the Unity Assets store.

Avatar finger tapping frontend

Figure 6 shows the screenshots of the avatar finger tapping frontend. It was inspired by the BOLD brain pong (Goebel et al.,

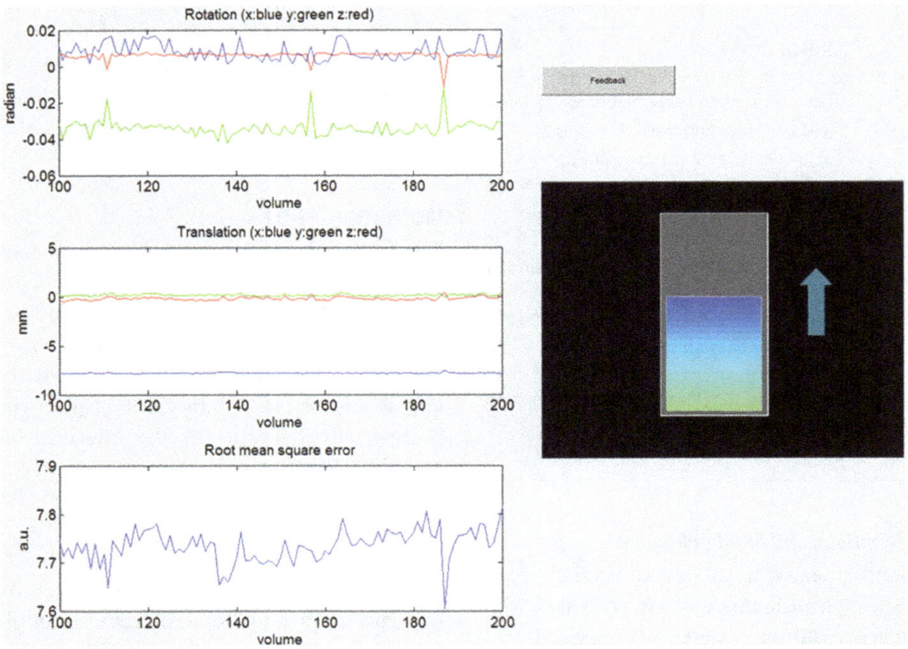

FIGURE 4 | Snapshot of a frontend designed with the Matlab® GUIDE tool, showing motion parameters (rotation, translation and root mean square error) and a thermometer indicating BOLD signal change as a feedback.

FIGURE 5 | Snapshots of the game like frontend designed in Unity, showing the path that the participant travels during the experiment. **(A)** Shows the situation where the rock is blocking the way; **(B)** shows the rock being "levitated," unblocking the way.

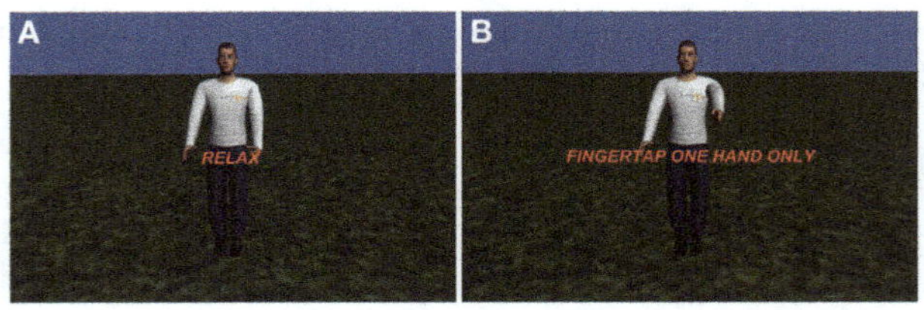

FIGURE 6 | Two situations of the avatar finger tapping scenario. (A) During a rest block and **(B)** during a finger tapping block.

2004). This is a finger tapping experiment with intercalating blocks of rest and finger tapping. Different from the previous examples, here we use two ROIs located in the primary motor cortex area of the left and right cerebral hemispheres. The participant is asked to perform finger tapping with either their left or right hand, alternating with resting blocks. This example employs the libMotor plug-in, which calculates the percent BOLD signal change in the left and right ROIs in the same way as the libROI plug-in in the single ROI example. The frontend compares the feedback values between ROIs, in such a way that the greater one will inform which hand of the avatar, showed by the frontend, will perform the finger tapping animation. If successfully performed, this conveys a clear impression that the participant is controlling the hands of the avatar with his/her own hands. The avatar and hand animations were implemented using the VR Hands Unity asset (https://serrarens.nl/passervr/downloads/vr-hands/).

DISCUSSION AND CONCLUSION

In this paper we introduced the FRIEND Engine framework, a reengineered implementation of our previous work (Sato et al., 2013) to provide a flexible and user-friendly framework that enables users to customize frontends and data processing pipelines for neurofeedback studies. For this aim, the standalone FRIEND software was re-implemented by breaking apart the core engine, which performs the basic data processing, the plug-in functionalities, which implement specifics of the neurofeedback study, and the frontend, which handles all the necessary graphic interfaces, external device inputs and sends commands to the engine.

The separation of the graphical interface from the data processing components provides a major advantage because users can implement virtually any type of feedback visualization strategy, such as images, audio, movie clips and virtual scenarios, by developing new frontends or connecting with standard stimulus presentation softwares and external devices. The use of the TCP/IP communication protocol between the frontend and the engine provides an interesting "weak connection," because the frontend does not need to make any assumptions about data processing other than the ones related to the feedback interpretation. This also enables users to more efficiently share frontends that can be used for different purposes. Computer processing time is always a critical concern, especially when real-time processing and feedback are needed. All frontends herein described were run on a different computer from the one running the FRIEND Engine application. The mean processing time for one volume (single-shot EPI, 64 × 64 to 80 × 80 matrix, 22–37 slices) was about 0.7 s in mid-/high-end workstations (PC, Quad-core i7, 8 GB RAM; Macintosh, quad-core Intel Core i5, 8 GB RAM). The performance of the game frontends was not affected by the communication with the engine, and no lags were noticed for the currently implemented routines and data types.

The FRIEND Engine framework flexibility was illustrated here by the game frontends. This implementation demonstrated the potential use of virtual reality in neurofeedback studies, which may increase engagement and compliance with the tasks. The economic push of commercial games and widely available software development kits facilitates constant updates and improvements that can be quickly embedded into new frontends for enhanced neurofeedback studies. The frontend implementation examples herein provided employed the Unity game engine (https://unity3d.com/), because of its user-friendliness, flexibility and availability for the three main operational systems (Windows®, Linux and Mac OSX).

Source code is available for all the software provided within the FRIEND Engine distribution, so that seamless customization is possible. From the user point of view, there is no apparent need to modify the exhaustively tested and well-established FRIEND Engine core functionalities, though these are open for improvement. Advanced users can also modify any existing plug-in (e.g., implementing ROI correlations using more than two ROIs) or create new ones (e.g., implementing simultaneous real-time fMRI and EEG neurofeedback). A few frontends and plug-ins are provided with this first distribution, but we expect that this can be substantially expanded whenever users share their developments, with a benefit for the growing scientific community interested in neurofeedback research (Sulzer et al., 2013).

Whereas the standalone FRIEND implementation includes quality controls mechanisms (e.g., a GUI that allows users to monitor details of the ongoing acquisition, such as motion parameters, visualization of ROIs transformed from the MNI space to subject space, the temporal variation of a ROI mean), FRIEND Engine still lacks a quality control module. While some of these functionalities are currently available on the Matlab® frontend (e.g., display of motion parameters), it is not the case for the game-like frontends. Toward this aim, we are currently developing an ancillary frontend for quality control, which will run independently from the main frontend. To access the motion parameters information and possibly feedback information, this frontend will only need the ID of the session workspace created by the main frontend. This ancillary frontend module also contains visualization capabilities for displaying anatomical and functional reference images, source MNI ROIs, ROIs transformed into subject space, visualization of active voxels prior to neurofeedback based on GLM thresholds or SVM feature-selection steps, among some other options. This frontend will operate in a largely generic way, as to be capable of working in conjunction with current or future frontends. In the short term, we are also planning to deliver a Python (https://www.python.org/) and a Presentation® (http://www.neurobs.com/) frontend.

In terms of usage and availability, currently AFNI (Cox, 1996) and Turbo Brain Voyager (Goebel, 2012) appear to be the leading packages for rtMRI neurofeedback. AFNI is a highly developed fMRI package that has pioneered work on real-time neurofeedback experiments. Turbo Brain Voyager is a user-friendly fMRI processing package containing a rtfMRI module that enjoys the benefits from a number of pre- and post-processing routines and an attractive graphic interface. Similarly, our package uses fMRI spatial and temporal processing routines that are largely based on the widely used and validated FSL package. Both AFNI and Brain Voyager allow ROI processing and thermometer-like feedback, as FRIEND Engine does. In a very recent publication, Cohen et al. (2014) employed Brain Voyager and the Unity environment to enable participants to control an avatar by hand and leg motion imagery, similarly as we report here. AFNI and Brain Voyager also provide interesting quality control functionalities, which are available in the standalone FRIEND version and which are currently being implemented and expanded in FRIEND Engine. For developers, Brain Voyager allows development of plug-ins for Windows®, MAC® and Linux platforms in C++ language whereas AFNI allows the addition of run-time functionalities in C language for MAC® and Linux. For FRIEND Engine, we recommend plug-ins to be developed in C++ for compatibility. Brain Voyager is a commercial package, thus source codes are not available, whereas AFNI and FRIEND Engine Framework are open source. An optimized FSL embedded functionality allows FRIEND to run seamlessly on Windows® (the official FSL package currently does not run on this platform), so there is no need for a virtual machine. AFNI requires Cygwin (https://www.cygwin.com) to run on Windows®, although with reduced functionality and possibly reduced performance. FRIEND Engine has the added advantage of providing full platform and language freedom for the development of frontends. A recent, freely available toolbox for rt-fMRI, implements similar capabilities as those described in FRIEND Engine, Turbo Brain Voyager and AFNI, and and adds the interesting feature of "subject-independent" multivariate pattern classification (Rana et al., 2013). However, so far it has not been made widely available for download, and we have not been able to evaluate and compare it to existing ones.

With respect to future developments in FRIEND Engine, one of our main goals is to encourage clinical applications. For this aim, streamlining routines for blind randomization procedures are under way. These will allow experimenters to run double-blind randomized controlled fMRI neurofeedback trials in a rigorous and straightforward manner.

The importance of building a repository for frontends and plug-ins is clear. A publicly accessible repository, with a discussion forum for implementations and strategies can be of great help for the development of new neurofeedback projects. To this aim, sharing of plug-ins and frontends will be possible through the NITRC repository (http://www.nitrc.org/projects/friend) and GitHub (https://github.com/InstitutoDOr/FriendENGINE). In summary, we believe that FRIEND Engine can be a valuable contribution to the thriving fMRI neurofeedback community, by providing an open and flexible collaborative platform for developing new solutions for fMRI neurofeedback research and clinical applications.

ACKNOWLEDGMENTS

The authors are thankful to colleagues from IDOR for helpful discussions and support in different stages of this work, in special to Ivanei E. Bramati, Fernando F. Paiva, Theo Marins, Patricia P. Bado, Julie Weingartner, Fernanda Tovar-Moll, Fernanda Meirelles, Luiz Felipe Costa, and Debora O. Lima. This work was supported from internal grants from the Cognitive and Behavioral Neuroscience Unit at IDOR, FAPERJ and MCT/INNT. Roland Zahn was funded by MRC fellowship (G0902304).

REFERENCES

Chang, C.-C., and Lin, C.-J. (2011). LIBSVM: a library for support vector machines. *ACM Trans. Intell. Syst. Technol.* 27, 1–27. doi: 10.1145/1961189.1961199

Cohen, O., Koppel, M., Malach, R., and Friedman, D. (2014). Controlling an avatar by thought using real-time fMRI. *J. Neural Eng.* 11:035006. doi: 10.1088/1741-2560/11/3/035006

Cox, R. W. (1996). AFNI: software for analysis and visualization of functional magnetic resonance neuroimages. *Comput. Biomed. Res. Int. J.* 29, 162–173. doi: 10.1006/cbmr.1996.0014

Goebel, R. (2012). BrainVoyager–past, present, future. *Neuroimage* 62, 748–756. doi: 10.1016/j.neuroimage.2012.01.083

Goebel, R., Sorger, B., Kaiser, J., Birbaumer, N., and Weiskopf, N. (2004). *BOLD Brain Pong: Self-Regulation of Local Brain Activity During Synchronously Scanned, Interacting Subjects.* San Diego, CA: Society for Neuroscience.

Green, S., Ralph, M. A. L., Moll, J., Deakin, J. F. W., and Zahn, R. (2012). Guilt-selective functional disconnection of anterior temporal and subgenual cortices in major depressive disorder. *Arch. Gen. Psychiatry* 69, 1014–1021. doi: 10.1001/archgenpsychiatry.2012.135

Jenkinson, M., Beckmann, C. F., Behrens, T. E., Woolrich, M. W., and Smith, S. M. (2012). FSL. *Neuroimage* 62, 782–790. doi: 10.1016/j.neuroimage.2011.09.015

LaConte, S. M. (2011). Decoding fMRI brain states in real-time. *Neuroimage* 56, 440–454. doi: 10.1016/j.neuroimage.2010.06.052

LaConte, S. M., Peltier, S. J., and Hu, X. P. (2007). Real-time fMRI using brain-state classification. *Hum. Brain Mapp.* 28, 1033–1044. doi: 10.1002/hbm.20326

Moll, J., Weingartner, J. H., Bado, P., Basilio, R., Sato, J. R., Melo, B. R., et al. (2014). Voluntary enhancement of neural signatures of affiliative emotion using FMRI neurofeedback. *PLoS ONE* 9:e97343. doi: 10.1371/journal.pone.0097343

Rana, M., Gupta, N., Dalboni Da Rocha, J. L., Lee, S., and Sitaram, R. (2013). A toolbox for real-time subject-independent and subject-dependent classification of brain states from fMRI signals. *Front. Neurosci.* 7:170. doi: 10.3389/fnins.2013.00170

Renaud, P., Joyal, C., Stoleru, S., Goyette, M., Weiskopf, N., and Birbaumer, N. (2011). Real-time functional magnetic imaging-brain-computer interface and virtual reality promising tools for the treatment of pedophilia. *Prog. Brain Res.* 192, 263–272. doi: 10.1016/B978-0-444-53355-5.00014-2

Sato, J. R., Basilio, R., Paiva, F. F., Garrido, G. J., Bramati, I. E., Bado, P., et al. (2013). Real-time fMRI pattern decoding and neurofeedback using FRIEND: an FSL-integrated BCI toolbox. *PLoS ONE* 8:e81658. doi: 10.1371/journal.pone.0081658

Sato, J. R., Thomaz, C. E., Cardoso, E. F., Fujita, A., Martin, M. da G., and Amaro, E. (2008). Hyperplane navigation: a method to set individual scores in fMRI group datasets. *Neuroimage* 42, 1473–1480. doi: 10.1016/j.neuroimage.2008.06.024

Sitaram, R., Lee, S., Ruiz, S., Rana, M., Veit, R., and Birbaumer, N. (2011). Real-time support vector classification and feedback of multiple emotional brain states. *Neuroimage* 56, 753–765. doi: 10.1016/j.neuroimage.2010.08.007

Sorger, B., Reithler, J., Dahmen, B., and Goebel, R. (2012). A real-time fMRI-based spelling device immediately enabling robust motor-independent communication. *Curr. Biol.* 22, 1333–1338. doi: 10.1016/j.cub.2012.05.022

Stoeckel, L. E., Garrison, K. A., Ghosh, S., Wighton, P., Hanlon, C. A., Gilman, J. M., et al. (2014). Optimizing real time fMRI neurofeedback for therapeutic discovery and development. *Neuroimage.* 5, 254–255. doi: 10.1016/j.nicl.2014.07.002

Stroustrup, B. (1988). What is object-oriented programming? *IEEE Softw.* 5, 10–20. doi: 10.1109/52.2020

Sulzer, J., Haller, S., Scharnowski, F., Weiskopf, N., Birbaumer, N., Blefari, M. L., et al. (2013). Real-time fMRI neurofeedback: progress and challenges. *Neuroimage* 76, 386–399. doi: 10.1016/j.neuroimage.2013.03.033

Weiskopf, N. (2012). Real-time fMRI and its application to neurofeedback. *Neuroimage* 62, 682–692. doi: 10.1016/j.neuroimage.2011.10.009

Zotev, V., Krueger, F., Phillips, R., Alvarez, R. P., Simmons, W. K., Bellgowan, P., et al. (2011). Self-regulation of amygdala activation using real-time FMRI neurofeedback. *PLoS ONE* 6:e24522. doi: 10.1371/journal.pone.0024522

4

Self-regulation of frontal-midline theta facilitates memory updating and mental set shifting

***Stefanie Enriquez-Geppert*[1,2]*, *René J. Huster*[1,3], *Christian Figge*[2] *and Christoph S. Herrmann*[1,3,4]**

[1] *Experimental Psychology Laboratory, Department of Psychology, European Medical School, Carl von Ossietzky University of Oldenburg, Oldenburg, Germany*
[2] *Karl-Jaspers Clinic, European Medical School Oldenburg-Groningen, Oldenburg, Germany*
[3] *Research Center Neurosensory Science, Carl von Ossietzky University, Oldenburg, Germany*
[4] *Center for Excellence 'Hearing4all', Carl von Ossietzky University of Oldenburg, Oldenburg, Germany*

Correspondence:
Stefanie Enriquez-Geppert, Experimental Psychology Laboratory, Department of Psychology, European Medical School, Carl von Ossietzky University of Oldenburg, A7, Ammerländer Heerstr. 114–118, 26129 Oldenburg, Germany
e-mail: s.geppert@uni-oldenburg.de

Frontal-midline (fm) theta oscillations as measured via the electroencephalogram (EEG) have been suggested as neural "working language" of executive functioning. Their power has been shown to increase when cognitive processing or task performance is enhanced. Thus, the question arises whether learning to increase fm-theta amplitudes would functionally impact the behavioral performance in tasks probing executive functions (EFs). Here, the effects of neurofeedback (NF), a learning method to self-up-regulate fm-theta over fm electrodes, on the four most representative EFs, memory updating, set shifting, conflict monitoring, and motor inhibition are presented. Before beginning and after completing an individualized, eight-session gap-spaced NF intervention, the three-back, letter/number task-switching, Stroop, and stop-signal tasks were tested while measuring the EEG. Self-determined up-regulation of fm-theta and its putative role for executive functioning were compared to an active control group, the so-called pseudo-neurofeedback group. Task-related fm-theta activity after training differed significantly between groups. More importantly, though, after NF significantly enhanced behavioral performance was observed. The training group showed higher accuracy scores in the three-back task and reduced mixing and shifting costs in letter/number task-switching. However, this specific protocol type did not affect performance in tasks probing conflict monitoring and motor inhibition. Thus, our results suggest a modulation of proactive but not reactive mechanisms of cognitive control. Furthermore, task-related EEG changes show a distinct pattern for fm-theta after training between the NF and the pseudo-neurofeedback group, which indicates that NF training indeed tackles EFs-networks. In sum, the modulation of fm-theta via NF may serve as potent treatment approach for executive dysfunctions.

Keywords: frontal-midline theta, neurofeedback, cognitive enhancement, executive functions, EEG, proactive and reactive control

INTRODUCTION

Time-frequency analyses of electroencephalographic (EEG) recordings reveal synchronous processes of neural networks known as neuronal oscillations. Nowadays, these neural oscillations are considered to provide a linkage of neural activity with behavior and thought. As such, they are supposed to coordinate neuronal spiking between and within brain circuits (e.g., Buzsáki, 2006; Buzsáki et al., 2013), whereby different neural oscillations may appear at the same time and interact with each other in a hierarchical way in order to implement perception and cognition (Herrmann et al., 2004; Canolty et al., 2006; Basar and Güntekin, 2008; Fingelkurts and Fingelkurts, 2014).

Regarding higher cognitive functions, frontal-midline (fm) theta oscillations are of particular interest. Fm-theta oscillations are recorded over fronto-medial brain regions at frequencies between 4–8 Hz and are suggested to be generated in the midcingulate cortex (MCC; Mitchell et al., 2008; Cavanagh and Frank, 2014), a highly interconnected brain structure (Beckmann et al., 2009; Vogt, 2009) that is part of the superordinate cognitive control network (Niendam et al., 2012). The MCC is known to be crucially involved in executive functioning (Cavanagh et al., 2012), which enables goal directed behavior (e.g., Lezak, 2012). Increases of fm-theta power have been associated with enhanced coupling between neuronal spikes and the phase of the population theta cycle, and thus are suggested to organize neural processes during decision points where executive functioning is needed and information is integrated to inform action selection (Cavanagh and Frank, 2014). Enhanced cognitive processing is accompanied with increases of fm-theta (Mitchell et al., 2008), specifically in tasks involving working memory (WM; Mitchell et al., 2008) and executive functions (EFs; Nigbur et al., 2011). In addition, fm-theta activity has been related to efficient WM maintenance (Tóth et al., 2014), and increases of fm-theta activity during task processing have been shown to predict successful behavioral performance

(Sederberg et al., 2003) and RTs in a Simon task involving conflict monitoring (Cohen and Donner, 2013). Correspondingly, the absence of fm-theta up-regulation, when executive functioning is required, has been reported to be associated with reduced performance (e.g., Donkers et al., 2011). In short, fm-theta has been proposed as a universal mechanism for EFs with the MCC acting as hub for the integration of relevant information (Cavanagh et al., 2012).

The possibility to modulate neural oscillations marks an important step beyond simply focusing on correlations between oscillations and cognitive performance. The feasibility to self-regulate endogenous neural activity has been nicely demonstrated in extracellular recordings for activity of single neurons (e.g., Olds and Olds, 1961), local field potentials (LFPs) in the animal model (e.g., Sterman et al., 1970), as well as for EEG activity measured on the scalp of humans (Kamiya, 1968). Nowadays the technique by which the modulation of neuronal activity is achieved in a reward-based fashion by giving feedback on the real-time status of the participants' brain activity who thereby learn to voluntarily control it, is termed neurofeedback (NF; Sherlin et al., 2011; Huster et al., 2014). NF-systems belong to a subclass of brain computer interfaces (BCIs) that aim at the regulation of oscillations and slow cortical potentials with EEG (Birbaumer et al., 2009) and magnetoencephalography (MEG; e.g., Sudre et al., 2011), or at the modulation of brain metabolism by functional magnetic resonance imaging (fMRI; e.g., Birbaumer et al., 2013; Ruiz et al., 2013) and near infrared spectroscopy (NIRS; e.g., Mihara et al., 2012; Kober et al., 2014). The modulation of neural oscillations by EEG-NF has been shown for diverse frequencies in association to different cognitive (sub) processes (see review of Gruzelier, 2014), for instance regarding enhanced upper alpha band and improved mental rotation (e.g., Hanslmayr et al., 2005; Zoefel et al., 2011), increased gamma-band activity and enhanced episodic retrieval (Keizer et al., 2010), or enhanced sensorimotor rhythm (SMR) and improved declarative learning (Hoedlmoser et al., 2008).

With respect to fm-theta oscillations, its basic modulability by NF has recently been demonstrated (e.g., Enriquez-Geppert et al., 2014). van Schie et al. (2014) designed a study to investigate effects of controlled fm-theta down-and up-regulation on WM performance. They demonstrated that the up-regulation led to increased, the down-regulation to attenuated performance. Concerning fm-theta NF training, positive effects on cognition have been shown for WM and attention (Wang and Hsieh, 2013). Notwithstanding this, effects of fm-theta modulation on EFs by NF remain to be elucidated.

The modulation of fm-theta by NF can be categorized within a broader framework of theta protocols. Generally, theta protocols can be performed at diverse electrode positions thereby focusing different neural networks (see review Gruzelier, 2014). A subdivision of protocols pertains to NF for theta up- or theta-downregulation. In case of the clinical application, down regulation of theta is most often combined with the modulation of other frequencies (e.g., theta-beta training, e.g., Gani et al., 2008; Arns et al., 2013), as for example seen with attention deficit hyperactivity disorder (ADHD). Here, EEG deviations have been observed during resting state compared to healthy controls, namely increased theta activity in context of beta activity (e.g., Chabot and Serfontein, 1996; Clarke et al., 2001). However, this deviation of theta measured at rest reflects a tonic condition that has to be dissociated from phasic theta responses, which in turn have been linked to specific cognitive functions. An important fact concerning the dissociation of tonic and phasic amplitude is the notion that successful behavior seems to be related to both of these EEG phenomena as good performance is related to a decrease in tonic and increased phasic theta activity (see review, Klimesch, 1999).

Taken together, NF seems perfectly suited to induce positive effects on EFs. This issue becomes imperative since EFs are crucial for success in daily life as they mediate learning processes (St Clair-Thompson et al., 2010), the control of emotions (e.g., Fikke et al., 2011), and predict academic achievement and social functioning (e.g., Miller et al., 2012b). Furthermore, age-related declines in EFs have been reported to lead to reduced success in everyday activities (Vaughan and Giovanello, 2010). Moreover, disturbances of EFs are associated with neurocognitive, and psychiatric impairments (e.g., Elliott, 2003).

The aim of this study is therefore to investigate the behavioral and neuronal effects of fm-theta NF on EFs. We set up an eight session personalized NF training for up-regulation of fm-theta and compared the achieved training effects to those of a pseudo NF training constituting an active control condition. A pre/post-test training design was implemented measuring the four most independent and representative EFs (Miyake et al., 2000; Miyake and Friedman, 2012) namely memory updating, set shifting, conflict monitoring, and motor inhibition, experimentally operationalized by a three-back, a number-letter task-switching, a Stroop-, and a stop-signal task. Concurrently, the participants' EEG was recorded. We hypothesized that NF for self-up-regulation of fm-theta would lead to enhanced performance in EFs at the behavioral level, and would also translate to enhanced fm-theta during executive functioning in the respective tasks compared to the pseudo NF group.

MATERIAL AND METHODS

PARTICIPANTS

40 students (19 men; mean age: 24.8, standard deviation: 3.3) participated in this study. Participants were pseudo-randomly assigned to the experimental (NF; n = 19, 8 men; mean age: 23.8, standard deviation: 2.7) or the active control group (pseudo-NF, n = 21, 11 men; mean age: 25.8, standard deviation: 3.8) in order to balance the groups according to age, education level and gender. All subjects were right handed, as indicated by the Edinburgh Handedness Inventory (Oldfield, 1971), and had normal or corrected to normal vision. None of them reported a history of psychiatric or neurological disorders. Before the experiment, all participants gave written consent to the protocol approved by the ethics committee of the University of Oldenburg. For study participation, participants were rewarded with 8 € per hour. The study was conducted in accordance with the Declaration of Helsinki.

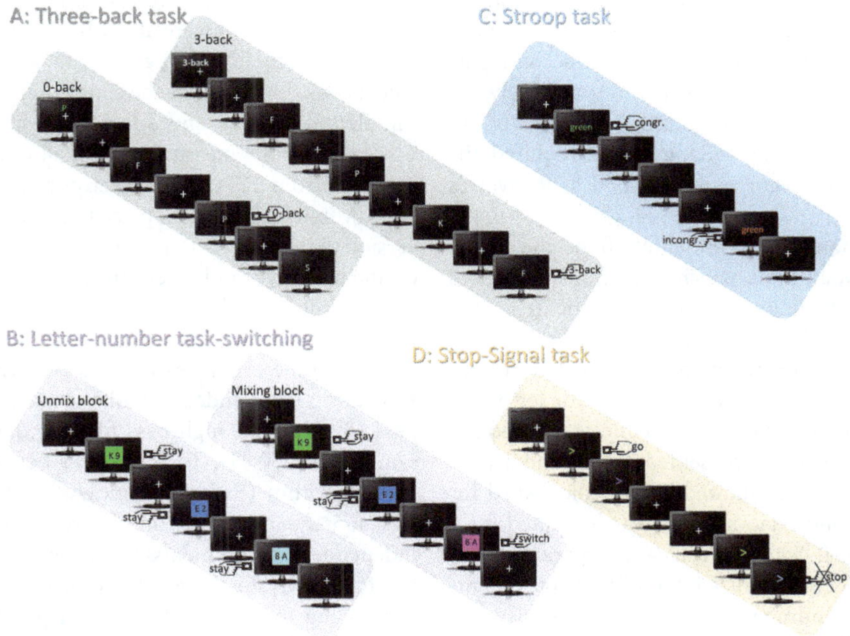

FIGURE 1 | Depicts all four tasks of the EFs test-battery. The graphic depicts the targets of each task by a left/right button-press icon. **(A)** Represents the trial sequence of the three-back tasks that consisted of the alternating presentation of the zero-back and the three-back sequence. Each sequence started with a fixation cross, above which either a green letter indicated the subjects to perform the zero-back task and to detect in the following sequence targets that matched to the green letter or above which "3-back" indicated to update every letter and to compare it to the identity of three trials before. **(B)** Represents the letter-number task switching. In the unmix-block, the colors green, blue and turquoise indicate that only one categorization task has to be performed, for instance only number categorization. In the example "unmix-block" depicted in the graphic, uneven numbers require a right hand button-press and even a left hand button-press. In the mixing-block the colors of the other category are also introduced and indicate that categorization has to be performed concerning both letters and numbers, each respectively. Thus, the third trial of the depicted example "mixing-block" requires a "switch" of number categorization to letter categorization and thereby leads to another required response, since vocals have to be responded with the right hand. **(C)** Represents the trials of the Stroop task requiring the categorization of the presentation color (e.g., right button press for presentation colors), but not the word-meaning. Consequently, although the word meaning in this example is the same, the required button-press is different because of the different presentation color of the word. **(D)** Shows exemplarily two trials of the visual stop-signal task, whereby the directions of the arrows are indicating the response side. In this example the color change into purple should be ignored, however, the change into blue indicates to stop the initiated response.

PRE-POST TRAINING DESIGN

To measure the effects of up-regulation of fm-theta on EFs, an individualized and adaptive eight session NF training was performed on consecutive working days within 2 weeks, comparing the effects to an active control group, the so-called pseudo-NF. One day before and one day after finishing the NF training, an EFs test-battery, assessing the four most important and independent EFs. The study was carried out at the Carl von Ossietzky University of Oldenburg.

Executive function test-battery, EEG recordings and preprocessing

In the first task of the EFs test-battery (see **Figure 1**), the visual three-back task, participants were presented with two kinds of letter sequences, the three-back and the zero-back sequence. In the three-back sequence, participants were instructed to respond via button press (using the right index finger), whenever a letter had already been presented three trials before the current one (three-back target condition). In the zero-back condition subjects were instructed to simply respond whenever a letter matched a target letter presented at the beginning of the letter sequence. In all other cases, participants were asked not to react. There were ten three-back and nine zero-back sequences that were presented in an alternating fashion with 24 white letters presented on a black background for 1000 ms, and followed by a fixation cross with a duration of 1000 ms (total trial length: 2000 ms; total trial number per sequence: 24; target numbers per sequence: 8). It is assumed that the three-back condition requires memory updating processes whereas the zero-back condition does not.

The number-letter task-switching consisted of number-letter pairs that were presented on a colored background. Participants were instructed to either classify the numbers (in even or odd numbers) or the letters (in vowels or consonants) by a right or left index button press. The classification depended of the specific background color (red, orange, pink vs. green, blue, and turquoise). Two versions with different number-color and letter-color assignments were utilized. Letter-number pairs were presented for 2000 ms followed by a white fixation cross presented for 1000 ms (trial length: 3000 ms). The task consisted of two parts. In the first part that included unmix-blocks, only the letters (unmix-block 1; 60 trials) had to be classified, followed by a second block during which only numbers (unmix-block 2; 60 trials) had to be processed. In the second part that included mixing blocks, participants had to switch between both classification types (trial number: 234; switches: 70). In contrast to the unmix-blocks, the mixing blocks required the switching between the two categorization tasks, thus it involves set-shifting.

The Stroop task contained the presentation of the color-words blue, green, yellow, and red, which were either presented congruently in colors matching the word meaning (e.g., the color-word "blue" presented in blue) or incongruently in an unmatching fashion (e.g., the color-word "blue" presented in red). Participants were instructed to indicate via a right or left index button press the presentation color, but not the word-color. A trial started with a fixation cross presented for a randomized duration of 1200–1400 ms, and followed by the color word for 500 ms. Afterwards a second fixation cross was presented for a randomized duration of 100–500 ms. Trials were separated by an inter-trial interval (ITI) of a randomized duration of 400–800 ms (total trial number: 128, number of incongruent trials: 64). Regarding the involved EFs, conflict-monitoring is supposed to detect the conflict associated with incongruent trials relative to the congruent condition.

In the visual stop-signal task, left- or rightward pointing arrows were presented that changed their color during presentation time from purple to green, blue, or orange. Participants were instructed to press the button of a two-button box according to the arrow direction either with the right or the left index in a fast and accurate way directly after beginning of the arrow presentation (go-trials). However, a specific color change (for instance from purple to orange) was indicating that participants had to abort their initiated response (stop-trials). Two versions with different color-response assignments were used. The timing of the color-change was adjusted dynamically via a certain stimulus onset asynchrony (SOA; Logan et al., 1997) such that participants could stop their response in 75% of the stop-trials. Every trial with a length of 2 s started with a fixation cross that was randomly set with a duration of 300–600 ms. Then, the arrow was presented with an initial duration of 250 ms (this SOA was adjusted by adding 50 ms after every second correct or subtracting 50 ms after every failed stop trial to reach the intended error rate) before the color changed. The color change remained on screen for another 200 ms. The trial was ended with the presentation of a fixation cross (total number of trials: 300; number of stop trials: 100). The stop-trials of this task require motor inhibition as EFs, in contrast to motor execution during go-trials.

Before each task, a short exercise period was implemented to familiarize participants with the task requirements and the presentation. The four tasks each had a duration of roughly eight to 18 min. All four EFs tasks were implemented using the Presentation software[1].

The measurements of the EFs test-battery, as well as the NF training, were conducted in an electrically shielded and sound attenuated room. EEG recordings were done using the Brain Vision Recorder software and a Brain Amp EEG amplifier (Brain Products GmbH, Filching, Germany). Electrode impendences were kept below 5 kΩ for the continuous EEG recording, data was sampled at 500 Hz, and a low-pass online filter of 250 Hz was used. During the measurement of all four EFs, EEG activity was recorded from 32 Ag/AgCl electrodes (Easycap, Falk Minov Services, Munich, Germany), placed in accordance with the extended version of the international 10–20 system, with a nose electrode as online reference, and an electrode attached beneath the right eye for recording the electrooculogram (EOG) and quantification of ocular artifacts.

The offline-preprocessing was performed using the EEGLAB software[2] and included the following steps. First, data were low-pass (80 Hz) and high-pass filtered (0.5 Hz), and then down-sampled to 250 Hz. To correct for ocular artifact, the Infomax ICA algorithm (Bell and Sejnowski, 1995; Makeig et al., 2004) was subsequently used on the continuous data. Blink-related independent components (ICs) were identified by comparing the IC activity to the eye blink artifacts in the EOG. The corresponding topographical maps of putative ICs had to show a frontal distribution. Eye-blink related ICs were then excluded from back-projection to the EEG channels. Afterwards, stimulus-locked epochs were computed comprising an interval of −1250 to +1250 ms corresponding to the stimulus presentation. Trials were then baseline-corrected. To correct for residual artifacts, a semi-automatic correction procedure was used based on the epoched data. Thereby single trials that crossed a self-set threshold (set to 60 μV) were marked automatically for visual inspection and rejection. Thereby 5.3 epochs were rejected on average per condition and task. Incorrect responses were discarded from further analyses.

Afterwards, so-called event-related spectral perturbations (ERSPs) were calculated for each task that represent log-transformed changes of power in dB relative to the baseline (Delorme and Makeig, 2004). For this time-frequency decomposition, a sinusoidal wavelet transform, using an increasing number of cycles with increasing frequency was used (range: 1–50 Hz; starting with 1 cycle at 1 Hz and increasing by 0.5 Hz per frequency; using 300 frequency steps). To visualize power changes relative to the pre-stimulus activity, the average power across the trials was divided by the frequency specific baseline values separately for each frequency. Mean ERSP values were calculated for the fm ROI over electrodes Fz, FC1, FC2, Cz.

Individualized and adaptive neurofeedback training

For up-regulating fm-theta by NF, eight 30-minutes training sessions were conducted. Because it was shown that fm-theta exhibits large inter-individual variability, but high intra-individual stability (e.g., Näpflin et al., 2008), a procedure for the detection of the individual fm-theta peak was used. Thus, the dominant individual fm-theta frequency peak was estimated based on the average of four peaks (+/−1 Hz), detected by the ERSPs computed from the four EF tasks. Fm-theta was shown to fall

[1] Version 14.8, www.neurobs.com

[2] freely available from http://www.sccn.ucsd.edu/eeglab/

into the time range of the N200/P300 complex (Huster et al., 2013), as well as fm-negativities (Huster et al., 2013), and furthermore to have a maximum at Fz (Ishihara et al., 1981; Cavanagh et al., 2012). Thus, the individual fm-theta frequency was determined from electrode Fz, between 4–8 Hz in the corresponding ERP time range of conditions requiring EFs. Each of the eight NF sessions furthermore consisted of six five-minute blocks of NF with self-paced breaks in-between. Before and after these blocks, a five minute start/end-baseline was measured to assess resting state activity. Frequency spectra were computed using a fast Fourier transformation and a hamming window for data segments of 2 s, shifted along the data in steps of 200 ms. For NF, the software NF Suite 1.0 (Huster et al., 2014) was used.

In the following, all five steps of the basic set-up for NF (Huster et al., 2014), forming the real-time processing pipeline, are described. First, the data acquisition was based on five electrodes placed at positions Fz, FC1, FC2, FCz, and Cz, thus covering the fm-brain region, with the nose as reference, and Fp1 and Fp2 for monitoring ocular activity. Before the start-baseline measurement, an EOG calibration method (3 min) was implemented that calculates the subject-specific, artifact-associated frequency band. This was used for all following measurements for eye blink detection and rejection during further measurements (for details see Huster et al., 2014). The second step refers to the data online-preprocessing. A crucial feature of this step is the monitoring of artifacts, specifically that of eye activity. This technique is important to avoid falsely modulating eye- rather than actual brain activity, since the power of eye activity unfolds in several frequency bands. Thus, the subject-specific artifact-associated frequency band that was calculated in the EOG calibration measure was monitored. Whenever the mean amplitudes of a 2 s segment was higher than the subject-specific artifact-associated frequency band (minus one standard deviation), the segment was rejected and not used for feedback. Third, for feature generation and selection, the raw power value of each 2 s segment for the individualized fm-theta frequency was compared to the baseline power of the same frequency. Fourth, to feed back the extracted feature to the participant, a visual procedure was used in form of a visual display of a colored square (range: highly saturated red over gray to highly saturated blue, each with 40 color steps). The color saturation depended on the fm-theta activity changes, and was updated every 200 ms. The color red indicated an fm-theta power increase, blue a decrease, and gray either an eye blink or no power change relative to the start-baseline of the specific NF session. The feedback saturation scale enclosed 95% of the amplitude range, whereby values above 97.5% or below 2.5% were indicated by a maximum red or blue saturation. Fifth, participants were instructed to color the square as red and as often as possible. To do so, they received a list of strategies based on the NF literature and were encouraged to find own self-invented strategies.

Participants of the pseudo-NF were matched to participants of the actual NF group according to age and gender. During a NF block, they received a playback of the same session and block of their matched participant. Thereby, both groups received a similar visual stimulation. To enhance the credibility of the pseudo manipulation, participants of the pseudo-NF received real feedback of their own eyeblink activity, by haltering the feedback replay and introducing the gray color feedback as it is done in the actual NF group.

DATA ANALYSIS

NF training effects

To analyze the self-upregulation of the individual fm-theta (ind-fm-th) by NF, the relative change of the fm-theta amplitude was quantified for all training sessions during training blocks as change in percent relative to the values of the first training session. This procedure was chosen because it minimizes some of the inter-subject variability caused by unspecific effects such as amplitude variability due to the visual stimulation during feedback. Thus, this specific calculation has the advantage to compare fm-theta increases relative to a condition in which subjects are also up-regulating their brain activity, but with lower success, thereby making sure that the same system or process is engaged. However, as a drawback, it attenuates some of the relevant inter-group variance (by essentially removing training effects of the first session), therefore reducing the likelihood to find a group by session interaction. Correspondingly, a main effect is expected, as the dependent variable represents a difference measure, indicating that proper NF induces increased fm-theta not seen with the pseudo-NF training. Consequently, NF training effects were investigated by a repeated-measures ANOVA with the factors SESSION (2–8) and GROUP (NF vs. pseudo-NF group). These calculations and analyzes were also performed for the alpha (ind-fm-th + 2 Hz to ind-fm-th + 7 Hz) and beta (ind-fm-th + 7 Hz to ind-fm-th + 15 Hz) frequency bands. In case of violations of sphericity, Greenhouse-Geisser corrections were performed, and corrected p-values and ϵ-values are reported.

Data analysis: behavioral performance of executive function tasks

To investigate transfer effects of NF training on cognitive performance, mean RT and mean accuracy of correct responses were calculated for all conditions of the four EFs tasks, namely for the three-back vs. zero-back conditions of the three-back task; the unmix vs. stay vs. switch conditions of the letter number task-switching task, the congruent vs. incongruent conditions of the Stroop-task, and the go vs. stop conditions of the stop-signal task. Extreme values exceeding the mean by more than 2.5 standard deviations were excluded for statistical analyses. To investigate performance gains after NF training, performance differences between pre- and post measurements were calculated for all the conditions of the four EF tasks. A stronger performance gain was expected in conditions requiring EFs. In other words, concerning the three-back task, performance gains are expected after NF in the three-back condition, because for this condition a higher load of memory-updating is involved compared to the zero-back condition (larger effects in NF compared to pseudo-NF training). Similarly, larger effects were expected in the stay and switch conditions compared to the unmix condition after NF-training relative to the pseudo-NF training. Likewise, stronger performance gains regarding conflict monitoring were expected after NF in the incongruent compared to the congruent condition of the Stroop task. Finally, behavioral performance gains were expected in the stop condition as reflected in reduced SSRT after proper NF. Thus, pre-post measurement differences were tested for by means of independent-samples t-tests comparing the training and the control group. To examine the range of significant results, Cohen's d (Cohen, 1988) was calculated for the pretest-posttest differences or the standardized mean difference in performance between pre- and post measurements (the difference was divided by the pooled standard deviation for the measurements occasions) for each group and corrected for small sample bias using the Hedges and Olkin (Hedges and Olkin, 1985) correction factor (d') only for significant results. As result, a pre-post measurement effect size (ES) of $d' = 1$ reflects a mean difference between pre-and post-measurements of one standard deviation.

Data analysis: effects of NF training on fm-theta in executive functions tasks

For the evaluation of NF effects on fm-theta during the four EFs tasks, ERSP values were extracted for the time range used for the detection of the individual fm-theta peaks (three-back task: 100–300 ms, number/letter task-switching: 100–300 ms, Stroop: 220–500 ms, stop-signal task: 300–500 ms) and the theta frequency range of 4–8 Hz. These values were then averaged for each condition, task and subject. Then, difference scores were calculated by subtracting the values before from values after training: (pre-post difference of letter number task-switching, the congruent and incongruent pre-post-differences of the Stroop-task, and the go and stop pre-post-differences of the stop-signal task. To investigate if these difference scores differed significantly between the NF and the pseudo-NF group, a MANOVA with the above-mentioned pre-post-difference scores as dependent variables and GROUP (NF vs. pseudo-NF group) as independent variable was run.

RESULTS

NF TRAINING EFFECTS

NF training effects on the fm-theta amplitude are depicted in **Figure 2**. The repeated-measures ANOVA resulted in a main effect of SESSION ($F_{(4.346,39)} = 6.487$, $\epsilon = 0.724$, $p < 0.001$) showing that every training session let to a change in fm-theta self-upregulation. The further expected main effect was the GROUP ($F_{(6,39)} = 6.225$, $p < 0.05$) effect, demonstrating the validity of the experimental manipulation resulting in stronger enhancements of activity in the NF group regarding fm-theta amplitude, starting already at the second training session when compared to the pseudo-NF group.

Regarding the alpha range, a trend for a main effect of SESSION ($F_{(6,37)} = 8.173$, $p < 0.1$) was observed, no further effects were detected. Similarly, within the beta frequency range also only a trend for the main effect of SESSION ($F_{(6,37)} = 3.157$, $\epsilon = 0.308$, $p < 0.1$) was observed.

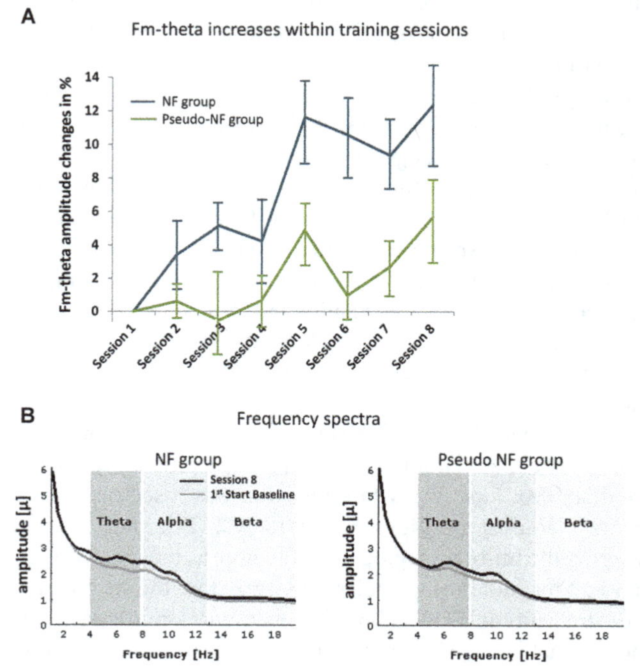

FIGURE 2 | shows frequency effects during NF. (A) Depicts the means of fm-theta increases of the NF (blue lines) and the pseudo-NF group (green) within the eight training sessions (error bars represent standard error of mean). In **(B)** the frequency spectra are shown for the start baseline measure of the first session (in gray) and during the last training session (S8, black) for each group (left side: NF, right side: pseudo-NF group). Unspecific alpha effects are observed in both groups, whereas fm-theta is specifically increased in the experimental group.

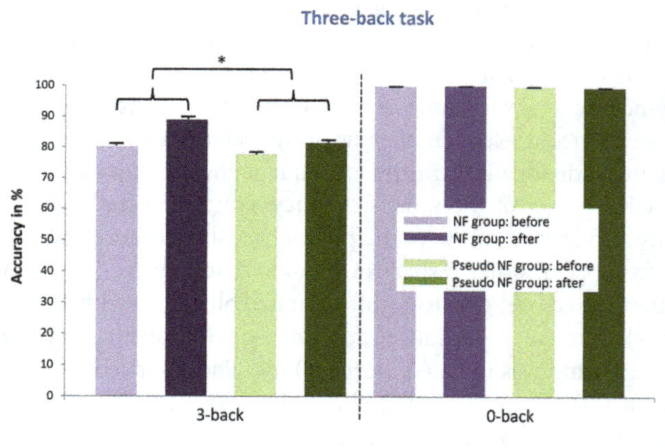

FIGURE 3 | Provides the mean accuracy scores (and standard error of mean) in the three-back task of the NF group (left) and the pseudo-NF group (right) for each condition (three-back vs. zero-back) before and after the training intervention. Significant differences (marked with a star) between accuracy enhancements (pre- post differences as depicted with curly brackets) were detected in the three-back condition between both groups showing stronger improvements after proper NF training.

BEHAVIORAL PERFORMANCE IN EXECUTIVE FUNCTIONS TASKS

The results of the pre- and post measurements (RTs and accuracy) are shown in **Figures 3–6** computed from correct responses of all conditions for the three-back, task-switch, Stroop-, and stop-signal tasks for both training types (NF and pseudo-NF). Descriptively, these figures hint to behavioral changes, particularly in the three-back and task-switching tasks. Although these enhancements are more pronounced in the NF group, behavioral

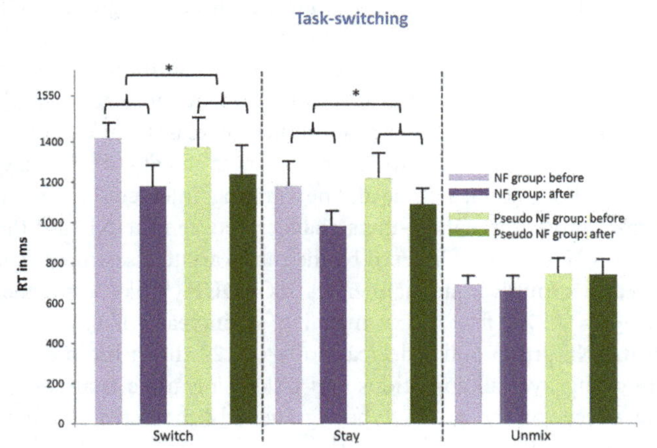

FIGURE 4 | Shows the behavioral results of the task-switching (mean RT and standard error of mean) for the NF group (left) and the pseudo-NF group (right) for all three conditions (unmix, stay, switch) before and after the training intervention. Significant differences (pre-post differences as depicted with curly brackets) are marked with stars and are depicted between both groups as training results. Stronger enhanced RTs can be observed for the NF group in the stay and switch condition.

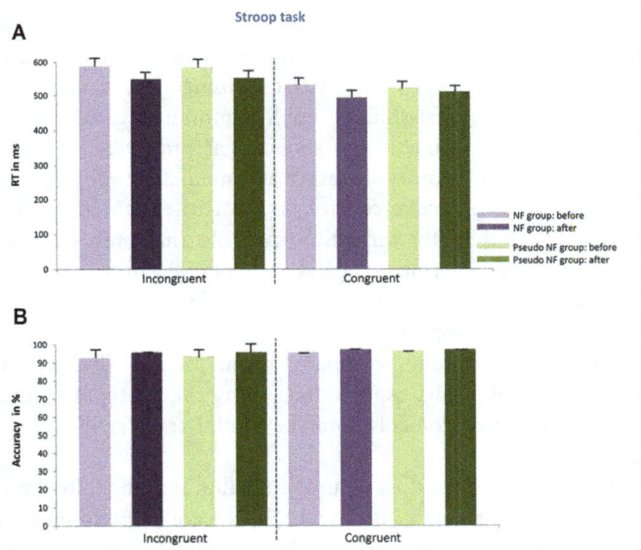

FIGURE 5 | Depicts the behavioral results of the Stroop task (mean RT in (A), accuracy scores in (B) including standard error of mean) for the NF group (left) and the pseudo-NF group (right) for both conditions (congruent, incongruent) before and after the training intervention. No behavioral differences between groups can be observed as a result of the training intervention neither concerning RTs nor accuracy scores.

changes appear also in the pseudo-NF group. However, any study that is using a pre-post design has to expect repetition-related effects that may simply arise from repeatedly testing a task. Such unspecific repetition-related effects are particularly well known in behavioral training studies and are found in all subjects, for instance in task-switching (e.g., Karbach and Kray, 2009) or three-back tasks (e.g., Schneiders et al., 2011). Therefore, the utilization of a control group is urgently needed

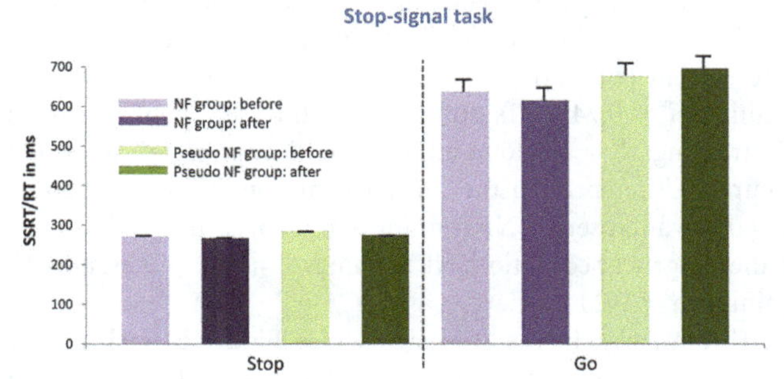

FIGURE 6 | Presents the mean RTs or the SSRT (as well as the standard error of mean) of the stop signal task for the NF group (left) and the pseudo-NF group (right) for the go and stop condition before and after the training intervention. No performance differences between groups due to the intervention were shown.

to dissociate such repetition-related or non-specific effects from true enhancements of cognitive functions, which in turn are reflected in stronger improvements in the intervention group than in the control group (Campbell and Stanley, 1963; Oken et al., 2008).

Concerning the three-back task, the expected stronger increases in accuracy was statistically confirmed in the three-back condition ($t_{(38)} = 1.786$; $p < 0.05$) after proper NF training when compared to the pseudo-NF training; such effects were absent in the zero-back condition (see **Figure 3**). These results were supported by the pretest-posttest ES. ES were larger after NF training (three-back: $d' = 1.059$) than after pseudo-NF training (three-back: $d' = 0.346$). For the zero-back condition, the following ES are reported (NF training: $d' = -0.076$; pseudo-NF training: $d' = -0.494$).

I. As expected, stronger RT decreases were observed in the switch condition ($t_{(38)} = 1.966$; $p < 0.05$), and in the stay condition ($t_{(38)} = 1.695$; $p < 0.05$) after proper NF training as compared to the pseudo intervention (see **Figure 4**). No differences were found for neither the unmix condition ($t_{(38)} = 1.036$; p = n.s.) between both training types nor for accuracy scores (switch: $t_{(38)} = 1.633$; p = n.s.; stay $t_{(38)} = -1.651$; p = n.s. unmix: $t_{(38)} = -0.388$; p = n.s.). These results were supported by the pretest-posttest ES. For both, switch and stay conditions, EF were larger after NF training (switch: $d' = 1.67$; stay: $d' = 1.09$) than after pseudo-NF training (switch: $d' = 0.582$; stay: $d' = 0.649$). However, no differences in performance gains were shown in accuracy (switch: $t_{(38)} = 1.633$, p = n.s.; stay: $t_{(38)} = -1.651$, p = n.s.). ES for the unmix condition were the following, NF training: $d' = -0.408$ and pseudo-NF training: $d' = -0.063$, (the ES for differences in accuracy scores are also given subsequently, NF training: switch $d' = 0.607$, stay $d' = 0.718$, unmix $d' = 0.091$; pseudo-NF training: switch $d' = 0.879$, stay $d' = 0.929$ unmix $d' = 0.142$).

II. Different from what was expected, no differences were observed when comparing NF to pseudo-NF training regarding the Stroop task, neither concerning RTs (incongruent: $t_{(34)} = 0.247$, p = n.s.; congruent: $t_{(38)} = 0.142$, p = n.s.) nor accuracy (incongruent: $t_{(38)} = 0.989$, p = n.s.; incongruent: $t_{(38)} = 0.81$,

p = n.s.), see **Figure 5**. Similarly, low ES values were recorded for the NF and the pseudo-NF training (RTs differences in the incongruent condition: NF training: $d' = 0.337$ and pseudo-NF training: $d' = 0.749$; RTs differences in the congruent condition: NF training: $d' = -0.469$ and pseudo-NF training: $d' = -0.143$; accuracy differences in the incongruent condition: NF training $d' = 0.846$ and pseudo-NF training $d' = 0.55$; accuracy differences in the congruent condition: NF training: $d' = 0.42$ and pseudo-NF training: $d' = 0.244$).

III. Similarly, in the stop-signal (see **Figure 6**) task no differences were observed comparing the pre-post difference of the NF- and the pseudo-NF-training groups neither concerning SSRTs of the stop condition ($t_{(38)} = -1.558$, p = n.s.) nor RTs of the go-condition ($t_{(36)} = 1.65$, p = n.s.). Accordingly, low ES scores were registered: differences in the stop condition: NF training $d' = 0.159$, pseudo-NF training $d' = 1.147$; differences in the go condition: NF training $d' = 0.159$, pseudo-NF training $d' = 0.147$.

EFFECTS OF NF ON FM-THETA IN EXECUTIVE FUNCTION TASKS

In the following, a descriptive overview will be given for each task and group before and after the training; thereafter the fm-theta effects will be reported, as computed within the multivariate analysis framework.

I. Irrespective of group, power enhancements can especially be observed in the delta and theta frequency range around 300 ms post stimulus onset, accompanied by power reductions in the beta and slight power enhancements in the gamma range in the three-back condition of the three-back task (see **Figure 7**), which are in agreement with those obtained by e.g., Pesonen et al. (2007). Slight frequency changes can be observed in both groups after training.

II. The ERSPs in the task-switching task before and after the training intervention are characterized by a distinct theta-alpha power enhancement at around 200 ms, accompanied by weaker effects with a similar time pattern in the beta and gamma frequency range with a duration of approximately 100 ms, in accordance with previous studies as Prada et al. (2014). In the subsequent time frame, the power enhancement of theta and delta remains stable and the beta power reduction (20 Hz) becomes apparent.

III. To turn to the ERSPs in the Stroop task, here theta and beta power enhancement effects are observed corresponding with prior finding in literature (e.g., Cavanagh et al., 2012) beginning at 180 ms, whereby the theta power enhancement becomes maximal at 300 ms and remains stable until the end of the analyses time window. Minor frequency changes can visually be detected after the training intervention for both groups.

IV. With respect to the stop-signal task, maximal theta power enhancements are detected starting at about 220 ms till 600 ms post stimulus, consistent with those reported in the review of Huster et al. (2013), these power enhancements are very similar before and after training.

V. To inspect training induced changes in fm-theta more closely, pre-post fm-theta difference scores, representing changes in fm-theta power after training compared to the initial power before training, are depicted in **Figure 7** (lower panels of A–D) for each EF condition of the four EFs task and groups (NF and pseudo-NF group). As can be seen in **Figure 7**, fm-theta is decreasing in the pseudo-NF group after the control intervention (an exception is the congruent condition in the Stroop task), whereas the NF group shows amplitude increases. An exception is the stop-signal task, in which the fm-theta activity was decreasing for both groups. Indeed, the training intervention led to significantly different fm-theta changes between the NF and the pseudo-NF group as indexed by the multivariate assessment that revealed a multivariate main effect of GROUP (Wilks' $\lambda = 0.468$, $F_{(9,25)} = 2.774$, $p < 0.05$), meaning an increase of 0.0036 dB in the NF group and a decrease of -0.2122 dB in the pseudo-NF group over all conditions and tasks. Univariate analyses for the effects of the group type significantly predicted fm-theta changes in the three-back task, such as significant fm-theta reductions were observed in the zero-back condition ($p < 0.05$) in the pseudo-NF group. A trend ($p < 0.1$) was furthermore observed within the univariate analyses for the prediction of group type concerning fm-theta power changes in the incongruent condition.

DISCUSSION

Since fm-theta has been proposed as neural "working language" of brain communication for EFs, the current study investigated the effects of an individualized and adaptive eight session NF training to up-regulate fm-theta compared to a pseudo-NF intervention by utilizing a pre/post-test training design, analyzing memory updating, set-shifting, conflict monitoring, and motor inhibition. As a result, it was shown that proper NF training led to facilitated memory updating and mental set shifting, two EFs relying on proactive control, but not to enhanced conflict monitoring and motor inhibition, two EFs that built on reactive control. Furthermore, analyses of neural effects after NF training demonstrated that learning to self-upregulate fm-theta during NF translated to fm-theta changes in tasks engaging EFs after proper training compared to the pseudo-NF intervention. In the following, aspects concerning the subtypes of EFs, the fm-theta NF protocols, and the neural transfer effects are discussed.

With regard to the dual nature of the findings, the differential NF training effects of this fm-theta NF protocol on EFs reflect the current qualitative distinction of cognitive control mechanisms into proactive and reactive control. Indeed, a dual mechanisms framework (DMS; Braver, 2012) has been suggested that works by means of these two distinct operating modes that probably differ concerning their temporal dynamics and relevant neural networks. As such, within the DMS, proactive control is conceptualized as an anticipatory mechanism, actively maintaining task goals that serve as a source of top-down bias, thus supporting facilitated processing of expected events with a high cognitive demand before they actually occur. For instance, in the three-back task, subjects can process upcoming targets by subvocally repeating the sequence they have to keep in WM, and comparing it with their mental representation of the target stimulus. In contrast, reactive control is conceptualized as a reactive bottom-up mechanism that is recruited only when it is required, for instance when interference is detected by a conflict monitoring

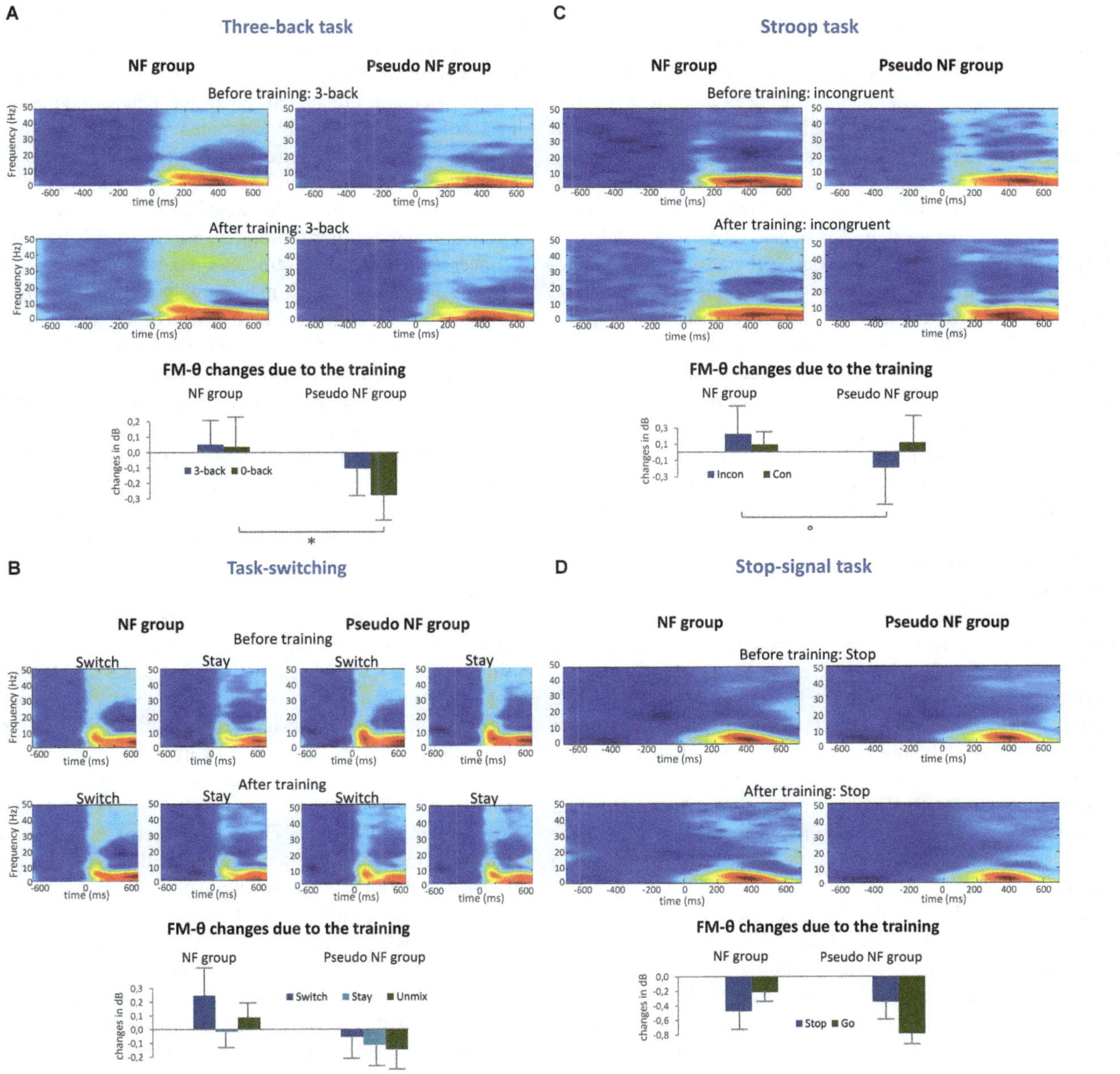

FIGURE 7 | Provides the mean ERSPs before and after training, as well as the extracted fm-theta changes (and standard error of mean) for all conditions as bar charts for the three-back condition in the three-back task (A), the switch and stay condition of the task-switching (B), the incongruent condition of the Stroop task (C), and the stop condition of the stop-signal task (D), significant univariate results are marked with a star, trends with a circle.

system or when a stop-signal requires the inhibition of an initiated response as is the case with the Stroop and the stop-signal tasks.

Interestingly, although all EFs, regardless of whether they require proactive or reactive control mechanisms, recruit the superordinate cognitive control network (Niendam et al., 2012), the subtypes seem to rely on different sub-networks. Menon (2011) distinguishes the central executive network, a fronto-parietal system, anchored in the dorsolateral prefrontal cortex (DLPFC) and lateral posterior parietal cortex (PPC), crucially involved in actively maintaining task goals, from the salience network, a cingulate-frontal-opercular system, reacting to detected task events. Similarly, Dosenbach et al. (2008) proposes a dual-network architecture for EFs based on graph analytic methods, differentiating the fronto-parietal from a cingulo-opercular network, implementing proactive and reactive cognitive control, respectively.

From the lack of behavioral effects in the Stroop- and stop-signal tasks, one might be tempted to conclude that fm-theta is not necessarily crucial for the implementation of reactive control. Yet, the current fm-theta protocol of this study might have primarily targeted fm-theta used in the proactive control network and might less effectively address the network implementing reactive control, as fm-theta might primarily affect the detection signals generated in the MCC and less the resolution activity or the compensatory mechanisms processed in other brain regions of the EFs network (Botvinick et al., 2004). Indeed, fm-theta is thought to enable the transmission of information over different cortical brain areas by entraining activity in disparate neural systems (Cavanagh and Frank, 2014). More precisely, the properties of theta oscillations showing high-amplitude-low-frequency modulations denote an ideal neural parameter for neural organization over distal brain regions (Buzsáki and Draguhn, 2004). Theta phase synchrony between the MCC and distal brain regions has been observed in different studies on EFs, such as the study of Cohen and Cavanagh (2011), who reported of single-trial phase synchrony between the MCC and lateral prefrontal brain areas that was modulated by RTs during conflict monitoring. Nigbur et al. (2011) presented enhanced synchrony in the theta range between fronto-medial and lateral frontal electrode sites, interpreted as cooperated work to allocate control during conflict monitoring, as well as between fronto-medial electrode sites with those over the contra-lateral motor area during conflict monitoring, possibly reflecting the renewed need of response selection during conflicts. Just recently, Oehrn et al. demonstrated by means of intra-cranial recordings that fm-theta originated from MCC as conflict detection signal, causally leading to entrained theta in the DLPFC, and finally accomplishing a coupling between DLPFC-gamma power and MCC oscillations for conflict resolution (Oehrn et al., 2014). Ultimately, accounting for the dual nature of EFs provides potentially new avenues for more elaborative feature extraction procedures concerning fm-theta NF protocols.

Apart from the beneficial behavioral effects of proactive control, the current study revealed an overall alteration of fm-theta in EF-tasks after proper NF training as compared to the active control intervention. This finding generally demonstrates that the targeted EF network has been affected by fm-theta NF. However, one would have expected EF-specific fm-theta effects in the proactive tasks to be paralleled by the above described behavioral effects. When looking more specifically at the neural effects, this does not seem to be the case, since results demonstrate that fm-theta effects between the proper NF group and the active control group are detected in the non EF-condition of memory updating, whereas no differences in fm-theta changes were found between both groups with task-switching. Although both the behavioral and the neural findings are interesting in itself, one should keep in mind that only one of the possible neural parameters, namely the fm-theta amplitude, has been assessed. It is conceivable that the fm-theta NF training could have influenced other neural parameters, such as coherence, frequency-coupling, or even myelination, paralleling the behavioral effects in proactive control in a more consistent way. The behavioral effects observed in proactive control could also correspond to structural changes within axonal pathways of relevant networks (e.g., changes in the integrity of white matter or the velocity of conductivity). In fact, glance at the EEG-NF literature indicates that the neural mechanisms underlying NF and putative transfer effects to neurocognition are still not well understood. Little is known about which specific network elements are changed and how the elements are altered due to NF. Behavioral performance increases aren't necessarily associated with increases in neural activity; rather, reduced neural activity may also result from stimulus and task repetition (see review Grill-Spector et al., 2006). Furthermore, associations between behavioral task proficiency and neural activity after training do not necessarily have to follow a linear function. For example, domain-proficient relative to domain-naive participants may show lower neural activity with simple tasks, but stronger neural processing with higher task difficulty (e.g., Prat and Just, 2011; Dunst et al., 2014). Hence, complex interactions of repetition-related performance changes, training-induced changes in neural responding and behavior, and task difficulty may exist.

Those functional and structural studies, on neural mechanism mediating behavioral improvements, undertaken so far either focus: (a) on immediate and long-lasting functional EEG effects, (b) on immediate fMRI effects and network activity; and finally (c) on long-lasting structural effects found in white matter pathways, usually examined via diffusion tensor imaging (DTI). For instance, Egner and Gruzelier (2001, 2004) were among the first to study neural changes induced by NF by using a protocol to increase activity in the 12–18 Hz frequency range. In their study EEG training effects were accompanied by improved attention. More importantly, after NF an increase of the oddball P300 was detected and interpreted as indicator for improved neural integration of relevant environmental stimuli. In order to investigate immediate neural effects after NF, Ros et al. (2010) examined possible changes of motor evoked potentials (MEP) by means of transcranial magnetic stimulation (TMS) to assess variations in the strength of neurotransmission from the motor cortex to the muscle. By using two types of TMS protocols (single vs. paired pulses), they could dissociate increases in cortico-spinal excitability (CSE), short-interval intra-cortical inhibition (SICI), and intra-cortical facilitation (ICF). This way, Ros et al. (2010) demonstrated that down-regulation of alpha oscillations, considered as a marker of cortical activation, indeed led to increased CSE and decreases of SICI. Similar increases of SICI were recently reported after completion of a 20 session theta/beta training (Studer et al., 2014). Here as well, a decreased P300 observed in the Attention Network Test (ANT) was considered to indicate increased efficiency of stimulus processing. Later on, Ros et al. (2013) conducted an independent component analysis (ICA) of brain activity recorded via fMRI during an oddball task to identify functionally coupled brain regions and to assess putative connectivity changes directly after a single session NF intervention. Immediately after alpha down-regulation, increased activation of brain regions belonging to the salience network were detected, namely within the MCC, the bilateral insular, thalamic, basal ganglia, cerebellar and ponto-mesencephalic regions. Structural changes after NF were assessed by DTI by Ghaziri et al. (2013) after a 3 months beta up-regulation training that resulted in enhanced sustained attention as evidenced in behavioral measures. Interestingly, microstructural changes were observed in three white matter pathways that are part of the sustained attention network, namely the cingulum bundle (a tract connecting the MCC with the DLPFC and the PPC), the anterior corona radiata (connecting the frontal cortex with the brainstem), and the splenium of the corpus callosum (a tract supporting inter-hemispheric processing), which seem not only to speak for enhanced neural transmission, but for increased myelination and faster conduction velocity (CV) underlying improved performance triggered by NF.

Regarding the relation between NF and myelination, participants learn to change oscillatory activity by recruiting and synchronizing the activity of neurons in a specific brain region, which again may affect myelination that preferable takes place at electrically active axons (e.g., Demerens et al., 1996; Ishibashi et al., 2006; Fields, 2010; Wake et al., 2011). Myelin plasticity has been furthermore suggested as an experience and learning dependent mechanisms (Wang and Young, 2014), which is thought to be relevant throughout adulthood (Miller et al., 2012a). Overall, myelin plasticity seems to crucially reflect an important lifelong process of relevance for oscillatory activity and cross-regional coupling (e.g., Pajevic et al., 2014; O'Rourke et al., 2014), and thus may also represent important mechanisms underlying NF-induced neural modulations.

Altogether, self-regulation of endogenous fm-theta increases capacities of EFs and represent a feasible neuroscientific training approach. Theta protocols may also be adapted according to the specific needs of the participants, with a focus on enhancing general EFs or proactive and reactive subtypes, in neurological and psychiatric disorders. Given that age-related changes of fm-theta seem to be related to EFs declines in age (Kardos et al., 2014), fm-theta NF protocols may also serve as an ideal tool to decelerate aging effects.

REFERENCES

Arns, M., Conners, C. K., and Kraemer, H. C. (2013). A decade of EEG theta/beta ratio research in ADHD: a meta-analysis. *J. Atten. Disord.* 17, 374–383. doi: 10.1177/1087054712460087

Basar, E., and Güntekin, B. (2008). A review of brain oscillations in cognitive disorders and the role of neurotransmitters. *Brain Res.* 1235, 172–193. doi: 10.1016/j.brainres.2008.06.103

Beckmann, M., Johansen-Berg, H., and Rushworth, M. F. S. (2009). Connectivity-based parcellation of human cingulate cortex and its relation to functional specialization. *J. Neurosci.* 29, 1175–1190. doi: 10.1523/jneurosci.3328-08.2009

Bell, A. J., and Sejnowski, T. J. (1995). An information-maximization approach to blind separation and blind deconvolution. *Neural Comput.* 7, 1129–1159. doi: 10.1162/neco.1995.7.6.1129

Birbaumer, N., Ramos Murguialday, A., Weber, C., and Montoya, P. (2009). Neurofeedback and brain-computer interface clinical applications. *Int. Rev. Neurobiol.* 86, 107–117. doi: 10.1016/S0074-7742(09)86008-X

Birbaumer, N., Ruiz, S., and Sitaram, R. (2013). Learned regulation of brain metabolism. *Trends Cogn. Sci.* 17, 295–302. doi: 10.1016/j.tics.2013.04.009

Botvinick, M. M., Cohen, J. D., and Carter, C. S. (2004). Conflict monitoring and anterior cingulate cortex: an update. *Trends Cogn. Sci.* 8, 539–546. doi: 10.1016/j.tics.2004.10.003

Braver, T. S. (2012). The variable nature of cognitive control: a dual mechanisms framework. *Trends Cogn. Sci.* 16, 106–113. doi: 10.1016/j.tics.2011.12.010

Buzsáki, G. (2006). *Rhythms of the Brain.* Oxford, NY: Oxford University Press.

Buzsáki, G., and Draguhn, A. (2004). Neuronal oscillations in cortical networks. *Science* 304, 1926–1929. doi: 10.1126/science.1099745

Buzsáki, G., Logothetis, N., and Singer, W. (2013). Scaling brain size, keeping timing: evolutionary preservation of brain rhythms. *Neuron* 80, 751–764. doi: 10.1016/j.neuron.2013.10.002

Campbell, D. T., and Stanley, J. C. (1963). *Experimental and Quasi-Experimental Designs for Research.* Chicago: Rand McNally, 84.

Canolty, R. T., Edwards, E., Dalal, S. S., Soltani, M., Nagarajan, S. S., Kirsch, H. E., et al. (2006). High gamma power is phase-locked to theta oscillations in human neocortex. *Science* 313, 1626–1628. doi: 10.1126/science.1128115

Cavanagh, J. F., and Frank, M. J. (2014). Frontal theta as a mechanism for cognitive control. *Trends Cogn. Sci.* 18, 414–421. doi: 10.1016/j.tics.2014.04.012

Cavanagh, J. F., Zambrano-Vazquez, L., and Allen, J. J. B. (2012). Theta lingua franca: a common mid-frontal substrate for action monitoring processes. *Psychophysiology* 49, 220–238. doi: 10.1111/j.1469-8986.2011.01293.x

Chabot, R. J., and Serfontein, G. (1996). Quantitative electroencephalographic profiles of children with attention deficit disorder. *Biol. Psychiatry* 40, 951–963. doi: 10.1016/0006-3223(95)00576-5

Clarke, A. R., Barry, R. J., McCarthy, R., and Selikowitz, M. (2001). EEG-defined subtypes of children with attention-deficit/hyperactivity disorder. *Clin. Neurophysiol.* 112, 2098–2105. doi: 10.1016/s1388-2457(01)00668-x

Cohen, J. (1988). *Statistical Power Analysis for The Behavioral Sciences.* 2nd Edn. Hillsdale, N.J.: L. Erlbaum Associates.

Cohen, M. X., and Cavanagh, J. F. (2011). Single-trial regression elucidates the role of prefrontal theta oscillations in response conflict. *Front. Psychol.* 2:30. doi: 10.3389/fpsyg.2011.00030

Cohen, M. X., and Donner, T. H. (2013). Midfrontal conflict-related theta-band power reflects neural oscillations that predict behavior. *J. Neurophysiol.* 110, 2752–2763. doi: 10.1152/jn.00479.2013

Delorme, A., and Makeig, S. (2004). EEGLAB: an open source toolbox for analysis of single-trial EEG dynamics including independent component analysis. *J. Neurosci. Methods* 134, 9–21. doi: 10.1016/j.jneumeth.2003.10.009

Demerens, C., Stankoff, B., Logak, M., Anglade, P., Allinquant, B., Couraud, F., et al. (1996). Induction of myelination in the central nervous system by electrical activity. *Proc. Natl. Acad. Sci. U S A* 93, 9887–9892.

Donkers, F. C. L., Schwikert, S. R., Evans, A. M., Cleary, K. M., Perkins, D. O., and Belger, A. (2011). Impaired neural synchrony in the theta frequency range in adolescents at familial risk for schizophrenia. *Front. Psychiatry* 2:51. doi: 10.3389/fpsyt.2011.00051

Dosenbach, N. U. F., Fair, D. A., Cohen, A. L., Schlaggar, B. L., and Petersen, S. E. (2008). A dual-networks architecture of top-down control. *Trends Cogn. Sci.* 12, 99–105. doi: 10.1016/j.tics.2008.01.001

Dunst, B., Benedek, M., Jauk, E., Bergner, S., Koschutnig, K., Sommer, M., et al. (2014). Neural efficiency as a function of task demands. *Intelligence* 42, 22–30. doi: 10.1016/j.intell.2013.09.005

Egner, T., and Gruzelier, J. H. (2001). Learned self-regulation of EEG frequency components affects attention and event-related brain potentials in humans. *Neuroreport* 12, 4155–4159. doi: 10.1097/00001756-200112210-00058

Egner, T., and Gruzelier, J. H. (2004). EEG biofeedback of low beta band components: frequency-specific effects on variables of attention and event-related brain potentials. *Clin. Neurophysiol.* 115, 131–139. doi: 10.1016/s1388-2457(03)00353-5

Elliott, R. (2003). Executive functions and their disorders. *Br. Med. Bull.* 65, 49–59. doi: 10.1093/bmb/65.1.49

Enriquez-Geppert, S., Huster, R. J., Scharfenort, R., Mokom, Z. N., Zimmermann, J., and Herrmann, C. S. (2014). Modulation of frontal-midline theta by neurofeedback. *Biol. Psychol.* 95, 59–69. doi: 10.1016/j.biopsycho.2013.02.019

Fields, R. D. (2010). Neuroscience. Change in the brain's white matter. *Science* 330, 768–769. doi: 10.1126/science.1199139

Fikke, L. T., Melinder, A., and Landrø, N. I. (2011). Executive functions are impaired in adolescents engaging in non-suicidal self-injury. *Psychol. Med.* 41, 601–610. doi: 10.1017/s0033291710001030

Fingelkurts, A. A., and Fingelkurts, A. A. (2014). EEG oscillatory states: universality, uniqueness and specificity across healthy-normal, altered and pathological brain conditions. *PloS One* 9:e87507. doi: 10.1371/journal.pone.0087507

Gani, C., Birbaumer, N., and Strehl, U. (2008). Long term effects after feedback of slow cortical potentials and of theta-beta-amplitudes in children with Attention Deficit Hyperactivity Disorder (ADHD). *Int. J. Bioelectromagn.* 10, 209–232.

Ghaziri, J., Tucholka, A., Larue, V., Blanchette-Sylvestre, M., Reyburn, G., Gilbert, G., et al. (2013). Neurofeedback training induces changes in white and gray matter. *Clin. EEG Neurosci.* 44, 265–272. doi: 10.1177/1550059413476031

Grill-Spector, K., Henson, R., and Martin, A. (2006). Repetition and the brain: neural models of stimulus-specific effects. *Trends Cogn. Sci.* 10, 14–23. doi: 10.1016/j.tics.2005.11.006

Gruzelier, J. H. (2014). EEG-neurofeedback for optimising performance. I: a review of cognitive and affective outcome in healthy participants. *Neurosci. Biobehav. Rev.* 44C, 124–141. doi: 10.1016/j.neubiorev.2013.09.015

Hanslmayr, S., Sauseng, P., Doppelmayr, M., Schabus, M., and Klimesch, W. (2005). Increasing individual upper alpha power by neurofeedback improves cognitive performance in human subjects. *Appl. Psychophysiol. Biofeedback* 30, 1–10. doi: 10.1007/s10484-005-2169-8

Hedges, L. V., and Olkin, I. (1985). *Statistical Methods for Meta-analysis.* Orlando: Academic Press.

Herrmann, C. S., Munk, M. H. J., and Engel, A. K. (2004). Cognitive functions of gamma-band activity: memory match and utilization. *Trends Cogn. Sci.* 8, 347–355. doi: 10.1016/j.tics.2004.06.006

Hoedlmoser, K., Pecherstorfer, T., Gruber, G., Anderer, P., Doppelmayr, M., Klimesch, W., et al. (2008). Instrumental conditioning of human sensorimotor rhythm (12–15 Hz) and its impact on sleep as well as declarative learning. *Sleep* 31, 1401–1408.

Huster, R. J., Enriquez-Geppert, S., Lavallee, C. F., Falkenstein, M., and Herrmann, C. S. (2013). Electroencephalography of response inhibition tasks: functional networks and cognitive contributions. *Int. J. Psychophysiol.* 87, 217–233. doi: 10.1016/j.ijpsycho.2012.08.001

Huster, R. J., Mokom, Z. N., Enriquez-Geppert, S., and Herrmann, C. S. (2014). Brain-computer interfaces for EEG neurofeedback: peculiarities and solutions. *Int. J. Psychophysiol.* 91, 36–45. doi: 10.1016/j.ijpsycho.2013.08.011

Ishibashi, T., Dakin, K. A., Stevens, B., Lee, P. R., Kozlov, S. V., Stewart, C. L., et al. (2006). Astrocytes promote myelination in response to electrical impulses. *Neuron* 49, 823–832. doi: 10.1016/j.neuron.2006.02.006

Ishihara, T., Hayashi, H., and Hishikawa, Y. (1981). Distribution of frontal midline theta rhythm (Fm0) on the scalp in different states (mental calculation, resting and drowsiness). *Electroencephalogr. Clin. Neurophysiol.* 52, 19. doi: 10.1016/0013-4694(81)92408-1

Kamiya, J. (1968). Conscious control of brain waves: st study of alpha and nonalpha states of the brain; indicates possibility of teaching man to perceive and control some of this brain functions. *Psychology Today* 1, 56–60. doi: 10.1037/e400092009-006

Karbach, J., and Kray, J. (2009). How useful is executive control training? Age differences in near and far transfer of task-switching training. *Dev. Sci.* 12, 978–990. doi: 10.1111/j.1467-7687.2009.00846.x

Kardos, Z., Tóth, B., Boha, R., File, B., and Molnár, M. (2014). Age-related changes of frontal-midline theta is predictive of efficient memory maintenance. *Neuroscience* 273, 152–162. doi: 10.1016/j.neuroscience.2014.04.071

Keizer, A. W., Verment, R. S., and Hommel, B. (2010). Enhancing cognitive control through neurofeedback: a role of gamma-band activity in managing episodic retrieval. *NeuroImage* 49, 3404–3413. doi: 10.1016/j.neuroimage.2009.11.023

Klimesch, W. (1999). EEG alpha and theta oscillations reflect cognitive and memory performance: a review and analysis. *Brain Res. Brain Res. Rev.* 29, 169–195. doi: 10.1016/s0165-0173(98)00056-3

Kober, S. E., Wood, G., Kurzmann, J., Friedrich, E. V. C., Stangl, M., Wippel, T., et al. (2014). Near-infrared spectroscopy based neurofeedback training increases specific motor imagery related cortical activation compared to sham feedback. *Biol. Psychol.* 95, 21–30. doi: 10.1016/j.biopsycho.2013.05.005

Lezak, M. D. (2012). *Neuropsychological Assessment.* 5th Edn. Oxford, New York: Oxford University Press.

Logan, G. D., Schachar, R. J., and Tannock, R. (1997). Impulsivity and inhibitory control. *Psychol. Sci.* 8, 60–64.

Makeig, S., Debener, S., Onton, J., and Delorme, A. (2004). Mining event-related brain dynamics. *Trends Cogn. Sci.* 8, 204–210. doi: 10.1016/j.tics.2004.03.008

Menon, V. (2011). Large-scale brain networks and psychopathology: a unifying triple network model. *Trends Cogn. Sci.* 15, 483–506. doi: 10.1016/j.tics.2011.08.003

Mihara, M., Miyai, I., Hattori, N., Hatakenaka, M., Yagura, H., Kawano, T., et al. (2012). Neurofeedback using real-time near-infrared spectroscopy enhances motor imagery related cortical activation. *PloS One* 7:e32234. doi: 10.1371/journal.pone.0032234

Miller, D. J., Duka, T., Stimpson, C. D., Schapiro, S. J., Baze, W. B., McArthur, M. J., et al. (2012a). Prolonged myelination in human neocortical evolution. *Proc. Natl. Acad. Sci. U S A* 109, 16480–16485. doi: 10.1073/pnas.1117943109

Miller, M., Nevado-Montenegro, A. J., and Hinshaw, S. P. (2012b). Childhood executive function continues to predict outcomes in young adult females with and without childhood-diagnosed ADHD. *J. Abnorm. Child Psychol.* 40, 657–668. doi: 10.1007/s10802-011-9599-y

Mitchell, D. J., McNaughton, N., Flanagan, D., and Kirk, I. J. (2008). Frontal-midline theta from the perspective of hippocampal "theta". *Prog. Neurobiol.* 86, 156–185. doi: 10.1016/j.pneurobio.2008.09.005

Miyake, A., and Friedman, N. P. (2012). The nature and organization of individual differences in executive functions: four general conclusions. *Curr. Dir. Psychol. Sci.* 21, 8–14. doi: 10.1177/0963721411429458

Miyake, A., Friedman, N. P., Emerson, M. J., Witzki, A. H., Howerter, A., and Wager, T. D. (2000). The unity and diversity of executive functions and their contributions to complex "Frontal lobe" tasks: a latent variable analysis. *Cogn. Psychol.* 41, 49–100. doi: 10.1006/cogp.1999.0734

Näpflin, M., Wildi, M., and Sarnthein, J. (2008). Test-retest reliability of EEG spectra during a working memory task. *NeuroImage* 43, 687–693. doi: 10.1016/j.neuroimage.2008.08.028

Niendam, T. A., Laird, A. R., Ray, K. L., Dean, Y. M., Glahn, D. C., and Carter, C. S. (2012). Meta-analytic evidence for a superordinate cognitive control network subserving diverse executive functions. *Cogn. Affect. Behav. Neurosci.* 12, 241–268. doi: 10.3758/s13415-011-0083-5

Nigbur, R., Ivanova, G., and Stürmer, B. (2011). Theta power as a marker for cognitive interference. *Clin. Neurophysiol.* 122, 2185–2194. doi: 10.1016/j.clinph.2011.03.030

Oehrn, C. R., Hanslmayr, S., Fell, J., Deuker, L., Kremers, N. A., Do Lam, A. T., et al. (2014). Neural communication patterns underlying conflict detection, resolution and adaptation. *J. Neurosci.* 34, 10438–10452. doi: 10.1523/jneurosci.3099-13.2014

Oken, B. S., Flegal, K., Zajdel, D., Kishiyama, S., Haas, M., and Peters, D. (2008). Expectancy effect: impact of pill administration on cognitive performance in healthy seniors. *J. Clin. Exp. Neuropsychol.* 30, 7–17. doi: 10.1080/13803390701775428

Oldfield, R. C. (1971). The assessment and analysis of handedness: the Edinburgh inventory. *Neuropsychologia* 9, 97–113. doi: 10.1016/0028-3932(71)90067-4

Olds, J., and Olds, M. E. (Eds) (1961). *Brain Mechanisms and Learning. Interference and Learning in Paleocortical Systems.* London: Blackwell Scientific Publication.

O'Rourke, M., Gasperini, R., and Young, K. M. (2014). Adult myelination: wrapping up neuronal plasticity. *Neural Regen. Res.* 9, 1261–1264. doi: 10.4103/1673-5374.137571

Pajevic, S., Basser, P. J., and Fields, R. D. (2014). Role of myelin plasticity in oscillations and synchrony of neuronal activity. *Neuroscience* 276, 135–147. doi: 10.1016/j.neuroscience.2013.11.007

Pesonen, M., Hämäläinen, H., and Krause, C. M. (2007). Brain oscillatory 4–30 Hz responses during a visual n-back memory task with varying memory load. *Brain Res.* 1138, 171–177. doi: 10.1016/j.brainres.2006.12.076

Prada, L., Barceló, F., Herrmann, C. S., and Escera, C. (2014). EEG delta oscillations index inhibitory control of contextual novelty to both irrelevant distracters and relevant task-switch cues. *Psychophysiology* 51, 658–672. doi: 10.1111/psyp.12210

Prat, C. S., and Just, M. A. (2011). Exploring the neural dynamics underpinning individual differences in sentence comprehension. *Cerebral cortex* 21, 1747–1760. doi: 10.1093/cercor/bhq241

Ros, T., Munneke, M. A. M., Ruge, D., Gruzelier, J. H., and Rothwell, J. C. (2010). Endogenous control of waking brain rhythms induces neuroplasticity in humans. *Eur. J. Neurosci.* 31, 770–778. doi: 10.1111/j.1460-9568.2010.07100.x

Ros, T., Théberge, J., Frewen, P. A., Kluetsch, R., Densmore, M., Calhoun, V. D., et al. (2013). Mind over chatter: plastic up-regulation of the fMRI salience network directly after EEG neurofeedback. *NeuroImage* 65, 324–335. doi: 10.1016/j.neuroimage.2012.09.046

Ruiz, S., Lee, S., Soekadar, S. R., Caria, A., Veit, R., Kircher, T., et al. (2013). Acquired self-control of insula cortex modulates emotion recognition and brain network connectivity in schizophrenia. *Hum. Brain Mapp.* 34, 200–212. doi: 10.1002/hbm.21427

Schneiders, J. A., Opitz, B., Krick, C. M., and Mecklinger, A. (2011). Separating intra-modal and across-modal training effects in visual working memory: an fMRI investigation. *Cereb. Cortex* 21, 2555–2564. doi: 10.1093/cercor/bhr037

Sederberg, P. B., Kahana, M. J., Howard, M. W., Donner, E. J., and Madsen, J. R. (2003). Theta and gamma oscillations during encoding predict subsequent recall. *J. Neurosci.* 23, 10809–10814.

Sherlin, L. H., Arns, M., Lubar, J., Heinrich, H., Kerson, C., Strehl, U., et al. (2011). Neurofeedback and basic learning theory: implications for research and practice. *J. Neurother.* 15, 292–304. doi: 10.1080/10874208.2011.623089

St Clair-Thompson, H., Stevens, R., Hunt, A., and Bolder, E. (2010). Improving children's working memory and classroom performance. *Educ. Psychol.* 30, 203–219. doi: 10.1080/01443410903509259

Sterman, M. B., Howe, R. C., and Macdonald, L. R. (1970). Facilitation of spindle-burst sleep by conditioning of electroencephalographic activity while awake. *Science* 167, 1146–1148. doi: 10.1126/science.167.3921.1146

Studer, P., Kratz, O., Gevensleben, H., Rothenberger, A., Moll, G. H., Hautzinger, M., et al. (2014). Slow cortical potential and theta/beta neurofeedback training in adults: effects on attentional processes and motor system excitability. *Front. Hum. Neurosci.* 8:555. doi: 10.3389/fnhum.2014.00555

Sudre, G., Parkkonen, L., Bock, E., Baillet, S., Wang, W., and Weber, D. J. (2011). rtMEG: a real-time software interface for magnetoencephalography. *Comput. Intell. Neurosci.* 2011:327953. doi: 10.1155/2011/327953

Tóth, B., Kardos, Z., File, B., Boha, R., Stam, C. J., and Molnár, M. (2014). Frontal midline theta connectivity is related to efficiency of WM maintenance and is affected by aging. *Neurobiol. Learn. Mem.* 114, 58–69. doi: 10.1016/j.nlm.2014.04.009

van Schie, H. T., Whitmarsh, S., Wouters, J., and Jensen, O. (2014). "Neurofeedback as an experimental technique: controlled theta oscillations modulate reaction times in a Sternberg working memory task," in *Conference Program and Abstracts SAN/NIHC 2014 Meeting* (Society of Applied Neuroscience).

Vaughan, L., and Giovanello, K. (2010). Executive function in daily life: age-related influences of executive processes on instrumental activities of daily living. *Psychol. Aging* 25, 343–355. doi: 10.1037/a0017729

Vogt, B. A. (2009). *Cingulate Neurobiology and Disease.* Oxford, New York: Oxford University Press.

Wake, H., Lee, P. R., and Fields, R. D. (2011). Control of local protein synthesis and initial events in myelination by action potentials. *Science* 333, 1647–1651. doi: 10.1126/science.1206998

Wang, J.-R., and Hsieh, S. (2013). Neurofeedback training improves attention and working memory performance. *Clin. Neurophysiol.* 124, 2406–2420. doi: 10.1016/j.clinph.2013.05.020

Wang, S., and Young, K. M. (2014). White matter plasticity in adulthood. *Neuroscience* 276, 148–160. doi: 10.1016/j.neuroscience.2013.10.018

Zoefel, B., Huster, R. J., and Herrmann, C. S. (2011). Neurofeedback training of the upper alpha frequency band in EEG improves cognitive performance. *NeuroImage* 54, 1427–1431. doi: 10.1016/j.neuroimage.2010.08.078

5

Down-regulation of amygdala activation with real-time fMRI neurofeedback in a healthy female sample

Christian Paret[1,2]*, Rosemarie Kluetsch[2], Matthias Ruf[1], Traute Demirakca[1], Steffen Hoesterey[1], Gabriele Ende[1†] and Christian Schmahl[2†]

[1] *Department Neuroimaging, Central Institute of Mental Health Mannheim, Medical Faculty Mannheim/Heidelberg University, Mannheim, Germany*
[2] *Department of Psychosomatic Medicine and Psychotherapy, Central Institute of Mental Health Mannheim, Medical Faculty Mannheim/Heidelberg University, Mannheim, Germany*

Oxford, UK

Correspondence:
Christian Paret, Department Neuroimaging, Central Institute of Mental Health, J5, Mannheim, D-68159, Germany
e-mail: christian.paret@zi-mannheim.de

Psychiatric conditions of emotion dysregulation are often characterized by difficulties in regulating the activity of limbic regions such as the amygdala. Real-time functional magnetic resonance imaging (rt-fMRI) allows to feedback brain activation and opens the possibility to establish a neurofeedback (NF) training of amygdala activation, e.g., for subjects suffering from emotion dysregulation. As a first step, we investigated whether feedback of the amygdala response to aversive scenes can improve down-regulation of amygdala activation. One group of healthy female participants received amygdala feedback ($N = 16$) and a control group was presented with feedback from a control region located in the basal ganglia [$N(\text{sum}) = 32$]. Subjects completed a one-session rt-fMRI-NF training where they viewed aversive pictures and received continuous visual feedback on brain activation (REGULATE condition). In a control condition, subjects were advised to respond naturally to aversive pictures (VIEW), and a neutral condition served as the non-affective control (NEUTRAL). In an adjacent run, subjects were presented with aversive pictures without feedback to test for transfer effects of learning. In a region of interest (ROI) analysis, the VIEW and the REGULATE conditions were contrasted to estimate brain regulation success. The ROI analysis was complemented by an exploratory analysis of activations at the whole-brain level. Both groups showed down-regulation of the amygdala response during training. Feedback from the amygdala but not from the control region was associated with down-regulation of the right amygdala in the transfer test. The whole-brain analysis did not detect significant group interactions. Results of the group whole-brain analyses are discussed. We present a proof-of-concept study using rt-fMRI-NF for amygdala down-regulation in the presence of aversive scenes. Results are in line with a potential benefit of NF training for amygdala regulation.

Keywords: affective disorders, amygdala, emotion regulation, mPFC, emotions, real-time fMRI neurofeedback, affective symptoms, instrumental learning

INTRODUCTION

The amygdala constitutes a core structure of emotion processing (Phan et al., 2002; Kober et al., 2008). It plays a major role in the generation and modulation of emotional responses in animals (LaBar and LeDoux, 1996) and humans (LaBar et al., 1995; Hermans et al., 2012; Haaker et al., 2013). Accumulating data indicate a close relationship between psychiatric symptoms and an exaggerated amygdala response to emotional material. An excessive response of this structure to emotional information has been shown for borderline personality disorder (BPD) (Niedtfeld et al., 2010; Schulze et al., 2011), depression (Sheline et al., 2001; Victor et al., 2010), phobias (Phan et al., 2006; Goossens et al., 2007), and post-traumatic stress disorder (PTSD) (Fonzo et al., 2010; Simmons et al., 2011)—all of which involve emotional dysregulation. Consequently, improving emotion regulation is one of the central goals of psychotherapy. On the neural level, there is evidence for normalization of the amygdala response with psychotherapy (Sheline et al., 2001; Goossens et al., 2007; Godlewska et al., 2012; Lipka et al., 2013). This is in line with a recent meta-analysis by Buhle et al. (2013), who identified the amygdala as a robust target of cognitive emotion regulation. The decrease of amygdala activation by cognitive reappraisal has been shown to correlate with perceived emotion regulation success (Wager et al., 2008). The neural top-down control of the amygdala is achieved by prefrontal-limbic coupling: specifically, a decrease in amygdala activation is associated with activation in lateral and medial regions of the prefrontal cortex (PFC) (Urry et al., 2006; Wager et al., 2008; Erk et al., 2010; Diekhof et al., 2011). In addition to amygdala hyperactivity, individuals with the aforementioned disorders have previously shown dysfunctional amygdala-prefrontal coupling (Johnstone et al., 2007; Fonzo et al., 2010; Schulze et al., 2011; Simmons et al., 2011; Lang et al., 2012).

Taken together, improving amygdala self-regulation might constitute a pathway to mental health. Hence, there is a need to develop effective therapeutic interventions which could help patients to better control amygdala activation. Several studies have begun to test real-time functional magnetic resonance imaging (rt-fMRI) as a potential therapeutic tool in psychiatric conditions (Linden et al., 2012; Ruiz et al., 2013). With rt-fMRI, a volume of brain data can be processed as soon as it has been scanned. This enables the estimation of the activation in a brain region-of-interest (ROI) for each newly acquired volume. In rt-fMRI neurofeedback (NF), the patient is supplied e.g., with a visual display indicating the current activation level in a ROI. There is increasing evidence that the control of neural circuits of emotion can be achieved by rt-fMRI-NF in healthy individuals as well as psychiatric populations. For example, Young et al. (2014) recently showed that depressed subjects who received feedback from the left amygdala during recall of positive autobiographical memories were able to up-regulate their amygdala response. This corroborates earlier findings in healthy male volunteers (Zotev et al., 2011), who showed a significant Blood Oxygenation Level Dependent (BOLD) signal increase in the left amygdala, which was not found in a control group receiving sham feedback. Another study by Brühl et al. (2014) investigated amygdala down-regulation by rt-fMRI-NF. Specifically, the authors instructed a group of healthy subjects to down-regulate a region in their right amygdala while viewing faces with different emotional expressions. Their results demonstrated an increasing down-regulation effect over the course of four scanning sessions. However, due to the lack of a control group it is not possible to rule out unspecific effects that may have influenced learning, like task repetition or rehearsal of a regulation strategy (Sulzer et al., 2013).

In this proof-of-concept study, we aimed to assess whether subjects can profit from a rt-fMRI-NF training of the amygdala with the aim of down-regulating their amygdala response to aversive scenes, and whether such a training effect can be attributed specifically to having received contingent amygdala feedback. Previous results of our group have shown that the amygdala responds with sustained BOLD activation in aversive picture viewing and identified this region as a potential target region for down-regulation by a rt-fMRI-NF training (Paret et al., 2014). While the reduction of the amygdala response emerges from the literature as one consistent effect of successful emotion regulation (see Diekhof et al., 2011; Buhle et al., 2013 for meta-analyses), the precise prefrontal structures involved in regulation may differ with the cognitive strategy applied (Ochsner et al., 2004; Kalisch et al., 2006; McRae et al., 2010; Kanske et al., 2011; Opialla et al., 2014). We assume, that choosing the signal from the amygdala opposed to a prefrontal region allows for flexibility in strategy-selection. Studies on down-regulation of the amygdala response to aversive material either endorse preferential involvement of the left (Diekhof et al., 2011), right (Brühl et al., 2014), or bilateral (Buhle et al., 2013) amygdala. We combined an anatomical delineation of the bilateral amygdala with a functional voxel selection based on the activation profile during the experiment. This procedure was flexible for including voxels from the right as well as the left amygdala, depending on their activation to the experimental stimuli.

Only female participants were included to control for variance due to potential effects of gender. We chose to elicit emotional activation by presenting aversive pictures which are widely used in the neuroimaging literature of emotion regulation (Kalisch, 2009). A one-session learning protocol was used, closing with a transfer test without NF, where subjects were again presented with aversive pictures and instructed to regulate, but did not receive any feedback. We hypothesized a decrease of the BOLD signal amplitude of the amygdala in blocks where subjects of the experimental group were instructed to regulate vs. view aversive pictures. This finding was expected to be more pronounced in the experimental group compared to a control group receiving feedback from a region located in another part of the brain. Further, we expected the experimental group to show stronger down-regulation of amygdala activation during the transfer run compared to the control group.

Given previous reports of run-to-run improvements during NF training (Zotev et al., 2011; Lawrence et al., 2013), we also evaluated our data for an improvement in amygdala down-regulation over the course of the training.

Veit et al. (2012) have recently used the anterior insula response to aversive pictures as a NF signal for a training of brain self-regulation. The authors found a modulation of the anterior insula response consistent with the instruction to up-regulate and down-regulate a thermometer, which displayed the activation of the region. Together with the amygdala, the anterior insula plays an important role in the processing of emotional information (Damasio et al., 2000; Phan et al., 2002; Kober et al., 2008). To explore the specifity of amygdala NF training on the regulation of brain structures of the affective brain system, we investigated the effect of the training on the activation of the anterior insula.

Finally, we conducted a whole-brain analysis to explore the involvement of other regions.

METHODS

SAMPLE

$N = 32$ right-handed female participants ($N = 16$ per group) were tested. There were no significant differences in age between the experimental (24.19 ± 4.17, range: 19–34) and the control group (24.94 ± 3.87, range: 20 to 34) [$T_{(30)} = 0.53$]. 14 participants of the experimental group and 15 participants of the control group had a university entrance diploma (German Abitur) (Fisher's Exact Test: $p = 1.000$). Participants reported no current and past DSM-IV Axis I and II disorder or family history of neurological or psychiatric disorders, as confirmed by the Structured Clinical Interview for DSM-IV (SCID; First et al., 1997) as well as the International Personality Disorder Examination (IPDE; Loranger, 1999), which had been conducted before inviting subjects for the experiment. The study was approved by the Ethics Committee of the Medical Faculty Mannheim of the University of Heidelberg, and all subjects provided written informed consent before participation. Compensation for expenses was 24 Euro.

GROUP ASSIGNMENT

Subject assignment to groups was randomized and blinded to both the participant and the investigator welcoming and instructing the participant before training. Subjects were informed before the investigation that part of the experiment was to find out which of two regions would be best suited for the training.

INSTRUCTION AND VISUAL FEEDBACK PRESENTATION

Subjects were instructed to regulate "the feeling center" of their brains and were told that this brain region is involved in the "perception and processing of emotions." No further instructions on the use of a specific regulation strategy were provided. During training, feedback on brain activation was given by the level of a thermometer displayed to both sides of the picture stimulus. The bilateral presentation was chosen to ensure high visibility of the thermometer regardless of gaze orientation. Participants were presented with the following instruction in German language: "If you see the statement "Regulate," an unpleasant image will be shown. Your task is to regulate the number of bars in the thermometer." Additionally, subjects were briefed that an orange line in the lower half of the thermometer indicated "the activation of the feeling center under rest or non-emotional conditions" and the aim is "that the bars remain at or below the baseline." In terms of activation magnitude, one bar of the thermometer display corresponded to 0.2% signal change. The orange line divided the thermometer in an upper part displaying activation (maximum of 2.8% signal change, derived from reported BOLD signal changes in the literature, Zotev et al., 2011 and confirmed by piloting experiments in our group) and a lower part indicating deactivation from baseline (maximum of 1.2% signal change, since we expected more positive signal change compared to baseline in the REGULATE and VIEW conditions, we chose to leave more space for thermometer bars above compared to below). To prevent regulation by just looking at the thermometer or non-emotional details of the picture, participants were advised not to avert their gaze or keep their eyes closed, nor to focus exclusively on the thermometer, but rather to look at the picture for its entire presentation. The participants' eyes were tracked by a camera system (MRC Systems, Heidelberg, Germany) to encourage subjects to adhere to the instructions and to control for drowsiness during training. Data were not statistically analyzed. Subjects were also instructed to consider the temporal latency of the BOLD signal amplitude when evaluating the success of regulating their brain activation.

When a NF run was finished, subjects rated perceived regulation success. They were asked whether they had been able to regulate the thermometer on a 9-point scale (0 = not at all, 9 = very much).

EXPERIMENTAL CONDITIONS

In addition to the "regulate"-condition (REGULATE), the protocol included two control conditions: a "view-negative" (VIEW) and a "view-neutral" (NEUTRAL) condition. Subjects were instructed to refrain from controlling the thermometer during the control conditions. While aversive pictures were presented in VIEW trials, scrambled pictures with no meaningful content were presented during NEUTRAL trials. Trials were separated by an inter-trial interval (ITI) with a fixation cross displayed on the screen.

The structure of an experimental trial is shown in **Figure 1A**. An experimental run lasted approximately 9 min and consisted of 15 trials, with 5 of each condition. Each subject participated in 3 consecutive NF training runs, followed by 1 transfer run.

STIMULUS MATERIAL AND PRESENTATION

Stimuli were taken from standardized picture series (Lang et al., 2008; Wessa et al., 2010) and were chosen to elicit moderate to high negative valence and arousal. Pictures included in the training runs had a valence level of 2.17 ± 0.49 (mean ± standard deviation (SD), values were taken from the original reports by Lang and colleagues and Wessa and colleagues) and an arousal level of 6.35 ± 0.70. Stimuli included in the transfer run were matched to training stimuli with a valence of 2.12 ± 0.54 and arousal values of 6.26 ± 0.71. Stimuli were assigned to the REGULATE and VIEW conditions matching valence and arousal between runs and conditions (significance value of $p < 0.05$ in a comparison of means) and the stimulus-to-condition assignment was counterbalanced (picture numbers can be obtained from the corresponding author). The condition order was semi-randomized with the restriction of ≤ 2 consecutive stimuli of the same condition. Each subject of the control group received the same version of the experiment as another subject from the experimental group. An overview on the experimental procedure can be obtained from **Figure 1B**. Stimuli were presented with Presentation software (Neurobehavioral Systems, Berkeley, CA). After completion of the experiment, subjects rated the pictures outside the MRI suite.

DELINEATION OF BRAIN AREA AND REAL-TIME DATA PROCESSING

The anatomical scans were imported into BrainVoyager software (version QX2.4, Brain Innovations, Maastricht, Netherlands), skull-stripped and transformed into Talairach space. Normalization parameters were loaded into TurboBrainVoyager (TBV) (version 3.0, Brain Innovations, Maastricht, Netherlands). Depending on group assignment, an anatomical mask of the bilateral amygdala or a mask of a region located in the rostral part of the basal ganglia (control region) was loaded (**Figure 2**). Due to a technical problem, the Talairach transformation failed in three subjects of the control group. Instead of the control region, these subjects received feedback from a manually drawn square region of variable size (thickness: 5 axial slices), covering parts of the corpus callosum, gray matter, and ventricular areas.

The initial 2 volumes of the functional scans were discarded before real-time processing started. A motion correction feature implemented in TBV was enabled to correct for head movements and spatial smoothing with a 4 mm kernel (full width at half maximum, FWHM) was applied. For the calculation of the BOLD signal amplitude, the "best voxel selection" tool implemented in TBV was used to identify the 33% voxels with beta-values discriminating best between VIEW and NEUTRAL conditions. The voxels were dynamically determined by a score defined by Goebel (2014) based "(a) on the maximum condition beta value and (b) on the amount of deviation from the mean of all condition betas. The first criterion selects those voxels, which have the largest beta value. The second criterion calculates first the mean of all betas and then adds the absolute differences of each beta value from the mean. This deviation index biases the selection to those voxels with a "irregular" profile, i.e., which will show high values for contrasts between betas." The overall voxel-score is calculated by: voxel-score = (b_max + b_dev)/b_constant. Thereby, the selection of voxels within the spatial region was dynamically

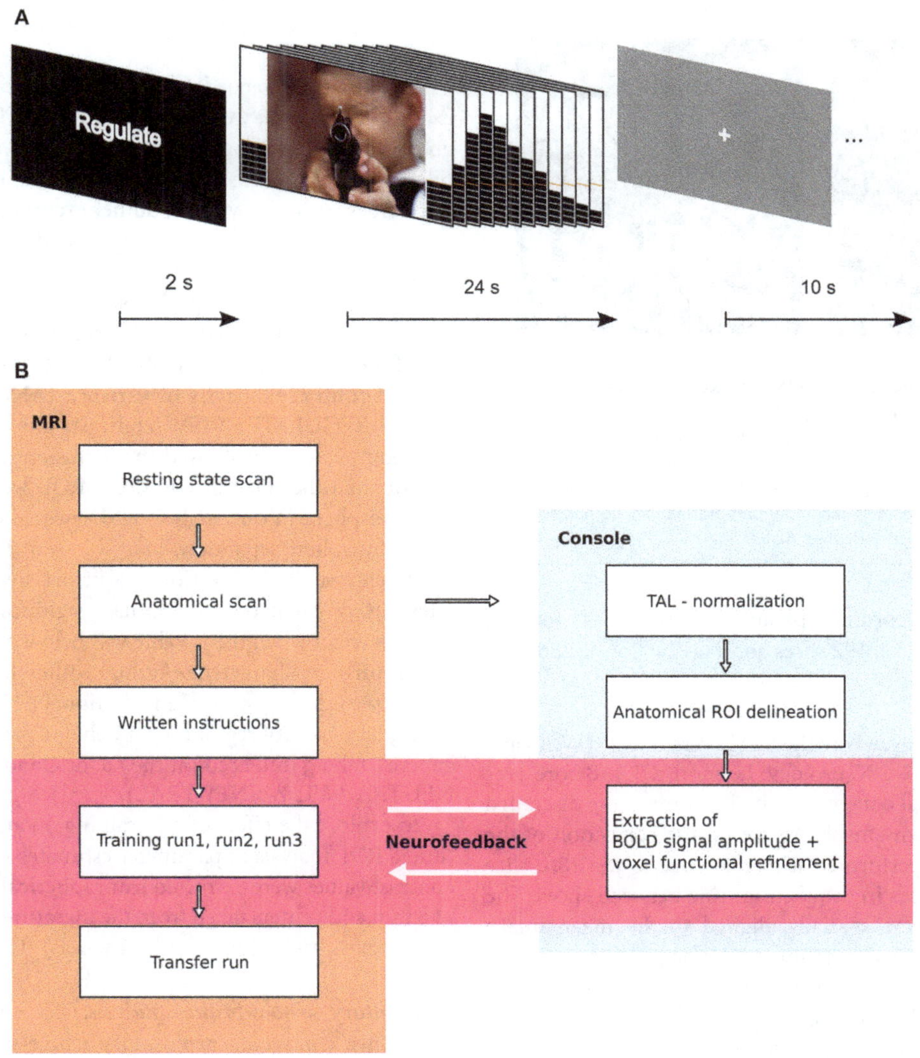

FIGURE 1 | Experimental design. (A) Trial structure. A trial started with a 2 s instruction slide indicating trial type (REGULATE, VIEW, NEUTRAL). In the following block, participants either saw an aversive or a scrambled picture with a thermometer at both sides. The thermometer displayed the change in brain activation and was updated every 2 s. After 24 s, the screen changed to gray with a white fixation cross (ITI), and 10 s later, the next trial started. **(B)** Flow Chart of experimental procedure. Results from resting state data are published elsewhere.

refined along the course of training and counterbalanced moderate shifts of the anatomical delineation due to alignment errors across successive runs as well as movement-related slice shifts. Furthermore, the procedure guaranteed that there was no difference in the number of voxels used for signal extraction between subjects and groups. To permit an initial selection of voxels based on their response patterns during VIEW and NEUTRAL, the first two trials of each NF run consisted of those conditions.

The BOLD signal amplitude was passed to Presentation as soon as a new volume had been processed. For each trial, the mean of the last 4 data points before picture onset was taken as a baseline. The signal was smoothed by calculating the mean of the current and the preceding 3 data points. The subtraction of the baseline resulted in the feedback signal amplitude $[(X + [X - 1] + [X - 2] + [X - 3])/4\text{-baseline};\ X =$ current data point]. The feedback display was updated as soon as information of a new volume had been available. Thus, the latency of the feedback was composed of the TR (2 s) plus the time needed for real-time calculation and display actualization by the presentation software (about half a second).

DATA ACQUISTION AND *POST-HOC* ANALYSIS OF IMAGING DATA

Image acquisition

For brain imaging, a 3 Tesla MRI Scanner (Trio, Siemens Medical Solutions, Erlangen, Germany) with a 32 channel head coil was used. Functional images of the BOLD contrast were acquired with a gradient echo T2* weighted echo-planar-imaging sequence ($TE = 30$ ms, $TR = 2$ s, $FOV = 192 \times 192$ mm, flip angle $= 80°$). One volume comprised 36 slices in AC-PC orientation with a thickness of 3 mm and slice gap of 1 mm. Participants' heads were lightly restrained using soft pads. The four experimental runs comprised 284 volumes each. The T1-weighted

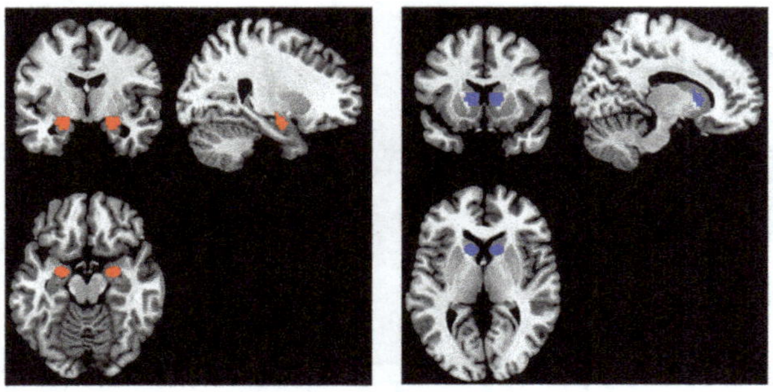

FIGURE 2 | Regions of interest (ROIs) for the extraction of the neurofeedback signal during training. The amygdala mask was prepared using the Talairach Daemon (Lancaster et al., 2000) and included voxels which were exclusively assigned to the amygdala by the online tool. The mask delineating the control region was the same size and shape as the amygdala mask, but was located in another part of the brain, comprising parts of rostral basal ganglia, and white matter.

anatomical image recording parameters were as follows: $TE = 3.03$ ms, $TR = 2.3$ s, 192 slices and $FOV = 256 \times 256$ mm.

Preprocessing

FMRI data were analyzed with SPM version 8 (Wellcome Department of Cognitive Neurology, London, UK). Before preprocessing of functional data, nine initial volumes were discarded to avoid T1-equilibrium effects. A slice timing correction of the functional scans was performed with reference to the 18th slice to correct for differences in acquisition time between slices. The functional volumes were spatially aligned to the mean image using a rigid body transformation and images were resliced. Functional images were coregistered to the anatomical image, normalized to the SPM standard template and brought into Montreal Neurological Institute (MNI) coordinate space. Finally, images were smoothed with a kernel of 6 mm (FWHM).

Statistical analysis

First-level analysis. We formulated separate models in SPM for the NF training and the transfer run. The three NF runs were modeled as separate sessions. Three experimental conditions were modeled (REGULATE, VIEW, NEUTRAL) and the movement vectors taken from the spatial realignment procedure were included in the model as nuisance variables. All events were modeled as blocks of brain activation and were convolved with the hemodynamic response function. Data were high-pass filtered (128 s) and a correction for serial correlations was implemented by autoregressive modeling.

ROI analysis. To test our hypotheses, voxel-wise T-tests of parameter estimates for the contrasts VIEW>REGULATE, REGULATE>NEUTRAL, and VIEW>NEUTRAL were conducted on the subject level. The mean contrast value was then extracted from all voxels of the amygdala and from the control region. Anatomical templates were used as provided by the Wake Forest University (WFU) PickAtlas toolbox (Maldjian et al., 2003) to delineate the amygdala (left: 71 voxels, right: 76 voxels). To assess results of the control region, we extracted mean contrast values using the control region mask (left and right: 43 voxels each).

Values were screened for outliers before the analysis. As an exclusion criterion, we set a 3 SD threshold below and above the group mean, based on the mean contrast value taken from the bilateral region masks. When outliers were identified, we report test-values with and without outlier exclusion.

Extracted contrast values were passed to SPSS version 20 for statistical analyses.

To test our main hypothesis regarding down-regulation of brain activation (REGULATE) as contrasted with natural viewing of the aversive stimulus (VIEW), a Region (2) × Hemisphere (2) × Group (2) analysis of variance (ANOVA) was calculated for the REGULATE>VIEW contrast. Since the dynamic voxel selection principally allowed the inclusion of more voxels of the one or the other laterality into the ROI, we included the factor of Hemisphere in our analysis and assessed down-regulation for each hemisphere separately.

Where we had directional a-priori hypotheses, one-tailed t-tests were calculated to estimate significance ($p < 0.05$). We report a trend when the p-value was below $p = 0.10$.

To further characterize group differences and condition-effects, we report results of an additional ANOVA for each region (amygdala, control region; separately for the left and right hemisphere), taking into account the factor Condition (REGULATE>NEUTRAL, VIEW>NEUTRAL).

To explore the effect of NF training on anterior insula regulation, a ROI analysis of parameter estimates was calculated. Mean contrast values were extracted from spherical masks with a radius of 8 mm and centers taken from the literature (left peak: [−33, 20, 0], 82 voxels; right: [36, 26, 6], 81 voxels) (Caria et al., 2007).

Exploratory whole-brain analysis. To elucidate task-related effects, we conducted exploratory whole-brain random effects analyses for both groups independently on the t-contrasts VIEW>REGULATE, REGULATE>NEUTRAL and VIEW>NEUTRAL. Additionally we explored group differences, assuming independent measurements and equal variances of errors. To protect against false positives, we used Monte-Carlo simulations to estimate the cluster-extend at a voxel-threshold of $p < 0.001$ and a cluster-threshold of $p < 0.05$. Simulations were performed with 3dClustSim, implemented in AFNI (Cox, 1996). Estimation of cluster-extend was determined in 10.000 iterations, based on the number of voxels included in the masks and the smoothness (FWHM) of the residuals of the second-level SPM8-analyses. The resulting number of voxels (k) is indicated in the results tables.

ANALYSIS OF RATING DATA

Picture-rating data of 2 participants was lost. We looked for group differences in subjective arousal and valence elicited by picture viewing and conducted Group × Condition (VIEW, REGULATE) ANOVAs for pictures presented during training and transfer. To further determine whether groups differed in their perceived regulation success, we conducted a repeated measures ANOVA on regulation success, with "Run" as the within-subjects factor and "Group" as the between-subjects factor.

ANALYSIS OF THERMOMETER VARIABILITY

To compare the dynamics of the thermometer display between the groups, the number of bars presented to a subject at any given time point in the experiment was derived from the data. The variance of the number of bars as a measure of thermometer variability was calculated for each subject and each condition, and was taken to a Condition (3) × Run (3) × Group (2) ANOVA.

RESULTS

ROI ANALYSIS

Since three participants of the control group did not receive feedback from the standardized control region due to a technical error, we additionally report results of an analysis leaving out these subjects.

Neurofeedback training

Neither the Region × Hemisphere × Group ANOVA nor the Hemisphere × Group ANOVA of the amygdala revealed significant interactions. The main effect of Region was significant [$F_{(1, 31)} = 33.163$, $p < 0.001$]. Subjects from the experimental group showed down-regulation of the left amygdala in the REGULATE>VIEW contrast [-0.25 ± 0.38 (mean ± *SD*), $T_{(15)} = 2.675$, $p = 0.009$, one-tailed] in the hypothesized direction (**Figure 3**). The effect was less pronounced in the right amygdala [-0.15 ± 0.34, $T_{(15)} = 1.684, p = 0.057$]. The control group showed a similar effect in the left [-0.31 ± 0.53, $T_{(15)} = 2.324$, $p = 0.018$] and right amygdala [-0.36 ± 0.62, $T_{(15)} = 2.338$, $p = 0.017$]. All *t*-tests were not significant when correcting for multiple comparisons.

An exploratory ANOVA of the run-to-run change in the REGULATE>VIEW contrast revealed a trend for a Hemisphere by Group interaction [$F_{(1, 30)} = 3.164$, $p = 0.085$] and a significant main effect of Region [$F_{(1, 30)} = 33.394$, $p < 0.001$]. Since a visual inspection did not suggest a linear trend of the outcome measure in the experimental group, we did not further explore within-group run-to-run changes in parameter estimates.

Excluding subjects who did not receive feedback from the standardized control region did not change significance of the test values.

To further elucidate condition effects, we analyzed the REGULATE>NEUTRAL and VIEW>NEUTRAL contrasts (**Table 1**). Consistent with the previous results, we detect a significant main effect of Condition in the analysis of the left and right amygdala, while Group-interactions were not significant.

Transfer run

The screening for outlier values had identified one outlier in the control group (i.e., contrast-value of 3 SD below the group mean). The Region by Hemisphere by Group interaction was significant [$F_{(1, 29)} = 4.550, p < 0.05$], with outlier inclusion there was still a trend [$F_{(1, 30)} = 3.452, p = 0.073$] (**Figure 4**). There was a main effect of Region [$F_{(1, 29)} = 5.172, p < 0.05$; including the outlier: $F_{(1, 30)} = 5.701$, $p < 0.05$] and Hemisphere [$F_{(1, 29)} = 19.012$, $p < 0.001$, including the outlier: $F_{(1, 30)} = 21.023$, $p < 0.001$]. When excluding subjects who had received feedback from a non-standardized control region, the results did not change in terms of significance regarding the three-way interaction [$F_{(1, 26)} = 4.618$,

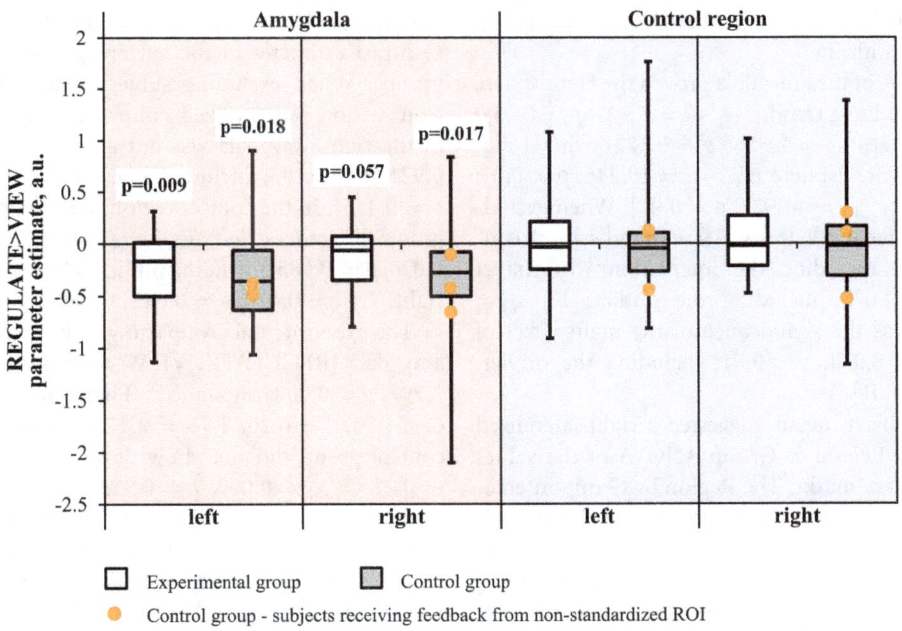

FIGURE 3 | Results of the region-of-interest analysis of the neurofeedback training. Negative values indicate a decrease of the BOLD signal amplitude in the regulate condition (REGULATE) compared to natural responding toward aversive pictures (VIEW). White box plots: participants receiving feedback from the amygdala during training (experimental group). Gray box plots: participants receiving feedback from a standardized control region during training (control group). Orange dots: participants who had received feedback from a non-standardized control region during training due to a technical error ($N = 3$). *P*-values indicate probability of the findings for each group and mask under the null-hypothesis. *T*-tests were not significant when correcting for multiple comparisons. A.u., artificial units.

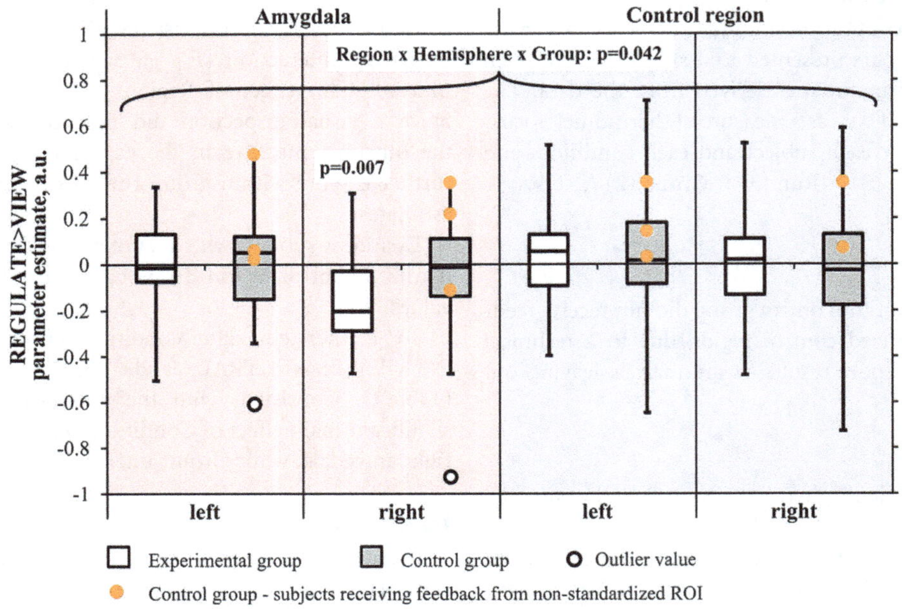

FIGURE 4 | Results of the region-of-interest analysis of the transfer run. Negative values indicate a decrease of the BOLD signal amplitude in the regulate condition (REGULATE) compared to natural responding toward aversive pictures (VIEW). White box plots: participants receiving feedback from the amygdala during training (experimental group). Gray box plots: participants receiving feedback from a standardized control region during training (control group). Orange dots: participants who had received feedback from a non-standardized control region during training due to a technical error ($N = 3$). *P*-values indicate probability of the findings for each group and mask under the null-hypothesis. Tests were not significant when correcting for multiple comparisons. Black circle: outlier value (3 standard deviations > group mean). A.u., artificial units.

$p < 0.05$; including the outlier: $F_{(1, 27)} = 3.339, p = 0.079$]. The main effects of Region [$F_{(1, 26)} = 5.675, p < 0.05$; including the outlier: $F_{(1, 27)} = 6.326, p < 0.05$] and Hemisphere [$F_{(1, 26)} = 18.314, p < 0.001$; including the outlier: $F_{(1, 27)} = 20.942, p < 0.001$] were still significant.

The two-way ANOVA of the amygdala proved the Hemisphere by Group interaction to be at trend [$F_{(1, 29)} = 3.921, p = 0.057$; including the outlier: $F_{(1, 30)} = 2.526, p = 0.122$] with a significant main effect of Hemisphere [$F_{(1, 29)} = 10.246, p < 0.01$; including the outlier: $F_{(1, 30)} = 11.922, p < 0.01$]. When excluding subjects receiving feedback from a non-standardized control region, the trend regarding the interaction was robust [$F_{(1, 26)} = 3.435, p = 0.075$; including the outlier: $F_{(1, 27)} = 2.016, p = 0.167$] as was the significance of the main effect of Hemisphere [$F_{(1, 26)} = 8.934, p < 0.01$; including the outlier: $F_{(1, 27)} = 10.944, p < 0.01$].

An inspection of subject means suggested a right-lateralized effect. We conducted a Region × Group ANOVA of the values from the right hemisphere masks. The Region by Group interaction was found at trend level [$F_{(1, 29)} = 3.491, p = 0.072$; including the outlier: $F_{(1, 30)} = 3.046, p = 0.091$] and the main effect of Region was significant [$F_{(1, 29)} = 7.765, p < 0.01$; including the outlier: $F_{(1, 30)} = 9.028, p < 0.01$], also when excluding subjects who had received feedback from a non-standardized control region [Region by Group interaction: $F_{(1, 26)} = 2.956, p = 0.097$; including the outlier: $F_{(1, 27)} = 2.500, p = 0.125$; main effect of Hemisphere: $F_{(1, 26)} = 7.468, p < 0.05$; including the outlier: $F_{(1, 27)} = 8.964, p < 0.01$]. The Region × Group ANOVA did not indicate a significant interaction effect in the left hemisphere.

When contrasting groups, we observed a trend for lower values in the experimental group compared to the control group in the right amygdala [$T_{(29)} = 1.522, p = 0.070$, one-tailed; including the outlier subject: $T_{(30)} = 0.648, p = 0.261$, one-tailed]. Contrast estimates in the left amygdala did not differ between groups. When excluding subjects who had received feedback from a non-standardized control region, the group difference in the right amygdala was not anymore at trend level [$T_{(26)} = 0.921, p = 0.183$; including the outlier subject: $T_{(27)} = 0.062, p = 0.476$]. In the control region, we did not find any significant group differences [left: $T_{(29)} = 0.391, p = 0.698$, right: $T_{(29)} = 0.020, p = 0.985$; including outlier: left: $T_{(30)} = 0.073, p = 0.942$, right: $T_{(30)} = 0.470, p = 0.642$].

The experimental group showed down-regulation of the right amygdala [REGULATE>VIEW contrast: -0.14 ± 0.20, $T_{(15)} = 2.797, p = 0.007$, one-tailed] (**Figure 5A**) but not the left amygdala [-0.01 ± 0.20, $T_{(15)} = 0.178, p = 0.$ 861, two-tailed]. The control group did not show down-regulation in the left [0.01 $\pm$ 0.22, $T_{(15)} = 0.099, p = 0.923$, two-tailed; including outlier subject: -0.03 ± 0.26, $T_{(15)} = 0.506, p = 0.310$, one-tailed] and right amygdala [-0.03 ± 0.22, $T_{(14)} = 0.451, p = 0.330$, one-tailed; including the outlier subject: -0.08 ± 0.31, $T_{(15)} = 1.056, p = 0.154$, one-tailed]. However, all *t*-tests were not significant after correcting for multiple comparisons.

Results didn't change in terms of significance when excluding subjects from the analysis who had received feedback from a non-standardized ROI [left amygdala: -0.07 ± 0.20, $T_{(11)} = 0.708, p = 0.247$; including the outlier subject: -0.08 ± 0.24, $T_{(12)} = 1.235, p = 0.120$, one-tailed; right amygdala: -0.14 ± 0.31,

Table 1 | Group statistics and ANOVA results of neurofeedback training.

(A)		**Amygdala**					
	Hemisphere:		**Left**			**Right**	
	Run:	**1**	**2**	**3**	**1**	**2**	**3**
GROUP STATISTICS (MEAN ± *SD*)							
Experimental group	REG>NEU	0.23 ± 0.16	0.13 ± 0.27	0.14 ± 0.20	0.21 ± 0.18	0.19 ± 0.27	0.22 ± 0.20
(*N* = 16)	VIEW>NEU	0.35 ± 0.20	0.19 ± 0.23	0.21 ± 0.21	0.30 ± 0.17	0.23 ± 0.22	0.23 ± 0.20
Control group	REG>NEU	0.25 ± 0.21	0.19 ± 0.18	0.11 ± 0.29	0.22 ± 0.22	0.18 ± 0.16	0.15 ± 0.27
(*N* = 16)	VIEW>NEU	0.29 ± 0.13	0.27 ± 0.29	0.29 ± 0.27	0.31 ± 0.22	0.28 ± 0.28	0.32 ± 0.31
ANOVA RESULTS (*P*-VALUES)							
Interaction effects	Run × condition × group		0.308			0.271	
	Condition × group		0.747			0.229	
	Run × group		0.628			0.994	
	Run × condition		0.581			0.887	
Main effects	Group		0.578			0.776	
	Run		0.104			0.669	
	Condition		0.002			0.008	

(B)		**Control region**					
	Hemisphere:		**Left**			**Right**	
	Run:	**1**	**2**	**3**	**1**	**2**	**3**
GROUP STATISTICS (MEAN ± *SD*)							
Experimental group	REG>NEU	0.16 ± 0.18	0.12 ± 0.27	0.22 ± 0.18	0.18 ± 0.19	0.15 ± 0.25	0.22 ± 0.19
(*N* = 16)	VIEW>NEU	0.22 ± 0.16	0.14 ± 0.20	0.17 ± 0.19	0.23 ± 0.19	0.11 ± 0.20	0.15 ± 0.19
Control group	REG>NEU	0.24 ± 0.33	0.22 ± 0.30	0.10 ± 0.24	0.24 ± 0.32	0.22 ± 0.25	0.13 ± 0.29
(*N* = 16)	VIEW>NEU	0.21 ± 0.20	0.19 ± 0.38	0.17 ± 0.29	0.20 ± 0.18	0.22 ± 0.34	0.20 ± 0.32
ANOVA RESULTS (*P*-VALUES)							
Interaction effects	Run × condition × group		0.098			0.144	
	Condition × group		0.942			0.642	
	Run × group		0.492			0.592	
	Run × condition		0.942			0.922	
Main effects	Group		0.720			0.623	
	Run		0.714			0.718	
	Condition		0.890			0.866	

Table shows parameter-estimate-contrast values from the regions of interest. ***(A)*** *Amygdala,* ***(B)*** *Control region. SD, standard deviation; REG, regulate; NEU, neutral.*

$T_{(12)} = 1.602$, $p = 0.068$, including outlier subject: -0.07 ± 0.20, $T_{(11)} = 1.200$, $p = 0.127$].

We examined training effects on activation of the control region and did not find significant regulation in the REGULATE>VIEW contrast in both groups, as well as no group-differences of the contrast values.

The results of the Condition × Group ANOVA can be obtained from **Table 2**. Descriptively, subjects of the experimental group showed lower activations in both REGULATE and VIEW trials compared to the control group (**Figure 5B**). In the right amygdala, the main effect of Group showed a trend and the main effect of Condition was significant, however, the Condition × Group interaction was not significant. *Post-hoc t*-tests of group differences in the single conditions brought a trend for the experimental group showing lower values than the control group when instructed to regulate. In line with the results presented above, the experimental group and not the control group did show a significant reduction of the right amygdala response in the REGULATE vs. the VIEW condition in the transfer run. Regarding the control region, we detected a significant effect of Group, with participants of the control group showing higher values than the experimental group during both conditions.

Anterior insula: neurofeedback training and transfer run

Results from the Run × Condition × Group ANOVA can be obtained from **Table 3A**. There was a significant main effect of Condition with higher anterior insula activation during REGULATE vs. VIEW (**Figure 6A**). None of the interactions were significant. The Run × Group interaction was found at trend level. A linear decrease of anterior insula activation, however, was not visible from the data of both groups.

Table 3B lists the results of the transfer run. The Condition × Group effect was found at trend-level. The main effect of Condition was significant with higher anterior insula activation in the REGULATE vs. the VIEW condition. *Post-hoc t*-tests paralleled the findings from the amygdala ROI analysis: the experimental group showed less right anterior insula activation compared to the control group in the REGULATE condition. This difference was not present in the VIEW condition. Increased activation in the REGULATE vs. VIEW contrast was revealed in the bilateral anterior insula in the control group. The experimental group, however, did not significantly increase right anterior insula activation (**Figure 6B**).

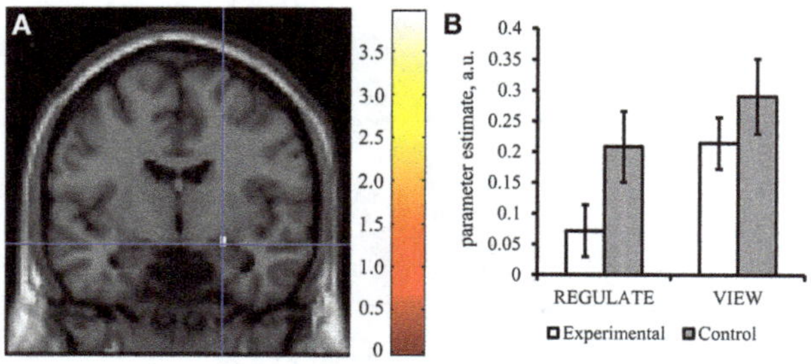

FIGURE 5 | The experimental group down-regulated the right amygdala response in the transfer run. (A) Voxels were found activated at $p < 0.05$ (family-wise error corrected for multiple comparisons) in an anatomical mask of the right amygdala (Tzourio-Mazoyer et al., 2002) for the contrast VIEW>REGULATE in the experimental group. Crosshairs indicate location of the peak voxel at [24, −7, −14], Montreal Neurological Institute coordinate space. Activation is displayed on a coronal view of the SPM8 canonical standard template. Left is left. Scale indicates *t*-values of the parameter estimate. **(B)** Mean parameter estimate of all voxels within the right amygdala mask of the REGULATE>NEUTRAL and VIEW>NEUTRAL contrast, taken from the transfer run. White bars: experimental group ($N = 16$), gray bars: control group ($N = 16$). Error bars indicate standard error of mean. A.u., artificial units.

EXPLORATORY WHOLE-BRAIN ANALYSIS

Neurofeedback training

No significant group comparisons were detected with a whole-brain analysis. When inspecting brain activation associated with natural responding to aversive picture viewing (VIEW>NEUTRAL), the experimental (Supplementary Table 1A) and the control group (Supplementary Table 1B) showed a similar pattern of activated brain regions, including the occipital lobe, the inferior temporal lobe and medial temporal areas. Activations were also found in the ventrolateral cortex, extending to the anterior insula. An analysis of brain areas implicated in regulation (REGULATE>NEUTRAL) brought only one significant cluster for the experimental group in the medial parietal lobe. In contrast, the analysis of the control group showed activated clusters covering occipital, parietal, inferior temporal, and prefontal areas. Activations were also detected in the anterior insula and in the medial temporal lobe. The analysis of brain regions with reduced responding during regulation with amygdala NF (VIEW>REGULATE) brought an activation cluster in the ventromedial PFC and another one in the medial occipital/temporal lobes. In contrast, no significant clusters were detected for the control group. The inspection of areas activated by regulation compared to natural responding (REGULATE>VIEW) in the experimental group brought one significant cluster in the right dorsolateral PFC. The control group, in contrast, activated an area in the dorsomedial frontal cortex and the thalamus.

Transfer run

Again, no group differences were found for neither of the contrasts. Supplementary Table 2 summarizes the findings of the

Table 2 | Group statistics and ANOVA results of the transfer run.

	Hemisphere:	Amygdala		Control region	
		Left	Right	Left	Right
GROUP STATISTICS (MEAN ± *SD*)					
Experimental group	REG>NEU	0.19 ± 0.04	0.07 ± 0.04	0.02 ± 0.06	0.00 ± 0.06
($N = 16$)	VIEW>NEU	0.20 ± 0.05	0.21 ± 0.04	−0.02 ± 0.04	−0.01 ± 0.04
Control group	REG>NEU	0.20 ± 0.07	0.21 ± 0.06	0.20 ± 0.06	0.18 ± 0.05
($N = 16$)	VIEW>NEU	0.24 ± 0.05	0.29 ± 0.06	0.18 ± 0.06	0.22 ± 0.06
ANOVA RESULTS (*P*-VALUE)					
Interaction effect	Condition × group	0.774	0.522	0.823	0.614
Main effects	Group	0.677	0.067	0.003	0.003
	Condition	0.611	0.022	0.595	0.798
Post-hoc t-test (*p*-value, two-tailed)	REG>NEU:control vs. experimental	0.845	0.067	0.042	0.045
	VIEW>NEU:control vs. experimental	0.600	0.308	0.011	0.007
	Experimental group:REG vs. VIEW	0.861	0.014	0.540	0.842
	Control group:REG vs. VIEW	0.620	0.308	0.847	0.632

Table shows parameter-estimate-contrast values from the regions of interest. SD, standard deviation; REG, regulate; NEU, neutral.

Table 3 | Group statistics and ANOVA results of the anterior insula analysis.

(A)		**Neurofeedback training**					
	Hemisphere:	**Left**			**Right**		
	Run:	**1**	**2**	**3**	**1**	**2**	**3**
GROUP STATISTICS (MEAN ± *SD*)							
Experimental group	REG>NEU	0.40 ± 0.35	0.35 ± 0.30	0.34 ± 0.34	0.30 ± 0.23	0.36 ± 0.25	0.27 ± 0.28
(*N* = 16)	VIEW>NEU	0.23 ± 0.24	0.08 ± 0.21	0.18 ± 0.28	0.15 ± 0.16	0.08 ± 0.26	0.14 ± 0.20
Control group	REG>NEU	0.43 ± 0.32	0.28 ± 0.39	0.22 ± 0.33	0.48 ± 0.43	0.15 ± 0.37	0.42 ± 0.47
(*N* = 16)	VIEW>NEU	0.24 ± 0.33	0.10 ± 0.43	0.17 ± 0.32	0.24 ± 0.40	0.00 ± 0.41	0.25 ± 0.37
ANOVA RESULTS (*P*-VALUES)							
Interaction effects	Run × condition × group		0.660			0.285	
	Condition × group		0.465			0.972	
	Run × group		0.841			0.072	
	Run × condition		0.257			0.601	
Main effects	Group		0.714			0.595	
	Run		0.164			0.067	
	Condition		0.000			0.000	

(B)		**Transfer run**	
	Hemisphere:	**Left**	**Right**
Group statistics (mean ± *SD*)			
Experimental group	REG>NEU	0.31 ± 0.39	0.24 ± 0.28
(*N* = 16)	VIEW>NEU	0.03 ± 0.32	0.13 ± 0.35
Control group	REG>NEU	0.45 ± 0.23	0.47 ± 0.30
(*N* = 16)	VIEW>NEU	0.09 ± 0.36	0.12 ± 0.30
ANOVA RESULTS (*P*-VALUES)			
Interaction effect	Condition × group	0.593	0.095
Main effects	Group	0.333	0.219
	Condition	0.000	0.002
Post-hoc t-test	REG>NEU:control vs. experimental	0.258	0.037
(*p*-value, two-tailed)	VIEW>NEU:control vs. experimental	0.592	0.954
	Experimental group:REG vs. VIEW	0.010	0.270
	Control group:REG vs. VIEW	0.001	0.001

Table shows parameter-estimate-contrast values from the anterior insula spheres. ***(A)*** *Neurofeedback training,* ***(B)*** *Transfer run. SD, standard deviation; REG, regulate; NEU, neutral.*

single-group analyses. Taken together, activations were largely congruent in the VIEW>NEUTRAL contrast. Brain regions involved were found in the occipital lobe, inferior temporal lobe (including the fusiform gyrus) and medial temporal lobe (including the bilateral amygdala). At the whole-brain, both groups also responded similar when instructed to regulate (REGULATE>NEUTRAL). Besides activation clusters spanning the occipital lobe and inferior temporal lobe, both groups activated the dorsomedial frontal cortex and the dorsolateral PFC. Consistent with the ROI analysis, the experimental group showed activation in the left but not right amygdala in this contrast. No activations were found in the VIEW>REGULATE contrast. While control participants activated clusters in the dorsomedial frontal cortex, anterior insula and left ventrolateral PFC contrasting REGULATE vs. VIEW, no activations exceeded the cluster-threshold in the experimental group.

RATING DATA

A repeated measures ANOVA for arousal and valence ratings of the stimuli used in the training neither showed significant group differences nor within-subjects effects (VIEW vs. REGULATE). There was also no significant Group interaction or main effect of Group found. An analysis of the arousal and valence ratings of the stimuli used in the transfer run also did not show significant group or within-subjects effects.

In terms of perceived regulation success, we did not find any significant differences between the experimental group [3.04 ± 1.89 (mean ± *SD*)] and the control group [3.85 ± 1.82; $T_{(30)}$ =

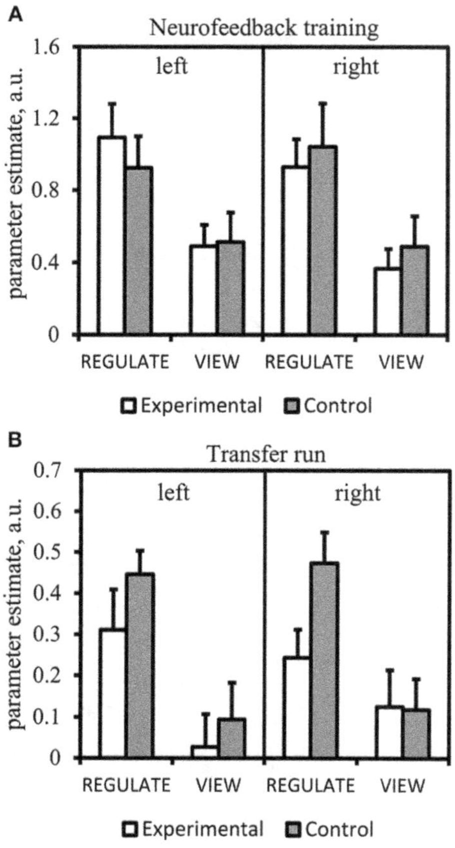

FIGURE 6 | Results of the region-of-interest analysis of the anterior insula. Mean parameter estimate of all voxels within the anterior insula masks of the REGULATE>NEUTRAL and VIEW>NEUTRAL contrast. Error bars indicate standard error of mean. A.u., artificial units. **(A)** Neurofeedback training (mean over all runs). **(B)** Transfer run.

1.530, $p = 0.226$]. Results did not change significantly when participants' ratings were compared on a run-by-run basis.

THERMOMETER VARIABILITY

The three-way ANOVA did not indicate an effect of Group on the variance of the number of bars displayed during the experimental runs (interactions: Condition × Run × Group: $p = 0.949$, Run × Group: $p = 0.149$, Condition × Group: $p = 0.582$; main effect of Group: $p = 0.685$).

DISCUSSION

Within one session of rt-fMRI-NF training, subjects receiving contingent amygdala feedback were successful in down-regulating amygdala activation in response to aversive pictures. In a subsequent run, subjects were able to decrease right amygdala activation without the feedback signal, which is in line with the hypothesis of a transfer of learned amygdala down-regulation. A control group receiving feedback from a standardized control region located in the rostal caudate did also reduce amygdala activation during training. A significant Region by Hemisphere by Group interaction indicated a specific effect of rt-fMRI-NF training on brain self-regulation in the transfer test. A trend in the two-way interactions of the amygdala (Hemisphere by Group) and right hemisphere (Region by Group) may suggest that this effect was lateralized to the right side. This proof of concept study is in line with previous reports on rt-fMRI-NF training of amygdala regulation (Zotev et al., 2011; Brühl et al., 2014) and extends the existing literature by providing evidence for the feasibility to use affective pictures as stimulus material to train amygdala down-regulation.

To provide evidence for a specificity of the treatment, the effect of the intervention needs to exceed the effect of a sham treatment which mimics external aspects of the real treatment. In other words, a placebo control is needed. In our study, we used the signal of a spatially well-defined control region located at the rostral caudate. We chose this region for its similarity with the experimental region in tissue composition and we matched the number of voxels taken to extract the NF signal for both groups. Furthermore, the literature does not indicate a function of the caudate comparable to the amygdala in emotion processing. This suggests that feedback from the control region may not specifically help in down-regulating amygdala activation in response to aversive stimuli. *Post-hoc* tests of the training phase illustrate, that the control region showed a positive change in BOLD signal amplitude in response to aversive pictures during REGULATE and VIEW (Supplementary Figure 1) and an analysis on the dynamics of the thermometer display does not indicate a significant difference between groups. The belief of receiving contingent feedback of affective brain activation may have prevented control subjects to become suspicious of a sham treatment or to become frustrated because of failure during the course of training. Due to the instructions, subjects knew that they would somehow have to engage in emotion regulation. Since we tested healthy participants, it is conceivable that all subjects were equipped with effective strategies to control their emotions in everyday life, and they may have employed these strategies to try to regulate the thermometer during training. Subjects of both groups may have applied strategies they had evaluated as successful based on their interpretation of the feedback signal and this may have impeded the detection of significant group differences during training. In this context it is not surprising that ratings of regulation success do not indicate a group difference. However, regulation-success was only estimated to be in the medium to low range. The lack of a difference in subjective success is in line with a previous report by Lawrence et al. (2013), who had trained one group with anterior insula NF and a control group with feedback from a control region located in the parietal lobe. It may be that a retrospective evaluation of regulation success is not sensible to capture between-group differences, especially when using placebo-feedback as a control. A better way to assess group differences may be via behavioral measures which are associated with the specific psychological function the intervention is thought to modulate. Regarding amygdala NF, future studies could let participants rate the subjective arousal and valence after regulation vs. natural viewing, which is known to be associated with amygdala activation to affective pictures (Zald, 2003; Anders et al., 2004).

The results of the transfer run provide first evidence that a rt-fMRI-NF training of amygdala down-regulation can have a differential effect on brain self-regulation in a placebo-controlled study. Further, results indicate a hemispheric asymmetry of brain self-regulation. There is an ongoing debate on a functional differentiation between left and right amygdala (Baas et al., 2004; Costafreda et al., 2008; Sergerie et al., 2008). However, methodological issues have been raised on interpreting laterality differences (LaBar et al., 2001; Mathiak et al., 2012) and no consistent laterality difference of amygdala activation has been reported in the emotion regulation literature (Buhle et al., 2013). A possible but rather speculative explanation for a lateralized transfer effect may state that subjects had tried different emotion regulation strategies during training which may have been successful in down-regulating the right as well as left amygdala. In the transfer run, however, participants may have used a strategy they had evaluated during training as most successful. Strategies approved as most successful may have preferentially involved neural processes of top-down control of the right amygdala. This interpretation endorses the choice of Brühl et al. (2014) to use the right amygdala for NF training.

The results of the anterior insula analysis largely complemented the results of the amygdala analysis. In the transfer run, the experimental group did not show a significant difference of right anterior insula responding when comparing the REGULATE to the VIEW condition, while the control group significantly up-regulated the anterior insula when instructed to regulate. In the group comparison, the experimental group showed less activation during REGULATE than the control group, which is in support of improved regulation of affective brain structures after amygdala NF. The group interaction, however, did only show a trend. As opposed to a training effect on the regulation of a rather circumscribed component of the brain's affective system, this result suggests that amygdala NF training may extend to the self-regulation of other brain regions in the domain of emotional processing. Future studies are needed to corroborate this finding.

To evaluate general effects of training and transfer, we conducted a whole-brain analysis between and within groups. The between-group analysis did not show significant group interactions. When instructed to naturally respond to aversive picture presentation, both groups congruently activated regions of the medial temporal lobe and the anterior insula, which are consistently found to be involved in the processing of emotion stimuli (Phan et al., 2002; Kober et al., 2008). This finding was consistent across the training and the transfer phase. When contrasting the REGULATE-condition against the non-affective control condition, both groups showed highly overlapping brain regions in the analysis of the transfer run. Results indicate that subjects from both groups had engaged in the top-down control of limbic and para-limbic regions when instructed to regulate their brain responses to aversive stimuli after training. The involvement of lateral PFC (Kalisch, 2009; Buhle et al., 2013), medial PFC/anterior cingulate cortex (Etkin et al., 2011; Paret et al., 2011), and anterior insula (Dosenbach et al., 2006; Hollmann et al., 2012; Veit et al., 2012) in emotion regulation and cognitive control is consistent with the existing fMRI literature. The single-group analyses of the REGULATE condition differed, however, regarding the rt-fMRI-NF training. Contrasting regulation with natural viewing of aversive pictures in the experimental group brought an acitivation cluster in the right lateral PFC, while the control group displayed activation of the dorsomedial frontal cortex. In the transfer run, the dorsomedial frontal cortex was again found activated only by the control group, indicating the involvement of similar brain structures during training and transfer in this group. The results may give a hint for the neural patterns implicated in down-regulation of the amygdala with and without contingent amygdala NF training. However, between-group differences may result from voxel-thresholding and may not reflect real differences in the involvement of brain regions between groups. Since we did not find significant group interactions, between-group differences remain descriptive and should be interpreted with caution.

We did not find evidence for a run-to-run improvement of amygdala down-regulation in the experimental group. This could have had several reasons, like exhaustion due to the duration of the scanning session or task difficulty. Future studies should try to improve the task design in order to make the NF training more efficient.

There are several limitations for this study. Regarding our hypotheses, we cannot conclude from the results that rt-fMRI-NF had a specific effect on the down-regulation of the BOLD signal amplitude of the amygdala response during the training phase. Additionally, we did not include a pre-training test to evaluate pre-post comparisons in amygdala regulation success. However, without any experience of rt-fMRI-NF, the instruction to regulate a brain region (the "feeling center") may be difficult to follow. Therefore, and to prevent exhaustion due to long scanning duration, we decided against a run similar to the transfer run before the training. Data from pre-post comparisons, however, could advance our understanding of whether and to what extent amygdala NF training can change the activation of neural circuitries of emotion regulation and may be easier to implement with another experimental design. Another potential limitation may be the display of contingent feedback during the control conditions (VIEW and NEUTRAL). First, subjects of both groups reported that the thermometer did sometimes rise during the NEUTRAL condition. Signal increases without an external aversive stimulus may have had several reasons, such as affective responses to internal stimuli or signal noise. This may have confused participants and could have made them suspicious of receiving a sham feedback. Second, contingent amygdala feedback during VIEW may have triggered evaluation and control processes similar as in the REGULATE condition. An at-trend main effect of the factor Group in the Condition × Group ANOVA of the right amygdala is in line with this interpretation and may result from the generalization of learned regulation to the natural viewing condition. Future studies are needed for replication and should consider the potential confound of a feedback display during the control condition in the study design. In this study only healthy female subjects were tested. There are fMRI studies reporting gender differences in the involvement of prefrontal and limbic regions during emotion regulation (McRae et al., 2008; Mak et al., 2009; Domes et al., 2010). Thus, the results reported here may not generalize to samples of male participants.

In conclusion, this study shows that contingent rt-fMRI-NF from the amygdala may improve the regulation of amygdala activation in response to aversive pictures. A test of transfer effects showed an influence of amygdala feedback vs. feedback from a control region on brain self-regulation. This study is a starting point for further research toward the application of rt-fMRI-NF of the amygdala as a potential intervention in psychiatric populations. In particular, down-regulation of the amygdala as demonstrated in the current study and elsewhere (Brühl et al., 2014) may be helpful for disorders characterized by problems in emotion regulation and elevated amygdala activity such as borderline personality disorder. In these patients, training skills for emotion regulation is a decisive aspect of successful psychotherapies (Stoffers et al., 2012). NF may be used to test and train individual emotion regulation skills and therefore provide an excellent tool to increase efficacy and time-to-success of psychotherapy in such conditions.

AUTHOR CONTRIBUTIONS

Christian Paret, Rosemarie Kluetsch, Matthias Ruf, Traute Demirakca, Gabriele Ende, and Christian Schmahl were involved in the design and conception of the work. Rosemarie Kluetsch, Steffen Hoesterey, and Christian Paret conducted the data acquisition. Christian Paret analyzed the fMRI data and wrote the manuscript. All authors (Christian Paret, Rosemarie Kluetsch, Matthias Ruf, Traute Demirakca, Steffen Hoesterey, Gabriele Ende, Christian Schmahl) were involved in the interpretation of data and revised the draft critically for important intellectual content. All authors approved the final version to be published and agreed to be accountable for all aspects of the work.

ACKNOWLEDGMENTS

We would like to thank Lydia Robnik and Martin Jungkunz for their support in study organization, Rebekka Knies, Kathrin Haeussler, and Marie-Luise Zeitler for recruitment and conducting the diagnostic interviews, Anja Voigt for her help with the preparation of figures, and Bettina Kirr for assisting in data acquisition. The study was part of the clinical research unit 256, funded by the German Research Foundation (DFG, SCHM 1526/14-1, EN 361/13-1).

REFERENCES

Anders, S., Lotze, M., Erb, M., Grodd, W., and Birbaumer, N. (2004). Brain activity underlying emotional valence and arousal: a response-related fMRI study. *Hum. Brain Mapp.* 23, 200–209. doi: 10.1002/hbm.20048

Baas, D., Aleman, A., and Kahn, R. S. (2004). Lateralization of amygdala activation: a systematic review of functional neuroimaging studies. *Brain Res. Brain Res. Rev.* 45, 96–103. doi: 10.1016/j.brainresrev.2004.02.004

Brühl, A. B., Scherpiet, S., Sulzer, J., Stämpfli, P., Seifritz, E., and Herwig, U. (2014). Real-time neurofeedback using functional MRI could improve down-regulation of amygdala activity during emotional stimulation: a proof-of-concept study. *Brain Topogr.* 27, 138–148. doi: 10.1007/s10548-013-0331-9

Buhle, J. T., Silvers, J. A., Wager, T. D., Lopez, R., Onyemekwu, C., Kober, H., et al. (2013). Cognitive reappraisal of emotion: a meta-analysis of human neuroimaging studies. *Cereb. Cortex.* doi: 10.1093/cercor/bht154. [Epub ahead of print].

Caria, A., Veit, R., Sitaram, R., Lotze, M., Weiskopf, N., Grodd, W., et al. (2007). Regulation of anterior insular cortex activity using real-time fMRI. *Neuroimage* 35, 1238–1246. doi: 10.1016/j.neuroimage.2007.01.018

Costafreda, S. G., Brammer, M. J., David, A. S., and Fu, C. H. Y. (2008). Predictors of amygdala activation during the processing of emotional stimuli: a meta-analysis of 385 PET and fMRI studies. *Brain Res. Rev.* 58, 57–70. doi: 10.1016/j.brainresrev.2007.10.012

Cox, R. W. (1996). AFNI: software for analysis and visualization of functional magnetic resonance neuroimages. *Comput. Biomed. Res.* 29, 162–173.

Damasio, A. R., Grabowski, T. J., Bechara, A., Damasio, H., Ponto, L. L., Parvizi, J., et al. (2000). Subcortical and cortical brain activity during the feeling of self-generated emotions. *Nat. Neurosci.* 3, 1049–1056. doi: 10.1038/79871

Diekhof, E. K., Geier, K., Falkai, P., and Gruber, O. (2011). Fear is only as deep as the mind allows: a coordinate-based meta-analysis of neuroimaging studies on the regulation of negative affect. *Neuroimage* 58, 275–285. doi: 10.1016/j.neuroimage.2011.05.073

Domes, G., Schulze, L., Böttger, M., Grossmann, A., Hauenstein, K., Wirtz, P. H., et al. (2010). The neural correlates of sex differences in emotional reactivity and emotion regulation. *Hum. Brain Mapp.* 31, 758–769. doi: 10.1002/hbm.20903

Dosenbach, N. U. F., Visscher, K. M., Palmer, E. D., Miezin, F. M., Wenger, K. K., Kang, H. C., et al. (2006). A core system for the implementation of task sets. *Neuron* 50, 799–812. doi: 10.1016/j.neuron.2006.04.031

Erk, S., Mikschl, A., Stier, S., Ciaramidaro, A., Gapp, V., Weber, B., et al. (2010). Acute and sustained effects of cognitive emotion regulation in major depression. *J. Neurosci.* 30, 15726–15734. doi: 10.1523/JNEUROSCI.1856-10.2010

Etkin, A., Egner, T., and Kalisch, R. (2011). Emotional processing in anterior cingulate and medial prefrontal cortex. *Trends Cogn. Sci.* 15, 85–93. doi: 10.1016/j.tics.2010.11.004

First, M. B., Spitzer, R. L., Gibbon, M., and Williams, J. B. W. (1997). *User's Guide for the Structured Clinical Interview for Dsm-IV Axis I Disorders: Scid-1 Clinician Version.* 1st Edn. Arlington: American Psychiatric Publishing.

Fonzo, G. A., Simmons, A. N., Thorp, S. R., Norman, S. B., Paulus, M. P., and Stein, M. B. (2010). Exaggerated and disconnected insular-amygdalar blood oxygenation level-dependent response to threat-related emotional faces in women with intimate-partner violence posttraumatic stress disorder. *Biol. Psychiatry* 68, 433–441. doi: 10.1016/j.biopsych.2010.04.028

Godlewska, B. R., Norbury, R., Selvaraj, S., Cowen, P. J., and Harmer, C. J. (2012). Short-term SSRI treatment normalises amygdala hyperactivity in depressed patients. *Psychol. Med.* 42, 2609–2617. doi: 10.1017/S0033291712000591

Goebel, R. (2014). *Dynamic ROIs. TBVUsersGuide.* Available online at: http://download.brainvoyager.com/tbv/TBVUsersGuide/Neurofeedback/DynamicROIs.html [Accessed July 10, 2014].

Goossens, L., Sunaert, S., Peeters, R., Griez, E. J. L., and Schruers, K. R. J. (2007). Amygdala hyperfunction in phobic fear normalizes after exposure. *Biol. Psychiatry* 62, 1119–1125. doi: 10.1016/j.biopsych.2007.04.024

Haaker, J., Gaburro, S., Sah, A., Gartmann, N., Lonsdorf, T. B., Meier, K., et al. (2013). Single dose of L-dopa makes extinction memories context-independent and prevents the return of fear. *Proc. Natl. Acad. Sci. U.S.A.* 110, E2428–E2436. doi: 10.1073/pnas.1303061110

Hermans, E. J., Henckens, M. J. A. G., Roelofs, K., and Fernández, G. (2012). Fear bradycardia and activation of the human periaqueductal grey. *Neuroimage* 66C, 278–287. doi: 10.1016/j.neuroimage.2012.10.063

Hollmann, M., Hellrung, L., Pleger, B., Schlögl, H., Kabisch, S., Stumvoll, M., et al. (2012). Neural correlates of the volitional regulation of the desire for food. *Int. J. Obes. (Lond.)* 36, 648–655. doi: 10.1038/ijo.2011.125

Johnstone, T., van Reekum, C. M., Urry, H. L., Kalin, N. H., and Davidson, R. J. (2007). Failure to regulate: counterproductive recruitment of top-down prefrontal-subcortical circuitry in major depression. *J. Neurosci.* 27, 8877–8884. doi: 10.1523/JNEUROSCI.2063-07.2007

Kalisch, R. (2009). The functional neuroanatomy of reappraisal: time matters. *Neurosci. Biobehav. Rev.* 33, 1215–1226. doi: 10.1016/j.neubiorev.2009.06.003

Kalisch, R., Wiech, K., Herrmann, K., and Dolan, R. J. (2006). Neural correlates of self-distraction from anxiety and a process model of cognitive emotion regulation. *J. Cogn. Neurosci.* 18, 1266–1276. doi: 10.1162/jocn.2006.18.8.1266

Kanske, P., Heissler, J., Schönfelder, S., Bongers, A., and Wessa, M. (2011). How to regulate emotion? Neural networks for reappraisal and distraction. *Cereb. Cortex* 21, 1379–1388. doi: 10.1093/cercor/bhq216

Kober, H., Barrett, L. F., Joseph, J., Bliss-Moreau, E., Lindquist, K., and Wager, T. D. (2008). Functional grouping and cortical-subcortical interactions in emotion: a meta-analysis of neuroimaging studies. *Neuroimage* 42, 998–1031. doi: 10.1016/j.neuroimage.2008.03.059

LaBar, K. S., Gitelman, D. R., Mesulam, M. M., and Parrish, T. B. (2001). Impact of signal-to-noise on functional MRI of the human amygdala. *Neuroreport* 12, 3461–3464. doi: 10.1097/00001756-200111160-00017

LaBar, K. S., and LeDoux, J. E. (1996). Partial disruption of fear conditioning in rats with unilateral amygdala damage: correspondence with unilateral temporal lobectomy in humans. *Behav. Neurosci.* 110, 991–997.

LaBar, K. S., LeDoux, J. E., Spencer, D. D., and Phelps, E. A. (1995). Impaired fear conditioning following unilateral temporal lobectomy in humans. *J. Neurosci.* 15, 6846–6855.

Lancaster, J. L., Woldorff, M. G., Parsons, L. M., Liotti, M., Freitas, C. S., Rainey, L., et al. (2000). Automated Talairach atlas labels for functional brain mapping. *Hum. Brain Mapp.* 10, 120–131. doi: 10.1002/1097-0193(200007)10:3<120::AID-HBM30>3.0.CO;2-8

Lang, P. J., Bradley, M. M., and Cuthbert, B. N. (2008). *International Affective Picture System (IAPS): Affective Ratings of Pictures and Instruction Manual. Technical Report A-8.* Gainsville, FL: University of Florida.

Lang, S., Kotchoubey, B., Frick, C., Spitzer, C., Grabe, H. J., and Barnow, S. (2012). Cognitive reappraisal in trauma-exposed women with borderline personality disorder. *Neuroimage* 59, 1727–1734. doi: 10.1016/j.neuroimage.2011.08.061

Lawrence, E. J., Su, L., Barker, G. J., Medford, N., Dalton, J., Williams, S. C. R., et al. (2013). Self-regulation of the anterior insula: reinforcement learning using real-time fMRI neurofeedback. *Neuroimage* 88C, 113–124. doi: 10.1016/j.neuroimage.2013.10.069

Linden, D. E. J., Habes, I., Johnston, S. J., Linden, S., Tatineni, R., Subramanian, L., et al. (2012). Real-time self-regulation of emotion networks in patients with depression. *PLoS ONE* 7:e38115. doi: 10.1371/journal.pone.0038115

Lipka, J., Hoffmann, M., Miltner, W. H. R., and Straube, T. (2013). Effects of cognitive-behavioral therapy on brain responses to subliminal and supraliminal threat and their functional significance in specific phobia. *Biol. Psychiatry.* doi: 10.1016/j.biopsych.2013.11.008. [Epub ahead of print].

Loranger, A. (1999). *International Personality Disorder Examination (IPDE): DSM-IV and ICD-10 Modules.* Odessa, FL: Psychological Assessment Resources.

Mak, A. K. Y., Hu, Z., Zhang, J. X. X., Xiao, Z., and Lee, T. M. C. (2009). Sex-related differences in neural activity during emotion regulation. *Neuropsychologia* 47, 2900–2908. doi: 10.1016/j.neuropsychologia.2009.06.017

Maldjian, J. A., Laurienti, P. J., Kraft, R. A., and Burdette, J. H. (2003). An automated method for neuroanatomic and cytoarchitectonic atlas-based interrogation of fMRI data sets. *Neuroimage* 19, 1233–1239. doi: 10.1016/S1053-8119(03)00169-1

Mathiak, K. A., Zvyagintsev, M., Ackermann, H., and Mathiak, K. (2012). Lateralization of amygdala activation in fMRI may depend on phase-encoding polarity. *MAGMA* 25, 177–182. doi: 10.1007/s10334-011-0285-4

McRae, K., Hughes, B., Chopra, S., Gabrieli, J. D. E., Gross, J. J., and Ochsner, K. N. (2010). The neural bases of distraction and reappraisal. *J. Cogn. Neurosci.* 22, 248–262. doi: 10.1162/jocn.2009.21243

McRae, K., Ochsner, K. N., Mauss, I. B., Gabrieli, J. J. D., and Gross, J. J. (2008). Gender differences in emotion regulation: an fMRI study of cognitive reappraisal. *Group Process. Intergroup Relat.* 11, 143–162. doi: 10.1177/1368430207088035

Niedtfeld, I., Schulze, L., Kirsch, P., Herpertz, S. C., Bohus, M., and Schmahl, C. (2010). Affect regulation and pain in borderline personality disorder: a possible link to the understanding of self-injury. *Biol. Psychiatry* 68, 383–391. doi: 10.1016/j.biopsych.2010.04.015

Ochsner, K. N., Ray, R. D., Cooper, J. C., Robertson, E. R., Chopra, S., Gabrieli, J. D. E., et al. (2004). For better or for worse: neural systems supporting the cognitive down- and up-regulation of negative emotion. *Neuroimage* 23, 483–499. doi: 10.1016/j.neuroimage.2004.06.030

Opialla, S., Lutz, J., Scherpiet, S., Hittmeyer, A., Jäncke, L., Rufer, M., et al. (2014). Neural circuits of emotion regulation: a comparison of mindfulness-based and cognitive reappraisal strategies. *Eur. Arch. Psychiatry Clin. Neurosci.* doi: 10.1007/s00406-014-0510-z. [Epub ahead of print].

Paret, C., Brenninkmeyer, J., Meyer, B., Yuen, K. S. L., Gartmann, N., Mechias, M.-L., et al. (2011). A test for the implementation-maintenance model of reappraisal. *Front. psychol.* 2:216. doi: 10.3389/fpsyg.2011.00216

Paret, C., Kluetsch, R., Ruf, M., Demirakca, T., Kalisch, R., Schmahl, C., et al. (2014). Transient and sustained BOLD signal time courses affect the detection of emotion-related brain activation in fMRI. *Neuroimage.* doi: 10.1016/j.neuroimage.2014.08.054. (in press).

Phan, K. L., Fitzgerald, D. A., Nathan, P. J., and Tancer, M. E. (2006). Association between amygdala hyperactivity to harsh faces and severity of social anxiety in generalized social phobia. *Biol. Psychiatry* 59, 424–429. doi: 10.1016/j.biopsych.2005.08.012

Phan, K. L., Wager, T., Taylor, S. F., and Liberzon, I. (2002). Functional neuroanatomy of emotion: a meta-analysis of emotion activation studies in PET and fMRI. *Neuroimage* 16, 331–348. doi: 10.1006/nimg.2002.1087

Ruiz, S., Lee, S., Soekadar, S. R., Caria, A., Veit, R., Kircher, T., et al. (2013). Acquired self-control of insula cortex modulates emotion recognition and brain network connectivity in schizophrenia. *Hum. Brain Mapp.* 34, 200–212. doi: 10.1002/hbm.21427

Schulze, L., Domes, G., Krüger, A., Berger, C., Fleischer, M., Prehn, K., et al. (2011). Neuronal correlates of cognitive reappraisal in borderline patients with affective instability. *Biol. Psychiatry* 69, 564–573. doi: 10.1016/j.biopsych.2010.10.025

Sergerie, K., Chochol, C., and Armony, J. L. (2008). The role of the amygdala in emotional processing: a quantitative meta-analysis of functional neuroimaging studies. *Neurosci. Biobehav. Rev.* 32, 811–830. doi: 10.1016/j.neubiorev.2007.12.002

Sheline, Y. I., Barch, D. M., Donnelly, J. M., Ollinger, J. M., Snyder, A. Z., and Mintun, M. A. (2001). Increased amygdala response to masked emotional faces in depressed subjects resolves with antidepressant treatment: an fMRI study. *Biol. Psychiatry* 50, 651–658. doi: 10.1016/S0006-3223(01)01263-X

Simmons, A. N., Matthews, S. C., Strigo, I. A., Baker, D. G., Donovan, H. K., Motezadi, A., et al. (2011). Altered amygdala activation during face processing in Iraqi and Afghanistani war veterans. *Biol. Mood Anxiety Disord.* 1, 6. doi: 10.1186/2045-5380-1-6

Stoffers, J. M., Völlm, B. A., Rücker, G., Timmer, A., Huband, N., and Lieb, K. (2012). Psychological therapies for people with borderline personality disorder. *Cochrane Database Syst. Rev.* 8:CD005652. doi: 10.1002/14651858.CD005652.pub2.

Sulzer, J., Haller, S., Scharnowski, F., Weiskopf, N., Birbaumer, N., Blefari, M. L., et al. (2013). Real-time fMRI neurofeedback: progress and challenges. *Neuroimage* 76, 386–399. doi: 10.1016/j.neuroimage.2013.03.033

Tzourio-Mazoyer, N., Landeau, B., Papathanassiou, D., Crivello, F., Etard, O., Delcroix, N., et al. (2002). Automated anatomical labeling of activations in SPM using a macroscopic anatomical parcellation of the MNI MRI single-subject brain. *Neuroimage* 15, 273–289. doi: 10.1006/nimg.2001.0978

Urry, H. L., van Reekum, C. M., Johnstone, T., Kalin, N. H., Thurow, M. E., Schaefer, H. S., et al. (2006). Amygdala and ventromedial prefrontal cortex are inversely coupled during regulation of negative affect and predict the diurnal pattern of cortisol secretion among older adults. *J. Neurosci.* 26, 4415–4425. doi: 10.1523/JNEUROSCI.3215-05.2006

Veit, R., Singh, V., Sitaram, R., Caria, A., Rauss, K., and Birbaumer, N. (2012). Using real-time fMRI to learn voluntary regulation of the anterior insula in the presence of threat-related stimuli. *Soc. Cogn. Affect. Neurosci.* 7, 623–634. doi: 10.1093/scan/nsr061

Victor, T. A., Furey, M. L., Fromm, S. J., Ohman, A., and Drevets, W. C. (2010). Relationship of emotional processing to masked faces in the amygdala to mood state and treatment in major depressive disorder. *Arch. Gen. Psychiatry* 67, 1128–1138. doi: 10.1001/archgenpsychiatry.2010.144

Wager, T. D., Davidson, M. L., Hughes, B. L., Lindquist, M. A., and Ochsner, K. N. (2008). Prefrontal-subcortical pathways mediating successful emotion regulation. *Neuron* 59, 1037–1050. doi: 10.1016/j.neuron.2008.09.006

Wessa, M., Kanske, P., Neumeister, P., Bode, K., Heissler, J., and Schönfelder, S. (2010). EmoPics: Subjektive und psychophysiologische Evaluation neuen Bildmaterials für die klinisch-bio-psychologische Forschung. *Zeitschrift für Klinische Psychologie und Psychotherapie, (Suppl. 1/11),* 77.

Young, K. D., Zotev, V., Phillips, R., Misaki, M., Yuan, H., Drevets, W. C., et al. (2014). Real-time FMRI neurofeedback training of amygdala activity in patients with major depressive disorder. *PLoS ONE* 9:e88785. doi: 10.1371/journal.pone.0088785

Zald, D. H. (2003). The human amygdala and the emotional evaluation of sensory stimuli. *Brain Res. Brain Res. Rev.* 41, 88–123. doi: 10.1016/S0165-0173(02)00248-5

Zotev, V., Krueger, F., Phillips, R., Alvarez, R. P., Simmons, W. K., Bellgowan, P., et al. (2011). Self-regulation of amygdala activation using real-time FMRI neurofeedback. *PLoS ONE* 6:e24522. doi: 10.1371/journal.pone.0024522

6

Estimating cognitive load during self-regulation of brain activity and neurofeedback with therapeutic brain-computer interfaces

Robert Bauer[1,2]* and Alireza Gharabaghi[1,2]*

[1] Division of Functional and Restorative Neurosurgery and Division of Translational Neurosurgery, Department of Neurosurgery, Eberhard Karls University Tuebingen, Tuebingen, Germany
[2] Neuroprosthetics Research Group, Werner Reichardt Centre for Integrative Neuroscience, Eberhard Karls University Tuebingen, Tuebingen, Germany

Correspondence:
Robert Bauer and Alireza Gharabaghi, Division of Functional and Restorative Neurosurgery and Division of Translational Neurosurgery, Department of Neurosurgery, Eberhard Karls University Tuebingen, Otfried-Mueller-Str.45, 72076 Tuebingen, Germany
e-mail: robert.bauer@cin.uni-tuebingen.de;
e-mail: alireza.gharabaghi@uni-tuebingen.de

Neurofeedback (NFB) training with brain-computer interfaces (BCIs) is currently being studied in a variety of neurological and neuropsychiatric conditions in an aim to reduce disorder-specific symptoms. For this purpose, a range of classification algorithms has been explored to identify different brain states. These neural states, e.g., self-regulated brain activity vs. rest, are separated by setting a threshold parameter. Measures such as the maximum classification accuracy (CA) have been introduced to evaluate the performance of these algorithms. Interestingly enough, precisely these measures are often used to estimate the subject's ability to perform brain self-regulation. This is surprising, given that the goal of improving the tool that differentiates between brain states is different from the aim of optimizing NFB for the subject performing brain self-regulation. For the latter, knowledge about mental resources and work load is essential in order to adapt the difficulty of the intervention accordingly. In this context, we apply an analytical method and provide empirical data to determine the zone of proximal development (ZPD) as a measure of a subject's cognitive resources and the instructional efficacy of NFB. This approach is based on a reconsideration of item-response theory (IRT) and cognitive load theory for instructional design, and combines them with the CA curve to provide a measure of BCI performance.

Keywords: neurofeedback, cognitive load theory, zone of proximal development, workload, instructional design, brain-computer interface

INTRODUCTION

Brain-computer interfaces (BCIs) support reinforcement learning of brain self-regulation by feedback and reward. While assistive BCIs aim to replace lost functions by controlling external devices (Yanagisawa et al., 2011; Hochberg et al., 2012; Collinger et al., 2013; Wang et al., 2013), the ultimate goal of restorative or therapeutic approaches is to improve specific functions by neurofeedback (NFB) training, e.g., hand and arm control following a stroke (Ang et al., 2010; Shindo et al., 2011; Buch et al., 2012; Ramos-Murguialday et al., 2013; Gharabaghi et al., 2014a,b). The fundamental approach of NFB is based on the idea that physiological signals during restful waking (Mantini et al., 2007; Albert et al., 2009; De Vico Fallani et al., 2011) are contrasted to the signals during the task condition, using classification algorithms to weight the respective features (Theodoridis and Koutroumbas, 2009). In this regard, restorative BCI is similar to assistive BCI. However, unlike assistive BCI approaches, which select features on the basis of their ability to maximally contrast the two states, the feature space for restorative BCI and NFB training is constrained in accordance with the specific treatment rationale. In stroke rehabilitation, for example, the feature space might be restricted to power in the β-range (15–30 Hz), since decreased movement-related desynchronization in this frequency range is related to the amount of motor impairment after the insult (Rossiter et al., 2014). During restorative BCI training, the power of the frequency band is therefore estimated, and the desired modulation of this feature space is reinforced using appropriate visual, auditory or haptic feedback (Gharabaghi et al., 2014a,b). The feature weights are deliberately constrained during these interventions and the modality of feedback is designed to maximize the reinforcing effect of NFB (Sherlin et al., 2011; Vukelić et al., 2014). By contrast, during assistive BCI, the feature weights are calculated so as to allow maximal separation (Blankertz et al., 2008; Theodoridis and Koutroumbas, 2009) and the classification output is used for communication or robotic control (Wolpaw et al., 2002). While the primary goal for assistive BCI is accuracy and speed, the main goal for restorative BCI is reinforcement and learning. A theoretical difference therefore exists between the self-regulation of brain activity and the classification algorithm (Wood et al., 2014). However, although there are several ways of measuring the performance of an assistive BCI (Thomas et al., 2013; Thompson et al., 2013), similar appropriate measures for restorative BCI and NFB are currently not available. The most common measure for BCI is classification accuracy (CA). While the magnitude of CA has been used to estimate subject's ability to perform brain self-regulation, this interpretation currently lacks theoretical foundation (Blankertz et al., 2010; Buch et al., 2012; Hammer et al., 2012). What is more, there is no consensus regarding what approaches are appropriate for disentangling the performance of subject and classifier from each other, nor is there any theory as to how they are connected with each other.

By integrating classification theory (Theodoridis and Koutroumbas, 2009) with item response theory (Safrit et al., 1989), we describe how the relationship between the classification algorithm and the ability for self-regulation can be understood. In addition, on the basis of the theory of cognitive load for instructional design (Sweller, 1994; Schnotz and Kürschner, 2007), we will describe how the CA can be interpreted within the framework of NFB training. Our argument is based on the fact that it is possible to make an off-line calculation of the positive rates for different classifiers and thresholds. We will argue that the true positive and the false positive curve provide information about the subject's ability and his/her performance when support is provided. Moreover, since the shape of CA depends on the difference between true and false positive rate (FPR), we propose that it contains information about the subject's zone of proximal development (ZPD). Therefore, on the basis of the theory of cognitive learning, the ZPD may serve as an indirect measure of the subject's cognitive resources (Allal and Ducrey, 2000; Schnotz and Kürschner, 2007).

In this respect, the goal of this paper is to provide a measurement theory for subjects' abilities and ZPD during NFB training. We support this theory by mathematical models and by evidence from empirical data.

EMPIRICAL DATASET

Exemplary data is based on two right-handed, healthy subjects, one female (age 19) and one male (age 31), who presented different abilities for brain self-regulation. They each performed 75 trials of cued motor imagery. The trial structure consisted of consecutive preparatory (2 s), motor imagery (6 s) and rest (6 s) phases, each of which was initiated by a specific auditory cue. Electroencephalography (EEG) was recorded at 64 channels in accordance with the 10–20 system with Brain Products amplifiers and analyzed offline with custom-written scripts and Fieldtrip in Matlab (Oostenveld et al., 2011) according to the following steps. Data was down-sampled to 200 Hz and band-pass filtered between 14 and 26 Hz using a Butterworth filter. Wavelet transformation was used to perform a time-frequency analysis for time steps of 50 ms for the power in the β-range (15–25 Hz) over sensorimotor regions (FC3, C3 and CP3). For each trial, the power at each time point was normalized by z-scoring based on the mean and standard deviation of the power distribution in the rest and preparatory phase. Both subjects gave written, informed consent prior to participation. The study was approved by the local ethics committee.

LINKING SUBJECT'S ABILITY FOR BRAIN SELF-REGULATION WITH THE CLASSIFICATION PERFORMANCE

In the following section, we will propose a link between the ability for brain self-regulation, as estimated by the item function, with the classifier performance, as estimated by the rate function. This integration will enable us to apply off-line analysis of the positive rate across different thresholds to determine the subjects' ability for brain self-regulation.

RATE FUNCTIONS

When applying NFB for therapeutic purposes, a two-class separation of brain states is usually performed, i.e., rest vs. learned self-regulation of brain activity. Due to the fact that most of the classifiers used in NFB are based on supervised learning algorithms employing linear discriminant analysis, the sensitivity and specificity of the classifier can be calculated relatively easily. The sensitivity informs us how often the classifier detects sufficient self-regulation while the subject is performing brain self-regulation (true positive rate or TPR). The specificity informs us how often the classifier detects rest while the subject is performing insufficient brain self-regulation (true negative rate or TNR). Since the probabilities of each conditional classification must add up to 1 within each class, the false negative rate (FNR) is equal to 1-TPR, and the FPR is equal to 1-TNR. CA is based on the average of TPR and TNR.

$$CA = \frac{(\text{TPR} + \text{TNR})}{2}$$

THRESHOLD-BASED RATE FUNCTIONS

These rates are functions of the threshold θ (Theodoridis and Koutroumbas, 2009). During the training, the threshold θ usually remains fixed, and the rates therefore also remain fixed. However, provided that the electrophysiological signals have been recorded and stored, the positive rate can be calculated offline after the training for any threshold. We exemplify this by the empirical dataset (see **Figure 1**): the higher—i.e., the more challenging—the threshold, the stronger the desynchronization must be if it is to be classified as positive (see **Figure 1A**). The examples also reveal how subjects vary in their ability for brain self-regulation, e.g., sensorimotor beta-band desynchronization. The first subject shows stronger desynchronization and is thus able to reach more challenging thresholds (see **Figure 1A**) than the second subject, who has less pronounced brain self-regulation (see **Figure 1C**).

In parallel, this data enables us to characterize the classifier performance: detecting "positive" during the motor imagery phase (second 0 to 6) is a true positive, whereas "positive" during the preparatory phase (second −2 to 0) is a false positive. The average rate of positives for each phase is a suitable measure for characterizing a classifier's performance, i.e., true and FPRs are expressed as probabilities in the range between 0 and 1 (see **Figures 1B/D**). The first subject has higher TPRs for all thresholds (see **Figure 1B**) than the second subject (see **Figure 1D**).

For most classifiers, the rate functions result in sigmoidal rate curves. We show this sigmoidal shape for the TPR

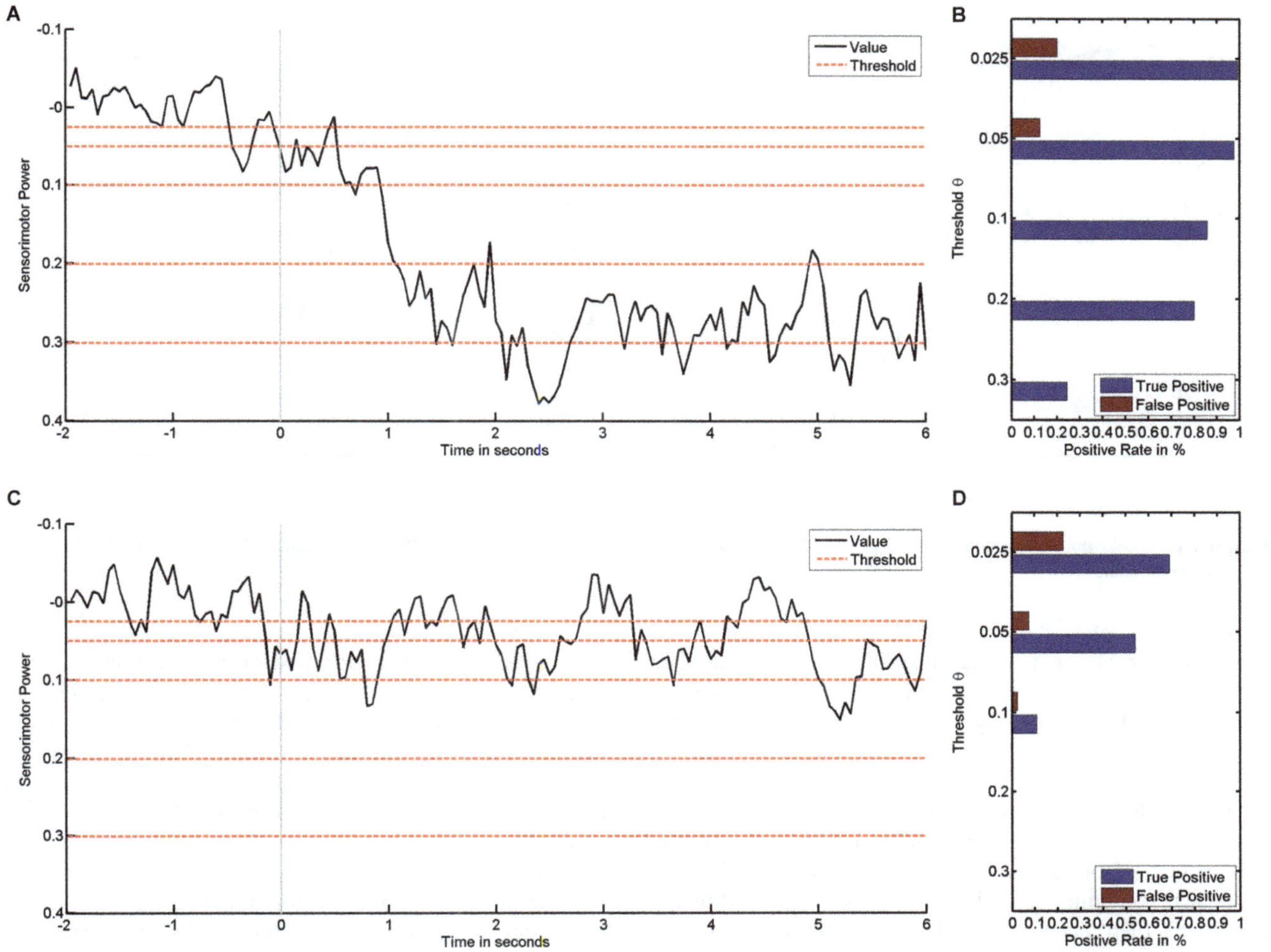

FIGURE 1 | It shows how sensorimotor beta power values are transformed into positive rates by threshold. Left subplots show time course of sensorimotor power in black and different threshold levels in red for subject #1 **(A)** and subject #2 **(C)**. The respective rates of false and true positives for the first **(B)** and second subject **(D)** show how rates decrease as the threshold increases.

of the empirical dataset (see **Figure 2A**). The higher the thresholds, the more the probability of success decreases in a logistic fashion. Accordingly, the location of the first subject's true positive curve is further to the right, indicating a generally higher success rate. However, the shape of the respective curves for the first and the second subject are highly similar.

ITEM FUNCTIONS

The *rate functions* described resemble the *item functions* used in the psychometric item-response theory (IRT). In various fields of research, such as in assessment psychology (De Champlain, 2010) or motor behavior research (Safrit et al., 1989), the parameters of the item functions are usually estimated across datasets of several subjects and items. This enables us to quantify the respective variability of subject's ability and task difficulty necessary for fitting algorithms. If, for example a mathematical test battery is distributed to a school class, the marginal success rates enable us to estimate the difficulty of a specific test and the ability of a single subject. Generally speaking, students with a higher mathematical ability achieve a higher success rate, and easier tests should result in higher average success rates. This information about the relative ranks based on success rates can be used for parameter estimation. More specifically, the shape of these success curves can be approximated by a two-parameter logistic model (2PLM) using the following function (Safrit et al., 1989; De Champlain, 2010):

$$P = \frac{1}{1 + e^{-D(\alpha - \theta)}}$$

In this function, e is Euler's number and D is the slope of the curve. The parameter θ, generally known as the threshold parameter in rate functions, now represents the difficulty of the task. Ability α and difficulty θ are located on the same axis. They can therefore be measured in one dimension. The location of the curve depends on the difference between the difficulty of a task and the subject's ability α. The shape of the curve depends on the slope parameter D, and a value of ~1.7 would result in

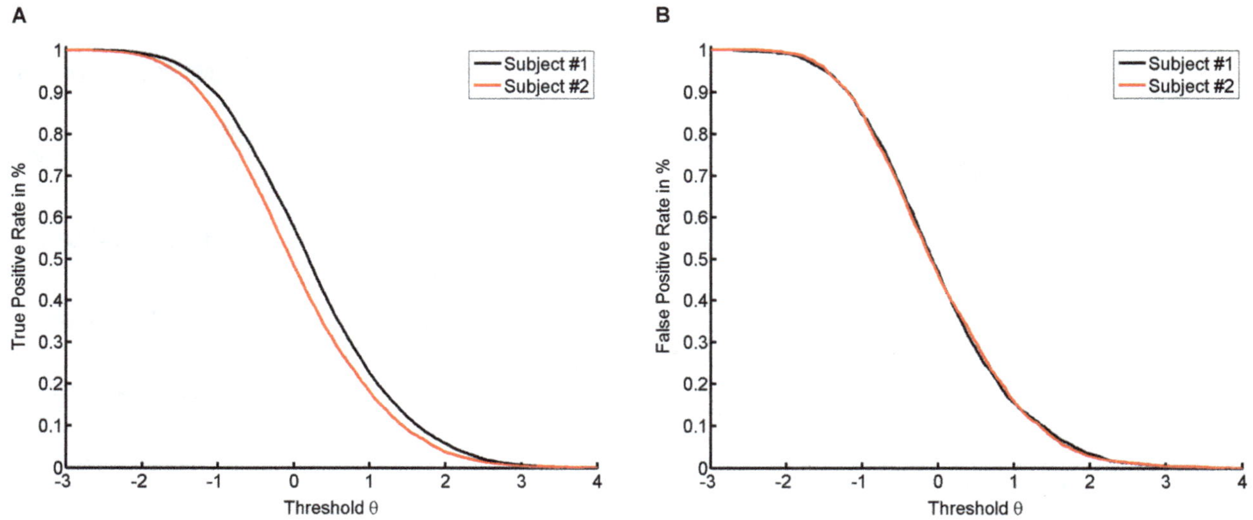

FIGURE 2 | It shows the numerical results with true positive rate (TPR) (A) and false positive rate (FPR) (B) for both subjects on the basis of the average across trials.

an approximate fit for a normal distribution (De Champlain, 2010). If the slope is identical for all curves, all item function are parallel and the difficulty level θ is the only changeable parameter.

SIMILARITY OF RATE AND ITEM FUNCTIONS

For dichotomous items, the probability of success is modeled as a function of the difficulty of the item and the ability of the subject. Assuming that the latter is stable, the difficulty of an item then depends on the design of the task. The combination of NFB task, i.e., the classification algorithm, the trial structure, the cues and any instructions or extraneous aspects constitute the phrasing of such an item. By way of example: in NFB training, our aim is to differentiate between sufficient and insufficient modulation of brain activity. If we were to use a questionnaire instead of EEG and BCI, we might phrase an item: "Are you currently performing sufficient brain self-regulation?" to which the possible answers would be "yes" and "no". However, since the decision about "yes" or "no" is based on physiological recordings during the task, a *post hoc* reassessment for different thresholds is possible. This recalculation enables us to apply virtually the same items over a range of difficulties. In addition, threshold-based recalculation modifies only one aspect of the "item", namely the difficulty parameter; an aspect that lies in one clearly defined dimension. These properties (unidimensionality, off-line analysis) allow for an interpretation of the parameters that describe the positive rate curves on the threshold dimension within the framework of the item response theory.

INTERPRETATION OF CURVE PARAMETERS

TRUE POSITIVE CURVE REPORTS ON ABILITY

Due to the fact that the measurement of the subject's ability for brain self-regulation can be performed *post hoc*, NFB training is comparable to an action like videotaping a sports exercise such as long jump. The data acquired during the task can then be used later to estimate several aspects of the performance. As in sports training, the compound ability can be divided into subsets (e.g., sprinting, take-off, and landing in long jump). In this example, the coach would be ill-advised to reward any jump independent of the actual performance. Therefore, specificity matters.

NFB training has the ability to provide this specificity by selecting the appropriate features and classification algorithms. In addition to determining the threshold to be passed by the event-related desynchronisation (ERD), additional features might include the speed of the power dip in the first two seconds or continuity of desynchronization. This highlights the fact that the reinforced features must be carefully selected for their respective clinical or rehabilitative purpose.

In this respect, it is also important to note that functional improvement is a combination of several abilities and preconditions, of which for instance, brain self-regulation of sensorimotor beta-rhythms is only one example. Others, such as reaching out and holding a certain position with the upper limb, as assessed in the Fugl-Meyer assessment (Deakin et al., 2003), or interacting with an object, as assessed in the Broetz hand assessment (Brötz et al., 2014), necessitate the involvement of parieto-frontal circuits for motor planning (Andersen and Cui, 2009) and sensorimotor circuits for execution (Chouinard and Paus, 2006). Along these lines, stroke survivors who train to modulate the activity of the primary motor cortex (Kaiser et al., 2011; Kilavik et al., 2012) show improvements in this ability only if the fronto-parietal integrity is preserved (Buch et al., 2012). Training such ability of brain-self-regulation may therefore be related both directly and indirectly to the respective function, e.g., moving the upper extremity. However, improving brain self-regulation does not necessarily lead to functional improvements, since these may also depend on abilities and preconditions that are not influenced by the NFB training. Improvements are therefore required with regard to the clinical efficacy of such a training (Ramos-Murguialday et al., 2013; Ang et al., 2014) by researching the feedback modality (Gomez-Rodriguez et al., 2011) or using it in combination with simultaneous cortical stimulation (Gharabaghi et al., 2014a). Screening examinations might also be necessary to determine the eligibility of subjects for a specific intervention (Stinear et al., 2012; Burke Quinlan et al., 2014; Vukelić et al., 2014). In addition, the validity of functional assessment scores requires re-evaluation in the light of biomarkers of sub-clinical improvement.

We therefore conclude that the location of the TPR can be interpreted as a subject's ability for brain self-regulation, regardless of the potential influence of this ability on a specific function. In this respect, the location of the true positive curve—mathematically speaking, the point of maximal slope and halfway between success and failure—provides information about the subject's ability to perform the task which is defined by the features and the classifier.

FALSE POSITIVE CURVE REPORTS ON ATTEMPT

According to our previous example, a long jump coach would be ill-advised not to reward any jump. To be more precise, for reasons of motivation, even attempts should sometimes be rewarded, or support is required to transform an attempt into a success. In the case of NFB, specificity and sensitivity also have to be balanced according to their importance for learning. If the task remains identical, such a balance can only be achieved by changing the threshold. Decreasing the threshold increases the number of false positives (see **Figure 2B**). Since the classifier normalizes to rest, there is no apparent difference in the location of the FPR between the two subjects (see **Figure 2B**). This indicates that the subjects have the same opportunity to try to perform the task. This theory is supported by the following line of argument. In this context, "support" or "help" can be formalized by assuming that the subject with the current level of ability α is unable to perform the task at the given level of difficulty θ, whereas providing help will lead to success. If we then detect a success, this will be a "false positive" result, since the subject's current ability is too low for him/her to actually succeed. If no help is provided, the success achieved will be a "true positive" result. This approach will lead to a range of thresholds which are defined by two limits. The lower limit will be marked by the most difficult task that the subject can perform when help is provided. The upper limit is defined by the most difficult task that can be performed by the subject without help (see **Figure 3A**). Once the subject no longer benefits from help, e.g., due to overly high intrinsic or extrinsic load, he can no longer benefit from the training.

SHAPE OF CLASSIFICATION ACCURACY SHEDS LIGHT ON THE ZONE OF PROXIMAL DEVELOPMENT

The range between the most difficult tasks that can be achieved by the subject with and without help, respectively, can be defined as the ZPD. Cognitive load theory argues that mental load can be divided into three categories: intrinsic load, extrinsic load and germane load (Jong, 2009). Intrinsic load resembles the difficulty of the task and is mainly caused by the element interactivity of the task. Extraneous load is mainly caused by irrelevant information. Germane load is caused by the construction and subsequent automation of schemas, i.e., learning. Lower difficulty results in a reduction of intrinsic load while extrinsic load will increase, since the instructional material now contains irrelevant information. If a task is too easy (i.e., $\theta \ll \alpha$) or too difficult (i.e., $\theta \gg \alpha$) for a given ability, the extrinsic or the intrinsic load of the task would be too high.

For every given level of difficulty and ability for a task, there is therefore a ZPD, where learning is possible (Schnotz and Kürschner, 2007). The cognitive load theory thus provides a feasible explanation as to why the boundaries of ZPD are characterized by TPR and FPR (Allal and Ducrey, 2000; see **Figure 3B**). A second line of argumentation considers the likelihood of reward. Since a subject cannot discern a reward with identical qualities, the only way of differentiating between a true and a false reward is to determine the relative probability of their occurrence. The difference between the true and FPR might therefore be a good approximation of the difference with respect to the informational content of the two reward rates. Although more elaborate measures might be better suited to this divergence (MacKay, 2003), the most straightforward approach would consider the magnitude and the shape of ZPD as estimated by a linear transformation of CA in accordance with the following equations:

$$
\begin{aligned}
CA &= \frac{TPR + TNR}{2} \\
ZPD &= TPR - FPR \\
TNR &= 1 - FPR \\
CA &= \frac{TPR + (1 - FPR)}{2} = \frac{TPR - FPR + 1}{2} \\
(2 * CA) - 1 &= TPR - FPR \\
ZPD &= (2 * CA) - 1
\end{aligned}
$$

CONCLUSION AND OUTLOOK

In the sections above, we have shown how the true and false positives rates of brain self-regulation can be interpreted within the framework of NFB. We have demonstrated that there is a natural relationship between classification of rate functions and item response functions. We have revealed the connection between applying a threshold to ERD signals and estimating the ability to perform ERD. In this respect, the true positive curve provides information as to the brain's ability to perform brain self-regulation in a NFB task. In addition, we showed that not only can the false positive curve provide information about attempts to perform the task but it can also set the lower limit of the ZPD. Below, we will illustrate how the ZPD, in its capacity as a transformation of CA, can support the instructional design of NFB interventions.

CONCLUSION REGARDING CLASSIFICATION ACCURACY

The ZPD can be used to compare different classification algorithms. In BCI approaches, classification algorithms are often trained to maximize CA. This can result in a peaky but narrow ZPD (see **Figure 4A**) instead of a flat but broad ZPD (see **Figure 4B**), although the area of ZPD is equal in both cases. A

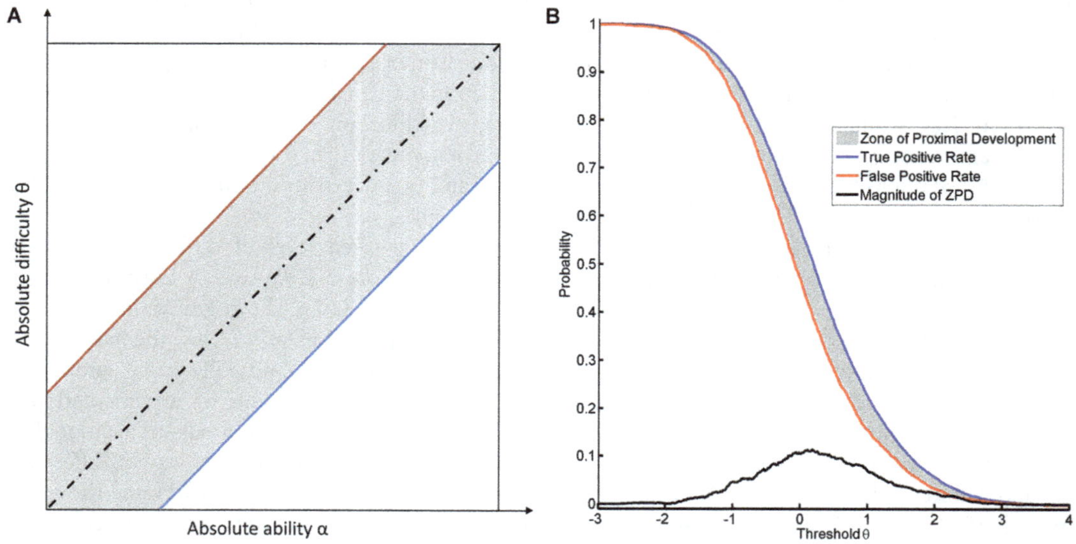

FIGURE 3 | It illustrates the concept of ZPD. (A) shows the dependance of the location of the ZPD from the absolute difficulty and the absolute ability. The ZPD width is based on the between the true and false positive rate. The blue line indicates the success rate of the task when performed without help (true positive rate) and the red line indicates the success rate due to help (false positive rate). The dotted black line indicates the equality of difficulty and ability. The area of ZPD is shown in gray. **(B)** shows the ZPD based on FPR and TPR over different thresholds for the first subject.

more broadly shaped ZPD indicates that learning can occur over a larger range of thresholds, whereas a peaky shape means that maximal help is available only for a narrow range of thresholds. This being the case, slight misalignments might have significant adverse effects. The shape of CA may therefore serve as a measure to evaluate whether or not a NFB task is instructionally effective. While the best general instructional efficacy is obviously achieved by NFB training with a high *and* broad ZPD, interpreting the shape enables us to apply tailored approaches. These might be more effective with regard to instructional needs for specific subjects and environments. A broad ZPD might be more robust for home-based training with low availability of supervision and the possibility of noisy measurements. A peaky ZPD might be more suitable for environments where professionals can perform alignments, i.e., adapt the classification algorithm or correct noisy measurements. Shaping the ZPD can thus support instructional design of NFB interventions. The approach presented here will also be applicable to classification algorithms resulting in non-normal distributions where TPR and TNR are calculated numerically (see **Figure 3B**), since the interpretation is also supported by non-parametric IRT-models provided that TPR and FPR are monotonic functions (Mokken and Lewis, 1982; Rost, 2004).

RELATIONSHIP TO ALTERNATIVE MEASURES OF PERFORMANCE AND FEEDBACK

CA is by far the most widely reported measure of performance for BCIs and can be used for both synchronized (e.g., cued) and self-paced interventions (Thomas et al., 2013). However, for some clinical applications, additional measures of performance that are regarded as relevant for the treatment goal have been developed. These include the latency to movement onset or the maximum consecutive movement time in stroke rehabilitation (Ramos-Murguialday et al., 2013) and the path efficiency for a high degree of freedom prosthetic control in tetraplegia (Collinger et al., 2013). How does the ZPD now relate to these alternative performance measures?

These alternative measures may sometimes be translated into one of the basic measures used for calculating the ZPD, e.g., the average movement rate could also be understood as a TPR. However, such measures are much more liable to contain unique information about additional abilities that are required for the given task to be performed, such as already mentioned in the paragraph on the interpretation of the true positive curve.

Since learning is conceptually linked to the accuracy of feedback, we propose that a NFB task should be characterized by its instructional efficacy with regard to the action to be trained. This instructional efficacy is characterized by the feedback curves. In this context, the CA changes as soon as the coupling of the feedback to the action changes. The shape of the ZPD will therefore be useful for the instructional design of the intervention and tends to be independent of other task-specific measures. If, for example, the subject receives feedback to alternative actions, any improvement in these actions will be caused by the task's instructional design. In this respect, a ZPD, e.g., for latency of movement onset or path efficiency, may also exist. Estimating the ZPD for these measures would be similar to the approach illustrated above.

It should be borne in mind that the theory presented here is based on the classical binary feedback, the distance between feedback and no feedback being one bit of information, i.e., reward (Ortega and Braun, 2010). Alternative approaches such as

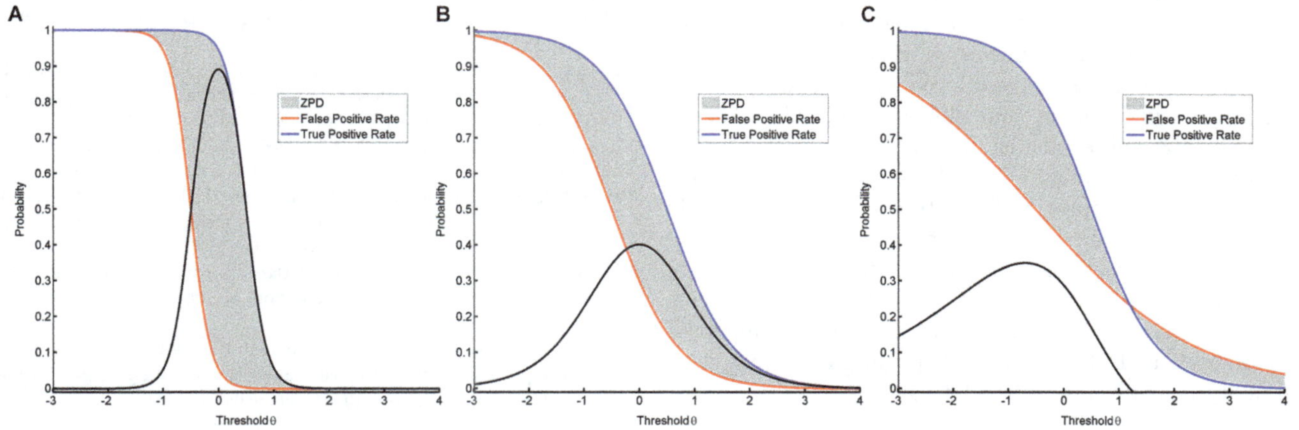

FIGURE 4 | It visualizes different shapes of ZPD. In the first two models **(A, B)**, the discrimination is different despite the distance between the two conditions being equal, resulting in ZPDs with equal areas. **(A)** shows success rates for a peaky but narrow ZPD based on a two-parametric model with equal but high discrimination values for both positive functions. **(B)** shows success rates for a broad but flat ZPD based on a two-parametric model with equal but low discrimination values. **(C)** shows success rates for a ZPD with a break-point based on a two-parametric model with unequal discrimination values.

continuous feedback (e.g., the frequency of an auditory signal) or psychophysical perception rules (e.g., the perception of the duration of binary feedback in a log-linear fashion) do, of course, affect the bit-rate and may thus increase the achievable speed of learning. However, since the ZPD is based on a single bit as a distance metric, adequate mapping of the ZPD for alternative feedback approaches will probably be mathematically demanding. In order to interpret the curves under such conditions, further research and specific transformations might be necessary. A system analytical perspective, where continuous feedback can be understood as a pattern of step functions, and a complex-valued ZPD might help to solve such aspects. Nonetheless, the real-valued ZPD based on the single bit of feedback will also remain a fundamental building block of such advanced approaches.

CONCLUSION WITH REGARD TO COGNITIVE RESOURCES

The ZPD may also act as a measure to compare different subjects with regard to their cognitive resources for a NFB task. If two subjects perform the very same NFB training, one might show a peaky and narrow ZPD (see **Figure 4A**) while the other has a broad and flat ZPD (see **Figure 4B**). Since in this case both curves indicate equal abilities, this difference in the respective shapes requires an alternative explanation. On the basis of the relevance of cognitive resources for the ZPD (Schnotz and Kürschner, 2007), we postulate that the shape of ZPD can also be applied to measure a subject's cognitive resources for coping with the mental load that occurs during a misalignment between ability and difficulty. Such an interpretation would, furthermore, permit a different view on the discussion about BCI illiteracy (Vidaurre and Blankertz, 2010). In particular, when the curves of TPR and FPR cross, they provide information about the specific break-points of that task. At this point, any support provided by the instructional design of the training will cease to be beneficial and will begin to be detrimental for the performance (see **Figure 4C**). This would be indicated by a negative value for the ZPD.

However, these concepts require validation by future research. Measurements of cognitive resources are currently based on psychophysiological recordings (e.g., heart rate variability, blink rate, electrodermal response), which are highly variable and very difficult to generalize across task conditions (Cegarra and Chevalier, 2008; Novak et al., 2010). Motor imagery itself can also cause vegetative effects related to the imagined movement, e.g., subjects imagining running at 12 km/h had an increased heart rate and pulmonary ventilation as compared to walking at 5 km/h (Decety et al., 1991). Mental imagery might therefore affect psychophysiological biomarkers, masking the measurement of the mental effort unrelated to the imagery content. One alternative to psychophysiological measures is the application of self-rating questionnaires. However, from the subject's point of view, it is often not possible to distinguish between the intrinsic, extrinsic and germane load (Cegarra and Chevalier, 2008). What is more, many psychophysiological measures and questionnaires can be sampled only at a very low rate. For example, the low frequency part of the heart rate commences at 0.04 Hz (Malik et al., 1996), meaning that at least 25 s of clean data have to be recorded for adequate frequency resolution of the Fourier transformation. Furthermore, slow frequency fluctuations in the EEG (<0.1 Hz) can correlate with psychophysiological performance, but they require similarly large time windows. In addition, slow fluctuations in the EEG measurements appear to be highly masked by imagery-related fluctuations, e.g., movement-related cortical potentials (Shibasaki and Hallett, 2006). This is also an issue if higher frequency components of the EEG are used to estimate cognitive resources, e.g., in the gamma range (Grosse-Wentrup et al., 2011), since they need to be disentangled from pure motor-related fluctuations in the same frequency band (de Lange et al., 2008; Miller et al., 2012).

In this context, the shape of ZPD might prove useful for disentangling the multitude of interacting and complex psychophysiological measurements in challenging tasks. This perspective is in agreement with the understanding that a proper alignment of ability and difficulty will reduce mental effort (Schnotz and Kürschner, 2007). Future studies might focus on psychophysiological correlates of the shape of the ZPD. Furthermore, improving the instructional material should help to reduce extrinsic load. NFB training could similarly be supported by "instructions", e.g., by providing haptic feedback (Gomez-Rodriguez et al., 2011) or visual and auditory cueing (Heremans et al., 2009). Systematic research on the impact of these feedback modalities on the ZPD might provide insight on their utility in guiding instructional design.

ACKNOWLEDGMENTS

Robert Bauer was supported by the Graduate Training Centre of Neuroscience, International Max Planck Research School, Tuebingen, Germany. Alireza Gharabaghi was supported by grants from the German Research Council and from the Federal Ministry for Education and Research [BFNT 01GQ0761, BMBF 16SV3783, BMBF 03160064B, BMBF V4UKF014]. We wish to thank Valerio Raco for fruitful discussions regarding the concept of cognitive load theory.

REFERENCES

Albert, N. B., Robertson, E. M., Mehta, P., and Miall, R. C. (2009). Resting state networks and memory consolidation. *Commun. Integr. Biol.* 2, 530–532. doi: 10.4161/cib.2.6.9612

Allal, L., and Ducrey, G. P. (2000). Assessment of—or in—the zone of proximal development. *Learn. Instr.* 10, 137–152. doi: 10.1016/s0959-4752(99)00025-0

Andersen, R. A., and Cui, H. (2009). Intention, action planning and decision making in parietal-frontal circuits. *Neuron* 63, 568–583. doi: 10.1016/j.neuron.2009.08.028

Ang, K. K., Guan, C., Chua, K. S. G., Ang, B. T., Kuah, C., Wang, C., et al. (2010). Clinical study of neurorehabilitation in stroke using EEG-based motor imagery brain-computer interface with robotic feedback. *Conf. Proc. IEEE Eng. Med. Biol. Soc.* 2010, 5549–5552. doi: 10.1109/iembs.2010.5626782

Ang, K. K., Guan, C., Phua, K. S., Wang, C., Zhou, L., Tang, K. Y., et al. (2014). Brain-computer interface-based robotic end effector system for wrist and hand rehabilitation: results of a three-armed randomized controlled trial for chronic stroke. *Front. Neuroeng.* 7:30. doi: 10.3389/fneng.2014.00030

Blankertz, B., Sannelli, C., Halder, S., Hammer, E. M., Kübler, A., Müller, K.-R., et al. (2010). Neurophysiological predictor of SMR-based BCI performance. *Neuroimage* 51, 1303–1309. doi: 10.1016/j.neuroimage.2010.03.022

Blankertz, B., Tomioka, R., Lemm, S., Kawanabe, M., and Muller, K. (2008). Optimizing spatial filters for robust EEG single-trial analysis. *IEEE Signal Process. Mag.* 25, 41–56. doi: 10.1109/msp.2008.4408441

Brötz, D., Del Grosso, N. A., Rea, M., Ramos-Murguialday, A., Soekadar, S. R., and Birbaumer, N. (2014). A new hand assessment instrument for severely affected stroke patients. *NeuroRehabilitation* 34, 409–427. doi: 10.3233/NRE-141063

Buch, E. R., Modir Shanechi, A., Fourkas, A. D., Weber, C., Birbaumer, N., and Cohen, L. G. (2012). Parietofrontal integrity determines neural modulation associated with grasping imagery after stroke. *Brain* 135, 596–614. doi: 10.1093/brain/awr331

Burke Quinlan, E., Dodakian, L., See, J., McKenzie, A., Le, V., Wojnowicz, M., et al. (2014). Neural function, injury and stroke subtype predict treatment gains after stroke. *Ann. Neurol.* 77, 132–145. doi: 10.1002/ana.24309

Cegarra, J., and Chevalier, A. (2008). The use of Tholos software for combining measures of mental workload: toward theoretical and methodological improvements. *Behav. Res. Methods* 40, 988–1000. doi: 10.3758/brm.40.4.988

Chouinard, P. A., and Paus, T. (2006). The primary motor and premotor areas of the human cerebral cortex. *Neurosci. Rev. J. Bringing Neurobiol. Neurol. Psychiatry* 12, 143–152. doi: 10.1177/1073858405284255

Collinger, J. L., Wodlinger, B., Downey, J. E., Wang, W., Tyler-Kabara, E. C., Weber, D. J., et al. (2013). High-performance neuroprosthetic control by an individual with tetraplegia. *Lancet* 381, 557–564. doi: 10.1016/S0140-6736(12)61816-9

Deakin, A., Hill, H., and Pomeroy, V. M. (2003). Rough guide to the fugl-meyer assessment. *Physiotherapy* 89, 751–763. doi: 10.1016/s0031-9406(05)60502-0

Decety, J., Jeannerod, M., Germain, M., and Pastene, J. (1991). Vegetative response during imagined movement is proportional to mental effort. *Behav. Brain Res.* 42, 1–5. doi: 10.1016/s0166-4328(05)80033-6

De Champlain, A. F. (2010). A primer on classical test theory and item response theory for assessments in medical education. *Med. Educ.* 44, 109–117. doi: 10.1111/j.1365-2923.2009.03425.x

de Lange, F. P., Jensen, O., Bauer, M., and Toni, I. (2008). Interactions between posterior gamma and frontal alpha/beta oscillations during imagined actions. *Front. Hum. Neurosci.* 2:7. doi: 10.3389/neuro.09.007.2008

De Vico Fallani, F., Vecchiato, G., Toppi, J., Astolfi, L., and Babiloni, F. (2011). Subject identification through standard EEG signals during resting states. *Conf. Proc. IEEE Eng. Med. Biol. Soc.* 2011, 2331–2333. doi: 10.1109/iembs.2011.6090652

Gharabaghi, A., Kraus, D., Leão, M. T., Spüler, M., Walter, A., Bogdan, M., et al. (2014a). Coupling brain-machine interfaces with cortical stimulation for brain-state dependent stimulation: enhancing motor cortex excitability for neurorehabilitation. *Front. Hum. Neurosci.* 8:122. doi: 10.3389/fnhum.2014.00122

Gharabaghi, A., Naros, G., Walter, A., Grimm, F., Schuermeyer, M., Roth, A., et al. (2014b). From assistance towards restoration with an implanted brain-computer interface based on epidural electrocorticography: a single case study. *Restor. Neurol. Neurosci.* 32, 517–525. doi: 10.3233/RNN-140387

Gomez-Rodriguez, M., Peters, J., Hill, J., Schölkopf, B., Gharabaghi, A., and Grosse-Wentrup, M. (2011). Closing the sensorimotor loop: haptic feedback facilitates decoding of motor imagery. *J. Neural Eng.* 8:036005. doi: 10.1088/1741-2560/8/3/036005

Grosse-Wentrup, M., Schölkopf, B., and Hill, J. (2011). Causal influence of gamma oscillations on the sensorimotor rhythm. *Neuroimage* 56, 837–842. doi: 10.1016/j.neuroimage.2010.04.265

Hammer, E. M., Halder, S., Blankertz, B., Sannelli, C., Dickhaus, T., Kleih, S., et al. (2012). Psychological predictors of SMR-BCI performance. *Biol. Psychol.* 89, 80–86. doi: 10.1016/j.biopsycho.2011.09.006

Heremans, E., Helsen, W. F., De Poel, H. J., Alaerts, K., Meyns, P., and Feys, P. (2009). Facilitation of motor imagery through movement-related cueing. *Brain Res.* 1278, 50–58. doi: 10.1016/j.brainres.2009.04.041

Hochberg, L. R., Bacher, D., Jarosiewicz, B., Masse, N. Y., Simeral, J. D., Vogel, J., et al. (2012). Reach and grasp by people with tetraplegia using a neurally controlled robotic arm. *Nature* 485, 372–375. doi: 10.1038/nature11076

Jong, T. (2009). Cognitive load theory, educational research and instructional design: some food for thought. *Instr. Sci.* 38, 105–134. doi: 10.1007/s11251-009-9110-0

Kaiser, V., Kreilinger, A., Müller-Putz, G. R., and Neuper, C. (2011). First steps toward a motor imagery based stroke BCI: new strategy to set up a classifier. *Front. Neurosci.* 5:86. doi: 10.3389/fnins.2011.00086

Kilavik, B. E., Zaepffel, M., Brovelli, A., MacKay, W. A., and Riehle, A. (2012). The ups and downs of beta oscillations in sensorimotor cortex. *Exp. Neurol.* 245, 15–26. doi: 10.1016/j.expneurol.2012.09.014

MacKay, D. J. C. (2003). *Information Theory, Inference and Learning Algorithms.* Cambridge, UK: Cambridge University Press.

Malik, M., Bigger, J. T., Camm, A. J., Kleiger, R. E., Malliani, A., Moss, A. J., et al. (1996). Heart rate variability. *Eur. Heart J.* 17, 354–381. doi: 10.1093/eurheartj/17.suppl_2.28

Mantini, D., Perrucci, M. G., Del Gratta, C., Romani, G. L., and Corbetta, M. (2007). Electrophysiological signatures of resting state networks in the human brain. *Proc. Natl. Acad. Sci. U S A* 104, 13170–13175. doi: 10.1073/pnas.0700668104

Miller, K. J., Hermes, D., Honey, C. J., Hebb, A. O., Ramsey, N. F., Knight, R. T., et al. (2012). Human motor cortical activity is selectively phase-entrained on underlying rhythms. *PLoS Comput. Biol.* 8:e1002655. doi: 10.1371/journal.pcbi.1002655

Mokken, R. J., and Lewis, C. (1982). A nonparametric approach to the analysis of dichotomous item responses. *Appl. Psychol. Meas.* 6, 417–430. doi: 10.1177/014662168200600404

Novak, D., Mihelj, M., and Munih, M. (2010). Psychophysiological responses to different levels of cognitive and physical workload in haptic interaction. *Robotica* 29, 367–374. doi: 10.1017/s0263574710000184

Oostenveld, R., Fries, P., Maris, E., and Schoffelen, J.-M. (2011). FieldTrip: open source software for advanced analysis of MEG, EEG and invasive electrophysiological data. *Comput. Intell. Neurosci.* 2011, 1–9. doi: 10.1155/2011/156869

Ortega, P. A., and Braun, D. A. (2010). A conversion between utility and information. *Proc. Third Conf. Artif. Gen. Intell.* 115–120. doi: 10.2991/agi.2010.10

Ramos-Murguialday, A., Broetz, D., Rea, M., Läer, L., Yilmaz, O., Brasil, F. L., et al. (2013). Brain-machine-interface in chronic stroke rehabilitation: a controlled study. *Ann. Neurol.* 74, 100–108. doi: 10.1002/ana.23879

Rossiter, H. E., Boudrias, M.-H., and Ward, N. S. (2014). Do movement-related beta oscillations change following stroke? *J. Neurophysiol.* 112, 2053–2058. doi: 10.1152/jn.00345.2014

Rost, J. (2004). *Lehrbuch Testtheorie - Testkonstruktion.* Bern: Huber.

Safrit, M. J., Cohen, A. S., and Costa, M. G. (1989). Item response theory and the measurement of motor behavior. *Res. Q. Exerc. Sport* 60, 325–335. doi: 10.1080/02701367.1989.10607459

Schnotz, W., and Kürschner, C. (2007). A reconsideration of cognitive load theory. *Educ. Psychol. Rev.* 19, 469–508. doi: 10.1007/s10648-007-9053-4

Sherlin, L. H., Arns, M., Lubar, J., Heinrich, H., Kerson, C., Strehl, U., et al. (2011). Neurofeedback and basic learning theory: implications for research and practice. *J. Neurother.* 15, 292–304. doi: 10.1080/10874208.2011.623089

Shibasaki, H., and Hallett, M. (2006). What is the bereitschaftspotential? *Clin. Neurophysiol. Off. J. Int. Fed. Clin. Neurophysiol.* 117, 2341–2356. doi: 10.1016/j.clinph.2006.04.025

Shindo, K., Kawashima, K., Ushiba, J., Ota, N., Ito, M., Ota, T., et al. (2011). Effects of neurofeedback training with an electroencephalogram-based brain-computer interface for hand paralysis in patients with chronic stroke: a preliminary case series study. *J. Rehabil. Med.* 43, 951–957. doi: 10.2340/16501977-0859

Stinear, C. M., Barber, P. A., Petoe, M., Anwar, S., and Byblow, W. D. (2012). The PREP algorithm predicts potential for upper limb recovery after stroke. *Brain* 135, 2527–2535. doi: 10.1093/brain/aws146

Sweller, J. (1994). Cognitive load theory, learning difficulty and instructional design. *Learn. Instr.* 4, 295–312. doi: 10.1016/0959-4752(94)90003-5

Theodoridis, S., and Koutroumbas, K. (2009). *Pattern Recognition.* Burlington, MA: Academic Press.

Thomas, E., Dyson, M., and Clerc, M. (2013). An analysis of performance evaluation for motor-imagery based BCI. *J. Neural Eng.* 10:031001. doi: 10.1088/1741-2560/10/3/031001

Thompson, D. E., Blain-Moraes, S., and Huggins, J. E. (2013). Performance assessment in brain-computer interface-based augmentative and alternative communication. *Biomed. Eng. Online* 12:43. doi: 10.1186/1475-925x-12-43

Vidaurre, C., and Blankertz, B. (2010). Towards a cure for BCI illiteracy. *Brain Topogr.* 23, 194–198. doi: 10.1007/s10548-009-0121-6

Vukelić, M., Bauer, R., Naros, G., Naros, I., Braun, C., and Gharabaghi, A. (2014). Lateralized alpha-band cortical networks regulate volitional modulation of beta-band sensorimotor oscillations. *Neuroimage* 87, 147–153. doi: 10.1016/j.neuroimage.2013.10.003

Wang, W., Collinger, J. L., Degenhart, A. D., Tyler-Kabara, E. C., Schwartz, A. B., Moran, D. W., et al. (2013). An electrocorticographic brain interface in an individual with tetraplegia. *PloS One* 8:e55344. doi: 10.1371/journal.pone.0055344

Wolpaw, J. R., Birbaumer, N., McFarland, D. J., Pfurtscheller, G., and Vaughan, T. M. (2002). Brain-computer interfaces for communication and control. *Clin. Neurophysiol. Off. J. Int. Fed. Clin. Neurophysiol.* 113, 767–791. doi: 10.1016/S1388-2457(02)00057-3

Wood, G., Kober, S. E., Witte, M., and Neuper, C. (2014). On the need to better specify the concept of "control" in brain-computer-interfaces/neurofeedback research. *Front. Syst. Neurosci.* 8:171. doi: 10.3389/fnsys.2014.00171

Yanagisawa, T., Hirata, M., Saitoh, Y., Goto, T., Kishima, H., Fukuma, R., et al. (2011). Real-time control of a prosthetic hand using human electrocorticography signals. *J. Neurosurg.* 114, 1715–1722. doi: 10.3171/2011.1.jns101421

7

Comparison of anterior cingulate vs. insular cortex as targets for real-time fMRI regulation during pain stimulation

Kirsten Emmert[1,2*†], Markus Breimhorst[3†], Thomas Bauermann[4], Frank Birklein[3], Dimitri Van De Ville[1,2] and Sven Haller[1]

[1] Department of Radiology and Medical Informatics, University of Geneva, Geneva, Switzerland
[2] Medical Image Processing Laboratory, Institute of Bioengineering, Ecole Polytechnique Fédérale de Lausanne, Lausanne, Switzerland
[3] Department of Neurology, University Medical Center of the Johannes Gutenberg-University Mainz, Mainz, Germany
[4] Institute of Neuroradiology, University Medical Center of the Johannes Gutenberg-University Mainz, Mainz, Germany

***Correspondence:**
Kirsten Emmert, Department of Radiology and Medical Informatics, Hôpitaux Universitaires de Genève, University of Geneva, Rue Gabrielle Perret-Gentil 4, 1211 Genève 14, Switzerland
e-mail: emmert.kirsten@gmail.com

Real-time functional magnetic resonance imaging (rt-fMRI) neurofeedback allows learning voluntary control over specific brain areas by means of operant conditioning and has been shown to decrease pain perception. To further increase the effect of rt-fMRI neurofeedback on pain, we directly compared two different target regions of the pain network, notably the anterior insular cortex (AIC) and the anterior cingulate cortex (ACC). Participants for this prospective study were randomly assigned to two age-matched groups of 14 participants each (7 females per group) for AIC and ACC feedback. First, a functional localizer using block-design heat pain stimulation was performed to define the pain-sensitive target region within the AIC or ACC. Second, subjects were asked to down-regulate the BOLD activation in four neurofeedback runs during identical pain stimulation. Data analysis included task-related and functional connectivity analysis. At the behavioral level, pain ratings significantly decreased during feedback vs. localizer runs, but there was no difference between AIC and ACC groups. Concerning neuroimaging, ACC and AIC showed consistent involvement of the caudate nucleus for subjects that learned down-regulation (17/28) in both task-related and functional connectivity analysis. The functional connectivity toward the caudate nucleus is stronger for the ACC while the AIC is more heavily connected to the ventrolateral prefrontal cortex. Consequently, the ACC and AIC are suitable targets for real-time fMRI neurofeedback during pain perception as they both affect the caudate nucleus, although functional connectivity indicates that the direct connection seems to be stronger with the ACC. Additionally, the caudate, an important area involved in pain perception and suppression, could be a good rt-fMRI target itself. Future studies are needed to identify parameters characterizing successful regulators and to assess the effect of repeated rt-fMRI neurofeedback on pain perception.

Keywords: real-time fMRI neurofeedback, realtime fMRI, pain, anterior cingulate cortex (ACC), anterior insular cortex, insular cortex

INTRODUCTION

Pain perception has a great impact on individual emotional health as pain is associated with anxiety (Asmundson and Katz, 2009), anger (Trost et al., 2012), fear (Leeuw et al., 2007a,b; Vlaeyen and Linton, 2012), and worry (Eccleston and Crombez, 2007; Linton, 2013). Thus, not surprisingly, chronic pain increases the risk of depression and suicide (Turk et al., 1995; Geisser et al., 2000; Bair et al., 2003; Ilgen et al., 2008; Denkinger et al., 2014). Pharmacological intervention remains the mainstay of chronic pain treatment. As most chronic pain patients are treated with a combination of pain medications and over long periods of time (Muller-Schwefe et al., 2011), cumulative drug-related side effects pose a considerable risk of adverse effects for these patients (Jouini et al., 2014), highlighting the importance of alternative and supplementary pain therapies.

One novel technique that shows potential in the treatment of chronic pain is real-time functional magnetic resonance imaging (rt-fMRI), which allows volitionally influencing activation of a targeted brain area by means of operant conditioning when being supplied with a corresponding feedback signal. This technique could be employed to reduce brain activation in pain network target areas with the aim to decrease the subjective pain perception.

Abbreviations: ACC, anterior cingulate cortex; AIC, anterior insular cortex; aMCC, anterior mid-cingulate cortex; ANOVA, analysis of variance; BOLD, blood oxygenation level dependent; fMRI, functional magnetic resonance imaging; GLM, general linear model; ICA, independent component analysis; MELODIC, multivariate exploratory linear optimized decomposition into independent components; MPRAGE, magnetization prepared rapid gradient echo; NRS, numeric rating scale; PIC, posterior insular cortex; PFC, prefrontal cortex; ROI, region of interest; rt-fMRI, real-time fMRI; SEM, standard error of the mean.

A pilot study showed that it is possible to regulate the anterior cingulate cortex (ACC) as a target brain region using rt-fMRI for chronic pain patients as well as healthy participants during pain perception (Decharms et al., 2005). However, according to subsequent reports of the same group, these findings could not be replicated (Decharms, 2012). In line with this observation, rt-fMRI is generally still in its early days, facing some limitations and confounds. High inter-individual differences in regulation success and small effect sizes make it difficult to assess the therapeutic use of this method. In an attempt to optimize the choice of the target region, which is a key factor of the rt-fMRI experiment, this study compares two possible target brain regions for feedback involved in pain processing in healthy subjects. The effect of the feedback on these target regions and other brain regions within the pain-responsive network will be assessed.

Acute pain perception starts with an external stimulus that activates peripheral receptors such as the vanilloid receptor (TRPV1), which is sensitive to temperatures above 43°C (Cesare and McNaughton, 1996) eliciting a depolarization of peripheral sensory neurons synapsing onto second-order dorsal horn neurons (Basbaum and Jessell, 2000) in the spinal cord. These fibers ascend to the thalamus relaying information to the somatosensory cortex, the ACC and the insular cortex (IC). Additional projection neurons from the dorsal horn to the parabrachial nucleus in the brainstem engage the ACC and the IC via the amygdala. Apart from this ascending connection, cortical pain areas such as the primary and secondary somatosensory cortex as well as the posterior insula (PIC), which are implicated in basic pain perception, are heavily interconnected (Apkarian et al., 2005). The same is true for higher-level areas involved in pain processing, including the ACC, the anterior insula (AIC) and prefrontal cortical areas exerting top-down regulation on the thalamus and the amygdala in turn. In addition, the basal ganglia are activated through multiple pathways including the thalamus, the amygdala and cortical areas (Borsook et al., 2010). While areas that are involved in basic sensory pain processing, such as the PIC, are predominantly activated contralateral to the pain stimulus, higher-level processing areas implicated in pain interpretation including the AIC are activated in a bilateral fashion (Brooks et al., 2002).

Ongoing nociceptive input from injuries leads to a hyperexcitability of the nervous system, in a process that resembles long-term potentiation called central sensitization (Drdla and Sandkuhler, 2008; Woolf, 2011), in addition to a decrease of tonic inhibition (Moore et al., 2002; Keller et al., 2007). This hyperalgesia has the purpose of facilitating the healing processes of the injured tissue. However, central sensitization can persist after tissue healing leading to chronic hyperalgesia and even pain perception in the absence of painful stimuli (Voscopoulos and Lema, 2010; Woolf, 2011). Furthermore, pathological changes in the descending modulatory pathways might also contribute to the emergence of chronic pain (Porreca et al., 2002; Ossipov et al., 2010).

Functional brain imaging showed abnormal activation in the rostral ACC and the frontal cortex in certain chronic pain populations (Baliki et al., 2006; Berman et al., 2008; Jensen et al., 2009; Burgmer et al., 2010). Additionally, chronic pain patients show altered functional connectivity of the prefrontal cortex (PFC) and the insula with the default mode network (Napadow et al., 2010; Baliki et al., 2011). Similarly, structural imaging revealed gray matter reductions within the PFC, the ACC and the IC (Bushnell et al., 2013). On a molecular level, chronic pain patients seem to show altered endogenous release for the glutamatergic and GABAergic system as well as a decrease in receptor binding of the opioidergic system in these areas (Bushnell et al., 2013). These anatomical and molecular changes might not only alter pain regulation, but also affect decision making (Grace et al., 1999; Leavitt and Katz, 2006; Munguia-Izquierdo and Legaz-Arrese, 2007).

Some studies also suggest that these changes can be partly reversed, for example, in cases where there is an underlying painful condition that can be removed after years (Gwilym et al., 2010; Seminowicz et al., 2011). Moreover, the pain modulation system consisting of the PFC, ACC, and AIC was shown to be modulated by cognitive measures such as meditation or cognitive behavior therapy (Grant et al., 2011; Gard et al., 2012; Jensen et al., 2012). Thus, it seems useful and feasible to regulate these areas using rt-fMRI neurofeedback. Before looking into possible neurofeedback effects for chronic pain patients, we aim to optimize target ROI selection for pain neurofeedback in healthy subjects during pain stimulation as a first step. Future studies are needed to make sure that these target ROIs can be regulated in chronic pain patients as well.

The ACC and the AIC seem to be particularly important in perceiving pain intensity (Favilla et al., 2014). Therefore, these two regions of the medial pain system (Treede et al., 1999) were considered the most promising rt-fMRI target regions for cortical pain processing. The ACC was also the subject of a recent rt-fMRI neurofeedback study testing feasibility of pain regulation for the rostral ACC and PIC (Rance et al., 2014). They postulated that sensory pain aspects might be more related to PIC activation while affective aspects are more related to ACC activation. In this context, it is interesting to investigate how the AIC—implicated in another aspect of pain, namely cognitive control processes—can be regulated.

The ACC has been associated to several functions relevant to pain processing including saliency (Seeley et al., 2007; Iannetti and Mouraux, 2010), attention (Bush et al., 2000; Weissman et al., 2005), and emotion (Bush et al., 2000; Shackman et al., 2011). It is furthermore linked to affective processing of painful stimuli (Vogt et al., 1996; Rainville et al., 1997). Studies already showed that it is possible to target the ACC in smokers (Canterberry et al., 2013; Hartwell et al., 2013; Li et al., 2013) and chronic pain patients as well as healthy participants during pain perception (Decharms et al., 2005). In the latter study, regulation of the ACC activation using rt-fMRI neurofeedback even resulted in a decrease of pain intensity ratings. Other behavioral interventions that have been shown to modulate ACC activation include hypnosis (Rainville et al., 1997; Faymonville et al., 2000), modulation of pain expectation (Sawamoto et al., 2000; Bingel et al., 2011), and distraction (Bantick et al., 2002; Valet et al., 2004).

The IC can be divided into the anterior and the PIC that serve distinct functions in pain processing. The PIC seems to be involved in basic pain and touch sensation (Greenspan and Winfield, 1992), receiving direct spinothalamic input

(Garcia-Larrea, 2012). Lesions in this area lead to pain and temperature deficits (Greenspan et al., 1999; Birklein et al., 2005). In contrast, AIC lesions usually do not seem to have a direct impact on pain perception *per se* (Greenspan et al., 1999). The AIC is implicated in a wide variety of functions, including visceral sensation and an integrative role in perception-action coupling possibly by mediating heightened alertness to prepare for action (Sterzer and Kleinschmidt, 2010). It seems to be engaged in affective-motivational processes of pain perception as a disconnection of the AIC from the PIC leads to a decrease of emotional pain reaction while nociceptive recognition remains intact (Berthier et al., 1988). Up-regulation of the AIC was shown to be possible (Caria et al., 2007; Veit et al., 2012) using recall of personal and affectively relevant events or focused attention on arising bodily sensations (Lawrence et al., 2013). It was shown that it is even possible to target subjects with clinical disorders such as schizophrenia (Ruiz et al., 2013) or depression (Linden et al., 2012). While these studies suggest that AIC regulation can be used to increase certain affective states and control, there is no specific data looking at the influence of the AIC down-regulation on pain perception.

In this work, we directly compared two possible target regions for rt-fMRI neurofeedback in pain, notably the AIC and the ACC, in order to determine the most efficient target region for future neurofeedback studies in pain processing.

MATERIALS AND METHODS

PARTICIPANTS

The local ethics committee in Mainz approved the study that adhered to the Declaration of Helsinki. Twenty-eight healthy subjects (mean age: 27.5 ± 2.3 years, 14 male, 14 female) gave written informed consent prior to participation. Participants were randomly split into two groups of $N = 14$ each, including seven male and seven female participants per group (group 1: 27.6 years ± 2.1, group 2: 27.4 ± 2.6 years). The first group received feedback from the left anterior insula (lAIC) as a target region, while the second group did so from the ACC. Exclusion criteria were defined by acute or chronic pain, pregnancy, severe neurological or internal disorders, intake of painkillers and contraindications for MR-measurements. Participants were paid for participation in the study.

REAL-TIME EXPERIMENT

The experiment consisted of two stages. First, a functional localizer run with an ON-OFF block design of eight blocks alternating between continuous painful stimulation for 30 s and rest for 30 s each was performed to identify the individual target regions. The target region was chosen based on significant activation within the lAIC/ACC during the functional localizer. Thereafter, four identical neurofeedback runs were performed consisting of a block design of four rest and regulation blocks (30 s each) preceded by 15 s of initial rest before the first block. Online data analysis was performed using TurboBrainVoyager version 2.8 (Brain Innovation, Maastricht, The Netherlands).

The target region was chosen based on significant activation within the lAIC/ACC during the functional localizer (summarized in Supplementary Table 1). Regulation blocks included the same pain stimulation as during the localizer. During this period of the neurofeedback runs, subjects were asked to decrease the blood oxygen level dependent (BOLD) activation level in the target region, which was visualized to them by a yellow line. The background color of the yellow line indicated to either keep the yellow line constant (black = rest blocks, no heat pain) or to decrease the amplitude of the yellow line (blue = down-regulation, heat pain). Subjects could freely choose their mental strategy to reach this objective.

PAIN STIMULATION AND RATING

An MR compatible thermode (TSA 2001, Medoc Ltd, Ramat Yishai, Israel), placed at middle of the lower right volar forearm, was used for pain stimulation. This 30 × 30 mm Peltier device has a default temperature of 32°C. Before the start of the experiment the thermode temperature was adjusted for each participant to elicit a subjective pain intensity of 7 out of 10 on the numeric rating scale (NRS). The thermode temperature for pain stimulation remained constant throughout the experiment [Ramp rate: 4°C/s, mean ramp and fall time for AIC-group: 3.83 s (*SD* 0.26) and for ACC-group: 3.64 s (*SD* 0.32), mean plateau for AIC-Group: 22.35 s (*SD* 0.53) and for ACC-Group: 22.71 s (*SD* 0.64), mean temperature for AIC-Group: 47.08°C (*SD* 1.1) and for ACC-group: 46.42°C (*SD* 1.4)]. After each run pain ratings were obtained using a 11-point NRS ranging from 0 (not painful) to 10 (most painful).

fMRI DATA ACQUISITION

Imaging was performed on a 3T MRI Scanner (Siemens Tim Trio, Erlangen, Germany) using a 32-channel head-coil. For functional data acquisition an echo-planar imaging sequence (EPI, $TR = 1500$ ms, $TE = 30$ ms, matrix size 64 × 64, 24 slices, slice thickness 3 mm without gap) was utilized. Additionally, a high-resolution T1-weighted anatomical scan [magnetization prepared rapid gradient echo (MPRAGE), 1 mm isotropic] was acquired for later co-registration with the lower resolution EPI images.

STATISTICAL ANALYSIS BETWEEN RUNS AND GROUPS

Statistical testing for differences between runs and groups [pain ratings, region of interest (ROI) activation, s-modes] was performed in MATLAB 2012b (The MathWorks, Inc., Natick, USA). First, parameters were tested for normality using D'Agostino K-squared test. As normality was rejected for all our parameters of interest (pain ratings, ROI beta values, s-mode values), we used the non-parametric Friedman test (comparison between all runs) and *post-hoc* Wilcoxon tests (comparison between groups, and comparison of two runs when the Friedman test showed significant results). Bonferroni correction was applied to correct for multiple comparisons in the s-mode analysis (i.e., the number of independent components).

POST-HOC GLM ACTIVATION ANALYSIS OF THE FUNCTIONAL LOCALIZER

Off-line analysis was performed with SPM 8 (UCL, London, UK) and FSL 5.0 (FMRIB Analysis Group, University of Oxford, UK). Functional data was spatially realigned, co-registered to the anatomical data, normalized and smoothed (8 mm kernel) before group analysis on the basis of a general linear model (GLM) using the block design described under Section Real-Time Experiment. For the fMRI analysis, family-wise error (FWE) corrected values of $p < 0.05$ are considered significant.

POST-HOC ROI ACTIVATION ANALYSIS OF THE NEUROFEEDBACK RUNS

GLM analysis for all four neurofeedback runs was performed analogous to the localizer run. As self-regulation was expected to increase with practice, we compared the first neurofeedback run with the subsequent runs in a ROI analysis for regions that were activated during the localizer run and known to be involved in pain processing, namely ACC, AIC, PIC. Based on our functional connectivity and ICA results in combination with its know implication in pain processing (Borsook et al., 2010), we included the caudate nucleus as an additional (a posteriori) ROI. Then, ROIs were defined as spheres with 1-cm diameter centered at the activation peaks within the relevant clusters from the group analysis of the functional localizer. This approach seemed more suitable than defining the ROIs on an individual level, as done for target ROI analysis, as not all subjects showed significant activation in all of the ROIs in the localizer run. Since regulation using rt-fMRI neurofeedback fails in some subjects, we restricted extensive *post-hoc* ROI analysis to those subjects who showed a decrease in activation in the target ROI; i.e., 9/14 for the AIC group and 8/14 subjects for the ACC group.

POST-HOC fMRI CONNECTIVITY ANALYSIS OF THE NEUROFEEDBACK RUNS

Using FSL 5.0, functional connectivity was assessed with a seed-based approach testing for correlation with the seed's time course orthogonalized to the global signal and the GLM regressor of main effect. Seed regions were both rt-fMRI targets, ACC and lAIC, respectively. The resulting connectivity maps of each subject were fed into a 2nd level GLM analysis to obtain group results.

In addition, an independent component analysis (ICA) was carried out in FSL using multi-session multivariate exploratory linear optimized decomposition into independent components (MELODIC) tensor ICA. So-called s-modes (i.e., measures of activation strength for every component in each subject) were compared between groups.

RESULTS

EFFECT OF NEUROFEEDBACK ON PAIN RATINGS

Pain ratings were lower in the neurofeedback runs compared to the localizer run [non-parametric, $p(\text{AIC group}) < 0.001$; $p(\text{ACC}) < 0.01$] in both groups, but did not show any significant differences between neurofeedback runs (see **Figure 1**, **Table 1**). Pain ratings did not differ between regulators and non-regulators ($p > 0.1$).

Neither pain ratings of the regulators nor the non-regulators changed significantly between neurofeedback runs.

FUNCTIONAL LOCALIZER

As expected, the functional localizer revealed significant activation within the insula, PFC and the ACC, all regions involved in pain processing (see **Figure 2**). Activation of the target region in each subject enabled the individual region of interest placement (see Supplementary Figure 1).

NEUROFEEDBACK RUNS

Seed-based connectivity of the left AIC and the ACC

Seed-based analysis at the group level showed the functional connectivity of the ACC and the AIC to other regions of the pain network (see **Figure 3A**). The analysis confirmed that ACC and

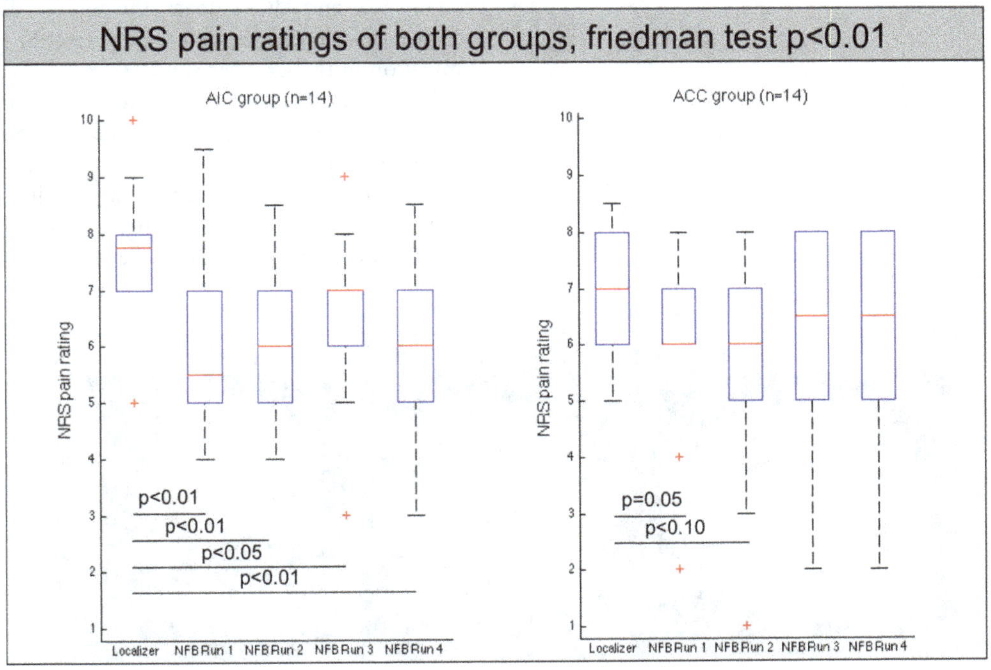

FIGURE 1 | Pain ratings of all participants (AIC-left, ACC-right) across localizer run and all neurofeedback runs. The red line indicates the mean value, the box indicates 25%/75% confidence intervals and the whiskers indicate the most extreme points within 1.5 times of the box length.

the AIC are strongly interconnected as well as showing connections to prefrontal areas. Interestingly, the ACC has high functional connectivity with the caudate nucleus that did not show up in the AIC connectivity map while the AIC group has an increased connectivity with the ventrolateral PFC (see **Figure 3B**).

Table 1 | Pain ratings on the numeric rating scale for all subjects.

Target ROI	Subject	Pain rating (0–10)				
		Localizer run	Run 1	Run 2	Run 3	Run 4
AIC	1	8.0	4.0	4.0	6.0	5.0
	2	7.0	5.0	6.0	6.0	6.0
	3	8.0	6.0	5.0	7.0	7.0
	4	7.0	5.0	6.0	6.0	4.0
	5	5.0	5.0	7.0	7.0	7.0
	6	9.0	7.0	6.0	7.0	4.0
	7	8.0	8.0	8.0	7.0	7.0
	8	7.0	5.0	5.0	7.0	6.0
	9	7.0	6.0	6.0	5.0	5.0
	10	7.5	7.0	6.0	7.0	6.0
	11	10.0	9.5	7.5	7.5	7.5
	12	9.0	7.5	8.5	9.0	8.5
	13	8.0	5.0	6.0	8.0	8.0
	14	7.0	5.0	4.0	3.0	3.0
ACC	15	6.0	6.0	7.0	8.0	8.0
	16	7.0	6.0	6.0	4.0	6.0
	17	8.0	8.0	8.0	8.0	8.0
	18	6.0	6.0	6.0	6.0	5.0
	19	8.0	7.0	7.0	8.0	8.0
	20	7.0	6.0	6.0	8.0	7.0
	21	8.5	6.0	6.0	6.0	6.0
	22	7.0	6.0	5.0	6.0	5.0
	23	7.0	6.0	5.0	5.0	6.0
	24	5.0	4.0	3.0	4.0	4.0
	25	8.0	7.0	7.0	7.0	7.0
	26	8.0	8.0	8.0	8.0	8.0
	27	8.0	6.0	7.0	8.0	7.0
	28	5.0	2.0	1.0	2.0	2.0

Effect of training (runs over time)

To assess a possible improvement in self-regulation over time, we looked for a decrease in activation in the later runs compared to the first run. To that aim, we first analyzed the activation within each individual target ROI (see **Table 2** and **Figure 4**). Data from subjects that showed a successful down-regulation (i.e., decrease of target region's activation level from the first to the average of the following runs) were used for a more extensive ROI analysis including the main brain areas involved in pain regulation (see **Table 3**).

The analysis of these regions showed that the decrease of the left AIC in the AIC group is accompanied by a similar significant decrease in the contralateral anterior insula ($p < 0.05$). In addition, both groups show a significant decrease of the caudate nucleus with the effect being more pronounced in the AIC group ($p < 0.01$, ACC: $p < 0.05$, see **Figure 5**).

Independent component analysis

Using ICA, we identified 33 components of which one is significantly different between groups according to its s-mode ($p < 0.05$, corrected for multiple comparison). This component includes AIC, ACC, and small portions of the occipital and parietal lobes (see **Figure 6**). In addition, we looked for components that exhibit a linear trend over runs and identified one component with slope significantly different from zero for the ACC group ($p < 0.05$, corrected for multiple comparison). This component includes thalamus and parts of the basal ganglia (see **Figure 7**).

DISCUSSION

In the current investigation, we compared the effectiveness in pain regulation using real-time fMRI neurofeedback from two different target regions, notably ACC and AIC. At the behavioral level, both for ACC and AIC feedback, the neurofeedback runs showed a decrease in pain perception with respect to the identical pain stimulation in the localizer runs. However, there was no significant behavioral difference in the direct comparison between ACC and AIC and between runs. Despite the absence of behavioral differences between runs, we found effects in neuroimaging for the two target regions. This observation is in line with the known higher sensitivity of neuroimaging, as compared to behavioral measures, in functional MRI studies investigating subtle effects

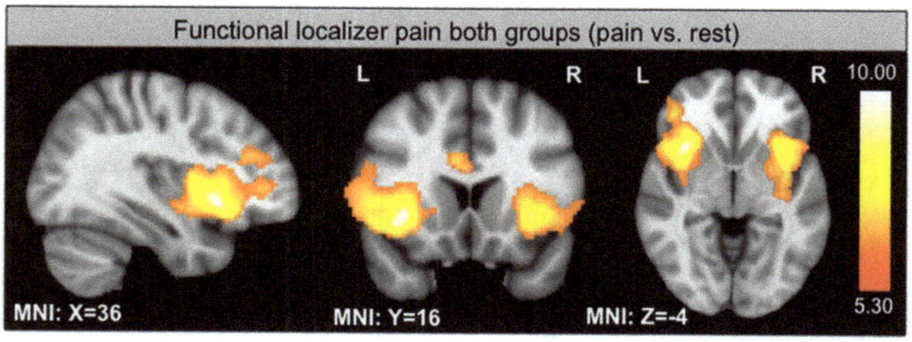

FIGURE 2 | GLM contrast localizer run: pain vs. rest in both groups threshold at $p < 0.05$ FWE.

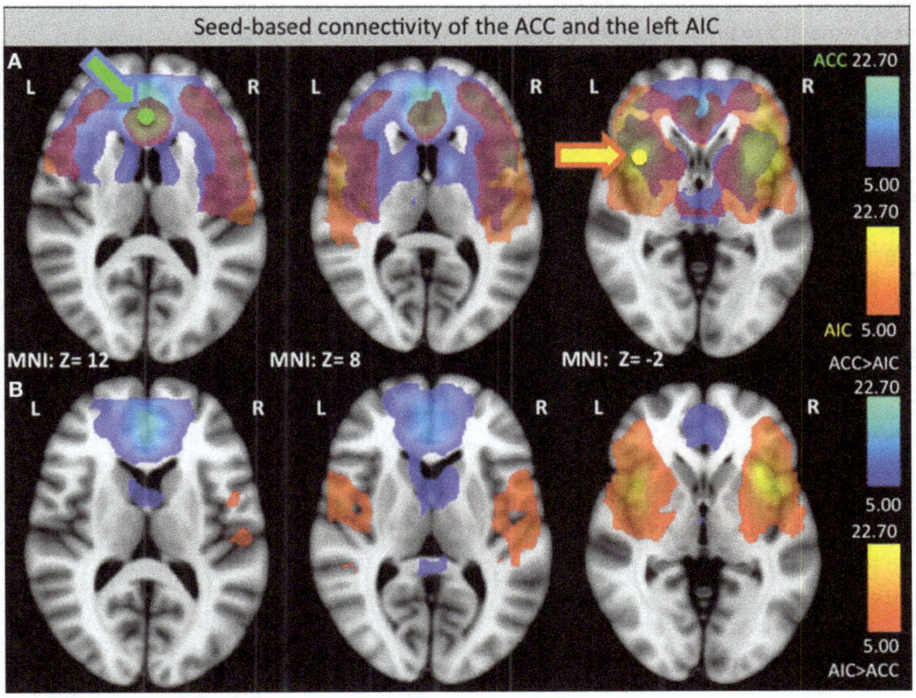

FIGURE 3 | Seed-based functional connectivity of the ACC (green, connectivity blue, A) and left AIC (yellow, connectivity orange, A). **(B)** Areas that had a significantly greater connection to the ACC than to the AIC (blue) or a significantly greater connection to the AIC than to the ACC (orange) in a direct comparison. Arrows indicate the target seed location.

(Weiskopf et al., 2003; Haller et al., 2005, 2013; Johnston et al., 2011).

At the neuroimaging level, AIC and ACC regulation led to a significant down-regulation of parts of the pain network with practice, notably the caudate nucleus for successful regulators.

Functional-connectivity analyses further demonstrated that both target regions are functionally well connected to other parts of the pain network. Therefore, based on this neuroimaging evidence, we found that both AIC and ACC influence the pain network in a similar fashion through the caudate nucleus.

ACC REGULATION DURING PAIN

Contrary to two previous studies about rt-fMRI ACC regulation of pain processing (Decharms et al., 2005; Rance et al., 2014), we did not find a significant down-regulation effect of ACC regulation over runs within the ACC for all subjects. This might be due to the different experimental paradigm that compared down-regulation vs. no regulation in our setting, while deCharms et al. compared up- vs. down-regulation. Considering that down-regulation might be harder to obtain than up-regulation, as it is easier to explicitly focus on acute pain than to find a strategy to decrease pain, the effect of down-regulation might be smaller. In addition, this particular finding could not be replicated by deCharms et al. in a later follow-up study; as publicly stated at the rt-fMRI conference in Zurich, 2012 (Decharms, 2012). One factor that possibly complicates ACC regulation is that the adjacent anterior mid-cingulate cortex (aMCC) is also thought to be involved in rt-fMRI neurofeedback regulation (Lee et al., 2012), inducing activation during the regulation and thus making it harder to detect the deactivation in nearby ACC, and possibly also confounding the participants' feedback signal itself to some extent. This possible confound is less strong in the recent study of Rance et al. as they used a more rostral part of the ACC leading to a significant down-regulation of this ROI. Therefore, future studies should preferably use a more rostral part of the ACC.

Nevertheless, ACC rt-fMRI neurofeedback did induce a down-regulation of the ACC in a large group of subjects (8/14) as well as a significant change within the caudate nucleus, a brain region involved in planning of goal directed actions (Grahn et al., 2008) and affective processing of pain (Borsook et al., 2010). This part of the basal ganglia is anatomically closely connected to the ACC, with functional relevance, for example, in pain avoidance behavior in monkeys (Koyama et al., 2000). Similarly, previous studies found caudate nucleus involvement when participants suppressed pain (Freund et al., 2009; Wunderlich et al., 2011). Thus, the caudate nucleus, regulated via the ACC, seems to be important in deliberate pain control. This result is supported by the seed-based functional connectivity analysis showing a strong ACC—caudate nucleus interaction and the ICA analysis that revealed a specific component including the caudate nucleus and thalamus that showed significantly decreasing s-modes as a function of runs. These results also indicate that the caudate, the thalamus or a combination of these regions could be considered as suitable targets for future pain real-time neurofeedback studies.

AIC REGULATION DURING PAIN

Similar to the ACC group, AIC down-regulation was not significant when looking at all subjects. This difficulty in AIC regulation

Table 2 | Beta values of the target ROI for all subjects, classification criteria (beta value decrease from run 1 to the average of run 2–4), and classification label (+, regulator; −, non-regulator).

Target ROI	Subject	Beta value				Beta value decrease	Regulator
		Run 1	Run 2	Run 3	Run 4		
AIC	1	0.156	0.097	0.400	0.285	−0.315	−
	2	0.332	−0.077	0.212	0.277	0.584	+
	3	0.436	0.274	0.227	0.162	0.643	+
	4	−0.125	−0.698	0.183	−0.862	1.002	+
	5	0.204	0.006	0.462	0.753	−0.608	+
	6	−0.481	−0.367	0.252	−0.290	−1.039	−
	7	0.325	0.224	0.157	0.201	0.395	+
	8	0.446	−0.099	0.274	0.319	0.843	+
	9	1.093	1.163	0.479	0.822	0.816	−
	10	0.268	0.056	−0.161	0.354	0.556	+
	11	1.026	−0.059	1.022	0.313	1.803	+
	12	0.201	0.104	0.149	−0.155	0.506	+
	13	0.257	0.413	0.825	0.353	−0.819	−
	14	−0.008	0.044	0.246	0.422	−0.737	−
ACC	15	0.1934	−0.0628	−0.1711	0.1088	0.705	+
	16	−0.147	−0.101	0.146	−0.162	−0.325	+
	17	0.072	−0.119	−0.502	−0.182	1.020	+
	18	−0.127	0.072	0.060	0.061	−0.575	−
	19	0.341	−0.379	1.795	−0.455	0.063	+
	20	0.281	0.221	0.178	0.013	0.432	−
	21	0.240	0.847	0.309	0.324	−0.760	−
	22	0.117	−0.071	0.097	0.146	0.179	+
	23	−0.008	0.429	−0.610	0.254	−0.097	+
	24	0.450	0.719	0.874	0.943	−1.186	−
	25	0.223	−0.046	−0.051	0.012	0.754	+
	26	0.713	0.476	−0.020	−0.085	1.766	+
	27	0.153	0.248	0.324	0.309	−0.424	−
	28	1.284	0.116	0.754	1.116	1.866	−

might be explained by competing processes within the AIC. On one hand, the AIC was selected as the target for down-regulation as it is a core component of the network involved in pain processing (Apkarian et al., 2005). On the other hand it is likely to be activated in neurofeedback regulation processes (Haller et al., 2010). In addition, the AIC is involved in many other cognitive processes such as saliency detection (Cauda et al., 2012) and emotion regulation and representation (Singer et al., 2004; Eippert et al., 2007). Due to the regulation procedure, saliency of the visual display (focus on the line and the lower part of the "scale") as well as saliency of the pain stimulus (less focus on pain) could be modulated. In addition, the feedback could induce emotions such as frustration or contentment, thus possibly increasing insula activation, thereby counteracting insula down-regulation. This might also explain why all previous studies only reported reliable up-regulation while voluntary down-regulation of the AIC by rt-fMRI neurofeedback was less successful (Veit et al., 2012). The possible interaction of cognitive and emotional processes within the AIC was also underlined by an fMRI study showing increased reaction times and error rates for cognitively demanding tasks during presentation of painful compared to non-painful pictures (Gu et al., 2013).

However, 9 out of 14 subjects showed a trend to down-regulation of the AIC. In these subjects the ROI analysis also showed a down-regulation of the contralateral AIC. This corresponding contralateral change could be expected, given the bilateral processing of higher-level pain functions and the high connectivity between the left and right AIC as confirmed in the functional connectivity analysis. Additionally, the left and right caudate nucleus showed a down-regulation when comparing the first and later feedback runs. The fact that in both groups successful target region regulation is accompanied by a decrease in caudate nucleus activation underlines its importance in pain regulation.

DIFFERENCES IN THE FUNCTIONAL CONNECTIVITY AND ICA BETWEEN GROUPS

Functional connectivity analysis revealed that the ACC shows a stronger functional connectivity to the caudate nucleus while the AIC is more heavily connected to the ventrolateral PFC. These differences might reflect different pathways of pain regulation. While the ACC might directly influence caudate nucleus activity, the AIC has a stronger connection to higher-level processing via the PFC that in turn might regulate caudate activity.

ICA revealed one functional connectivity ICA component involving the ACC and the AIC that showed significantly lower s-mode values (a measure of effect size) in the ACC group in comparison to the AIC group. This implies that AIC and ACC activity overall was higher in the AIC group. One possible explanation might be that AIC regulation is harder to obtain in the beginning due to competing processes within this brain region. This might lead to an increase in pain processing within the AIC and ACC that is compensated at a later phase when subjects learned down-regulation.

EFFECT OF rt-fMRI ON PAIN RATINGS

In addition to our main goal of comparing two targets for rt-fMRI neurofeedback, we also looked at the pain rating as a function of runs. The finding that pain ratings decreased in neurofeedback runs compared to the localizer run suggests that ACC and AIC down-regulation by means of rt-fMRI neurofeedback decreases pain perception. Two contradictory factors potentially confound the interpretation of decrease in pain perception. Habituation might reduce, while sensitization might increase subjective pain perception despite identical physical stimulation. The observed result of decreased pain ratings in feedback as compared to localizer runs would not be expected from a regular pain study as short-term repeated pain stimulation in general causes sensitization rather than habituation (Drdla and Sandkuhler, 2008; Breimhorst et al., 2012). The same trend was seen in another recent pain real-time neurofeedback study (Rance et al., 2014) where slightly higher pain intensity was applied and pain unpleasantness ratings were compared for the last against the first run, indicating a pain sensitization over run. However, we cannot exclude the possibility that the placebo effect, caused by the neurofeedback intervention, might have confounded pain ratings

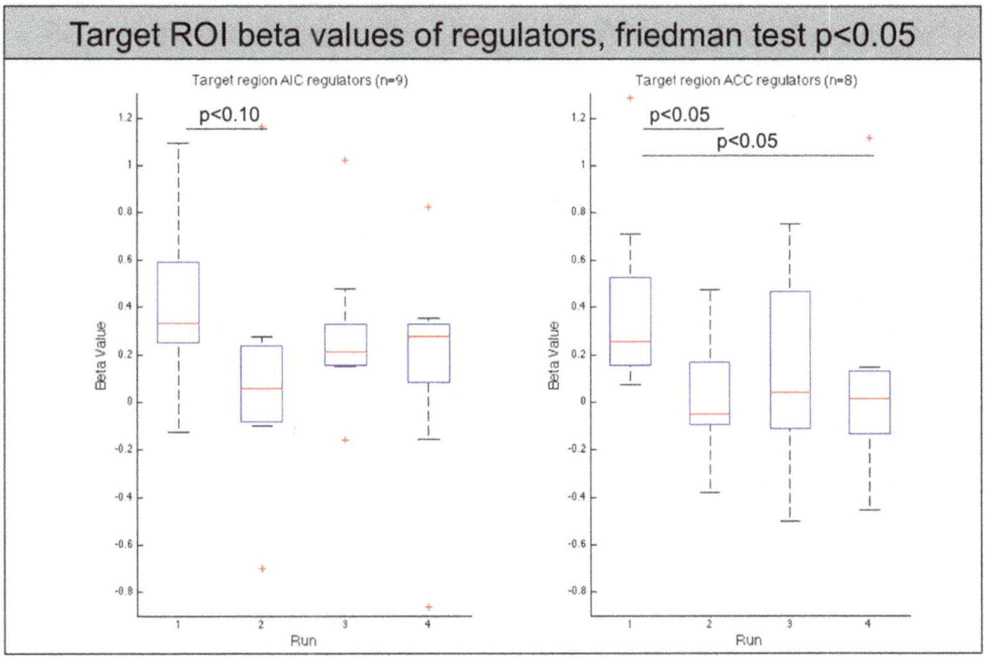

FIGURE 4 | Beta values of the target region (left AIC/ACC) for all regulators across neurofeedback runs (AIC-left, ACC-right). The red line indicates the mean value, the box indicates 25%/75% confidence intervals and the whiskers indicate the most extreme points within 1.5 times of the box length.

Table 3 | Overview of ROIs with their location and *p*-value of Friedman test for change in Beta-value across neurofeedback runs (AIC: *n* = 9, ACC: *n* = 8).

ROI	MNI coordinates			*p*-value—AIC regulators	*p*-value—ACC regulators
ACC	6	20	26	0.115	**0.016**
Left AIC	−34	6	−6	**0.020**	0.415
Left PIC	−38	−20	12	0.086	0.392
Left caudate	−14	−2	14	**0.008**	**0.044**
Right AIC	36	16	4	**0.024**	0.789
Right PIC	40	−16	10	0.091	0.494
Right caudate	16	2	12	**0.026**	0.187

Bold numbers indicate significant results (p < 0.05), values for the corresponding target area are highlighted red.

during neurofeedback runs. Pain perception is known to vary depending on the context (Rhudy and Meagher, 2000; Iannetti et al., 2008; Wang and Mitchell, 2011), therefore, making it hard to distinguish the factors that contribute to the pain reduction between localizer run and feedback runs. The fact that subjects were directing attention toward a cognitively demanding task itself could decrease pain perception as shown in a study working with different distraction tasks (Verhoeven et al., 2011). Both effects might be particularly high in the first neurofeedback runs when the task is new and subjects exert more effort than later on, thus possibly counteracting the desired effect of increasing regulation. The difference between localizer and neurofeedback pain rating in the AIC group can also be explained by competing processes within the ROI and the effect of cognitively highly demanding task engagement. These confounding effects might be similar in size to the effects of rt-fMRI, which are expected to be rather small, considering that pain perception has been experienced for years while cognitive modulation of pain has been practiced for minutes only. Some other neuroimaging studies already showed a similar phenomenon: significant neuroimaging effects were not accompanied by corresponding behavioral changes (Weiskopf et al., 2003; Haller et al., 2005, 2009, 2013, 2014; Johnston et al., 2011). This might indicate that objective fMRI data are more sensitive to small-scale changes within a rather small group than subjective behavioral measures. Therefore, it is not surprising that the decreased caudate activity over runs in the AIC and ACC group did not directly lead to a significant decrease in pain rating between feedback runs.

STRENGTH AND LIMITATIONS

The current investigation is a comparison of two possible target regions for rt-fMRI neurofeedback in pain. It clearly indicates that the AIC and the ACC could serve as a pain neurofeedback target in future studies. The following limitations should however be taken into account when interpreting the current results. First, this study did not aim at assessing the absolute behavioral effect of neurofeedback on pain ratings. Thus, further studies including sham feedback as well as modified pain stimulation are needed to separate specific effects of rt-fMRI neurofeedback from habituation/sensitization over time. Additionally, these studies should aim to compare neurofeedback to a sham method with a similar cognitive load, as a high cognitive load could influence pain ratings as well (Verhoeven et al., 2011). Second, as in previous real-time fMRI studies (Decharms et al., 2005;

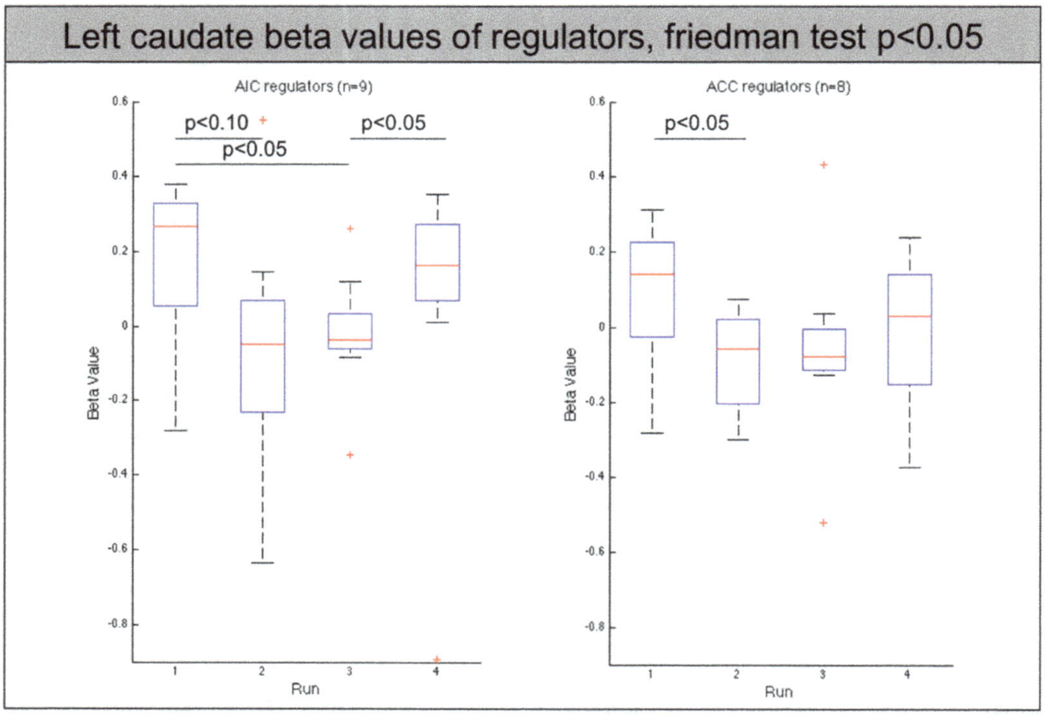

FIGURE 5 | Beta values of the left caudate nucleus for all regulators across neurofeedback runs (AIC-left, ACC-right). The red line indicates the mean value, the box indicates 25%/75% confidence intervals and the whiskers indicate the most extreme points within 1.5 times of the box length.

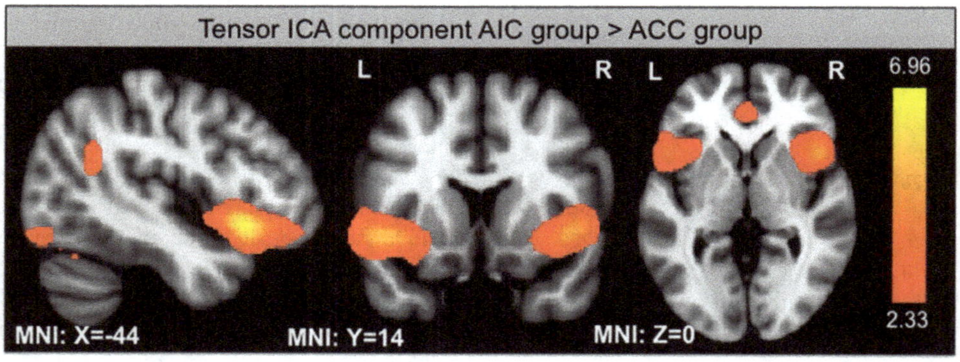

FIGURE 6 | Component from ICA that shows significantly different s-mode values between group.

Bray et al., 2007; Scharnowski et al., 2012; Robineau et al., 2014) not all subjects learned to down regulate the target area. Future studies should aim at identifying the parameters that lead to successful rtfMRI neurofeedback regulation in order to maximize the number of subjects that succeed. Another limitation lies in the use of a GLM on the basis of a box-type function convolved with the hemodynamic response function. Due to this hypothesis about the shape of the response, differently shaped responses such as a decrease in BOLD response after a certain period of pain stimulation, as it has been reported for the thalamus (Tran et al., 2010), would lead to underestimated statistical values.

The ACC and the AIC were judged as the most suitable neurofeedback targets based on literature (see Introduction). Based on our results the caudate nucleus and the thalamus or measures of the connectivity between the ACC and the caudate nucleus (e.g., intrinsic connectivity contrast degree) might be an additional target for future rt-fMRI neurofeedback studies in the domain of pain. As a next step, the potential long-term effects of neurofeedback training on pain perception should be assessed using the AIC, the ACC, thalamus or caudate nucleus as ROI in healthy subjects and as a next step also in chronic pain patients. Due to the possible involvement of the aMCC in neurofeedback regulation processes, the target area should be sufficiently separated

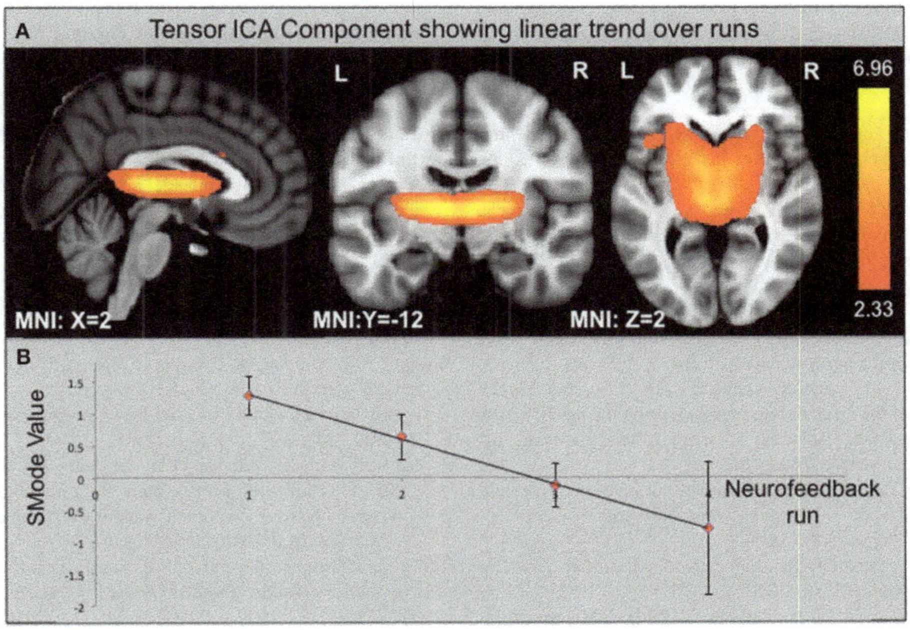

FIGURE 7 | Component from ICA that shows a significant linear trend over neurofeedback runs in the ACC group. (A) Component identified by ICA. **(B)** SMode Values of the component shown in **(A)** over runs. Error bars indicate the standard error of the mean (SEM).

from the aMCC. These future studies could be another important step toward a possible supplemental pain therapy to reduce the impact of pain on patients' life.

ACKNOWLEDGMENTS

This work was supported in part by the Swiss National Science Foundation (projects 320030_147126/1, 320030_127079/1 and PP00P2-146318), the foundation "Stiftung Rheinland-Pfalz" (Project 936) and the Center for Biomedical Imaging (CIBM).

REFERENCES

Apkarian, A. V., Bushnell, M. C., Treede, R. D., and Zubieta, J. K. (2005). Human brain mechanisms of pain perception and regulation in health and disease. *Eur. J. Pain* 9, 463–484. doi: 10.1016/j.ejpain.2004.11.001

Asmundson, G. J., and Katz, J. (2009). Understanding the co-occurrence of anxiety disorders and chronic pain: state-of-the-art. *Depress. Anxiety* 26, 888–901. doi: 10.1002/da.20600

Bair, M. J., Robinson, R. L., Katon, W., and Kroenke, K. (2003). Depression and pain comorbidity: a literature review. *Arch. Intern. Med.* 163, 2433–2445. doi: 10.1001/archinte.163.20.2433

Baliki, M. N., Baria, A. T., and Apkarian, A. V. (2011). The cortical rhythms of chronic back pain. *J. Neurosci.* 31, 13981–13990. doi: 10.1523/JNEUROSCI.1984-11.2011

Baliki, M. N., Chialvo, D. R., Geha, P. Y., Levy, R. M., Harden, R. N., Parrish, T. B., et al. (2006). Chronic pain and the emotional brain: specific brain activity associated with spontaneous fluctuations of intensity of chronic back pain. *J. Neurosci.* 26, 12165–12173. doi: 10.1523/JNEUROSCI.3576-06.2006

Bantick, S. J., Wise, R. G., Ploghaus, A., Clare, S., Smith, S. M., and Tracey, I. (2002). Imaging how attention modulates pain in humans using functional MRI. *Brain* 125, 310–319. doi: 10.1093/brain/awf022

Basbaum, A., and Jessell, T. (2000). *"The perception of pain," in Principles of Neural Science*, eds E. Kandel, J. Schwartz, and T. Jessell (New York, NY: McGraw-Hill), 472–491.

Berman, S. M., Naliboff, B. D., Suyenobu, B., Labus, J. S., Stains, J., Ohning, G., et al. (2008). Reduced brainstem inhibition during anticipated pelvic visceral pain correlates with enhanced brain response to the visceral stimulus in women with irritable bowel syndrome. *J. Neurosci.* 28, 349–359. doi: 10.1523/JNEUROSCI.2500-07.2008

Berthier, M., Starkstein, S., and Leiguarda, R. (1988). Asymbolia for pain: a sensory-limbic disconnection syndrome. *Ann. Neurol.* 24, 41–49. doi: 10.1002/ana.410240109

Bingel, U., Wanigasekera, V., Wiech, K., Mhuircheartaigh, R. N., Lee, M. C., Ploner, M., et al. (2011). The effect of treatment expectation on drug efficacy: imaging the analgesic benefit of the opioid remifentanil. *Sci. Transl. Med.* 3:70ra14. doi: 10.1126/scitranslmed.3001244

Birklein, F., Rolke, R., and Muller-Forell, W. (2005). Isolated insular infarction eliminates contralateral cold, cold pain, and pinprick perception. *Neurology* 65, 1381. doi: 10.1212/01.wnl.0000181351.82772.b3

Borsook, D., Upadhyay, J., Chudler, E. H., and Becerra, L. (2010). A key role of the basal ganglia in pain and analgesia–insights gained through human functional imaging. *Mol. Pain* 6:27. doi: 10.1186/1744-8069-6-27

Bray, S., Shimojo, S., and O'Doherty, J. P. (2007). Direct instrumental conditioning of neural activity using functional magnetic resonance imaging-derived reward feedback. *J. Neurosci.* 27, 7498–7507. doi: 10.1523/JNEUROSCI.2118-07.2007

Breimhorst, M., Hondrich, M., Rebhorn, C., May, A., and Birklein, F. (2012). Sensory and sympathetic correlates of heat pain sensitization and habituation in men and women. *Eur. J. Pain* 16, 1281–1292. doi: 10.1002/j.1532-2149.2012.00133.x

Brooks, J. C., Nurmikko, T. J., Bimson, W. E., Singh, K. D., and Roberts, N. (2002). fMRI of thermal pain: effects of stimulus laterality and attention. *Neuroimage* 15, 293–301. doi: 10.1006/nimg.2001.0974

Burgmer, M., Pogatzki-Zahn, E., Gaubitz, M., Stuber, C., Wessoleck, E., Heuft, G., et al. (2010). Fibromyalgia unique temporal brain activation during experimental pain: a controlled fMRI Study. *J. Neural Transm.* 117, 123–131. doi: 10.1007/s00702-009-0339-1

Bush, G., Luu, P., and Posner, M. I. (2000). Cognitive and emotional influences in anterior cingulate cortex. *Trends Cogn. Sci.* 4, 215–222. doi: 10.1016/S1364-6613(00)01483-2

Bushnell, M. C., Ceko, M., and Low, L. A. (2013). Cognitive and emotional control of pain and its disruption in chronic pain. *Nat. Rev. Neurosci.* 14, 502–511. doi: 10.1038/nrn3516

Canterberry, M., Hanlon, C. A., Hartwell, K. J., Li, X., Owens, M., Lematty, T., et al. (2013). Sustained reduction of nicotine craving with real-time neurofeedback: exploring the role of severity of dependence. *Nicotine Tob. Res.* 15, 2120–2124. doi: 10.1093/ntr/ntt122

Caria, A., Veit, R., Sitaram, R., Lotze, M., Weiskopf, N., Grodd, W., et al. (2007). Regulation of anterior insular cortex activity using real-time fMRI. *Neuroimage* 35, 1238–1246. doi: 10.1016/j.neuroimage.2007.01.018

Cauda, F., Costa, T., Torta, D. M., Sacco, K., D'Agata, F., Duca, S., et al. (2012). Meta-analytic clustering of the insular cortex: characterizing the meta-analytic connectivity of the insula when involved in active tasks. *Neuroimage* 62, 343–355. doi: 10.1016/j.neuroimage.2012.04.012

Cesare, P., and McNaughton, P. (1996). A novel heat-activated current in nociceptive neurons and its sensitization by bradykinin. *Proc. Natl. Acad. Sci. U.S.A.* 93, 15435–15439. doi: 10.1073/pnas.93.26.15435

Decharms, R. C. (2012). *1st Swiss rtfMRI Neurofeedback Conference.* Available online at: http://www.relab.ethz.ch/rtfMRI2012

Decharms, R. C., Maeda, F., Glover, G. H., Ludlow, D., Pauly, J. M., Soneji, D., et al. (2005). Control over brain activation and pain learned by using real-time functional MRI. *Proc. Natl. Acad. Sci. U.S.A.* 102, 18626–18631. doi: 10.1073/pnas.0505210102

Denkinger, M. D., Lukas, A., Nikolaus, T., Peter, R., Franke, S., and for the Acti, F.E.S.G. (2014). Multisite pain, pain frequency and pain severity are associated with depression in older adults: results from the ActiFE Ulm study. *Age Ageing* 43, 510–514. doi: 10.1093/ageing/afu013

Drdla, R., and Sandkuhler, J. (2008). Long-term potentiation at C-fibre synapses by low-level presynaptic activity *in vivo*. *Mol. Pain* 4:18. doi: 10.1186/1744-8069-4-18

Eccleston, C., and Crombez, G. (2007). Worry and chronic pain: a misdirected problem solving model. *Pain* 132, 233–236. doi: 10.1016/j.pain.2007.09.014

Eippert, F., Veit, R., Weiskopf, N., Erb, M., Birbaumer, N., and Anders, S. (2007). Regulation of emotional responses elicited by threat-related stimuli. *Hum. Brain Mapp.* 28, 409–423. doi: 10.1002/hbm.20291

Favilla, S., Huber, A., Pagnoni, G., Lui, F., Facchin, P., Cocchi, M., et al. (2014). Ranking brain areas encoding the perceived level of pain from fMRI data. *Neuroimage* 90, 153–162. doi: 10.1016/j.neuroimage.2014.01.001

Faymonville, M. E., Laureys, S., Degueldre, C., Delfiore, G., Luxen, A., Franck, G., et al. (2000). Neural mechanisms of antinociceptive effects of hypnosis. *Anesthesiology* 92, 1257–1267. doi: 10.1097/00000542-200005000-00013

Freund, W., Klug, R., Weber, F., Stuber, G., Schmitz, B., and Wunderlich, A. P. (2009). Perception and suppression of thermally induced pain: a fMRI study. *Somatosens. Mot. Res.* 26, 1–10. doi: 10.1080/08990220902738243

Garcia-Larrea, L. (2012). The posterior insular-opercular region and the search of a primary cortex for pain. *Neurophysiol. Clin.* 42, 299–313. doi: 10.1016/j.neucli.2012.06.001

Gard, T., Holzel, B. K., Sack, A. T., Hempel, H., Lazar, S. W., Vaitl, D., et al. (2012). Pain attenuation through mindfulness is associated with decreased cognitive control and increased sensory processing in the brain. *Cereb. Cortex* 22, 2692–2702. doi: 10.1093/cercor/bhr352

Geisser, M. E., Roth, R. S., Theisen, M. E., Robinson, M. E., and Riley, J. L. 3rd. (2000). Negative affect, self-report of depressive symptoms, and clinical depression: relation to the experience of chronic pain. *Clin. J. Pain* 16, 110–120. doi: 10.1097/00002508-200006000-00004

Grace, G. M., Nielson, W. R., Hopkins, M., and Berg, M. A. (1999). Concentration and memory deficits in patients with fibromyalgia syndrome. *J. Clin. Exp. Neuropsychol.* 21, 477–487. doi: 10.1076/jcen.21.4.477.876

Grahn, J. A., Parkinson, J. A., and Owen, A. M. (2008). The cognitive functions of the caudate nucleus. *Prog. Neurobiol.* 86, 141–155. doi: 10.1016/j.pneurobio.2008.09.004

Grant, J. A., Courtemanche, J., and Rainville, P. (2011). A non-elaborative mental stance and decoupling of executive and pain-related cortices predicts low pain sensitivity in Zen meditators. *Pain* 152, 150–156. doi: 10.1016/j.pain.2010.10.006

Greenspan, J. D., Lee, R. R., and Lenz, F. A. (1999). Pain sensitivity alterations as a function of lesion location in the parasylvian cortex. *Pain* 81, 273–282. doi: 10.1016/S0304-3959(99)00021-4

Greenspan, J. D., and Winfield, J. A. (1992). Reversible pain and tactile deficits associated with a cerebral tumor compressing the posterior insula and parietal operculum. *Pain* 50, 29–39. doi: 10.1016/0304-3959(92)90109-O

Gu, X., Liu, X., Van Dam, N. T., Hof, P. R., and Fan, J. (2013). Cognition-emotion integration in the anterior insular cortex. *Cereb. Cortex* 23, 20–27. doi: 10.1093/cercor/bhr367

Gwilym, S. E., Filippini, N., Douaud, G., Carr, A. J., and Tracey, I. (2010). Thalamic atrophy associated with painful osteoarthritis of the hip is reversible after arthroplasty: a longitudinal voxel-based morphometric study. *Arthritis Rheum.* 62, 2930–2940. doi: 10.1002/art.27585

Haller, S., Bartsch, A. J., Radue, E. W., Klarhofer, M., Seifritz, E., and Scheffler, K. (2005). Effect of fMRI acoustic noise on non-auditory working memory task: comparison between continuous and pulsed sound emitting EPI. *MAGMA* 18, 263–271. doi: 10.1007/s10334-005-0010-2

Haller, S., Birbaumer, N., and Veit, R. (2010). Real-time fMRI feedback training may improve chronic tinnitus. *Eur. Radiol.* 20, 696–703. doi: 10.1007/s00330-009-1595-z

Haller, S., Homola, G. A., Scheffler, K., Beckmann, C. F., and Bartsch, A. J. (2009). Background MR gradient noise and non-auditory BOLD activations: a data-driven perspective. *Brain Res.* 1282, 74–83. doi: 10.1016/j.brainres.2009.05.094

Haller, S., Montandon, M. L., Rodriguez, C., Moser, D., Toma, S., Hofmeister, J., et al. (2014). Acute caffeine administration effect on brain activation patterns in mild cognitive impairment. *J. Alzheimers Dis.* 41, 101–112. doi: 10.3233/JAD-132360

Haller, S., Rodriguez, C., Moser, D., Toma, S., Hofmeister, J., Sinanaj, I., et al. (2013). Acute caffeine administration impact on working memory-related brain activation and functional connectivity in the elderly: a BOLD and perfusion MRI study. *Neuroscience* 250, 364–371. doi: 10.1016/j.neuroscience.2013.07.021

Hartwell, K. J., Prisciandaro, J. J., Borckardt, J., Li, X., George, M. S., and Brady, K. T. (2013). Real-time fMRI in the treatment of nicotine dependence: a conceptual review and pilot studies. *Psychol. Addict. Behav.* 27, 501–509. doi: 10.1037/a0028215

Iannetti, G. D., Hughes, N. P., Lee, M. C., and Mouraux, A. (2008). Determinants of laser-evoked EEG responses: pain perception or stimulus saliency? *J. Neurophysiol.* 100, 815–828. doi: 10.1152/jn.00097.2008

Iannetti, G. D., and Mouraux, A. (2010). From the neuromatrix to the pain matrix (and back). *Exp. Brain Res.* 205, 1–12. doi: 10.1007/s00221-010-2340-1

Ilgen, M. A., Zivin, K., McCammon, R. J., and Valenstein, M. (2008). Pain and suicidal thoughts, plans and attempts in the United States. *Gen. Hosp. Psychiatry* 30, 521–527. doi: 10.1016/j.genhosppsych.2008.09.003

Jensen, K. B., Kosek, E., Petzke, F., Carville, S., Fransson, P., Marcus, H., et al. (2009). Evidence of dysfunctional pain inhibition in Fibromyalgia reflected in rACC during provoked pain. *Pain* 144, 95–100. doi: 10.1016/j.pain.2009.03.018

Jensen, K. B., Kosek, E., Wicksell, R., Kemani, M., Olsson, G., Merle, J. V., et al. (2012). Cognitive Behavioral Therapy increases pain-evoked activation of the prefrontal cortex in patients with fibromyalgia. *Pain* 153, 1495–1503. doi: 10.1016/j.pain.2012.04.010

Johnston, S., Linden, D. E., Healy, D., Goebel, R., Habes, I., and Boehm, S. G. (2011). Upregulation of emotion areas through neurofeedback with a focus on positive mood. *Cogn. Affect. Behav. Neurosci.* 11, 44–51. doi: 10.3758/s13415-010-0010-1

Jouini, G., Choiniere, M., Martin, E., Perreault, S., Berbiche, D., Lussier, D., et al. (2014). Pharmacotherapeutic management of chronic noncancer pain in primary care: lessons for pharmacists. *J. Pain Res.* 7, 163–173. doi: 10.2147/JPR.S56884.

Keller, A. F., Beggs, S., Salter, M. W., and De Koninck, Y. (2007). Transformation of the output of spinal lamina I neurons after nerve injury and microglia stimulation underlying neuropathic pain. *Mol. Pain* 3:27. doi: 10.1186/1744-8069-3-27

Koyama, T., Kato, K., and Mikami, A. (2000). During pain-avoidance neurons activated in the macaque anterior cingulate and caudate. *Neurosci. Lett.* 283, 17–20. doi: 10.1016/S0304-3940(00)00894-6

Lawrence, E. J., Su, L., Barker, G. J., Medford, N., Dalton, J., Williams, S. C., et al. (2013). Self-regulation of the anterior insula: reinforcement learning using real-time fMRI neurofeedback. *Neuroimage* 88C, 113–124. doi: 10.1016/j.neuroimage.2013.10.069

Leavitt, F., and Katz, R. S. (2006). Distraction as a key determinant of impaired memory in patients with fibromyalgia. *J. Rheumatol.* 33, 127–132.

Lee, J. H., Kim, J., and Yoo, S. S. (2012). Real-time fMRI-based neurofeedback reinforces causality of attention networks. *Neurosci. Res.* 72, 347–354. doi: 10.1016/j.neures.2012.01.002

Leeuw, M., Goossens, M. E., Linton, S. J., Crombez, G., Boersma, K., and Vlaeyen, J. W. (2007a). The fear-avoidance model of musculoskeletal pain: current state of scientific evidence. *J. Behav. Med.* 30, 77–94. doi: 10.1007/s10865-006-9085-0

Leeuw, M., Houben, R. M., Severeijns, R., Picavet, H. S., Schouten, E. G., and Vlaeyen, J. W. (2007b). Pain-related fear in low back pain: a prospective study in the general population. *Eur. J. Pain* 11, 256–266. doi: 10.1016/j.ejpain.2006.02.009

Li, X., Hartwell, K. J., Borckardt, J., Prisciandaro, J. J., Saladin, M. E., Morgan, P. S., et al. (2013). Volitional reduction of anterior cingulate cortex activity produces decreased cue craving in smoking cessation: a preliminary real-time fMRI study. *Addict. Biol.* 18, 739–748. doi: 10.1111/j.1369-1600.2012.00449.x

Linden, D. E., Habes, I., Johnston, S. J., Linden, S., Tatineni, R., Subramanian, L., et al. (2012). Real-time self-regulation of emotion networks in patients with depression. *PLoS ONE* 7:e38115. doi: 10.1371/journal.pone.0038115

Linton, S. J. (2013). A transdiagnostic approach to pain and emotion. *J. Appl. Biobehav. Res.* 18, 82–103. doi: 10.1111/jabr.12007

Moore, K. A., Kohno, T., Karchewski, L. A., Scholz, J., Baba, H., and Woolf, C. J. (2002). Partial peripheral nerve injury promotes a selective loss of GABAergic inhibition in the superficial dorsal horn of the spinal cord. *J. Neurosci.* 22, 6724–6731.

Muller-Schwefe, G., Jaksch, W., Morlion, B., Kalso, E., Schafer, M., Coluzzi, F., et al. (2011). Make a CHANGE: optimising communication and pain management decisions. *Curr. Med. Res. Opin.* 27, 481–488. doi: 10.1185/03007995.2010.545377

Munguia-Izquierdo, D., and Legaz-Arrese, A. (2007). Exercise in warm water decreases pain and improves cognitive function in middle-aged women with fibromyalgia. *Clin. Exp. Rheumatol.* 25, 823–830.

Napadow, V., Lacount, L., Park, K., As-Sanie, S., Clauw, D. J., and Harris, R. E. (2010). Intrinsic brain connectivity in fibromyalgia is associated with chronic pain intensity. *Arthritis Rheum.* 62, 2545–2555. doi: 10.1002/art.27497

Ossipov, M. H., Dussor, G. O., and Porreca, F. (2010). Central modulation of pain. *J. Clin. Invest.* 120, 3779–3787. doi: 10.1172/JCI43766

Porreca, F., Ossipov, M. H., and Gebhart, G. F. (2002). Chronic pain and medullary descending facilitation. *Trends Neurosci.* 25, 319–325. doi: 10.1016/S0166-2236(02)02157-4

Rainville, P., Duncan, G. H., Price, D. D., Carrier, B., and Bushnell, M. C. (1997). Pain affect encoded in human anterior cingulate but not somatosensory cortex. *Science* 277, 968–971. doi: 10.1126/science.277.5328.968

Rance, M., Ruttorf, M., Nees, F., Schad, L. R., and Flor, H. (2014). Real time fMRI feedback of the anterior cingulate and posterior insular cortex in the processing of pain. *Hum. Brain Mapp.* doi: 10.1002/hbm.22585. [Epub ahead of print].

Rhudy, J. L., and Meagher, M. W. (2000). Fear and anxiety: divergent effects on human pain thresholds. *Pain* 84, 65–75. doi: 10.1016/S0304-3959(99)00183-9

Robineau, F., Rieger, S. W., Mermoud, C., Pichon, S., Koush, Y., Van De Ville, D., et al. (2014). Self-regulation of inter-hemispheric visual cortex balance through real-time fMRI neurofeedback training. *Neuroimage* 100C, 1–14. doi: 10.1016/j.neuroimage.2014.05.072

Ruiz, S., Lee, S., Soekadar, S. R., Caria, A., Veit, R., Kircher, T., et al. (2013). Acquired self-control of insula cortex modulates emotion recognition and brain network connectivity in schizophrenia. *Hum. Brain Mapp.* 34, 200–212. doi: 10.1002/hbm.21427

Sawamoto, N., Honda, M., Okada, T., Hanakawa, T., Kanda, M., Fukuyama, H., et al. (2000). Expectation of pain enhances responses to nonpainful somatosensory stimulation in the anterior cingulate cortex and parietal operculum/posterior insula: an event-related functional magnetic resonance imaging study. *J. Neurosci.* 20, 7438–7445.

Scharnowski, F., Hutton, C., Josephs, O., Weiskopf, N., and Rees, G. (2012). Improving visual perception through neurofeedback. *J. Neurosci.* 32, 17830–17841. doi: 10.1523/JNEUROSCI.6334-11.2012

Seeley, W. W., Menon, V., Schatzberg, A. F., Keller, J., Glover, G. H., Kenna, H., et al. (2007). Dissociable intrinsic connectivity networks for salience processing and executive control. *J. Neurosci.* 27, 2349–2356. doi: 10.1523/JNEUROSCI.5587-06.2007

Seminowicz, D. A., Wideman, T. H., Naso, L., Hatami-Khoroushahi, Z., Fallatah, S., Ware, M. A., et al. (2011). Effective treatment of chronic low back pain in humans reverses abnormal brain anatomy and function. *J. Neurosci.* 31, 7540–7550. doi: 10.1523/JNEUROSCI.5280-10.2011

Shackman, A. J., Salomons, T. V., Slagter, H. A., Fox, A. S., Winter, J. J., and Davidson, R. J. (2011). The integration of negative affect, pain and cognitive control in the cingulate cortex. *Nat. Rev. Neurosci.* 12, 154–167. doi: 10.1038/nrn2994

Singer, T., Seymour, B., O'Doherty, J., Kaube, H., Dolan, R. J., and Frith, C. D. (2004). Empathy for pain involves the affective but not sensory components of pain. *Science* 303, 1157–1162. doi: 10.1126/science.1093535

Sterzer, P., and Kleinschmidt, A. (2010). Anterior insula activations in perceptual paradigms: often observed but barely understood. *Brain Struct. Funct.* 214, 611–622. doi: 10.1007/s00429-010-0252-2

Tran, T. D., Wang, H., Tandon, A., Hernandez-Garcia, L., and Casey, K. L. (2010). Temporal summation of heat pain in humans: evidence supporting thalamocortical modulation. *Pain* 150, 93–102. doi: 10.1016/j.pain.2010.04.001

Treede, R. D., Kenshalo, D. R., Gracely, R. H., and Jones, A. K. (1999). The cortical representation of pain. *Pain* 79, 105–111. doi: 10.1016/S0304-3959(98)00184-5

Trost, Z., Vangronsveld, K., Linton, S. J., Quartana, P. J., and Sullivan, M. J. (2012). Cognitive dimensions of anger in chronic pain. *Pain* 153, 515–517. doi: 10.1016/j.pain.2011.10.023

Turk, D. C., Okifuji, A., and Scharff, L. (1995). Chronic pain and depression: role of perceived impact and perceived control in different age cohorts. *Pain* 61, 93–101. doi: 10.1016/0304-3959(94)00167-D

Valet, M., Sprenger, T., Boecker, H., Willoch, F., Rummeny, E., Conrad, B., et al. (2004). Distraction modulates connectivity of the cingulo-frontal cortex and the midbrain during pain–an fMRI analysis. *Pain* 109, 399–408. doi: 10.1016/j.pain.2004.02.033

Veit, R., Singh, V., Sitaram, R., Caria, A., Rauss, K., and Birbaumer, N. (2012). Using real-time fMRI to learn voluntary regulation of the anterior insula in the presence of threat-related stimuli. *Soc. Cogn. Affect. Neurosci.* 7, 623–634. doi: 10.1093/scan/nsr061

Verhoeven, K., Van Damme, S., Eccleston, C., Van Ryckeghem, D. M., Legrain, V., and Crombez, G. (2011). Distraction from pain and executive functioning: an experimental investigation of the role of inhibition, task switching and working memory. *Eur. J. Pain* 15, 866–873. doi: 10.1016/j.ejpain.2011.01.009

Vlaeyen, J. W., and Linton, S. J. (2012). Fear-avoidance model of chronic musculoskeletal pain: 12 years on. *Pain* 153, 1144–1147. doi: 10.1016/j.pain.2011.12.009

Vogt, B. A., Derbyshire, S., and Jones, A. K. (1996). Pain processing in four regions of human cingulate cortex localized with co-registered PET and MR imaging. *Eur. J. Neurosci.* 8, 1461–1473. doi: 10.1111/j.1460-9568.1996.tb01608.x

Voscopoulos, C., and Lema, M. (2010). When does acute pain become chronic? *Br. J. Anaesth.* 105 Suppl. 1, i69–i85. doi: 10.1093/bja/aeq323

Wang, T., and Mitchell, C. J. (2011). Attention and relative novelty in human perceptual learning. *J. Exp. Psychol. Anim. Behav. Process.* 37, 436–445. doi: 10.1037/a0023104

Weiskopf, N., Veit, R., Erb, M., Mathiak, K., Grodd, W., Goebel, R., et al. (2003). Physiological self-regulation of regional brain activity using real-time functional magnetic resonance imaging (fMRI): methodology and exemplary data. *Neuroimage* 19, 577–586. doi: 10.1016/S1053-8119(03)00145-9

Weissman, D. H., Gopalakrishnan, A., Hazlett, C. J., and Woldorff, M. G. (2005). Dorsal anterior cingulate cortex resolves conflict from distracting stimuli by boosting attention toward relevant events. *Cereb. Cortex* 15, 229–237. doi: 10.1093/cercor/bhh125

Woolf, C. J. (2011). Central sensitization: implications for the diagnosis and treatment of pain. *Pain* 152, S2–S15. doi: 10.1016/j.pain.2010.09.030

Wunderlich, A. P., Klug, R., Stuber, G., Landwehrmeyer, B., Weber, F., and Freund, W. (2011). Caudate nucleus and insular activation during a pain suppression paradigm comparing thermal and electrical stimulation. *Open Neuroimag. J.* 5, 1–8. doi: 10.2174/1874440001105010001

8

Neurofeedback of the difference in activation of the anterior cingulate cortex and posterior insular cortex: two functionally connected areas in the processing of pain

Mariela Rance[1], Michaela Ruttorf[2], Frauke Nees[1], Lothar R. Schad[2] and Herta Flor[1]*

[1] *Department of Cognitive and Clinical Neuroscience, Medical Faculty Mannheim, Central Institute of Mental Health, Heidelberg University, Mannheim, Germany*
[2] *Computer Assisted Clinical Medicine, Medical Faculty Mannheim, Heidelberg University, Mannheim, Germany*

Correspondence:
Herta Flor, Department of Cognitive and Clinical Neuroscience, Central Institute of Mental Health, Square J5, D-68159 Mannheim, Germany
e-mail: herta.flor@zi-mannheim.de

The aim of this study was the analysis of the effect of a learned increase in the dissociation between the rostral anterior cingulate cortex (rACC) and the left posterior insula (pInsL) on pain intensity and unpleasantness and the contribution of each region to the effect, exploring the possibility to influence the perception of pain with neurofeedback methods. We trained ten healthy subjects to increase the difference in the blood oxygenation level-dependent response between the rACC and pInsL to painful electric stimuli. Subjects learned to increase the dissociation with either the rACC (state 1) or the pInsL (state 2) being higher. For feedback we subtracted the signal of one region from the other and provided feedback in four conditions with six trials each yielding two different states: [rACC—pInsL increase (state 1), rACC—pInsL decrease (state 2), pInsL—rACC increase (state 2), pInsL—rACC decrease (state 1)]. Significant changes in the dissociation from trial one to six were seen in all conditions. There were significant changes from trial one to six in the pInsL in three of the four conditions, the rACC showed no significant change. Pain intensity or unpleasantness ratings were unrelated to the dissociation between the regions and the activation in each region. Learning success in the conditions did not significantly correlate and there was no significant correlation between the two respective conditions of one state, i.e., learning to achieve a specific state is not a stable ability. The pInsL seems to be the driving force behind changes in the learned dissociation between the regions. Despite successful differential modulation of activation in areas responsive to the painful stimulus, no corresponding changes in the perception of pain intensity or unpleasantness emerged. Learning to induce different states of dissociation between the areas is not a stable ability since success did not correlate overall or between two conditions of the the same state.

Keywords: real-time fMRI, pain, anterior cingulate cortex, posterior insula, neuromodulation, connectivity

INTRODUCTION

The number of studies utilizing neuromodulation to alter behavior, cognition, and emotional processing has been growing in the past ten years. Applications include the modulation of the blood oxygenation level-dependent (BOLD) response in single brain regions such as altering motor function via modulation of the ventral or dorsal premotor cortex (Sitaram et al., 2012; Zhao et al., 2013), processing of emotional visual cues by modulating the anterior insula (Caria et al., 2010), craving in smokers by modulating the anterior cingulate cortex (Li et al., 2013), or improving working memory performance by modulating the dorsal lateral prefrontal cortex (Zhang et al., 2013). While in some studies altered brain activation was associated with changes in behavior, other studies showed that self-modulation of brain activation is possible in the absence of behavioral effects (Weiskopf et al., 2003; Johnston et al., 2011; McCaig et al., 2011; Birbaumer et al., 2013). More recently, real-time functional magnetic resonance imaging (rt-fMRI) has not only been used in the modulation of specific regions of the brain but of active networks defined by connectivity analyses or real-time pattern classification (Esposito et al., 2003; Laconte et al., 2007; Sitaram et al., 2011; Berman et al., 2013; Koush et al., 2013; Ruiz et al., 2013; Zotev et al., 2013; Scharnowski et al., 2014; Zilverstand et al., 2014). In the light of these results an important but so far under-investigated issue is the local specificity of neuromodulation of single regions, differential effects of up- or downregulation of BOLD activation and their influence on the active network and behavior.

Pain is a complex sensory and emotional experience and its alteration by rt-fMRI might be a challenge. It has been shown that pain perception involves a distributed network (Apkarian et al., 2005; Brodersen et al., 2012; Wager et al., 2013) that is, moreover, also involved in other functions (Iannetti and Mouraux, 2010; Legrain et al., 2011; Cauda et al., 2012b). Moreover, pain perception is subject of many modulating factors such as cognitive, emotional, and learning processes (Bingel et al., 2006; Diesch and Flor, 2007) that involve other brain circuits (Villemure and Bushnell, 2002, 2009; Wiech et al., 2006). Decharms et al. (2005) trained healthy controls while they received painful thermal stimulation to decrease and increase the BOLD signal in the rACC. The magnitude of the change in the activation was associated with the magnitude of the change in the ratings. The authors also transferred their design to chronic pain patients who subsequently reported pain relief. However, a replication of these results is still missing (Chapin et al., 2012).

We (Rance et al., 2014) previously examined and compared the effect of separately up- and downregulating two regions that are part of the pain processing network: the rACC, involved in the tonic aversive state elicited by pain (Apkarian et al., 2005; Qu et al., 2011) and the left posterior insula (pInsL), a region that processes the sensory aspect of pain perception (Rainville et al., 1997; Frot et al., 2007). In this study successful up- and downregulation of the rACC and pInsL was trained. The subjects acquired successful pInsL up- and downregulation and successful rACC down- but not upregulation. Successful modulation was not accompanied by a change in perceived pain intensity or unpleasantness. Modulation of one region also affected the second region, implying that the network seen active in the presence of the painful electrical stimulus was affected. Better learning was associated with higher dissociation between the two regions. Moreover, higher dissociation during upregulation of the pInsL correlated positively with an increase in pain unpleasantness ratings. These results suggest that the state of the pain-related network plays a role in the learning of self-modulation of the activation of single nodes.

In the light of these findings the current study aimed at examining and comparing the effects of a combined difference feedback of the two regions, rACC and pInsL, thus permitting to analyze the effect of the disruption of a part of the pain processing network. Similar to our previous study ten healthy subjects trained on four consecutive days. Two distinct states were trained: activation of the rACC higher than pInsL activation (state 1) or activation of pInsL higher than rACC activation (state 2). The goal of the training was to increase the difference. Each state was practiced in two distinct conditions; state 1A: rACC—pInsL increase (arrow up), state 1B: pInsL—rACC decrease (arrow down), state 2A: pInsL—rACC increase (arrow up), state 2B rACC—pInsL decrease (arrow down). For a detailed list of the balancing protocol see Supplementary Table SI. We assessed pain intensity and unpleasantness ratings after each training trial and recorded the strategy used. In the previous study we saw no differential contribution of the modulation of the two regions on the perception of pain intensity and unpleasantness. Based on our previous findings, we expected to find an effect of dissociating two functionally connected regions, which are part of a wider network active in the presence of painful stimulation, on pain intensity and unpleasantness ratings. We examined differences in the contributions of the two regions to the successful modulation of both. We thus compared within each condition (state) changes in the single regions of those subjects who were successful with those who did not learn the modulation of the combined regions.

MATERIALS AND METHODS

PARTICIPANTS

Ten healthy adults with a mean age of 27.8 years ($SD = 4.71$, range: 22–35), six females ($M = 29.0$, $SD = 5.25$) and four males ($M = 26.0$, $SD = 3.65$), were examined. All subjects were right-handed as assessed by the Edinburgh Handedness Inventory (Oldfield, 1971) and recruited by announcements at the local university. We defined cardiovascular or neurological disorders, brain injury, current or chronic pain, current analgesic medication, pregnancy, lifetime and current substance abuse or dependence, any mental disorder, and metallic implants as exclusion criteria. The study adhered to the Declaration of Helsinki and was approved by the Ethics Committee of the Medical Faculty Mannheim, Heidelberg University, Germany. All subjects gave written informed consent after a detailed description of the complete study and received a reimbursement of 60 €.

STIMULATION PROTOCOL

Painful monopolar transcutaneous electric stimuli (Digitimer, DS7A, Welwyn Garden City, UK) were applied to the base of the right fourth digit using a concentric stainless steel bipolar needle electrode (Nihon Kohden, Tokyo, Japan), which permitted the stimulation of Aδ nociceptive fibers located in the epidermis (Inui et al., 2002; Yoshino et al., 2010). Pulses lasted 1 ms and were applied with a frequency of 2 Hz. The method of limits was used to determine individual detection and pain thresholds, averaging over the last 2 of 3 ascending and descending stimulation sequences. Stimulation strength was set at 70% between pain threshold and pain tolerance and adjusted to be rated between 6 and 7 on an 11 point verbal rating scale (ranging from 0 = no pain to 10 = strongest imaginable pain). The individually adjusted mean stimulation current was 1.97 mA ($SD = 1.51$), the pre-baseline intensity of this stimulus was rated as 6.30 ($SD = 1.06$) and the unpleasantness as 5.80 ($SD = 1.23$). The post-baseline stimulus intensity was rated 6.10 ($SD = 2.44$) and the pain unpleasantness 6.50 ($SD = 2.69$) and served as reference for the ratings of the following training trials.

RT-fMRI FEEDBACK PROTOCOL

The neurofeedback protocol was identical to the one described in detail in our previous study (Rance et al., 2014): a baseline run accompanied by an anatomical scan on one day followed by 24 training trials spread over the course of four consecutive days. Each training day consisted of six successive training trials; each trial was composed of six regulation phases (45.0 s) and six non-regulation phases (22.5 s) evenly distributed across each session. During the regulation phases, painful electric stimuli were applied along with the real-time feedback (**Figure 1**). The feedback screen consisted of a moving blue or yellow ball on a black background accompanied by a stationary white arrow indicating the vertical direction in which the ball should be moved. Ball movements were calculated from changes in the computed BOLD signal of the regions (rACC and pInsL). The positions of the regions of interest (ROIs) were determined online and monitored throughout the trials. The criteria for the positions of the ROIs were a) lying in the most significant cluster active during the regulation phase and b) being in the respective areas in the rACC and pInsL. If

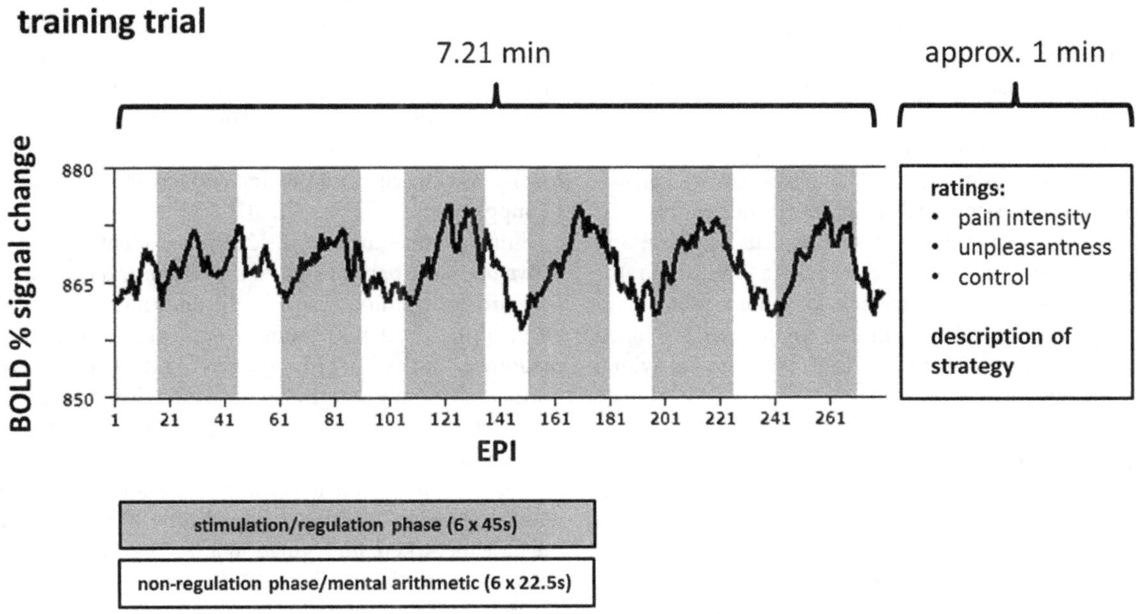

FIGURE 1 | Course of one training trial for one target region. Over the course of one training trial (290 echo planar imaging (EPI) sequences) the participants attempted either up- or downregulation of the difference in the activation of the rostral anterior cingulate cortex (rACC) and the left posterior insula (pInsL) during 6 regulation phases each lasting 45 s (gray) while receiving painful electrical stimulation. Between the regulation phases, i.e., in the non-regulation phases (white), each lasting 22.5 s, the subjects performed mental arithmetic. An exemplary blood oxygenation level-dependent (BOLD) time course of one target area is superimposed in black.

two foci of online activation in the rACC and pInsL were present, the location of the ROIs of the baseline run was used to guide the positioning. The feedback was updated every 1.5 s according to the repetition time of the fMRI protocol and calculated as the difference of the percent signal change in the two ROIs. The ball color was similar, blue or yellow, for state 1A/state 2B and state 1B/state 2A, ensuring that the two conditions of a state never had the same ball color or the same direction instruction. The trial sequence of the conditions and the color assignment were counterbalanced over the four days (see Supplementary Table SI) with the first training trial of each of the four states taking place on the first day and the last training trial on the last day. During the baseline session, a non-changing feedback screen with a stationary white ball was shown.

INSTRUCTIONS

Identical to our previous study (Rance et al., 2014), subjects were told that they could learn to control their own brain activity in previously defined brain regions, the vertical change of the blue or yellow ball being an indicator of the change in brain activation. They were informed that they would be able to observe these changes with a delay of a few seconds and that the two colors represented feedback of different brain regions. It was explained that the goal of the training was to assess if and to what extent it was possible to learn to alter brain activation in these brain areas. The function of the selected brain regions (pain processing) was not mentioned neither was the possibility of a relation between a change in activation to a change in the perception of pain intensity or unpleasantness. Subjects were also unaware that there were only two states and that two conditions per state were identical with regards to feedback computation but were presented in a different ball color. The subjects were advised to not use strategies involving body moment (e.g., muscle tension and relaxation), but were otherwise free to choose any other strategy in the regulation phases. During non-regulation phases, subjects were performing simple mental arithmetic. After each trial the subjects had to rate their perceived control over the ball movement on an 11 point verbal rating scale (ranging from 0 = no control to 10 = absolute control) and the average perceived pain intensity and unpleasantness of the nociceptive stimuli given during the regulation phases. The subjects were asked to report their individual regulation strategies verbally after each training trial.

RT-fMRI DATA ACQUISITION AND ONLINE ANALYSIS

The fMRI data were acquired on a 3 T MAGNETOM Trio whole body MR scanner using a standard 12-channel head coil (Siemens Medical Solutions, Erlangen, Germany). Imaging protocols and sequence parameters, as well as the scan procedure and preparation were identical to those used in our previous study (Rance et al., 2014). Before each training day for every subject a standard double gradient-echo field map to measure the static magnetic field was recorded. FMRI data were acquired with a gradient-echo echo planar imaging (EPI) sequence ($TR = 1500$ ms, echo time $TE = 22$ ms, matrix size = 96×96, voxel size = $2.2 \times 2.2 \times 3.5$ mm3, gap = 0.5 mm, flip angle $\alpha = 90°$, bandwidth $BW = 1270$ Hz/px, parallel acquisition technique GRAPPA acceleration factor 2) to record 24 axial slices aligned along the line connecting the anterior-posterior commissure. An anatomical scan was recorded using a three-dimensional (3D) fast low angle shot high-resolution T_1-weighted anatomical scan ($TR = 23$ ms, $TE =$

5.02 ms, matrix size = 448 × 448, $\alpha = 25°$, BW = 190 Hz/px, voxel size = 0.5 × 0.5 × 1.0 mm^3) from each subject. To ensure maximum comparability between all scans, all steps of the training, scanning, and feedback procedures were always performed by the same person.

Online data analysis was based on Turbo BrainVoyager Version 1.1 (Brain Innovation, Maastricht, The Netherlands) consisting of online preprocessing including linear detrending, 3D motion detection and correction, as well as drift removal, and computation of statistical maps for every scan based on the General Linear Model (GLM). Feedback computation and visualization was performed with in-house written scripts based on Presentation® Version 13.0 Build 01.23.09 (Neurobehavioral Systems Inc., Albany, CA, USA).

OFFLINE ANALYSES OF THE fMRI DATA

Offline data preprocessing of the fMRI scans was performed using BrainVoyager QX 2.3 (Brain Innovation, Maastricht, The Netherlands). Gradient field map based distortion correction was performed on the EPI images as well as 3D motion correction, spatial smoothing with a Gaussian kernel with a full width half maximum of 8 mm^3, linear detrending before high frequency artifacts were removed applying a highpass filter (0.006 Hz). Estimation of a response function was done by convolution of a condition box-car time course with a two-gamma hemodynamic response function.

Anatomical datasets were transformed into standard Talairach space and coregistered with their respective functional datasets applying the same transformation parameters using BrainVoyager. A group analysis based on the increase in BOLD percent signal change during the regulation phase with respect to the non-regulation phase was performed using a GLM. All results were Bonferroni corrected for multiple testing.

Offline time course data analysis of the feedback was automated with MATLAB R2011b (The MathWorks Inc., Natick, MA, USA), statistical analyses were performed with IBM SPSS Statistics Desktop (IBM, Armonk, NY, USA) for windows, version 21.0 using 2 (state) × 2 (direction) analysis of variance (ANOVA), paired samples t-tests, Pearson correlations, and the Friedman Test for ordinal data. A threshold of $p < 0.05$ was employed to determine statistical significance.

The ROI positions for each trial were equally sized (standard dimension of 12 × 12 × 1 voxels selected on the transverse slice). Time courses for the analyses of the change in the activation difference of the regions (feedback signal) were extracted from the ROI positions that were individually saved on every training trial of each subject for all conditions. For group analyses, the saved ROI positions were averaged per condition and region. For analyses of the activation of single regions requiring correction by an unrelated region to be comparable to the difference feedback, a ROI of equal size was determined after group analyses per condition at a location in Brodman area 39 that did not show activation or deactivation, analogous to our previous study (Rance et al., 2014). Time courses per training trial and subject for each condition were then extracted from this ROI and averaged according to regulation and non-regulation phases for each trial of each condition, leaving six single means per subject and condition for regulation and non-regulation phases. The averaged differences of these six single means were averaged into a resulting mean per subject and condition and trial. Later analyses employed one-tailed significance levels when a specific a priori hypothesis was present and two-tailed significance levels if we had no assumptions about the direction of an association. Group ROI activations for the baseline run and the first and last training trial are shown in Supplementary Tables SII, SIII.

Similarly to Rance et al. (2014) we identified brain regions active upon the painful stimulation alone and those active on the first and last training trial. For all conditions the success and the effect of the regulation training was assessed. We compared the magnitude of the learned regulation and the differential contribution of the single regions and assessed differences in the use of the chosen strategies. The effect of self-regulation (modulation effect) is seen in the BOLD percent signal change of the rACC, the pInsL, as well as the dissociation (difference between rACC and pInsL, constituting the feedback) in a training trial. In the baseline, where no regulation attempts took place, the BOLD percent signal change in the rACC and pInsL as well as their difference reflects the effect of the stimulation. The effect of the training can be seen in the change of the feedback from the first to the last training trial in a condition. Comparing the rACC and pInsL of the first and last training trial can determine whether both regions are similarly affected by the training. Paired samples t-tests were used to compare the feedback and single unrelated region corrected signal changes of the rACC and the pInsL of the first and last training trial of every condition to assess the training effect. The baseline stimulation effect was compared to the modulation effect of the first and the last training trial to assess the stability of the activation due to the stimulation as well as changes due to training (see **Figure 3** in the Results Section). To achieve state 1A and 1B rACC activation had to be higher than pInsL activation, state 2A and 2B required pInsL activation to be higher than rACC activation. In order to determine, whether successful regulation was possible for all subjects, the modulation effect was calculated for every training trial. To compare states regarding both successful and non-successful regulation attempts and to investigate possible effects of modulation as opposed to effects of non-successful modulation, within each condition subjects were additionally categorized as learners and non-learners. Analogously to our previous study, if the average difference of the activation of the two regions was in the right direction (i.e., the feedback was positive), and this was the case for at least four out of six training trials, and if the modulation effect for the specific condition improved from trial 1 to trial 6, a subject was considered a learner for the condition. The other subjects were categorized as non-learners.

RESULTS

ACTIVE REGIONS

A whole brain random effect analysis of the baseline session where no regulation attempts took place confirmed active clusters suitable for feedback in the rACC and the pInsL (**Figure 2**). Other active frontal regions were the left and right superior frontal gyrus, the left middle frontal gyrus, left and right inferior frontal gyrus. Parietal regions included the right posterior insula, the

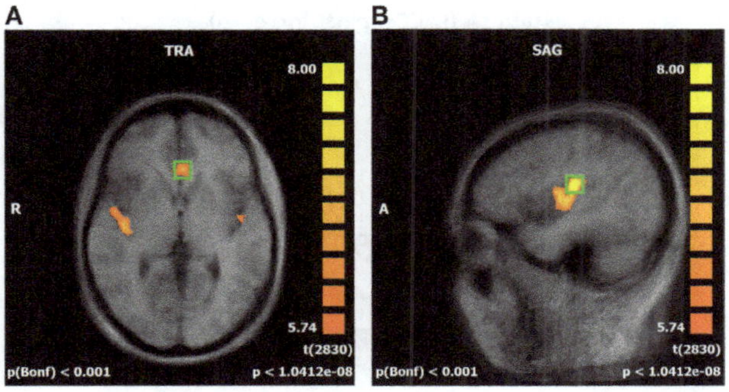

FIGURE 2 | (A,B) Offline statistical parametric mapping of the baseline run. Significant activations during the stimulation phases are superimposed over an averaged brain consisting of the ten T_1-weighted anatomical scans of the subjects, sagittal view (SAG). Red to yellow indicates significant activation in the regulation phases. Individual anatomical and functional scans were transformed into Talairach space. Average activation of the rostral anterior cingulate cortex **(A)** and the left posterior insula **(B)**.

secondary somatosensory cortex, the left supramarginal gyrus, and the right precuneus. The left thalamus and caudate nucleus region was also active (see Supplementary Table SII). With the exception of the right posterior insula in the state 1 pInsL—rACC decrease condition (trial 1), all regions found to show either activation or deactivation in the baseline run, were also active on the first training trial and the last training trial. An additional region in the left inferior gyrus was found to be significantly deactivated in all conditions on the first and last training trial but not significantly active in the baseline run. A region in the precuneus was found to be deactivated in the baseline run and activated on the first and last training trial. The right thalamus and caudate nucleus region was found to be active on the first and last training trial in four conditions. For a detailed overview of activated and deactivated regions in the baseline run and the first and last trial of all conditions see Supplementary Tables SII, SIII.

TRAINING EFFECTS

Subjects trained to achieve two states, each state had two conditions. For state 1 subjects trained to increase the difference between the rACC and pInsL activation with the rACC activation being higher. This state was trained in two conditions, each having a different ball color and an arrow pointing up in one condition and down in the other. State 2 was also trained in two separate conditions, with the goal of increasing the difference between the activation of the regions so that pInsL activation would be higher than rACC activation. The effect of the stimulation is seen in the activation of rACC and pInsL in the baseline. The modulation effect is seen in the activation of the single target regions and the difference of the rACC and pInsL activation of the training trials. This difference was translated into the vertical ball movement, i.e., the feedback signal. The training effect is seen in the magnitude of the difference of the two regions from the first to the last training trial. **Figure 3** summarizes the results separately for the four conditions, showing changes in the unrelated region corrected activation of both regions and the difference (feedback signal) for all ten subjects and the subgroups of *learners* and *non-learners*.

State 1A (rACC—pInsL increase)

There was a positive training effect with a significantly higher rACC-pInsL difference on the last training trial than on the first $[t_{(9)} = -1.974; p < 0.05]$ indicating that subjects had learned to significantly increase dissociation between the regions in the indicated direction from the first to the last training trial. The differential brain activation on the first training trial was significantly lower than the difference of the stimulation effects of the regions in the baseline $[t_{(9)} = 2.544; p < 0.05]$. The stimulation effect of the rACC and pInsL in the baseline did not differ significantly. The modulation effect of the regions did not differ significantly on the first and the last training trial. There was no significant change in the modulation effect of either the rACC or the pInsL from the first to the last training trial. In the *subgroup of the learners* there was a positive training effect with a significantly higher rACC-pInsL difference on the last training trial than on the first training trial $[t_{(5)} = -7.995; p < 0.001]$. The rACC-pInsL difference on the first training trial was significantly lower than the difference of the stimulation effects of the regions in the baseline $[t_{(5)} = 2.576; p < 0.05]$. The rACC-pInsL difference on the last training trial $[t_{(5)} = -8.029; p < 0.001]$ was significantly higher. There was no significant difference in the stimulation effect of the rACC and pInsL and no significant difference between the modulation effects of the regions on the first training trial. We observed a significant difference between the modulation effects of the regions on the last training trial $[t_{(5)} = 5.950; p < 0.01]$ with the activation in the pInsL being lower. The modulation effect in the pInsL was significantly lower on the last training trial than on the first $[t_{(5)} = 2.678; p < 0.05]$ and significantly lower than in the baseline $[t_{(5)} = 3.367; p < 0.05]$. The modulation effects of the rACC did not change significantly from the first to the last training trial. In the *subgroup of non-learners* there was no significant change modulation effects from the first to the last training trial. There was no significant difference between the stimulation effects of the regions in the baseline and no difference of the modulation effects between the regions on the first and on the last training trial. The modulation effects of the regions did not change from the first to the last training trial.

State 1B (pInsL—rACC decrease)

The pInsL-rACC difference on the last training trial was significantly lower than on the first training trial $[t_{(9)} = 1.860; p < 0.05]$, indicating a positive training effect. The stimulation effect in the baseline and the modulation effect on the first and last training trial of the regions did not differ significantly. There was a significant change in the modulation effect of the pInsL from the first to the last training trial $[t_{(9)} = 2.340; p < 0.05]$ with the activation being lower on the last training trial. The modulation effect of the pInsL on the last training trial was significantly lower than the stimulation effect in the baseline $[t_{(9)} = 2.502; p < 0.05]$. The modulation effect of the rACC did not change significantly from the first to the last training trial. For the *learners* there was a positive training effect with the pInsL-rACC difference on the last training trial being significantly lower than on the first $[t_{(4)} = 3.198; p < 0.05]$. The difference of the stimulation effect of the rACC and pInsL in the baseline was significantly lower than the

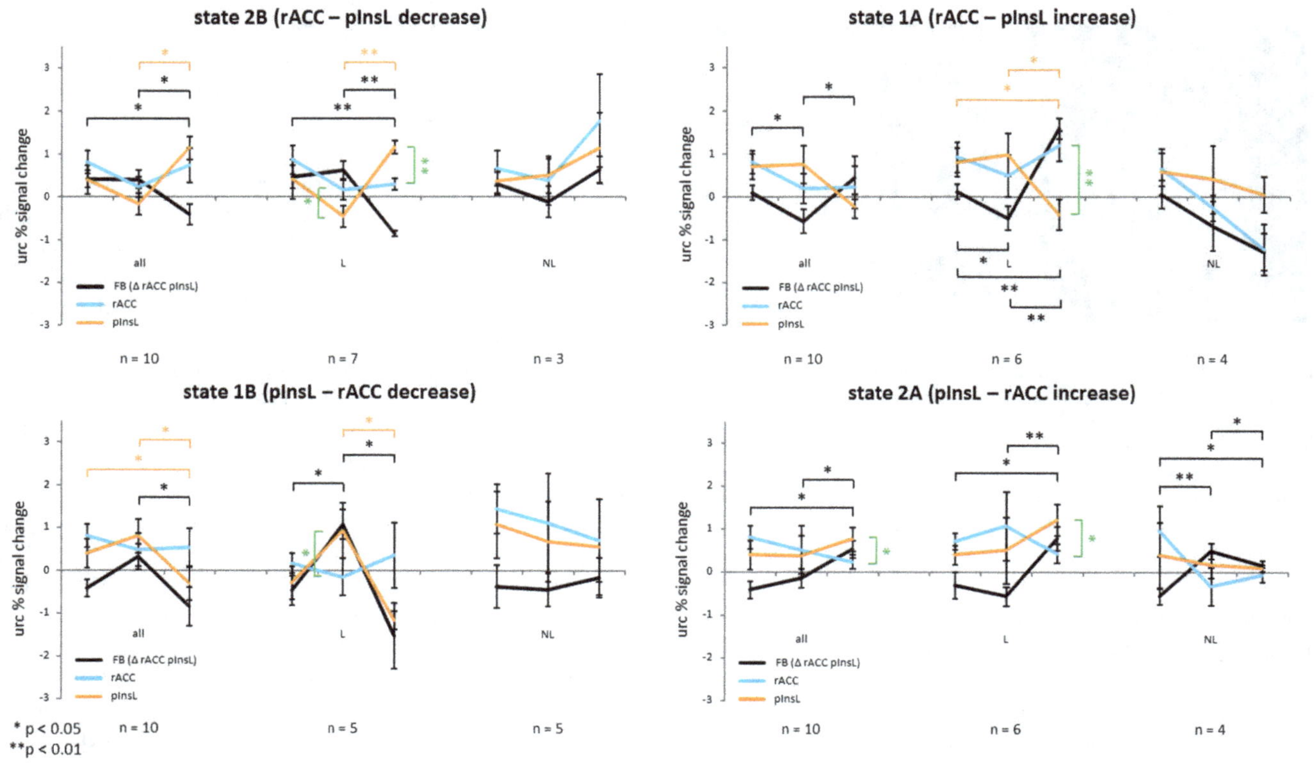

FIGURE 3 | Unrelated region corrected (urc) percent signal change of all ten subjects of the rostral anterior cingulate cortex (rACC), the left posterior insula (pInsL) and the feedback percent signal change consisting of the activation difference between the regions for the two directions of the two states. Black lines indicate the change of the feedback signal, red lines the change in the pInsL only, and the blue line the change in the rACC only. Significant changes in the feedback, rACC, and pInsL activation are indicated in brackets of the same color. A significant difference between the activation in the two regions is indicated by a green bracket. The first column depicts the development from the baseline run to the first and the last training trial for all ten subjects, the second for the learners (L) and the third for the non-learners (NL) only. A positive training effect is seen in the significant change of the differences between the regions (feedback) from the first to the last training trial in the right direction.

pInsL-rACC difference on the first training trial [$t_{(4)} = -2.881$; $p < 0.05$]. In the baseline there was no significant difference between the stimulation effects of the regions. There was a significant difference between the modulation effects between the regions on the first training trial [$t_{(4)} = -2.786$; $p < 0.05$] with pInsL being lower, but no significant difference between the modulation effects on the last training trial. The modulation effect of the pInsL was significantly lower on the last training trial than on the first training trial [$t_{(4)} = 3.514$; $p < 0.05$]. The modulation effect of the rACC did not change significantly between the trials. In the *subgroup of the non-learners* there was no significant change of the pInsL-rACC difference from the first to the last training trial, the stimulation effect in the baseline did not differ significantly between the regions, nor did the modulation effect differ between the regions on the first and the last training trial.

State 2A (pInsL—rACC increase)

There was a positive training effect with the pInsL-rACC difference on the last training trial being significantly higher than on the first training trial [$t_{(9)} = -2.268$; $p < 0.05$]. The modulation effect on the last training trial was significantly higher than the difference of the stimulation effect of the rACC and pInsL in the baseline [$t_{(9)} = 3.598$; $p < 0.01$]. The stimulation effect in the baseline did not differ significantly between the regions, nor did the modulation effect on the first training trial. On the last training trial the modulation effect was significantly higher in the pInsL than in the rACC [$t_{(9)} = -2.499$; $p < 0.05$]. There was no significant change in the modulation effect of the rACC and the pInsL from the first to the last training trial. In the *subgroup of the learners*, the pInsL-rACC difference on the last training trial was significantly higher than on the first [$t_{(5)} = -7.453$; $p < 0.01$] resulting in a positive training effect. The modulation effect on the last training trial was significantly higher than the difference of the stimulation effect of the region in the baseline [$t_{(5)} = -2.683$; $p < 0.05$]. There was no significant difference between the regions' stimulation effect in the baseline. There was a significant difference of the modulation effect between the regions on the last training trial [$t_{(5)} = 2.69$; $p < 0.05$], but no significant change in the modulation effects of either region from the first to the last training trial. For the *non-learners* there was a significant negative training effect with the pInsL-rACC difference in the last training trial being lower than on the first training trial [$t_{(3)} = 2.649$; $p < 0.05$]. The difference in the stimulation effect of the regions in the baseline was lower than the pInsL-rACC difference in the first training trial [$t_{(3)} = -4.788$; $p < 0.05$] and the pInsL-rACC difference in the last training trial

[$t_{(3)} = -2.687$; $p < 0.05$]. The stimulation effect in the baseline and the modulation effect on the first and last training trials did not differ between the rACC and pInsL. There was no significant change in the modulation effect of the regions from the first to the last training trial.

State 2B (rACC – pInsL decrease)

The rACC-pInsL difference on the last training trial was significantly lower than on the first training trial [$t_{(9)} = 2.024$; $p < 0.05$] resulting in a positive training effect, and significantly lower than the difference of the stimulation effect of the regions in the baseline [$t_{(9)} = 2.214$; $p < 0.05$]. There is no significant difference in the stimulation effect of the regions in the baseline and no significant difference between the modulation effects of the regions on the first and last training trial. The modulation effect of the pInsL is significantly higher on the last training trial than on the first [$t_{(9)} = -3.093$; $p < 0.05$]. The modulation effect of the rACC does not change significantly from the first to the last training trial. For the *subgroup of the learners* there was a significant positive training effect with the rACC-pInsL difference being lower on the last than on the first training trial [$t_{(6)} = 7.861$; $p < 0.001$] and significantly lower than the difference of the stimulation effect of the regions in the baseline [$t_{(6)} = 4.313$; $p < 0.01$]. The stimulation effect of the regions did not differ significantly in the baseline. The modulation effect of the regions differed significantly on the first [$t_{(6)} = 2.792$; $p < 0.05$] and on the last training trial [$t_{(6)} = -11.695$; $p < 0.001$]. The modulation effect of the pInsL was significantly higher on the last than on the first training trial [$t_{(6)} = -6.411$; $p < 0.01$], but the modulation effect was not significantly different for the rACC. In the group of the *non-learners*, there was no significant training effect. The stimulation effect in the baseline was not significantly different between the regions, nor was the modulation effect of the regions on the first and last training trial. For an overview of the results see **Figure 3**.

COMPARISON OF THE CONTROLLABILITY OF REGIONS

A correlation analysis between the training effects of the conditions showed that there was no correlation between the two conditions of state 1 and state 2. There was a significant negative correlation between the state 1 pInsL—rACC decrease and the state 2 rACC—pInsL decrease conditions [$r_{(8)} = -0.80$; $p < 0.01$].

To directly compare the controllability of the states and conditions, we compared the training effects of the two states and the two directions (increase, decrease). An analysis of variance revealed a significant effect of the regulation direction [$F_{(33.26, 0.87)} = 38.22$; $p < 0.001$]. There was no significant effect of the state and no significant interaction effect. Follow-up paired samples *t*-tests between the increase and decrease conditions of the different states, state 1 rACC—pInsL increase and state 2 rACC—pInsL decrease; state 1 pInsL—rACC increase and state 2 pInsL—rACC decrease revealed significant differences in the expected directions in both cases [$t_{(9)} = 3.14$; $p < 0.05$; $t_{(9)} = 2.48$; $p < 0.05$].

To examine whether one state was easier to achieve, the direction-independent magnitude of the training effect was compared (see **Figure 4**). There were no significant differences between the four conditions (both states and both directions).

We compared learner and non-learner for each condition. State 1 had six learners in the increase condition and five in the decrease condition, state 2 had six learners in the increase and seven in the decrease condition. Being a learner or a non-learner did not significantly correlate between the four conditions and was not correlated with other person-specific variables such as age, gender, stimulation current, or pain intensity and unpleasantness ratings.

EFFECTS ON PAIN INTENSITY AND UNPLEASANTNESS RATINGS

To identify a possible effect of the learned dissociation of the regions on the perception of pain intensity and unpleasantness, paired samples *t*-tests were used to compare the ratings of the first and the last training trial of every condition (see **Figure 5**). There was no significant difference between the ratings on the first and on the last training trial in any of the four conditions. The same was true for the subgroups of the learners and non-learners. Pain ratings from the baseline run and on the first and on the last training trial did not correlate with rACC and pInsL percent signal change or the difference between the activations.

To investigate the association of the dissociation of rACC and pInsL (training effect) and the evaluation of pain intensity and pain unpleasantness, a correlation analysis was performed. There was no significant correlation between the change in pain intensity and unpleasantness ratings [$\text{rating}_{(\text{training trial } 6-1)}$] and the respective activation difference between the regions [computed feedback $\text{signal}_{(\text{training trial } 6-1)}$] in the conditions, neither for the whole group nor for the respective subgroups. A similar

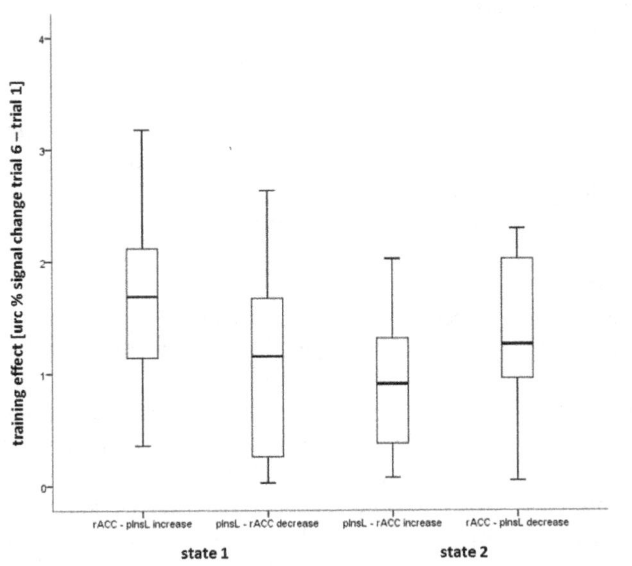

FIGURE 4 | Box plot showing the median, interquartile range, sample minimum and maximum of the direction independent magnitude of the training effect in the four conditions calculated from the unrelated region corrected (urc) difference of the rostral anterior cingulate gyrus (rACC) and the left posterior insula (pInsL) blood oxygenation level-dependent (BOLD) percent signal change.

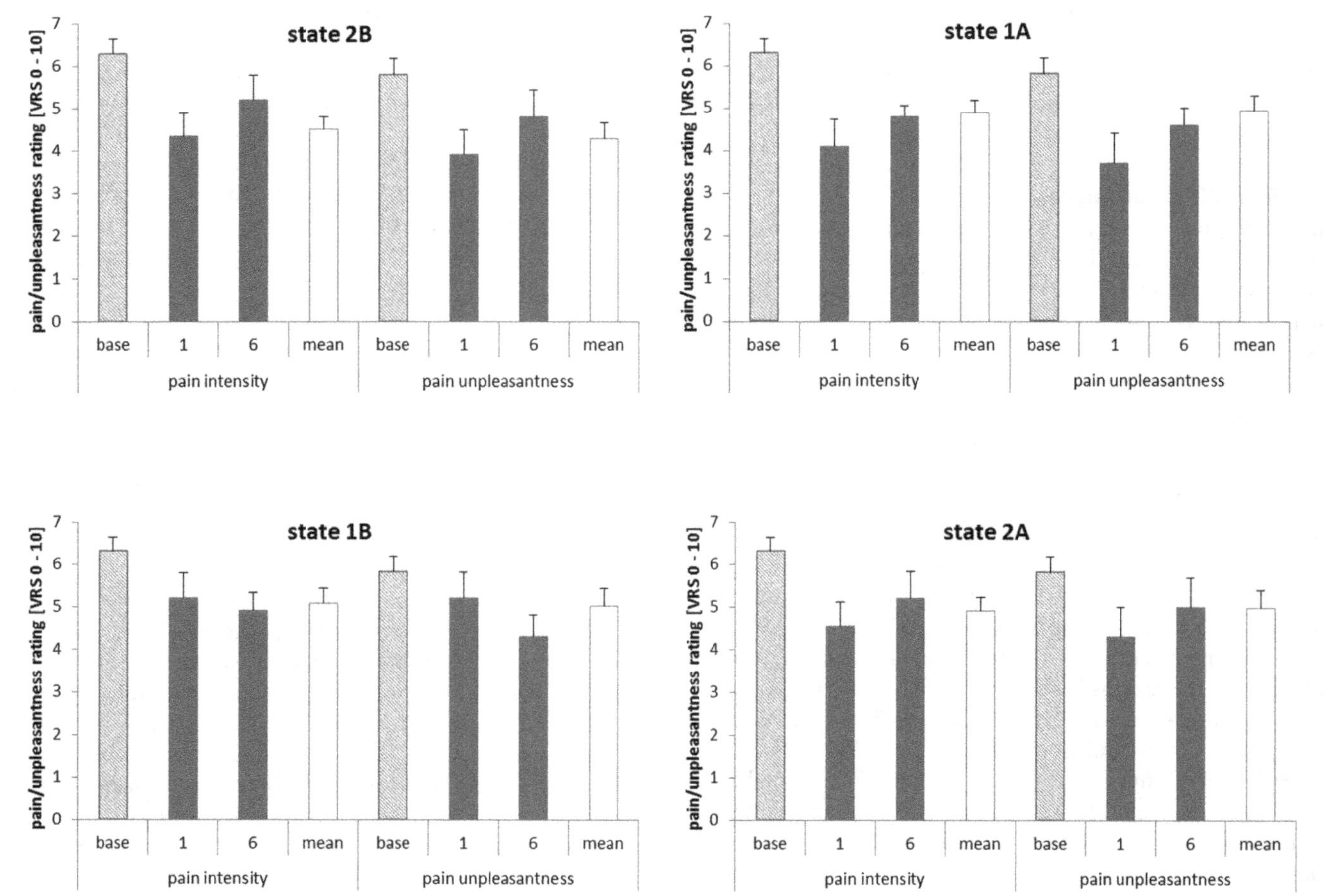

FIGURE 5 | Pain intensity and unpleasantness ratings in the baseline, on the first and last training trials (trials 1 and 6) and on average over all six training trials. The pain intensity and pain unpleasantness ratings relate to a verbal rating scale (VRS) with pain intensity ranging from 0 = no pain to 10 = strongest imaginable pain and pain unpleasantness ranging from 0 = not unpleasant to 10 = extremely unpleasant. State 1A, rostral anterior cingulate cortex (rACC) − left posterior insula (pInsL) increase condition; state 1B, pInsL − rACC decrease condition; state 2A, pInsL − rACC increase condition; state 2B, rACC − pInsL decrease condition.

correlation analysis between the activation change in the single regions [$rACC/pInsL_{(\text{training trial } 6-1)}$] from the first to the last training trial and change in the pain intensity and unpleasantness ratings also revealed no significant correlations.

STRATEGIES

The reported strategies were subsumed under four categories. Category 1: ball focus: picturing the ball in motion or silent verbal instructions to move the ball; Category 2: distraction: focusing on another body part, continuing with the mental arithmetic, imagining a scene that was not described as being particularly emotional or relaxing; Category 3: positive or negative emotional memories; Category 4: stimulus focus: imagined changing of the stimulus quality or intensity, the location or frequency. If a subject reported to have been using two strategies during one training trial, both were recorded and categorized.

We compared the frequency of the strategy use per category over all conditions using a Friedman test. There was no significant difference between the strategy use over all conditions [$\chi^2_{(3,\ 10)} = 9.255$; $p = 0.51$]. For a distribution of the strategies per trial over all conditions see Supplementary Figure S1.

DISCUSSION

ACTIVE REGIONS DURING STIMULATION AND MODULATION

A whole brain offline analysis of the baseline run when subjects received no feedback and did not attempt to modulate brain activation, showed that active regions generally consisted of areas involved in the processing of pain (Apkarian et al., 2005; Iannetti et al., 2005). They included the rACC and pInsL, which were the source of the feedback signal in the following training trials, and other regions that are frequently found to be involved in the processing of pain, including the right posterior insula, bilaterally the secondary somatosensory cortex, and the posterior cingulate cortex in accordance with our previous study (Rance et al., 2014). Additional regions found in the baseline run were the right thalamus and caudate nucleus region, several frontal regions in the mid, inferior, and superior frontal gyrus that showed either activation or deactivation. In the parietal lobe we found deactivation in the left primary somatosensory cortex, the left precuneus, and the left gyrus supramarginalis. Almost all regions found to be active in the baseline were also active on both the first and the last trials of all conditions. One region in the inferior frontal gyrus and the left thalamus and caudate nucleus region was additionally active on the first and last training trials. Similar to our previous study (Rance et al., 2014) the right posterior insula was significantly active in the baseline run, shifting to deactivation on the last training trial in all but one condition. Whereas in the previous study, on the first training trial the pInsR was mainly activated, here the results are mixed, with the pInsR being predominantly deactivated in two conditions of different states, not significantly activated or deactivated in one condition, and activated in one condition. The prevalent change from activation during the painful electric stimulation to deactivation on the last training trial of both regulation of single regions and the difference feedback suggests that this region is not only involved in the processing of pain but also in the regulation effort. Deactivation of this region is observed within the framework of task-induced deactivations seen in the default mode network (Harrison et al., 2011). It was also placed in the pattern of the deactivation of regions involved in the processing of pain during a reduction of pain perception through shifting attention away from the pain or placebo analgesia (Tracey and Mantyh, 2007; Amanzio et al., 2013). An increase in pInsR activation was seen during painful stimulation when subjects were in a state of mindfulness, an increased non-judgmental awareness of present experiences, thus effectively focusing attention on sensory aspects of the stimulus, such as the skin surface of the stimulated area (Gard et al., 2012). Taken together, the results of the present study suggest that during the course of the training the perception of painful stimulation was of increasingly lesser importance, consistent with the increased task demand of the training trials, i.e., finding and memorizing an adequate modulation strategy while observing the feedback and judging the success of the modulation efforts.

A region that was found to be deactivated in the baseline, the right precuneus, was consistently activated in all conditions on the first and the last training trial. The precuneus has been described to be involved in the process of integrating salient stimuli into self-relevant experiences. It is thus not necessarily involved in the processing of pain, but in the evaluation of a salient stimulus in the context of present experience (Cavanna and Trimble, 2006; Goffaux et al., 2014). Increased attention to the stimulation induced feedback might thus lead to an activation of the precuneus independent from the processing of the nociceptive quality of the stimulus.

MODULATION

In our previous study (Rance et al., 2014) the rACC and the pInsL were modulated separately, and subjects learned modulation of all but one condition. Using the same training paradigm in this study with the feedback consisting of a difference feedback of both regions, subjects successfully learned to achieve both states in the two respective conditions. In both studies, there was no significant correlation of the learning success between the conditions and states. When modulation efforts are focused on one region and direction, the absence of a significant correlation of the regulation success between the conditions suggests that subjects are not able to gain control over the activation of one of the regions better than the other and that there is no "easier" direction of modulation. In the present study, subjects trained to increase the difference in the activation of the two regions, with two seemingly different conditions per state. Here, we again did not find evidence that one state is achieved more easily. Moreover, even if one state is successfully learned in one condition, the same state is not necessarily achieved in another condition. We did find a difference in the utilization of the modulated regions. Regarding the regions separately, a significant change from the first to the last training trial was only evident in the pInsL in the state 1 pInsL—rACC decrease and the state 2 rACC—pInsL decrease in the pInsL activation. This was especially true in the subgroup of the learners, where this significant change was additionally observed in the state 1 rACC—pInsL increase condition. These results indicate that the target ROI in the insula was the driving force behind the change in the feedback consisting of the activation difference of the regions. There was also some evidence that the pInsL can be regulated in a more stable manner in our previous study (Rance et al., 2014), where the rACC could be trained overall, however, with a much larger range of training success, especially in the upregulation condition, where the group as a whole did not show a significant training effect. Both the rACC and the pInsL are implicated in a variety of functions. The posterior part of the insula is involved in interoception, emotional processing, and pain perception (Cauda et al., 2012a,b; Dowman, 2014; Uddin et al., 2014). In the presence of ongoing salient painful stimulation, activation in the posterior insula might be more readily accessible. The rACC on the other hand is involved in both emotional and cognitive-evaluative functions apart from playing a crucial role in the network active during pain perception (Bush et al., 2000; Li et al., 2013). It might be involved in both the modulation process itself and the processing of the painful stimulus, yielding it more difficult to regulate especially when the feedback does not depend on rACC activation alone.

Similar to our previous study (Rance et al., 2014), strategy use was equally distributed across the training trials. Together with the result that there also was no significant correlation between learning success between the regions or states, the regulation of rACC and pInsL in the presence of a painful stimulus does not require or favor a specific strategy. This might be connected to the multimodal nature of the regions. In other real-time neurofeedback studies, a concrete strategy has sometimes been linked to the modulation and the function of the modulated area such as emotion induction in the regulation of the right anterior insula (Caria et al., 2007). Because of the distributed nature of pain processing, there might not be generally useful strategies.

PAIN INTENSITY AND UNPLEASANTNESS RATINGS

In our previous study (Rance et al., 2014) no significant effect of the successful modulation of either the rACC or the pInsL on pain intensity or unpleasantness ratings was found. However, a connection between the modulation in the pInsL and unpleasantness ratings was observed when the difference between the target region (pInsL) and the rACC was high. In the present study, subjects successfully learned to increase the activation difference achieving two different states, however, there was no statistical evidence that the ability to dissociate the two regions was significantly correlated with a change in the pain intensity and unpleasantness ratings. This was also true in the subgroup of learners. Moreover, there was no significant correlation between either the differences of the activation of the target ROIs, or the unrelated region corrected activation of either region, and the pain intensity and unpleasantness ratings. The ratings were not significantly correlated with activation in either region or the combined feedback. Due to the exploratory nature of this study, we examined several specific aspects of feedback modulation and therefor refrained from an overall correction of the *p*-values. Our results are not in line with previous findings by deCharms et al. who found a correlation of the increase and decrease of rACC activation and a change in pain intensity and unpleasantness ratings, thus linking regulation of brain activation with changes in pain perception. One possible reason might be that activation in the rACC and pInsL are the result of both the stimulation or task and modulation efforts (Papageorgiou et al., 2009). In the current literature on neuromodulation there are mixed results on behavioral effects of modulation. Pain perception is a variable experience, involving many modulating cognitive, emotional, and physiological factors (Rhudy and Meagher, 2000; Bantick et al., 2002; Apkarian et al., 2005; Forys and Dahlquist, 2007; Tracey and Mantyh, 2007; Gard et al., 2012) and a wide network of contributing regions (Hofbauer et al., 2001; Tracey and Mantyh, 2007; Iannetti and Mouraux, 2010; Cauda et al., 2012b). The modulation of the perception of pain intensity and unpleasantness of a painful electrical stimulus does not seem possible by regulation of the rACC and pInsL either singularly or combined. Attempting modulation should thus involve the active network to a greater part. This has been suggested especially in the context of rt-fMRI since many connections between brain activation and behavior depend not only on the activity of single regions but on the connectivity of involved networks (Zilverstand et al., 2014). Connectivity feedback seems to be a more feasible method especially when attempting behavioral changes, since changes in connectivity go along with learning to regulate activation in brain areas (Berman et al., 2013; Zotev et al., 2013; Scharnowski et al., 2014). This approach might, moreover, help in identifying regions involved in the process of learning modulation. When considering employing rt-fMRI in the treatment of chronic pain, it is further important to distinguish experimental pain from ongoing chronic pain and the respective activated networks, which may be very different (Baliki et al., 2010). Taken together, rt-fMRI might be valuable in not only identifying regions involved in the processing of pain in pain disorders, but also help understanding the contribution to pain perception of single regions within the active network, which could be the targets of modulation in the treatment of chronic pain.

CONCLUSION

In our previous study we found that the state of the network played a crucial role in regulating pain-related activation and might be key in altering the perception of pain. In the present study we therefore explored the extent to which an increase in the difference in the activation of two functionally connected areas in response to a painful stimulus is possible and the effects on the perception of pain. We thus not only examined the results of the group but also looked at differences between subjects who learned regulation and those who did not, similar to the previous study. We found that subjects were able to increase the difference in all four conditions after six trainings trials, thus successfully achieving the two states of either the rACC or the pInsL BOLD percent signal change being higher. When looking at the contribution of the single regions to the combined difference feedback, the pInsL was found to be driving force in three out of the four conditions with significant changes in the activation from the first to the last training trial. Activation in the rACC did not change significantly. In our previous study we saw that control over rACC and pInsL in both directions can be acquired by the majority of subjects (Rance et al., 2014). Mirroring these results, learning success did not correlate between the conditions or states. This indicates that among our subjects, there is no overall ability to learn regulation to achieve the two states in general. This means that subjects who were successful in one or two conditions did not necessarily learn all, and that if a subject learned to establish one state in one condition the same subject did not always learn to establish the state in the other condition. Since the group as a whole did learn to establish both states in the conditions, our results suggest that, given enough training trials, both states can be successfully established. Furthermore, learning was unrelated to chosen strategies. In line with this, the magnitude of the feedback change was similar between all conditions. Despite successful modulation, there was no change in the perception of pain intensity or unpleasantness. Our results suggest that in the modulation of pain intensity and unpleasantness, both the rACC and pInsL either alone or combined, are not sufficient to alter perception of the painful experimental electric stimulus. However, it is possible that increasing automatization of the response would free the respective region from dual tasking and could thus have an effect. This could be tested by using extended training sessions. It is also necessary to identify networks not only involved in the processing of the stimulus but also in learning regulation of the network. It might then be possible to specifically modulate communication of parts of the network to alter perception and even correct altered states of the pain processing network in patients with chronic pain.

ACKNOWLEDGMENTS

The authors would like to thank Dr. C. Christmann from the Central Institute of Mental Health, Mannheim, Germany, for help with the set-up of the experimental hardware and the experimental procedure. We would also like to thank Professor K. Inui from National Institute for Physiological Sciences, Okazaki, Japan for providing the electrodes. This study was supported by a grant from the Deutsche Forschungsgemeinschaft (Fl 156/33) and the Prize for Basic Research of the State of Baden-Württemberg to Herta Flor.

REFERENCES

Amanzio, M., Benedetti, F., Porro, C. A., Palermo, S., and Cauda, F. (2013). Activation likelihood estimation meta-analysis of brain correlates of placebo analgesia in human experimental pain. *Hum. Brain Mapp.* 34, 738–752. doi: 10.1002/hbm.21471

Apkarian, A. V., Bushnell, M. C., Treede, R. D., and Zubieta, J. K. (2005). Human brain mechanisms of pain perception and regulation in health and disease. *Eur. J. Pain* 9, 463–484. doi: 10.1016/j.ejpain.2004.11.001

Baliki, M. N., Geha, P. Y., Fields, H. L., and Apkarian, A. V. (2010). Predicting value of pain and analgesia: nucleus accumbens response to noxious stimuli changes in the presence of chronic pain. *Neuron* 66, 149–160. doi: 10.1016/j.neuron.2010.03.002

Bantick, S. J., Wise, R. G., Ploghaus, A., Clare, S., Smith, S. M., and Tracey, I. (2002). Imaging how attention modulates pain in humans using functional MRI. *Brain* 125, 310–319. doi: 10.1093/brain/awf022

Berman, B. D., Horovitz, S. G., and Hallett, M. (2013). Modulation of functionally localized right insular cortex activity using real-time fMRI-based neurofeedback. *Front. Hum. Neurosci.* 7:638. doi: 10.3389/fnhum.2013.00638

Bingel, U., Lorenz, J., Schoell, E., Weiller, C., and Buchel, C. (2006). Mechanisms of placebo analgesia: rACC recruitment of a subcortical antinociceptive network. *Pain* 120, 8–15. doi: 10.1016/j.pain.2005.08.027

Birbaumer, N., Ruiz, S., and Sitaram, R. (2013). Learned regulation of brain metabolism. *Trends Cogn. Sci.* 17, 295–302. doi: 10.1016/j.tics.2013.04.009

Brodersen, K. H., Wiech, K., Lomakina, E. I., Lin, C. S., Buhmann, J. M., Bingel, U., et al. (2012). Decoding the perception of pain from fMRI using multivariate pattern analysis. *Neuroimage* 63, 1162–1170. doi: 10.1016/j.neuroimage.2012.08.035

Bush, G., Luu, P., and Posner, M. I. (2000). Cognitive and emotional influences in anterior cingulate cortex. *Trends Cogn. Sci.* 4, 215–222. doi: 10.1016/S1364-6613(00)01483-2

Caria, A., Sitaram, R., Veit, R., Begliomini, C., and Birbaumer, N. (2010). Volitional control of anterior insula activity modulates the response to aversive stimuli. a real-time functional magnetic resonance imaging study. *Biol. Psychiatry* 68, 425–432. doi: 10.1016/j.biopsych.2010.04.020

Caria, A., Veit, R., Sitaram, R., Lotze, M., Weiskopf, N., Grodd, W., et al. (2007). Regulation of anterior insular cortex activity using real-time fMRI. *Neuroimage* 35, 1238–1246. doi: 10.1016/j.neuroimage.2007.01.018

Cauda, F., Costa, T., Torta, D. M., Sacco, K., D'agata, F., Duca, S., et al. (2012a). Meta-analytic clustering of the insular cortex: characterizing the meta-analytic connectivity of the insula when involved in active tasks. *Neuroimage* 62, 343–355. doi: 10.1016/j.neuroimage.2012.04.012

Cauda, F., Torta, D. M., Sacco, K., Geda, E., D'agata, F., Costa, T., et al. (2012b). Shared "core" areas between the pain and other task-related networks. *PLoS ONE* 7:e41929. doi: 10.1371/journal.pone.0041929

Cavanna, A. E., and Trimble, M. R. (2006). The precuneus: a review of its functional anatomy and behavioural correlates. *Brain* 129, 564–583. doi: 10.1093/brain/awl004

Chapin, H., Bagarinao, E., and Mackey, S. (2012). Real-time fMRI applied to pain management. *Neurosci. Lett.* 520, 174–181. doi: 10.1016/j.neulet.2012.02.076

Decharms, R. C., Maeda, F., Glover, G. H., Ludlow, D., Pauly, J. M., Soneji, D., et al. (2005). Control over brain activation and pain learned by using real-time functional MRI. *Proc. Natl. Acad. Sci. USA.* 102, 18626–18631. doi: 10.1073/pnas.0505210102

Diesch, E., and Flor, H. (2007). Alteration in the response properties of primary somatosensory cortex related to differential aversive Pavlovian conditioning. *Pain* 131, 171–180. doi: 10.1016/j.pain.2007.01.016

Dowman, R. (2014). Neural mechanisms underlying pain's ability to reorient attention: evidence for sensitization of somatic threat detectors. *Cogn. Affect. Behav. Neurosci.* 14, 805–817. doi: 10.3758/s13415-013-0233-z

Esposito, F., Seifritz, E., Formisano, E., Morrone, R., Scarabino, T., Tedeschi, G., et al. (2003). Real-time independent component analysis of fMRI time-series. *Neuroimage* 20, 2209–2224. doi: 10.1016/j.neuroimage.2003.08.012

Forys, K. L., and Dahlquist, L. M. (2007). The influence of preferred coping style and cognitive strategy on laboratory-induced pain. *Health Psychol.* 26, 22–29. doi: 10.1037/0278-6133.26.1.22

Frot, M., Magnin, M., Mauguiere, F., and Garcia-Larrea, L. (2007). Human SII and posterior insula differently encode thermal laser stimuli. *Cereb. Cortex* 17, 610–620. doi: 10.1093/cercor/bhk007

Gard, T., Holzel, B. K., Sack, A. T., Hempel, H., Lazar, S. W., Vaitl, D., et al. (2012). Pain attenuation through mindfulness is associated with decreased cognitive control and increased sensory processing in the brain. *Cereb. Cortex* 22, 2692–2702. doi: 10.1093/cercor/bhr352

Goffaux, P., Girard-Tremblay, L., Marchand, S., Daigle, K., and Whittingstall, K. (2014). Individual differences in pain sensitivity vary as a function of precuneus reactivity. *Brain Topogr.* 27, 366–374. doi: 10.1007/s10548-013-0291-0

Harrison, B. J., Pujol, J., Contreras-Rodriguez, O., Soriano-Mas, C., Lopez-Sola, M., Deus, J., et al. (2011). Task-induced deactivation from rest extends beyond the default mode brain network. *PLoS ONE* 6:e22964. doi: 10.1371/journal.pone.0022964

Hofbauer, R. K., Rainville, P., Duncan, G. H., and Bushnell, M. C. (2001). Cortical representation of the sensory dimension of pain. *J. Neurophysiol.* 86, 402–411.

Iannetti, G. D., and Mouraux, A. (2010). From the neuromatrix to the pain matrix (and back). *Exp. Brain Res.* 205, 1–12. doi: 10.1007/s00221-010-2340-1

Iannetti, G. D., Zambreanu, L., Cruccu, G., and Tracey, I. (2005). Operculoinsular cortex encodes pain intensity at the earliest stages of cortical processing as indicated by amplitude of laser-evoked potentials in humans. *Neuroscience* 131, 199–208. doi: 10.1016/j.neuroscience.2004.10.035

Inui, K., Tran, T. D., Hoshiyama, M., and Kakigi, R. (2002). Preferential stimulation of Adelta fibers by intra-epidermal needle electrode in humans. *Pain* 96, 247–252. doi: 10.1016/S0304-3959(01)00453-5

Johnston, S., Linden, D. E., Healy, D., Goebel, R., Habes, I., and Boehm, S. G. (2011). Upregulation of emotion areas through neurofeedback with a focus on positive mood. *Cogn. Affect. Behav. Neurosci.* 11, 44–51. doi: 10.3758/s13415-010-0010-1

Koush, Y., Rosa, M. J., Robineau, F., Heinen, K., W Rieger, S., Weiskopf, N., et al. (2013). Connectivity-based neurofeedback: dynamic causal modeling for real-time fMRI. *Neuroimage* 81, 422–430. doi: 10.1016/j.neuroimage.2013.05.010

Laconte, S. M., Peltier, S. J., and Hu, X. P. (2007). Real-time fMRI using brain-state classification. *Hum. Brain Mapp.* 28, 1033–1044. doi: 10.1002/hbm.20326

Legrain, V., Iannetti, G. D., Plaghki, L., and Mouraux, A. (2011). The pain matrix reloaded: a salience detection system for the body. *Prog. Neurobiol.* 93, 111–124. doi: 10.1016/j.pneurobio.2010.10.005

Li, X., Hartwell, K. J., Borckardt, J., Prisciandaro, J. J., Saladin, M. E., Morgan, P. S., et al. (2013). Volitional reduction of anterior cingulate cortex activity produces decreased cue craving in smoking cessation: a preliminary real-time fMRI study. *Addict. Biol.* 18, 739–748. doi: 10.1111/j.1369-1600.2012.00449.x

McCaig, R. G., Dixon, M., Keramatian, K., Liu, I., and Christoff, K. (2011). Improved modulation of rostrolateral prefrontal cortex using real-time fMRI training and meta-cognitive awareness. *Neuroimage* 55, 1298–1305. doi: 10.1016/j.neuroimage.2010.12.016

Oldfield, R. C. (1971). The assessment and analysis of handedness: the Edinburgh inventory. *Neuropsychologia* 9, 97–113.

Papageorgiou, T. D., Curtis, W. A., Mchenry, M., and Laconte, S. M. (2009). Neurofeedback of two motor functions using supervised learning-based real-time functional magnetic resonance imaging. *Conf. Proc. IEEE Eng. Med. Biol. Soc.* 2009, 5377–5380. doi: 10.1109/IEMBS.2009.5333703

Qu, C., King, T., Okun, A., Lai, J., Fields, H. L., and Porreca, F. (2011). Lesion of the rostral anterior cingulate cortex eliminates the aversiveness of spontaneous neuropathic pain following partial or complete axotomy. *Pain* 152, 1641–1648. doi: 10.1016/j.pain.2011.03.002

Rainville, P., Duncan, G. H., Price, D. D., Carrier, B., and Bushnell, M. C. (1997). Pain affect encoded in human anterior cingulate but not somatosensory cortex. *Science* 277, 968–971.

Rance, M., Ruttorf, M., Nees, F., Schad, L. R., and Flor, H. (2014). Real time fMRI feedback of the anterior cingulate and posterior insular cortex in the processing of pain. *Hum. Brain Mapp.* doi: 10.1002/hbm.22585. [Epub ahead of print].

Rhudy, J. L., and Meagher, M. W. (2000). Fear and anxiety: divergent effects on human pain thresholds. *Pain* 84, 65–75. doi: 10.1016/S0304-3959(99)00183-9

Ruiz, S., Lee, S., Soekadar, S. R., Caria, A., Veit, R., Kircher, T., et al. (2013). Acquired self-control of insula cortex modulates emotion recognition and brain network connectivity in schizophrenia. *Hum. Brain Mapp.* 34, 200–212. doi: 10.1002/hbm.21427

Scharnowski, F., Rosa, M. J., Golestani, N., Hutton, C., Josephs, O., Weiskopf, N., et al. (2014). Connectivity changes underlying neurofeedback training of visual cortex activity. *PLoS ONE* 9:e91090. doi: 10.1371/journal.pone.0091090

Sitaram, R., Lee, S., Ruiz, S., Rana, M., Veit, R., and Birbaumer, N. (2011). Real-time support vector classification and feedback of multiple emotional brain states. *Neuroimage* 56, 753–765. doi: 10.1016/j.neuroimage.2010.08.007

Sitaram, R., Veit, R., Stevens, B., Caria, A., Gerloff, C., Birbaumer, N., et al. (2012). Acquired control of ventral premotor cortex activity by feedback training: an exploratory real-time FMRI and TMS study. *Neurorehabil. Neural Repair* 26, 256–265. doi: 10.1177/1545968311418345

Tracey, I., and Mantyh, P. W. (2007). The cerebral signature for pain perception and its modulation. *Neuron* 55, 377–391. doi: 10.1016/j.neuron.2007.07.012

Uddin, L. Q., Kinnison, J., Pessoa, L., and Anderson, M. L. (2014). Beyond the tripartite cognition-emotion-interoception model of the human insular cortex. *J. Cogn. Neurosci.* 26, 16–27. doi: 10.1162/jocn_a_00462

Villemure, C., and Bushnell, M. C. (2002). Cognitive modulation of pain: how do attention and emotion influence pain processing? *Pain* 95, 195–199. doi: 10.1016/S0304-3959(02)00007-6

Villemure, C., and Bushnell, M. C. (2009). Mood influences supraspinal pain processing separately from attention. *J. Neurosci.* 29, 705–715. doi: 10.1523/JNEUROSCI.3822-08.2009

Wager, T. D., Atlas, L. Y., Lindquist, M. A., Roy, M., Woo, C. W., and Kross, E. (2013). An fMRI-based neurologic signature of physical pain. *N. Engl. J. Med.* 368, 1388–1397. doi: 10.1056/NEJMoa1204471

Weiskopf, N., Veit, R., Erb, M., Mathiak, K., Grodd, W., Goebel, R., et al. (2003). Physiological self-regulation of regional brain activity using real-time functional magnetic resonance imaging (fMRI): methodology and exemplary data. *Neuroimage* 19, 577–586. doi: 10.1016/S1053-8119(03)00145-9

Wiech, K., Kalisch, R., Weiskopf, N., Pleger, B., Stephan, K. E., and Dolan, R. J. (2006). Anterolateral prefrontal cortex mediates the analgesic effect of expected and perceived control over pain. *J. Neurosci.* 26, 11501–11509. doi: 10.1523/JNEUROSCI.2568-06.2006

Yoshino, A., Okamoto, Y., Onoda, K., Yoshimura, S., Kunisato, Y., Demoto, Y., et al. (2010). Sadness enhances the experience of pain via neural activation in the anterior cingulate cortex and amygdala: an fMRI study. *Neuroimage* 50, 1194–1201. doi: 10.1016/j.neuroimage.2009.11.079

Zhang, G., Yao, L., Zhang, H., Long, Z., and Zhao, X. (2013). Improved working memory performance through self-regulation of dorsal lateral prefrontal cortex activation using real-time fMRI. *PLoS ONE* 8:e73735. doi: 10.1371/journal.pone.0073735

Zhao, X., Zhang, H., Song, S., Ye, Q., Guo, J., and Yao, L. (2013). Causal interaction following the alteration of target region activation during motor imagery training using real-time fMRI. *Front. Hum. Neurosci.* 7:866. doi: 10.3389/fnhum.2013.00866

Zilverstand, A., Sorger, B., Zimmermann, J., Kaas, A., and Goebel, R. (2014). Windowed correlation: a suitable tool for providing dynamic fMRI-based functional connectivity neurofeedback on task difficulty. *PLoS ONE* 9:e85929. doi: 10.1371/journal.pone.0085929

Zotev, V., Phillips, R., Young, K. D., Drevets, W. C., and Bodurka, J. (2013). Prefrontal control of the amygdala during real-time fMRI neurofeedback training of emotion regulation. *PLoS ONE* 8:e79184. doi: 10.1371/journal.pone.0079184

9

Fast mental states decoding in mixed reality

Daniele De Massari[1,2†], Daniel Pacheco[3†], Rahim Malekshahi[1,4], Alberto Betella[3], Paul F. M. J. Verschure[3,5], Niels Birbaumer[1,2] and Andrea Caria[1,2*]

[1] *Institut für Medizinische Psychologie und Verhaltensneurobiologie, Universität Tübingen, Tübingen, Germany*
[2] *Fondazione Ospedale San Camillo, Istituto di Ricovero e Cura a Carattere Scientifico, Venezia, Italy*
[3] *SPECS - Laboratory of Synthetic Perceptive, Emotive and Cognitive Systems, Department of Technology, Center of Autonomous Systems and Neurorobotics, Universitat Pompeu Fabra, Barcelona, Spain*
[4] *Graduate School of Neural & Behavioural Sciences, International Max Planck Research School, Tübingen, Germany*
[5] *Institució Catalana de Recerca i Estudis Avançats, Barcelona, Spain*

Correspondence:
Andrea Caria, Institute of Medical Psychology and Behavioural Neurobiology, Eberhard-Karls-University of Tübingen, Silcherstrasse 5, D-72076 Tübingen, Germany
e-mail: andrea.caria@uni-tuebingen.de

The combination of Brain-Computer Interface (BCI) technology, allowing online monitoring and decoding of brain activity, with virtual and mixed reality (MR) systems may help to shape and guide implicit and explicit learning using ecological scenarios. Real-time information of ongoing brain states acquired through BCI might be exploited for controlling data presentation in virtual environments. Brain states discrimination during mixed reality experience is thus critical for adapting specific data features to contingent brain activity. In this study we recorded electroencephalographic (EEG) data while participants experienced MR scenarios implemented through the eXperience Induction Machine (XIM). The XIM is a novel framework modeling the integration of a sensing system that evaluates and measures physiological and psychological states with a number of actuators and effectors that coherently reacts to the user's actions. We then assessed continuous EEG-based discrimination of spatial navigation, reading and calculation performed in MR, using linear discriminant analysis (LDA) and support vector machine (SVM) classifiers. Dynamic single trial classification showed high accuracy of LDA and SVM classifiers in detecting multiple brain states as well as in differentiating between high and low mental workload, using a 5 s time-window shifting every 200 ms. Our results indicate overall better performance of LDA with respect to SVM and suggest applicability of our approach in a BCI-controlled MR scenario. Ultimately, successful prediction of brain states might be used to drive adaptation of data representation in order to boost information processing in MR.

Keywords: mental states decoding, EEG, mixed reality, XIM

INTRODUCTION

Mixed Reality (MR) is a type of virtual reality-related technology where real and virtual worlds are merged so that real-time interaction with both physical and digital objects (Milgram, 1994; Bohil et al., 2011) is achievable. A particularly promising MR system is the eXperience Induction Machine (XIM) (Bernardet et al., 2011; Omedas et al., 2014). This technology permits to model representational elements analog to real phenomena as well as highly abstract non-representation forms describing complex high-dimensional data in a controlled environment. The exploration of data in XIM is conceptualized as an integrative narrative of varying forms where implicit and explicit responses as well as neurophysiological signals from the user can be utilized to modulate data representation (Bernardet et al., 2011; Lessiter et al., 2011; Verschure, 2011; Omedas et al., 2014).

It has been proposed that the combination of Brain-Computer Interface (BCI) technology, allowing online monitoring and decoding of mental states (Muller et al., 2008; Blankertz et al., 2010), with virtual reality systems may help to shape and guide implicit and explicit learning using ecological scenarios (Lécuyer et al., 2008; Lotte et al., 2013). Online analysis of specific brain activity has mainly been used in BCI applications for communication and control of external devices (Birbaumer and Cohen, 2007; Daly and Wolpaw, 2008), as well as for shaping behavior through neurofeedback paradigms (Delorme and Makeig, 2003; Shibata et al., 2011; Yoo et al., 2011; Caria et al., 2012; Scharnowski et al., 2012). Alternatively, the information acquired with BCI can be used to support human-computer interaction, in applications where its content is adapted to user's implicit interest, as well as for adaptive automation, affective computing, or video games (George, 2010). BCI-based real-time analysis of brain signals, with no need of participants to learn their control (sometimes referred to as "passive" BCI), can additionally be utilized to manipulate behavioral response by delivering information according to specific mental states.

Using this approach, enhancing and depressing learning and memory formation was demonstrated by triggering stimuli presentation during brain states favoring or reducing learning, which were assessed through online detection of activity in the bilateral parahippocampal areas with real-time fMRI (Yoo et al., 2011).

In a similar fashion, presentation of external inputs during specific phases of neuroelectric activity might enhance or reduce participant's response.

Successful electroencephalographic (EEG)-based detection of brain states predicting participants' errors during complex cognitive decision tasks has been shown (Eichele et al., 2010). Several studies also demonstrated that brain states preceding stimulus presentation significantly affect perception (Arieli et al., 1996; Boly et al., 2007; Fox and Raichle, 2007; Fox et al., 2007; Busch et al., 2009; Mathewson et al., 2009). Building on these results, real-time information of ongoing brain states might be exploited for controlling data presentation in MR in order to boost information processing. For instance, detection of specific brain states might be used to drive changes in the level of complexity of presented information to facilitate participants' perception.

Toward this aim, we assessed to what extent multiple brain states can be discriminated during MR experience. Previous studies in the visual domain showed that real-time analysis of visual evoked potentials can detect fluctuations of perceptual dominance of each eye during binocular rivalry (Brown and Norcia, 1997). In the field of motor imagery-based BCI Millán and colleagues proposed a simple local neural classifier for the recognition of multiple mental tasks from on-line spontaneous EEG signal that achieved a recognition rate of 70% in distinguishing between relaxation, left and right hand movement imagination (Millán et al., 2002).

However, to date, clear evidence of classification of brain states during different cognitive tasks for BCI control of virtual and MR environments is still lacking. Most of studies on the integration of BCI with virtual reality focused on motor imagery, P300 and steady-state visual evoked potentials (SSVEPs) (Lotte et al., 2013). In particular, SSVEPs, permitting high information transfer rates and minimal training, seem to be suitable for BCI in virtual and MR (Martinez et al., 2007; Faller et al., 2010). Though, BCI based on continuous EEG decoding might be more flexible for monitoring brain activity during natural behavior in virtual and MR applications.

In our study, we tested classification of continuous EEG signal during spatial navigation, calculation and reading toward the implementation of BCI-controlled XIM-based MR. Spatial navigation represents a typical category of actions in virtual reality (Lécuyer et al., 2008; Lotte et al., 2013), while calculation and reading are fundamental tasks performed during information processing and data mining, and are also common cognitive processes used for mental workload assessment (Kohlmorgen et al., 2007). In particular, we performed EEG data classification using supervised classifiers based on linear discriminant analysis (LDA) and support vector machine (SVM). Furthermore, we examined predictive accuracy of our classifiers of mental workload in XIM. Increased mental workload was expected during calculation and reading as compared to spatial navigation because of larger involvement of working memory (Mayes and Koonce, 2001; Destefano, 2004; Imbo et al., 2007).

Based on previous studies showing large inter-individual differences in single-trial EEG classification of mental states in real operational environments (Kohlmorgen et al., 2007), we have used a flexible approach and calibrated our classifiers to each participant. Dynamic single trial classification was conducted using a sliding time-window shifting every 200 ms to permit applicability in a BCI-controlled MR scenario.

MATERIALS AND METHODS

Five participants (29.60 ± 6.73 mean age ± *SD*, 1 female) underwent two consecutive sessions in a MR environment during which EEG signal was acquired continuously. The experiment was performed in the XIM (Bernardet et al., 2011; Omedas et al., 2014). The XIM architecture is an integrated framework that combines a sensing system to evaluate and measure complex psychological states with a number of actuators and effectors to coherently react to the user's actions (**Figure 1**). The internal processing of XIM is based on three main components. First, adaptive data mining that defines what data is presented to the user. Second, spatio-temporal structuring of the presented content in the form of narratives generated by the composition engines, and third an intentional, sentient agent, who controls the XIM interface and guides data exploration. XIM covers a surface area of 5.5 × 5.5 m, with a height of 4 m. Eight video projectors display the scenarios into four projection screens (2.25 × 5 m) surrounding the MR room. During each session participants experienced three different conditions, all involving the visual system: spatial navigation (SPN), reading (MER), and calculation (MEC). The user, sitting on a chair positioned in the middle of the XIM room, could navigate the virtual space by pressing the arrow keys of a keyboard. Participants were required to navigate a squared spiral labyrinth until the central point (indicated by a yellow sphere) (**Figure 2**). Nine different targets represented by red spheres were placed in alternating corners of the path. Proximity to red spheres triggered the beginning of a different condition. In the first session the condition consisted of a 30 s calculation task. When the participant reached the red sphere, screen went black and a random 3-digit

FIGURE 1 | The eXperience Induction Machine (XIM) architecture is a mixed reality integrated framework that combines a sensing system to evaluate and measure complex physiological and psychological states with a number of actuators and effectors to coherently react to the user's actions. It is mainly constituted of an immersive room that covers a surface area of 5.5 × 5.5 m, with a height of 4 m. Eight video projectors display the scenarios into four projection screens (2.25 × 5 m) surrounding the MR room. Reprinted with permission from Betella et al. (2014).

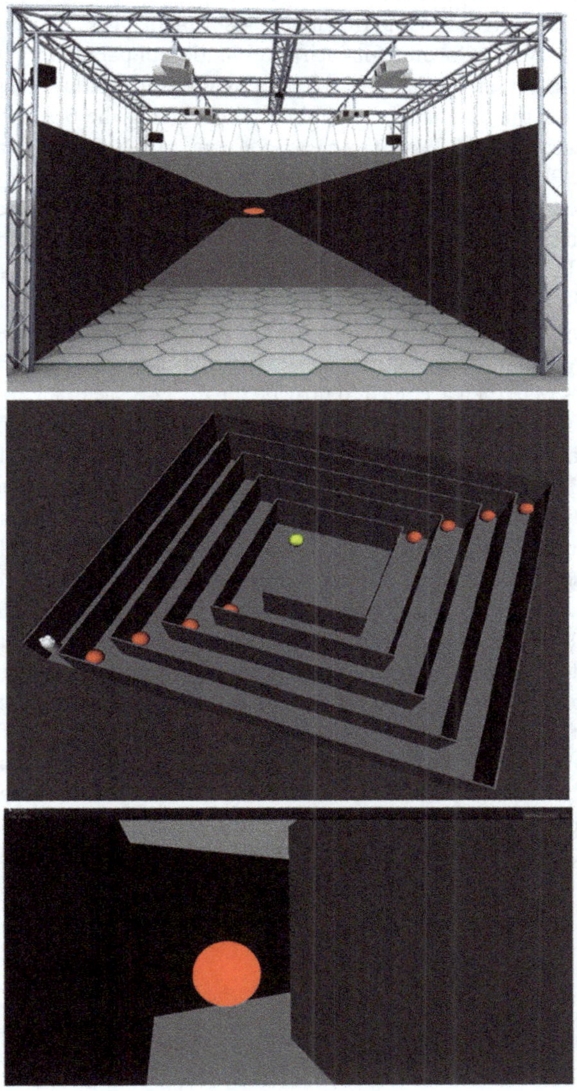

FIGURE 2 | Top: The immersive XIM modeling the virtual maze used in the experiment (left). **Center:** View from the top of the labyrinth and the nine different targets (red spheres) that were placed in alternating corners of the path. The labyrinth size was 10 × 10 VR units (meters). Participants were required to navigate the squared spiral labyrinth until the central point (yellow sphere). Proximity to red spheres triggered the beginning of a different condition. In the first session the condition consisted of a 30 s calculation task. When the participant reached the red sphere, screen went black and a random 3-digit number was displayed in the graphical interface. The participant was asked to iteratively subtract 17 from a given number. After 30 s, the black screen faded out and the participant was asked to continue spatial navigation. In the second session, the condition consisted of a 30 s reading. The introduction of a scientific article was displayed and the participant was required to read it and press the space keyboard command when finished. **Bottom:** First person perspective of the labyrinth and a red sphere.

number was displayed in the graphical interface. The participant was asked to iteratively subtract 17 from a given number. After 30 s, the black screen faded out and the participant was asked to continue spatial navigation. In the second session, the condition consisted of a 30 reading. The introduction of a scientific article was displayed and the participant was required to read it and press the space keyboard command when finished. In each session 9 SPN conditions were alternated to 8 MER or MEC conditions. An immersive 180° virtual reality application was developed and projected into the back screens of the XIM room. The VR application was developed using the Unity3D Game Engine, and adapted to fit the displays of XIM (Bernardet et al., 2011; Omedas et al., 2014). A virtual maze was modeled using Autodesk Maya (Autodesk Inc., San Rafael, CA, USA). The labyrinth size was 10 × 10 VR units (VR units permit to assign any type of units to objects' properties, e.g., weight, distance, etc., in our case they are defined as meters). The environment was constructed as an extension of the real physical space of the XIM—wall, floor, and other virtual objects were modeled so that they were perceived of real size (i.e., the point of view of the participant experiencing MR was equivalent to that of a person with average height). All participants were appropriately instructed about the experimental procedure. This study was approved by the ethics committee of the University of Tübingen.

EEG DATA ACQUISITION AND PREPROCESSING

EEG data were recorded using a 64-channels BrainAmp amplifier (Brain Products GmbH, Munich Germany). An actiCap 64-channels EEG cap (modified 10–20 system, Brain Products GmbH, Munich Germany) was used for data acquisition, referenced to the FCz, and grounded anteriorly to Fz. Only 28 surface active electrodes at the following locations were used: Fp1, Fp2, F7, F3, Fz, F4, F8, Fc5, Fc1, Fc2, Fc6, T7, C3, Cz, C4, T8, Cp5, Cp1, Cp2, Cp6, P7, P3, Pz, P4, P8, O1, Oz, O2. Electrodes impedance was reduced to 15 kΩ before data recording. EEG signals were sampled at 250 Hz.

EEG signal was first visually inspected to exclude channels affected by artifacts. Spectral analysis was then conducted on each channel to prevent our classifiers from being affected by large muscle and eye artifacts. To this aim we explored differences between SPN (low cognitive load) and MER + MEC (high cognitive load) conditions focusing on the frequencies above 20 Hz (typical of muscles artifacts) and below 6 Hz (typical of eye artifacts) (Kohlmorgen et al., 2007). The channels showing a significant difference between different workload conditions in the selected frequency bands were discarded (Kohlmorgen et al., 2007). As in Kohlmorgen et al. (2007), for each subject a customized feature selection—channel subsets, spatial filtering, frequency bands, and window lengths—was performed based on the following set of parameters: EEG channels subset {FC#, C#, P#, CP#}, {F#, FC#, C#, P#, CP#, O#}, {F#, FC#, C#, P#, CP#, O#, T7, T8}, {FC#, C#, P#, CP#, T7, T8}; spatial filter: common median reference or none; frequency band for spectral estimation: 3–15, 7–15, 10–15, 3–10 Hz; window length: 2 or 5 s. Feature extraction was performed by computing a spectral estimation within a dynamic sliding window approach shifting every 200 ms. EEG data analysis and classification were performed using MATLAB (The Mathworks, Natick, MA).

CLASSIFICATION AND PHYSIOLOGICAL ANALYSES

A SVM (from LIBSVM library, http://www.csie.ntu.edu.tw/~cjlin/libsvm/faq.html#f203) with non-linear kernel (radial basis function, rbf) and a LDA classifier were tested on each subject. For SVM classification, the regularization parameter C was set to 0.6 in order to prevent over-fitting, (Cherkassky and Ma, 2004). Two different classification schemes were used. In the first scheme, the classifiers aimed to distinguish between three different classes: spatial navigation, reading and calculation. The most common decomposing strategies for multiclass SVM are the "one against one" and "one against all" binary classification approaches. The former implies the training of k*(k–1)/2 different binary classifiers (where k is the number of classes); each new test sample is then labeled according to the class selected by the majority of classifiers. The latter implies to build a classifier per each class to distinguish the samples of the selected class from the samples of all remaining classes; a new test sample is labeled according to the maximum outcome of all trained SVMs. A comparison of several multi-class SVM methods showed similar performance for the "one-against-all," "one-against-one" and directed acyclic graph SVM (DAGSVM) (Hsu and Lin, 2002). However, the authors suggested that one-against-one and DAG approaches are more suitable for practical use due to reduced training time. Accordingly, we adopted the "one against one" strategy. For each subject 8 MEC, 8 MER, and 18 SPN blocks were recorded in the two sessions. A leave-one-out cross validation (CV) was used for performing feature selection and for measuring classifiers performance (see **Figure 3**). One MEC, one MER, and two SPN blocks were pseudo-randomly selected and retained for testing classifiers performance, while the remaining blocks were fed into a 7-fold cross-validation scheme for performing parameter selection. This procedure satisfies the requirement of independency between parameter selection samples and testing samples for classifier performance assessment. The 7-fold CV scheme was performed for each combination of parameters (i.e., channel subset, spatial filter, frequency band, and window length) to select the parameters' combination providing the best 7-fold CV accuracy (see **Table 1**). In each fold one MEC, one MER, and two SPN blocks were retained to compute the accuracy of the model trained on the other 6 MEC, 6 MER, and 14 SPN blocks. As duration of SPN blocks was approximately half the duration of MEC, a comparable number of samples was obtained by using for SPN double the number of MEC or MER blocks. For measuring classifiers performance the CV procedure was repeated 7 times with different training subset for each class. The 7 accuracy values were then averaged to provide the final CV accuracy.

A second classification scheme aimed to test generalization capability of the classifier in discriminating between high (MER and MEC) and low (SPN) workload (LW and HW) independently of the type of workload. This additional scheme consisted in the application of a 11-fold CV on the merged MEC and MER datasets. The merged dataset was divided into two parts: four blocks (1 LW and 1 HW block from the MEC dataset and 1 LW and 1 HW block from the MER dataset) were pseudo-randomly selected for estimating classifier performance; the remaining 16 LW and 14 HW were fed into a 11-fold CV scheme aiming to select the best parameter setting for each subject. During each fold 14 LW and 12 HW blocks were used for training and the remaining 2 LW and 2 HW blocks for testing. The 11-fold CV scheme was performed for each combination of parameters (i.e., channel subset, spatial filter, frequency band, and window length). The

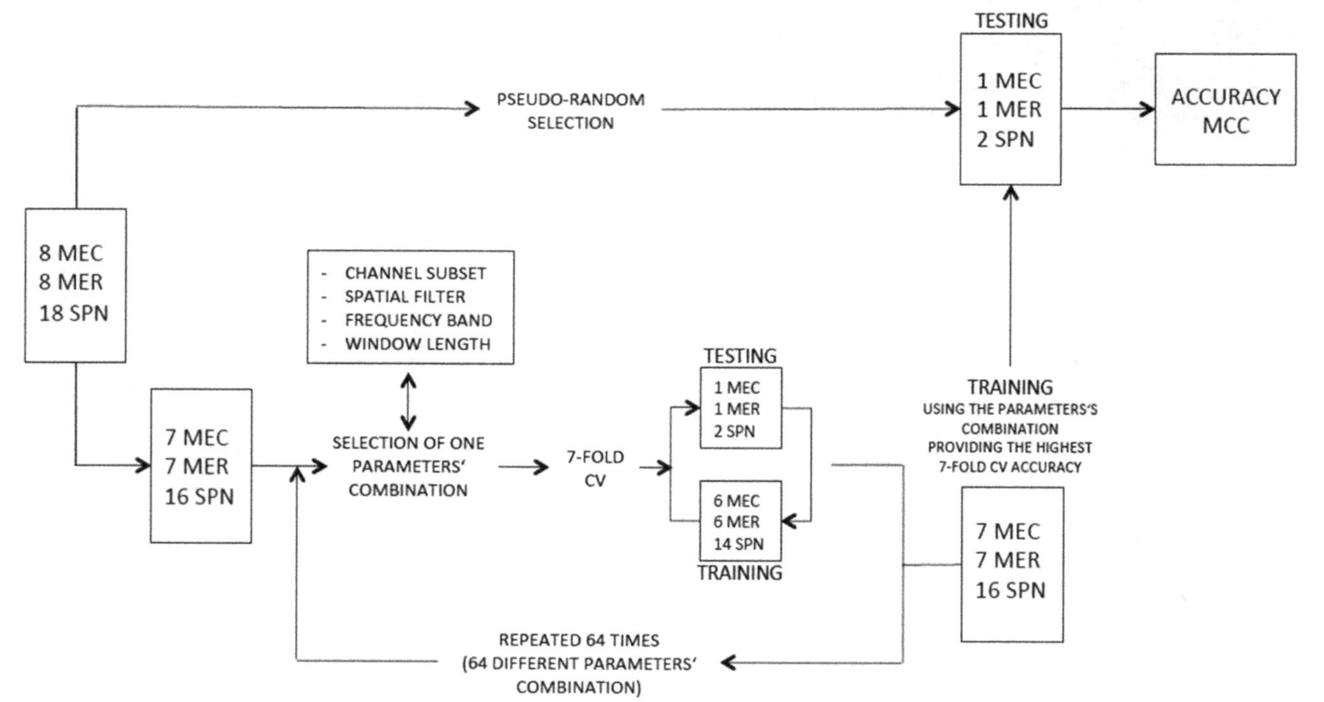

FIGURE 3 | Flow diagram depicting feature selection and estimation of classification performance for scheme 1. A similar flow diagram was used for scheme 2 but using a different numbers of blocks and classes (HW and LW conditions).

Table 1 | Selected parameters in scheme 1 (top) and scheme 2 for each subject (bottom).

Subjects	SVM				LDA			
	Channels	Spatial filtering	Window length (s)	Frequency band (Hz)	Channels	Spatial filtering	Window length (s)	Frequency band (Hz)
SCHEME 1								
Sub 1	{F#, FC#, C#, P#, CP#, O#}	Y	5	10–15	{F#, FC#, C#, P#, CP#, O#}	N	5	3–10
Sub 2	{F#, FC#, C#, P#, CP#, O#}	Y	5	7–15	{F#, FC#, C#, P#, CP#, O#}	Y	5	3–10
Sub 3	{F#, FC#, C#, P#, CP#, O#}	Y	5	10–15	{F#, FC#, C#, P#, CP#, O#, T7, T8}	Y	5	3–10
Sub 4	{F#, FC#, C#, P#, CP#, O#}	Y	5	10–15	{F#, FC#, C#, P#, CP#, O#, T7, T8}	Y	5	3–15
Sub 5	{F#, FC#, C#, P#, CP#, O#}	N	5	10–15	{F#, FC#, C#, P#, CP#, O#, T7, T8}	Y	5	3–10
SCHEME 2								
Sub 1	{F#, FC#, C#, P#, CP#, O#, T7, T8}	N	5	7–15	{F#, FC#, C#, P#, CP#, O#, T7, T8}	Y	5	3–10
Sub 2	{F#, FC#, C#, P#, CP#, O#, T7, T8}	Y	5	3–10	{F#, FC#, C#, P#, CP#, O#, T7, T8}	Y	5	3–15
Sub 3	{F#, FC#, C#, P#, CP#, O#, T7, T8}	Y	5	3–10	{F#, FC#, C#, P#, CP#, O#}	N	5	3–15
Sub 4	{F#, FC#, C#, P#, CP#, O#}	Y	5	3–15	{F#, FC#, C#, P#, CP#, O#}	Y	5	10–15
Sub 5	{F#, FC#, C#, P#, CP#, O#}	Y	5	3–10	{F#, FC#, C#, P#, CP#, O#}	N	5	3–10

parameters' combination providing the best 11-fold CV accuracy was then employed to test classifier performance on the retained four pseudo-randomly blocks (see **Table 1**). Features selection for the first and second classification scheme included a 5 s window length and the common median reference (in 15 out of 20 cases).

Feature selection process allowed to determine two most discriminant channels' subsets out of the four considered: {F#, FC#, C#, P#, CP#, O#} and {F#, FC#, C#, P#, CP#, O#, T7, T8} (see **Table 1**).

The Matthews correlation coefficient (MCC) was additionally computed, as it guarantees more robustness to performance variability in binary classification accuracy by taking into account differences in data dimensionality (Baldi et al., 2000). *MCC* ranges between -1 and 1, from total disagreement to agreement between prediction and observation, respectively, and with 0 indicating completely random prediction.

EEG spectral differences among the three conditions were inspected considering 3–7 and 8–12 Hz bands. Spectral differences between HW and LW conditions were assessed using a non-parametric Wilcoxon signed-rank test considering each of the 26 channels of all participants for 3–7 and 8–12 Hz bands separately.

Table 2 | Results of the classification of spatial navigation, reading, and calculation.

Subjects	SVM		LDA	
	Acc (%)	*MCC*	Acc (%)	*MCC*
Sub1	75.63	0.60	81.59	0.69
Sub2	54.76	0.36	89.72	0.84
Sub3	73.36	0.49	79.07	0.61
Sub4	60.35	0.36	76.56	0.62
Sub5	64.29	0.45	89.56	0.82
Average	65.68	0.45	83.30	0.72

The accuracy, MCC, and average values for LDA and SVM classifiers are reported for each participant.

Table 3 | Results of the classification between LW and HW.

Subjects	SVM		LDA	
	Acc (%)	*MCC*	Acc (%)	*MCC*
Sub1	87.59	0.61	96.92	0.92
Sub2	85.43	0.63	93.72	0.86
Sub3	90.89	0.75	87.12	0.69
Sub4	80.56	0.59	73.72	0.54
Sub5	88.46	0.59	91.3	0.68
Average	86.59	0.63	88.56	0.74

The accuracy, MCC, and average values for LDA and SVM classifiers are reported for each participant.

RESULTS

Classification performance of continuous EEG data during the three mental states SPN, MEC and MER is reported in **Table 2**. The LDA based classifier generated on average the highest accuracy (83.30%, $MCC = 0.72$) across all subjects, with peaks of 89.72% for accuracy and 0.84 for *MCC* in subject 2. The SVM based classifier generated on average the lower accuracy (65.68%, $MCC = 0.45$). The results of the classification between HW and LW are reported in **Table 3**. As for the first scheme, LDA yielded on average the highest accuracy (88.56%, $MCC = 0.74$) across all subjects, with peaks of 96.92% for accuracy and 0.92 for *MCC* in subject 1. SVM yielded on average a lower accuracy (86.59%) and a lower *MCC* value (0.63). Visual inspection of EEG power spectrum at representative discriminative channels (Fz and Pz, as they are usually less affected by muscle artifacts) showed power changes at theta frequencies (3–7 Hz) and at alpha band (8–12 Hz) among all three conditions (see **Figure 4A**). Moreover, increased alpha band power in frontal regions and theta band power in the frontal and parietal regions was measured during reading and calculation with respect to spatial navigation (see **Figure 4B**). Topographic distribution of the 8–12 Hz band power

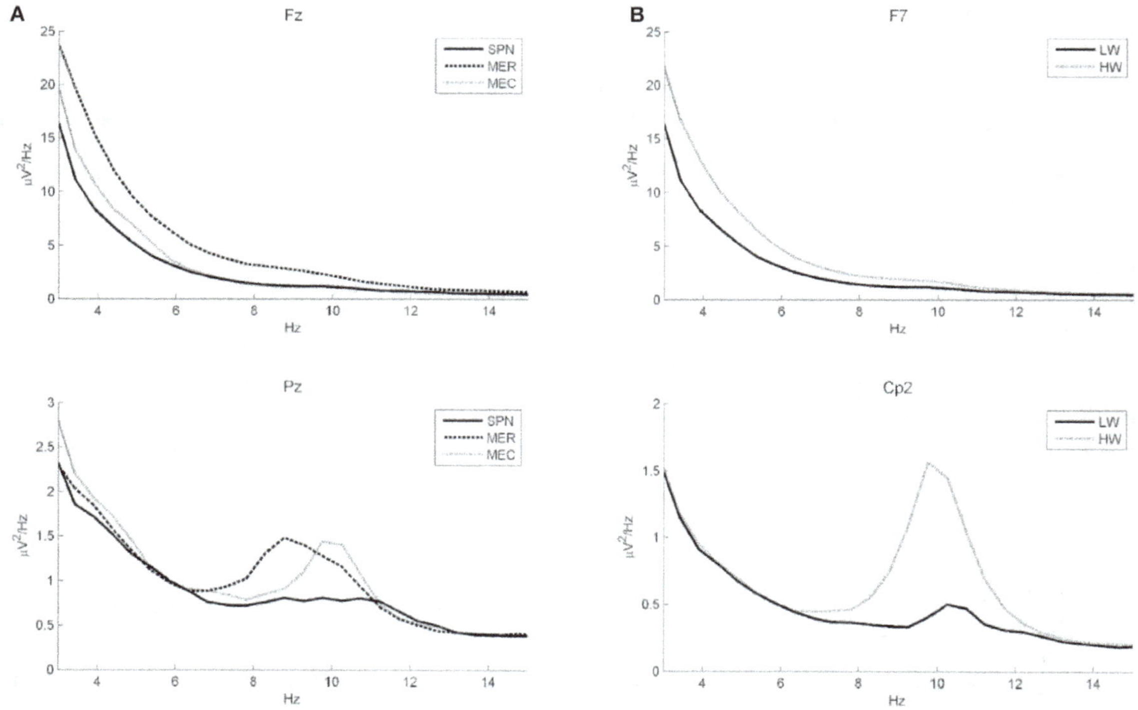

FIGURE 4 | (A) Power spectra (grand average across all subjects) of two discriminative channels of all conditions in frontal and parietal areas (Fz and Pz). Solid, dashed, and dotted lines represent the grand average power spectrum for SPN, MER, and MEC tasks, respectively. Fz shows a clear power difference among all conditions in the 3–7 Hz band, whereas Pz shows a clear power difference in the 8–12 Hz band. **(B)** Power spectra (grand average across all subjects) of channels showing positive peaks during high (HW) as compared to low (LW) mental workload (left frontal area, F7, and central parietal region, Cp2).

difference comparing HW to LW conditions showed positive peaks of neuroelectric activity in the left frontal area, F7, and bilateral parietal regions, Cp1 and Cp2 ($p < 0.001$, see larger dots in **Figure 5**, right). Topographic distribution of the 3–7 Hz band power difference comparing HW to LW conditions shows a significant positive peak in the left frontal area (F7) and several negative peaks in central and parietal areas ($p < 0.001$, see larger dots in **Figure 5**, left), except channels F8, Fc6, T7, C3, C4, T8, Cp1, Pz.

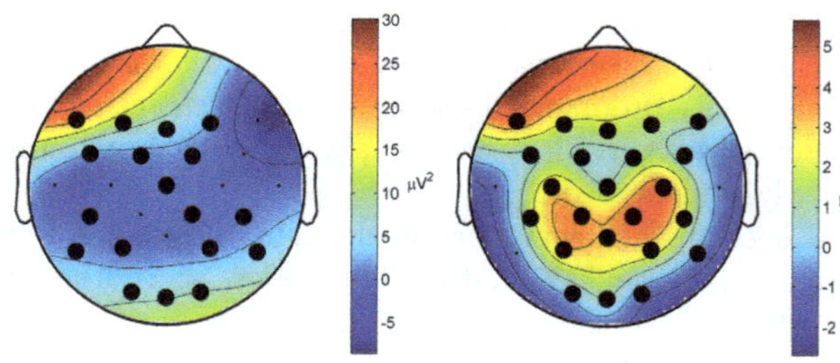

FIGURE 5 | Topographic distribution of the spectral difference in the 3–7 Hz band (left) and in the 8–12 Hz band (right) between HW and LW (grand average across all subjects). Larger dots indicate those channels where a significant difference was measured ($p < 0.001$). Distribution of the 8–12 Hz band power difference shows significant positive peaks in the left frontal area (F7) and bilateral parietal regions (Cp1 and Cp2). Distribution of the 3–7 Hz band power shows a significant positive peak in the frontal area (F7), and several negative peaks in central and parietal areas.

DISCUSSION

Our study investigated brain states classification during the execution of multiple cognitive processes in MR. To this end we explored continuous EEG data decoding during performance of MR relevant tasks such as spatial navigation, calculation and reading in XIM, using LDA and SVM based classifiers. Results of our first classification scheme, aiming to discriminate spatial navigation, calculation and reading, showed high performance of both LDA and SVM classifiers, with an average accuracy of around 83% for LDA and of around 65% for SVM. Results of our second classification scheme, aiming to decode mental workload independently on the workload task, showed high classification performance of both SVM and LDA (on average both above 86%). Successful decoding of all mental states was achieved considering a 5 s time-window shifting every 200 ms, permitting online applications with a bit-rate of about 5 bits/s.

Previous EEG-BCI mainly investigated mental states decoding considering different states separately, for instance motor imagery, attention, performance capability, emotional arousal, or brain activity prefiguring behavioral errors (Millán et al., 2002; Muller et al., 2008; Schubert et al., 2009; Eichele et al., 2010). However, the capability of decoding multiple brain states is particularly important for BCI-controlled MR as it would allow the implementation of more flexible scenarios with less behavioral constraints. A previous study aiming to implement a BCI for the recognition of multiple mental tasks from on-line spontaneous EEG signal reported a recognition rate of 70% in distinguishing between relaxation, left and right hand movement imagination using a simple local neural classifier (Millán et al., 2002). In addition, the authors performed a preliminary analysis in one subject to test generalization of two local neural classifiers in discriminating between three tasks—relaxation, arithmetic subtraction, and left hand movement imagination, as well as relaxation, cube rotation and left hand movement imagination; performance accuracy reached over 90% of correct prediction on the combined task (Millán et al., 2002). A more recent EEG classification study reported successful offline multi-class discrimination of several conditions, such as resting, mental calculation, mental writing and rotation, by combining wavelet transform decomposition for feature selection and a feed-forward neural network with one-step secant algorithm (Upadhyay, 2013).

Here, we tested a simpler approach using LDA and SVM, also on the basis of the results of a comparative analysis of multi-class EEG classifiers for BCI, such as LDA, Nearest Neighbor Classifier (NNC) and linear SVM, indicating that LDA provides the highest classification accuracy with low dimensional feature space (Lee et al., 2005). In line with these results both our classification schemes showed better performance of LDA with respect to SVM.

Increased accuracy of SVM classifier would also be achievable through additional optimization procedure applied to its parameters (i.e., C and γ), typically via cross-validation, but this would result in a substantial increase of the computational time. On the other hand, SVM can achieve higher performance as compared to LDA with high dimensional feature vectors (Lee et al., 2005).

Because of large intersubject variability of EEG data, subject-dependent classifiers, as those used here, guarantee better performance than subject-independent classifiers (Lotte and Ang, 2009) but they require an initial offline calibration during which the participants need to evoke specific mental state by performing appropriate tasks (supervised classifier). However, a subject-independent BCI system with no need of training, implemented using a combination of large datasets of subject-dependent classifiers into a single subject-independent classifier, demonstrated performance similar to that of subject-dependent methods (Fazli et al., 2009). In addition, Vidaurre and colleagues investigating co-adaptive learning using machine learning techniques implemented a subject-independent supervised classifier with no need of offline calibration procedure that showed good performance even in participants that are not able to control conventional BCI (Vidaurre et al., 2010). These promising findings suggest the possibility to extend to use of subject-independent classifiers in BCI applications.

Our subject-dependent LDA-based classifier provided the highest accuracy mostly using 3–10 and 3–15 Hz frequency power bands. Spectral analysis indicated changes at theta band (3–6 Hz) as well as at alpha band (8–12 Hz) between different mental states in frontoparietal regions. Alpha band increase in the frontal area was observed for all conditions, whereas both theta and alpha bands increase in the parietal regions was larger for reading and calculation with respect to spatial navigation. Accordingly, high workload, that included both reading and calculation, compared to low workload—spatial navigation—showed significant power differences at 3–6 and 8–12 Hz bands. In particular theta band maximum was observed in the left frontal area, while alpha band peaked in the left frontal and bilateral parietal regions.

Despite intersubject variability and our small sample size, the observed alpha band increase in the bilateral parietal areas is in line with previous results reporting alpha changes in bilateral parietal and occipital brain regions associated with mental workload, task engagement or attention (Humphrey and Kramer, 1994; Pope et al., 1995; Kohlmorgen et al., 2007). The measured changes in the theta band power are also in line with previous studies indicating that theta oscillations are related to spatial navigation as well as encoding and retrieval of spatial information (Kahana et al., 1999; Bischof and Boulanger, 2003). In particular, high amplitude theta activity, mainly in the left frontal and right temporal cortices, has been measured during navigation in a virtual maze (Kahana et al., 1999). Other studies corroborated these results and showed that the frequency of theta episodes is directly associated with the difficulty of maze navigation (Bischof and Boulanger, 2003). In light of previous studies our results indicate that indeed the here adopted reading and calculation tasks required increased allocation of mental resources with respect to spatial navigation.

In addition, we observed delta frequencies (3 Hz) power changes during all conditions in frontal regions. These results are in line with previous studies indicating increased EEG oscillations in the range 1–3.5 Hz in frontal regions associated with different cognitive processes (Harmony, 2013), in particular during internal concentration and calculation (Fernandez et al., 1995).

Our mental states classifiers can equally be employed for real-time analysis of frequency bands. Online monitoring of alpha and theta bands power would be important for assessing participants' performance as these bands reflect cognitive and memory processing (Klimesch, 1999). In online MR-combined BCI applications the information stream provided to the user could be adapted to the current workload as indicated by alpha and theta oscillations. Kohlmorgen et al. (2007) proposed the use of ratios of activity in alpha (8–12 Hz) or theta (3–7 Hz) bands to compute an index of the user task engagement.

Alpha band is also critical for visual perception, in particular medium and lower amplitudes can reflect improved performance in somatosensory and visual discrimination tasks (Pfurtscheller and Lopes Da Silva, 1999; Hanslmayr et al., 2005; Palva and Palva, 2007; Van Dijk et al., 2008). Moreover, decrease in the alpha frequencies (8–12 Hz) before target onset was associated with augmented visual target detection (Ergenoglu et al., 2004). Further studies confirmed this observation by showing that the amplitude of prestimulus ~10 Hz oscillations correlated with the detection of the upcoming target: the smaller the amplitude, the more likely the target would be detected (Van Dijk et al., 2008; Busch et al., 2009; Mathewson et al., 2009). On the contrary, stronger pre-stimulus alpha frequency band amplitude has been linked to increased cognitive performance (Neubauer and Freudenthaler, 1995; Klimesch, 1999). Thus, online inspection of alpha wave oscillations might be used for triggering stimuli presentation so as to optimize stimulus detection, as well as for improving interpretation of novel information and data mining since alpha band activity has also been associated with learning (Klimesch, 1999).

In conclusion, our LDA classifier is sufficiently flexible and powerful for the implementation of a MR-combined BCI system. Successful classification of mental states based on subject-specific single trials EEG indicates the possibility to combine BCI technology with the XIM so that brain activity could drive the adaptation of data representation. A possible way to refine our BCI in MR is the use of an asynchronous modality where participants do not need to follow a fixed repetitive scheme to switch from one mental task to another one. Asynchronous BCI, allowing individuals to decide when to perform a mental task and when to stop it and switch to another one, are more flexible and adaptive to different scenarios (Millán et al., 2002; Millan Jdel and Mourino, 2003). Ultimately, this approach would permit to model the user experience in the XIM as common product between the initial data representations and the changes made interactively as consequences of users' neurophysiological signals associated with spontaneous behavior.

ACKNOWLEDGMENTS

The present study was supported by EU grants: FP7-ICT-2009-258749 CEEDs: The Collective Experience of Empathic Data Systems; FP7-ICT-2013- 609593 BNCI Horizon 2020. The Future of Brain/Neural Computer Interaction: Horizon 2020; Italian Ministry of Health, GR-2009-1591908.

REFERENCES

Arieli, A., Sterkin, A., Grinvald, A., and Aertsen, A. (1996). Dynamics of ongoing activity: explanation of the large variability in evoked cortical responses. *Science* 273, 1868–1871. doi: 10.1126/science.273.5283.1868

Baldi, P., Brunak, S., Chauvin, Y., Andersen, C. A., and Nielsen, H. (2000). Assessing the accuracy of prediction algorithms for classification: an overview. *Bioinformatics* 16, 412–424. doi: 10.1093/bioinformatics/16.5.412

Bernardet, U., Valjamae, A., Inderbitzin, M., Wierenga, S., Mura, A., and Verschure, P. F. (2011). Quantifying human subjective experience and social interaction using the eXperience Induction Machine. *Brain Res. Bull.* 85, 305–312. doi: 10.1016/j.brainresbull.2010.11.009

Betella, A., Cetnarski, R., Zucca, R., Arsiwalla, X. D., Martinez, E., Omedas, P., et al. (2014). "BrainX3: embodied exploration of neural data," in *Proceedings of the 2014 Virtual Reality International Conference Article No. 37* (New York, NY: ACM). doi: 10.1145/2617841.2620726

Birbaumer, N., and Cohen, L. G. (2007). Brain-computer interfaces: communication and restoration of movement in paralysis. *J. Physiol.* 579, 621–636. doi: 10.1113/jphysiol.2006.125633

Bischof, W. F., and Boulanger, P. (2003). Spatial navigation in virtual reality environments: an EEG analysis. *Cyberpsychol. Behav.* 6, 487–495. doi: 10.1089/109493103769710514

Blankertz, B., Tangermann, M., Vidaurre, C., Fazli, S., Sannelli, C., Haufe, S., et al. (2010). The Berlin brain-computer interface: non-medical uses of BCI technology. *Front. Neurosci.* 4:198. doi: 10.3389/fnins.2010.00198

Bohil, C. J., Alicea, B., and Biocca, F. A. (2011). Virtual reality in neuroscience research and therapy. *Nat. Rev. Neurosci.* 12, 752–762. doi: 10.1038/nrn3122

Boly, M., Balteau, E., Schnakers, C., Degueldre, C., Moonen, G., Luxen, A., et al. (2007). Baseline brain activity fluctuations predict somatosensory perception in humans. *Proc. Natl. Acad. Sci. U.S.A.* 104, 12187–12192. doi: 10.1073/pnas.0611404104

Brown, R. J., and Norcia, A. M. (1997). A method for investigating binocular rivalry in real-time with the steady-state VEP. *Vision Res.* 37, 2401–2408. doi: 10.1016/S0042-6989(97)00045-X

Busch, N. A., Dubois, J., and Vanrullen, R. (2009). The phase of ongoing EEG oscillations predicts visual perception. *J. Neurosci.* 29, 7869–7876. doi: 10.1523/JNEUROSCI.0113-09.2009

Caria, A., Sitaram, R., and Birbaumer, N. (2012). Real-time fMRI: a tool for local brain regulation. *Neuroscientist* 18, 487–501. doi: 10.1177/1073858411407205

Cherkassky, V., and Ma, Y. (2004). Practical selection of SVM parameters and noise estimation for SVM regression. *Neural Netw.* 17, 113–126. doi: 10.1016/S0893-6080(03)00169-2

Daly, J. J., and Wolpaw, J. R. (2008). Brain-computer interfaces in neurological rehabilitation. *Lancet Neurol.* 7, 1032–1043. doi: 10.1016/S1474-4422(08)70223-0

Delorme, A., and Makeig, S. (2003). EEG changes accompanying learned regulation of 12-Hz EEG activity. *IEEE Trans. Neural Syst. Rehabil. Eng.* 11, 133–137. doi: 10.1109/TNSRE.2003.814428

Destefano, D. L. J. (2004). The role of working memory in mental arithmetic. *Eur. J. Cogn. Psychol.* 16, 353–386. doi: 10.1080/09541440244000328

Eichele, H., Juvodden, H. T., Ullsperger, M., and Eichele, T. (2010). Mal-adaptation of event-related EEG responses preceding performance errors. *Front. Hum. Neurosci.* 4:65. doi: 10.3389/fnhum.2010.00065

Ergenoglu, T., Demiralp, T., Bayraktaroglu, Z., Ergen, M., Beydagi, H., and Uresin, Y. (2004). Alpha rhythm of the EEG modulates visual detection performance in humans. *Brain Res. Cogn. Brain Res.* 20, 376–383. doi: 10.1016/j.cogbrainres.2004.03.009

Faller, J. M. L.-P. G., Schmalstieg, D., and Pfurtscheller, G. (2010). "An application framework for controlling an avatar in a desktop based virtual environment via a software SSVEP brain-computer interface," in *Presence: Teleoperators and Virtual Environments*, Vol. 19 (Cambridge, MA: MIT Press), 25–34.

Fazli, S., Popescu, F., Danoczy, M., Blankertz, B., Muller, K. R., and Grozea, C. (2009). Subject-independent mental state classification in single trials. *Neural Netw.* 22, 1305–1312. doi: 10.1016/j.neunet.2009.06.003

Fernandez, T., Harmony, T., Rodriguez, M., Bernal, J., Silva, J., Reyes, A., et al. (1995). EEG activation patterns during the performance of tasks involving different components of mental calculation. *Electroencephalogr. Clin. Neurophysiol.* 94, 175–182. doi: 10.1016/0013-4694(94)00262-J

Fox, M. D., and Raichle, M. E. (2007). Spontaneous fluctuations in brain activity observed with functional magnetic resonance imaging. *Nat. Rev. Neurosci.* 8, 700–711. doi: 10.1038/nrn2201

Fox, M. D., Snyder, A. Z., Vincent, J. L., and Raichle, M. E. (2007). Intrinsic fluctuations within cortical systems account for intertrial variability in human behavior. *Neuron* 56, 171–184. doi: 10.1016/j.neuron.2007.08.023

George, L. L. A. (2010). "An overview of research on "passive" brain-computer interfaces for implicit human-computer interaction," in *International Conference on Applied Bionics and Biomechanics ICABB* (Venice).

Hanslmayr, S., Sauseng, P., Doppelmayr, M., Schabus, M., and Klimesch, W. (2005). Increasing individual upper alpha power by neurofeedback improves cognitive performance in human subjects. *Appl. Psychophysiol. Biofeedback* 30, 1–10. doi: 10.1007/s10484-005-2169-8

Harmony, T. (2013). The functional significance of delta oscillations in cognitive processing. *Front. Integr. Neurosci.* 7:83. doi: 10.3389/fnint.2013.00083

Hsu, C. W., and Lin, C. J. (2002). A comparison of methods for multiclass support vector machines. *IEEE Trans. Neural Netw.* 13, 415–425. doi: 10.1109/72.991427

Humphrey, D. G., and Kramer, A. F. (1994). Toward a psychophysiological assessment of dynamic changes in mental workload. *Hum. Factors* 36, 3–26.

Imbo, I., Vandierendonck, A., and De Rammelaere, S. (2007). The role of working memory in the carry operation of mental arithmetic: number and value of the carry. *Q. J. Exp. Psychol. (Hove)* 60, 708–731. doi: 10.1080/17470210600762447

Kahana, M. J., Sekuler, R., Caplan, J. B., Kirschen, M., and Madsen, J. R. (1999). Human theta oscillations exhibit task dependence during virtual maze navigation. *Nature* 399, 781–784. doi: 10.1038/21645

Klimesch, W. (1999). EEG alpha and theta oscillations reflect cognitive and memory performance: a review and analysis. *Brain Res. Brain Res. Rev.* 29, 169–195. doi: 10.1016/S0165-0173(98)00056-3

Kohlmorgen, J. D. G., Braun, M., Blankertz, B., Müller, K. R., Curio, G., Hagemann, K., et al. (2007). "Improving human performance in a real operating environment through real-time mental workload detection," in *Toward Brain-Computer Interfacing,* eds J. D. R. M. G. Dornhege, T. Hinterberger, D. McFarland, and K.-R. Müller (Cambridge: MIT press), 409–422.

Lécuyer, A., Lotte, F., Reilly, R. B., Leeb, R., Hirose, M., and Slater, M. (2008). Brain–computer interfaces, virtual reality, and videogames. *Computer* 41, 66–72. doi: 10.1109/MC.2008.410

Lee, F. S. R., Leeb, R., Neuper, C., Bischof, H., and Pfurtscheller, G. (2005). "A comparative analysis of multi-class EEG classification for brain computer interface," in *Computer Vision Winter Workshop CVWW* (Graz: Austrian Computer Society).

Lessiter, J., Miotto, A., Freeman, J., Verschure, P., and Bernardet, U. (2011). CEEDs: unleashing the power of the subconscious. *Proc. Comput. Sci.* 7, 214–215. doi: 10.1016/j.procs.2011.09.069

Lotte, F. F. J., Guger, C., Renard, Y., Pfurtscheller, G., Lécuyer, A., and Leeb, R. (2013). "Combining BCI with virtual reality: towards new applications and improved BCI," in *Towards Practical Brain-Computer Interfaces,* eds S. D. Brendan, Z. Allison, R. Leeb, J. Del R. Millán, and A. Nijholt (Berlin; Heidelberg: Springer), 197–220.

Lotte, F. G. C., and Ang, K. K. (2009). Comparison of designs towards a subject-independent brain–computer interface based on motor imagery. *Conf. Proc. IEEE Eng. Med. Biol. Soc.* 2009, 4543–4546. doi: 10.1109/IEMBS.2009.5334126

Martinez, P., Bakardjian, H., and Cichocki, A. (2007). Fully online multicommand brain-computer interface with visual neurofeedback using SSVEP paradigm. *Comput. Intell. Neurosci.* 2007:94561. doi: 10.1155/2007/94561

Mathewson, K. E., Gratton, G., Fabiani, M., Beck, D. M., and Ro, T. (2009). To see or not to see: prestimulus alpha phase predicts visual awareness. *J. Neurosci.* 29, 2725–2732. doi: 10.1523/JNEUROSCI.3963-08.2009

Mayes, D. K. S. V. K., and Koonce, J. M. (2001). Comprehension and workload differences for VDT and paper-based reading. *Int. J. Ind. Ergon.* 28, 367–378. doi: 10.1016/S0169-8141(01)00043-9

Milgram, P. K. A. F. (1994). Taxonomy of mixed reality visual displays. *IEICE Trans. Inf. Syst.* E77-D, 1321–1329.

Millán Jdel, R., and Mouriño, J. (2003). Asynchronous BCI and local neural classifiers: an overview of the Adaptive Brain Interface project. *IEEE Trans. Neural Syst. Rehabil. Eng.* 11, 159–161. doi: 10.1109/TNSRE.2003.814435

Millán, J. D. R., Mouriño, J., Franzé, M., Cincotti, F., Varsta, M., Heikkonen, J., et al. (2002). A local neural classifier for the recognition of EEG patterns associated to mental tasks. *IEEE Transa. Neural Netw.* 13, 678–686. doi: 10.1109/TNN.2002.1000132

Muller, K. R., Tangermann, M., Dornhege, G., Krauledat, M., Curio, G., and Blankertz, B. (2008). Machine learning for real-time single-trial EEG-analysis: from brain-computer interfacing to mental state monitoring. *J. Neurosci. Methods* 167, 82–90. doi: 10.1016/j.jneumeth.2007.09.022

Neubauer, A. C., and Freudenthaler, H. H. (1995). Ultradian rhythms in cognitive performance: no evidence for a 1.5-h rhythm. *Biol. Psychol.* 40, 281–298. doi: 10.1016/0301-0511(95)05121-P

Omedas, P. B. A., Zucca, R., Arsiwalla, X., Pacheco, D., Wagner, J., Lingenfelser, F., et al. (2014). "XIM-Engine: a software framework to support the development of interactive applications that uses conscious and unconscious reactions in immersive mixed reality," in *Virtual Reality International Conference (VRIC)* (Laval).

Palva, S., and Palva, J. M. (2007). New vistas for alpha-frequency band oscillations. *Trends Neurosci.* 30, 150–158. doi: 10.1016/j.tins.2007.02.001

Pfurtscheller, G., and Lopes Da Silva, F. H. (1999). Event-related EEG/MEG synchronization and desynchronization: basic principles. *Clin. Neurophysiol.* 110, 1842–1857. doi: 10.1016/S1388-2457(99)00141-8

Pope, A. T., Bogart, E. H., and Bartolome, D. S. (1995). Biocybernetic system evaluates indices of operator engagement in automated task. *Biol. Psychol.* 40, 187–195. doi: 10.1016/0301-0511(95)05116-3

Scharnowski, F., Hutton, C., Josephs, O., Weiskopf, N., and Rees, G. (2012). Improving visual perception through neurofeedback. *J. Neurosci.* 32, 17830–17841. doi: 10.1523/JNEUROSCI.6334-11.2012

Schubert, R., Haufe, S., Blankenburg, F., Villringer, A., and Curio, G. (2009). Now you'll feel it, now you won't: EEG rhythms predict the effectiveness of perceptual masking. *J. Cogn. Neurosci.* 21, 2407–2419. doi: 10.1162/jocn.2008.21174

Shibata, K., Watanabe, T., Sasaki, Y., and Kawato, M. (2011). Perceptual learning incepted by decoded fMRI neurofeedback without stimulus presentation. *Science* 334, 1413–1415. doi: 10.1126/science.1212003

Upadhyay, D. (2013). Classification of eeg signals under different mental tasks using wavelet transform and neural network with one step secant algorithm. *Int. J. Sci. Eng. Technol.* 2, 256–259.

Van Dijk, H., Schoffelen, J. M., Oostenveld, R., and Jensen, O. (2008). Prestimulus oscillatory activity in the alpha band predicts visual discrimination ability. *J. Neurosci.* 28, 1816–1823. doi: 10.1523/JNEUROSCI.1853-07.2008

Verschure, P. F. (2011). "The complexity of reality and human computer confluence: stemming the data deluge by empowering human creativity," in *Proceedings of the 9th ACM SIGCHI Italian Chapter International Conference on Computer-Human Interaction: Facing Complexity* (New York, NY: ACM), 3–6.

Vidaurre, C., Sannelli, C., Muller, K. R., and Blankertz, B. (2010). Machine-learning-based coadaptive calibration for brain-computer interfaces. *Neural Comput.* 23, 791–816. doi: 10.1162/NECO_a_00089

Yoo, J. J., Hinds, O., Ofen, N., Thompson, T. W., Whitfield-Gabrieli, S., Triantafyllou, C., et al. (2011). When the brain is prepared to learn: enhancing human learning using real-time fMRI. *Neuroimage* 59, 846–852. doi: 10.1016/j.neuroimage.2011.07.063

10

A controlled study on the cognitive effect of alpha neurofeedback training in patients with major depressive disorder

Carlos Escolano[1,2]*, Mayte Navarro-Gil[3], Javier Garcia-Campayo[4,5], Marco Congedo[6], Dirk De Ridder[7] and Javier Minguez[1,3]

[1] Department of Robotics, Perception and Real Time Group, Aragon Institute of Engineering Research (I3A), University of Zaragoza, Zaragoza, Spain
[2] Department of Computer Science and Systems Engineering (DIIS), University of Zaragoza, Zaragoza, Spain
[3] BitBrain Technologies SL, Zaragoza, Spain
[4] Department of Mental Health in Primary Care, Aragon Health Sciences Institute (IACS), University of Zaragoza, Zaragoza, Spain
[5] Psychiatric Service in the Miguel Servet University Hospital, University of Zaragoza, Zaragoza, Spain
[6] GIPSA-Lab, Département Images et Signal, CNRS, University of Grenoble, Grenoble, France
[7] Department of Surgical Sciences, Dunedin School of Medicine, University of Otago, North Dunedin, New Zealand

***Correspondence:**
Carlos Escolano, Department of Robotics, Perception and Real Time Group, Aragon Institute of Engineering Research (I3A), University of Zaragoza, I+D+i Building, Mariano Esquillor, 50018 Zaragoza, Spain
e-mail: cescolan@unizar.es

Cognitive deficits are core symptoms of depression. This study aims to investigate whether neurofeedback (NF) training can improve working memory (WM) performance in patients with major depressive disorder (MDD). The NF group ($n = 40$) underwent eight NF sessions and was compared to a non-interventional control group ($n = 20$). The NF protocol aimed to increase the individual upper alpha power in the parieto-occipital area of the scalp. Main cognitive variable was WM, which was measured pre- and post- training along with other variables such as attention and executive functions. EEG was recorded in both eyes closed resting state and eyes open task-related activity, pre- and post- NF training, and pre- and post- the NF trials within each session. A power EEG analysis and an alpha asymmetry analysis were conducted at the sensor level. Frequency domain standardized low resolution tomography (sLORETA) was used to assess the effect at brain source level. Correlation analysis between the clinical/cognitive and EEG measurements was conducted at both the sensor and brain source level. The NF group showed increased performance as well as improved processing speed in a WM test after the training. The NF group showed pre-post enhancement in the upper alpha power after the training, better visible in task-related activity as compared to resting state. A current density increase appeared in the alpha band (8–12 Hz) for the NF group, localized in the subgenual anterior cingulate cortex (sgACC, BA 25). A positive correlation was found for the NF group between the improvement in processing speed and the increase of beta power at both the sensor and brain source level. These results show the effectiveness of this NF protocol in improving WM performance in patients with MDD.

Keywords: major depressive disorder (MDD), neurofeedback (NF), EEG, cognitive enhancement, working memory (WM), upper alpha (UA)

1. INTRODUCTION

Major depressive disorder (MDD) is a severe, chronic, mood disorder characterized by episodes of sadness, loss of interest and motivation, pessimism, and suicidal thoughts (DeRubeis et al., 2008). Depression affects each year 13–14 million citizens in the United States, with a lifetime prevalence of 16.2% (Kessler et al., 2003). MDD is estimated to become the second cause of burden of disease in 2030 (Mathers and Loncar, 2006). The current standard treatment for depression is antidepressant medication. Unfortunately with this treatment about 33% of patients fail to achieve remission (Anderson et al., 2008). Moreover, the patient compliance to the treatment can decrease due to the side effects such as sexual dysfunction, gastrointestinal problems, and weight gain (Brunoni et al., 2009). For this reason, the development of new treatments is constantly explored. In particular, recently there has been a renewed interest on neuromodulation techniques such as repetitive transcranial magnetic stimulation, transcranial direct current stimulation, and neurofeedback (DeRubeis et al., 2008; Brunoni et al., 2009).

The aim of neurofeedback (NF) is to allow the subjects to self-regulate brain activity. NF consists in measuring the brain activity and providing the subjects with real-time feedback covarying with the brain patterns of interest. Thus, the subjects may acquire a certain degree of awareness of the underlying brain processes and learn to regulate them (Congedo et al., 2004). Most of the NF protocols applied to date to depressive patients are based on EEG findings of frontal asymmetry in the alpha frequency band, with depressive patients showing left hypoactivation

(Henriques and Davidson, 1991; Davidson, 1998, 2004; Coan and Allen, 2004). These findings are interpreted as a dysfunction of the prefrontal cortex (PFC) and a predisposition toward negative emotions and behavioral withdrawal (Davidson, 2004; DeRubeis et al., 2008). While some studies support this theory (Gotlib, 1998; Lubar et al., 2003), controversial results have also been reported (Reid et al., 1998). Furthermore, some studies found asymmetry changes over recording sessions not related to the clinical symptoms of the patients (Allen et al., 2004b), thus its consideration as a marker for depression remains unclear to date (Allen and Cohen, 2010). Some NF studies have tried to reduce the alpha asymmetry in an attempt to alleviate the depressive symptoms, reporting promising results (Baehr et al., 1997, 2001; Hammond, 2000, 2005). However, to the best of our knowledge, none of the early studies were appropriately controlled. The first controlled study of this kind reported a reduction in depressive symptoms and an improvement in executive functions (Choi et al., 2011).

The present work is based on a different rationale. Our objective is to alleviate the cognitive symptoms of depression. Cognitive deficits are core symptoms of depressive disorders with a clear-cut impact on social and occupational functioning, with patients showing decreased performance in working memory (WM) and attention, among others (Austin et al., 2001; Castaneda et al., 2008; Gotlib and Joormann, 2010). Furthermore, depressive patients show biases in the processing of emotional contents in WM (Gotlib and Joormann, 2010; Levens and Gotlib, 2010). For example, Levens and Gotlib (2010) performed an emotion n-back WM task in which depressive and control individuals had to match the valence of stimuli (happy, neutral, or sad). Comparing the depressive vs. control individuals they found in the 2-back task that depressive individuals were slower to match emotional stimuli in WM (regardless of the valence), and they integrated faster and removed slower the sad stimuli from WM. Recent evidences thus suggest that cognitive deficits may not only be correlates of depression, but they may also increase the risk for depression (Gotlib and Joormann, 2010; Levens and Gotlib, 2010).

We hereby explore WM entrainment by means of a NF protocol aimed to up-regulate the alpha power in posterior locations of the scalp. A large body of research has highlighted the relation between alpha oscillations and WM performance through inhibitory mechanisms (Klimesch et al., 2007; Freunberger et al., 2011). Recent evidences suggest that the inhibition of irrelevant information (filtering efficiency to WM contents) is a key factor in WM performance (Vogel et al., 2005; McNab and Klingberg, 2007), whereas the neuronal substrates of inhibitory mechanisms is hypothetized to be related to alpha oscillations (Klimesch et al., 2007; Sauseng et al., 2009; Freunberger et al., 2011). For example, Sauseng et al. (2009) performed a visuospatial WM task in which a memory array displayed either on the right or left visual hemifield had to be retained. During the retention interval of the task, repetitive transcranial magnetic stimulation (rTMS) was delivered (at 10 Hz to increase alpha amplitude) in either contralateral or ipsilateral parietal sites to the items to be retained. Increased performance was found when rTMS was applied ipsilaterally to the items to be retained, suggesting that enhanced alpha oscillations effectively suppressed irrelevant information. In this line, some NF studies have reported higher cognitive performance in healthy users after regulating the alpha oscillations, specifically measured in WM (Escolano et al., 2011; Nan et al., 2012), visuospatial rotation (Hanslmayr et al., 2005; Zoefel et al., 2011), and procedural learning (Ros et al., 2014). The reader is directed to Gruzelier (2013) for a review on NF studies on cognitive enhancement.

To the best of our knowledge, this is the first NF study exploring the cognitive effect of WM entrainment in patients with MDD. Some preliminary results of the current study have been published in Escolano et al. (2013). The trained parameter was the power in the individual upper alpha band, since the upper part of alpha has been suggested to respond to cognitive demands (Klimesch, 1999) and is the direction followed by several alpha-based NF studies (Hanslmayr et al., 2005; Escolano et al., 2011; Zoefel et al., 2011; Nan et al., 2012).

2. MATERIALS AND METHODS

2.1. PARTICIPANTS

Seventy-four participants diagnosed with major depressive disorder (MDD) were allocated to the NF group ($n = 50$) or to the control group ($n = 24$). Participants were not randomly allocated to groups (see Section 4). Patients were recruited from different health centers in the city of Zaragoza (Spain). The inclusion criteria were age range (18–65 years), Spanish as the native language, diagnosis of MDD according to DSM-IV, and stable pharmacological/psychological treatment. The exclusion criteria were diagnosis of comorbid disorders (e.g., schizophrenia, drug addiction, dementia). The experimental design was approved by the Ethical Review Board of the regional health authority and followed the Declaration of Helsinki. All participants signed an informed consent. Five participants dropped out the study due to the inability to perform the cognitive assessments or recording sessions, four of whom belonging to the NF group. Among the remaining participants who completed the study, six subjects in the NF group and three in the control group were excluded due to excessive artifacts in the EEG. Thus, the final sample consisted of 40 participants in the NF group and 20 in the control group. Demographic and clinical variables for both groups are reported in **Table 1**. There were no significant differences between groups in any variable.

2.2. EXPERIMENTAL DESIGN

The design of the study is shown in **Figure 1**. The severity of depressive symptoms was evaluated in a semi-structured interview using the Beck Depression Inventory (BDI-II, Beck et al., 1996) and the Patient Health Questionnaire (PHQ-9, Kroenke et al., 2001). After that, both groups performed a cognitive assessment and an EEG screening at the beginning and at the end of the study (5-week time interval). Cognitive assessments lasted approximately 1 h. The NF group performed eight NF sessions over 4 weeks (two sessions per week). Each session was composed of five trials of 4 min each for a total of 20 min of training, and a pre- and post- EEG screening. For each EEG screening we recorded 3-min of eyes closed resting state activity and 3-min of eyes open task-related activity. In the latter, participants faced a computer screen showing a square that changed saturation color randomly from gray to red or blue (gradually). Participants were instructed to count the number of saturation changes from gray to red as a cognitive challenge (Zoefel et al., 2011). A power EEG analysis and an alpha asymmetry analysis were conducted at the sensor level. Frequency domain standardized low resolution tomography (sLORETA) was used to assess the effect of training at the brain source level. Finally, a correlation analysis between the clinical/cognitive and EEG measurements was conducted at both the sensor and brain source level.

2.3. COGNITIVE PERFORMANCE

Pre- and post- cognitive assessments were carried out at the beginning and at the end of the study. The main outcome variable was WM, which was measured using the Paced Auditory Serial Addition Task (PASAT, Gronwall, 1977) along with the processing speed. This test is sensitive to minimal changes in neurocognitive performance and presents high levels of internal consistency and test-retest reliability (Tombaugh, 2006). The test scores were the number of errors and elapsed time. Episodic memory, attention, and executive functions were also assessed using the following tests: (i) Rey Auditory Verbal Learning Test (RAVLT, Rey, 1964) evaluated episodic memory and the test score was the number of recognized words. (ii) Stroop Color-Word Test (STROOP, Stroop, 1992) evaluated attention and concentration. The test score was the interference, which was standardized across age groups. (iii) Trail Making Test (TMT, Reitan, 1958) evaluated executive functions and was composed of parts A and B. The scores were the elapsed time to complete each part of the test. (iv) Fluency Verbal Test (FAS, Benton and Hamsher, 1976) evaluated verbal phonetic fluency. The test score was the number of evoked words. To determine statistical significance, Two-Way repeated-measures ANOVA (rm-ANOVA) was separately conducted for each score with the between-subject factor Group (NF, Control) and the within-subject factor Time (Pre, Post). Paired samples t-tests were performed for within-group (pre vs. post) comparisons.

Table 1 | Demographic and clinical variables of the participants at study entry.

	NF group $n = 40$	Control group $n = 20$	NF vs. Control p-value
Gender (male/female)	15/25	4/16	0.24
Age, years (mean ± SD)	53.70 ± 10.87	49.50 ± 10.18	0.16
Antidepressant medication (yes/no)	37/3	18/2	1.00
Comorbidity of anxiety (yes/no)	33/7	15/5	0.51
BDI-II score (mean ± SD)	23.70 ± 13.51	22.25 ± 11.74	0.68
PHQ-9 score (mean ± SD)	13.33 ± 6.84	15.65 ± 5.96	0.21

Between-group differences were assessed by Fisher's exact test and independent samples t-tests for categorical and continuous variables, respectively.

2.4. EEG RECORDING AND NEUROFEEDBACK PROCEDURE

EEG data was recorded from 16 electrodes placed at FP1, FP2, F3, Fz, F4, C3, Cz, C4, P7, P3, Pz, P4, P8, O1, Oz, and O2 (subset of the 10/10 system), with the ground and reference electrodes on FPz and on the left earlobe, respectively. EEG was amplified and digitized using a g.tec amplifier (Guger Technologies, Graz, Austria) at a sampling rate of 256 Hz, power-line notch-filtered at 50 Hz and (0.5–60) Hz band-pass filtered. EEG recording and the NF procedure were developed using software of *Bit & Brain Technologies, SL.*

The NF training focused on the increase of the individual upper alpha (UA) power averaged over parieto-occipital locations (P3, Pz, P4, O1, and O2, referred to as feedback electrodes). EEG power was calculated through a short-term fast Fourier transform (FFT) with 1 s hamming window, 30 ms of overlapping, and zero-padded to 1024 points (0.25 Hz resolution). For each session, the pre-NF EEG screening was recorded and then used to calibrate the training for each participant and session. In this calibration step, we automatically filtered out the blinking component from the task-related activity by Independent Component Analysis (ICA), using the FastICA algorithm (Hyvarinen, 1999). Furthermore, we removed the epochs with amplitude larger than 200 μV at any electrode. The Individual Alpha Frequency (IAF) was computed for each electrode on the power spectra of the reconstructed EEG data as the frequency bin with the maximum power value in the extended (7–13 Hz) alpha range (Klimesch, 1999). Note that when no clear alpha peak was found, the IAF was computed on resting state instead. The UA band was thus

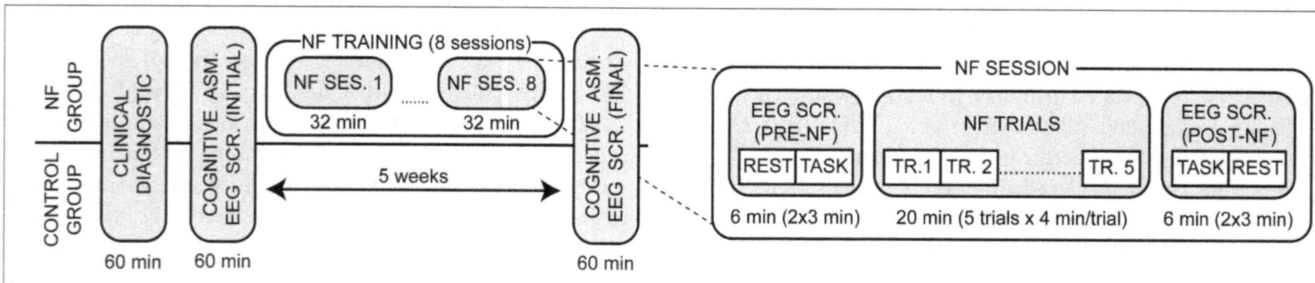

FIGURE 1 | Experimental design of the study. After an intake diagnostic both groups executed a pre- and post- cognitive assessment and EEG screening within a 5-week time interval. The NF group performed a total of eight NF sessions (two sessions per week), which were composed of a pre- and post-EEG screening (6 min each) and five training trials (4 min each). The EEG screenings included eyes closed resting state and eyes open task-related activity.

defined as the (IAF, IAF+2) Hz interval (Klimesch, 1999). Finally, the baseline was computed in task-related activity as the mean UA power averaged across the feedback electrodes, and (*5th–95th*) percentiles established the lower and upper limits, respectively. After the calibration, the participants performed the training trials. During online training, EEG data was online filtered from blinking artifacts (through the aforementioned ICA filter) and a visual feedback was then displayed every 30 ms on a computer screen in the form of a square with changing saturation colors. A linear mapping was used to convert between the UA power and the square color. Power values above the baseline were displayed in a red color scale with increasing saturation. Similarly, power values below the baseline were displayed in a blue color scale. The color scales ranged from 0% saturation (baseline in gray color) to 100% saturation in both blue and red color scales set by the lower and upper limits, respectively. No additional information was displayed during training.

Participants in the NF group were instructed to turn the square into red color with the maximum possible saturation, and to maintain it as long as possible. They were not given any mental strategy nor they were aware of the EEG trained parameter. Instead, they were encouraged to try different mental strategies guided by the feedback. To the best of our knowledge, the effect of different mental strategies in the ability to self-regulate brain activity is unclear to date, which is the focus of recent NF studies (Kober et al., 2013).

2.5. OFFLINE EEG PRE-PROCESSING

EEG data from the initial and final EEG screenings was carefully inspected for the presence of artifacts such as eye blinks, eye movements, body movements, and electrocardiogram artifacts. Initially, the extended infomax ICA (Lee et al., 1999) was applied to the task-related activity to remove the eye blinking component. Then, both resting state and task-related activity were imported into EureKa! software (Congedo, 2002) to reject the contaminated data by visual inspection. Participants with at least 30 s of artifact-free data were included in the analysis. EEG spectrum was computed following the same procedure as in the NF procedure. The EEG data of each NF session was cleaned from artifacts using a three-step automatic procedure: filtering of the blinking component by the extended infomax ICA (Lee et al., 1999), epoch rejection by a time-domain threshold ($>200\,\mu$V) at any electrode, and epoch rejection by a frequency-domain threshold. In the latter step, we computed the power values for each epoch in the bands (1–3 Hz) and (20–30 Hz), commonly affected by ocular and muscular artifacts (Delorme et al., 2007). Then, we converted the log-transformed power values to *z*-scores and removed the outliers (>2.5) at any electrode. Note that the automatic procedure was only used to compute the alpha power in parieto-occipital locations, and no significant differences were found between the two procedures in either resting state [paired samples *t*-test: $t_{(59)} = -0.77, p = 0.44$] or task-related activity [$t_{(59)} = 0.26, p = 0.79$].

2.6. POWER EEG ANALYSIS IN THE TRAINED PARAMETER

Power EEG analysis was conducted in the trained parameter: power in the individual UA band, averaged across the feedback electrodes (P3, Pz, P4, O1, O2). The pre-post enhancement was measured as the power change between the initial and final EEG screenings in resting state and task-related activity for both groups. The across- and within-session enhancement were also measured (for the NF group). Across-session enhancement was assessed by a linear trend analysis of the power values in the pre-NF screenings of all sessions and the final screening. The within-session enhancement comprised two measurements, computed in the power values averaged across the NF sessions: a power change comparison between the pre- and post- EEG screenings, and a linear trend analysis of the power values in the pre-NF task-related EEG screening and the five training trials. To determine statistical significance of pre- and post- comparisons, log-transformed power values were entered into a Two-Way rm-ANOVA with the factors Group (NF, Control) and Time (Pre, Post). Paired samples *t*-tests were performed for within-group (pre vs. post) comparisons. Trend analysis consisted in the computation of the slope of a fitted regression line for each participant, and a *t*-test to test the hypothesis of a null slope. The type I error was set at $\alpha = 0.05$.

2.7. POWER EEG ANALYSIS IN THE SENSOR X FREQUENCY DOMAIN

Power analysis was conducted for all sensors and frequencies in the (1–30 Hz) interval, separately applied for the resting state and task-related activity. The NF training effects were measured as the log-transformed power spectra comparison between the initial and final EEG screening: a between-group comparison (NF vs. control group) on the change power values, and a within-group comparison (pre vs. post) for each group. A cluster-based non-parametric randomization method (Nichols and Holmes, 2002; Maris and Oostenveld, 2007) was used, as implemented in the Fieldtrip toolbox (FC Donders Centre for Cognitive Neuroimaging, Nijmegen, The Netherlands; see http://www.ru.nl/fcdonders/fieldtrip). This method first computes the difference between two conditions by performing *t*-tests in the (sensor, frequency)-pairs. Those pairs exceeding a threshold *q* are clustered on the basis of spatial and spectral adjacency, and then cluster-level statistics are calculated as the sum of the *t*-values within every cluster. The threshold was set to ($q = 0.05$) for resting state and to ($q = 0.01$) for task-related activity. Finally, the significance probability at the cluster-level was estimated by a permutation method (Pesarin, 2001). The distribution of the cluster values was constructed under the null hypothesis by 5000 random permutations and then the observed values were tested against the $(1 - \alpha)$th percentile of the null distribution. This method controls for the type I error rate and corrects for multiple comparisons both across sensors and frequencies. The type I error at cluster-level was set to $\alpha = 0.05$.

2.8. ALPHA ASYMMETRY ANALYSIS

Initial and final scores of alpha (8–12 Hz) asymmetry were computed in resting state and task-related activity. EEG data was re-referenced to Cz and asymmetry scores were computed as the normalized power difference between homologous right- and left-side locations, (R−L)/(R+L). See Allen et al. (2004a) for a review on methodological considerations. This score indicates the relative activation of the left over right locations. Thus positive scores indicate left-lateralized activation, i.e., more power over right-side locations due to the inverse relation between alpha power and brain activation (Coan and Allen, 2004). Alpha asymmetry scores were computed in five areas of the scalp: prefrontal (FP: FP2-FP1), frontal (F: F4-F3), central (C: C4-C3), parietal (P: (P7+P3)/2-(P8+P4)/2), and occipital (O: O2-O1). Independent samples t-tests were conducted to test for between-group differences in initial scores. We applied t-tests on the initial scores (for each group and area of the scalp) to test for null asymmetry scores. Two-Way rm-ANOVA with the factors Group (NF, Control) and Time (Pre, Post) was separately conducted for each area of the scalp to test for pre-post study changes. Bonferroni correction was applied to correct for multiple areas so as to keep the FWER at $\alpha = 0.05$.

2.9. EEG ANALYSIS AT THE BRAIN SOURCE LEVEL

Frequency domain standardized low resolution tomography, sLORETA (Pascual-Marqui, 2002, 2007) was used to estimate the current density of brain sources in resting state and task-related activity. The current density changes were compared between groups (NF vs. control group) as well as within groups (pre vs. post) for each group. EEG data was re-referenced to a common average reference and Fourier cross-spectral matrices were computed for the following frequency bands: delta (1–4 Hz), theta (4.5–7 Hz), alpha (8–12 Hz), beta1 (12–15 Hz), beta2 (15–20 Hz), and beta3 (20–30 Hz). These bands were defined according to the results obtained in the clustering analysis at the sensor level (Section 2.7). After that, sLORETA estimated the current density values in 6239 voxels (5 mm^3 spatial resolution). sLORETA applies the boundary element method on the MNI-152 (Montreal Neurological Institute, Canada) template of Mazziotta et al. (2001), and the anatomical labeling is based on probabilities returned by the Daemon Atlas (Lancaster et al., 2000). Finally, current density values were log-transformed and statistical significance of each voxel was determined by a non-parametric randomization procedure using the t-max statistic to control the familywise type I error rate (FWER, Holmes et al., 1996). Following this procedure, the null distribution was estimated by 5000 random permutations under the null hypothesis of the maximum absolute t-value across all voxels. Then the absolute observed t-value for each voxel was tested against the $(1 - \alpha)$th percentile of the null distribution. Bonferroni correction was applied to correct for multiple bands so as to keep the FWER at $\alpha = 0.05$.

2.10. CORRELATION ANALYSIS: EEG vs. BEHAVIORAL VARIABLES

Spearman correlation was employed to test for a correlation in the initial scores between the clinical/cognitive and EEG variables, as well as in the change scores between the cognitive and EEG variables (clinical variables were not measured after NF training). A total of two clinical variables (Section 2.2) and seven cognitive variables (Section 2.3) were tested. The EEG variables were assessed in resting state and task-related activity and can be divided into two groups: power variables at the sensor level, and current density variables at the brain source level. In both cases, the analysis was conducted in the aforementioned frequency bands (delta, theta, alpha, beta1, beta2, beta3). In the case of the sensor level, power values in each band were averaged across five areas: prefrontal (FP: FP1, FP2), frontal (F: F3, Fz, F4), central (C: C3, Cz, C4), parietal (P: P7, P3, Pz, P4, P8), and occipital (O: O1, Oz, O2). In the case of the brain source level, a randomization procedure (similar to the one used in previous Section 2.9) was used to control the FWER (Holmes et al., 1996). Five-thousand random permutations were performed to construct a distribution of the maximum of the absolute r-value across all voxels under the null hypothesis. In both cases the Bonferroni correction was applied to keep the FWER at $\alpha = 0.05$.

3. RESULTS

3.1. COGNITIVE PERFORMANCE

Table 2 summarizes the scores in the cognitive assessments. A significant *Group* × *Time* ANOVA interaction appeared in the PASAT test [# errors: $F_{(1, 46)} = 5.42, p = 0.024$; time: $F_{(1, 46)} = 4.97, p = 0.031$], showing an improvement in WM performance and processing speed for the NF group only [# errors: $t_{(30)} = -5.21, p < 0.001$; time: $t_{(30)} = -4.91, p < 0.001$]. Cohen's d effect size (Cohen, 1988) revealed a medium-large effect for both the number of errors ($d = 0.703$) and elapsed time ($d = 0.673$). Note that 9 participants in the NF group did not complete the PASAT test in the initial assessment due to excessive cognitive effort, four of whom completed the final assessment. Three participants in the control group did not complete the PASAT test in both initial and final assessments. No significant ANOVA interaction appeared in the other variables. Regarding the within-group (pre vs. post) changes, the number of recognized words increased in the RAVLT test for the NF group [$t_{(39)} = 3.28, p < 0.005$]. Interference score in the STROOP test was not significantly modified for any group. Both parts of the TMT test improved for the NF group [part A: $t_{(37)} = -1.95, p = 0.059$; part B: $t_{(37)} = -2.85, p < 0.01$]. The NF group also improved the number of evoked words in the FAS test [$t_{(38)} = 2.61, p < 0.05$]. No significant changes were found for the control group.

3.2. POWER EEG ANALYSIS IN THE TRAINED PARAMETER

The analysis of the pre-post enhancement in the trained parameter (power in the individual UA band averaged across the feedback electrodes: P3, Pz, P4, O1, O2) revealed a no significant *Group* × *Time* ANOVA interaction for the resting state activity. However, a statistical trend between the pre and post measurements was found in the NF group [$t_{(39)} = -1.72, p = 0.093$], with an average increase of 22%. Regarding the task-related activity, a significant *Group* × *Time* interaction appeared [$F_{(1, 58)} = 14.88; p < 0.001$]. *Post-hoc* t-tests showed a significant pre vs. post difference for the NF group only [$t_{(39)} = -5.44, p < 0.001$], with an average increase of 56%. No significant change was found for the control group in either resting state or task-related activity. Note that groups did not differ statistically in initial IAF. Mean ± SD IAF measured in resting state activity was 9.81 ± 0.17 Hz for the NF group and 9.79 ± 0.25 Hz for the control group [t-test for independent samples, $t_{(58)} = 0.075, p = 0.94$]; in task-related activity it was 9.71 ± 0.19 Hz for the NF group and 9.64 ± 0.24 Hz for the control group [$t_{(58)} = 0.21, p = 0.83$]. Furthermore, IAF did not change significantly pre-post the study for either group. The across- and within- session enhancement was measured for the NF group (see **Figure 2**). Trend analysis

Table 2 | Cognitive performance at the beginning and at the end of the study for each group.

Test	NF			Control			Paired samples *t*-test		ANOVA
scores	Pre mean (s.e.m.)	Post mean (s.e.m.)	Change mean (s.e.m.)	Pre mean (s.e.m.)	Post mean (s.e.m.)	Change mean (s.e.m.)	NF *p*-value	Control *p*-value	*G* × *T* *p*-value
PASAT									
# errors	13.45 (1.09)	10.13 (1.08)	−3.32 (0.64)	11.59 (2.22)	11.18 (2.21)	−0.41 (1.23)	**<0.001**	0.742	**0.024**
time (s)	253.23 (13.25)	213.68 (12.13)	−39.55 (8.05)	249.76 (20.40)	246.06 (23.77)	−3.71 (16.08)	**<0.001**	0.821	**0.031**
RAVLT									
# recognized words	12.25 (0.43)	13.15 (0.30)	0.90 (0.27)	11.55 (0.65)	11.90 (0.50)	0.35 (0.65)	**0.002**	0.597	0.363
STROOP									
interference	51.64 (1.23)	53.38 (1.00)	1.74 (1.20)	54.60 (1.80)	54.80 (1.87)	0.20 (1.52)	0.154	0.897	0.443
TMT									
part A, time (s)	44.66 (3.03)	38.29 (3.80)	−6.37 (3.26)	41.35 (3.02)	37.95 (2.81)	−3.40 (2.43)	0.059	0.178	0.543
part B, time (s)	101.50 (14.57)	84.87 (11.91)	−16.63 (5.83)	84.90 (11.60)	73.40 (13.51)	−11.50 (10.55)	**0.007**	0.289	0.645
FAS									
# evoked words	43.74 (1.87)	46.85 (1.90)	3.10 (1.19)	38.70 (2.68)	39.80 (2.74)	1.10 (1.54)	**0.013**	0.482	0.319

Mean ± s.e.m. scores in pre and post cognitive assessments are shown, as well as the change scores (post-pre). The p-values of the paired samples t-tests are shown for each group (pre vs. post changes), as well as the p-values of the Group × Time interaction in the rm-ANOVAs. Significant effects are marked bold (p < 0.05), statistical trends are underlined (p < 0.1).

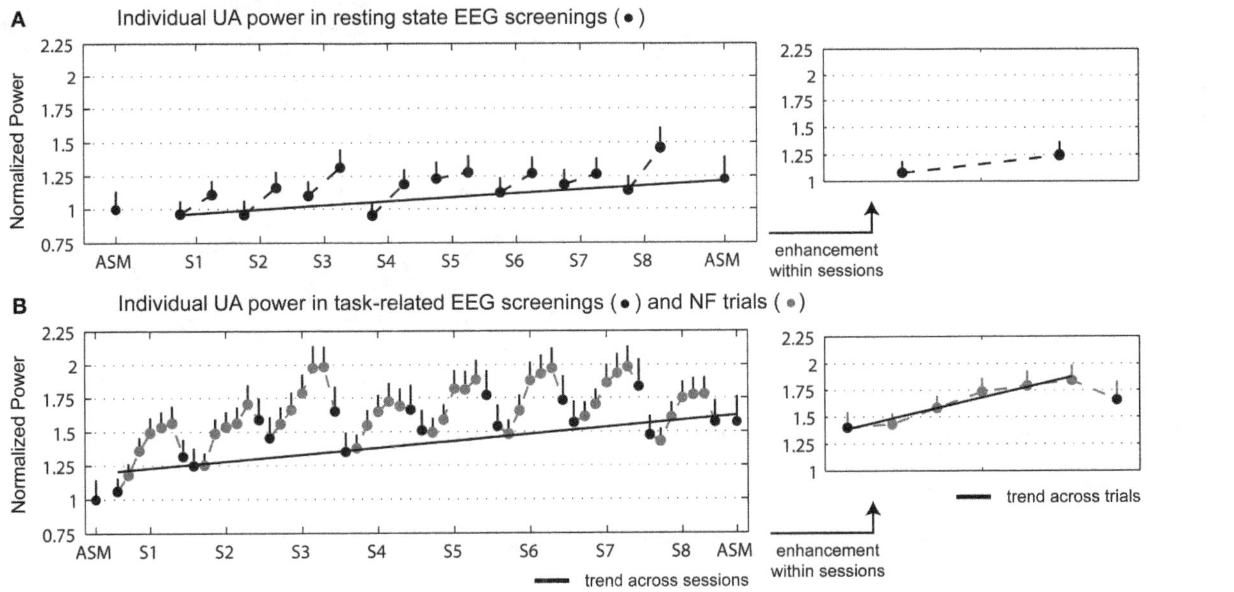

FIGURE 2 | Individual UA power (mean + s.e.m.) averaged across the feedback electrodes (P3, Pz, P4, O1, O2) for the NF group in the initial and final EEG screenings, and during the NF sessions. **(A)** Displays the resting state EEG screenings, and **(B)** the task-related EEG screenings and NF trials. Data was normalized to the power in the initial screening. Right figures display the power enhancement within sessions, in which in the EEG data of the NF sessions was averaged across sessions. Dark and light gray dots depict EEG screenings and NF trials, respectively, and gray line the relevant trend measurements.

revealed a significant UA power increase across the NF sessions in both resting state [$t_{(39)} = 2.56, p = 0.014$] and task-related activity [$t_{(39)} = 4.04, p < 0.001$]. Regarding the within-session enhancement, a significant power increase between the pre- and post- NF screenings appeared in resting state [$t_{(39)} = -3.10$, $p < 0.005$], with an average increase of 15.1%; as well as in task-related activity [$t_{(39)} = -5.72$, $p < 0.001$], with an average increase of 16.1%. Trend analysis revealed a significant power increase across the NF trials [$t_{(39)} = 7.81$, $p < 0.001$].

3.3. POWER EEG ANALYSIS IN THE SENSOR X FREQUENCY DOMAIN

We have adjusted the frequency bands according to the results obtained in this analysis as follows: delta (1–4 Hz), theta

(4.5–7 Hz), alpha (8–12 Hz), beta1 (12–15 Hz), beta2 (15–20 Hz), and beta3 (20–30 Hz). Regarding the power changes in the between-group (NF vs. control) comparison, a cluster appeared in the (5–9 Hz) frequency range for the resting state activity ($p = 0.008$), indicating a power increase for the NF group in theta, apparent in frontal and central locations, and lower part of alpha (8–10 Hz), in frontal, central and parietal locations. A cluster appeared in task-related activity covering the (5.5–12 Hz) range ($p < 0.0001$), indicating a power increase for the NF group in theta, apparent in frontal locations, and alpha, in frontal, central and parietal locations. **Figure 3** displays sensor x frequency maps of the power changes (pre vs. post NF training) for the NF group. Note that no significant clusters were found pre vs. post for the control group. Resting state activity showed a cluster in the (7–9.5 Hz) range at a trend level ($p = 0.073$), indicating a power increase in lower alpha in all the scalp areas. A cluster in the (4.5–20 Hz) range appeared for the task-related activity ($p < 0.0001$), indicating a power increase in theta, apparent in frontal locations, alpha and beta1 in all the scalp areas, and beta2, apparent in frontal, central, and parietal locations.

3.4. ALPHA ASYMMETRY ANALYSIS

No significant differences were found between groups in the initial asymmetry scores. We applied t-tests on the initial scores (for each area of the scalp) to test for null asymmetry scores within each group. No significant results appeared after strict control of the type I error (see Section 4). Regarding the pre-post changes in asymmetry scores, no significant *Group* × *Time* ANOVA interaction was found in any area of the scalp, as well as no significant pre vs. post differences within each group.

3.5. EEG ANALYSIS AT THE BRAIN SOURCE LEVEL

A significant effect was found for the NF group only (pre vs. post NF training) in task-related activity, measured in the alpha band (8–12 Hz), see **Figure 4**. Forty-two voxels showed a current density increase (threshold $t = 3.37$, $\alpha = 0.05$). The current density

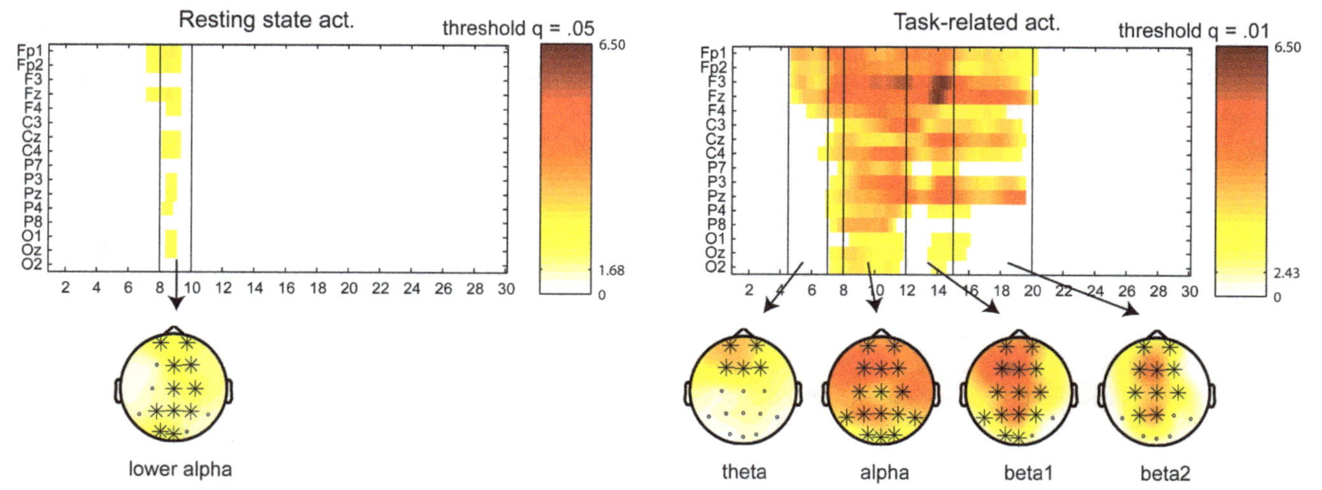

FIGURE 3 | Sensor x frequency maps displaying the significant clusters (in the power spectra) for the NF group in the within-group (pre vs. post) comparison. Left figure displays the resting state activity, and right figure the task-related activity. Significant clusters are shown at a given q threshold. X axis shows the frequency bins in the (1–30 Hz) frequency range, whereas Y axis shows the sensor locations. Topoplots are displayed in the frequency bands with power changes above the q threshold (in significant clusters), and the involved sensors are marked with a cross. Color scale represent t-values, indicating a power increase after the NF training.

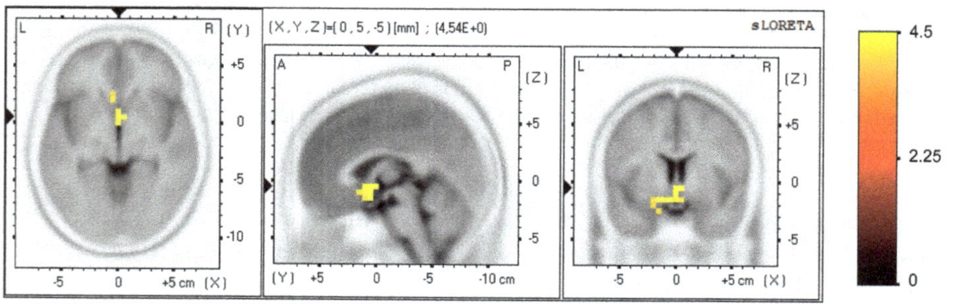

FIGURE 4 | Effect of the NF training at brain source level for the NF group. Voxels showing a significant current density increase (pre vs. post NF training) are displayed, measured in alpha band (8–12 Hz) in task-related activity. Axial (left), sagittal (middle), and coronal (right) sections of sLORETA are displayed through the voxel with maximal t-value. Color scale represent t-values, indicating a current density increase after NF training.

increase was localized in the subgenual anterior cingulate cortex, sgACC (BA 25; XYZ[1] = 0, 5, −5; $t = 4.54$), subcallosal gyrus (BA 34; XYZ = −10, 5, −15; $t = 4.35$), parahippocampal gyrus (BA 28; XYZ = −15, −5, −15; $t = 4.13$), anterior cingulate cortex, ACC (BA 32; XYZ = −5, 20, −10; $t = 4.11$), and rectal gyrus (BA 11; XYZ = −5, 15, −20; $t = 4.02$).

3.6. CORRELATION ANALYSIS: EEG vs. BEHAVIORAL VARIABLES

No significant correlation was found between the clinical and EEG variables at study entry. Significant correlations were found between the elapsed time variable of the PASAT test and EEG variables at both the sensor and brain source level for the NF group only, measured in task-related activity. Regarding the sensor level, a positive correlation appeared in the initial scores between the beta2 (15–20 Hz) power in parietal area (P: P7, P3, Pz, P4, P8) and the elapsed time [$r_{(29)} = 0.64, p = 0.029$], i.e., higher beta2 power in parietal locations correlated with slower processing speed. The analysis of the pre vs. post change scores revealed negative correlations between the power increase in each beta sub-band in prefrontal area (FP: FP1, FP2) and the increment in elapsed time: beta1 [12–15 Hz, $r_{(29)} = -0.68, p = 0.007$], beta2 [15–20 Hz, $r_{(29)} = -0.65, p = 0.019$)], and beta3 [20–30 Hz, $r_{(29)} = -0.79, p < 0.0001$]. Thus, the beta enhancement in prefrontal locations correlated with the improvement in processing speed. Regarding the brain source level, the analysis of the pre vs. post change scores revealed a negative correlation between the current density increase measured in the beta3 band (20–30 Hz) and the increment in elapsed time, see **Figure 5**. One hundred and thirty-three voxels were significant ($\alpha = 0.05$), which were localized in the ACC (BA 32; XYZ = −5, 40, −10; $r = -0.761$), medial frontal gyrus (BA 11; XYZ = −5, 35, −15; $r = -0.757$), medial frontal gyrus (BA 10; XYZ = −10, 40, −10; $r = -0.755$), pregenual ACC, pgACC (BA 24; XYZ = −5, 30, −5; $r = -0.747$), and subgenual ACC, sgACC (BA 25; XYZ = −5, 25, −20; $r = -0.741$). Thus, the current density increase in the aforementioned regions correlated with the improvement in processing speed. No significant correlations were found for the control group.

[1]MNI (Montreal Neurological Institute, Canada) coordinates are used throughout this paper.

4. DISCUSSION

The objective of the current work was to explore whether the cognitive symptoms of patients with major depressive disorder (MDD) can be alleviated by EEG-based NF training. Depression is associated with cognitive deficits such as decreased working memory (WM) and attention, among others, which have a clear-cut impact on social and occupational functioning (Austin et al., 2001; Castaneda et al., 2008; Gotlib and Joormann, 2010). We hereby explored the application of a NF protocol based on upper alpha up-regulation to improve WM performance in patients with MDD. The rationale beyond this protocol consists in evidences showing the relation between alpha oscillations and WM performance through inhibitory mechanisms (Klimesch et al., 2007; Freunberger et al., 2011). This NF protocol has obtained promising results in healthy users (Escolano et al., 2011; Nan et al., 2012). Recent evidences suggest that the WM deficits in depression (biases toward negative emotions) may not only be correlates of depression but also increase the vulnerability and recurrence to depression (Gotlib and Joormann, 2010; Levens and Gotlib, 2010). Thus this NF protocol has potential to improve depressive symptoms.

4.1. COGNITIVE PERFORMANCE

WM performance and processing speed (PASAT test) were improved for the NF group in comparison with the control group, showing medium-large effect sizes. While positive findings had been already reported in healthy users (Escolano et al., 2011; Nan et al., 2012) this paper supports the effectiveness of such a protocol in improving WM performance in patients with MDD. Episodic memory, executive functions, and verbal fluency were also improved for the NF group only as revealed by the RAVLT, TMT, and FAS tests. However the improvement in these cognitive functions was not significantly superior to the improvement observed in the control group. These results suggest that the stronger effect of the NF training is specifically found in WM performance and processing speed, whereas the improvement in the

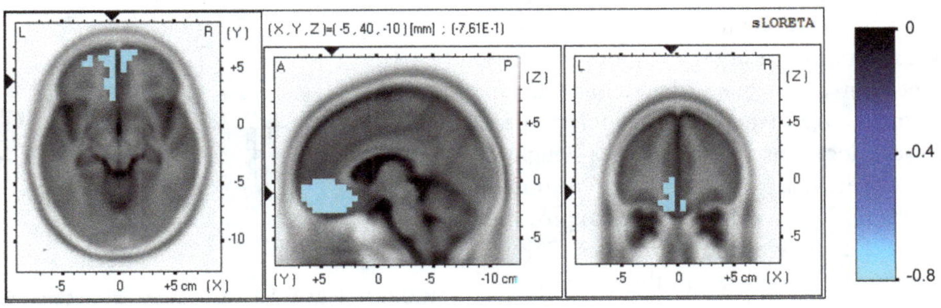

FIGURE 5 | Correlation analysis for the NF group at the brain source level between the pre vs. post increase in the elapsed time variable of the PASAT test and the increase in current density, measured in beta3 band (20–30 Hz) in task-related activity. Axial (left), sagittal (middle), and coronal (right) sections of sLORETA are displayed through the voxel with maximal absolute r-value. Color scale represent r-values, with negative values indicating a positive correlation between the current density increase and the improvement in processing speed (note the inverse relation between the elapsed time in the PASAT test and processing speed).

latter cognitive functions is marginal and may be explained by an enhancement of cognitive processing as a whole.

4.2. EEG ANALYSIS

A pre-post enhancement was found in the trained parameter: power in the individual upper alpha band averaged across parieto-occipital locations. The NF group showed an average increase of 56% in task-related activity after the NF training. Resting state activity was also increased for the NF group, with an average increase of 22%, but failed to reach statistical significance in comparison to the control group. No significant changes were found for the control group. In addition to that, upper alpha power in both resting state and task-related activity showed an increase with the number of sessions, as well as an increase (pre vs. post) within each session. Bruder et al. (2008) showed alpha power differences between responders and non-responders to selective serotonin reuptake inhibitor (SSRI), with responders showing greater alpha power in resting state at study entry, specifically measured at occipital locations. While these findings show the potential utility of the present NF protocol in improving the responsiveness to antidepressant medication, it should be confirmed in future studies.

Some NF studies assess the effects of the training not only in the trained parameter, but typically in a small number of pre-determined frequency bands (Escolano et al., 2011; Zoefel et al., 2011; Nan et al., 2012). Here we extended that analysis to assess the power changes in all sensors in the (1–30 Hz) frequency range by a clustering analysis, obtaining sensor x frequency maps of the power changes. We believe that the present analysis can offer a clearer insight of the electrophysiological effects. This analysis was separately applied for the two recording conditions: resting state and task-related activity. Since stronger effects were found in task-related activity in comparison to resting state, we adapted the q threshold to each recording condition to get clearer sensor x frequency maps. Please note that q threshold does not determine the type I error at cluster-level, which was set to ($\alpha = 0.05$) for both conditions. Significant clusters were found for the NF group only, showing a power increase after the NF training. The strongest effect in resting state activity appeared in the lower part of alpha (8–10 Hz). Task-related activity showed stronger effects in the (4.5–20 Hz) range, covering theta, alpha, and the lower part of beta. These effects were apparent in anterior, central, and posterior locations. Our results show the common finding that the effects of the NF training on the spectral power are not spatially or spectrally restricted to the trained locations and frequency bands, instead the training engenders profound changes of the homeostatic properties of the brain involving several locations and frequencies (Hughes and John, 1999). The strong effect in task-related activity illustrates the importance of recording EEG in several conditions to provide additional information of the underlying brain processes. This is in contrast to the common practice to study only the resting state, either eyes closed or eyes open.

Alpha asymmetry scores did not differ between groups at study entry and it did not change pre-post the study for any group. Note that this study can-not assess the commonly found frontal asymmetry in depression since it involves the comparison with a control group of non-depressive participants (Davidson, 2004). We investigated the initial alpha asymmetry scores for null scores, measured in five areas of the scalp (prefrontal, frontal, central, parietal, and occipital). Strong asymmetry scores were found although they failed to reach statistical significance after strict control of the type I error (Bonferroni correction). Here we summarize the significant results when not correcting for the multiple areas (see **Figure 6**). Significant scores were found in posterior areas (parietal and occipital). Left-lateralized activation (more alpha power over right locations) was found in resting state in the parietal area at a trend level for both the NF group [$t_{(39)} = 1.76, p = 0.086$] and the control group [$t_{(19)} = 1.86, p = 0.077$]. These results are in line with previous studies (Kemp et al., 2010). Interestingly, the opposite effect was found in task-related activity. Right-lateralized activation (more alpha power over left locations) was found in task-related activity in the occipital area at a trend level for the NF group [$t_{(39)} = -1.98, p = 0.054$], significant for the control group [$t_{(19)} = -2.71, p = 0.014$]. Please note that EEG data was recorded using a single earlobe reference, but re-referenced offline to Cz. The most common approach to measure brain asymmetry to date is the use of computer-averaged ears/mastoids reference, or Cz reference (Davidson, 1998; Coan and Allen, 2004; Allen and Cohen, 2010). Although there is no agreement about a preferred montage, reference placement might be a critical issue (Hagemann et al., 2001; Allen et al., 2004b; Davidson, 2004), with unilateral references being discouraged. Thus, the alpha asymmetry effects herein reported should be taken with caution and confirmed in future studies using one of the aforementioned recording approaches.

The analysis at the brain source level (using sLORETA) revealed significant changes in current density after the NF training for the NF group only. The stronger effect was found in task-related activity for the alpha band (8–12 Hz), localized in the subgenual ACC (sgACC, BA 25) extending to the entorhinal cortex (BAs 28, 34), ventromedial prefrontal cortex (BA 32) and orbitofrontal cortex (BA 11). Notice that we are controlling for the familywise type I error rate using a conservative method for correcting also for the multiple frequency bands (t-max permutation tests were further corrected using a Bonferroni correction for the multiple bands). Strong effects were also found

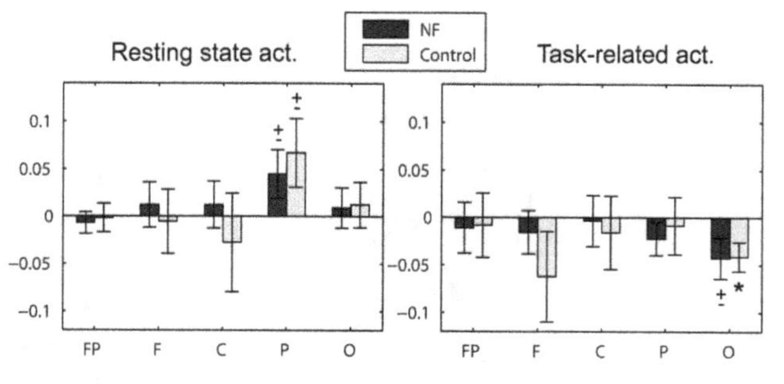

FIGURE 6 | Initial alpha asymmetry scores measured in prefrontal (FP: FP2–FP1), frontal (F: F4–F3), central (C: C4–C3), parietal (P: (P7+P3)/2–(P8+P4)/2), and occipital (O: O2–O1) areas of the scalp. Positive asymmetry scores denote left over right activation, i.e., more alpha power in right hemisphere locations. * significant effect ($p < 0.05$), ± statistical trend ($p < 0.1$). Note that statistical results are not corrected for the multiple areas.

in other brain structures although they failed to reach statistical significance after such a strict control of the type I error. Here we summarize the significant results when not correcting for the multiple frequency bands, which appeared for the NF group only. Regarding the resting state activity, a current density increase appeared in the pregenual ACC, pgACC (BA 24; XYZ $= -5, 35, 10$; $t = 3.25$) measured in alpha band. Regarding the task-related activity, a current density increase appeared in the sgACC (BA 25; XYZ $= 0, 5, -5$; $t = 3.03$) measured in delta (1–4 Hz), in the pgACC (BA 24; XYZ $= -5, 30, 0$; $t = 3.01$) in theta (4.5–7 Hz), and in the pgACC (BA 24; XYZ $= -5, 25, 15$; $t = 3.27$) in beta1 (12–15 Hz).

4.3. CORRELATION ANALYSIS: EEG vs. BEHAVIORAL VARIABLES

A strong correlation was found between the processing speed (elapsed time variable in the PASAT test) and the power in task-related activity measured in the beta frequency band. The power EEG analysis revealed that higher power in beta2 band (15–20 Hz) in parietal locations positively correlated with slower processing speed at study entry. We also found that the power increase in beta band (specifically in each one of the three beta sub-bands analyzed, ranging from 12 to 30 Hz) in prefrontal locations positively correlated with the improvement in processing speed (pre vs. post NF training). These results suggest that beta band is related to processing speed in different ways according to the area of the scalp involved. Furthermore, a strong correlation was found at the brain source level: the increase in current density measured in beta3 band (20–30 Hz) positively correlated with the improvement in processing speed (pre vs. post NF training). This correlation was localized in the pgACC (BA 24) and sgACC (BA 25) extending to the ventromedial prefrontal cortex (BA 32) and further into the orbitofrontal cortex (BA 11) and frontopolar cortex (BA 10).

Beta band activity has been traditionally linked to somatosensory and motor functions but its functional role is not well understood to date (see Engel and Fries, 2010, for a review). Regarding its perceptual-cognitive role, it has been recently associated with the active continuation of the current cognitive set in tasks involving a strong top-down component (Engel and Fries, 2010). According to this theory, the brain makes predictions in beta oscillations about what it will encounter in the internal and external environment, and updates this by measuring prediction errors, which are encoded by gamma oscillations (Arnal and Giraud, 2012). A large body of research has highlighted the relation of the ACC in error monitoring and prediction of errors (Rushworth and Behrens, 2008; Holroyd et al., 2009). The improvement in processing speed after NF training may be thus explained by this relation.

4.4. THE INVOLVEMENT OF THE ANTERIOR CINGULATE CORTEX

The ACC is known to be linked to cognitive and emotional processes (Bush et al., 2000). Based on cytoarchitecture, lesion, and electrophysiological studies the ACC has been divided into two major functional sub-divisions: a cognitive and an affective sub-divisions (Bush et al., 2000). The cognitive division is localized in the dorsal ACC (areas 24′, 32′), and the affective one is localized in the rostral-ventral ACC (rostral areas 24 and 32, and ventral areas 25 and 33). Functional differences in the ACC between depressive and non-depressive subjects have been repeatedly reported (Mayberg, 1997; Pizzagalli et al., 2001; Davidson et al., 2002). On one hand, decreased activation has been reported in the dorsal ACC (dorsal region of area 32; areas 24′, 32′). On the other hand, increased pre-treatment activation has been found in responders (vs. non-responders) to antidepressant medication in the rostral and ventral ACC (including pregenual areas 24 and 32), and it has been suggested as a predictor of treatment response (Mayberg et al., 1999; Pizzagalli et al., 2001). Pizzagalli et al. (2001) compared depressive participants showing better response to nortriptyline treatment to responders showing worse response. Participants showing a better response had higher pre-treatment theta (6.5–8 Hz) activity localized in the rostral ACC (BA 24, 32), estimated using sLORETA. In this line, the current study showed a current density increase in the rostral ACC (BA 24; XYZ $= -5, 30, 0$; $t = 3.01$) measured in the theta band (4.5–7 Hz), suggesting that the present NF protocol may increase the response to antidepressant medication. Regarding the correlation between the cognitive and EEG variables, the pregenual ACC (BA 24) and subgenual ACC (BA 25) were positively correlated with the improvement in processing speed. Interestingly, the subgenual ACC has not been traditionally linked to cognitive processing. However, recent studies demonstrate that there is an overlap of autonomic, sensorimotor, affective, and cognitive processing in the midcingulate gyrus (Beissner et al., 2013) suggesting that the functional-anatomical parcellation of the cingulate gyrus is not as simple as has been assumed. The present study suggests that the subgenual ACC, apart from its well-known involvement in autonomic (Beissner et al., 2013) and emotional (Mayberg et al., 1999; Bush et al., 2000) regulation, it also is implicated in cognitive processing. Thus analogous to the midcingulate gyrus also the subgenual ACC may be involved in multiple overlapping functions.

4.5. LIMITATIONS

Due to the novelty and the exploratory character of the study, the control group designed in the present study was not optimal. On one hand, the number of subjects in the NF and control group was not balanced. We decided to use an allocation ratio 2:1 between the NF and control group. On the other hand, participants were not randomly assigned to the experimental condition nor they were blinded with respect to the experimental condition. Nonetheless, the control group used in the present study can account for practice effects in the cognitive assessments and for electrophysiological changes before and after the study. Regarding the demographic characteristics, around 90% of the participants of the study followed a stable pharmacological antidepressant treatment during the study, 75% of whom consisted either on selective serotonin reuptake inhibitors (SSRI), benzodiazepines, or serotonin-norepinephrine reuptake inhibitors (SNRI). Also, 80% of the participants presented comorbidity with anxiety. Further research is needed to elucidate to what extent the obtained results can be translated to a drug-free population or to a population without anxiety symptoms. The averaged severity of depression was "moderate" for both the NF and control group according to the BDI-II. However, the averaged PHQ-9 scores were slightly lower for the NF group ("moderate") than for the control group ("moderately severe"). Nonetheless, there were no significant differences between groups in severity of depression as measured by either BDI-II or PHQ-9. The current study estimated the effects at brain source level using sLORETA (MNI-152 template). The spatial resolution and precision of sLORETA method could be improved by computing individual head models based on magnetic resonance imaging (MRI). A comparison of the cognitive performance with healthy subjects would have been an interesting analysis to estimate the significance of the observed effects. This analysis should be taken into account for future studies. Finally, although we have stated that the present NF protocol has the potential to improve depressive symptoms, such hypothesis can-not be corroborated in the present study since clinical variables were not assessed after NF training. Due to the positive cognitive effects, the present NF protocol should be evaluated in future studies using stricter control conditions such as active control conditions (e.g., psychotherapy) or sham feedback. However, a sham feedback control condition may lead to ethical concerns when effective standard treatments are available (La Vaque and Rossiter, 2001).

ACKNOWLEDGMENTS

This research has been partially supported by Spanish Ministry of Science projects HYPER-CSD2009-00067 and DPI2009-14732-C02-01, DGA-FSE, grupo T04. Author Marco Congedo was partly supported by the European project ERC-2012-AdG-320684-CHESS.

REFERENCES

Allen, J. J., Coan, J. A., and Nazarian, M. (2004a). Issues and assumptions on the road from raw signals to metrics of frontal EEG asymmetry in emotion. *Biol. Psychol.* 67, 183–218. doi: 10.1016/j.biopsycho.2004.03.007

Allen, J. J., Urry, H. L., Hitt, S. K., and Coan, J. A. (2004b). The stability of resting frontal electroencephalographic asymmetry in depression. *Psychophysiology* 41, 269–280. doi: 10.1111/j.1469-8986.2003.00149.x

Allen, J. J., and Cohen, M. X. (2010). Deconstructing the resting state: exploring the temporal dynamics of frontal alpha asymmetry as an endophenotype for depression. *Front. Hum. Neurosci.* 4:232. doi: 10.3389/fnhum.2010.00232

Anderson, I. M., Ferrier, I. N., Baldwin, R. C., Cowen, P. J., Howard, L., Lewis, G., et al. (2008). Evidence-based guidelines for treating depressive disorders with antidepressants: a revision of the 2000 British Association for Psychopharmacology guidelines. *J. Psychopharmacol.* 22, 343–396. doi: 10.1177/0269881107088441

Arnal, L. H., and Giraud, A. L. (2012). Cortical oscillations and sensory predictions. *Trends Cogn. Sci.* 16, 390–398. doi: 10.1016/j.tics.2012.05.003

Austin, M. P., Mitchell, P., and Goodwin, G. M. (2001). Cognitive deficits in depression possible implications for functional neuropathology. *Br. J. Psychiatry* 178, 200–206. doi: 10.1192/bjp.178.3.200

Baehr, E., Rosenfeld, J. P., and Baehr, R. (1997). The clinical use of an alpha asymmetry protocol in the neurofeedback treatment of depression. *J. Neurother.* 2, 10–23. doi: 10.1300/J184v02n03_02

Baehr, E., Rosenfeld, J. P., and Baehr, R. (2001). Clinical use of an alpha asymmetry neurofeedback protocol in the treatment of mood disorders: follow-up study one to five years post therapy. *J. Neurother.* 4, 11–18. doi: 10.1300/J184v04n04_03

Beck, A. T., Steer, R. A., and Brown, G. K. (1996). *Manual for the Beck Depression Inventory-II.* San Antonio, TX: Psychological Corporation.

Beissner, F., Meissner, K., Bär, K. J., and Napadow, V. (2013). The autonomic brain: an activation likelihood estimation meta-analysis for central processing of autonomic function. *J. Neurosci.* 33, 10503–10511. doi: 10.1523/JNEUROSCI.1103-13.2013

Benton, A. L., and Hamsher, K. (1976). *Multilingual Aphasia Examination.* Iowa City: University of Iowa.

Bruder, G. E., Sedoruk, J. P., Stewart, J. W., McGrath, P. J., Quitkin, F. M., and Tenke, C. E. (2008). Electroencephalographic alpha measures predict therapeutic response to a selective serotonin reuptake inhibitor antidepressant: pre-and post-treatment findings. *Biol. Psychiatry* 63, 1171–1177. doi: 10.1016/j.biopsych.2007.10.009

Brunoni, A. R., Fraguas, R. Jr., and Fregni, F. (2009). Pharmacological and combined interventions for the acute depressive episode: focus on efficacy and tolerability. *Ther. Clin. Risk Manage.* 5, 897. doi: 10.2147/TCRM.S5751

Bush, G., Luu, P., and Posner, M. I. (2000). Cognitive and emotional influences in anterior cingulate cortex. *Trends Cogn. Sci.* 4, 215–222. doi: 10.1016/S1364-6613(00)01483-2

Castaneda, A. E., Tuulio-Henriksson, A., Marttunen, M., Suvisaari, J., and Lönnqvist, J. (2008). A review on cognitive impairments in depressive and anxiety disorders with a focus on young adults. *J. Affect. Disord.* 106, 1–27. doi: 10.1016/j.jad.2007.06.006

Choi, S. W., Chi, S. E., Chung, S. Y., Kim, J. W., Ahn, C. Y., and Kim, H. T. (2011). Is alpha wave neurofeedback effective with randomized clinical trials in depression? A pilot study. *Neuropsychobiology* 63, 43–51. doi: 10.1159/000322290

Coan, J. A., and Allen, J. J. (2004). Frontal EEG asymmetry as a moderator and mediator of emotion. *Biol. Psychol.* 67, 7–50. doi: 10.1016/j.biopsycho.2004.03.002

Cohen, J. (1988). *Statistical Power Analysis for the Behavioral Sciences.* Hillsdale, NJ: Erlbaum.

Congedo, M. (2002). *Eureka!(Version 3.0)[Computer Software].* Knoxville, TN: NovaTech EEG Inc. Available online at: www.NovaTechEEG

Congedo, M., Lubar, J. F., and Joffe, D. (2004). Low-resolution electromagnetic tomography neurofeedback. *IEEE Trans. Neural Syst. Rehabil. Eng.* 12, 387–397. doi: 10.1109/TNSRE.2004.840492

Davidson, R. J. (1998). Anterior electrophysiological asymmetries, emotion, and depression: conceptual and methodological conundrums. *Psychophysiology* 35, 607–614. doi: 10.1017/S0048577298000134

Davidson, R. J. (2004). What does the prefrontal cortex do in affect: perspectives on frontal EEG asymmetry research. *Biol. Psychol.* 67, 219–234. doi: 10.1016/j.biopsycho.2004.03.008

Davidson, R. J., Pizzagalli, D., Nitschke, J. B., and Putnam, K. (2002). Depression: perspectives from affective neuroscience. *Annu. Rev. Psychol.* 53, 545–574. doi: 10.1146/annurev.psych.53.100901.135148

Delorme, A., Sejnowski, T., and Makeig, S. (2007). Enhanced detection of artifacts in EEG data using higher-order statistics and independent component analysis. *Neuroimage* 34, 1443–1449. doi: 10.1016/j.neuroimage.2006.11.004

DeRubeis, R. J., Siegle, G. J., and Hollon, S. D. (2008). Cognitive therapy versus medication for depression: treatment outcomes and neural mechanisms. *Nat. Rev. Neurosci.* 9, 788–796. doi: 10.1038/nrn2345

Engel, A. K., and Fries, P. (2010). Beta-band oscillations-signalling the status quo? *Curr. Opin. Neurobiol.* 20, 156–165. doi: 10.1016/j.conb.2010.02.015

Escolano, C., Aguilar, M., and Minguez, J. (2011). "EEG-based upper alpha neurofeedback training improves working memory performance," in *International Conference of the IEEE Engineering in Medicine and Biology Society (EMBC)*, (Boston, MA), 2327–2330.

Escolano, C., Navarro-Gil, M., Garcia-Campayo, J., and Minguez, J. (2013). "EEG-based Upper-Alpha neurofeedback for cognitive enhancement in major depressive disorder: a preliminary, uncontrolled study," in *International Conference of the IEEE Engineering in Medicine and Biology Society (EMBC)*, (Osaka), 6293–6296.

Freunberger, R., Werkle-Bergner, M., Griesmayr, B., Lindenberger, U., and Klimesch, W. (2011). Brain oscillatory correlates of working memory constraints. *Brain Res.* 1375, 93–102. doi: 10.1016/j.brainres.2010.12.048

Gotlib, I. H. (1998). EEG alpha asymmetry, depression, and cognitive functioning. *Cogn. Emot.* 12, 449–478. doi: 10.1080/026999398379673

Gotlib, I. H., and Joormann, J. (2010). Cognition and depression: current status and future directions. *Annu. Rev. Clin. Psychol.* 6:285. doi: 10.1146/annurev.clinpsy.121208.131305

Gronwall, D. M. A. (1977). Paced auditory serial-addition task: a measure of recovery from concussion. *Percept. Motor Skills* 44, 367–373. doi: 10.2466/pms.1977.44.2.367

Gruzelier, J. H. (2013). EEG-neurofeedback for optimising performance. I: a review of cognitive and affective outcome in healthy participants. *Neurosci. Biobehav. Rev.* 44, 124–141. doi: 10.1016/j.neubiorev.2013.09.015

Hagemann, D., Naumann, E., and Thayer, J. F. (2001). The quest for the EEG reference revisited: a glance from brain asymmetry research. *Psychophysiology* 38, 847–857. doi: 10.1111/1469-8986.3850847

Hammond, D. C. (2000). Neurofeedback treatment of depression with the Roshi. *J. Neurother.* 4, 45–56. doi: 10.1300/J184v04n02_06
Hammond, D. C. (2005). Neurofeedback treatment of depression and anxiety. *J. Adult Dev.* 12, 131–137. doi: 10.1007/s10804-005-7029-5
Hanslmayr, S., Sauseng, P., Doppelmayr, M., Schabus, M., and Klimesch, W. (2005). Increasing individual upper alpha power by neurofeedback improves cognitive performance in human subjects. *Appl. Psychophysiol. Biofeedback* 30, 1–10. doi: 10.1007/s10484-005-2169-8
Henriques, J. B., and Davidson, R. J. (1991). Left frontal hypoactivation in depression. *J. Abnorm. Psychol.* 100:535. doi: 10.1037/0021-843X.100.4.535
Holmes, A. P., Blair, R. C., Watson, G., and Ford, I. (1996). Nonparametric analysis of statistic images from functional mapping experiments. *J. Cereb. Blood Flow Metab.* 16, 7–22. doi: 10.1097/00004647-199601000-00002
Holroyd, C. B., Krigolson, O. E., Baker, R., Lee, S., and Gibson, J. (2009). When is an error not a prediction error? An electrophysiological investigation. *Cogn. Affect. Behav. Neurosci.* 9, 59–70. doi: 10.3758/CABN.9.1.59
Hughes, J. R., and John, E. R. (1999). Conventional and quantitative electroencephalography in psychiatry. *J. Neuropsychiatry Clin. Neurosci.* 11, 190–208.
Hyvarinen, A. (1999). Fast and robust fixed-point algorithms for independent component analysis. *IEEE Trans. Neural Netw.* 10, 626–634. doi: 10.1109/72.761722
Kemp, A. H., Griffiths, K., Felmingham, K. L., Shankman, S. A., Drinkenburg, W., Arns, M., et al. (2010). Disorder specificity despite comorbidity: resting EEG alpha asymmetry in major depressive disorder and post-traumatic stress disorder. *Biol. Psychol.* 85, 350–354. doi: 10.1016/j.biopsycho.2010.08.001
Kessler, R. C., Berglund, P., Demler, O., Jin, R., Koretz, D., Merikangas, K. R., et al. (2003). The epidemiology of major depressive disorder. *JAMA* 289, 3095–3105. doi: 10.1001/jama.289.23.3095
Klimesch, W. (1999). EEG alpha and theta oscillations reflect cognitive and memory performance: a review and analysis. *Brain Res. Rev.* 29, 169–195. doi: 10.1016/S0165-0173(98)00056-3
Klimesch, W., Sauseng, P., and Hanslmayr, S. (2007). EEG alpha oscillations: the inhibition-timing hypothesis. *Brain Res. Rev.* 53, 63–88. doi: 10.1016/j.brainresrev.2006.06.003
Kober, S. E., Witte, M., Ninaus, M., Neuper, C., and Wood, G. (2013). Learning to modulate one's own brain activity: the effect of spontaneous mental strategies. *Front. Hum. Neurosci.* 7:695. doi: 10.3389/fnhum.2013.00695
Kroenke, K., Spitzer, R. L., and Williams, J. B. (2001). The PHQ-9. *J. Gen. Int. Med.* 16, 606–613. doi: 10.1046/j.1525-1497.2001.016009606.x
Lancaster, J. L., Woldorff, M. G., Parsons, L. M., Liotti, M., Freitas, C. S., Rainey, L., et al. (2000). Automated Talairach atlas labels for functional brain mapping. *Hum. Brain Mapp.* 10, 120–131. doi: 10.1002/1097-0193(200007)10:3<120::AID-HBM30>3.0.CO;2-8
La Vaque, T. J., and Rossiter, T. (2001). The ethical use of placebo controls in clinical research: the Declaration of Helsinki. *Appl. Psychophysiol. Biofeedback* 26, 23–37. doi: 10.1023/A:1009563504319
Lee, T. W., Girolami, M., and Sejnowski, T. J. (1999). Independent component analysis using an extended infomax algorithm for mixed subgaussian and supergaussian sources. *Neural Comput.* 11, 417–441. doi: 10.1162/089976699300016719
Levens, S. M., and Gotlib, I. H. (2010). Updating positive and negative stimuli in working memory in depression. *J. Exp. Psychol. Gen.* 139:654. doi: 10.1037/a0020283
Lubar, J. F., Congedo, M., and Askew, J. H. (2003). Low-resolution electromagnetic tomography (LORETA) of cerebral activity in chronic depressive disorder. *Int. J. Psychophysiol.* 49, 175–185. doi: 10.1016/S0167-8760(03)00115-6
Maris, E., and Oostenveld, R. (2007). Nonparametric statistical testing of EEG- and MEG-data. *J. Neurosci. Methods* 164, 177–190. doi: 10.1016/j.jneumeth.2007.03.024
Mathers, C. D., and Loncar, D. (2006). Projections of global mortality and burden of disease from 2002 to 2030. *PLoS Med.* 3:e442. doi: 10.1371/journal.pmed.0030442
Mayberg, H. S. (1997). Limbic-cortical dysregulation: a proposed model of depression. *J. Neuropsychiatry Clin. Neurosci.* 9:471.
Mayberg, H. S., Liotti, M., Brannan, S. K., McGinnis, S., Mahurin, R. K., Jerabek, P. A., et al. (1999). Reciprocal limbic-cortical function and negative mood: converging PET findings in depression and normal sadness. *Am. J. Psychiatry* 156, 675–682.
Mazziotta, J., Toga, A., Evans, A., Fox, P., Lancaster, J., Zilles, K., et al. (2001). A probabilistic atlas and reference system for the human brain: International Consortium for Brain Mapping (ICBM). *Philos. Trans. R. Soc. Lond. B Biol. Sci.* 356, 1293–1322. doi: 10.1098/rstb.2001.0915
McNab, F., and Klingberg, T. (2007). Prefrontal cortex and basal ganglia control access to working memory. *Nat. Neurosci.* 11, 103–107. doi: 10.1038/nn2024
Nan, W., Rodrigues, J. P., Ma, J., Qu, X., Wan, F., Mak, P. I., et al. (2012). Individual alpha neurofeedback training effect on short term memory. *Int. J. Psychophysiol.* 86, 83–87. doi: 10.1016/j.ijpsycho.2012.07.182
Nichols, T. E., and Holmes, A. P. (2002). Nonparametric permutation tests for functional neuroimaging: a primer with examples. *Hum. Brain Mapp.* 15, 1–25. doi: 10.1002/hbm.1058
Pascual-Marqui, R. D. (2007). Discrete, 3D distributed, linear imaging methods of electric neuronal activity. Part 1: exact, zero error localization. arXiv preprint arXiv:0710.3341. Available online at: http://arxiv.org/pdf/0710.3341
Pascual-Marqui, R. D. (2002). Standardized low-resolution brain electromagnetic tomography (sLORETA): technical details. *Methods Find. Exp. Clin. Pharmacol.* 24(Suppl. D), 5–12.
Pesarin, F. (2001). *Multivariate Permutation Tests: With Applications In Biostatistics*, Vol. 240. New York, NY: Wiley.
Pizzagalli, D., Pascual-Marqui, R. D., Nitschke, J. B., Oakes, T. R., Larson, C. L., Abercrombie, H. C., et al. (2001). Anterior cingulate activity as a predictor of degree of treatment response in major depression: evidence from brain electrical tomography analysis. *Am. J. Psychiatry* 158, 405–415. doi: 10.1176/appi.ajp.158.3.405
Reid, S. A., Duke, L. M., and Allen, J. J. (1998). Resting frontal electroencephalographic asymmetry in depression: inconsistencies suggest the need to identify mediating factors. *Psychophysiology* 35, 389–404. doi: 10.1111/1469-8986.3540389
Reitan, R. M. (1958). Validity of the Trail Making Test as an indicator of organic brain damage. *Percept. Motor Skills* 8, 271–276. doi: 10.2466/pms.1958.8.3.271
Rey, A. (1964). *L'examen Clinique en Psychologie.* Presses Universitaires de France, Paris.
Ros, T., Munneke, M. A. M., Parkinson, L. A., and Gruzelier, J. H. (2014). Neurofeedback facilitation of implicit motor learning. *Biol. Psychol.* 95, 54–58. doi: 10.1016/j.biopsycho.2013.04.013
Rushworth, M. F., and Behrens, T. E. (2008). Choice, uncertainty and value in prefrontal and cingulate cortex. *Nat. Neurosci.* 11, 389–397. doi: 10.1038/nn2066
Sauseng, P., Klimesch, W., Heise, K. F., Gruber, W. R., Holz, E., Karim, A., et al. (2009). Brain oscillatory substrates of visual short-term memory capacity. *Curr. Biol.* 19, 1846–1852. doi: 10.1016/j.cub.2009.08.062
Stroop, J. R. (1992). Studies of interference in serial verbal reactions. *J. Exp. Psychol. Gen.* 121:15.
Tombaugh, T. N. (2006). A comprehensive review of the Paced Auditory Serial Addition Test (PASAT). *Arch. Clin. Neuropsychol.* 21, 53–76. doi: 10.1016/j.acn.2005.07.006
Vogel, E. K., McCollough, A. W., and Machizawa, M. G. (2005). Neural measures reveal individual differences in controlling access to working memory. *Nature* 438, 500–503. doi: 10.1038/nature04171
Zoefel, B., Huster, R. J., and Herrmann, C. S. (2011). Neurofeedback training of the upper alpha frequency band in EEG improves cognitive performance. *Neuroimage* 54, 1427–1431. doi: 10.1016/j.neuroimage.2010.08.078

11

Volitional control of the anterior insula in criminal psychopaths using real-time fMRI neurofeedback

Ranganatha Sitaram[1,2,3]*, Andrea Caria[1], Ralf Veit[1], Tilman Gaber[1], Sergio Ruiz[1,4] and Niels Birbaumer[1,5]

[1] Institute of Medical Psychology and Behavioral Neurobiology, University of Tübingen, Tübingen, Germany
[2] Department of Biomedical Engineering, University of Florida, Gainesville, FL, USA
[3] Sri Chitra Tirunal Institute of Medical Sciences and Technology, Thiruvananthapuram, Kerala, India
[4] Departamento de Psiquiatría, Escuela de Medicina, Centro Interdisciplinario de Neurociencias, Pontificia Universidad Católica de Chile, Santiago, Chile
[5] Ospedale San Camillo, Istituto di Ricovero e Cura a Carattere Scientifico (IRCCS), Venezia, Italy

***Correspondence:**
Ranganatha Sitaram, Department of Biomedical Engineering, University of Florida, P.O. Box 116131, Gainesville, FL 32611-6131, USA
e-mail: ranganatha.sitaram@bme.ufl.edu

This pilot study aimed to explore whether criminal psychopaths can learn volitional regulation of the left anterior insula with real-time fMRI neurofeedback. Our previous studies with healthy volunteers showed that learned control of the blood oxygenation-level dependent (BOLD) signal was specific to the target region, and not a result of general arousal and global unspecific brain activation, and also that successful regulation modulates emotional responses, specifically to aversive picture stimuli but not neutral stimuli. In this pilot study, four criminal psychopaths were trained to regulate the anterior insula by employing negative emotional imageries taken from previous episodes in their lives, in conjunction with contingent feedback. Only one out of the four participants learned to increase the percent differential BOLD in the up-regulation condition across training runs. Subjects with higher Psychopathic Checklist-Revised (PCL:SV) scores were less able to increase the BOLD signal in the anterior insula than their lower PCL:SV counterparts. We investigated functional connectivity changes in the emotional network due to learned regulation of the successful participant, by employing multivariate Granger Causality Modeling (GCM). Learning to up-regulate the left anterior insula not only increased the number of connections (causal density) in the emotional network in the single successful participant but also increased the difference between the number of outgoing and incoming connections (causal flow) of the left insula. This pilot study shows modest potential for training psychopathic individuals to learn to control brain activity in the anterior insula.

Keywords: real-time fMRI, brain-computer interface, neurofeedback, criminal psychopathy, antisocial behavior, anterior insula

INTRODUCTION

Psychopathy is a personality disorder described by a constellation of affective, interpersonal and behavioral characteristics such as callousness, a marked lack of empathy, egocentricity and impulsivity. Psychopaths engage in more criminal behavior and institutional misconduct than their non-psychopathic counterparts. Central to psychopathy is the deficient processing of emotions. These include shallowness and profound lack of remorse or empathy. Hare et al. (1991) subsumed those features under the term "emotional detachment". Lykken (1957), using questionnaires and electrodermal responses, investigated the hypothesis that psychopaths fail to develop anxiety. Lykken found reduced anxiety levels in the subjective evaluations and low electrodermal responses to conditioned stimuli that were previously associated with shock in the autonomic indices. Cleckley (1951) suggested that psychopaths exhibit discordance in the verbal and experiential components of emotion. Empirical evidence indicates that psychopathic individuals have less intense aversive emotional reactions to many everyday situations than do non-psychopaths (Day and Wong, 1996). Other investigators suggested that the inability of psychopaths to anticipate the negative consequences of their behavior results from an insufficient capacity to develop anticipatory fear (Hare, 1978). Hence, psychopathy may be characterized by a faulty modulation of associative links between external stimuli and internal reactions (Patrick, 1994; Patrick et al., 1994). Neuroimaging studies investigating the affective processing of psychopathy will potentially lead to an understanding of neural mechanisms and elements that maintain this disorder (Porter, 1996). We have reported that the absence of conditioned fear in psychopathic individuals is reflected in a virtually complete lack of activation of the fear circuitry in the brain (i.e., insula, anterior cingulate, amygdala, orbital frontal cortex) (Birbaumer et al., 2005).

The amygdala plays a central role in emotional processing, particularly in fear conditioning (Kim and Jung, 2006). However, fear retention is not necessarily at the same site as fear association, and hence it is unclear whether the amygdala is the permanent storage site for long-term fear memory. Fear retention is abolished after amygdala lesion 1 day after, but not after many days, of inhibitory avoidance training, suggesting that long-term fear memory is not stored in amygdala (Liang et al., 1982; McGaugh et al., 1982). Electrical stimulation of the amygdala can have positive and negative emotional effects (Aggleton, 2000), and amygdala is active in conditions involving both positive and negative stimuli. In addition to the amygdala, a network of structures that includes insula, anterior cingulate gyrus and medial orbitofrontal cortex is suggested as important in identifying the emotional significance of the stimulus, and regulate the affective state (Adolphs, 2003a,b; Phillips et al., 2003). The insula has afferent and efferent connections to the medial and orbitofrontal cortices, anterior cingulate and amygdala (Augustine, 1996). Stein et al. (2007) maintain that the insula may have been relatively neglected compared with amygdala in the literature.

Insula activation is involved in several types of emotional processes, including differential positive vs. negative emotional processing (Büchel et al., 1998; Morris et al., 1998a,b), pain perception (Gelnar et al., 1999; Peyron et al., 2000), anticipation and viewing of aversive images (Simmons et al., 2004; Phan et al., 2006), and the making of judgments about emotions (Gorno-Tempini et al., 2001). Blair et al. (2006) propose that psychopathic individuals receive markedly reduced augmentation of the representation of the conditioned stimulus (CS) from the reciprocal connections of the amygdala and insula. Response to the CS will be impaired in individuals with psychopathy relative to controls (i.e., a weaker representation should be less able to control behavior). On the other hand, if the CS functions only as a distracter to ongoing behavior, performance will be superior in individuals with psychopathy relative to comparison individuals (i.e., a weaker representation will be a less of a competitor for the stimulus that should be controling behavior). Furthermore, insula is instrumental in the detection and interpretation of certain internal bodily states (Critchley et al., 2002, 2004), and is part of an interconnected subcortical network involved in empathic behavior (Decety et al., 2013).

Recent studies have provided new information on insula's role in criminal and psychopathic behavior. de Oliveira-Souza et al. (2008) observed bilateral gray matter reductions in mid-anterior insula of community patients high on psychopathy scores compared with healthy individuals. Tiihonen et al. (2008) compared violent offenders with healthy subjects showing that the first group, and specially those with a diagnosis of psychopathy, had reductions of focal gray matter volumes in right insula. Similarly, Cope et al. (2012) examined a large sample of individuals from community correction centers observing that psychopathic traits were negatively associated with gray matter volumes in right insula. Schiffer et al. (2011) observed that violent offenders displayed smaller gray matter volume in the left insula, compared with non-offenders. Congruently with previous reports, left insula was the area of greatest difference between psychopath and non-psychopath prison inmates (psychopaths displayed significant insula cortical thinning) in a recent study by Ly et al. (2012). These findings are in line with a series of functional MRI studies that have shown hypoactivity of insula cortex on psychopathic individuals during classical fear conditioning as compared with healthy subjects (Veit et al., 2002; Birbaumer et al., 2005), that could act as a marker of psychopathy.

Until present it is unclear whether the defective brain fear circuitry of psychopaths can be modified at all. The stability of the psychopathic personality trait and its strong genetic determination (Tielbeek et al., 2012; Yildirim and Derksen, 2013) would argue against the possibility to self-regulate brain activity in fear-related regions. On the other hand, social and developmental factors also play a fundamental role in psychopathic behavior (Viding, 2004; Moffitt, 2005). These environmental factors suggest that modification of the fear circuitry is possible. In view of the above line of argument, we asked the following questions: could psychopaths be trained to regulate the BOLD activity in the insula, and does volitional increase of BOLD in insula have any effect on emotional processing? In this pilot study, we also wanted to test whether training to regulate the insular cortex changes the functional connectivity of the emotional network. We hypothesized that with learned increase of activity in the insula, connectivity to the other areas of the fear circuitry will improve.

We implemented a Functional Magnetic Resonance Imaging based Brain-Computer Interface (fMRI-BCI) for this study. An fMRI-BCI is a non-invasive system that can be used for on-line neurofeedback of the BOLD signal to learn regulation of localized changes in brain activity, and to study related behavioral effects of regulation of specific brain regions and their connectivity (Sitaram et al., 2007, 2009; Weiskopf et al., 2007; Caria et al., 2012; Birbaumer et al., 2013; Ruiz et al., 2013a, 2014; Sulzer et al., 2013). In a series of studies on healthy individuals, we investigated the self-regulation of anterior insula and its behavioral effects (Caria et al., 2007, 2010; Veit et al., 2012). The present pilot study employs a similar paradigm of feedback-guided regulation of left anterior insula and a subsequent evaluation of emotional and neutral pictures. Statistical parametric mapping and region of interest (ROI1) analyses were carried out to assess the brain activation during regulation, picture presentation and rating conditions. Statistical analysis was also carried out on the valence and arousal ratings of pictures to test for the influence of regulation of insular activity on picture processing.

For analyzing the functional connectivity of the emotional network due to regulation training, we used Granger Causality Modeling (GCM). Granger Causality Modeling is a method of vector autoregressive modeling using the theory of Granger causality to analyze directed influences (Goebel et al., 2003; Roebroeck et al., 2005; Seth, 2005, 2010; Abler et al., 2006). The method works by using temporal information in one or more time-series of brain regions to predict signal time courses in another region. These predictions can be used to arrive at temporally directed influences rather than only correlations in activity between brain regions. Directed influences of one neural system on another, called effective connectivity (Büchel and Friston, 2000;

Friston and Büchel, 2000), could be generated for one or more regions of interest to develop a circuit diagram that could replicate the observed timing relationships between brain regions. We tested whether different stages of self-regulation training would indicate a change in the functional connectivity of the network.

METHODS

PARTICIPANTS

Four psychopaths with criminal records participated in the study. Mean age of the psychopaths was 31.5 years (SD = 3.5 years, see **Table 1**). The criminal psychopaths were sexual offenders out on bail and waiting for their trial or out of jail and on parole, all of whom were screened from a larger sample using the Psychopathy Checklist: Screening Version (PCL:SV, Hart et al., 1995) and Levenson Self-Report Psychopathy Scale (LSRP; Levenson et al., 1995; Miller et al., 2008). The screening version of the PCL consists of 12 items and was developed to measure psychopathy in civic or forensic settings. Participants' PCL:SV scores, including, emotional detachment aspects (PCL-SV F1) and antisocial behavior aspects (PCL-SV F2); and the LSRP scores, including, interpersonal and affective aspects (LSRP F1), and the social deviance aspects (LSRP F2) are listed in the **Table 1**. These values are much lower than the scores for the American population of psychopaths but are in accordance with the lower values for the German norms (Ullrich et al., 2003). The PCL:SV and LSRP scores were obtained by structured interviews conducted by the certified clinical psychologist of this study (author Niels Birbaumer). Written instructions were provided to all participants and informed written consent was obtained. The ethics committee of the Faculty of Medicine of the University of Tübingen approved the study.

fMRI DATA ACQUISITION

Functional images were acquired on a 3.0 T whole body scanner, with standard 12-channel head coil (Siemens Magnetom Trio Tim, Siemens, Erlangen, Germany). A standard echo-planar imaging sequence was used (EPI; TR = 1.5 s, matrix size = 64 × 64, effective echo time TE = 30 ms, flip angle α = 70°, bandwidth = 1.954 kHz/pixel). Sixteen slices (voxel size = 3.3 × 3.3 × 5.0 mm^3, slice gap = 1 mm), AC/PC aligned in axial orientation were acquired. For superposition of functional maps upon brain anatomy a high-resolution T1-weighted structural scan of the whole brain was collected from each subject (MPRAGE, matrix size = 256 × 256, 160 partitions, 1 mm^3 isotropic voxels, TR = 2300 ms, TE = 3.93 ms, TI = 1100 ms, α = 8°). In order to reduce movement artefacts, two foam cushions were used to immobilize the participant's head.

LOCALIZATION OF REGION OF INTEREST

A localizer run was used to delineate the target ROI1, the left anterior insula. A block-based paradigm was used for the localizer run consisting of four blocks (22.5 s each) during which the subjects had to use mental imagery to recall emotionally relevant personal experiences alternating with five baseline blocks (22.5 s each) during which they had to count in a reverse order from number 100. No verbal cues for the direction of emotional valence of mental strategies and imagery were given. Region of Interest, consisting of a rectangular area encompassing 5 × 5 voxels (~20 × 20 mm) on a single slice (5 mm), was selected based on the activation maps generated on-line during the task by means of Turbo-BrainVoyager (Goebel, 2001) and saved for the following training runs. The reference ROI2 was a large background ROI1 selected from a slice positioned distant from ROI1 encompassing a complete slice, selected with the intent to cancel global effects and to average out any unspecific activations. The ROI2 was chosen closer to the motor cortical surface to subtract movement related activations and further away from the anterior insula and other subcortical emotional brain regions.

EXPERIMENTAL PROTOCOL

Feedback training

Each participant was conducted through three different types of protocols in this chronological order: a pretest on the first day; four feedback runs per day for 1–3 days depending on the availability of the subject; and a final day of a post-test. Each feedback run consisted of seven baseline blocks and six up-regulation blocks, each block of 30 s duration, presented in an alternating manner. During the up-regulation subjects had to increase the BOLD response in the ROI1 (left anterior insula) and during the baseline block return it to original value by watching the feedback presented in the form of an animated graphical thermometer. Normalized average BOLD signal from the left anterior insula was used to generate animated images of the varying thermometer bars. The feedback signal was computed as $(\text{BOLDupreg} - \text{BOLDbaseline})_{\text{ROI1}} - (\text{BOLDupreg} - \text{BOLDbaseline})_{\text{ROI2}}$. Where BOLDupreg and

Table 1 | The table reports for each participant his/her name, age, psychopathy score based on Psychopathy Checklist: Screening Version (PCL:SV, Hart et al., 1995) for factors emotional detachment (F1) and antisocial behavioral aspect (F2), and Levenson Self-Report Psychopathy Scale (LSRP, Levenson et al., 1995) for interpersonal and affective factor (LSRP F1), the social deviance factor (LSRP F2) and the total LSRP score.

Participant	Age	PCL:SV Total	PCL:SV F1	PCL:SV F2	LSRP F1	LSRP F2	LSRP Total
GM	35	21	11	10	46	17	63
WE	35	7	3	4	31	16	47
RS	28	14	6	8	41	28	69
AK	28	6	2	4	20	26	46
Mean	**31.5**	**12**	**5.5**	**6.5**	**34.5**	**21.75**	**56.25**

BOLDbaseline constituted the BOLD signal during the current scan of up-regulation, and the average BOLD signal from the previous baseline block, respectively. The up-regulation and baseline blocks were cued with red and blue colored backgrounds, respectively. Each run of the feedback training took 6.75 min to complete. At the end of each training run monetary reward was computed and presented to the subject proportional to the aggregate valid differential BOLD increase or decrease at every time point with respect to the previous time points. For computing monetary reward, percent BOLD change was counted as valid only if there was a BOLD increase but not decrease during the up-regulation block, and a percent BOLD decrease but not increase during the baseline block. Each valid percent increase and decrease of BOLD earned 10 European cents. Maximum reward for a feedback run was limited to 10 Euros.

Pre-test and post-test

The pre-test and post-test were similar in structure and only differed in the stimulus material used. The intent of the tests was to measure the effect of volitional regulation of the left anterior insula on aversive and neutral picture evaluation. Each run of the pre-test or post-test consisted of five alternating up-regulation and baseline runs, totally lasting 9 m. Each run consisted of a 30 s up-regulation or baseline block performed by watching the feedback of the moving thermometer bars as described before, followed by a 9 s emotional picture presentation block, that in turn was followed by a 12 s picture rating block (**Figure 1A**).

During picture presentation blocks, one emotional or neutral picture from the International Affective Picture System (IAPS; Lang et al., 2008, NIMH Center for the Study of Emotion and Attention, see **Table 2**) was presented. The pictures presented to the participants consisted of 20 aversive and 20 neutral pictures from IAPS. Valence and arousal ratings for aversive pictures were based on ratings from a large representative reference sample (Lang et al., 2008, NIMH Center for the Study of Emotion and Attention) with mean values of 3.26 ± 0.78 SD and 4.93 ± 0.47 SD, respectively. Valence and arousal ratings for neutral pictures had mean values of 4.84 ± 0.32 SD and 2.33 ± 0.40 SD, respectively. Pictures were pseudo-randomized such that no significant difference in standard ratings of valence and arousal was present between pictures after up-regulation and baseline blocks and between runs.

During the evaluation blocks subjects had to rate the picture for valence and arousal using a button-based control device inside the MRI scanner. Pictures were rated in terms of subjective emotional valence and arousal using the

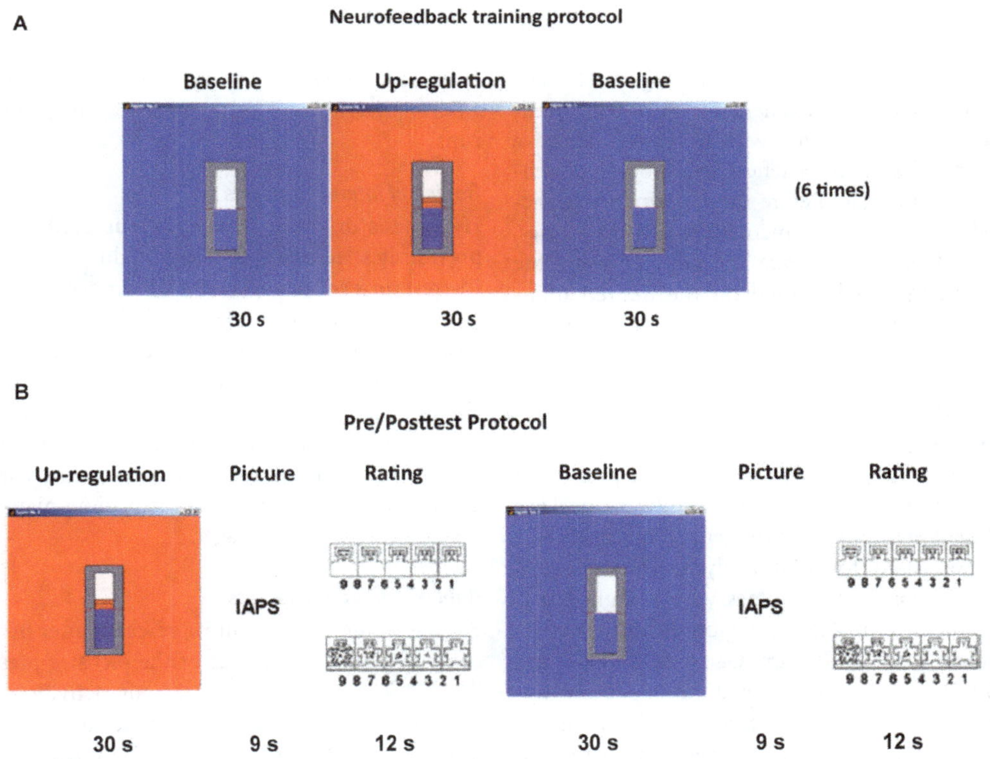

FIGURE 1 | Experimental design. (A) RtfMRI feedback Training: Each feedback run consisted of seven baseline blocks and six up-regulation blocks, each block of 30 s duration, presented in an alternating manner. **(B)** Pre/Posttests: Each pre- or post-test consisted of five regulation blocks (30 s) alternating with six baseline blocks (30 s) both followed by an International Affective Picture System (31) picture presentation block (9 s) and a rating block (12 s). During rating blocks, participants were shown the Self-Assessment Manikin (34), which allows them to evaluate emotional valence and arousal. Both valence and arousal dimensions vary along a 9-point scale. Selection of the subjective rating was performed by positioning a red outline on the chosen number on each of the two scales, presented in close succession. Subjects were provided with two buttons allowing movements of the cursor in the left and right direction. (IAPS = International Affective Picture System).

Table 2 | Valence and arousal ratings of emotion and neutral pictures shown during pre- and post-tests (Lang et al., 2008, NIMH Center for the Study of Emotion and Attention).

Pictorial stimuli from the International Affective Pictures System (IAPS)							
Aversive pictures				Neutral pictures			
IAPS number	Description	Valence	Arousal	IAPS number	Description	Valence	Arousal
9421	Soldier	2,47	4,86	5740	Plant	5,07	2,36
9430	Burial	3,1	4,81	7175	Lamp	4,78	1,55
9432	Mastectomy	3,29	4,12	7002	Towel	4,91	2,99
9433	Dead man	2,39	5	7950	Tissue	4,62	2,3
9440	Skulls	4,42	4,71	7020	Fan	5,02	2,15
9452	Gun	3,62	4,5	7025	Stool	4,46	2,44
9470	Ruins	3,62	4,53	7031	Shoes	4,2	1,67
9480	Skull	4,06	5,15	7010	Basket	4,95	1,55
9490	Corpse	4,2	5,41	7004	Spoon	4,89	2,09
9500	Porpoises	2,85	5,65	7224	File cabinets	4,38	2,55
9520	Kids	2,14	5,45	7217	Clothes rack	4,63	2,31
9530	Boys	3,65	4,74	7705	Cabinet	4,75	2,4
9560	Duck in oil	2,07	5,46	7080	Fork	5,43	1,98
9561	Sick kitty	3,2	4,18	7009	Mug	4,96	2,69
9570	Dog	1,9	5,84	7030	Iron	4,82	2,76
9571	Cat	2,65	4,68	7035	Mug	4,81	2,56
9582	Dental exam	4,09	5,15	7040	Dust pan	4,72	2,46
9584	Dental exam	3,44	4,65	7050	Hair dryer	4,81	2,59
9592	Injection	4	5,11	7140	Bus	5,59	2,67
9594	Injection	4,08	4,55	7233	Plate	5,01	2,51

Self-Assessment Manikin (SAM; Bradley and Lang, 1994). The SAM is a non-verbal pictorial assessment for measuring pleasure, aversion and arousal associated with a person's affective reaction to a variety of stimuli. Valence and arousal dimensions vary along a 9-point scale. Before the experiment, participants were briefed about the experimental tasks, SAM ratings, and were also trained on how to rate the pictures using the two buttons. Positioning a red outline on the desired number of the SAM scale selected the appropriate subjective rating (**Figure 1B**).

OFF-LINE DATA ANALYSIS

SPM analysis of brain images

Off-line image post-processing and data analysis were performed using SPM2 statistical parametric mapping software package (Wellcome Department of Imaging Neuroscience, London), while BrainVoyager QX was used for ROI analysis. During signal preprocessing, the functional EPI volumes were realigned spatially, normalized into Montreal Neurological Institute (MNI) space, and smoothed spatially (9-mm Gaussian kernel) and temporally (0.0039 Hz, 1/(2.5 times the duration of the up-regulation and baseline block)) to remove high frequency artefacts. Hemodynamic response amplitudes were estimated using standard regressors, constructed by convolving a box-car function, representing the block duration, with a canonical hemodynamic response function using standard SPM2 parameters. Motion parameters were also included into the general linear model (GLM) as covariates to take account for variance caused by head motion. Signal change during increase blocks with respect to the decrease blocks was evaluated by SPM2. Areas showing training related changes were analyzed with t-test comparisons of BOLD magnitude over runs.

Region of interest analysis

Hypothesis driven ROI analysis was performed using the ROI previously selected for each subject during the training. Region of Interest time series underwent the same preprocessing and model estimation using the GLM for whole brain analysis. The percent signal change during up-regulation blocks with respect to the baseline blocks was calculated for each run separately, and then also averaged across subjects. The training effect was evaluated by computing paired t-test on all subjects of percent signal changes in the target ROI run by run. Activation maps produced by offline analysis matched and validated activations maps produced in real-time by Turbo-BrainVoyager.

Analysis of picture ratings

Ratings of the IAPS pictures presented after increase blocks were compared with the ratings of the pictures presented after baseline blocks across runs. Local brain activity was also compared between pictures presented after increase blocks with respect to those presented after baseline blocks across runs.

Effective connectivity analysis

Granger Causality Modeling (Granger, 1969, 1980) is a method originally developed in economics for causal interaction between multiple events from time-series data. Recently, GCM has been applied in conjunction with Vector Autoregressive Models (VAR) to fMRI data also (Roebroeck et al., 2005; Abler et al., 2006) to investigate directed influences between neuronal populations. In this study, GCM analysis was carried out to evaluate the network dynamics during self-regulation during three different training runs: a run of weak regulation (2nd training run), a run of intermediate regulation (5th training run), and a run of strongest regulation (11th training run). Time-series of ROIs, known to be involved in self-induced or stimulus-induced emotions from literature (Phan et al., 2002) and also passed the height threshold of $P < 0.05$ (Bonferroni corrected) and a cluster threshold of 50 voxels were used as input to the GCM analysis for each stage of regulation. We implemented a multivariate GCM by adapting the Causal Connectivity Matlab (Mathworks Inc., USA) Toolkit from Seth (2005) to work with fMRI signals and our design protocols. Multivariate GCM was applied to multiple time-series of selected ROIs (varying from 5–10) at three different stages of regulation under consideration.

Two important measures of connectivity, namely, *causal density* and *causal flow* were adapted from Seth (2005) and Seth and Edelman (2007) for comparison of functional connectivity across feedback training runs.

Causal Density: The *causal density* (*cd*) of a functional network is defined as the fraction of interactions among ROIs that are causally significant. Causal density is given by the relation $cd = gc/(n(n-1))$, where gc is the total number of causal connections observed and n is the network size. A set of unconnected ROIs will have low *cd*.

Causal Flow: The *causal flow* (*cf*) of an ROI i in Granger-causality graph is defined as difference between the number of outgoing connections and the number of incoming connections. An ROI with highly positive *cf* exerts a strong causal influence over the network and so acts as a *causal source*. An ROI with a negative *cf* can be called a *causal sink* of the network.

RESULTS

Participants reported using the following mental imageries for up-regulation of BOLD signal in the anterior insula: fight with the landlord, death of parents, experience in jail, memories of grand mother, negative memories of a stay in a detention center and pronouncement of judgment in the courtroom. We used the percent BOLD difference between up-regulation and baseline rather than actual values in order to rule out effects of baseline drift and inter-subject differences. Only one participant (Subject-AK) learned to increase the BOLD activity in the anterior insula with training (**Figure 2A**), while the other participants did not increase their activation levels and in some cases even reduced them (subjects RS and GM). Mean BOLD change in the left anterior insula in the up-regulation condition across the training runs for all participants correlated negatively with the participants' PCL:SV ratings (Pearson Correlation = −0.7, **Figure 2B**). Only subject AK had the most consistent increase of BOLD in the up-regulation blocks, and also underwent the most number of training runs (12 runs in 4 days) compared to (4 runs in 1 day) other participants (**Figure 2B**). To correct for the difference in the training runs, we recalculated the correlation using only data from first four training runs, the corrected Pearson Correlation Coefficient is −0.67.

Because, only subject AK showed consistent activation increases in the up-regulation blocks, further analysis on behavioral data, and effective connectivity from fMRI data were performed in this participant alone. Whole brain analysis for participant AK showed an increased activation cluster in the left anterior insula in the last run when the subject had learned to regulate strongly in comparison to the first day run. The Talairach coordinate for the activated cluster of the left anterior insula for subject AK was (−37, 27, 0; **Figure 3**).

For subject AK, mean subjective ratings of valence and arousal of aversive images from the IAPS, after all the up-regulation conditions, decreased from the pretest to the posttest, and became closer in value to the healthy subject ratings reported by Lang et al. (2008) (**Figure 4A**). This indicates that in the pretest the participant rated aversive images to be more positive in emotional valence and more arousing compared to the standard healthy ratings for the same images. However, during the posttest (conducted after neurofeedback training), the same participant rated the images as being less positive (more negative) and less arousing, and similar to the IAPS healthy ratings.

In the successful subject AK, percent BOLD increase and the *causal density* (*cd*; the number of interactions that are causally significant in the brain network involved in up-regulation) increased proportionately, from the early stage to the final stage of training, in the subject AK (**Figure 4B**). A high correlation coefficient of 0.987 was observed between the percent BOLD and the causal density.

Figure 5 shows results of connectivity analysis for three different strengths of regulation in the successful subject AK. Left column of the figure contains schematic depictions of the directed influences among different ROIs; the right column shows bar charts of causal flow (*cf*) for the ROIs.

Connectivity during the early stage of training: Figures 5A,D show the brain network and the causal flow, respectively, during the early stage (2nd training run) of the subject AK. Regulation at this stage is driven by the posterior part of the brain, mainly involving the posterior cingulate, which has significant directed influences to left insula, anterior cingulate cortex (ACC) and hippocampus. The posterior cingulate is the major causal source at this stage followed by the left medial prefrontal cortex. At this stage one can see a very sparse network involving interactions among very few ROIs in the emotional network indicated by the low causal density.

Connectivity during the mid stage of training: Figures 5B,E show the brain network and the causal flow, respectively, during mid stage of training (5th training run) of the subject AK. Regulation at this stage continues to be driven by the posterior cingulate, which has significant directed influences to left insula, ACC, medial prefrontal cortex and hippocampus. In addition, the hippocampus directs its influence to the left insula. The posterior cingulate is still the major causal source followed by hippocampus at this stage. The causal density of the network has slightly increased compared to the early stage of training.

Connectivity during the final stage of training: Figures 5C,F show the brain network and the causal flow, respectively, during the final stage of training (11th training run) of the subject AK.

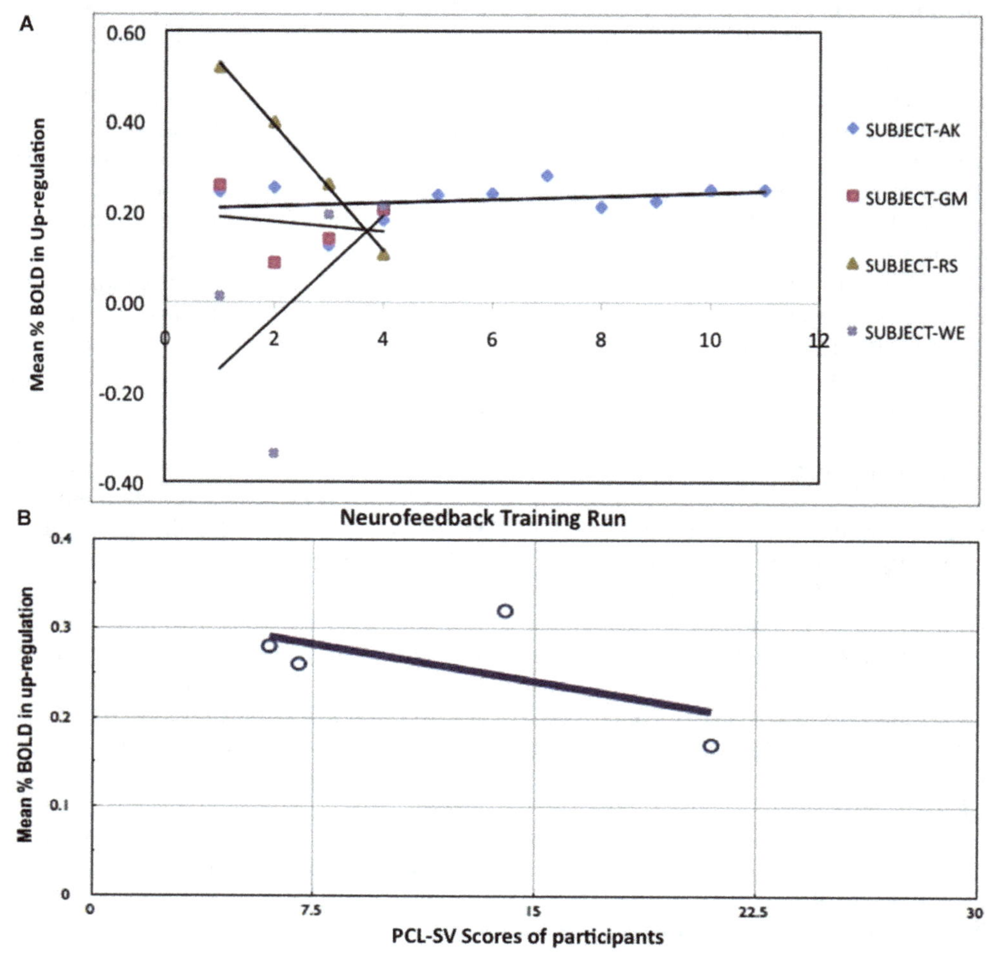

FIGURE 2 | Results of rtfMRI training. **(A)** Percent BOLD change between up-regulation and baseline in all participants across training runs. **(B)** Relationship between psychopathy (PCL:SV) ratings and percent BOLD increase during up-regulation. Negative correlation of percent BOLD change with PCL:SV scores of the subjects (Pearson Correlation = −0.7), indicating that subjects with higher Psychopathic Checklist-Revised (PCL:SV) scores are less successful at self-regulation than their lower PCL:SV counterparts, when compared across equal number of training runs.

Now, the anterior portion of the brain drives the network, with left insula taking a major share. Left insula is the predominant causal source with directed influences to superior medial frontal cortex, right insula, medial prefrontal cortex and posterior cingulate. Right insula and the posterior cingulate are the major causal sinks. At this stage, a great number of ROIs in the network (high causal density) have been recruited into the regulation function, mainly mediated by the left insula, superior medial frontal cortex and hippocampus. The anterior cingulate now has reciprocal connections with hippocampus. New influences from midtemporal gyrus and amygdale towards insula are also observed.

DISCUSSION

This pilot study explored the possibility of training criminal psychopaths to volitionally control the BOLD signal in the left anterior insula with the help of an fMRI Brain-Computer Interface developed in our laboratory (Sitaram et al., 2009, 2011). Our previous studies with healthy volunteers (Caria et al., 2007) had shown that learned control of the anterior insula was specific to the region, and not a result of general arousal and global unspecific brain activation, as demonstrated by a control group trained with a non-contingent feedback. From a follow-up study (Caria et al., 2010), we had reported that regulation of left anterior insula modulates the emotional response specific to aversive pictures but not neutral picture stimuli. Both studies had shown that mental imagery alone is not sufficient, and that real-time feedback of the BOLD signal extracted from the target region enhances participants' ability to achieve regulation. These studies naturally led to the question as to whether patients suffering from clinical conditions characterized by emotion deficits could learn to volitionally regulate anterior insula. In the present study, four criminal psychopaths underwent rtfMRI neurofeedback training. Three psychopathic criminals could only complete four runs of training and were not very successful in learning to control the BOLD signal in the insula. Only one participant (AK) participated

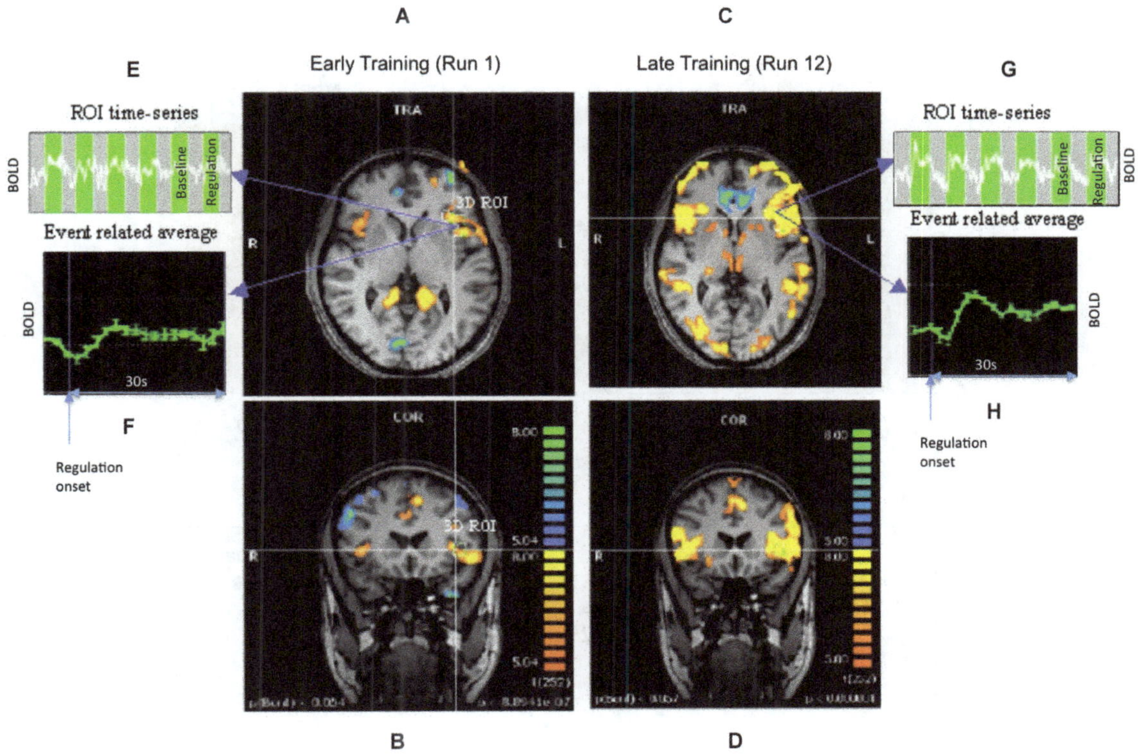

FIGURE 3 | Results of offline SPM analysis for representative subject AK. Statistical parametric maps showing the contrast up-regulation vs. baseline during early and late runs. Panels **(A,B)** show the transversal and coronal views of the contrast during an early run when the regulation was still weak. Panels **(C,D)** show the same views for a later run when a stronger regulation was achieved. Maps are all obtained at the same height threshold ($P = 0.05$, Bonferroni corrected). A precise, 3-dimensional ROI was delineated in the left anterior insula. Panels **(E,F)** show the time-series of BOLD signal and its event related average (ERA) in the ROI during weak regulation. The up- and baseline blocks are shown as alternating green and gray rectangles in the time-series. The ERA plots the percent BOLD change in the up-regulation block with respect to the baseline block after averaging across all the blocks of the run. The panels **(G,H)** show similar plots for the stronger regulation.

in extending neurofeedback training (12 in total) and also learned to successfully control the insula.

In comparison to the low success rate of psychopathic criminals to up-regulate the anterior insula in this study, an earlier study in our lab in 15 healthy participants showed significant increase in the BOLD signal in the anterior insula with five neurofeedback training runs (Caria et al., 2007). Linear regression across all runs showed significant increase of activity in the anterior insula [$y = 0.174 + 0.127$, $P < 0.012$]. Percent BOLD signal change in the region between up-regulation and baseline averaged across all the participants resulted in a clear monotonic increase across the first three runs (repeated measures ANOVA, $F_{(2,7)} = 10.32$, $P = 0.001$). In a subsequent study in our lab, a group of healthy individuals given real-time, veridical feedback learned to increase BOLD activity in bilateral anterior insula while two groups of healthy participants, one with sham feedback and another with no feedback did not learn to increase activity in the region (Caria et al., 2010).

In comparison, the results of the current study, although modest in the number of participants being successful, are still in line with a recent study from our laboratory in schizophrenia patients, and indicates that insula self-regulation can be achieved with fMRI-BCI, even in severe chronic brain disorders (Ruiz et al., 2013b).

A number of reasons could have potentially affected learning in the majority of our psychopathic participants: general lack of motivation to participate in the experiments in spite of the monetary reward, failure to understand and follow experimental instructions, inability to perform emotional imagery and lack of attention to the task. In more basic terms, the inability to learn up-regulation of insula could be attributed to faulty modulation of associative links between external stimuli and internal reactions (Patrick, 1994; Patrick et al., 1994). As per earlier reports, the absence of conditioned fear in psychopathic individuals and the reduced activation of the fear circuitry in the brain (i.e., insula, anterior cingulate, amygdala, orbital frontal cortex, Birbaumer et al., 2005) may be the fundamental reason for the ineffective learning.

In the present study, one psychopathic criminal learned to regulate anterior insula by employing negative emotional imageries in conjunction with contingent feedback, despite a widespread scientific view that the psychopathic brain is resistant to change. We have also extended previous experimental protocols

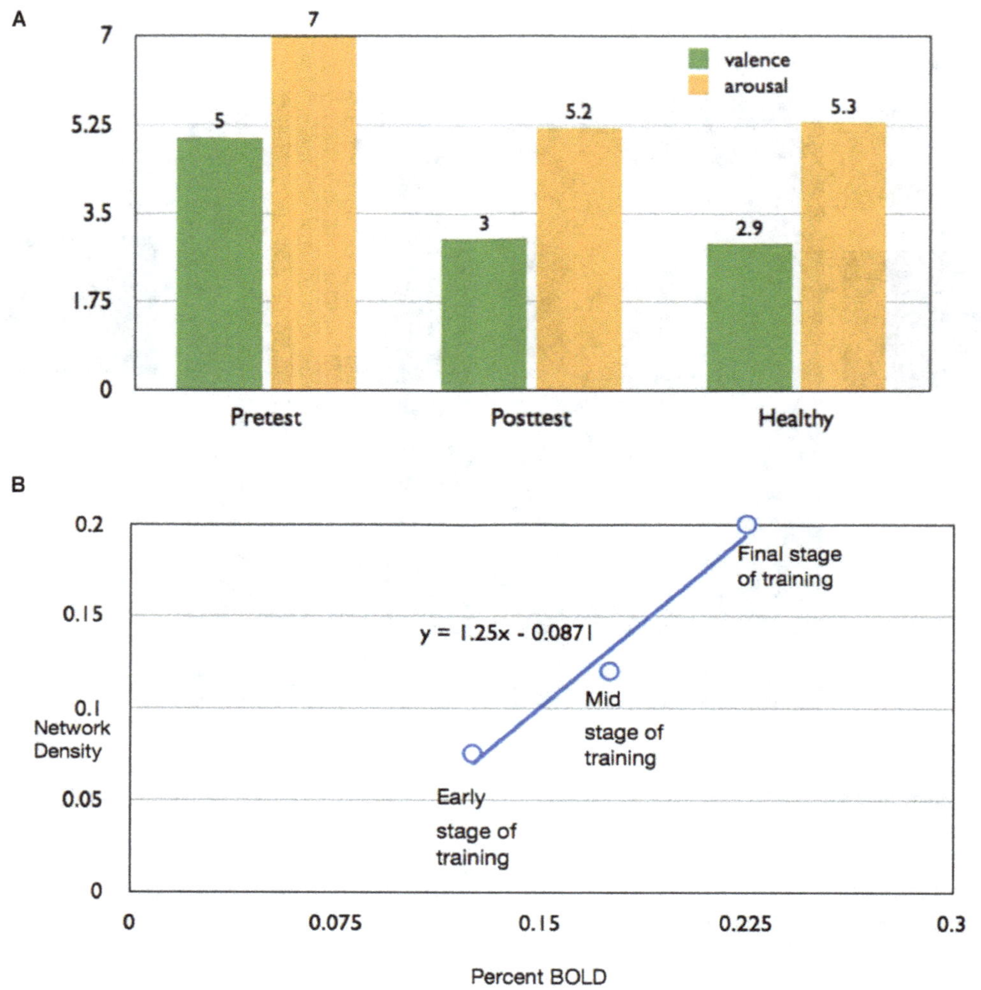

FIGURE 4 | Effect of rtfMRI training on subjective ratings of aversive pictures and **(A)** Bar chart of valence and arousal to aversive ratings of subject AK to pictures from the IAPS presented immediately after up-regulation blocks, in the pretest (left bar graphs) and posttest (middle bar graphs), in comparison with mean ratings for healthy individuals reported by Lang et al. (2008). **(B)** Scatter plot showing high correlation (r = 0.987) percent BOLD increase in insula and the corresponding values for density of the functional connectivity of the network computed by the Granger Causality Mapping (GCM) method.

by providing monetary reward after every run. Monetary reward was computed proportional to the percent BOLD increase in the target region to motivate these difficult-to-recruit experimental subjects to continue feedback training. In the successful participant, continued training enhanced the percent differential BOLD in the up-regulation condition compared to the down-regulation condition. Overall, subjects with higher PCL:SV scores were less successful at up-regulation than their lower PCL:SV counterparts. The severity of psychopathic features and different symptom clusters of psychopathy as measured by the PCL:SV have been linked to different emotional processing deficits (Hicks and Patrick, 2006; Hansen et al., 2008; Gao et al., 2012). The current results, although limited due to the results from a single participant, are in line with these studies and with the existing notion that psychopathy consists of a neurobiological trait deficit of aversive anticipatory conditioning responsible for socialization and regulation of negative affect and instrumental aggression (Birbaumer et al., 2005). Alternatively, as psychopathic traits have been associated with insula abnormalities (de Oliveira-Souza et al., 2008; Tiihonen et al., 2008; Schiffer et al., 2011; Ly et al., 2012), the difficulty to learn self-regulation in individuals with higher PCL:SV scores could reflect the abnormality of the insular structure, hypothesis that can be tested in future studies. Although observed in only criminal psychopath, it is nevertheless interesting that the volitional up-regulation of insula was associated with changes in the subjective ratings of valence and arousal of aversive stimuli in this participant. More tests are needed to confirm this finding. This behavioral modulation is congruent with the evidence from previous studies in healthy participants (Caria et al., 2007, 2010) indicating that insula self-regulation modifies the appraisal of emotional picture stimuli, particularly of negative valence. Considering the abnormal

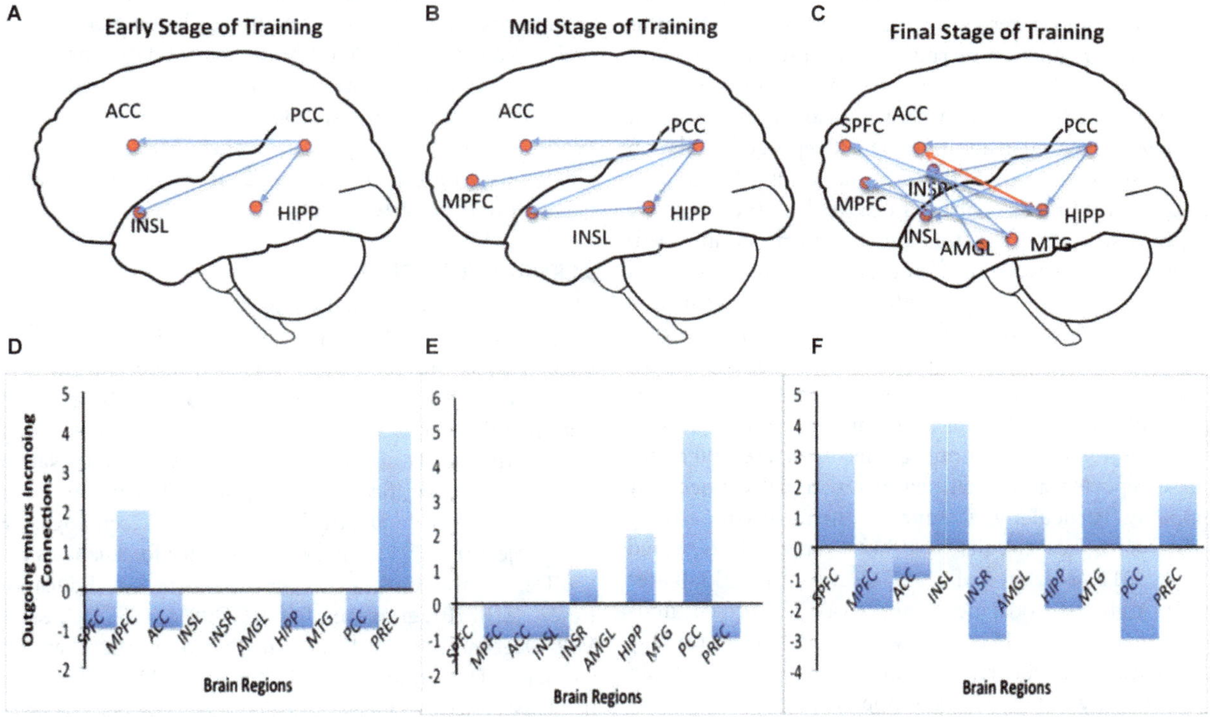

FIGURE 5 | Effective connectivity analysis of self-regulation of insula for subject AK. Panels **(A–C)** show directed influence maps (DIMs) and panels **(D–F)** show the bar charts of the causal flow (CF; defined as the net difference between outgoing and incoming connections) in the brain regions (the emotional network) involved in the self-regulation of insula. Panels are arranged from top to bottom from the early through mid to the final stage of training: from early stage of training (top), mid stage of training (middle) to final stage of training (bottom). As the training proceeds, the number of directed influences in the emotional network also increases as shown by the DIMs. During the final stage of training, many regions in the emotional network, including medial prefrontal cortex (MPFC), right insula, anterior cingulate cortex (ACC), amygdala and posterior cingulate cortex are seen to become connected with insula. The CF diagram of the early stage shows that the activations are driven predominantly from the posterior portion of the brain (especially by the posterior cingulate cortex) and that the CF in the left insula is close to zero. However, more training, insula and the anterior regions of the brain seem to drive the network activation to a greater extent as shown by their increasing CF.

autonomic reactivity to aversive stimuli, consistently reported in literature on psychopathy (Lorber, 2004; Gao and Raine, 2010), it would be interesting to assess whether the observed changes in the appraisal of emotional stimuli are accompanied by modifications of physiological measures related to anxiety or other emotional states (e.g., electrodermal response, heart rate, and so forth).

The main purpose of the present study was not only to ascertain whether criminal psychopaths can learn to regulate the BOLD signal in the left anterior insula but also to investigate the changes in effective connectivity in the brain of criminal psychopaths due to successful regulation. In particular, we wanted to compare the effective connectivity changes with varying strength of the regulation. To this end, we employed the multivariate GCM adapted from the Causal Connectivity Toolkit from Seth (2005) to work with fMRI data. A recent study on insula self-regulation showed that fMRI-BCI training is associated with an enhancement in the numbers of effective connections in the emotional network in a successful regulation run, compared with an unsuccessful regulation run (Ruiz et al., 2013b). In the present study, multivariate GCM was applied to time-series of 8–10 ROIs from the emotional network separately for three different levels of regulation, namely, weak, intermediate and strong, determined based on the average percent BOLD increase in up-regulation blocks compared down-regulation blocks. The results show that, firstly, the level of up-regulation is proportional to the causal density of the network, in other words, the extent of "connectedness" of the functional network purportedly involved in the regulation process. Secondly, the results show that during early training, up-regulation is driven mainly from the posterior cingulate, which acts as the main causal source, while right insula and the posterior cingulate are the major causal sinks. With more training, the source of the network moves towards the anterior of the brain finally settling in the left anterior insula during the final stage of up-regulation. During the final stage of training, the left insula directs its influence outwardly to superior medial frontal cortex, right insula, medial prefrontal cortex and posterior cingulate, indicated by the high value of the causal flow. In addition, the hippocampus, amygdala and midtemporal gyrus are introduced into the causal network during the final stage of training. Our results are supported by previous reports of emotional regulation and processing. Ochsner et al. (2004) have shown that up- and down-regulating negative emotion recruited prefrontal and anterior cingulate regions implicated in cognitive control. Further, they reported that self-focussed regulation recruited medial prefrontal regions implicated in internally focused processing, whereas situation-focussed regulation recruited lateral prefrontal regions implicated in externally focused processing. In our study, the predominance of medial prefrontal activation and its involvement in the causal network, and in addition the self-report of regulation strategies by subjects (e.g., fight with the landlord, death of parents, experience in jail, memories of grand mother, negative memories of a stay in a detention center and pronouncement of judgment in the courtroom) indicate the employment of self-focussed imagery, and thus further corroborate Ochsner's findings of the critical role of medial prefrontal cortex in self-focussed emotional appraisal (Ochsner et al., 2004).

The modulation of brain functional connectivity and the enhanced involvement of frontal areas during the final stage of training could have important implications. In fact, several recent studies have reported abnormal neural functional connectivity in psychopathy. Particularly, a reduced functional connectivity in prefrontal-amygdala circuits have been repeatedly observed (Marsh et al., 2011; Motzkin et al., 2011; Osumi et al., 2012; Juárez et al., 2013; Contreras-Rodríguez et al., 2014). The present findings suggest that fMRI-BCI could serve to modulate abnormally activated cortical and subcortical brain circuits, including brain systems purportedly abnormal in psychopaths, e.g., "the circuitry of empathy" (Decety and Svetlova, 2012; Decety et al., 2012). Interestingly, Ly et al. (2012) reported that psychopath inmates exhibit a reduction in functional connectivity between insula and the dorsal ACC, which could be a neural correlate of the abnormalities in the flexibility of goal-directed attention observed in psychopath. In light of this, future studies for training control of functional or effective connectivity between brain regions, e.g., insula and ACC, could serve to explore specific hypothesis regarding the link between neural substrates and psychopathology (Ruiz et al., 2013a).

Our results question a position emphasizing the resistance to change of psychopathic traits and its heritability. If the brain defect in psychopathy (evident from the neuroimaging literature on classical aversive conditioning) is genetically determined, then the modification of that circuit would not be possible at all. Our pilot study indicates to the contrary that criminal psychopaths could learn to volitionally control brain activity pertaining to emotion and that might have brain and behavioral consequences. Of particular interest are the results of GCM in the course of regulation improvement. The more a psychopathic individual regains control over the deficient activity of the anterior insular cortex, the greater is the restoration of the brain network of emotion.

The study has limitations. Firstly, there are obvious challenges to recruiting this very special population of study participants, and then motivating them to undergo multiple days of neurofeedback training. Secondly, it is difficult to ascertain how much of the variability observed in the capability to self-regulate can be explained by differences in motivation, compliance with the instructions, and other factors that might be playing a role in a population with psychopathic traits. Also, as a preliminary report, no long-term behavioral effects were explored. Future studies with larger samples will serve to generalize our results.

In summary, this pilot study shows modest feasibility that criminal psychopaths can learn self-regulation of a circumscribed brain area with fMRI-BCI, leading to modifications in the functional emotional network. Considering the limited evidence of effective treatment of psychopathy (Salekin et al., 2010) this proof-of principle study suggests that fMRI-BCI could offer a new valuable tool for modulating abnormal brain activations and behavior in this severe condition.

ACKNOWLEDGMENTS

This work was supported by by the Deutschen Forschungsgemeinschaft (DFG; BI 195/64-1 and and Reinhard Kosseleck support to Niels Birbaumer); SFB 437 "Kriegserfahrungen" of the DFG; the Marie Curie Host Fellowship for Early Stage Researchers Training; the Center for Integrative Neuroscience (CIN), Tübingen, Germany (Pool-Project 2011-08); Comisión Nacional de Investigación Científica y Tecnológica de Chile (Conicyt) through Fondo Nacional de Desarrollo Científico y Tecnológico Fondecyt (project n°11121153); German Center for Diabetes Research (DZDe.V.); the German Federal Ministry of Education and Research (BMBF, grant number 01GQ0831, 16SV5838K); and the Volkswagenstiftung (VW) and the Baden-Württemberg Stiftung, Germany. The authors are indebted to Dr. Michael Erb for technical assistance in data acquisition.

REFERENCES

Abler, B., Roebroeck, A., Goebel, R., Höse, A., Schönfeldt-Lecuona, C., Hole, G., et al. (2006). Investigating directed influences between activated brain areas in a motor-response task using fMRI. *Magn. Reson. Imaging* 24, 181–185. doi: 10.1016/j.mri.2005.10.022

Adolphs, R. (2003a). Cognitive neuroscience of human social behavior. *Nat. Rev. Neurosci.* 4, 165–178. doi: 10.1038/nrn1056

Adolphs, R. (2003b). Investigating the cognitive neuroscience of social behavior. *Neuropsychologia* 41, 119–126. doi: 10.1016/s0028-3932(02)00142-2

Aggleton, J. P. (2000). *The Amygdala: A Functional Analysis.* New York: Oxford University Press.

Augustine, J. R. (1996). Circuitry and functional aspects of the insular lobe in primates including humans. *Brain Res. Brain Res. Rev.* 22, 229–244. doi: 10.1016/s0165-0173(96)00011-2

Birbaumer, N., Ruiz, S., and Sitaram, R. (2013). Learned regulation of brain metabolism. *Trends Cogn. Sci.* 17, 295–302. doi: 10.1016/j.tics.2013.04.009

Birbaumer, N., Veit, R., Lotze, M., Erb, M., Hermann, C., Grodd, W., et al. (2005). Deficient fear conditioning in psychopathy: a functional magnetic resonance imaging study. *Arch. Gen. Psychiatry* 62, 799–805. doi: 10.1001/archpsyc.62.7.799

Blair, R. J., Peschardt, K. S., Budhani, S., Mitchell, D. G., and Pine, D. S. (2006). The development of psychopathy. *J. Child Psychol. Psychiatry* 47, 262–276. doi: 10.1111/j.1469-7610.2006.01596.x

Bradley, M. M., and Lang, P. J. (1994). Measuring emotion: the self-assessment manikin and the semantic differential. *J. Behav. Ther. Exp. Psychiatry* 25, 49–59. doi: 10.1016/0005-7916(94)90063-9

Büchel, C., and Friston, K. (2000). Assessing interactions among neuronal systems using functional neuroimaging. *Neural Netw.* 13, 871–882. doi: 10.1016/s0893-6080(00)00066-6

Büchel, C., Morris, J., Dolan, R. J., and Friston, K. J. (1998). Brain systems mediating aversive conditioning: an event-related fMRI study. *Neuron* 20, 947–957. doi: 10.1016/s0896-6273(00)80476-6

Caria, A., Sitaram, R., and Birbaumer, N. (2012). Real-time fMRI: a tool for local brain regulation. *Neuroscientist* 18, 487–501. doi: 10.1177/1073858411407205

Caria, A., Sitaram, R., Veit, R., Begliomini, C., and Birbaumer, N. (2010). Volitional control of anterior insula activity modulates the response to aversive stimuli. A real-time functional magnetic resonance imaging study. *Biol. Psychiatry* 68, 425–432. doi: 10.1016/j.biopsych.2010.04.020

Caria, A., Veit, R., Sitaram, R., Lotze, M., Weiskopf, N., Grodd, W., et al. (2007). Regulation of anterior insular cortex activity using real-time fMRI. *Neuroimage* 35, 1238–1246. doi: 10.1016/j.neuroimage.2007.01.018

Cleckley, H. M. (1951). The mask of sanity. *Postgrad. Med.* 9, 193–197.

Contreras-Rodríguez, O., Pujol, J., Batalla, I., Harrison, B. J., Bosque, J., Ibern-Regàs, I., et al. (2014). Disrupted neural processing of emotional faces in psychopathy. *Soc. Cogn. Affect. Neurosci.* 9, 505–512. doi: 10.1093/scan/nst014

Cope, L. M., Shane, M. S., Segall, J. M., Nyalakanti, P. K., Stevens, M. C., Pearlson, G. D., et al. (2012). Examining the effect of psychopathic traits on gray matter volume in a community substance abuse sample. *Psychiatry Res.* 204, 91–100. doi: 10.1016/j.pscychresns.2012.10.004

Critchley, H. D., Mathias, C. J., and Dolan, R. J. (2002). Fear conditioning in humans: the influence of awareness and autonomic arousal on functional neuroanatomy. *Neuron* 33, 653–663. doi: 10.1016/S0896-6273(02)s00588-3

Critchley, H. D., Wiens, S., Rotshtein, P., Ohman, A., and Dolan, R. J. (2004). Neural systems supporting interoceptive awareness. *Nat. Neurosci.* 7, 189–195. doi: 10.1038/nn1176

Day, R., and Wong, S. (1996). Anomalous perceptual asymmetries for negative emotional stimuli in the psychopath. *J. Abnorm. Psychol.* 105, 648–652. doi: 10.1037/0021-843x.105.4.648

Decety, J., Norman, G. J., Berntson, G. G., and Cacioppo, J. T. (2012). A neurobehavioral evolutionary perspective on the mechanisms underlying empathy. *Prog. Neurobiol.* 98, 38–48. doi: 10.1016/j.pneurobio.2012.05.001

Decety, J., Skelly, L. R., and Kiehl, K. A. (2013). Brain response to empathy-eliciting scenarios involving pain in incarcerated individuals with psychopathy. *JAMA Psychiatry* 70, 638–645. doi: 10.1001/jamapsychiatry.2013.27

Decety, J., and Svetlova, M. (2012). Putting together phylogenetic and ontogenetic perspectives on empathy. *Dev. Cogn. Neurosci.* 2, 1–24. doi: 10.1016/j.dcn.2011.05.003

de Oliveira-Souza, R., Hare, R. D., Bramati, I. E., Garrido, G. J., Azevedo Ignácio, F., Tovar-Moll, F., et al. (2008). Psychopathy as a disorder of the moral brain: fronto-temporo-limbic grey matter reductions demonstrated by voxel-based morphometry. *Neuroimage* 40, 1202–1213. doi: 10.1016/j.neuroimage.2007.12.054

Friston, K. J., and Büchel, C. (2000). Attentional modulation of effective connectivity from V2 to V5/MT in humans. *Proc. Natl. Acad. Sci. U S A* 97, 7591–7596. doi: 10.1073/pnas.97.13.7591

Gao, Y., and Raine, A. (2010). Successful and unsuccessful psychopaths: a neurobiological model. *Behav. Sci. Law* 28, 194–210. doi: 10.1002/bsl.924

Gao, Y., Raine, A., and Schug, R. A. (2012). Somatic aphasia: mismatch of body sensations with autonomic stress reactivity in psychopathy. *Biol. Psychol.* 90, 228–233. doi: 10.1016/j.biopsycho.2012.03.015

Gelnar, P. A., Krauss, B. R., Sheehe, P. R., Szeverenyi, N. M., and Apkarian, A. V. (1999). A comparative fMRI study of cortical representations for thermal painful, vibrotactile and motor performance tasks. *Neuroimage* 10, 460–482. doi: 10.1006/nimg.1999.0482

Goebel, R. (2001). Cortex—based real-time fMRI. *Neuroimage* 62, 748–756. doi: 10.1016/j.neuroimage.2012.01.083

Goebel, R., Roebroeck, A., Kim, D. S., and Formisano, E. (2003). Investigating directed cortical interactions in time-resolved fMRI data using vector autoregressive modeling and Granger causality mapping. *Magn. Reson. Imaging* 21, 1251–1261. doi: 10.1016/j.mri.2003.08.026

Gorno-Tempini, M. L., Pradelli, S., Serafini, M., Pagnoni, G., Baraldi, P., Porro, C., et al. (2001). Explicit and incidental facial expression processing: an fMRI study. *Neuroimage* 14, 465–473. doi: 10.1006/nimg.2001.0811

Granger, C. (1969). Investigating causal relations by econometric models and cross-spectral methods. *Econometrica* 37, 424–438. doi: 10.2307/1912791

Granger, C. (1980). Testing for causality: a personal viewpoint. *J. Econ. Dyn. Control* 2, 329–352. doi: 10.1016/0165-1889(80)90069-X

Hansen, A. L., Johnsen, B. H., Hart, S., Waage, L., and Thayer, J. F. (2008). Brief communication: psychopathy and recognition of facial expressions of emotion. *J. Pers. Disord.* 22, 639–644. doi: 10.1521/pedi.2008.22.6.639

Hare, R. D. (1978). Psychopathy and electrodermal responses to nonsignal stimulation. *Biol. Psychol.* 6, 237–246. doi: 10.1016/0301-0511(78)90026-1

Hare, R. D., Hart, S. D., and Harpur, T. J. (1991). Psychopathy and the DSM-IV criteria for antisocial personality disorder. *J. Abnorm. Psychol.* 100, 391–398. doi: 10.1037//0021-843x.100.3.391

Hart, S. D., Cox, D. N., and Hare, R. D. (1995). *Manual for the Psychopathy Checklist: Screening Version (PCL:SV)*. Toronto: Multi-Health Systems.

Hicks, B. M., and Patrick, C. J. (2006). Psychopathy and negative emotionality: analyses of suppressor effects reveal distinct relations with emotional distress, fearfulness and anger-hostility. *J. Abnorm. Psychol.* 115, 276–287. doi: 10.1037/0021-843x.115.2.276

Juárez, M., Kiehl, K. A., and Calhoun, V. D. (2013). Intrinsic limbic and paralimbic networks are associated with criminal psychopathy. *Hum. Brain Mapp.* 34, 1921–1930. doi: 10.1002/hbm.22037

Kim, J. J., and Jung, M. W. (2006). Neural circuits and mechanisms involved in Pavlovian fear conditioning: a critical review. *Neurosci. Biobehav. Rev.* 30, 188–202. doi: 10.1016/j.neubiorev.2005.06.005

Lang, P. J., Bradley, M. M., and Cuthbert, B. N. (2008). *International Affective Picture System (IAPS): Affective Ratings of Pictures and Instruction Manual. Technical Report A-8*. (Gainesville, FL: University of Florida).

Levenson, M. R., Kiehl, K. A., and Fitzpatrick, C. M. (1995). Assessing psychopathic attributes in a noninstitutionalized population. *J. Pers. Soc. Psychol.* 68, 151–158. doi: 10.1037//0022-3514.68.1.151

Liang, K. C., McGaugh, J. L., Martinez, J. L. Jr., Jensen, R. A., Vasquez, B. J., and Messing, R. B. (1982). Post-training amygdaloid lesions impair retention of an inhibitory avoidance response. *Behav. Brain Res.* 4, 237–249. doi: 10.1016/0166-4328(82)90002-x

Lorber, M. F. (2004). Psychophysiology of aggression, psychopathy and conduct problems: a meta-analysis. *Psychol. Bull.* 130, 531–552. doi: 10.1037/0033-2909.130.4.531

Ly, M., Motzkin, J. C., Philippi, C. L., Kirk, G. R., Newman, J. P., Kiehl, K. A., et al. (2012). Cortical thinning in psychopathy. *Am. J. Psychiatry* 169, 743–749. doi: 10.1176/appi.ajp.2012.11111627

Lykken, D. T. (1957). A study of anxiety in the sociopathic personality. *J. Abnorm. Psychol.* 55, 6–10. doi: 10.1037/h0047232

Marsh, A. A., Finger, E. C., Fowler, K. A., Jurkowitz, I. T., Schechter, J. C., Yu, H. H., et al. (2011). Reduced amygdala-orbitofrontal connectivity during moral judgments in youths with disruptive behavior disorders and psychopathic traits. *Psychiatry Res.* 194, 279–286. doi: 10.1016/j.pscychresns.2011.07.008

McGaugh, J. L., Martinez, J. L. Jr., Messing, R. B., Liang, K. C., Jensen, R. A., Vasquez, B. J., et al. (1982). Role of neurohormones as modulators of memory storage. *Adv. Biochem. Psychopharmacol.* 33, 123–130.

Miller, J. D., Gaughan, E. T., and Pryor, L. R. (2008). The levenson self-report psychopathy scale: an examination of the personality traits and disorders associated with the LSRP factors. *Assessment* 15, 450–463. doi: 10.1177/1073191108316888

Moffitt, T. E. (2005). Genetic and environmental influences on antisocial behaviors: evidence from behavioral-genetic research. *Adv. Genet.* 55, 41–104. doi: 10.1016/s0065-2660(05)55003-x

Morris, J. S., Friston, K. J., Büchel, C., Frith, C. D., Young, A. W., Calder, A. J., et al. (1998a). A neuromodulatory role for the human amygdala in processing emotional facial expressions. *Brain* 121, 47–57. doi: 10.1093/brain/121.1.47

Morris, J. S., Ohman, A., and Dolan, R. J. (1998b). Conscious and unconscious emotional learning in the human amygdala. *Nature* 393, 467–470. doi: 10.1038/30976

Motzkin, J. C., Newman, J. P., Kiehl, K. A., and Koenigs, M. (2011). Reduced prefrontal connectivity in psychopathy. *J. Neurosci.* 31, 17348–17357. doi: 10.1523/JNEUROSCI.4215-11.2011

Ochsner, K. N., Ray, R. D., Cooper, J. C., Robertson, E. R., Chopra, S., Gabrieli, J. D., et al. (2004). For better or for worse: neural systems supporting the cognitive down- and up-regulation of negative emotion. *Neuroimage* 23, 483–499. doi: 10.1016/j.neuroimage.2004.06.030

Osumi, T., Nakao, T., Kasuya, Y., Shinoda, J., Yamada, J., and Ohira, H. (2012). Amygdala dysfunction attenuates frustration-induced aggression in psychopathic individuals in a non-criminal population. *J. Affect. Disord.* 142, 331–338. doi: 10.1016/j.jad.2012.05.012

Patrick, C. J. (1994). Emotion and psychopathy: startling new insights. *Psychophysiology* 31, 319–330. doi: 10.1111/j.1469-8986.1994.tb02440.x

Patrick, C. J., Cuthbert, B. N., and Lang, P. J. (1994). Emotion in the criminal psychopath: fear image processing. *J. Abnorm. Psychol.* 103, 523–534. doi: 10.1037//0021-843x.103.3.523

Peyron, R., Laurent, B., and García-Larrea, L. (2000). Functional imaging of brain responses to pain. A review and meta-analysis (2000). *Neurophysiol. Clin.* 30, 263–288. doi: 10.1016/s0987-7053(00)00227-6

Phan, K. L., Fitzgerald, D. A., Nathan, P. J., and Tancer, M. E. (2006). Association between amygdala hyperactivity to harsh faces and severity of social anxiety in generalized social phobia. *Biol. Psychiatry* 59, 424–429. doi: 10.1016/j.biopsych.2005.08.012

Phan, K. L., Wager, T., Taylor, S. F., and Liberzon, I. (2002). Functional neuroanatomy of emotion: a meta-analysis of emotion activation studies in PET and fMRI. *Neuroimage* 16, 331–348. doi: 10.1006/nimg.2002.1087

Phillips, M. L., Drevets, W. C., Rauch, S. L., and Lane, R. (2003). Neurobiology of emotion perception II: implications for major psychiatric disorders. *Biol. Psychiatry* 54, 515–528. doi: 10.1016/s0006-3223(03)00171-9

Porter, S. (1996). Without conscience or without active conscience? The etiology of psychopathy revisited. *Aggress. Violent Behav.* 1, 179–189. doi: 10.1016/1359-1789(95)00010-0

Roebroeck, A., Formisano, E., and Goebel, R. (2005). Mapping directed influence over the brain using Granger causality and fMRI. *Neuroimage* 25, 230–242. doi: 10.1016/j.neuroimage.2004.11.017

Ruiz, S., Birbaumer, N., and Sitaram, R. (2013a). Abnormal neural connectivity in schizophrenia and fMRI-brain-computer interface as a potential therapeutic approach. *Front. Psychiatry* 4:17. doi: 10.3389/fpsyt.2013.00017

Ruiz, S., Buyukturkoglu, K., Rana, M., Birbaumer, N., and Sitaram, R. (2014). Real-time fMRI brain computer interfaces: self-regulation of single brain regions to networks. *Biol. Psychol.* 95, 4–20. doi: 10.1016/j.biopsycho.2013.04.010

Ruiz, S., Lee, S., Soekadar, S. R., Caria, A., Veit, R., Kircher, T., et al. (2013b). Acquired self-control of insula cortex modulates emotion recognition and brain network connectivity in schizophrenia. *Hum. Brain Mapp.* 34, 200–212. doi: 10.1002/hbm.21427

Salekin, R. T., Worley, C., and Grimes, R. D. (2010). Treatment of psychopathy: a review and brief introduction to the mental model approach for psychopathy. *Behav. Sci. Law* 28, 235–266. doi: 10.1002/bsl.928

Schiffer, B., Müller, B. W., Scherbaum, N., Hodgins, S., Forsting, M., Wiltfang, J., et al. (2011). Disentangling structural brain alterations associated with violent behavior from those associated with substance use disorders. *Arch. Gen. Psychiatry* 68, 1039–1049. doi: 10.1001/archgenpsychiatry.2011.61

Seth, A. K. (2005). Causal connectivity of evolved neural networks during behavior. *Network* 16, 35–54. doi: 10.1080/09548980500238756

Seth, A. K. (2010). A MATLAB toolbox for Granger causal connectivity analysis. *J. Neurosci. Methods* 186, 262–273. doi: 10.1016/j.jneumeth.2009.11.020

Seth, A. K., and Edelman, G. M. (2007). Distinguishing causal interactions in neural populations. *Neural Comput.* 19, 910–933. doi: 10.1162/neco.2007.19.4.910

Simmons, A., Matthews, S. C., Stein, M. B., and Paulus, M. P. (2004). Anticipation of emotionally aversive visual stimuli activates right insula. *Neuroreport* 15, 2261–2265. doi: 10.1097/00001756-200410050-00024

Sitaram, R., Caria, A., and Birbaumer, N. (2009). Hemodynamic brain-computer interfaces for communication and rehabilitation. *Neural Netw.* 22, 1320–1328. doi: 10.1016/j.neunet.2009.05.009

Sitaram, R., Caria, A., Veit, R., Gaber, T., Rota, G., Kuebler, A., et al. (2007). FMRI brain-computer interface: a tool for neuroscientific research and treatment. *Comput. Intell. Neurosci.* 2007: 25487. doi: 10.1155/2007/25487

Sitaram, R., Lee, S., Ruiz, S., Rana, M., Veit, R., and Birbaumer, N. (2011). Real-time support vector classification and feedback of multiple emotional brain states. *Neuroimage* 56, 753–765. doi: 10.1016/j.neuroimage.2010.08.007

Stein, M. B., Simmons, A. N., Feinstein, J. S., and Paulus, M. P. (2007). Increased amygdala and insula activation during emotion processing in anxiety-prone subjects. *Am. J. Psychiatry* 164, 318–327. doi: 10.1176/appi.ajp.164.2.318

Sulzer, J., Haller, S., Scharnowski, F., Weiskopf, N., Birbaumer, N., Blefari, M. L., et al. (2013). Real-time fMRI neurofeedback: progress and challenges. *Neuroimage* 76C, 386–399. doi: 10.1016/j.neuroimage.2013.03.033

Tielbeek, J. J., Medland, S. E., Benyamin, B., Byrne, E. M., Heath, A. C., Madden, P. A., et al. (2012). Unraveling the genetic etiology of adult antisocial behavior: a genome-wide association study. *PLoS One* 7:e45086. doi: 10.1371/journal.pone.0045086

Tiihonen, J., Rossi, R., Laakso, M. P., Hodgins, S., Testa, C., Perez, J., et al. (2008). Brain anatomy of persistent violent offenders: more rather than less. *Psychiatry Res.* 163, 201–212. doi: 10.1016/j.pscychresns.2007.08.012

Ullrich, S., Paelecke, M., Kahle, I., and Marneros, A. (2003). Categorical and dimensional assessment of "psychopathy" in German offenders. Prevalence, gender differences and age factors. *Nervenarzt* 74, 1002–1008. doi: 10.1007/s00115-003-1495-4

Veit, R., Flor, H., Erb, M., Hermann, C., Lotze, M., Grodd, W., et al. (2002). Brain circuits involved in emotional learning in antisocial behavior and social phobia in humans. *Neurosci. Lett.* 328, 233–236. doi: 10.1016/s0304-3940(02)00519-0

Veit, R., Singh, V., Sitaram, R., Caria, A., Rauss, K., and Birbaumer, N. (2012). Using real-time fMRI to learn voluntary regulation of the anterior insula in the presence of threat-related stimuli. *Soc. Cogn. Affect. Neurosci.* 7, 623–634. doi: 10.1093/scan/nsr061

Viding, E. (2004). On the nature and nurture of antisocial behavior and violence. *Ann. N Y Acad. Sci.* 1036, 267–277. doi: 10.1196/annals.1330.017

Weiskopf, N., Sitaram, R., Josephs, O., Veit, R., Scharnowski, F., Goebel, R., et al. (2007). Real-time functional magnetic resonance imaging: methods and applications. *Magn. Reson. Imaging* 25, 989–1003. doi: 10.1016/j.mri.2007.02.007

Yildirim, B. O., and Derksen, J. J. (2013). Systematic review, structural analysis and new theoretical perspectives on the role of serotonin and associated genes in the etiology of psychopathy and sociopathy. *Neurosci. Biobehav. Rev.* 37, 1254–1296. doi: 10.1016/j.neubiorev.2013.04.009

12

Learned EEG-based brain self-regulation of motor-related oscillations during application of transcranial electric brain stimulation: feasibility and limitations

Surjo R. Soekadar[1,2,3]*, Matthias Witkowski[1,2,3], Eliana G. Cossio[2,3], Niels Birbaumer[3,4] and Leonardo G. Cohen[1]

[1] *Human Cortical Physiology and Neurorehabilitation Section, NINDS, NIH, Bethesda, MD, USA*
[2] *Applied Neurotechnology Lab, Department of Psychiatry and Psychotherapy, University Hospital Tübingen, Tübingen, Germany*
[3] *Institute of Medical Psychology and Behavioral Neurobiology, University of Tübingen, Tübingen, Germany*
[4] *Ospedale san Camillo, IRCCS, Venice, Italy*

Correspondence:
Surjo R. Soekadar, Applied Neurotechnology Lab, Department of Psychiatry and Psychotherapy, University Hospital of Tübingen, Calwerstr. 14, 72076 Tübingen, Germany
e-mail: surjo.soekadar@uni-tuebingen.de

Objective: Transcranial direct current stimulation (tDCS) improves motor learning and can affect emotional processing and attention. However, it is unclear whether learned electroencephalography (EEG)-based brain-machine interface (BMI) control during tDCS is feasible, how application of transcranial electric currents during BMI control would interfere with feature-extraction of physiological brain signals and how it affects brain control performance. Here we tested this combination and evaluated stimulation-dependent artifacts across different EEG frequencies and stability of motor imagery-based BMI control.

Approach: Ten healthy volunteers were invited to two BMI-sessions, each comprising two 60-trial blocks. During the trials, learned desynchronization of mu-rhythms (8–15 Hz) associated with motor imagery (MI) recorded over C4 was translated into online cursor movements on a computer screen. During block 2, either sham (session A) or anodal tDCS (session B) was applied at 1 mA with the stimulation electrode placed 1 cm anterior of C4.

Main results: tDCS was associated with a significant signal power increase in the lower frequencies most evident in the signal spectrum of the EEG channel closest to the stimulation electrode. Stimulation-dependent signal power increase exhibited a decay of 12 dB per decade, leaving frequencies above 9 Hz unaffected. Analysis of BMI control performance did not indicate a difference between blocks and tDCS conditions.

Conclusion: Application of tDCS during learned EEG-based self-regulation of brain oscillations above 9 Hz is feasible and safe, and might improve applicability of BMI systems.

Keywords: brain-machine interface (BMI) control, motor imagery, EEG, transcranial electric stimulation (TES), stimulation artifacts

INTRODUCTION

Brain-machine interfaces (BMI) translate physiological features of brain activity associated with the user's intention or state into control signals of a particular device or computer (Birbaumer and Cohen, 2007). BMIs are increasingly used in the context of neurorehabilitation, e.g., after stroke (Ang et al., 2011; Ramos-Murguialday et al., 2013) with two main purposes: (1) to drive assistive devices or computers that surrogate a lost or impeded function, or (2) to facilitate motor recovery related to BMI-based neurofeedback training (Wang et al., 2010; Soekadar et al., 2011). The best-established BMI in stroke is based on volitional modulation of mu-rhythm (8–15 Hz, also called sensorimotor rhythm, SMR) recorded over the sensori-motor cortex using electro- or magnetoencephalography (EEG/MEG) (Buch et al., 2008; Ramos-Murguialday et al., 2013). Motor planning, imagery or execution is associated with a decrease in amplitude of mu-rhythm (Pfurtscheller and Neuper, 1997; Llanos et al., 2013). This decrease can be quantified as event-related desynchronization (ERD) (Pfurtscheller and Aranibar, 1979) and used by a BMI system to control an exoskeleton moving a patient's paralyzed hand (Soekadar et al., 2011).

Depending on the physiological features, several sessions of BMI training are typically required to achieve stable and reliable BMI control (Soekadar et al., 2011). Training-related BMI learning, however, is often substantially impeded in patients with brain lesions, such as stroke, traumatic brain injury or other brain disorders resulting in compromised learning capacity (Buch et al., 2008). Thus, it would be desirable to identify strategies to improve BMI learning and performance in these populations.

Several studies suggest that the application of weak electric currents in the form of transcranial direct current stimulation (tDCS) can improve motor learning (Zimerman et al., 2012), cognition (Metuki et al., 2012), memory consolidation (Dockery et al., 2009; Reis et al., 2009) and emotional processing (Nitsche et al., 2012). While the underlying physiological mechanisms of these effects are still unknown, it has been shown that tDCS can result in polarity-dependent shifts of membrane potentials and modulate cortical excitability (Nitsche and Paulus, 2000; Pellicciari et al., 2013). Recent work indicates that anodal tDCS applied before a motor imagery-based BMI session might improve BMI control (Wei et al., 2013) and modulate motor imagery-related mu-ERD (Matsumoto et al., 2010). A series of experiments suggests that learning is faster when tDCS is applied during a task compared to when it is applied prior to the task (Stagg et al., 2011). It was concluded that such timing-dependency might be of particular importance for the development of plasticity-inducing stimulation protocols (Nitsche et al., 2007). Furthermore, in addition to being time-saving in the clinical context when applied during motor or BMI training, direct effects of tDCS on brain oscillatory activity in the context of such training can be assessed, allowing for a better understanding of how transcranial electric currents modulate task-related brain activity.

While a novel strategy using magnetoencephalography (MEG) for *in vivo* assessment of neuromagnetic brain oscillations during transcranial electric brain stimulation was recently introduced (Soekadar et al., 2013a), the immobility and costs of MEG constrains broader clinical applications, e.g., for BMI training in the context of neurorehabilitation. EEG, in contrast, is inexpensive and widely used in clinical environments. However, the application of electric currents at voltages of up to 20 volts to the human head while recording EEG in the range of millivolts is particularly challenging. This is due to two main reasons: (1) Most EEG systems use wet electrodes to improve conduction between electrodes and the skin. Likewise, the application of electric currents to the head also requires good conduction, mostly provided by using electrolyte gels or pastes. If the conductive agents used for the EEG electrodes and stimulating electrodes are in direct contact, the stimulation currents will saturate the EEG amplifier and impede any physiological recordings. (2) Electric stimulation of the head can be associated with additional stimulation-depended signals picked up by the EEG amplifiers that might reduce classification accuracy in BMI control. This would be disadvantageous for both assistive and neurofeedback BMI applications. While denoting any stimulation-dependent signal during neurophysiological recordings of brain activity as artifacts or noise (i.e., an irregular fluctuation of the measured signal that does not contain meaningful information or obscures the information of interest) is somewhat appealing, it should be emphasized that the separation between the physiological responses or effects of the stimulation and stimulator-dependent noise is difficult. While recently systems were introduced that integrate electric stimulation and recording of EEG (e.g., Starstim® by Neuroelectrics, Barcelona, Spain) allowing for simultaneous EEG monitoring during tDCS (Schestatsky et al., 2013), it remained unclear how EEG signals across different frequency bands recorded at different distances from the stimulating electrode are affected by tDCS, and whether learned electroencephalography (EEG)-based brain-machine interface (BMI) control e.g., using motor imagery (MI) during tDCS is feasible, reliable, and safe.

Here, we investigated such a combination choosing an electrode montage that places the stimulation electrode as close as 1 cm to the EEG electrode recording brain oscillations used for BMI control (see **Figure 1A**). To allow generalization to other BMI paradigms, we first characterized stimulation-dependent signals at different EEG locations. We then compared the signal power in different frequencies (delta: 0.1–4 Hz; theta: 4–9 Hz; alpha: 9–15 Hz; and beta: 15–30 Hz) before stimulation and during stimulation, and identified those frequencies significantly influenced by stimulation-dependent signals. Finally, we calculated the effect size of the stimulation conditions for each frequency band. Potential side effects of stimulation, like tingling, itching or burning (Brunoni et al., 2011) were assessed throughout the sessions.

MATERIALS AND METHODS

PARTICIPANTS AND EXPERIMENTAL DESIGN

Ten healthy volunteers (5 males, 5 females, mean age: 26.7 years ± 4.3) exhibiting reliable and stable motor imagery-based BMI control in a previous investigation (Soekadar et al., 2011) were invited for two BMI sessions on consecutive days. All participants were right handed according to the Edinburgh Handedness Inventory (Oldfield, 1971). Each session was divided into two blocks of 60 trials (block 1, block 2). While no stimulation was delivered during block 1 of both sessions, either sham stimulation (session A) or anodal stimulation (session B) was applied during block 2. Sessions were conducted in random order. All participants gave written informed consent before entering the study. The study protocol was approved by the National Institute of Neurologic Disorders and Stroke Institutional Review Board (NINDS IRB).

ELECTROENCEPHALOGRAPHIC (EEG)-RECORDINGS AND FEEDBACK OF mu-EVENT-RELATED DESYNCHRONIZATION (mu-ERD)

Participants were seated comfortably in an armchair facing a computer monitor. EEG was recorded from the following conventional EEG-recording sites (F3, FC5, C3, P3, Fz, AFz, Cz, FCz, F4, FC6, C4, P4 according to the international 10/20 system) using a 12-channel active electrode EEG system (Acti-cap® and BrainAmp MRplus®, BrainProducts, Gilching, Germany) with the reference electrode placed at FCz and the ground electrode at AFz. For translation of neurophysiological signals into visual feedback, BCI2000, a multipurpose standard BCI platform, was used (Schalk et al., 2004).

All participants were instructed to use visuo-kinesthetic MI of moving their left hand modulating right-hemispheric mu-rhythms when they saw the visual cue indicating the initialization of each trial.

To rule out overt movements during MI, electromyography (EMG) was recorded from the first dorsal interosseus muscle (FDI), extensor digitorum communis (EDC), extensor carpi ulnaris (ECU) and flexor carpi radialis (FCR) during the sessions. Skin/electrode resistance was kept below 10 kΩ. EMG signals were recorded at a sampling rate of 1 kHz and high-pass filtered at 2 Hz (BrainAmp ExG®, Brainproducts, Gilching, Germany). Trials in which EMG activity exceeded that recorded during rest by two standard deviations were interrupted and excluded from further analysis. The number of excluded trials in which

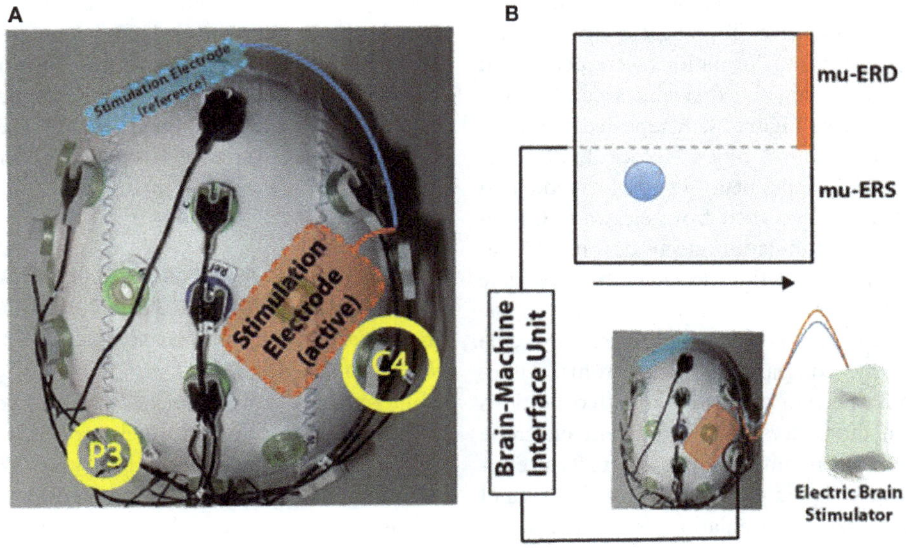

FIGURE 1 | (A) Experimental setup for simultaneous transcranial electric current stimulation during electroencephalography (EEG). The active stimulation electrode was placed immediately anterior to the EEG electrode C4 used for online brain-machine interface (BMI) control (right yellow circle). The reference stimulation electrode was placed over the left supraorbital region (blue). **(B)** BMI paradigm. Electric brain activity recorded at electrode C4 was translated into visual feedback. Event-related desynchronization of mu-rhythms (9–15 Hz, mu-ERD) was indicated by upward movements of a blue ball, while mu-event-related synchronization was indicated by downward movements (mu-ERS). Participants were instructed to keep the ball above the dotted horizontal line during the task to hit the target (indicated by red bar).

EMG activity was present was comparable across participants and ranged between 5 and 10%.

Amplitude of mu-rhythm event-related desynchronization (mu-ERD) and synchronization (mu-ERS) was visually fed back to the participants during each trial (see **Figure 1B**). While increasing mu-ERD was indicated by up-movements of a ball above the horizontal midline of the screen, mu-ERS resulted in down-movements below the midline. Visual feedback was continuously updated every 100 ms. Computation of mu-ERD/mu-ERS included the power spectrum estimation (an autoregressive model of order 16 using the Yule–Walker algorithm) of each incoming sample at the optimal frequency for mu-ERD detection. The optimal frequency was identified in a screening run before the first session (11 Hz in all participants). Resulting values were compared with mean power values of the preceding inter-trial-intervals (ITI) that were continuously updated during BMI control according to the method of Pfurtscheller and Aranibar (1979) and as previously implemented into a mu-ERD BMI system (Soekadar et al., 2011):

$$\overline{R} = \frac{1}{N}\sum_{t=1}^{N} R_t \tag{1}$$

$$ERD\,(t) = \frac{T_t}{\overline{R}} - 1 \tag{2}$$

Where t represents the recorded sample block, T_t the event-related task condition period and R_t the power estimate in a given frequency band of t. $\overline{R}$ (reference value) represents power estimates during the rest (task-free) condition.

Each session consisted of 2 blocks with 60 trials. After the first block either sham stimulation (session A) or anodal stimulation (session B) was applied during the following 60 trials in a randomized order.

TRANSCRANIAL DIRECT CURRENT STIMULATION (tDCS)

tDCS was applied via two conducting 4 × 6 cm rubber electrodes and attached to the participant's head using a conductive paste (Ten20®, D.O. Deaver, Aurora, CO, USA). The adhesive features of this paste prevented any sliding or dislocation of the electrodes during the attachment of the EEG cap. A bipolar electrode montage (right M1 and left supraorbital area) was used (see **Figure 1A**) to deliver a current of 1 mA (current density 0.04 mA/cm^2; total charge 0.048 C/cm^2 using the DC-STIMULATOR PLUS, neuroConn GmbH, Germany). During sham stimulation, the DC stimulator was set up to apply an anodal current for 15 s and—at the offset—decrease stimulation intensity in a ramp-like fashion, a method shown to achieve a good level of blinding (Gandiga et al., 2006). Prior to the first block of the first session, the M1 hand-area was localized in all participants based on the motor evoked potential (MEP) hotspot of the first digit's interosseus muscle (FDI) using transcranial magnetic stimulation (TMS). After the end of block 2 of sessions A and B, all participants rated possible discomfort, pain, tingling, itching or burning associated with the stimulation on visual analog scales (VAS) to assess safety and tolerability of tDCS during BMI control.

OFFLINE ANALYSIS

For all outcome measures, assumption of a normal distribution (Shapiro–Wilk test of normality) was tested. Parametric tests were corrected by Greenhouse-Geisser estimates if Mauchly's sphericity test indicated significance. To compare signal power across conditions, fast Fourier transformations were performed for all EEG data collected during the first and second blocks of session A and session B (see **Figure 2**). A repeated-measures ANOVA (rmANOVA) with factors "block" (block 1, block 2) and "frequency" (delta, theta, alpha, beta) was performed based on the raw EEG signal power recorded from electrode C4 (in immediate proximity to the stimulation electrode) and P3 (at ~8–10 cm distance from the stimulation electrode) to investigate stimulation-dependent changes in different EEG channels. *Post-hoc* paired-samples Students *t*-tests were used when applicable and corrected for multiple comparisons (Bonferroni). Time-frequency representations (TFR) were plotted for both conditions and tested for statistical differences at two different electrode positions (C4 in immediate proximity of the stimulation electrode, and P3) using a cluster-based permutation test (Maris and Oostenveld, 2007). Effect size of stimulation-dependent signal differences in each frequency band was calculated using Cohen's *d* transformed into a regression coefficient *r* where $r < 0.3$ is considered a small, $r < 0.5$ is considered a medium, and $r > 0.5$ is considered a large effect (Cohen, 1988). A rmANOVA with factors "session" (session A, session B) and "block" (block 1, block 2) was used to evaluate changes of BMI control across sessions in the absence (block 1) and presence (block 2) of anodal tDCS. BMI control was defined as the time during each trial in which the ball was above midline (indicating mu-ERD). All analyses were performed in SPSS 17.0. Significance level was set to $p < 0.05$. Variance is defined as the standard error of the mean.

RESULTS

STIMULATION-DEPENDENT CHANGES OF SIGNAL POWER ACROSS DIFFERENT FREQUENCY BANDS AND CONDITIONS

Stimulation electrode in close proximity (~1 cm) to the recording EEG channel (C4)

While rmANOVA of data recorded during session A (sham stimulation during block 2) from electrode C4 (**Figure 2A**) showed a main effect for "frequency" [$F_{(1, 27)} = 37.156$, $p < 0.0001$], indicating an expected difference between power values across the investigated frequency bands, there was no effect for "block" [$F_{(1, 27)} = 0.233$, $p = 0.641$] and no interaction between the factors ($p = 0.188$). *Post-hoc t*-tests showed no significant differences between power values of block 1 and 2 in any frequency band (delta: $p = 0.729$; theta: $p = 0.963$; alpha: $p = 0.946$; beta: $p = 0.784$).

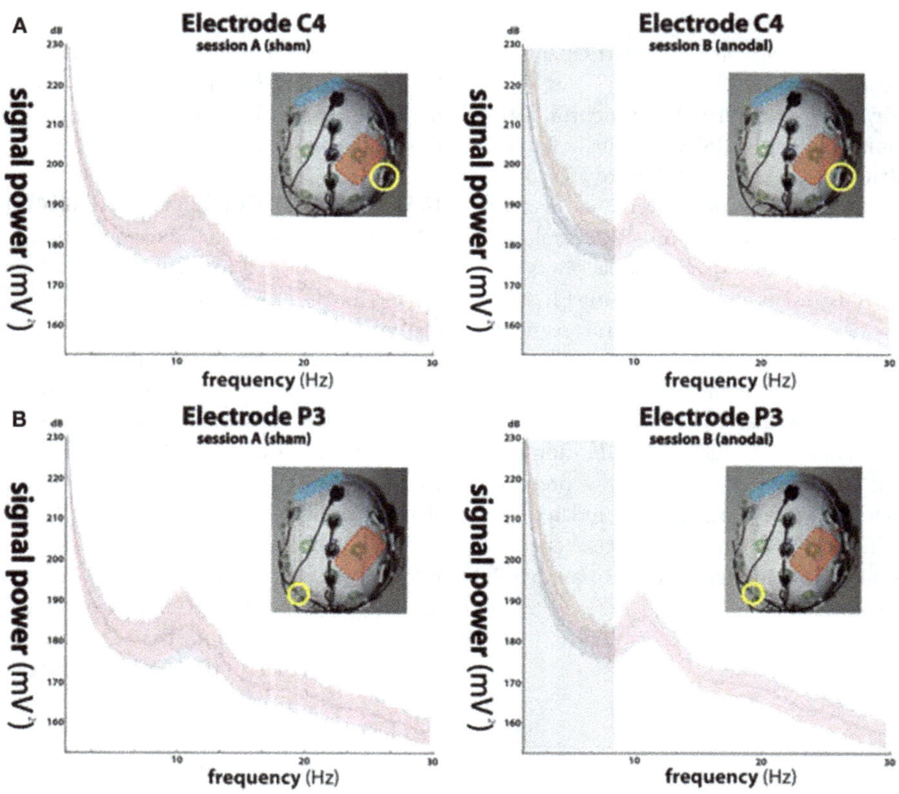

FIGURE 2 | Power spectra of the electroencephalographic (EEG) signals recorded from electrode C4 (A) indicated by yellow circles in the upper panels and P3 (B) during sham stimulation (left column, red curve) and anodal stimulation (right column, red curve). Power spectra of trials in absence of stimulation (block 1) are shown in blue. While not significant during sham stimulation (left column), anodal stimulation resulted in significant signal changes in delta (0–4 Hz) and theta (4–9 Hz) oscillations at electrode position C4 (indicated by the gray underlay in the upper right panel), equally present in delta, and in trend in theta oscillations recorded at P3 (indicated by the gray underlay in the lower right panel), while alpha (9–15 Hz) and beta (15–30 Hz) frequencies showed no difference between conditions.

When analyzing data of session B (anodal stimulation during block 2) from the same location, we found a main effect for both "frequency" [$F_{(1, 27)} = 77.536, p < 0.0001$] and "block" [$F_{(1, 27)} = 33.16, p < 0.0001$] and an interaction between the two [$F_{(1, 3)} = 39.584, p < 0.0001$]. *Post-hoc t*-tests showed a significant difference between power values of block 1 and 2 in the delta band ($p < 0.0001$) and a trend in the theta band ($p = 0.068$), but no significant differences in the alpha ($p = 0.482$) or beta (beta: $p = 0.336$) bands.

Stimulation electrode at ~8–10 cm distance to the recording EEG channel (P3)

Analysis of EEG data recorded ~8–10 cm away from the stimulation electrode (P3) (**Figure 2B**) during session A, revealed a main effect for "frequency" [$F_{(1, 27)} = 28.28, p < 0.0001$], but no effect for "block" [$F_{(1, 27)} = 1.202, p = 0.301$] and no interaction between the factors ($p = 0.056$). We found no significant differences between power values of block 1 and 2 in any frequency band (delta: $p = 0.655$; theta: $p = 0.984$; alpha: $p = 0.937$; beta: $p = 0.923$).

The same analysis performed for data acquired during session B (anodal stimulation during block 2) at electrode position P3, showed a main effect for both, "frequency" [$F_{(1, 27)} = 34.39, p < 0.0001$] and "block" [$F_{(1, 27)} = 11.34, p < 0.01$] and a significant interaction between the two [$F_{(1, 3)} = 14.152, p < 0.0001$]. *Post-hoc t*-tests indicated a significant difference between power values of block 1 and 2 in the delta band ($p < 0.05$), but not in the theta ($p = 0.217$), alpha ($p = 0.445$) or beta (beta: $p = 0.482$) bands.

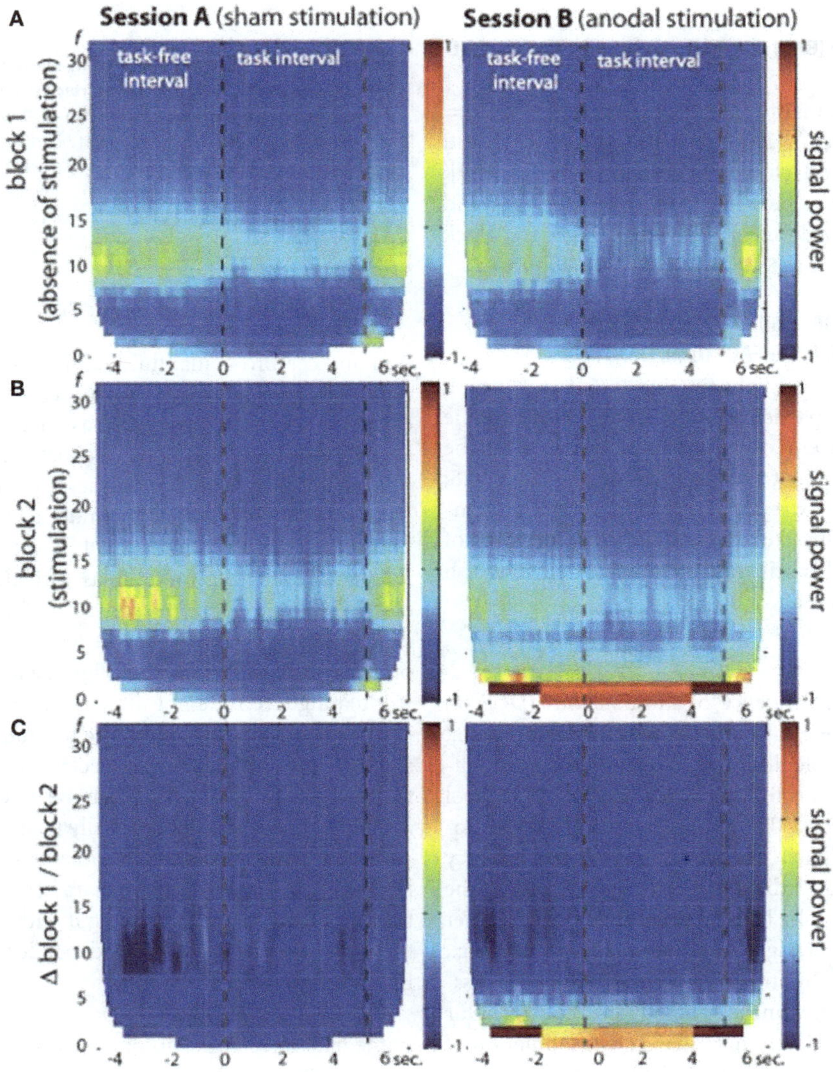

FIGURE 3 | Time-frequency representation (TFR) of brain oscillations recorded from EEG electrode position C4 at 1 cm distance from the active electric brain stimulation electrode. (A) Block 1 of session A (left) and session B (right) in absence of electric brain stimulation. **(B)** Block 2 of session A (left, during sham stimulation) and session B (right, during anodal stimulation). Note the signal power increase in frequencies below 9 Hz in block 2 of session B (during anodal stimulation) across task-free and task intervals. **(C)** Signal power differences between block 1 and block 2 are plotted separately for both sessions (session A: left graph; session B: right graph), indicating no significant stimulation-dependent signal changes above 9 Hz.

Fourier transformations and TFR calculated for both sessions and blocks separately showed an increase in signal power during the second block of session B (see **Figures 2, 3**), which was highest in the slow frequency bands showing a decay of ~12 dB per decade. While not significant, we found a slight increase in broadband noise across all frequencies during anodal stimulation (second block, session B; see **Figure 3B**, right panel). Statistical analysis using a non-parametric cluster-based permutation test indicated significant stimulation-dependent changes of signal power in frequencies below 8 Hz (**Figure 3C**, right panel), but not in frequencies above 9 Hz. Calculation of the stimulation-dependent signal difference's effect size on each frequency band indicated a large effect on the delta band ($d = 0.9893$, $r = 0.443$) which was weaker in the theta band ($d = 0.5721$, $r = 0.275$) and small in the alpha ($d = 0.2988$, $r = 0.122$) as well as beta band ($d = 0.2791$, $r = 0.115$).

BRAIN-MACHINE INTERFACE (BMI) CONTROL ACROSS SESSIONS AND CONDITIONS

RmANOVA indicated no main effects for "session" [$F_{(1, 9)} = 0.30$, $p = 0.597$] or "block" [$F_{(1, 9)} = 1.097$, $p = 0.322$] and no interaction between the factors [$F_{(1, 1)} = 0.349$, $p = 0.569$]. There also was no difference between block 1 of session A and session B ($p = 0.541$), nor a difference between block 1 and block 2 of session A ($p = 0.880$) or session B ($p = 0.470$) (**Figure 4**).

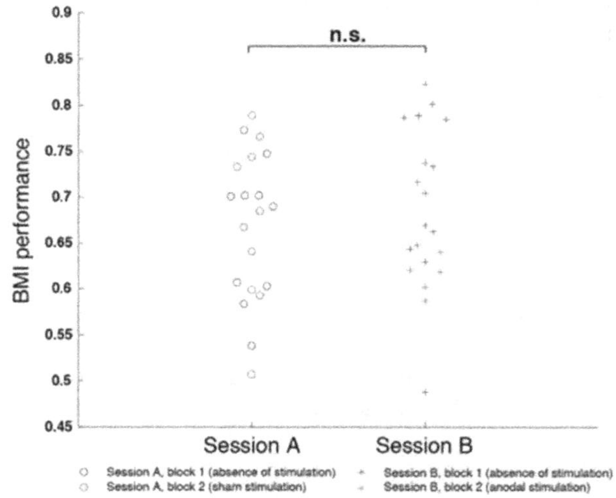

FIGURE 4 | Motor imagery (mu-event-related desynchronization, mu-ERD)-based brain-machine interface (BMI) performance was defined as the percentage of time mu-ERD was detected during trials. BMI performance was comparable between both sessions and did not exhibit differences between block 1 and block 2. There was neither a difference between block 1 of session A and session B ($p = 0.541$), nor a difference between block 1 and block 2 of session A ($p = 0.880$) or session B ($p = 0.470$).

SAFETY AND TOLERABILITY OF SIMULTANEOUS tDCS DURING EEG-BASED BRAIN-MACHINE INTERFACE (BMI) CONTROL

Six of ten participants reported light tingling (rated at 2–3 on a VAS, mean value across all participants 1.6 ± 0.4 with $0 =$ none and $10 =$ unbearable, extreme tingling) in at least one of the sessions, and five reported light itching (mean value 1.4 ± 0.8; $0 =$ none, $10 =$ unbearable, extreme itching), mainly at the beginning of block 2. None of the participants reported any form of severe discomfort or pain. Participants were unable to distinguish sensations between session A and session B.

DISCUSSION

Our study investigated the influence of simultaneous tDCS on EEG recordings across different frequency bands and shows that online extraction of physiological signals during learned self-regulation of brain oscillations for online MI-based BMI control is feasible and safe. We found that application of tDCS is associated with a significant signal increase across slower frequency bands below 9 Hz (delta and theta) in direct proximity of the stimulation electrode, and delta band (<4 Hz) recorded at larger distance (>~8 cm). However, signals oscillating above 9 Hz (e.g., 11 Hz) were not influenced by stimulation and could be successfully used for reliable, motor imagery-based BMI control. Our results indicate that any BMI paradigm driven by modulation of brain oscillations in the alpha (9–15 Hz) or beta range (15–30 Hz) or even higher frequencies (>30 Hz) is possible, given that the signal/noise ratio allows proper linear or non-linear classification of the neurophysiological features used for BMI control.

An important aspect in the combination of tDCS and BMI control is the stimulation montage. Due to the conduction properties of the human head, most electric currents pass through the skin and cerebro-spinal fluid (CSF), while only a fraction enters the gray or white matter (Sadleir et al., 2012). The path of the electric currents in any given case depends on many individual characteristics, such as bone thickness, shape of the skull, density of bone-passing veins or volume of the outer CSF space (which is increased, for instance, in brain atrophy). Various computational models were developed to calculate intracranial current flow and to identify brain areas with the highest magnitude of cortical electric fields (Bikson et al., 2012; Sadleir et al., 2012). Depending on the montage, the area with the highest magnitude of the cortical electrical field might be in larger distance from the stimulating electrode not directly underlying the current source (Edwards et al., 2013). Thus, the technique described here which allows for the application of electric currents as close as 1 cm to the EEG recording channel might be used for modulating cortical activity of brain areas functionally related to BMI control.

When using a different stimulator than the one used in this investigation, corresponding characteristics of this device should be tested first before combining it with EEG-based BMI systems to rule out other stimulation-dependent contaminations of the EEG signal.

While some previous studies suggested that tDCS can have immediate effects on motor imagery-related ERD (Matsumoto et al., 2010) and BMI control (Wei et al., 2013), we did not find such immediate effects. This might be due to the fact that participants were not BMI-naïve and exhibited already high and stable BMI control before admission to the study. tDCS, here applied as anodal tDCS, might not have improved BMI performance further, as a ceiling in BMI control may have been reached in these participants. Another reason could be the montage of the stimulation electrode placed 1 cm anterior of the C4, which might have resulted in the highest magnitude of cortical electrical fields in brain areas not related to motor imagery-based BMI control. A different placement of the stimulation electrode might have led to other results.

The immediate effects of electric currents on oscillatory activity in the human brain and their relatedness to behavior are still poorly understood (Dayan et al., 2013). As noted previously, a sensor-space based approach does not allow unambiguous differentiation between signals with a physiological origin opposed to stimulation-dependent signals deriving from the electric circuit of the stimulator. It is conceivable that the observed slow frequency signal power elevation during tDCS is in part of physiological origin and might reflect mechanisms that also underlie the previously well-described after-effects of tDCS, for instance polarity-specific modulation of cortical excitability and improvements of cognition and learning. Due to the design of the paradigm, the effect of tDCS on slow cortical potentials (SCP) could not be investigated here, but might be of interest in future studies to improve general understanding of the physiological effects of tDCS in the context of learned brain self-regulation during motor imagery-based BMI control. Implementation of algorithms with noise-canceling features, e.g., online source-reconstruction using beamformers (Soekadar et al., 2013b) might help to further investigate these mechanisms. The combination of electrical stimulation during multimodal EEG-MEG recordings in the context of brain self-regulation might help to shed light on these issues and further improve understanding of the exact neural substrates and mechanisms underlying the learning of abstract skills, like volitional modulation of brain oscillatory activity in the context of BMI control (Koralek et al., 2012).

CONCLUSION

tDCS delivered at 1 mA in close proximity (1 cm) to an EEG channel used for learned self-regulation of brain oscillatory activity above 9 Hz is feasible and safe. While associated with a signal power elevation across slower frequencies, brain signals above 9 Hz were unaffected by the stimulation allowing simultaneous application of electric currents during motor imagery-based online BMI control. Such combination might substantially improve the applicability and practicality of BMI use in patient populations, for instance, in the context of neurorehabilitation, and allow systematic investigation of the relatedness between learned brain self-regulation, brain oscillatory activity and behavior.

ACKNOWLEDGMENTS

This work was supported by the Intramural Research Program (IRP) of the National Institute of Neurological Disorders and Stroke (NINDS), USA; the Center for Neuroscience and Regenerative Medicine (CNRM), Uniformed Services University of Health Sciences, USA; the Advanced Convergence Research Center at the Daegu Gyeongbuk Institute of Science and Technology, Korea; the German Federal Ministry of Education and Research (BMBF, grant number 01GQ0831, 16SV5838K to Surjo R. Soekadar and Niels Birbaumer); the Deutsche Forschungsgemeinschaft (DFG, grant number SO932-1 to Surjo R. Soekadar and Reinhart Koselleck Project support to Niels Birbaumer); the European Commission under the project WAY (grant number 288551 to Surjo R. Soekadar and Niels Birbaumer); the Volkswagenstiftung and the Baden-Württemberg Stiftung, Germany. We thank Sook-Lei Liew and Birgit Teufel for their assistance in preparing the manuscript.

REFERENCES

Ang, K. K., Guan, C., Chua, K. S. G., Ang, B. T., Kuah, C. W. K., Wang, C., et al. (2011). A large clinical study on the ability of stroke patients to use an EEG-based motor imagery brain-computer interface. *Clin. EEG Neurosci.* 42, 253–258. doi: 10.1177/155005941104200411

Bikson, M., Rahman, A., and Datta, A. (2012). Computational models of transcranial direct current stimulation. *Clin. EEG Neurosci.* 43, 176–183. doi: 10.1177/1550059412445138

Birbaumer, N., and Cohen, L. G. (2007). Brain-computer interfaces: communication and restoration of movement in paralysis. *J. Physiol. (Lond.)* 579, 621–636. doi: 10.1113/jphysiol.2006.125633

Brunoni, A. R., Amadera, J., Berbel, B., Volz, M. S., Rizzerio, B. G., and Fregni, F. (2011). A systematic review on reporting and assessment of adverse effects associated with transcranial direct current stimulation. *Int. J. Neuropsychopharmacol.* 14, 1133–1145. doi: 10.1017/S1461145710001690

Buch, E., Weber, C., Cohen, L. G., Braun, C., Dimyan, M. A., Ard, T., et al. (2008). Think to move: a neuromagnetic brain-computer interface (BCI) system for chronic stroke. *Stroke* 39, 910–917. doi: 10.1161/STROKEAHA.107.505313

Cohen, J. (1988). *Statistical Power Analysis for the Behavioral Sciences, 2nd Edn.* Hillsdale, NJ: Lawrence Erlbaum.

Dayan, E., Censor, N., Buch, E. R., Sandrini, M., and Cohen, L. G. (2013). Noninvasive brain stimulation: from physiology to network dynamics and back. *Nat. Neurosci.* 16, 838–844. doi: 10.1038/nn.3422

Dockery, C.A., Hueckel-Wenig, R., Birbaumer, N., and Plewnia, C. (2009). Enhancement of planning ability by transcranial direct current stimulation. *J. Neurosci.* 29, 7271–7277. doi: 10.1523/JNEUROSCI.0065-09.2009

Edwards, D., Cortes, M., Datta, A., Minhas, P., Wassermann, E.M., and Bikson, M. (2013). Physiological and modeling evidence for focal transcranial electrical brain stimulation in humans: a basis for high-definition tDCS. *Neuroimage* 74, 266–275. doi: 10.1016/j.neuroimage.2013.01.042

Gandiga, P. C., Hummel, F. C., and Cohen, L. G. (2006). Transcranial DC stimulation (tDCS): a tool for double-blind sham-controlled clinical studies in brain stimulation. *Clin. Neurophysiol.* 117, 845–850. doi: 10.1016/j.clinph.2005.12.003

Koralek, A. C., Jin, X., Long, J. D. 2nd., Costa, R. M., and Carmena, J. M. (2012). Corticostriatal plasticity is necessary for learning intentional neuroprosthetic skills. *Nature* 483, 331–335. doi: 10.1038/nature10845

Llanos, C., Rodriguez, M., Rodriguez-Sabate, C., Morales, I., and Sabate, M. (2013). Mu-rhythm changes during the planning of motor and motor imagery actions. *Neuropsychologia* 51, 1019–1026. doi: 10.1016/j.neuropsychologia.2013.02.008

Maris, E., and Oostenveld, R. (2007). Nonparametric statistical testing of EEG-and MEG-data. *J. Neurosci. Methods* 164, 177–190. doi: 10.1016/j.jneumeth.2007.03.024

Matsumoto, J., Fujiwara, T., Takahashi, O., Liu, M., Kimura, A., and Ushiba, J. (2010). Modulation of mu rhythm desynchronization during motor imagery by transcranial direct current stimulation. *J. Neuroeng. Rehabil.* 7:27. doi: 10.1186/1743-0003-7-27

Metuki, N., Sela, T., and Lavidor, M. (2012). Enhancing cognitive control components of insight problems solving by anodal tDCS of the left dorsolateral prefrontal cortex. *Brain Stimul.* 5, 110–115. doi: 10.1016/j.brs.2012.03.002

Nitsche, M.A., Koschack, J., Pohlers, H., Hullemann, S., Paulus, W., and Happe, S. (2012). Effects of frontal transcranial direct current stimulation on emotional state and processing in healthy humans. *Front. Psychiatry* 3:58. doi: 10.3389/fpsyt.2012.00058

Nitsche, M. A., and Paulus, W. (2000). Excitability changes induced in the human motor cortex by weak transcranial direct current stimulation. *J. Physiol. (Lond.)* 527, 633–639. doi: 10.1111/j.1469-7793.2000.t01-1-00633.x

Nitsche, M. A., Roth, A., Kuo, M. F., and Fischer, A. K. (2007). Timing-dependent modulation of associative plasticity by general network excitability in the human motor cortex. *J. Neurosci.* 27, 3807–3812. doi: 10.1523/JNEUROSCI.5348-06.2007

Oldfield, R. C. (1971). The assessment and analysis of handedness: the Edinburgh inventory. *Neuropsychologia* 9, 97–113. doi: 10.1016/0028-3932(71)90067-4

Pellicciari, M. C., Brignani, D., and Miniussi, C. (2013). Excitability modulation of the motor system induced by transcranial direct current stimulation: a multimodal approach. *Neuroimage* 83, 569–580. doi: 10.1016/j.neuroimage.2013.06.076

Pfurtscheller, G., and Aranibar, A. (1979). Evaluation of event-related desynchronization (ERD) preceding and following voluntary self-paced movement. *Electroencephalogr. Clin. Neurophysiol.* 46, 138–146. doi: 10.1016/0013-4694(79)90063-4

Pfurtscheller, G., and Neuper, C. (1997). Motor imagery activates primary sensorimotor area in humans. *Neurosci. Lett.* 239, 65–68. doi: 10.1016/S0304-3940(97)00889-6

Ramos-Murguialday, A., Broetz, D., Rea, M., Läer, L., Yilmaz, O., Brasil, F. L., et al. (2013). Brain-machine interface in chronic stroke rehabilitation: a controlled study. *Ann. Neurol.* 74, 100–108. doi: 10.1002/ana.23879

Reis, J., Schambra, H. M., Cohen, L. G., Buch, E. R., Fritsch, B., Zarahn, E., et al. (2009). Noninvasive cortical stimulation enhances motor skill acquisition over multiple days through an effect on consolidation. *Proc. Natl. Acad. Sci.* 106, 1590–1595. doi: 10.1073/pnas.0805413106

Sadleir, R. J., Vannorsdall, T. D., Schretlen, D. J., and Gordon, B. (2012). Target optimization in transcranial direct current stimulation. *Front. Psychiatry* 3:90. doi: 10.3389/fpsyt.2012.00090

Schalk, G., McFarland, D. J., Hinterberger, T., Birbaumer, N., and Wolpaw, J. R. (2004). BCI2000: a general-purpose brain-computer interface (BCI) system. *IEEE Trans. Biomed. Eng.* 51, 1034–1043. doi: 10.1109/TBME.2004.827072

Schestatsky, P., Morales-Quezada, L., and Fregni, F. (2013). Simultaneous EEG monitoring during transcranial direct current stimulation. *J. Vis. Exp.* 76:50426. doi: 10.3791/50426

Soekadar, S. R., Witkowski, M., Cossio, E. G., Birbaumer, N., Robinson, S. E., and Cohen, L. G. (2013a). *In vivo* assessment of human brain oscillations during application of transcranial electric currents. *Nat. Commun.* 4:2032. doi: 10.1038/ncomms3032

Soekadar, S. R., Witkowski, M., Mellinger, J., Ramos, A., Birbaumer, N., and Cohen, L. G. (2011). ERD-based online brain-machine interfaces (BMI) in the context of neurorehabilitation: optimizing BMI learning and performance. *IEEE Trans. Neural Syst. Rehabil. Eng.* 19, 542–549. doi: 10.1109/TNSRE.2011.2166809

Soekadar, S. R., Witkowski, M., Robinson, S. E., and Birbaumer, N. (2013b). Combining electric brain stimulation and source-based brain-machine interface (BMI) training in neurorehabilitation of chronic stroke. *J. Neurol. Sci.* 333:e542. doi: 10.1016/j.jns.2013.07.1906

Stagg, C. J., Jayaram, G., Pastor, D., Kincses, Z. T., Matthews, P. M., and Johansen-Berg, H. (2011). Polarity and timing-dependent effects of transcranial direct current stimulation in explicit motor learning. *Neuropsychologia* 49, 800–804. doi: 10.1016/j.neuropsychologia.2011.02.009

Wang, W., Collinger, J. L., Perez, M. A., Tyler-Kabara, E. C., Cohen, L. G., Birbaumer, N., et al. (2010). Neural interface technology for rehabilitation: exploiting and promoting neuroplasticity. *Phys. Med. Rehabil. Clin. N. Am.* 21, 157–178. doi: 10.1016/j.pmr.2009.07.003

Wei, P., He, W., Zhou, Y., and Wang, L. (2013). Performance of motor imagery brain-computer interface based on anodal transcranial direct current stimulation modulation. *IEEE Trans. Neural Syst. Rehabil. Eng.* 21, 404–415. doi: 10.1109/TNSRE.2013.2249111

Zimerman, M., Heise, K.F., Hoppe, J., Cohen, L.G., Gerloff, C., and Hummel, F.C. (2012). Modulation of training by single-session transcranial direct current stimulation to the intact motor cortex enhances motor skill acquisition of the paretic hand. *Stroke* 43. 2185–2191. doi: 10.1161/STROKEAHA.111.645382

13

Learned self-regulation of the lesioned brain with epidural electrocorticography

Alireza Gharabaghi[1,2]*, Georgios Naros[1,2], Fatemeh Khademi[1,2], Jessica Jesser[1,2], Martin Spüler[3], Armin Walter[3], Martin Bogdan[3,4], Wolfgang Rosenstiel[3] and Niels Birbaumer[5,6,7]

[1] *Division of Functional and Restorative Neurosurgery and Division of Translational Neurosurgery, Department of Neurosurgery, Eberhard Karls University Tuebingen, Tuebingen, Germany*
[2] *Neuroprosthetics Research Group, Werner Reichardt Centre for Integrative Neuroscience, Eberhard Karls University Tuebingen, Tuebingen, Germany*
[3] *Department of Computer Engineering, Wilhelm-Schickard Institute for Computer Science, Eberhard Karls University Tuebingen, Tuebingen, Germany*
[4] *Department of Computer Engineering, University of Leipzig, Leipzig, Germany*
[5] *Institute for Medical Psychology and Behavioural Neurobiology, Eberhard Karls University Tuebingen, Tuebingen, Germany*
[6] *Ospedale San Camillo, IRCCS, Venice, Italy*
[7] *DZD, Eberhard Karls University Tuebingen, Tuebingen, Germany*

***Correspondence:**
Alireza Gharabaghi, Division of Functional and Restorative Neurosurgery and Division of Translational Neurosurgery, Department of Neurosurgery, Eberhard Karls University Tuebingen, Otfried-Mueller-Str. 45, 72076 Tuebingen, Germany
e-mail: alireza.gharabaghi@uni-tuebingen.de

Introduction: Different techniques for neurofeedback of voluntary brain activations are currently being explored for clinical application in brain disorders. One of the most frequently used approaches is the self-regulation of oscillatory signals recorded with electroencephalography (EEG). Many patients are, however, unable to achieve sufficient voluntary control of brain activity. This could be due to the specific anatomical and physiological changes of the patient's brain after the lesion, as well as to methodological issues related to the technique chosen for recording brain signals.

Methods: A patient with an extended ischemic lesion of the cortex did not gain volitional control of sensorimotor oscillations when using a standard EEG-based approach. We provided him with neurofeedback of his brain activity from the epidural space by electrocorticography (ECoG).

Results: Ipsilesional epidural recordings of field potentials facilitated self-regulation of brain oscillations in an online closed-loop paradigm and allowed reliable neurofeedback training for a period of 4 weeks.

Conclusion: Epidural implants may decode and train brain activity even when the cortical physiology is distorted following severe brain injury. Such practice would allow for reinforcement learning of preserved neural networks and may well provide restorative tools for those patients who are severely afflicted.

Keywords: electrocorticography, neuroprosthetics, epidural implant, brain-machine interface, neurofeedback, cortical lesion, stroke

INTRODUCTION

Specific feedback and reward of brain activity allows learning of self-regulation strategies. Operant conditioning of electroencephalography (EEG) and of blood-oxygen-level-dependent (BOLD) signal activity has been applied to reduce disorder-specific symptoms in a variety of neurological and neuropsychiatric conditions (Wyckhoff and Birbaumer, 2014). When neurofeedback is coupled to external devices such as brain-machine interfaces (BMI), the volitional control of brain activity can often be attained, opening up novel training opportunities for the very severely brain-injured and even paralyzed (Buch et al., 2008, 2012; Ang et al., 2011, 2014; Gomez-Rodriguez et al., 2011; Ramos-Murguialday et al., 2012, 2013); first results using EEG-based BMI were promising (Ang et al., 2011, 2014; Ramos-Murguialday et al., 2013). Some -even healthy- participants, however, fail to achieve volitional control of brain activity (Vidaurre and Blankertz, 2010) because of subject-specific anatomical (Halder et al., 2011; Buch et al., 2012; Várkuti et al., 2013) and physiological (Blankertz et al., 2010; Grosse-Wentrup et al., 2011; Vukelić et al., 2014) limitations of the brain, or methodological issues of brain signal recording (Leuthardt et al., 2009). In the context of rehabilitation, additional neurophysiological considerations might contribute to limitations of EEG-based BMI: previous approaches have chosen those frequency bands and algorithms which differentiated best between "motor imagery" and "rest", e.g., the mu/alpha-band and/or modified common spatial filter algorithms to optimize the selection of temporo-spatial discriminative EEG characteristics (Buch et al., 2008, 2012; Ang et al., 2011, 2014; Ramos-Murguialday et al., 2013). Although even larger groups of stroke patients have participated in BMI training with this approach, a more restricted feature space, e.g., perturbations in the beta-band over selected sensorimotor electrode contacts, might be preferred as a reinforced therapeutic target for restorative purposes (Gharabaghi et al., 2014a,b), despite the fact that they might be less optimal from classification purposes, e.g., to differentiate movement-related brain states in stroke patients (Gomez-Rodriguez et al., 2011; Rossiter et al., 2014).

In general, EEG-based approaches have a characteristically low spatial resolution and a low signal-to-noise ratio because of signal attenuation caused by the skull, possible contamination by muscle artifacts and external electrical activity. These approaches might therefore be specifically challenged in cases of an intentionally limited feature space due to therapeutic purposes. Moreover, they often require a relatively long period of training before subjects can gain real-time control of devices (Birbaumer et al., 1999; Leuthardt et al., 2009; Gharabaghi et al., 2014b).

By contrast, electrocorticographic (ECoG) neurofeedback approaches may be able to surmount such difficulties thanks to their proximity to the neural signal source. We recently proposed a new approach which is less invasive than the classical implanted approaches with *subdural* grids (Yanagisawa et al., 2011, 2012; Wang et al., 2013) or even brain penetrating electrodes (Hochberg et al., 2012; Collinger et al., 2013). This novel approach entailed the application of *epidural* ECoG to decode volitional brain activity in patients with locked-in syndrome suffering from amyotrophic lateral sclerosis (Bensch et al., 2014), with chronic pain as a result of upper limb amputation (Gharabaghi et al., 2014c), and with hemiparesis following subcortical hemorrhagic stroke (Gharabaghi et al., 2014b). In all of these cases, however, most of the cortical tissue of the patients was preserved.

Essential questions with regard to the clinical usefulness of implantable brain-computer interfaces based on epidural ECoG remain unanswered. For instance, would this technique also be applicable in patients with extended cortical lesions? Are these patients able to learn consistent online-control of brain activity? Would high intensity neurofeedback training in these patients be possible? Would ECoG neurofeedback be applicable in patients who are not using volitional control of their brain oscillations with a standard EEG-based approach?

We therefore investigated a brain-machine interface based on epidural ECoG and examined its practicability for neurofeedback training in a patient with an extended ischemic lesion of motor cortical areas who did otherwise not adequately engage in voluntary modulation of brain activity based on EEG recordings.

METHODS

PATIENT

The patient, a 52-year-old man, had suffered an ischemic stroke of the right hemisphere with extended cortical lesions (see **Figure 1**) 13 years prior to implantation. This caused a persistent severe hemiparesis and he no longer had control of his left upper extremity (Medical Research Council motor scale < 2).

Several months before surgery, the patient underwent twenty sessions of EEG-based BMI neurofeedback similar to the training described earlier (Ramos-Murguialday et al., 2012; Vukelić et al., 2014) with the same study design that was later used for ECoG-based BMI neurofeedback (see Section Experimental Procedure and **Figure 2**). Offline evaluation of the EEG data revealed artifacts in the recorded brain signals induced by muscle contraction, i.e., showing EEG amplitudes which exceeded the mean cortical activity by at least two standard deviations. For each feedback electrode (FC4, C4 and CP4) we calculated, separately for the "move" and "rest" period of each trial, the percentage of artifacted samples per session and compared their evolution over time with the respective BMI performance evaluated by the area under the recipient operating characteristics curve (AUC).

Several months later, the patient participated in a different, long-term study for motor cortex stimulation with epidural implants simultaneously with rehabilitation training to improve upper limb motor function following the stroke. The study protocol, approved by the ethics committee of the Medical Faculty of the University of Tuebingen, also involved a four-week evaluation period immediately subsequent to implantation, with electrodes externalized with percutaneous extensions to assess the patient's cortical physiology for optimization of stimulation. The data shown below is derived from this period.

Following implantation of the electrode array, i.e., several months after the preoperative evaluation with EEG, the patient was subjected to several different experiments for parameter selection and optimization of motor cortex stimulation (not part of the present report) which included altogether 30 ECoG-based neurofeedback sessions with a mean of ~108 feedback trials per session. Due to their heterogeneity these sessions are not suited to evaluate the evolution of BMI performance during this period, however, they may serve as a valuable source of information for estimating the influence of muscle artifacts, which were visually detected during offline analysis, and the feasibility and reliability of ECoG-based neurofeedback.

EPIDURAL ELECTROCORTICOGRAPHY

The epidurally implanted 4 × 4 electrode array consisted of four electrode leads for chronic application (Resume II, Medtronic, Minneapolis, USA) with four platinum iridium electrode contacts, each (4 mm diameter, 10 mm center-to-center distance) covering parts of the right primary motor, somatosensory cortex and premotor cortex. During the evaluation period, the electrode grid was externalized with percutaneous extensions which were connected to a recording and processing unit and a robotic hand orthosis. A monopolar amplifier (BrainAmp MR plus, BrainProducts, Munich, Germany) with 1 kHz sampling rate and a high-pass filter (cutoff frequency at 0.16 Hz) and a low-pass filter (cutoff frequency at 1000 Hz) was used for ECoG recording. Online processing of brain signals was performed using the BCI 2000 framework (Schalk et al., 2004) extended with custom-built features to control an electromechanical hand orthosis (Amadeo, Tyromotion GmbH, Graz, Austria). The data was collected batch-wise, i.e., every 40 ms, the recording computer received a batch of data that contained 40 samples per channel (Walter et al., 2012; Gharabaghi et al., 2014a). The reference electrode was chosen from the contacts on the somato-sensory

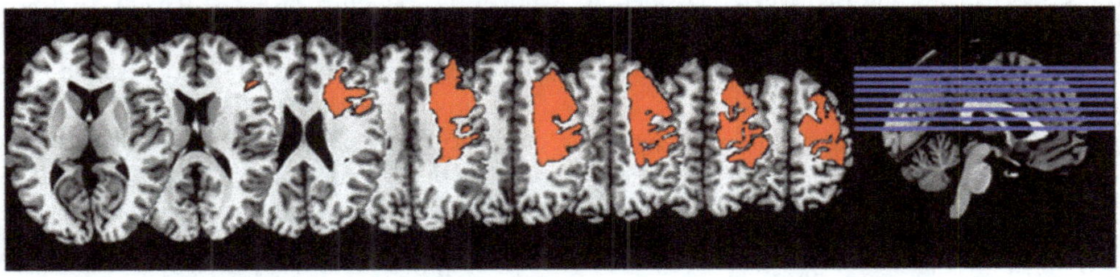

FIGURE 1 | Lesion mask: Normalized lesion mask displayed on MNI (Montreal neurological institute) brain in standard space (Fonov et al., 2009).

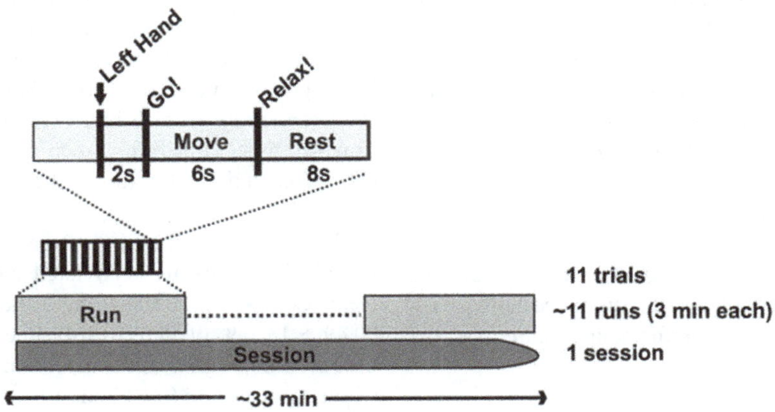

FIGURE 2 | Study design.

cortex, i.e., medio-posterior or latero-posterior corner of the grid.

EXPERIMENTAL PROCEDURE

We used closed-loop, orthosis-assisted opening of the paralyzed left hand which was triggered online by ipsilesional oscillatory brain activity during cued kinesthetic motor imagery of hand opening (Walter et al., 2012; Gharabaghi et al., 2014a). Each session contained 4–16 runs (average 10.86 ± 4.5 runs). Each of the runs had a duration of circa 3 min and consisted of 11 trials. Each trial began with a preparation phase of 2 s, followed by a 6 s movement imagination phase and an 8 s rest phase (see **Figure 3**). Preparation, imagination and rest phases were instigated by a recorded female voice that gave the commands "left hand", "go" and "rest" respectively.

A hand orthosis passively opened the affixed left hand as soon as motor imagery-related event-related desynchronization (ERD) in the beta-band (17–23 Hz) was identified during the movement imagination phase. An epoch was regarded as ERD-positive only when the output of the classifier exceeded a threshold. The latter and the electrode selection were determined individually from three training runs before the test sessions (Walter et al., 2012; Gharabaghi et al., 2014a). The spectral power was calculated using an autoregressive model with an order of 16 (McFarland and Wolpaw, 2008) over a normalized 500 ms sliding window shifting every 40 ms. In order to sidestep a noisy control signal

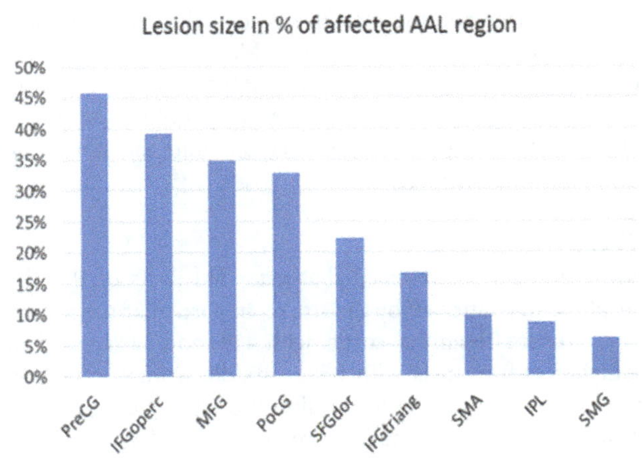

FIGURE 3 | Lesion size in percentage of affected cortical AAL (=automated anatomical labeling) region (Tzourio-Mazoyer et al., 2002): Affected cortical regions are named according to the AAL brain atlas labels: PreCG = precentral gyrus, IFGoperc = pars opercularis of inferior frontal gyrus, MFG = middle frontal gyrus, PoCG = postcentral gyrus, SFGdor = superior frontal gyrus, dorsolateral, IFGtriang = pars triangularis of inferior frontal gyrus, SMA = supplementary motor area, IPL = inferior parietal lobule, SMG = supramarginal gyrus.

for the orthosis, i.e., giving robust and harmonic feedback, we initiated or discontinued orthosis-assisted movement only when five consecutive 40 ms epochs (i.e., 200 ms) where classified as ERD-positive or negative, respectively.

PERFORMANCE EVALUATION

To determine the patient's ability to modulate his brain activity contingent on the BMI feedback task, we determined the percentage of trials with orthosis movement (i.e., ERD) and the average time with orthosis movement (i.e., ERD) divided by the total feedback duration phase (Gharabaghi et al., 2014b,c).

We also measured a baseline condition to supervise spontaneous perturbations of brain activity which could cause fluctuations in the online performance during the feedback task, i.e., could start the orthosis movement independent of motor-imagery. This baseline condition entailed several ECoG recordings which were taken while the patient rested, i.e., one run with eyes open and one run with eyes closed before each session throughout the whole study period. All in all, we recorded approximately 20 min of such spontaneous baseline ECoG activity for offline analysis, segmented it into trials of the same structure and processed it in the same way as in the feedback sessions (Gharabaghi et al., 2014b,c). For statistical analysis, we used the Matlab toolbox (Wilcoxon rank-sum test) to compare the distribution of performance values per run in each feedback session with the distribution of performance values for the baseline data.

IMAGING EVALUATION

Before implantation magnetic resonance imaging (MRI) was performed on a 3.0-Tesla Siemens Trio Scanner (TR 1.95 s, TE 2.26 ms, 176 slices of 1 mm slice thickness). For lesion segmentation MRIcron software[1] was used to manually delineate the lesion. The anatomical image and the mask were normalized to MNI space using SPM 8 (Statistical Parametric Mapping, The Wellcome Department of Imaging Neuroscience, Institute of Neurology, University College London, UK). The overlap of the Automated Anatomical Labeling (AAL) atlas regions and the normalized lesion mask were calculated.

RESULTS

Lesion segmentation revealed that extended parts of the right hemisphere were affected by the stroke, in particular the primary motor and somatosensory cortex with 45% and 33% lesion size and higher motor areas with 35% (middle frontal gyrus) and 22% (superior frontal gyrus) lesion size with respect to the AAL atlas. The basal ganglia were not affected by the lesion (**Figure 3**).

EEG analysis of the non-invasive training showed a systematic change of the number of muscle artifacts. In the course of the training, there was an increase of artifacted samples in the "rest" period of each trial and a decrease in the respective "move" periods. The patient learned to increase and decrease muscle tension in the rest period and in the move period of each trial, respectively (see **Figures 4A,B**).

These changes correlated significantly ($p < 0.05$) with the BMI performance for all channels and both conditions (rest and move), i.e., channel FC4 $r = 0.8905$ for rest and $r = -0.8254$ for move; channel C4: $r = 0.7045$ for rest and $r = -0.8447$ for move; channel CP4: $r = 0.8878$ for rest and $r = -0.8386$ for move (Pearsons correlation coefficient). As a result of the increasing difference between the rest and move condition, there was an increase of BMI control (see **Figure 4B**), i.e., the increased baseline activity in "rest" made it easier to reach the desynchronization threshold in the "move" period for controlling the BMI. Thus, the patient did not volitionally control his oscillatory brain activity for the neurofeedback training.

In contrast, ECoG analysis of the implant based training showed no systematic change in the number of muscle artifacts. Due to the low distance of the two recording channels, the number of artifacted samples was identical. In the course of the training, there was a fluctuating amount of artifacted samples both in the "rest" period and in the "move". Similar to the EEG experiment there were more artifacts in the rest period, but showed no evolution over time. Thus, although muscle tension was not completely eliminated, it did not influence the volitional control of oscillatory brain activity (see **Figure 5**).

Accordingly, in the ECoG-based approach, the patient modulated his motor-imagery related ERD contingent on the BMI feedback task, i.e., initiated the orthosis movement in a mean of 90.49 ± 13.73% of all trials (baseline condition: 32.72 ± 9.77%), thus retaining significant control of brain activity throughout the whole study period (see **Figure 6**).

In fact, he controlled the orthosis movement (i.e., ERD) for a mean of 37.15 ± 15.27% of the feedback duration in each trial. Thus, his performance in this online closed-loop paradigm was constant and significantly higher than in the baseline condition (14.52 ± 7.30%) throughout the study period (see **Figure 7**).

DISCUSSION

The patient presented here—with an extended ischemic lesion of the cortex—learned control of high intensity neurofeedback training based on self-regulation of brain oscillations recorded from the epidural space by ECoG. Although the ECoG based approach enabled the patient to maintain consistent control of his sensorimotor rhythms in the beta-band in an online closed-loop paradigm throughout the study period, his performance in controlling the neurofeedback device in ~30–40% of the feedback duration was—while significantly better than baseline (~15%)—nonetheless markedly lower than comparable ECoG-based (Gharabaghi et al., 2014b) or EEG-based (Ramos-Murguialday et al., 2013) approaches in other similarly affected patients who had attained control rates of ~50–60% of the feedback duration. These variations in performance might be explained by physiological and morphological differences: The respective patients showed strikingly different baseline conditions, i.e., spontaneous perturbations of brain activity in the beta-band could start the orthosis movement independent of motor-imagery during ~15% vs. ~30% of the feedback period in the present and in previous cases (e.g., Gharabaghi et al., 2014b), respectively. These physiological baseline differences could be explained by the different lesion characteristics, namely extended cortical vs. circumscribed subcortical lesions, respectively. Since this brain activity is known to originate from primary motor and

[1] http://www.mccauslandcenter.sc.edu/mricro/mricron/install.html

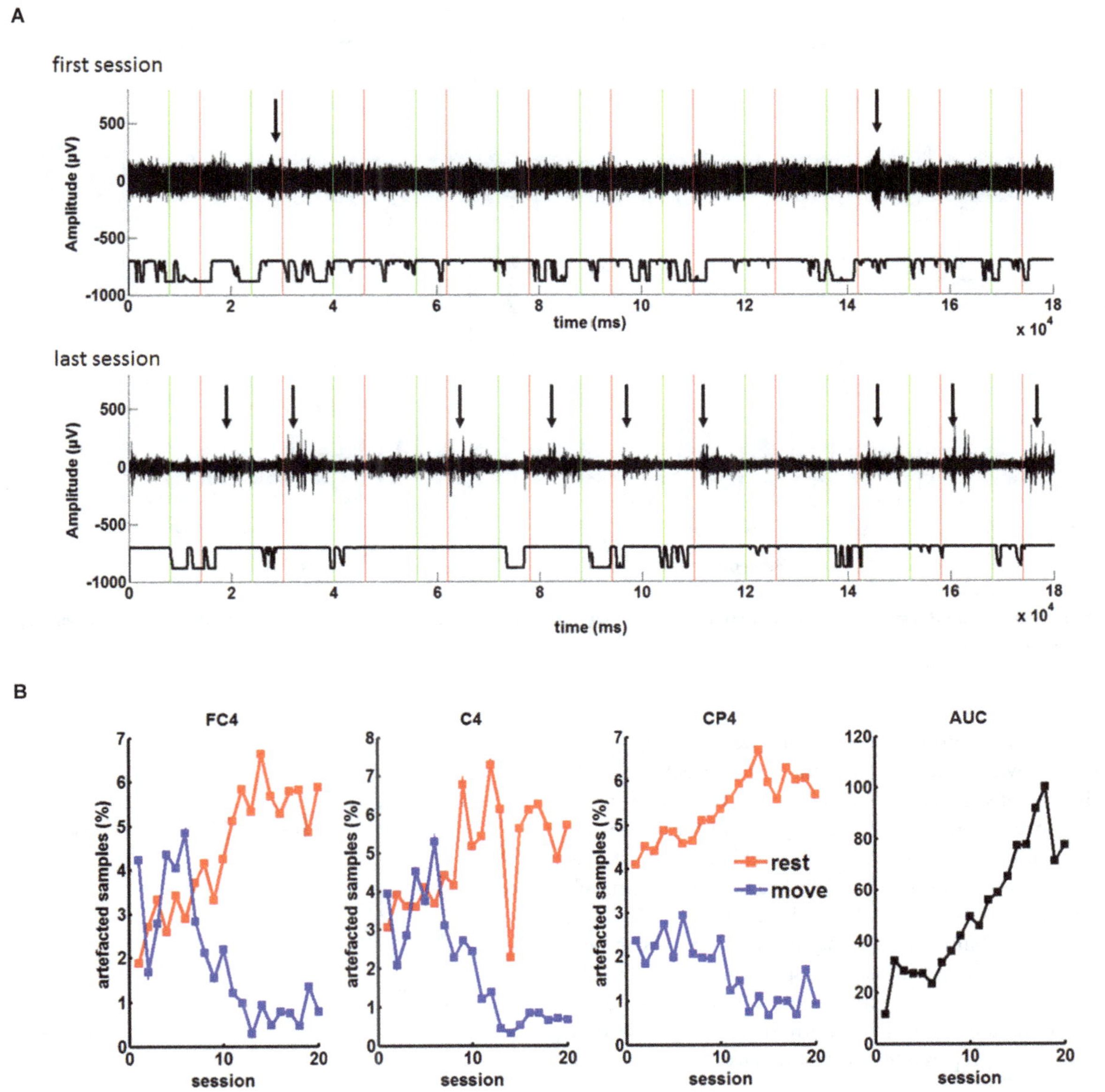

FIGURE 4 | (A) EEG recordings during the feedback task with the orthosis before grid implantation: Green and red lines indicate "Go" and "Rest" cues during each trial, respectively. Arrows highlight muscle artifacts during the run. From the first to the last session the number of the artifacts in the rest period of each trial increased. **(B)** Percentage of artifacted samples during the rest and move condition for the three feedback electrodes (FC4, C4, CP4) in the course of twenty sessions. As a result of the increasing difference of artifacts in the rest and the move condition, there was an increase of BCI control measured by the area under the recipient operating characteristics curve (AUC).

somatosensory as well as from secondary motor areas, the most plausible explanation for the decrease of spontaneous perturbations in the presented case is that they have been affected by the lesion. Our results are in line with recent findings that movement-related beta desynchronization in the contralateral primary motor cortex was found to be significantly reduced in stroke patients compared to controls, while within this patient group, smaller desynchronization has been seen in those with more motor impairment (Rossiter et al., 2014). Moreover, these observations support our general strategy, applied in the present case as well, to choose beta-band desynchronisation as a therapeutic target for restorative interventions in severely affected stroke patients (Gharabaghi et al., 2014a,b).

An intriguing insight gained in this study was that the epidural ECoG technique enabled the patient to engage in feedback exercises based on voluntary modulation of brain activity despite the fact that he did otherwise not use properly a standard EEG-based approach. Interestingly enough, prior to using the implanted brain interface, the patient learned to increase and decrease muscle tension in the rest period and in the move period of each trial, respectively, for BMI control. This alternative conditioning probably occurred because the extent of his

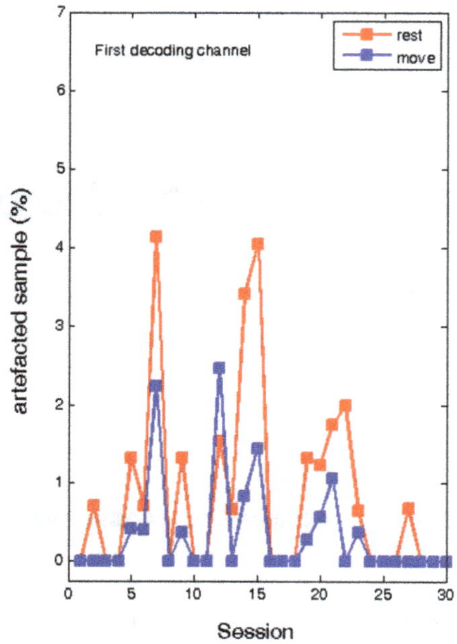

FIGURE 5 | Percentage of artifacted samples during the rest and move condition of the ECoG recordings for two epidural feedback electrodes in the course of thirty sessions.

own voluntary modulation of brain activity was too insignificant to be detected by EEG whereas the muscle contractions could sufficiently be detected and were reinforced by feedback and reward. This alternative control strategy applied by the patient was unexpected. The participants in this study and in previous studies with healthy subjects (Vukelić et al., 2014) and similarly severely affected stroke patients (Ramos-Murguialday et al., 2012) were instructed to avoid blinking, chewing, head and body compensation movements. Along with visual inspection and feedback by an experienced examiner this approach proved to be a sufficient method to prevent alternative BMI control in the past. Moreover, the examiners were prepared to detect compensatory movements *during* the "move" phase of the feedback task as this is the most commonly observed strategy to pretend volitional modulation of ERD, and not *before* the actual task in the "rest" phase. Therefore, increasing baseline activity in "rest" through elevated muscle tension and concurrent reduced muscle tension in the "move" period, have in future to be considered as subtle bypassing strategies to reach the desynchronization threshold more easily.

For this purpose, online detection of EMG contamination with dedicated spectral and topographical analyses might be necessary to prevent alternative BMI control in future. Previous work in this field was conducted without such precautions most probably due to the fact that lower frequency bands were applied for BMI control, which are usually less affected by muscle artifacts (Goncharova et al., 2003). However, due to their relevance for sensorimotor control (Kilavik et al., 2013; Brittain et al., 2014), motor learning (Herrojo Ruiz et al., 2014) and corticospinal excitability (Takemi et al., 2013) as well as due to their correlation with the extent of functional impairments after stroke (Rossiter et al., 2014), higher frequency bands in the beta

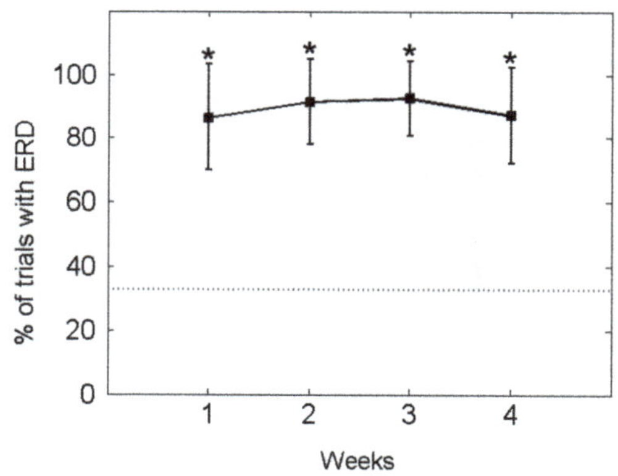

FIGURE 6 | Percentage of EcoG trials with orthosis movement (i.e., event-related desynchronisation [ERD] in the beta-band): The mean ± standard deviation of the performance measure per week is indicated by solid lines. The mean of the baseline data is indicated as a dotted line. An asterisk (*) marks weeks in which the mean of the performance measure differs significantly ($p < 0.05$) from the mean of the baseline value.

range might be considered in future more often as therapeutic targets for restorative EEG neurofeedback and motor rehabilitation (Gharabaghi et al., 2014a,b), necessitating the consideration of even subtle EMG contamination as observed in the presented case. EMG artifact detection may include relatively simple methods such as rejection of EEG segments that exceed a predefined amplitude threshold or more sophisticated methods such as factor decomposition using principal component or independent component analysis with or without source reconstruction algorithms (Goncharova et al., 2003; Hipp and Siegel, 2013). In any case,

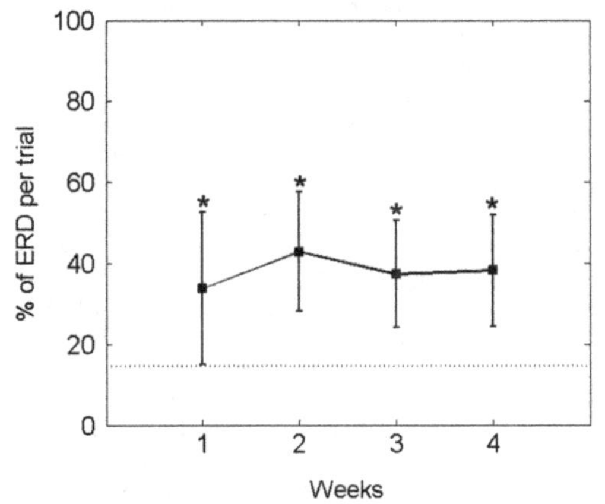

FIGURE 7 | Percentage of average ECoG-based orthosis movement (i.e., event-related desynchronisation [ERD] in the beta-band) divided by the total feedback duration phase: The mean ± standard deviation of the performance measure per week is indicated by solid lines. The mean of the baseline data is indicated as a dotted line. An asterisk (*) marks weeks in which the mean of the performance measure differs significantly ($p < 0.05$) from the mean of the baseline value.

applicable approaches need to work even with only few available channels within a narrow frequency band and have to provide real time processing and low computational complexity (Tiganj et al., 2010).

Should EMG artifacts turn out to be too difficult to mitigate (yet not explicitly addressed by this study) or should the targeted physiological brain state, e.g., motor imagery-related beta-band desynchronisation, be too weak to be robustly detected in the EEG of severely affected stroke patients, implantable approaches might provide an alternative. In this context, the ECoG approach has two advantages over EEG: On account of its proximity to the neural signal source, it surmounts difficulties related to signal attenuation caused by the skull. It is also less susceptible to contamination by muscle artifacts, and, in this case, benefits from the signal attenuation caused by the skull. In this vein, simultaneously recorded ECoG and EEG activity in motor cortical areas revealed that invasively measured signals had a twenty to hundred times better brain signal quality than signals that were acquired non-invasively (Ball et al., 2009).

The technique presented here is limited by the necessity to connect the intracranial implant to an external online processing framework for recording and neurofeedback training via extension leads which are externalized through the skin (Gharabaghi et al., 2014b,c). Future applications of this brain self-regulation approach will require wireless devices capable of fast and reliable information transfer (Borton et al., 2013; Piangerelli et al., 2014). This would facilitate the application of this intervention on a day-patient basis or even in the patient's home environment.

However, before drawing definite conclusions regarding effectiveness of various neurofeedback approaches, future studies need to directly compare ECoG-based techniques to EEG-based methods which control for EMG artifacts. This research needs to consider further aspects such as direct and indirect costs, complications, learning curve, motivation, applicability for long-term use and the possibility of performing training independent of professional support. Based on the respective findings, patients with different impairment levels might then be referred to the specific treatment modality best suited for the individual pathophysiological state.

In conclusion, epidural implants could provide reliable feedback interfaces for brain self-regulation in patients in whom non-invasive approaches fail on account of signal attenuation caused by the skull or due to the underlying pathophysiology. This could establish them as valuable tools in the context of reinforcement learning in a variety of neurological and neuropsychiatric conditions.

ACKNOWLEDGMENTS

Alireza Gharabaghi is supported by grants from the German Research Council, Deutsche Forschungsgemeinschaft [DFG GH 94/2-1, DFG EC 307], and from the Federal Ministry for Education and Research [BFNT 01GQ0761, BMBF 16SV3783, BMBF 03160064B, BMBF V4UKF014]. Fatemeh Khademi is supported by the Graduate Training Centre of Neuroscience, International Max Planck Research School, Tuebingen, Germany. Niels Birbaumer is supported by the Deutsche Forschungsgemeinschaft (Reinhard Koselleck Project) and by Brain Products GmbH, Munich, Germany. We thank Ramin Azodi Avval for his support with the figures and Dr. Mathias Vukelić and Vladislav Royter for fruitful discussions.

REFERENCES

Ang, K. K., Chua, K. S. G., Phua, K. S., Wang, C., Chin, Z. Y., Kuah, C. W. K., et al. (2014). A randomized controlled trial of EEG-based motor imagery brain-computer interface robotic rehabilitation for stroke. *Clin. EEG Neurosci.* 42, 253–258. doi: 10.1177/1550059414522229

Ang, K. K., Guan, C., Chua, K. S. G., Ang, B. T., Kuah, C. W. K., Wang, C., et al. (2011). A large clinical study on the ability of stroke patients to use EEG-based motor imagery brain-computer interface. *Clin. EEG Neurosci.* 42, 253–258. doi: 10.1177/155005941104200411

Ball, T., Kern, M., Mutschler, I., Aertsen, A., and Schulze-Bonhage, A. (2009). Signal quality of simultaneously recorded invasive and non-invasive EEG. *Neuroimage* 46, 708–716. doi: 10.1016/j.neuroimage.2009.02.028

Bensch, M., Martens, S., Halder, S., Hill, J., Nijboer, F., Ramos, A., et al. (2014). Assessing attention and cognitive function in completely locked-in state with event-related brain potentials and epidural electrocorticography. *J. Neural Eng.* 11:026006. doi: 10.1088/1741-2560/11/2/026006

Birbaumer, N., Ghanayim, N., Hinterberger, T., Iversen, I., Kotchoubey, B., Kübler, A., et al. (1999). A spelling device for the paralysed. *Nature* 398, 297–298. doi: 10.1038/18581

Blankertz, B., Sannelli, C., Halder, S., Hammer, E. M., Kübler, A., Müller, K. R., et al. (2010). Neurophysiological predictor of SMR-based BCI performance. *Neuroimage* 51, 1303–1309. doi: 10.1016/j.neuroimage.2010.03.022

Borton, D. A., Yin, M., Aceros, J., and Nurmikko, A. (2013). An implantable wireless neural interface for recording cortical circuit dynamics in moving primates. *J. Neural Eng.* 10:026010. doi: 10.1088/1741-2560/10/2/026010

Brittain, J.-S., Sharott, A., and Brown, P. (2014). The highs and lows of beta activity in cortico-basal ganglia loops. *Eur. J. Neurosci.* 39, 1951–1959. doi: 10.1111/ejn.12574

Buch, E. R., Modir Shanechi, A., Fourkas, A. D., Weber, C., Birbaumer, N., and Cohen, L. G. (2012). Parietofrontal integrity determines neural modulation associated with grasping imagery after stroke. *Brain* 135, 596–614. doi: 10.1093/brain/awr331

Buch, E., Weber, C., Cohen, L. G., Braun, C., Dimyan, M. A., Ard, T., et al. (2008). Think to move: a neuromagnetic brain-computer interface (BCI) system for chronic stroke. *Stroke* 39, 910–917. doi: 10.1161/STROKEAHA.107.505313

Collinger, J. L., Wodlinger, B., Downey, J. E., Wang, W., Tyler-Kabara, E. C., Weber, D. J., et al. (2013). High-performance neuroprosthetic control by an individual with tetraplegia. *Lancet* 381, 557–564. doi: 10.1016/S0140-6736(12)61816-9

Fonov, V. S., Evans, A. C., McKinstry, R. C., Almli, C. R., and Collins, D. L. (2009). Unbiased nonlinear average age-appropriate brain templates from birth to adulthood. *Neuroimage* 47(Suppl. 1), S102. doi: 10.1016/s1053-8119(09)70884-5

Gharabaghi, A., Kraus, D., Leão, M. T., Spüler, M., Walter, A., Bogdan, M., et al. (2014a). Coupling brain-machine interfaces with cortical stimulation for brain-state dependent stimulation: enhancing motor cortex excitability for neurorehabilitation. *Front. Hum. Neurosci.* 8:122. doi: 10.3389/fnhum.2014.00122

Gharabaghi, A., Naros, G., Walter, A., Grimm, F., Schuermeyer, M., Roth, A., et al. (2014b). From assistance towards restoration with epidural brain-computer interfacing. *Restor. Neurol. Neurosci.* 32, 517–525. doi: 10.3233/RNN-140387

Gharabaghi, A., Naros, G., Walter, A., Roth, A., Bogdan, M., Rosenstiel, W., et al. (2014c). Epidural electrocorticography of phantom hand movement following long-term upper-limb amputation. *Front. Hum. Neurosci.* 8:285. doi: 10.3389/fnhum.2014.00285

Gomez-Rodriguez, M., Peters, J., Hill, J., Schölkopf, B., Gharabaghi, A., and Grosse-Wentrup, M. (2011). Closing the sensorimotor loop: haptic feedback facilitates decoding of motor imagery. *J. Neural Eng.* 8:036005. doi: 10.1088/1741-2560/8/3/036005

Goncharova, I. I., McFarland, D. J., Vaughan, T. M., and Wolpaw, J. R. (2003). EMG contamination of EEG: spectral and topographical characteristics. *Clin. Neurophysiol.* 114, 1580–1593. doi: 10.1016/s1388-2457(03)00093-2

Grosse-Wentrup, M., Schölkopf, B., and Hill, J. (2011). Causal influence of gamma oscillations on the sensorimotor rhythm. *Neuroimage* 56, 837–842. doi: 10.1016/j.neuroimage.2010.04.265

Halder, S., Agorastos, D., Veit, R., Hammer, E. M., Lee, S., Varkuti, B., et al. (2011). Neural mechanisms of brain-computer interface control. *Neuroimage* 55, 1779–1790. doi: 10.1016/j.neuroimage.2011.01.021

Herrojo Ruiz, M., Brücke, C., Nikulin, V. V., Schneider, G.-H., and Kühn, A. A. (2014). Beta-band amplitude oscillations in the human internal globus pallidus support the encoding of sequence boundaries during initial sensorimotor sequence learning. *Neuroimage* 85, 779–793. doi: 10.1016/j.neuroimage.2013.05.085

Hipp, J. F., and Siegel, M. (2013). Dissociating neuronal gamma-band activity from cranial and ocular muscle activity in EEG. *Front. Hum. Neurosci.* 7:338. doi: 10.3389/fnhum.2013.00338

Hochberg, L. R., Bacher, D., Jarosiewicz, B., Masse, N. Y., Simeral, J. D., Vogel, J., et al. (2012). Reach and grasp by people with tetraplegia using a neurally controlled robotic arm. *Nature* 485, 372–375. doi: 10.1038/nature11076

Kilavik, B. E., Zaepffel, M., Brovelli, A., MacKay, W. A., and Riehle, A. (2013). The ups and downs of beta oscillations in sensorimotor cortex. *Exp. Neurol.* 245, 15–26. doi: 10.1016/j.expneurol.2012.09.014

Leuthardt, E. C., Schalk, G., Roland, J., Rouse, A., and Moran, D. W. (2009). Evolution of brain-computer interfaces: going beyond classic motor physiology. *Neurosurg. Focus* 27:E4. doi: 10.3171/2009.4.FOCUS0979

McFarland, D. J., and Wolpaw, J. R. (2008). Sensorimotor rhythm-based brain-computer interface (BCI): model order selection for autoregressive spectral analysis. *J. Neural Eng.* 5, 155–162. doi: 10.1088/1741-2560/5/2/006

Piangerelli, M., Ciavarro, M., Paris, A., Marchetti, S., Cristiani, P., Puttilli, C., et al. (2014). A fully integrated wireless system for intracranial direct cortical stimulation, real-time electrocorticography data transmission and smart cage for wireless battery recharge. *Front. Neurol.* 5:156. doi: 10.3389/fneur.2014.00156

Ramos-Murguialday, A., Broetz, D., Rea, M., Läer, L., Yilmaz, O., Brasil, F. L., et al. (2013). Brain-machine interface in chronic stroke rehabilitation: a controlled study. *Ann. Neurol.* 74, 100–108. doi: 10.1002/ana.23879

Ramos-Murguialday, A., Schürholz, M., Caggiano, V., Wildgruber, M., Caria, A., Hammer, E. M., et al. (2012). Proprioceptive feedback and brain computer interface (BCI) based neuroprostheses. *PLoS One* 7:e47048. doi: 10.1371/journal.pone.0047048

Rossiter, H. E., Boudrias, M. H., and Ward, N. S. (2014). Do movement-related beta oscillations change following stroke? *J. Neurophysiol.* 30, 2053–2058. doi: 10.1152/jn.00345.2014

Schalk, G., McFarland, D. J., Hinterberger, T., Birbaumer, N., and Wolpaw, J. R. (2004). BCI2000: a general-purpose brain-computer interface (BCI) system. *IEEE Trans. Biomed. Eng.* 51, 1034–1043. doi: 10.1109/tbme.2004.827072

Takemi, M., Masakado, Y., Liu, M., and Ushiba, J. (2013). Is event-related desynchronization a biomarker representing corticospinal excitability? *Conf. Proc. IEEE Eng. Med. Biol. Soc.* 2013, 281–284. doi: 10.1109/EMBC.2013.6609492

Tiganj, Z., Mboup, M., Pouzat, C., and Belkoura, L. (2010). "An algebraic method for eye blink artifacts detection in single channel EEG recordings," in *17th International Conference on Biomagnetism Advances in Biomagnetism-Biomag* (Springer Berlin Heidelberg), 175–178.

Tzourio-Mazoyer, N., Landeau, B., Papathanassiou, D., Crivello, F., Etard, O., Delcroix, N., et al. (2002). Automated anatomical labeling of activations in SPM using a macroscopic anatomical parcellation of the MNI MRI single-subject brain. *Neuroimage* 15, 273–289. doi: 10.1006/nimg.2001.0978

Várkuti, B., Guan, C., Pan, Y., Phua, K. S., Ang, K. K., Kuah, C. W., et al. (2013). Resting state changes in functional connectivity correlate with movement recovery for BCI and robot-assisted upper-extremity training after stroke. *Neurorehabil. Neural Repair* 27, 53–62. doi: 10.1177/1545968312445910

Vidaurre, C., and Blankertz, B. (2010). Towards a cure for BCI illiteracy. *Brain Topogr.* 23, 194–198. doi: 10.1007/s10548-009-0121-6

Vukelić, M., Bauer, R., Naros, G., Naros, I., Braun, C., and Gharabaghi, A. (2014). Lateralized alpha-band cortical networks regulate volitional modulation of beta-band sensorimotor oscillations. *Neuroimage* 87, 147–153. doi: 10.1016/j.neuroimage.2013.10.003

Walter, A., Ramos Murguialday, A., Spüler, M., Naros, G., Leão, M. T., Gharabaghi, A., et al. (2012). Coupling BCI and cortical stimulation for brain-state-dependent stimulation: methods for spectral estimation in the presence of stimulation after-effects. *Front. Neural Circuits* 6:87. doi: 10.3389/fncir.2012.00087

Wang, W., Collinger, J. L., Degenhart, A. D., Tyler-Kabara, E. C., Schwartz, A. B., Moran, D. W., et al. (2013). An electrocorticographic brain interface in an individual with tetraplegia. *PLoS One* 8:e55344. doi: 10.1371/journal.pone.0055344

Wyckhoff, S., and Birbaumer, N. (2014). "Neurofeedback and brain-computer interfaces," in *The Handbook of Behavioural Medicine*, ed D. I. Mostofsky (Hoboken, NJ: Wiley-Blackwell), 275–312.

Yanagisawa, T., Hirata, M., Saitoh, Y., Goto, T., Kishima, H., Fukuma, R., et al. (2011). Real-time control of a prosthetic hand using human electrocorticography signals. *J. Neurosurg.* 114, 1715–1722. doi: 10.3171/2011.1.JNS101421

Yanagisawa, T., Hirata, M., Saitoh, Y., Kishima, H., Matsushita, K., Goto, T., et al. (2012). Electrocorticographic control of a prosthetic arm in paralyzed patients. *Ann. Neurol.* 71, 353–361. doi: 10.1002/ana.22613

14

Resting state functional connectivity predicts neurofeedback response

Dustin Scheinost[1], Teodora Stoica[1], Suzanne Wasylink[2], Patricia Gruner[2], John Saksa[2], Christopher Pittenger[2,3,4] and Michelle Hampson[1]*

[1] Magnetic Resonance Research Center (MRRC), Department of Diagnostic Radiology, Yale School of Medicine, New Haven, CT, USA
[2] Department of Psychiatry, Yale School of Medicine, New Haven, CT, USA
[3] Department of Psychology, Yale University, New Haven, CT, USA
[4] Child Study Center, Yale School of Medicine, New Haven, CT, USA

***Correspondence:**
Michelle Hampson, Magnetic Resonance Research Center (MRRC), Department of Diagnostic Radiology, Yale School of Medicine, The Anlyan Center, N121, 300 Cedar Street, New Haven, CT 06520-8043, USA
e-mail: michelle.hampson@yale.edu

Tailoring treatments to the specific needs and biology of individual patients—personalized medicine—requires delineation of reliable predictors of response. Unfortunately, these have been slow to emerge, especially in neuropsychiatric disorders. We have recently described a real-time functional magnetic resonance imaging (rt-fMRI) neurofeedback protocol that can reduce contamination-related anxiety, a prominent symptom of many cases of obsessive-compulsive disorder (OCD). Individual response to this intervention is variable. Here we used patterns of brain functional connectivity, as measured by baseline resting-state fMRI (rs-fMRI), to predict improvements in contamination anxiety after neurofeedback training. Activity of a region of the orbitofrontal cortex (OFC) and anterior prefrontal cortex, Brodmann area (BA) 10, associated with contamination anxiety in each subject was measured in real time and presented as a neurofeedback signal, permitting subjects to learn to modulate this target brain region. We have previously reported both enhanced OFC/BA 10 control and improved anxiety in a group of subclinically anxious subjects after neurofeedback. Five individuals with contamination-related OCD who underwent the same protocol also showed improved clinical symptomatology. In both groups, these behavioral improvements were strongly correlated with baseline whole-brain connectivity in the OFC/BA 10, computed from rs-fMRI collected several days prior to neurofeedback training. These pilot data suggest that rs-fMRI can be used to identify individuals likely to benefit from rt-fMRI neurofeedback training to control contamination anxiety.

Keywords: neurofeedback, real-time fMRI, resting state connectivity, obsessive-compulsive disorder, orbitofrontal cortex

INTRODUCTION

Dysregulation of anxiety is a core component of many neuropsychiatric conditions. Obsessive-compulsive disorder (OCD) is characterized by intrusive obsessions, which are often associated with anxiety, and with repetitive compulsions that seek to control that anxiety (Jenike, 2004). One common presentation of OCD is characterized by extreme contamination anxiety, often triggered by thoughts or images of, or contact with, potential contaminates such as dirt, body secretions, or mold (Bloch et al., 2008). Improving control of contamination anxiety is a key step in improving the quality of life for many individuals with OCD.

Treatments for contamination anxiety and for OCD exist, but none are universally effective (Franklin and Foa, 2011). For individuals who do not respond to standard behavioral and pharmacological treatments, interventions that more directly modulate the specific brain regions whose dysfunction is implicated in the disorder may be of benefit. In extreme cases, this modulation is sometimes done through invasive procedures such as deep brain stimulation (Greenberg et al., 2010). Targeted brain modulation using neurofeedback via real-time functional magnetic resonance (rt-fMRI) may prove to be an alternative (Scheinost et al., 2013).

rt-fMRI neurofeedback involves monitoring the blood oxygenation level dependent (BOLD) signal, a measure of brain activity, and providing immediate feedback to the subject showing them how specific brain activity patterns are changing over time. This form of feedback can facilitate learned control over brain activity and associated behaviors (Sulzer et al., 2013; Ruiz et al., 2014). Neurofeedback training has shown promise as a potential treatment in several clinical disorders including addiction (Hanlon et al., 2013; Li et al., 2013), tinnitus (Haller et al., 2010), stroke (Sitaram et al., 2012), depression (Linden et al., 2012; Young et al., 2014), Parkinson's Disease (Subramanian et al., 2011), and schizophrenia (Ruiz et al., 2013a,b). rt-fMRI neurofeedback can produce changes in brain function (Hampson et al., 2011; Harmelech et al., 2013) and related behaviors (Shibata et al., 2011). In individuals with significant but subclinical contamination anxiety, we have shown that neurofeedback of activity in the orbitofrontal cortex (OFC) and anterior prefrontal cortex Brodmann area (BA) 10 can reorganize functional brain networks associated with anxiety and reduce the anxiety produced by contamination-related stimuli (Scheinost et al., 2013).

Clinically, a trial of an intervention that ultimately proves ineffective carries substantial cost, in both time, resources, and ongoing patient suffering. How best to match an individual to an intervention is therefore a crucially important question. Predictors of response that can help with treatment selection in neuropsychiatric conditions such as OCD would be of enormous clinical value but have been slow to emerge.

Here, we ask whether resting-state fMRI (rs-fMRI) can predict response to neurofeedback training and, thus, potentially guide treatment selection in the future. Previous research suggests that imaging-based biomarkers can be used to predict performance with a brain-computer interface (Halder et al., 2013). rs-fMRI, in particular, provides a great opportunity for identifying biomarkers to aid clinical decisions, given that it can be collected in clinical populations without requiring any task performance and yet provides a wealth of information about brain function (Constable et al., 2013; Lee et al., 2013). To investigate whether brain connectivity at rest can predict reduction in contamination anxiety induced during a neurofeedback intervention, we correlated a voxel-wise measure of functional connectivity, computed from rs-fMRI collected prior to neurofeedback training, with behavioral response to the neurofeedback intervention in a cohort of healthy subjects with subclinical contamination anxiety (Scheinost et al., 2013). We then examined whether a similar relationship existed in a small cohort of patients.

METHODS

Data were from studies performed at Yale University School of Medicine, New Haven, CT. All protocols were reviewed and approved by Human Research Protection Program at Yale University. Written informed consent was obtained. All scans were obtained and analyzed at Yale University.

SUBJECTS

Two cohorts of subjects were used in this study. The first cohort has been described previously (Scheinost et al., 2013) and consisted of 10 subjects without any clinical diagnosis of OCD, but with high levels of contamination anxiety. Only the 10 subjects who received true neurofeedback in our previous study—not the 10 who received sham neurofeedback in the control condition—are included in the present analysis. The second cohort consisted of five OCD patients with moderate symptom severity (**Table 1**) and prominent contamination obsessions.

NEUROFEEDBACK TRAINING

Healthy subjects and OCD patients received neurofeedback training following a previously detailed protocol (Hampson et al., 2012a). Of the five OCD patients, the first two underwent only a single neurofeedback session, without pre- or post-neurofeedback resting-state scans. All other individuals participated in four separate MRI scanning sessions, spaced several days apart. In the first session, rs-fMRI data were collected and a functional localizer was used to identify the target area of the OFC/BA 10 region to be used for neurofeedback. The second and third sessions involved rt-fMRI neurofeedback training based on the target OFC/BA 10 region. A final session (not of relevance to this work) involved collecting post-intervention rs-fMRI data. The rs-fMRI data were always collected before any other functional scans in a given session to avoid possible effects of previous task on the rs-fMRI data.

The overlap of the target area for feedback for all 15 subjects is shown in **Figure 1**. Overlap was calculated by (1) smoothing the target region of each individual with a 6 mm Gaussian smoothing kernel to account for differences in functional anatomy and registration errors; (2) warping the target regions to a common reference; and (3) averaging across subjects the likelihood of a voxel being included in the target region.

BEHAVIORAL MEASURES

Behavioral measures of control over contamination anxiety (for the first cohort) and clinical measures (for the second cohort) were collected before and after neurofeedback training. The pre-intervention assessment data was collected before the first neurofeedback session (second overall imaging session), immediately prior to the start of neurofeedback training. The post-intervention assessment data was collected several days after the completion of neurofeedback training, either in a separate session with no imaging (for the first two OCD patients) or in conjunction with the fourth fMRI session (for all other patients). Finally, midpoint assessment data was collected in between the first and second neurofeedback sessions for the subjects who received two sessions of neurofeedback.

For the healthy subjects, with subclinical contamination anxiety we used a behavioral measure designed to assess the subjects' ability to control their anxiety. Subjects were instructed to try to control their anxiety while viewing 25 contamination-related images and to indicate their experienced anxiety for each image on a 1–5 scale. A rating of one indicated the least anxiety and a rating of five indicated the most anxiety. The ratings for the 25 contamination-related images were then averaged yielding a single measure of anxiety. Different sets of images were used before and after the intervention, but the sets were designed to induce similar levels of contamination related anxiety and piloted to verify that they were balanced in this respect (Hampson et al., 2012a).

For the patients, we administered a modified version of the Yale–Brown Obsessive Compulsive Scale (Y-BOCS), in which they were instructed to report on their symptoms over the last 3 days, rather than over the past week as in the traditional Y-BOCS (Goodman et al., 1989a,b). The Y-BOCS ranges from 0–40, with higher scores representing more severe symptoms, and measures the frequency, intrusiveness, and distress associated with obsessions and compulsions. Scores in the mid-twenties, as these patients had (**Table 1**), correspond to moderate to severe disease.

Table 1 | Clinical characteristics and symptom improvement in five OCD patients who underwent rt-fMRI biofeedback.

	Subject					Average
	1	2	3†	4†	5†	
Sex	F	M	F	M	M	3M/2F
Age	33	41	65	43	46	46
Handedness	R	L	R	R	R	4R/1L
Other dx	None	MDD Panic D/O GAD Past SUD	Past MDD	None	MDD BDD Motor tic	
Psychiatric medications	None	None	fluoxetine Synthroid Immitrex*	None	None	
Y-BOCS						
Baseline	27	28	25	26	28	26.8
Midpoint	24	21	23	25	23	23.2
Final	–	–	19	23	20	20.6
Improvement	11%	25%	24%	11.5%	28.5%	20%

*MDD—major depressive disorder. Panic D/O—panic disorder, with agoraphobia. GAD—generalized anxiety disorder. SUD—substance use disorder (in remission). BDD—body dysmorphic disorder. * taken occasionally, as needed. † rs-fMRI data collected prior to neurofeedback and used in connectivity analysis; see **Figure 2**.*

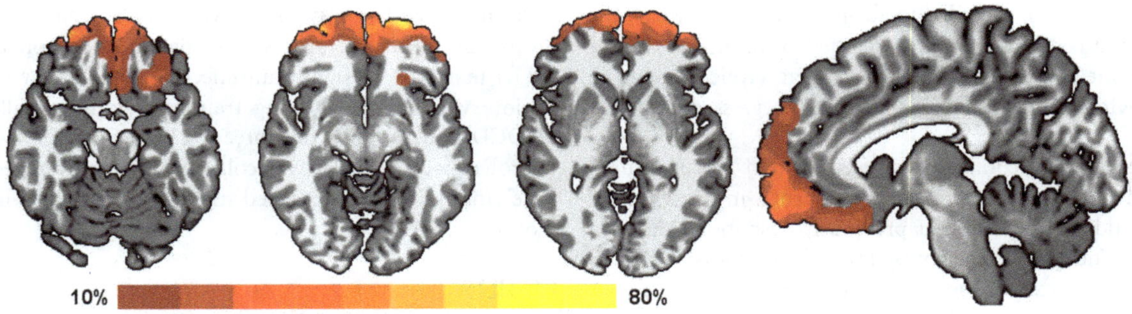

FIGURE 1 | Overlap of target regions for neurofeedback. All subjects received neurofeedback from a region in the OFC/BA 10 (Hampson et al., 2012a). These target regions were determined on individual basis from a functional localizer task allowing for differences in individual functional anatomy. The percent overlap of all these target regions is shown on a template brain using Radiological convention (left is on the right for axial slices). Warmer colors indicate that the voxel was included in a greater number of individual target regions.

For both groups, change in behavior measures were calculated as score prior to neurofeedback minus score after neurofeedback, such that a positive change indicates an improvement in anxiety.

IMAGING PARAMETERS

All imaging was done on a 1.5-T Siemens Sonata scanner (Siemens Medical Systems, Erlangen, Germany). A sequence designed to optimize signal in the OFC was used for all functional data collection (repetition time = 2000 ms, echo time = 30 ms, flip angle = 80, bandwidth = 2604, 200 mm field of view for 3.1 mm isotropic voxels, 31 axial-oblique slices covering almost the whole cerebrum and most of the cerebellum). Two 5 min resting data runs were collected.

RESTING-STATE CONNECTIVITY

Images were preprocessed using a previously detailed pipeline (Hampson et al., 2012b). All images were slice time and motion corrected using SPM.[1] Unless otherwise specified, all further analysis was performed using BioImage Suite (Joshi et al., 2011). Several covariates of no interest were regressed from the data including linear and quadratic drift, six rigid-body motion parameters, mean cerebrospinal fluid (CSF) signal, mean white-matter signal, and mean global signal. The data were low-pass filtered via temporal smoothing with a 0 mean unit variance Gaussian filter (approximate cutoff frequency = 0.12 Hz). Finally, a gray matter mask was applied to the preprocessed data so that only voxels in the gray matter were used in subsequent calculations. After preprocessing, all resting-state runs were concatenated and the connectivity for each voxel was then calculated in each subject's individual brain space.

The gray and white matter and CSF masks were defined on a template brain (Holmes et al., 1998), and warped to individual subject space using a series of transformations, described below.

[1] http://www.fil.ion.ucl.ac.uk/spm/

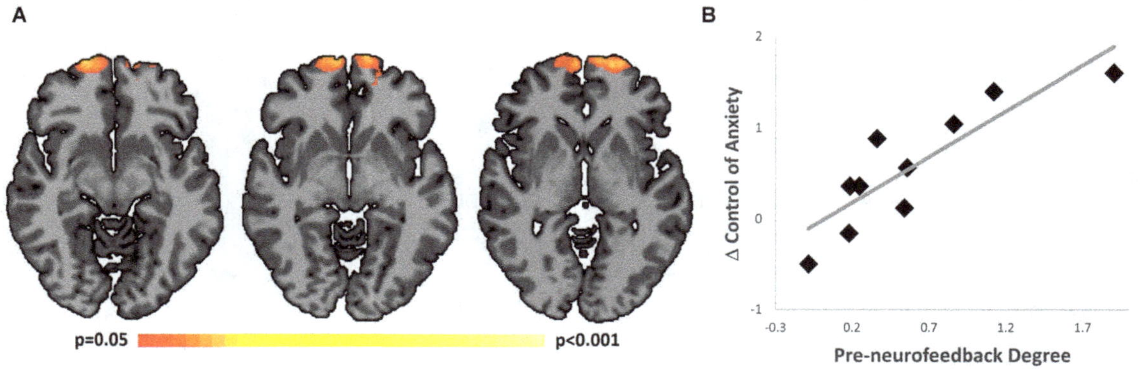

FIGURE 2 | Correlation of improved control over anxiety and rs-fMRI. (A) Subjects with the highest connectivity in the OFC/BA 10 (MNI coordinate of peak voxel: 0, 66, −4) prior to neurofeedback training had the largest improvement in control over anxiety over the course of the intervention. Results shown using Radiological convention at $p < 0.05$ level, corrected for multiple comparisons. **(B)** Scatterplot showing improved control over anxiety and pre-neurofeedback rs-fMRI.

The gray matter mask was dilated to ensure full coverage of the gray matter after warping into individual subject space. Regions that were not included in all subjects' data (for e.g., the bottom of the cerebellum) were excluded from analysis. Likewise, the white matter and CSF masks were eroded to ensure only pure white matter or CSF signal were regressed from the data.

Global functional connectivity of each voxel was measured from rs-fMRI data using the network theory measure *degree* (Bullmore and Sporns, 2009) as previously described (Martuzzi et al., 2011). The BOLD time course for each voxel was correlated with every other voxel in the gray matter. Two voxels were considered connected if correlation of their timecourses was greater than $r = 0.25$; the *degree* of each voxel was defined as the number of such connections. The process was repeated for every voxel in the gray matter. Each subject's degree map was normalized by subtracting the mean across all voxels and dividing by the standard deviation across all voxels. This normalization has been shown to reduce the impact of confounds related to motion (Yan et al., 2013).

To facilitate comparisons of imaging data, all degree maps were spatially smoothed with a 6 mm Gaussian filter and then warped to a common template space through the concatenation of a series of linear and non-linear registrations, as previously described (Scheinost et al., 2013). All transformations were computed using the intensity-based registration algorithms in BioImage Suite (Papademetris et al., 2004).

EVALUATING THE RELATIONSHIP BETWEEN RESPONSE TO INTERVENTION AND rs-fMRI DATA

To identify which brain regions predicted response to neurofeedback training, we related the rs-fMRI data acquired before any neurofeedback training with changes in the behavioral measure of control over contamination anxiety (for the healthy subjects) and changes in clinical severity (for the patients). For the healthy subjects, we performed a data-driven, whole-brain analysis by correlating the change in control of anxiety with the *degree* maps in a voxel-wise manner. Significance was assessed at a $p < 0.05$ level after correcting for multiple comparisons across the gray matter via AFNI's AlphaSim program. From this voxel-wise analysis, we defined a region of interest (ROI) that showed significant effects in the healthy subjects to explore whether this finding translated to the smaller cohort of OCD patients. For the three OCD patients on whom pre-neurofeedback rs-fMRI was collected, *degree* averaged over all voxels in this ROI was extracted and related to changes in Y-BOCS scores.

RESULTS

IMAGING PREDICTORS OF BEHAVIOR IN SUBCLINICALLY ANXIOUS SUBJECTS

As reported previously (Scheinost et al., 2013), healthy subjects with subclinical contamination anxiety showed a significant ($p < 0.05$) increase in control over anxiety after neurofeedback training. Whole-brain connectivity analysis revealed a single significant cluster ($p < 0.05$ corrected; MNI coordinate of peak voxel: 0, 66, −4, max t-value = 5.84, cluster size = 5857 mm^3) in which *degree* prior to neurofeedback training was significantly correlated with improved control over anxiety (**Figure 2A**). This cluster was located in the OFC/BA 10 target region. Subjects with the highest connectivity in this region prior to neurofeedback training exhibited the most improvement in post-treatment anxiety. A scatterplot of the average connectivity change in this region vs. the change in control of anxiety is shown in **Figure 2B**. As the choice of threshold used to consider whether two voxels are connected can impact connectivity results (Scheinost et al., 2012), we repeated this analysis over a range of thresholds ($0.10 < r < 0.65$). This produced no qualitative change in the findings. Additionally, as motion has been shown to confound functional connectivity results, average frame to frame displacement was calculated for each group (Van Dijk et al., 2012). Motion was not correlated with improved control of anxiety ($r = 0.18$, $p > 0.60$) and adding motion as a covariate in the group analysis did not change the presented results.

CLINICAL IMPROVEMENT AFTER NEUROFEEDBACK IN SUBJECTS WITH OCD

Five patients with moderate-to-severe OCD and prominent contamination symptoms underwent one or two sessions of neurofeedback (**Table 1**). All five tolerated the procedure well and exhibited reduced symptoms, as evaluated by the Y-BOCS several days after the last neurofeedback session. Average symptom improvement was 20%. Of the OCD patients, the three with the greatest symptom improvements also had a co-diagnosis or a history of major depressive disorder (MDD). Demographic and clinical details are given in **Table 1**.

IMAGING PREDICTORS OF CLINICAL IMPROVEMENT

Next, we tested whether a similar relationship between connectivity and behavioral improvements would be found in OCD patients. Pre-neurofeedback rs-fMRI was not measured on the first two subjects; this analysis was therefore performed only on the three subjects who underwent the full two-session neurofeedback protocol. To maximize power in this very limited dataset, we used the OFC/BA 10 region defined in the first cohort as an *a priori* ROI, Average *degree* in this ROI prior to neurofeedback training was related to clinical improvement for the three patients. Consistent with the pattern seen in the healthy subjects, a strong linear relationship was observed ($r = 0.99$). Thus, in both groups, increased connectivity in the OFC/BA 10 measured from rs-fMRI data collected prior to neurofeedback training was associated with greater behavioral improvements.

DISCUSSION

Advances in understanding individual differences motivate a new approach to health care in which treatment is tailored to the specific needs and biology of an individual patient. This "personalized medicine" approach has been endorsed by the National Institute of Mental Health, NIMH,[2] but its adoption depends critically on our ability to identify which patients are likely to respond to which interventions. rs-fMRI holds great promise as a tool for providing this information. It is easy to collect, does not require patients to perform any difficult tasks, and yet is a rich source of potentially clinically relevant information about brain function (Constable et al., 2013; Lee et al., 2013).

In a pilot study, we demonstrate, for the first time, that rs-fMRI can be a useful tool to predict response to neurofeedback training via rt-fMRI. After receiving two sessions of neurofeedback training, healthy subjects showed improved control over anxiety and OCD patients showed a reduction in OCD symptom severity. For both groups, these behavioral improvements were strongly correlated with the pre-intervention level of whole-brain connectivity in the anterior prefrontal cortex.

The resting state functional connectivity analysis used in this study was unbiased by *a priori* expectations regarding regions of interest. Therefore, it is striking that the region that emerged from our whole-brain analysis as most relevant for predicting improvements in contamination anxiety was in our target area of the OFC/BA 10. Taken together with a large body of data highlighting the importance of the OFC and anterior prefrontal cortex in obsessive-compulsive symptoms (Swedo et al., 1992; Chamberlain et al., 2008; Menzies et al., 2008; Harrison et al., 2009; Sakai et al., 2011; Anticevic et al., 2014; Beucke et al., 2013), this gives us confidence that we are targeting a biologically relevant brain area.

Notably, OFC/BA 10 connectivity predicted the response to the intervention in both healthy subjects and OCD patients, suggesting a shared neurobiological mechanism for improved control over contamination anxiety across groups. It is possible that the phenomenon of contamination anxiety is a dimensional construct, differing in a quantitative rather than a qualitative sense in patients when compared to healthy individuals. Supporting this view are previous reports of OFC/BA 10 activations to contamination related imagery in both healthy subjects and OCD patients (Mataix-Cols et al., 2003, 2004).

To the extent that neurobiology of a phenomenon is shared across patients and healthy subjects, interventions developed in the healthy group are likely to translate into the patient population. In this particular intervention, based on our preliminary patient data, translational potential appears high. A variety of other applications of rt-fMRI neurofeedback trainings have been developed in healthy populations (Hampson et al., 2011; Shibata et al., 2011; Chiew et al., 2012; Garrison et al., 2013). It will be interesting to see how well the findings from these studies translate into clinical populations. If the dimensional approach implicit in NIMHs Research Domain Criteria[3] is an accurate description of pathological brain dysfunction, many of these studies may successfully translate into the respective patient groups.

An important consideration for predictive validity is the reliability of rs-fMRI. Overall, graph theory measures have been shown to be reliable (Telesford et al., 2010; Braun et al., 2012) and, in particular, voxel-wise degree has shown good test-retest reproducibility across different sites and scanners (Tomasi and Volkow, 2010). While generally reliable, a variety of factors can reduce the predictive power of rs-fMRI. Medications and other drugs such as caffeine can alter connectivity patterns (Rack-Gomer et al., 2009; Martuzzi et al., 2010). Sleep also changes connectivity patterns (Tagliazucchi et al., 2013) which can be an issue if subjects are falling asleep and not reporting it. Finally, factors related to subject comfort such as hunger may reduce data quality and prediction accuracy due to motion artifacts and effects on subject compliance. The degree to which all these variables are controlled is likely to affect the power of future studies to identify clinically relevant biomarkers that predict treatment response.

The major limitation of this pilot study is the small number of subjects, particularly in the patient group, in which we only had three subjects with resting data. Although the finding in the healthy subject group is statistically significant, the finding in the patient group must be considered preliminary. However, the tight correspondence between connectivity and intervention response in our modest clinical sample, and its similarity to the relationship seen in healthy subjects, are promising. Future studies are needed

[2]http://www.nimh.nih.gov/about/strategic-planning-reports/index.shtml

[3]http://www.nimh.nih.gov/research-priorities/rdoc/nimh-research-domain-criteria-rdoc.shtml

to rigorously examine whether this biomarker is an effective predictor of response in the clinical group. A large study that can examine possible modulating variables would be particularly valuable. For example, the data in our small sample suggest that patients with a current co-diagnosis or a history of MDD show the greatest improvement in clinical symptoms, but we were unable to investigate this given our limited data in the patient group. A study with the power to test that possibility could yield interesting insights.

CONCLUSION

These pilot data provide evidence that rs-fMRI connectivity can be used to identify individuals likely to benefit from rt-fMRI neurofeedback interventions for training control over contamination anxiety. Specifically, we have identified a biomarker that may be useful in developing personalized treatment programs in patients with OCD. More generally, these findings illustrate the potential utility of rs-fMRI data for identifying biomarkers of treatment response and thereby facilitating a personalized medicine approach to treating mental illness.

ACKNOWLEDGMENTS

This research was supported by NIH grant R21 MH090384, The Taylor Foundation for Chronic Disease, and this publication was made possible by CTSA Grant Number UL1 TR000142 from the National Center for Advancing Translational Science (NCATS), a component of the National Institutes of Health (NIH). Its contents are solely the responsibility of the authors and do not necessarily represent the official view of NIH. We thank H. Sarofin for her technical assistance and E. Billingslea for her assistance with coordinating OCD patient recruitment, characterization, and logistics.

REFERENCES

Anticevic, A., Hu, S., Zhang, S., Savic, A., Billingslea, E., Wasylink, S., et al. (2014). Global resting-state functional magnetic resonance imaging analysis identifies frontal cortex, striatal and cerebellar dysconnectivity in obsessive-compulsive disorder. *Biol. Psychiatry* 75, 595–605. doi: 10.1016/j.biopsych.2013.10.021

Beucke, J. C., Sepulcre, J., Talukdar, T., Linnman, C., Zschenderlein, K., Endrass, T., et al. (2013). Abnormally high degree connectivity of the orbitofrontal cortex in obsessive-compulsive disorder. *JAMA Psychiatry* 70, 619–629. doi: 10.1001/jamapsychiatry.2013.173

Bloch, M. H., Landeros-Weisenberger, A., Rosario, M. C., Pittenger, C., and Leckman, J. F. (2008). Meta-analysis of the symptom structure of obsessive-compulsive disorder. *Am. J. Psychiatry* 165, 1532–1542. doi: 10.1176/appi.ajp.2008.08020320

Braun, U., Plichta, M. M., Esslinger, C., Sauer, C., Haddad, L., Grimm, O., et al. (2012). Test-retest reliability of resting-state connectivity network characteristics using fMRI and graph theoretical measures. *Neuroimage* 59, 1404–1412. doi: 10.1016/j.neuroimage.2011.08.044

Bullmore, E., and Sporns, O. (2009). Complex brain networks: graph theoretical analysis of structural and functional systems. *Nat. Rev. Neurosci.* 10, 186–198. doi: 10.1038/nrn2575

Chamberlain, S. R., Menzies, L., Hampshire, A., Suckling, J., Fineberg, N. A., del Campo, N., et al. (2008). Orbitofrontal dysfunction in patients with obsessive-compulsive disorder and their unaffected relatives. *Science* 321, 421–422. doi: 10.1126/science.1154433

Chiew, M., LaConte, S. M., and Graham, S. J. (2012). Investigation of fMRI neurofeedback of differential primary motor cortex activity using kinesthetic motor imagery. *Neuroimage* 61, 21–31. doi: 10.1016/j.neuroimage.2012.02.053

Constable, R. T., Scheinost, D., Finn, E. S., Shen, X., Hampson, M., Winstanley, F. S., et al. (2013). Potential use and challenges of functional connectivity mapping in intractable epilepsy. *Front. Neurol.* 4:39. doi: 10.3389/fneur.2013.00039

Franklin, M. E., and Foa, E. B. (2011). Treatment of obsessive compulsive disorder. *Annu. Rev. Clin. Psychol.* 7, 229–243. doi: 10.1146/annurev-clinpsy-032210-104533

Garrison, K. A., Scheinost, D., Worhunsky, P. D., Elwafi, H. M., Thornhill, T. A., Thompson, E., et al. (2013). Real-time fMRI links subjective experience with brain activity during focused attention. *Neuroimage* 81, 110–118. doi: 10.1016/j.neuroimage.2013.05.030

Goodman, W. K., Price, L. H., Rasmussen, S. A., Mazure, C., Delgado, P., Heninger, G. R., et al. (1989a). The yale-brown obsessive compulsive scale. II. Validity. *Arch. Gen. Psychiatry* 46, 1012–1016. doi: 10.1001/archpsyc.1989.01810110054008

Goodman, W. K., Price, L. H., Rasmussen, S. A., Mazure, C., Fleischmann, R. L., Hill, C. L., et al. (1989b). The yale-brown obsessive compulsive scale. I. Development, use and reliability. *Arch. Gen. Psychiatry* 46, 1006–1011. doi: 10.1001/archpsyc.1989.01810110048007

Greenberg, B. D., Rauch, S. L., and Haber, S. N. (2010). Invasive circuitry-based neurotherapeutics: stereotactic ablation and deep brain stimulation for OCD. *Neuropsychopharmacology* 35, 317–336. doi: 10.1038/npp.2009.128

Halder, S., Varkuti, B., Bogdan, M., Kübler, A., Rosenstiel, W., Sitaram, R., et al. (2013). Prediction of brain-computer interface aptitude from individual brain structure. *Front. Hum. Neurosci.* 7:105. doi: 10.3389/fnhum.2013.00105

Haller, S., Birbaumer, N., and Veit, R. (2010). Real-time fMRI feedback training may improve chronic tinnitus. *Eur. Radiol.* 20, 696–703. doi: 10.1007/s00330-009-1595-z

Hampson, M., Scheinost, D., Qiu, M., Bhawnani, J., Lacadie, C. M., Leckman, J. F., et al. (2011). Biofeedback of real-time functional magnetic resonance imaging data from the supplementary motor area reduces functional connectivity to subcortical regions. *Brain Connect.* 1, 91–98. doi: 10.1089/brain.2011.0002

Hampson, M., Stoica, T., Saksa, J., Scheinost, D., Qiu, M., Bhawnani, J., et al. (2012a). Real-time fMRI biofeedback targeting the orbitofrontal cortex for contamination anxiety. *J. Vis. Exp.* 3535. doi: 10.3791/3535

Hampson, M., Tokoglu, F., Shen, X., Scheinost, D., Papademetris, X., and Constable, R. T. (2012b). Intrinsic brain connectivity related to age in young and middle aged adults. *PLoS One* 7:e44067. doi: 10.1371/journal.pone.0044067

Hanlon, C. A., Hartwell, K. J., Canterberry, M., Li, X., Owens, M., Lematty, T., et al. (2013). Reduction of cue-induced craving through realtime neurofeedback in nicotine users: the role of region of interest selection and multiple visits. *Psychiatry Res.* 213, 79–81. doi: 10.1016/j.pscychresns.2013.03.003

Harmelech, T., Preminger, S., Wertman, E., and Malach, R. (2013). The day-after effect: long term, Hebbian-like restructuring of resting-state fMRI patterns induced by a single epoch of cortical activation. *J. Neurosci.* 33, 9488–9497. doi: 10.1523/JNEUROSCI.5911-12.2013

Harrison, B. J., Soriano-Mas, C., Pujol, J., Ortiz, H., López-Solà, M., Hernández-Ribas, R., et al. (2009). Altered corticostriatal functional connectivity in obsessive-compulsive disorder. *Arch. Gen. Psychiatry* 66, 1189–1200. doi: 10.1001/archgenpsychiatry.2009.152

Holmes, C. J., Hoge, R., Collins, L., Woods, R., Toga, A. W., and Evans, A. C. (1998). Enhancement of MR images using registration for signal averaging. *J. Comput. Assist. Tomogr.* 22, 324–333. doi: 10.1097/00004728-199803000-00032

Jenike, M. A. (2004). Clinical practice. Obsessive-compulsive disorder. *N. Engl. J. Med.* 350, 259–265. doi: 10.1056/NEJMcp031002

Joshi, A., Scheinost, D., Okuda, H., Belhachemi, D., Murphy, I., Staib, L. H., et al. (2011). Unified framework for development, deployment and robust testing of neuroimaging algorithms. *Neuroinformatics* 9, 69–84. doi: 10.1007/s12021-010-9092-8

Lee, M. H., Smyser, C. D., and Shimony, J. S. (2013). Resting-state fMRI: a review of methods and clinical applications. *AJNR Am. J. Neuroradiol.* 34, 1866–1872. doi: 10.3174/ajnr.A3263

Li, X., Hartwell, K. J., Borckardt, J., Prisciandaro, J. J., Saladin, M. E., Morgan, P. S., et al. (2013). Volitional reduction of anterior cingulate cortex activity produces decreased cue craving in smoking cessation: a preliminary real-time fMRI study. *Addict. Biol.* 18, 739–748. doi: 10.1111/j.1369-1600.2012.00449.x

Linden, D. E., Habes, I., Johnston, S. J., Linden, S., Tatineni, R., Subramanian, L., et al. (2012). Real-time self-regulation of emotion networks in patients with depression. *PLoS One* 7:e38115. doi: 10.1371/journal.pone.0038115

Martuzzi, R., Ramani, R., Qiu, M., Rajeevan, N., and Constable, R. T. (2010). Functional connectivity and alterations in baseline brain state in humans. *Neuroimage* 49, 823–834. doi: 10.1016/j.neuroimage.2009.07.028

Martuzzi, R., Ramani, R., Qiu, M., Shen, X., Papademetris, X., and Constable, R. T. (2011). A whole-brain voxel based measure of intrinsic connectivity contrast reveals local changes in tissue connectivity with anesthetic without a priori assumptions on thresholds or regions of interest. *Neuroimage* 58, 1044–1050. doi: 10.1016/j.neuroimage.2011.06.075

Mataix-Cols, D., Cullen, S., Lange, K., Zelaya, F., Andrew, C., Amaro, E., et al. (2003). Neural correlates of anxiety associated with obsessive-compulsive symptom dimensions in normal volunteers. *Biol. Psychiatry* 53, 482–493. doi: 10.1016/s0006-3223(02)01504-4

Mataix-Cols, D., Wooderson, S., Lawrence, N., Brammer, M. J., Speckens, A., and Phillips, M. L. (2004). Distinct neural correlates of washing, checking and hoarding symptom dimensions in obsessive-compulsive disorder. *Arch. Gen. Psychiatry* 61, 564–576. doi: 10.1001/archpsyc.61.6.564

Menzies, L., Williams, G. B., Chamberlain, S. R., Ooi, C., Fineberg, N., Suckling, J., et al. (2008). White matter abnormalities in patients with obsessive-compulsive disorder and their first-degree relatives. *Am. J. Psychiatry* 165, 1308–1315. doi: 10.1176/appi.ajp.2008.07101677

Papademetris, X., Jackowski, A., Schultz, R., Staib, L., Duncan, J., Barillot, C., et al. (2004). "Integrated intensity and point-feature nonrigid registration," in *Medical Image Computing and Computer-Assisted Intervention-MICCAI 2004*, eds C. Barillot, D. R. Haynor and P. Hellier (Berlin/Heidelberg: Springer), 763–770.

Rack-Gomer, A. L., Liau, J., and Liu, T. T. (2009). Caffeine reduces resting-state BOLD functional connectivity in the motor cortex. *Neuroimage* 46, 56–63. doi: 10.1016/j.neuroimage.2009.02.001

Ruiz, S., Birbaumer, N., and Sitaram, R. (2013a). Abnormal neural connectivity in schizophrenia and fMRI-brain-computer interface as a potential therapeutic approach. *Front. Psychiatry* 4:17. doi: 10.3389/fpsyt.2013.00017

Ruiz, S., Buyukturkoglu, K., Rana, M., Birbaumer, N., and Sitaram, R. (2014). Real-time fMRI brain computer interfaces: self-regulation of single brain regions to networks. *Biol. Psychol.* 95, 4–20. doi: 10.1016/j.biopsycho.2013.04.010

Ruiz, S., Lee, S., Soekadar, S. R., Caria, A., Veit, R., Kircher, T., et al. (2013b). Acquired self-control of insula cortex modulates emotion recognition and brain network connectivity in schizophrenia. *Hum. Brain Mapp.* 34, 200–212. doi: 10.1002/hbm.21427

Sakai, Y., Narumoto, J., Nishida, S., Nakamae, T., Yamada, K., Nishimura, T., et al. (2011). Corticostriatal functional connectivity in non-medicated patients with obsessive-compulsive disorder. *Eur. Psychiatry* 26, 463–469. doi: 10.1016/j.eurpsy.2010.09.005

Scheinost, D., Benjamin, J., Lacadie, C. M., Vohr, B., Schneider, K. C., Ment, L. R., et al. (2012). The intrinsic connectivity distribution: a novel contrast measure reflecting voxel level functional connectivity. *Neuroimage* 62, 1510–1519. doi: 10.1016/j.neuroimage.2012.05.073

Scheinost, D., Stoica, T., Saksa, J., Papademetris, X., Constable, R. T., Pittenger, C., et al. (2013). Orbitofrontal cortex neurofeedback produces lasting changes in contamination anxiety and resting-state connectivity. *Transl. Psychiatry* 3:e250. doi: 10.1038/tp.2013.24

Shibata, K., Watanabe, T., Sasaki, Y., and Kawato, M. (2011). Perceptual learning incepted by decoded fMRI neurofeedback without stimulus presentation. *Science* 334, 1413–1415. doi: 10.1126/science.1212003

Sitaram, R., Veit, R., Stevens, B., Caria, A., Gerloff, C., Birbaumer, N., et al. (2012). Acquired control of ventral premotor cortex activity by feedback training: an exploratory real-time FMRI and TMS study. *Neurorehabil. Neural Repair* 26, 256–265. doi: 10.1177/1545968311418345

Subramanian, L., Hindle, J. V., Johnston, S., Roberts, M. V., Husain, M., Goebel, R., et al. (2011). Real-time functional magnetic resonance imaging neurofeedback for treatment of Parkinson's disease. *J. Neurosci.* 31, 16309–16317. doi: 10.1523/JNEUROSCI.3498-11.2011

Sulzer, J., Haller, S., Scharnowski, F., Weiskopf, N., Birbaumer, N., Blefari, M. L., et al. (2013). Real-time fMRI neurofeedback: progress and challenges. *Neuroimage* 76, 386–399. doi: 10.1016/j.neuroimage.2013.03.033

Swedo, S. E., Leonard, H. L., Kruesi, M. J., Rettew, D. C., Listwak, S. J., Berrettini, W., et al. (1992). Cerebrospinal fluid neurochemistry in children and adolescents with obsessive-compulsive disorder. *Arch. Gen. Psychiatry* 49, 29–36. doi: 10.1001/archpsyc.1992.01820010029004

Tagliazucchi, E., von Wegner, F., Morzelewski, A., Brodbeck, V., Jahnke, K., and Laufs, H. (2013). Breakdown of long-range temporal dependence in default mode and attention networks during deep sleep. *Proc. Natl. Acad. Sci. U S A* 110, 15419–15424. doi: 10.1073/pnas.1312848110

Telesford, Q. K., Morgan, A. R., Hayasaka, S., Simpson, S. L., Barret, W., Kraft, R. A., et al. (2010). Reproducibility of graph metrics in FMRI networks. *Front. Neuroinform.* 4:117. doi: 10.3389/fninf.2010.00117

Tomasi, D., and Volkow, N. D. (2010). Functional connectivity density mapping. *Proc. Natl. Acad. Sci. U S A* 107, 9885–9890. doi: 10.1073/pnas.1001414107

Van Dijk, K. R., Sabuncu, M. R., and Buckner, R. L. (2012). The influence of head motion on intrinsic functional connectivity MRI. *Neuroimage* 59, 431–438. doi: 10.1016/j.neuroimage.2011.07.044

Yan, C. G., Cheung, B., Kelly, C., Colcombe, S., Craddock, R. C., Di Martino, A., et al. (2013). A comprehensive assessment of regional variation in the impact of head micromovements on functional connectomics. *Neuroimage* 76, 183–201. doi: 10.1016/j.neuroimage.2013.03.004

Young, K. D., Zotev, V., Phillips, R., Misaki, M., Yuan, H., Drevets, W. C., et al. (2014). Real-time FMRI neurofeedback training of amygdala activity in patients with major depressive disorder. *PLoS One* 9:e88785. doi: 10.1371/journal.pone.0088785

15

Internet addictive individuals share impulsivity and executive dysfunction with alcohol-dependent patients

Zhenhe Zhou*, Hongmei Zhu, Cui Li and Jun Wang

Department of Psychiatry, Wuxi Mental Health Center, Wuxi, China

Correspondence:
Zhenhe Zhou, Department of Psychiatry, Wuxi Mental Health Center, 156 QianRong Road, Wuxi City, Jiangsu Province 214151, China
e-mail: zhouzhenhe1970@gmail.com

Internet addiction disorder (IAD) should belong to a kind of behavioral addiction. Previous studies indicated that there are many similarities in the neurobiology of behavior and substance addictions. Up to date, although individuals with IAD have difficulty in suppressing their excessive online behaviors in real life, little is known about the patho-physiological and cognitive mechanisms responsible for IAD. Neuropsychological test studies have contributed significantly to our understanding of the effect of IAD on the cognitive function. The purpose of the present study was to examine whether Internet addictive individuals share impulsivity and executive dysfunction with alcohol-dependent individuals. Participants include 22 Internet addictive individuals, 22 patients with alcohol dependence (AD), and 22 normal controls (NC). All participants were measured with BIS-11, go/no-go task, Wisconsin Card Sorting Test, and Digit span task under the same experimental condition. Results showed that Barratt impulsiveness scale 11 scores, false alarm rate, the total response errors, perseverative errors, failure to maintain set of IAD and AD group were significantly higher than that of NC group, and hit rate, percentage of conceptual level responses, the number of categories completed, forwards scores, and backwards scores of IAD and AD group were significantly lower than that of NC group, however, no differences in above variables between IAD group and AD group were observed. These results revealed that the existence of impulsivity, deficiencies in executive function and working memory in an IAD and an AD sample, namely, Internet addictive individuals share impulsivity and executive dysfunction with alcohol-dependent patients.

Keywords: Internet addiction disorder, alcohol dependence, impulsivity, executive function, working memory

INTRODUCTION

Internet addiction disorder (IAD) originates from the phenomenon of the Internet now being a part of the common person's daily life. It is well known that the Internet provides persons with the abilities to easily acquire information, learn new knowledge, gain and maintain relationships, and even make money. In short, the Internet has been instrumental in improving people quality of life. IAD is defined as a person's inability to control his or her use of the Internet, which eventually leads to psychological, social, school, and work difficulties or dysfunction in an individual's life (Young and Rogers, 1998; Davis, 2001). Because IAD is recognized internationally and is known to be linked with academic and social dysfunction, it has been increasingly recognized as a mental disorder. Recent investigations of its high prevalence in youth populations, combined with evidence that IAD is a maladaptive behavior with potentially serious occupational and mental health consequences, support the validity of the diagnosis (Ko et al., 2012). A previous study that investigated deficient inhibitory control in persons with IAD using a go/no-go task by event-related potentials (ERPs) indicated adult individuals with IAD were more impulsive than controls and shared neuropsychological and ERPs characteristics of compulsive–impulsive spectrum disorder (Zhou et al., 2010). Another study using the cue-related go/no-go switching task showed that individuals with IAD present cognitive biases toward information related to Internet gaming and poor executive functioning skills (lower mental flexibility as well as response inhibition) (Zhou et al., 2012). Impairments in executive functioning, including response monitoring, have been suggested as a hallmark feature of impulse control disorders. The error-related negativity (ERN) reflects person's ability to monitor behavior. A recent study examines whether individuals with IAD display response monitoring functional deficit characteristics in a modified Eriksen flanker task (Zhou et al., 2013). In the study, subjects and controls completed the modified Eriksen flanker task while measured with ERPs. Results showed that the mean ERN amplitudes of total error response conditions at frontal electrode and central electrode sites of subjects were reduced compared with controls. These results indicated that individuals with IAD display response monitoring functional deficit characteristics and share ERN characteristics of individuals with compulsive–impulsive spectrum disorder. Subtypes of IAD include excessive gaming, sexual preoccupations, and e-mail/text messaging. Three subtypes share the common components, i.e., preoccupation, mood modification, unplanned use, withdrawal, tolerance, and functional impairment (Block, 2008). By using the Diagnostic and Statistical Manual of Mental Disorders (Fourth Edition, DSM-IV) criteria, some scholars suggest that IAD is an impulse disorder or at least related to impulse control disorder (Beard and Wolf, 2001; Shaw and Black, 2008).

Behavioral addiction is a form of addiction not caused by the usage of drugs. It consists of a compulsion to repeatedly engage in an action until it causes negative consequences to the person's physical, mental, and social well-being. Behavior persisting in spite of these consequences can be taken as a sign of addiction (Potenza, 2006; Parashar and Varma, 2007). According to above interpretation, IAD should belong to a kind of behavioral addiction. The drug based reinforcement and reward based learning processes are the most important mechanism of addictions. Impulsivity is considered as the tendency to act prematurely without foresight (Dalley et al., 2011). According to both animal and human studies, there are two forms of impulsivity: one depends on the temporal discounting of reward; another on motor or response disinhibition (Buckholtz et al., 2010). Barratt impulsiveness scale 11 (BIS-11) is considered more of a trait measure of impulsivity (Patton and Stanford, 1995). The go/no-go task is used for operational measures of impulsivity. Studies displayed that impulsivity is commonly associated with addiction to drugs from different pharmacological classes (Dick et al., 2010; Ersche et al., 2011; Molander et al., 2011; Economidou et al., 2012).

Executive function and working memory are critical features of cognition. The Wisconsin Card Sorting Test (WCST) is a neuropsychological test of "set-shifting," i.e., the ability to display flexibility in the face of changing schedules of reinforcement (Monchi et al., 2001). WCST is employed to assess the "frontal" lobe functions including strategic planning, organized searching, utilizing environmental feedback to shift cognitive sets, directing behavior toward achieving a goal, and modulating impulsive responding. Because of its reported sensitivity to frontal lobe dysfunction, WCST has been considered a measure of executive function. Individuals with substance dependence present working memory impairments as well as executive dysfunctions, which include reasoning, problem solving, inhibitory controlling, and decision-making (Crean et al., 2011; Hanson et al., 2011; Kiluk et al., 2011; Thoma et al., 2011; Yücel et al., 2012). Working memory refers to a brain system that provides temporary storage and manipulation of the information necessary for such complex cognitive tasks as language comprehension, learning, and reasoning. Digit span task (forwards/backwards) from the Wechsler Adult Intelligence Scale was used to index the maintenance and manipulation of verbal information in working memory (Baddeley, 1992).

Many studies displayed that individual with IAD present executive dysfunctions and reward/punishment sensitivities. For example, a study, which used a gambling task to simulate extreme win/lose situations to find the reward/punishment sensitivities after continuous wins and losses, showed that higher superior frontal gyrus activations after continuous wins for IAD subjects than for normal controls (NC). The brain activities in IAD subjects were not disturbed by their losses. In addition, IAD participants showed decreased posterior cingulate activation compared to NC after continuous losses. These results indicated that IAD subjects showed enhanced sensitivity to win and decreased sensitivity to lose (Dong et al., 2013a). Studies on neuroimaging indicated that individuals with IAD present executive dysfunctions including attentional selections and decision-making (Sun et al., 2009; Pawlikowski and Brand, 2011; Dong et al., 2013b).

Diminished control is a core defining concept of substance dependence or addiction. The concept of behavioral addictions has some scientific and clinical heuristic value, but remains controversial. Several behavioral addictions, such as pathological gambling, pathological kleptomania, and pathological shopping, have been hypothesized as having similarities to substance addictions. Additionally, these behavioral addictions are classified as impulse control disorders, a separate category from substance use disorders. However, not all impulse control disorders should be considered behavioral addictions (Grant et al., 2010). For example, intermittent explosive disorder is a behavioral disorder characterized by extreme expressions of anger, often to the point of uncontrollable rage, that are disproportionate to the situation at hand. Impulsive aggression is unpremeditated, and is defined by a disproportionate reaction to any provocation, real or perceived. Intermittent explosive disorder does not share characters of behavioral addictions. Previous studies indicated that there are many similarities in the neurobiology of behavior and substance addictions (Leeman and Potenza, 2012). Behavioral and substance addictions have many similarities in natural history, adverse consequences, and phenomenology. Individuals with behavioral addictions and those with substance use disorders both score high on self-report measures of impulsivity and sensation-seeking and generally low on measures of harm avoidance (Lejoyeux et al., 1997; Kim and Grant, 2001; Grant and Kim, 2002). Prevalence studies showed that individuals with IAD or substance dependence display common characteristics including high novelty-seeking behavior and low reward dependence (Ko et al., 2012). Adolescents with alcohol dependence were more likely to have IAD and show certain psychosocial characters including high behavior activation, low self-esteem, low family function, and life satisfaction (Ko et al., 2008). Substance dependence has been associated with sensation-seeking (Sargent et al., 2010), which has also been positively correlated with IAD (Chiu et al., 2004; Mehroof and Griffiths, 2010).

In research work, Internet Addiction Test (IAT, Young, 1999), Diagnostical Questionnaire (DQ, Young, 1996), the modified Diagnostic Questionnaire for Internet Addiction (YDQ, Beard and Wolf, 2001), and the Compulsive Internet Use Scale (CIUS, Meerkerk et al., 2009) are usually used as diagnosis instruments. It is becoming a common opinion that the IAT is not completely reliable and valid psychometric instrument nowadays. DQ is a significant contribution in providing a concrete basis for establishing problematic Internet use. However, there is limited research on Internet addiction including a representative sample to use as a comparison for those being diagnosed. As a result, no reliable and valid diagnostic criteria have been determined. Although YDQ does not solve all of the previously mentioned problems, it may help strengthen Young's proposed criteria (Beard and Wolf, 2001). CIUS showed good factorial stability across time and across different samples and subsamples. The internal consistency is high, and high correlations with concurrent and criterion variables demonstrate good validity (Meerkerk et al., 2009).

Being a non-invasive method, neuroimaging plays important roles in the investigation of neurobiological mechanism and adequate treatments of IAD and drug abuse. Until now, there are several neuroimaging studies on IAD. Studies indicated that individuals with IAD shared impulsivity features of individuals with substance dependence (Dong et al., 2011, 2012, 2014; Yuan et al., 2011; Zhou et al., 2013).

Up to date, although individuals with IAD have difficulty suppressing their excessive online behaviors in real life, little is known about the patho-physiological and cognitive mechanisms responsible for IAD (Weinstein and Lejoyeux, 2010). Neuropsychological test studies have contributed significantly to our understanding of the effect of IAD on the cognitive function. Under the same experimental condition to assess impulsivity and executive function of IAD and substance dependence (such as alcohol dependence) may not only help guide decisions as to whether or not IAD should be grouped together with substance use disorders, but also play important roles in the investigation of neurobiological mechanism and adequate treatments of IAD. In this study, participants are individuals with IAD, patients with alcohol dependence (AD) and NC. All participants were measured with BIS-11, go/no-go task, WCST, and Digit span task under the same experimental condition. The purpose of the present study was to examine whether Internet addictive individuals share impulsivity and executive dysfunction with alcohol-dependent individuals.

MATERIALS AND METHODS

TIME AND SETTING

The experiment was completed in the Department of Psychology and the Department of Psychiatry at Wuxi Mental Health Center, China, from May 2011 to October 2013.

DIAGNOSTIC APPROACHES AND PARTICIPANTS

IAD group

The diagnostic criteria of IAD group included: (i) met the criteria of the modified Diagnostic Questionnaire for Internet Addiction (YDQ) (Beard and Wolf, 2001), i.e., individuals who answered "yes" to questions one through five and at least any one of the remaining three questions were classified as suffering from IAD; (ii) whose age were more than 18 years old; (iii) did not meet criteria of any DSM-IV axis I disorder or personality disorders by administering a structured clinical interview (Chinese version); (iv) were not smokers; and (v) had not a diagnosis of alcohol or substance dependence, neurological disorders, all kinds of head injury, or systemic disease that might affect the central nervous system. The duration of the disorder was confirmed via a retrospective diagnosis. Subjects were asked to recall their life-style when they were initially addicted to the Internet. In order to confirm that they were suffering from Internet addiction, we retested them with the criteria of the modified YDQ. The reliability of these self-reports from the IAD subjects were confirmed by talking with their parents via telephone. The IAD subjects spent 11.20 ± 1.81 h/day on online activities (including gaming, Internet shopping, pornography, Internet social interaction, virtual society, and obtaining information). The days of Internet use per week was 6.41 ± 0.6. We verified this information from the roommates and co-workers of the IAD subjects that they often insisted being on the Internet late at night, disrupting others' lives despite the consequences. IAD group was recruited from Psychology Department of Wuxi Mental Health Center. They have regulated sleep patterns and did not ingest large quantities of caffeinated and energetic drinks by medical staffs' management. Twenty-two subjects were recruited as IAD group.

AD group

The diagnostic criteria of AD group included: (i) met the criteria of DSM-IV for alcohol dependence; (ii) no medication was received before 2 weeks; (iii) were not smokers; and (iv) had not a diagnosis of comorbid psychiatric illness (with the exception of depression in the alcohol-dependent group), history of head injury or neurological disorder. Alcohol-dependent subjects were in-patients at Psychiatry Department of Wuxi Mental Health Center. Sobriety at time of testing was confirmed by breath alcohol readings $\leq$0.01 mg/l. All subjects were abstinent for >1 week. The mean duration of abstinence was 15 days.

NC group

The controls were selected from citizens lived in Wuxi city, Jiangsu Province, China through local advertisement. Controls were excluded from the study if they were smokers; or had a diagnosis of alcohol or substance dependence, neurological disorders, all kinds of head injury, or systemic disease that might affect the central nervous system. Twenty-two healthy persons were recruited as NC group. Referred from a previous IAD study (Ko et al., 2009a), we chose NC who spent <2 h/day on the Internet. The NC were tested with the YDQ criteria modified by Beard and Wolf to certificate they were not suffering from IAD. All participants were Chinese.

All participants underwent a clinical assessment by a psychiatric residency to collect information on medication, sociodemographic data, and to confirm/exclude an IAD and AD diagnosis. In this study, we gave all participants a written informed consent to participate and all were paid. The protocol for the research project was approved by the Ethics Committee of Wuxi Mental Health Center, China.

The demographic characteristics of the sample are detailed in **Table 1**.

TASKS AND PROCEDURE

All participants completed the Hamilton Depression Scale (HAMD) (version of 17 items) (Hamilton, 1967) to measure depressive symptoms and BIS-11 to measure impulsivity. BIS-11 is a questionnaire on which participants rate their frequency of several common impulsive or non-impulsive behaviors/traits on a scale from 1 (rarely/never) to 4 (almost always/always). BIS-11 includes 30 items and is divided into three subscales including attentional key, motor key, and non-planning key, to determine overall impulsiveness scores, all items are summed, with higher scores indicating greater impulsivity. The AD group completed the Severity of Alcohol Dependence Questionnaire (SADQ) (Stockwell et al., 1983).

The Neuropsychological tests included the following measures.

Go/no-go task

E-Prime software 2.0 (Psychology Software Tools Inc., Sharpsburg, NC, USA) was used for the go/no-go task. The task, referred from pervious study (Zhou et al., 2010), involved the serial presentation on a computer screen of eight different two-digit numerical stimuli (four go stimuli and four no-go stimuli), displayed white on

Table 1 | Demographic characteristics and clinical data of the sample.

	IAD	AD	NC	Test statistic	*Post hoc* analyses
Sex ratio (M/F)	22 (16/6)	22 (18/4)	22 (15/7)	$\chi^2=5.64$, $P=0.12$, NS	–
Mean age (SD)	28 (7)	30 (6)	28 (7)	$F(2,66)=2.32$, NS	–
Age range	21–36	23–38	21–36	–	–
Education (SD)	9 (3)	9 (3)	9 (3)	$F(2,66)=3.21$, NS	–
Years of addiction (SD)	4 (3)	3 (3)	–	$t=1.355$, $P=0.62$, NS	–
SADQ (SD)	–	32.2 (17.3)	–	–	–
HAMD (SD)	9.1 (3.1)	8.9 (3.5)	5.1 (3.6)	$F(2,65)=5.88$, $P=0.23$, NS	–

IAD, internet addictive individual group; AD, alcohol-dependent individual group; NC, normal control group; M, male; F, female; SD, standard deviation; SADQ, severity of alcohol dependence questionnaire; HAMD, Hamilton depression scale; NS, not significant.

black background (1.5 cm × 1.5 cm in size). A total of 160 stimuli were presented in 20 blocks. Each block included eight trials, and pseudo-randomly presented with no more than three consecutive trials with either a go or no-go stimulus so that withholding a response involved overcoming an established response tendency. The go stimuli in any blocks were "08," "63," "74," and "25"; the no-go were "58," "19," "14," and "79." Subjects were told that the task involved learning when to go (bar press as quickly as possible) or not to go (withhold response) and that responses after some numbers would result in winning money ($0.16 per trial) but responses after others would result in losing money ($0.16 per response). The response window was 1000 ms and the inter-trial interval (ITI) was 1500 ms. Reward contingencies (green background with +$0.16 in white) or punishment contingencies (red background with −$0.16 in white) were presented on the computer screen for 1000 ms immediately after a response (within the 1500 ms ITI). The experiment included a practice phase and a recording phase. The practice phase consisted of 16 go and no-go trials. The percentage of hits and reactive time (RT) to go stimuli and the percentage of false alarms to no-go stimuli were used for analysis. When the button was pressed within 200–1000 ms after the presentation of a go stimulus, the response was confirmed as correct. Lack of a response in this latency window was defined as a miss, whereas responses made within this window to no-go stimuli were defined as false alarms. False alarms were defined for each modality separately. The percentage of correct responses to go stimuli was confirmed as 100 × N (target detections) divided by the total number of go stimuli. The percentage of false alarms to no-go stimuli was confirmed as 100 × N divided by the sum of no-go stimuli presented. RT was measured from the onset of the go stimulus to the button press.

Wisconsin card sorting test

The WCST (Beijing Ka Yip Wise Development Co., Ltd, computerized version VI) was present graphically on a computer screen. The WCST entailed matching stimulus cards with one of four category cards, in which the stimuli were multidimensional according to color, shape, and number, each dimension determining a sorting rule. By trial and error, the participant has to decide a preordained sorting rule given just the feedback ("Right" or "Wrong") on the screen after each sort. After 10 consecutive correct sorts the rule changed. There were up to six attempts to derive a rule, providing five rule shifts in the following sequence (color – shape – number – color – shape number), with each rule attainment referred to as "completing a category." Participants were not informed of the correct sorting principle and that the sorting principal shifts during the measurement; measuring continues until all 128 cards were sorted and irrespective of whether the participant achieved completes all the rule shifts. Two types of errors were possible, perseverative errors, in which the participant made a response in which they persist with a wrong sorting rule, and non-perseverative errors. In this study, five main types of WSCT were used for analysis: (i) the total response errors; (ii) perseverative errors; (iii) percentage of conceptual level responses; (iv) the number of categories completed; and (v) failure to maintain set.

Digit span task

Wechsler Adult Intelligence Scale-Revised China (WAIS-RC, Beijing Ka Yip Wise Development Co., Ltd, computerized version) was used for measurement of Digit span task. All participants are given sets of digits to repeat initially forwards then backwards. This is a test of immediate auditory recall and freedom from distraction. The participant was told to listen carefully because he or she will say a series of numbers and ask him or her to repeat them back in the same order. The first series is three numbers, such as "3, 9, 2." Each number is said in a monotone voice, one second apart. The person repeats those numbers back. The next step is to speak a series of four numbers, such as, "4, 7, 3, 1." Again, the individual repeats those back. Continue in the same manner by increasing the series of numbers to five and asking the participant to repeat the numbers back.

STATISTICAL ANALYSIS

Data were analyzed using SPSS (SPSS, Chicago, IL, USA). Sex ratio among IAD group, AD group, and NC group were analyzed with χ^2 tests. Comparisons of years of addiction between IAD group and AD group were done using independent-sample t-tests. Comparisons of HAMD scores, BIS-11 scores, data of go/no-go task, WSCT, and Digit span task among IAD group, AD group, and NC group were done using one-way analysis of variance (ANOVA). Least square difference (LSD) tests were performed as *post hoc* analyses if indicated. Alpha values of 0.05 were considered significant throughout.

RESULTS

COMPARISONS OF BIS-11 SCORES AMONG IAD GROUP, AD GROUP, AND NC GROUP

Using attentional key scores, motor key scores, non-planning key scores, and BIS-11 total scores as dependent variable, respectively, a one-way ANOVA revealed a significant main effect of Group (IAD group, AD group, and NC group). *Post hoc* LSD tests showed that attentional key scores, motor key scores, non-planning key scores, and BIS-11 total scores of IAD and AD group were significantly higher than that of NC group (for attentional key scores, $p = 0.038$ and 0.028, respectively; for motor key scores, $p = 0.030$ and 0.036, respectively; for non-planning key scores, $p = 0.017$ and 0.049, respectively; for BIS-11 total scores, $p = 0.022$ and 0.035, respectively), while above four main type data were not significantly different between IAD and AD group (all $p > 0.05$) (**Table 2**).

COMPARISONS OF RTs, HIT RATE, AND FALSE ALARM RATE AMONG IAD GROUP, AD GROUP, AND NC GROUP

Using RTs as dependent variable, a one-way ANOVA revealed no main effect of Group (IAD group, AD group, and NC group). Using hit rate and false alarm rate as dependent variable, respectively, a one-way ANOVA revealed a significant main effect of Group (IAD group, AD group, and NC group). *Post hoc* LSD tests showed that false alarm rate of IAD and AD group were significantly higher than that of NC group, and hit rate was significantly lower than that of NC group (for false alarm rate, $p = 0.027$ and 0.034, respectively; for hit rate, $p = 0.017$ and 0.020, respectively), while false alarm rate and hit rate was not significantly different between IAD and AD group (all $p > 0.05$) (**Table 3**).

COMPARISONS OF WSCT DATA AMONG IAD GROUP, AD GROUP, AND NC GROUP

Using total response errors, perseverative errors, percentage of conceptual level responses, the number of categories completed, and failure to maintain set as dependent variable respectively, a one-way ANOVA revealed a significant main effect of Group (IAD group, AD group, and NC group). *Post hoc* LSD tests showed that total response errors, perseverative errors, and failure to maintain set of IAD and AD group were significantly higher than that of NC group, and percentage of conceptual level responses and the number of categories completed of IAD and AD group were significantly lower than that of NC group (for total response errors, $p = 0.041$ and 0.022, respectively; for perseverative errors, $p = 0.039$ and 0.040, respectively; for failure to maintain set, $p = 0.024$ and 0.027, respectively; for percentage of conceptual level responses, $p = 0.011$ and 0.021, respectively; for the number of categories completed, $p = 0.043$ and 0.0391, respectively), while above five main type data were not significantly different between IAD and AD group (all $p > 0.05$) (**Table 4**).

COMPARISONS OF DIGIT SPAN TASK SCORES AMONG IAD GROUP, AD GROUP, AND NC GROUP

Using forwards scores and backwards scores as dependent variable, respectively, a one-way ANOVA revealed a significant main effect of Group (IAD group, AD group, and NC group). *Post hoc* LSD tests showed that forwards scores and backwards scores of IAD and AD group were significantly lower than that of NC group (for forwards scores, $p = 0.016$ and 0.025, respectively; for backwards scores, $p = 0.017$ and 0.041, respectively), while above two main type data were not significantly different between IAD and AD group (all $p > 0.05$) (**Table 5**).

Table 2 | BIS-11 scores [mean (SD)] in IAD group ($n = 22$), AD group ($n = 22$), and NC group ($n = 22$).

Variable	IAD	AD	NC	Test statistic
Attentional key	32.5 (2.6)	33.0 (3.7)	29.6 (2.8)	$F(2,65) = 10.98$, $P = 0.012$, Cohen's $d = 0.98$
Motor key	23.3 (3.1)	23.9 (4.2)	21.4 (3.9)	$F(2,65) = 12.57$, $P = 0.020$, Cohen's $d = 0.76$
Non-planning key	22.0 (3.1)	22.7 (1.1)	20.8 (3.1)	$F(2,65) = 9.67$, $P = 0.038$, Cohen's $d = 0.62$
Total scores	77.5 (8.1)	73.8 (9.2)	71.2 (7.5)	$F(2,65) = 62.50$, $P = 0.001$, Cohen's $d = 1.18$

IAD, internet addictive individual group; AD, alcohol-dependent individual group; NC, normal control group; SD, standard deviation.

Table 3 | RTs, hit rate, and false alarm rate [mean (SD)] in IAD group ($n = 22$), AD group ($n = 22$), and NC group ($n = 22$).

Variable	IAD	AD	NC	Test statistic
RT (ms)	541 (59)	542 (63)	539 (68)	$F(2,65) = 4.37$, $P = 0.13$, Cohen's $d = 0.00$
Hit rate	0.902 (0.003)	0.903 (0.002)	0.915 (0.002)	$F(2,65) = 15.61$, $P = 0.019$, Cohen's $d = 0.89$
False alarm rate	0.043 (0.057)	0.042 (0.058)	0.016 (0.015)	$F(2,65) = 13.25$, $P = 0.023$, Cohen's $d = 0.81$

IAD, internet addictive individual group; AD, alcohol-dependent individual group; NC, normal control group; SD, standard deviation.

Table 4 | WSCT data [mean (SD)] in IAD group ($n = 22$), AD group ($n = 22$), and NC group ($n = 22$).

Variable	IAD	AD	NC	Test statistic
Total response errors (%)	35.8 (20.6)	36.1 (23.2)	19.6 (21.8)	$F(2,65) = 21.28$, $P = 0.001$, Cohen's $d = 1.43$
Perseverative errors (%)	21.3 (12.1)	22.9 (14.2)	13.4 (13.0)	$F(2,65) = 18.55$, $P = 0.001$, Cohen's $d = 1.27$
Conceptual level responses (%)	53.0 (6.1)	54.7 (7.2)	60.8 (8.0)	$F(2,65) = 5.77$, $P = 0.040$, Cohen's $d = 0.56$
Number of categories completed	5.7 (2.1)	5.8 (3.3)	6.5 (3.5)	$F(2,65) = 10.50$, $P = 0.001$, Cohen's $d = 1.09$
Failure to maintain set	0.8 (0.6)	0.8 (1.2)	0.3 (0.5)	$F(2,65) = 3.50$, $P = 0.011$, Cohen's $d = 0.99$

IAD, internet addictive individual group; AD, alcohol-dependent individual group; NC, normal control group; SD, standard deviation.

Table 5 | Digit span scores [mean (SD)] in IAD group ($n = 22$), AD group ($n = 22$), and NC group ($n = 22$).

Variable	IAD	AD	NC	Test statistic
Forwards scores	8.5 (1.6)	8.1 (1.2)	11.6 (1.5)	$F(2,65) = 8.28$, $P = 0.014$, Cohen's $d = 0.86$
Backwards scores	8.3 (3.8)	7.9 (4.2)	10.1 (3.0)	$F(2,65) = 4.59$, $P = 0.026$, Cohen's $d = 0.59$

IAD, internet addictive individual group; AD, alcohol-dependent individual group; NC, Normal control group; SD, standard deviation.

DISCUSSION

This study is the first to test impulsivity, executive function, and working memory between Internet addictive individuals and with alcohol-dependent patients under the same experimental condition. In this study, impulsivity was measured with BIS-11 and a go/no-go task, executive function was assessed with WCST and working memory was tested with Digit span task. Our results indicate the existence of impulsivity in an IAD group and an AD group, deficiencies in executive function and working memory in an IAD and an AD sample.

Internet addiction disorder and alcohol dependence involve continued use of alcohol and Internet, respectively despite negative consequences, i.e., loss of behavioral control of alcohol and Internet use. Impulsivity refers to premature, unduly risky, and poorly conceived actions. Dysfunctional impulsivity includes deficits in attention, lack of reflection, or insensitivity to consequences, all of which may occur in addiction (Evenden, 1999; de Wit, 2009).

A recent study using traditional neuropsychological tests including the Stroop and computerized neuropsychological tests showed that IAD group exhibited more trait impulsivity than the healthy control group, Furthermore, IAD group performed more poorly than the healthy control group in a computerized stop signal test, and no group differences appeared for other neuropsychological tests, which indicated that individuals with IAD exhibited impulsivity as a core personality trait and in their neuropsychological functioning (Choi et al., 2014). Many studies displayed that alcohol-dependent patients present neurocognitive deficits in memory, learning, visuospatial functions, psychomotor speed processing, executive functions and decision-making, and the cognitive alterations are directly related to compliance with treatment and maintenance of withdrawal (Parsons, 1998). In our study, there were significant differences in BIS-11 scores among IAD group, AD group, and NC group; however, no differences in BIS-11 scores between IAD group and AD group were observed. Simultaneously, in go/no-go task, there were significant differences in false alarm rate and hit rate among IAD group, AD group, and NC group, and no differences in false alarm rate and hit rate between IAD group and AD group were observed. Above two tests indicate that both IAD and AD are more impulsive than controls, and Internet addictive individuals share impulsivity with alcohol-dependent patients.

Executive functions include abstract thinking, motivation, decision-making, planning, attention to tasks, and inhibition of impulsive responses. Although WCST exists some acknowledged weaknesses in interpretation of the profiles, i.e., difficulties in task performance could be caused by set-shifting, poor abstraction and conceptualization, or attentional problems, this procedure integrates multiple measurements of executive processes and is the most widely reported neuropsychological task. WCST commonly was used for neuropsychological measure of cognitive flexibility (or set-shifting ability). Our study results displayed that the total response errors, perseverative errors, and failure to maintain set of IAD and AD group were significantly higher than that of NC group, while above three main type data were not significantly different between IAD and AD group. Additionally, percentage of conceptual level responses and the number of categories completed of IAD and AD group were significantly lower than that of NC group, while above two main type data were not significantly different between IAD and AD group. These results indicate that both Internet addictive individuals and alcohol-dependent patients present the same property of executive dysfunctions. Many previous neuropsychological researches indicated that Internet-related cues interfere with control processes mediated by the prefrontal cortex and prefrontal brain areas, and Internet-related stimuli interfere with decision-making and other prefrontal functions, such as working memory and further executive functions (Brand et al., 2014). Our results support that the reductions of prefrontal control processes play a major role in developing and maintaining an addictive use of the Internet.

Working memory is the system that actively holds multiple pieces of transitory information in the mind, where they can be manipulated. Working memory is generally used synonymously with short-term memory, and it depends on how the two forms of memory are defined (Cowan, 2008). The cognitive processes needed to achieve this include the executive and attention control of short-term memory, which permit interim integration, processing, disposal, and retrieval of information (Rouder et al., 2011). This study results showed that by measurement of Digit span task, there were significant differences in forwards scores and backwards scores among IAD group, AD group, and NC group. Forwards scores and backwards scores of IAD and AD group were significantly lower than that of NC group, however, forwards scores and backwards scores were not significantly different between IAD and AD group. These results manifest that Internet addictive individuals share impairment of working memory with alcohol-dependent patients.

In conclusion, the results of this study clearly show that the existence of impulsivity, deficiencies in executive function, and working memory in an IAD and an AD sample, namely, Internet addictive individuals share impulsivity and executive dysfunction with alcohol-dependent individuals. Understanding the biological effects and characters of cognitive function of IAD on the human brain may provide insight into the pathogenesis of IAD and treatment. Up to date, although there is much argument on the diagnostic definition of IAD, numerous neuroimaging studies had highlighted structural and functional abnormalities in individuals with IAD similar to other type of addictive disorders, such as substance addiction and behavioral addiction (Fischl and Dale, 2000; Ko et al., 2009b). Our study using neuropsychological test proved that cognitive dysfunction in individuals with IAD similar to alcohol-dependent individuals. Neurocognitive assessment may be a useful tool for the detection and assessment of the progress of these alterations, as well as for the cognitive rehabilitation and psychosocial reinsertion of individuals with IAD.

A limitation of this study is that this study used the modified Diagnostic Questionnaire for Internet Addiction scores of higher than six as an indicator of IAD. Although this questionnaire is a frequently used instrument for assessing IAD, its validity as a diagnostic instrument has been questioned (Beard, 2005). Future studies may utilize other measures of assessing diagnostic criteria or severity of IAD to assess impulsivity, executive function, and working memory between Internet addictive individuals and alcohol-dependent patients. Additionally, this study results are preliminary because of the small sample size. Further studies with larger sample sizes are needed to replicate these findings.

ACKNOWLEDGMENTS

This study was supported by the Nature Science Foundation of Jiangsu Province, China (No. BK2007024).

REFERENCES

Baddeley, A. (1992). Working memory. *Science* 255, 556–559. doi:10.1126/science.1736359

Beard, K. W. (2005). Internet addition: a review of current assessment techniques and potential assessment questions. *Cyberpsychol. Behav.* 8, 7–14. doi:10.1089/cpb.2005.8.7

Beard, K. W., and Wolf, E. M. (2001). Modification in the proposed diagnostic criteria for Internet addiction. *Cyberpsychol. Behav.* 4, 377–383. doi:10.1089/109493101300210286

Block, J. (2008). Issues for DSM-V: Internet addiction. *Am. J. Psychiatry* 165, 306–307. doi:10.1176/appi.ajp.2007.07101556

Brand, M., Young, K. S., and Laier, C. (2014). Prefrontal control and Internet addiction: a theoretical model and review of neuropsychological and neuroimaging findings. *Front. Hum. Neurosci* 8:375. doi:10.3389/fnhum.2014.00375

Buckholtz, J. W., Treadway, M. T., Cowan, R. L., Woodward, N. D., Li, R., Ansari, M. S., et al. (2010). Dopaminergic network differences in human impulsivity. *Science* 329, 532–532. doi:10.1126/science.1185778

Chiu, S. I., Lee, J. Z., and Huang, D. H. (2004). Video game addiction in children and teenagers in Taiwan. *Cyberpsychol. Behav.* 7, 571–581. doi:10.1089/cpb.2004.7.571

Choi, J. S., Park, S. M., Roh, M. S., Lee, J. Y., Park, C. B., Hwang, J. Y., et al. (2014). Dysfunctional inhibitory control and impulsivity in Internet addiction. *Psychiatry Res.* 215, 424–428. doi:10.1016/j.psychres.2013.12.001

Cowan, N. (2008). What are the differences between long-term, short-term, and working memory? *Prog. Brain Res.* 169, 323–338. doi:10.1016/S0079-6123(07)00020-9

Crean, R. D., Crane, N. A., and Mason, B. J. (2011). An evidence based review of acute and long-term effects of cannabis use on executive cognitive functions. *J. Addict. Med.* 5, 1. doi:10.1097/ADM.0b013e31820c23fa

Dalley, J. W., Everitt, B. J., and Robbins, T. W. (2011). Impulsivity, compulsivity, and top-down cognitive control. *Neuron* 69, 680–694. doi:10.1016/j.neuron.2011.01.020

Davis, R. A. (2001). A cognitive-behavioral model of pathological Internet use. *Comput. Human Behav.* 17, 187–195. doi:10.1016/S0747-5632(00)00041-8

de Wit, H. (2009). Impulsivity as a determinant and consequence of drug use: a review of underlying processes. *Addict. Biol.* 14, 22–31. doi:10.1111/j.1369-1600.2008.00129.x

Dick, D., Smith, G., Olausson, P., Mitchell, S. H., Leeman, R. F., O'Malley, S. S., et al. (2010). Review: understanding the construct of impulsivity and its relationship to alcohol use disorders. *Addict. Biol.* 15, 217–226. doi:10.1111/j.1369-1600.2009.00190.x

Dong, G., Devito, E. E., Du, X., and Cui, Z. (2012). Impaired inhibitory control in "Internet addiction disorder": a functional magnetic resonance imaging study. *Psychiatry Res.* 203, 153–158. doi:10.1016/j.pscychresns.2012.02.001

Dong, G., Hu, Y., and Lin, X. (2013a). Reward/punishment sensitivities among Internet addicts: implications for their addictive behaviors. *Prog. Neuropsychopharmacol. Biol. Psychiatry* 46, 139–145. doi:10.1016/j.pnpbp.2013.07.007

Dong, G., Hu, Y., Lin, X., and Lu, Q. (2013b). What makes Internet addicts continue playing online even when faced by severe negative consequences? Possible explanations from an fMRI study. *Biol. Psychol.* 94, 282–289. doi:10.1016/j.biopsycho.2013.07.009

Dong, G., Huang, J., and Du, X. (2011). Enhanced reward sensitivity and decreased loss sensitivity in Internet addicts: an fMRI study during a guessing task. *J. Psychiatr. Res.* 45, 1525–1529. doi:10.1016/j.jpsychires.2011.06.017

Dong, G., Lin, X., Zhou, H., and Lu, Q. (2014). Cognitive flexibility in Internet addicts: fMRI evidence from difficult-to-easy and easy-to-difficult switching situations. *Addict. Behav.* 39, 677–683. doi:10.1016/j.addbeh.2013.11.028

Economidou, D., Theobald, D. E., Robbins, T. W., Everitt, B. J., and Dalley, J. W. (2012). Norepinephrine and dopamine modulate impulsivity on the five-choice serial reaction time task through opponent actions in the shell and core subregions of the nucleus accumbens. *Neuropsychopharmacology* 37, 2057–2066. doi:10.1038/npp.2012.53

Ersche, K. D., Barnes, A., Jones, P. S., Morein-Zamir, S., Robbins, T. W., and Bullmore, E. T. (2011). Abnormal structure of frontostriatal brain systems is associated with aspects of impulsivity and compulsivity in cocaine dependence. *Brain* 134, 2013–2024. doi:10.1093/brain/awr138

Evenden, J. L. (1999). Varieties of impulsivity. *Psychopharmacology* 146, 348–361. doi:10.1007/PL00005481

Fischl, B., and Dale, A. M. (2000). Measuring the thickness of the human cerebral cortex from magnetic resonance images. *Proc. Natl. Acad. Sci. U.S.A.* 97, 11050–11055. doi:10.1073/pnas.200033797

Grant, J. E., and Kim, S. W. (2002). Temperament and early environmental influences in kleptomania. *Compr. Psychiatry* 43, 223–228. doi:10.1053/comp.2002.32353

Grant, J. E., Potenza, M. N., Weinstein, A., and Gorelick, D. A. (2010). Introduction to behavioral addictions. *Am. J. Drug Alcohol Abuse* 36, 233–241. doi:10.3109/00952990.2010.491884

Hamilton, M. (1967). Development of a rating scale for primary depressive illness. *Br. J. Soc. Clin. Psychol.* 6, 278–296. doi:10.1111/j.2044-8260.1967.tb00530.x

Hanson, K. L., Cummins, K., Tapert, S. F., and Brown, S. A. (2011). Changes in neuropsychological functioning over 10 years following adolescent substance abuse treatment. *Psychol. Addict. Behav.* 25, 127. doi:10.1037/a0022350

Kiluk, B. D., Nich, C., and Carroll, K. M. (2011). Relationship of cognitive function and the acquisition of coping skills in computer assisted treatment for substance use disorders. *Drug Alcohol Depend.* 114, 169–176. doi:10.1016/j.drugalcdep.2010.09.019

Kim, S. W., and Grant, J. E. (2001). Personality dimensions in pathological gambling disorder and obsessive compulsive disorder. *Psychiatry Res.* 104, 205–212. doi:10.1016/S0165-1781(01)00327-4

Ko, C. H., Liu, G. C., Hsiao, S., Yen, J. Y., Yang, M. J., Lin, W. C., et al. (2009a). Brain activities associated with gaming urge of online gaming addiction. *J. Psychiatr. Res.* 43, 739–747. doi:10.1016/j.jpsychires.2008.09.012

Ko, C. H., Yen, J. Y., Liu, S. C., Huang, C. F., and Yen, C. F. (2009b). The associations between aggressive behaviors and Internet addiction and online activities in adolescents. *J. Adolesc. Health* 44, 598–605. doi:10.1016/j.jadohealth.2008.11.011

Ko, C. H., Yen, J. Y., Yen, C. F., Chen, C. S., and Chen, C. C. (2012). The association between Internet addiction and psychiatric disorder: a review of the literature. *Eur. Psychiatry* 27, 1–8. doi:10.1016/j.eurpsy.2010.04.011

Ko, C. H., Yen, J. Y., Yen, C. F., Chen, C. S., Weng, C. C., and Chen, C. C. (2008). The association between Internet addiction and problematic alcohol use in adolescents: the problem behavior model. *Cyberpsychol. Behav.* 11, 571–576. doi:10.1089/cpb.2008.0199

Leeman, R. F., and Potenza, M. N. (2012). Similarities and differences between pathological gambling and substance use disorders: a focus on impulsivity and compulsivity. *Psychopharmacology* 219, 469–490. doi:10.1007/s00213-011-2550-7

Lejoyeux, M., Tassain, V., Solomon, J., and Adès, J. (1997). Study of compulsive buying in depressed patients. *J. Clin. Psychiatry* 58, 169–173. doi:10.4088/JCP.v58n0406

Meerkerk, G. J., Van Den Eijnden, R. J., Vermulst, A. A., and Garretsen, H. F. (2009). The Compulsive Internet Use Scale (CIUS): some psychometric properties. *Cyberpsychol. Behav.* 12, 1–6. doi:10.1089/cpb.2008.0181

Mehroof, M., and Griffiths, M. D. (2010). Online gaming addiction: the role of sensation seeking, self-control, neuroticism, aggression, state anxiety, and trait anxiety. *Cyberpsychol. Behav. Soc. Netw.* 13, 313–316. doi:10.1089/cyber.2009.0229

Molander, A. C., Mar, A., Norbury, A., Steventon, S., Moreno, M., Caprioli, D., et al. (2011). High impulsivity predicting vulnerability to cocaine addiction in rats: some relationship with novelty preference but not novelty reactivity, anxiety or stress. *Psychopharmacology* 215, 721–731. doi:10.1007/s00213-011-2167-x

Monchi, O., Petrides, M., Petre, V., Worsley, K., and Dagher, A. (2001). Wisconsin card sorting revisited: distinct neural circuits participating in different stages of the task identified by event-related functional magnetic resonance imaging. *J. Neurosci.* 21, 7733–7741.

Parashar, A., and Varma, A. (2007). Behavior and substance addictions: is the world ready for a new category in the DSM-V? *CNS Spectr.* 12, 257.

Parsons, O. A. (1998). Neurocognitive deficits in alcoholics and social drinkers: a continuum? *Alcoh. Clin. Exp. Res.* 22, 954–961. doi:10.1111/j.1530-0277.1998.tb03895.x

Patton, J. H., and Stanford, M. S. (1995). Factor structure of the Barratt impulsiveness scale. *J. Clin. Psychol.* 51, 768–774. doi:10.1002/1097-4679(199511)51:6<768::AID-JCLP2270510607>3.0.CO;2-1

Pawlikowski, M., and Brand, M. (2011). Excessive Internet gaming and decision making: do excessive world of Warcraft-players have problems in decision making under risky conditions? *Psychiatry Res.* 188, 428–433. doi:10.1016/j.psychres.2011.05.017

Potenza, M. N. (2006). Should addictive disorders include non-substance-related conditions? *Addiction* 101(Suppl. 1), 142–151. doi:10.1111/j.1360-0443.2006.01591.x

Rouder, J. N., Morey, R. D., Morey, C. C., and Cowan, N. (2011). How to measure working memory capacity in the change detection paradigm. *Psychon. Bull. Rev.* 18, 324–330. doi:10.3758/s13423-011-0055-3

Sargent, J. D., Tanski, S., Stoolmiller, M., and Hanewinkel, R. (2010). Using sensation seeking to target adolescents for substance use interventions. *Addiction* 105, 506–514. doi:10.1111/j.1360-0443.2009.02782.x

Shaw, M., and Black, D. W. (2008). Internet addiction. *CNS Drugs* 22, 353–365. doi:10.2165/00023210-200822050-00001

Stockwell, T., Murphy, D., and Hodgson, R. (1983). The severity of alcohol dependence questionnaire: its use, reliability and validity. *Br. J. Addict.* 78, 145–155. doi:10.1111/j.1360-0443.1983.tb05502.x

Sun, D. L., Chen, Z. J., Ma, N., Zhang, X. C., Fu, X. M., and Zhang, D. R. (2009). Decision-making and prepotent response inhibition functions in excessive Internet users. *CNS Spectr.* 14, 75–81.

Thoma, R. J., Monnig, M. A., Lysne, P. A., Ruhl, D. A., Pommy, J. A., Bogenschutz, M., et al. (2011). Adolescent substance abuse: the effects of alcohol and marijuana on neuropsychological performance. *Alcohol. Clin. Exp. Res.* 35, 39–46. doi:10.1111/j.1530-0277.2010.01320.x

Weinstein, A., and Lejoyeux, M. (2010). Internet addiction or excessive Internet use. *Am. J. Drug Alcohol Abuse* 36, 277–283. doi:10.3109/00952990.2010.491880

Young, K. (1999). The research and controversy surrounding Internet addiction. *Cyberpsychol. Behav.* 2, 381–383. doi:10.1089/cpb.1999.2.381

Young, K. S. (1996). Addictive use of the Internet: a case that breaks the stereotype. *Psychol. Rep.* 79, 899–902. doi:10.2466/pr0.1996.79.3.899

Young, K. S., and Rogers, R. C. (1998). The relationship between depression and Internet addiction. *Cyberpsychol. Behav.* 1, 25–28. doi:10.1089/cpb.1998.1.25

Yuan, K., Qin, W., Liu, Y., and Tian, J. (2011). Internet addiction: neuroimaging findings. *Commun. Integr. Biol.* 4, 637–639. doi:10.4161/cib.17871

Yücel, M., Bora, E., Lubman, D. I., Solowij, N., Brewer, W. J., Cotton, S. M., et al. (2012). The impact of cannabis use on cognitive functioning in patients with schizophrenia: a meta-analysis of existing findings and new data in a first-episode sample. *Schizophr. Bull.* 38, 316–330. doi:10.1093/schbul/sbq079

Zhou, Z. H., Li, C., and Zhu, H. M. (2013). An error-related negativity potential investigation of response monitoring function in individuals with Internet addiction disorder. *Front. Behav. Neurosci.* 2013:7. doi:10.3389/fnbeh.2013.00131

Zhou, Z. H., Yuan, G. Z., and Yao, J. J. (2012). Cognitive biases toward Internet game-related pictures and executive deficits in individuals with an Internet game addiction. *PLoS ONE* 7:e48961. doi:10.1371/journal.pone.0048961

Zhou, Z. H., Yuan, G. Z., Yao, J. J., Li, C., and Cheng, Z. H. (2010). An event-related potential investigation of deficient inhibitory control in individuals with pathological Internet use. *Acta Neuropsychiatr.* 22, 228–236. doi:10.1111/j.1601-5215.2010.00444.x

16

Is neural hyperpolarization by cathodal stimulation always detrimental at the behavioral level?

Cornelia Pirulli[1†], Anna Fertonani[1†] and Carlo Miniussi[1,2]*

[1] Cognitive Neuroscience Section, IRCCS Istituto Centro San Giovanni di Dio Fatebenefratelli, Brescia, Italy
[2] Neuroscience Section, Department of Clinical and Experimental Sciences, University of Brescia, Brescia, Italy

***Correspondence:**
Carlo Miniussi, Department of Clinical and Experimental Sciences, University of Brescia, Viale Europa 11, 25123 Brescia, Italy
e-mail: carlo.miniussi@cognitiveneuroscience.it

†These authors have contributed equally to this work.

Cathodal transcranial direct current stimulation (c-tDCS) is usually considered an inhibitory stimulation. From a physiological perspective, c-tDCS induces hyperpolarization at the neural level. However, from a behavioral perspective, c-tDCS application does not always result in performance deterioration. In this work, we investigated the role of several important stimulation parameters (i.e., timing, presence of pauses, duration, and intensity) in shaping the behavioral effects of c-tDCS over the primary visual cortex. In Experiment 1, we applied c-tDCS at two different times (before or during an orientation discrimination task). We also studied the effects of pauses during the stimulation. In Experiments 2 and 3, we compared different durations (9 vs. 22 min) and intensities (0.75 vs. 1.5 mA) of stimulation. c-tDCS applied before task execution induced an improvement of performance, highlighting the importance of the activation state of the cortex. However, this result depended on the duration and intensity of stimulation. We suggest that the application of c-tDCS induces depression of cortical activity over a specific stimulated area; but to keep reactivity within given limits, the brain react in order to restore the equilibrium and this might result in increased sensitivity in visual performance. This is a further example of how the nervous system dynamically maintains a condition that permits adequate performance in different environments.

Keywords: transcranial direct current stimulation, perceptual learning, metaplasticity, facilitation, cathodal tDCS, homeostasis, NIBS, neural noise

INTRODUCTION

Transcranial direct current stimulation (tDCS) is a technique that allows the modulation of cortical excitability. A direct current of low-level intensity (~2 mA) is applied to electrodes that sit on the subject's scalp. This current passes through the scalp and crosses the extra cortical layers to reach the cortex, modulating the membrane polarity of neurons within a region of underlying neural tissue. The low strength of the current is not able to induce depolarization at a threshold level of "inactive" neurons (i.e., inducing an action potential). However, if there is ongoing activity (i.e., background activity determined by state or task-induced activity), the change in membrane potential induced by tDCS can promote more effective "excitation" or "inhibition" in a polarity-specific manner (Creutzfeldt et al., 1962; Bindman et al., 1964; Stagg and Nitsche, 2011). These tDCS-induced changes in the neuronal threshold during stimulation result from changes in membrane permeability, including depolarization of the soma by anodal stimulation (a-tDCS) and hyperpolarization by cathodal stimulation (c-tDCS) (Liebetanz et al., 2002; Nitsche et al., 2003b, 2004a,b). Polarization effects outlast the tDCS period (Nitsche and Paulus, 2000, 2001), and these after-effects are due to changes in receptor activity at the synaptic level, in addition to membrane polarity shifts (Nitsche et al., 2003a, 2004a,b).

From a behavioral standpoint, strong *a priori* assumptions are often made in neuromodulation studies using tDCS where physiological effects are directly mapped on to behavioral effects. The application of a-tDCS during a task is thought to induce facilitation, while c-tDCS is assumed to induce inhibition of performance. While the concept of a-tDCS facilitating and c-tDCS worsening performance seems well established, these effects are mainly valid for tDCS in the motor system (Nitsche et al., 2008, but see Wiethoff et al., 2014). Behavioral effects of tDCS have been identified in several functional areas, but the relationship between facilitation and inhibition is often quite complex (Jacobson et al., 2012; Miniussi et al., 2013). tDCS is thought to prime the behavioral system by increasing/decreasing cortical excitability and producing behavioral effects in the cognitive system. Nevertheless, the final effect depends on the stimulated area and on its involvement in a given task (i.e., the type of process and the final goal of the task) (Dockery et al., 2009; Nitsche and Paulus, 2011; Vallar and Bolognini, 2011; Berryhill and Jones, 2012; Jacobson et al., 2012; Tseng et al., 2012; Weiss and Lavidor, 2012; Filmer et al., 2013; Hsu et al., 2014; Nozari et al., 2014).

Several examples of contradictory final behavioral outcomes for c-tDCS can be found at different processing levels (Jacobson et al., 2012). Monti et al. (2008) found facilitation in a naming task using c-tDCS over Broca's area. Antal et al. (2004b) found that c-tDCS applied to the visual middle temporal area improved performance in a visuomotor coordination task. In a different study from the same group (Antal et al., 2001) using a Gabor patch stimulus, only c-tDCS showed a significant change in static and dynamic contrast sensitivities. Vicario et al. (2013) showed that c-tDCS applied to the posterior parietal cortex enhanced temporal accuracy in a time reproduction task compared to sham stimulation (see also Dockery et al., 2009; Moos et al., 2012; Weiss and Lavidor, 2012; Filmer et al., 2013). Moreover, several studies reported no effect of c-tDCS on task performance (e.g., Kincses et al., 2004; Iyer et al., 2005; Sparing et al., 2008; Cerruti and Schlaug, 2009; Fertonani et al., 2010; Kraft et al., 2010). Contrasting effects of c-DCS have also been found at the neurophysiological level (see Matsunaga, 2004; Pellicciari et al., 2013). A magnetoencephalography study has reported that the two tDCS polarities induce the same cortical EEG power density (Venkatakrishnan et al., 2011). Antal et al. (2004a) showed that c-tDCS over the primary visual cortex (V1) decreased the amplitude of an early visual evoked potential (N70), whereas Accornero et al. (2007) reported the opposite result with an increased amplitude of the early P100 potential.

This complex pattern of results may be explained by the fact that the ability or the efficacy of tDCS to induce modifications of membrane polarity—and consequently behavioral performance—depends on several methodological and technical parameters: current density, duration, timing of application, and pauses between stimulations (for a review, see Brunoni et al., 2012). Clearly, all these methodological aspects will determine the "reaction of the brain" to the DC stimulation in relation to the subject's state and task/protocol. As an example, the importance of duration and of the presence of pauses during the period of stimulation has been recently demonstrated by Fricke et al. (2011). These authors measured the motor evoked potential (MEP) amplitude after repeated tDCS. The authors found that 5 or 10 min of c-tDCS decreased excitability and suppressed MEP amplitude for 5 and 30 min, respectively, indicating the importance of tDCS duration. However, if a pause of 3 min was inserted between two stimulations of 5 min, there was an inversion of the effect, resulting in MEP amplitude enhancement (see also Monte-Silva et al., 2010). The stimulation intensity is also an important factor. Batsikadze et al. (2013) showed that 1 mA c-tDCS decreased MEP amplitude, but the application of 2 mA resulted in increased cortical excitability (see also Teo et al., 2011; Moos et al., 2012; Hoy et al., 2013). In addition, behavioral performance induced by tDCS depends on the timing of application in relation to task execution (Stagg et al., 2011; Pirulli et al., 2013; Fertonani et al., 2014). Several studies have shown that the same type of stimulation may have different behavioral effects (facilitation vs. inhibition vs. null-effect) depending on whether it is applied before or during the task execution.

Given the heterogeneity of the effects induced by c-tDCS, the aim of this work was to explore the outcome of applying c-tDCS on V1. We chose an orientation discrimination task (ODT) because it is a well established task to study visual perceptual learning (Vogels and Orban, 1985; Shiu and Pashler, 1992), and it has been showed to involves primarily V1 (Schoups et al., 2001; Li et al., 2004). Nevertheless it should be considered that we cannot be totally sure that stimulation delivered by tDCS is focalized only under the stimulation electrode (Miranda et al., 2006; Wagner et al., 2007). We applied c-tDCS before or during the execution of ODT, with or without pauses during stimulation, and at different intensities and durations. Based on the previous reports, our expectation was that the final outcome of the tDCS in terms of response facilitation or inhibition would depend on the interaction between the brain state and when and how c-tDCS was applied. Therefore, c-tDCS would not necessarily induce a univocal behavioral inhibition. Given that the brain is constructed to keep certain important parameters within given limits, the brain would react proportionally when it is shifted from these limits in order to restore the equilibrium, as suggested by the concept of homeostasis (see Bernard, 1878 and Cannon, 1929 in Cooper, 2008). Therefore, an initial down-regulation induced by an inhibitory stimulation, given for a longer time, at higher intensity can be reverted, rendering the involved neurons more easily responsive. Nevertheless to explain the effects of tDCS during a behavioral task it has been proposed that a neural noise framework should be consider (see non-linear systems and stochastic resonance; Miniussi et al., 2013), suggesting that the outcome of applying tDCS depends on the noise present in the system and the level of tDCS and task -induced activity, rather than solely on the stimulation polarity.

MATERIALS AND METHODS

ORIENTATION DISCRIMINATION TASK

We chose an ODT that is a widely studied VPL task and involves V1 neurons (Vogels and Orban, 1985; Shiu and Pashler, 1992). This task has been previously described in detail by our group (Fertonani et al., 2011; see Pirulli et al., 2013). Given the ODT characteristics, is likely that a local (i.e., V1) circuit of neuronal populations is dedicated to execute the task, nevertheless we cannot exclude that tDCS effects are due to a more complex neuronal network, involving others parietal areas. Briefly, throughout the experiment, participants were comfortably seated in an armchair in a quiet, dimly illuminated room. The subjects had to decide as quickly and accurately as possible whether the presented stimulus (a target line) was tilted clockwise or counter clockwise relative to the previously presented stimulus (reference line) (see trial structure in **Figure 1**). After each response an auditory feedback informed the subjects about the correctness of their responses (an high tone indicated the right response while a low tone the wrong response).

Each block of the ODT consisted of 64 trials and lasted approximately 4 min. The ODT consisted of 5 experimental blocks plus a training block. The training block contained 8 trials and an increased rotation angle between the two stimuli (10° clockwise or counter clockwise). In Experiments 1 and 2, the angular difference between the reference and the target was ±1.10, 1.21, 1.33, and 1.46°. All of the experimental parameters were balanced and randomized between blocks. In Experiment 3 (control experiment), the task was made easier by replacing the smallest degree of rotation (1.10°) with 1.60° (1.21, 1.33, 1.46, and 1.60°). All of the other task characteristics were unchanged, except for the presence of a baseline block before the stimulation.

TRANSCRANIAL DIRECT CURRENT STIMULATION

tDCS was delivered by a battery-driven current stimulator (Eldith-Plus, NeuroConn GmbH, Ilmenau, Germany) through

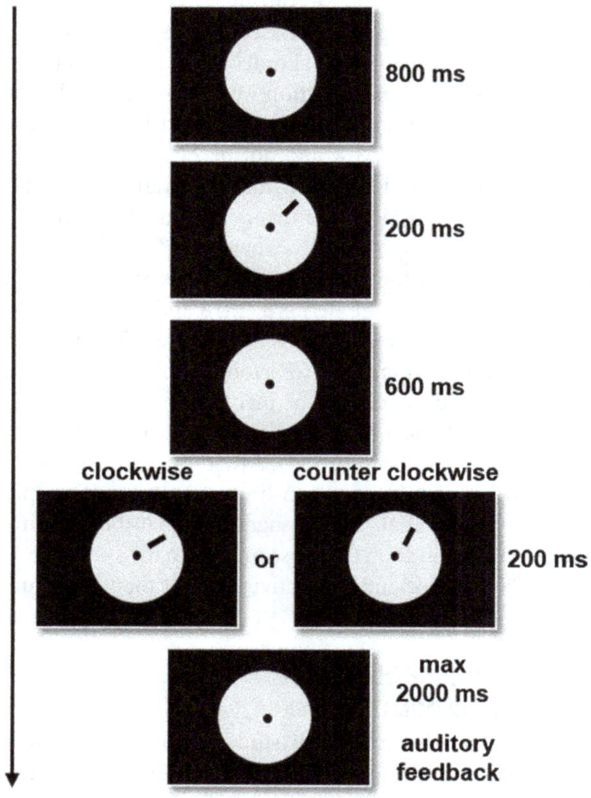

FIGURE 1 | Example of an ODT trial with the reference and target stimuli presented in the upper right hemifield. The line can turn clockwise or counter clockwise. The subjects were asked to decide whether the presented stimulus was tilted clockwise or counter clockwise relative to the previously presented stimulus.

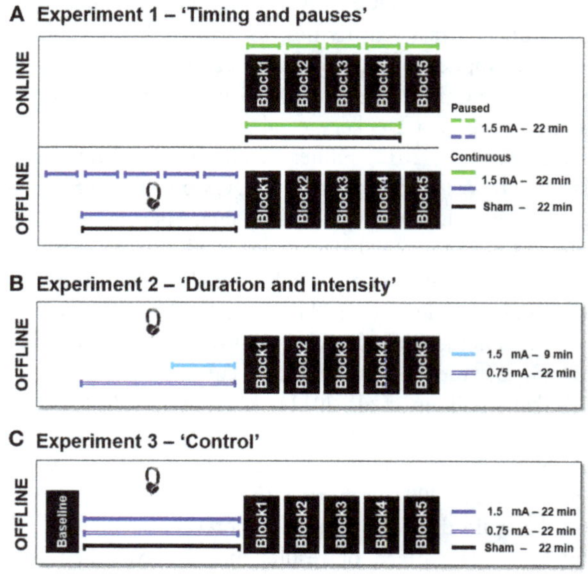

FIGURE 2 | Experimental procedure. (A) Experiment 1: in the top panel, the green lines represent the online conditions. In the bottom panel, the blue lines represent the offline conditions. The dashed lines represent the paused stimulations, whereas the continuous lines the continuous stimulations. The sham condition is shown in black lines. **(B)** Experiment 2 (offline conditions): the short turquoise line represents 1.5 mA for 9 min, and the double blue line represents 0.75 mA for 22 min. **(C)** Experiment 3 (offline conditions): the blue line represents 1.5 mA for 22 min, the double blue line represents 0.75 mA for 22 min, and the black line represents sham for 22 min.

a pair of saline-soaked surface sponge electrodes. The "active" electrode (16 cm^2) was placed over the occipital cortex in the area corresponding to V1, which was defined as 10% of the nasion-inion distance above the inion (mean position = 3.5 ± 0.2 cm above the inion). The reference electrode (60 cm^2) was fixed extra-cephalically on the right arm. The electrodes were kept in place with elastic bands, and an electro-conductive gel was applied under the electrodes to help reduce impedance to the electrical current. When tDCS was applied, the polarity of the active electrode over V1 was always cathodal. For active tDCS, the current was ramped up over 8 s (fade-in phase), held constant for the experimental time, and then ramped down over 8 s (fade-out phase). In the sham c-tDCS, the current was ramped up (8 s) and down (8 s) and stayed at level for 15 s.

Experiment 1—"Timing and pauses"

In this experiment, we investigated the effect of the timing of stimulation during task execution, either online or offline (before task execution), and the presence of pauses during the stimulation (intervals of 2 min between blocks). In all conditions, we applied c-tDCS for 22 min at 1.5 mA (current density of the active electrode 0.094 mA/cm^2 of the reference 0.025 mA/cm^2) as shown in **Figure 2A**. In the continuous stimulation, current was administered without pauses, while in the paused stimulation condition, the stimulation was turned on at the beginning of each experimental block and maintained until the end of the block. c-tDCS was applied for approximately 4 min during each of the 5 experimental blocks, with 2 min of pauses between blocks (i.e., 4 min of stimulation—2 min of pause—4 min of stimulation, and so on). In the online condition, the stimulation was applied during the task execution. In the offline condition, stimulation was applied before task execution while the subjects were listening to an audio book played on an audio device, maintaining the same time intervals used in the online condition. The duration of the entire experimental session was approximately 30 min for the online conditions and approximately 60 min for the offline conditions. The procedure is described in **Figure 2A**.

Experiment 2—"Duration and intensity"

In this experiment, we investigated the effect of the duration and intensity of stimulation for the offline condition, as shown in **Figure 2B**. Subjects were stimulated for 9 min at an intensity of 1.5 mA or for 22 min at an intensity of 0.75 mA (current density of the active electrode 0.047 mA/cm^2 of the reference 0.013 mA/cm^2). Data were compared with those for 22 min of stimulation at an intensity of 1.5 mA in the offline condition collected in Experiment 1 (see **Figure 2B**).

Experiment 3—Control experiment

In Experiment 3, we corroborated the effects of the stimulation intensity for the offline protocol with a modified experimental design (see the description of the ODT task, above). We facilitated the ODT and added a baseline block before the beginning of the offline stimulation. The stimulation was applied continuously for 22 min with an intensity of 1.5 or 0.75 mA (see **Figure 2C**).

Sensation questionnaire

In all of the experiments, at the end of the experimental session, we asked all subjects to complete a questionnaire (Fertonani et al., 2010) about the tDCS-induced sensations that they experienced during the different conditions so that we could evaluate if different stimulation protocols (e.g., active vs. sham) induced different sensations.

SUBJECTS

A total of 139 healthy subjects participated in the three experiments. All of the participants were right-handed except for 6 subjects tested in Experiment 3, who were equally distributed in the experimental groups. All participants had normal or corrected-to-normal vision. Subjects with a history of seizures, implanted metal objects, heart problems or any neurological disease were not recruited. Moreover, subjects who had a task performance below chance (no learning) were excluded from the study. Based on these criteria, 17 participants were excluded. The remaining 122 subjects (61 males, mean age ± standard deviation 22.0 ± 2.9 years; range 19–33 years) participated in the experiments.

Experiment 1—"Timing and pauses"

Seventy-two subjects were assigned to one of the five groups stimulated for 22 min at 1.5 mA: online paused (14 subjects, 7 males; 21.7 ± 2.6 years), offline paused (14 subjects, 7 males; 21.6 ± 2.6 years), online continuous (10 subjects, 5 males; 21.7 ± 0.8 years), offline continuous (10 subjects, 5 males; 23.0 ± 3.6 years) and placebo stimulation (sham, 24 subjects, 12 males; 21.7 ± 3.6 years). In the sham group, 14 subjects were stimulated online and 10 subjects were stimulated offline. The data for the online conditions were collected in a previous experiment (Fertonani et al., 2011; for details see Pirulli et al., 2013).

Experiment 2—"Duration and intensity"

We tested two additional groups (20 Subjects): 10 subjects (5 males; 22.1 ± 2.0 years) stimulated for 9 min at 1.5 mA (offline-9 min) and 10 subjects (5 males; 21.4 ± 2.0 years) stimulated for 22 min at 0.75 mA (offline-0.75 mA). We compared these two groups with the offline and sham groups of Experiment 1.

Experiment 3—Control experiment

We tested three new groups (30 Subjects) stimulated for 22 min at 0.75 mA (10 subjects, 5 males, 23.0 ± 4.4 years), 1.5 mA (10 subjects, 5 males, mean age 20.8 ± 1.8 years) and sham (10 subjects, 5 males; 23.6 ± 4.1 years).

The study was approved by the Ethics Committee of the IRCCS Centro San Giovanni di Dio Fatebenefratelli, Brescia, Italy. Safety procedures were used in accordance with non-invasive brain stimulation indications (Iyer et al., 2005; Poreisz et al., 2007; Rossi et al., 2009), and written informed consent was obtained from all participants prior to the beginning of the experiments.

DATA ANALYSIS

The average orientation sensitivity was calculated as a d prime value (d′) from measurements of the hit rate and false-alarm rate, for each subject and each block separately for each stimulation condition. We have chosen the d′ as a measure of accuracy because it is roughly invariant when response bias is manipulate, whereas simple indexes such as proportion correct don't have this property. As a first index of learning rate, we analyzed the relationship between d′ values and block numbers using linear regression analysis. This analysis allowed us to associate a slope value with each subject. A second index called the "learning index" was calculated, for Experiment 3, by subtracting the mean baseline d′ value from the mean d′ value of block 5 for each subject.

The Kolmogorov-Smirnov test confirmed the normality of the distribution of all data (d′ values, slope, learning index), and subsequently data were analyzed using a repeated-measures analysis of variance (ANOVA). The data sphericity was tested using the Mauchly test, where appropriate. When the test results were statistically significant, the data were corrected using the Huynh-Feldt correction. The effect size is reported using the partial Eta squared value. A p-value < 0.05 was considered significant for all statistical analyses. For multiple comparisons, we used Fisher's Least Significant Difference (LSD) method to test our specific "a priori" hypotheses (i.e., to compare different timings of application, intensities and durations). For all other comparisons, the p-values were corrected using a Tukey correction.

Data from the sensations induced by c-tDCS were analyzed using the Kruskal–Wallis one-way analysis of variance and, subsequently, with multiple comparisons.

RESULTS

ORIENTATION SENSITIVITY—d′

Experiment 1—"Timing and pauses"

We performed a repeated-measure ANOVA with *block* (from 1 to 5) as a within-subjects factor and *stimulation* (online paused, online continuous, offline paused, offline continuous, and sham) as a between-subjects factor. We observed a significant main effect for *block* [$F_{(4,\ 268)} = 24.105$; $p < 0.001$; $\eta_p^2 = 0.265$] and *stimulation* [$F_{(4,\ 67)} = 3.272$; $p = 0.016$; $\eta_p^2 = 0.163$]. The interaction between *block* and *stimulation* was not statistically significant [$F_{(16,\ 268)} = 1.005$; $p = 0.452$].

For *block*, multiple *post-hoc* comparisons revealed a statistically significant difference between block 1 and blocks 2, 3, 4, and 5 (all $p < 0.01$), between block 2 and blocks 4, and 5 (all $p < 0.001$), and between block 3 and block 5 ($p = 0.043$).

For *stimulation*, multiple *post-hoc* comparisons revealed that the offline paused (mean d′ ± standard error of the mean—s.e.m. = 0.615 ± 0.122) and offline continuous (0.623 ± 0.114) conditions were significantly different from the online paused (0.304 ± 0.121), online continuous (0.346 ± 0.118), and sham (0.368 ± 0.083) (all $p < 0.05$) conditions (see **Figure 3**).

These results support the initial hypothesis that c-tDCS, applied before the ODT, modulates behavior, while c-tDCS applied during the task does not modify the final outcome. We found an improvement in the subject's accuracy when c-tDCS was applied offline.

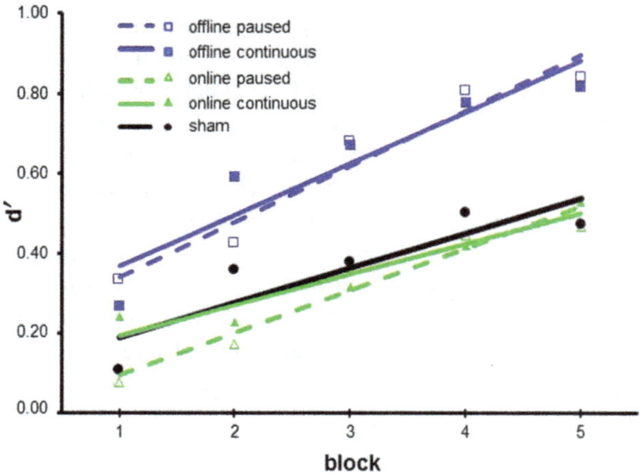

FIGURE 3 | Results of Experiment 1. Data are presented as the mean d′ values. The lines represent the fit of each condition. The blue lines represent the offline conditions, and the green lines represent online conditions. The dashed lines represent the paused stimulations, whereas the continuous lines represent the continuous stimulations. The sham condition is shown in black.

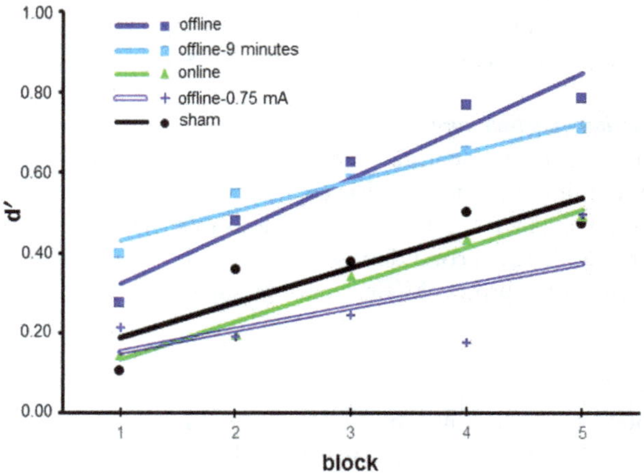

FIGURE 4 | Results of Experiment 2. Data are presented as the mean d′ values. The lines represent the fit of each condition. The blue line represents the offline 1.5 mA for the 22 min condition, the green line represents the online 1.5 mA for the 22 min condition, the turquoise line represents offline 1.5 mA for the 9 min condition, and the double blue line represents the offline-0.75 mA for the 22 min condition. The sham condition is shown in black.

These data highlight the absence of a difference between the conditions with or without pauses. Confirmation was obtained with an ANOVA with *block* (from 1 to 5) as a within-subjects factor and *timing* (online vs. offline) and presence of *pauses* (paused vs. continuous) as between-subjects factors. We observed a significant main effect of *block* [$F_{(4, 176)} = 18.438$; $p < 0.001$; $\eta_p^2 = 0.295$] and *timing* [$F_{(1, 44)} = 11.026$; $p = 0.002$; $\eta_p^2 = 0.200$]. The factor *pauses* was not statistically significant [$F_{(1, 44)} = 0.077$; $p = 0.782$]. No interaction was statistically significant. For *block*, multiple *post-hoc* comparisons revealed a statistically significant difference between block 1 and blocks 3, 4, and 5 (all $p < 0.001$) and between block 2 and block 3 ($p = 0.042$), 4 ($p < 0.001$), 5 ($p < 0.001$) (see **Figure 3**).

Having verified that the presence of pauses during stimulation does not influence the effect of stimulation, we collapsed the two online conditions (continuous and paused) and the two offline conditions (continuous and paused) into one online and one offline condition (hereafter, all conditions with the initial parameters, i.e., 22 min duration and 1.5 mA intensity, will be called "online" and "offline").

Experiment 2—"Duration and intensity"

We performed a repeated-measure ANOVA with *block* (from 1 to 5) as a within-subjects factor and *stimulation* (online, offline, offline-9 min, offline-0.75 mA, and sham) as a between-subjects factor. We observed a significant main effect for *block* [$F_{(4, 348)} = 20.286$; $p < 0.001$; $\eta_p^2 = 0.189$] and *stimulation* [$F_{(4, 87)} = 4.727$; $p = 0.002$; $\eta_p^2 = 0.163$]. The interaction between *block* and *stimulation* was not statistically significant [$F_{(16, 348)} = 1.512$; $p = 0.092$].

For *block*, multiple *post-hoc* comparisons revealed a statistically significant difference between block 1 and blocks 2, 3, 4, and 5 (all $p < 0.001$), between block 2 and blocks 4, and 5 (all $p < 0.001$), and between block 3 and block 5 ($p = 0.003$).

For *stimulation*, multiple *post-hoc* comparisons revealed that offline (0.618 ± 0.085) was different from sham (0.368 ± 0.083), online (0.321 ± 0.086) and offline-0.75 mA (0.264 ± 0.109). Moreover, offline-9 min (0.577 ± 0.123) was different from online and offline-0.75 mA and showed a marginally significant difference from sham ($p = 0.069$, all other $p < 0.05$) (see **Figure 4**).

Experiment 3—Control experiment

We performed a repeated-measure ANOVA with *block* (from baseline to 5) as a within-subjects factor and *stimulation* (offline, offline-0.75 mA, and sham) as a between-subjects factor. We observed a significant main effect for *block* [$F_{(5, 135)} = 7.843$; $p < 0.001$; $\eta_p^2 = 0.225$] and an interaction between *block* and *stimulation* [$F_{(10, 135)} = 1.980$; $p = 0.128$]. The factor *stimulation* was not statistically significant [$F_{(2, 27)} = 1.434$; $p = 0.256$].

For *block*, multiple *post-hoc* comparisons revealed a statistically significant difference between block baseline and blocks 1, 2, 3, 4, and 5 (all $p < 0.01$). The interaction between *block* and *stimulation* revealed that stimulation influences the block trend. In the offline condition, block baseline was different from blocks 1, 2, 3, 4, and 5; block 1 was different from blocks 4 and 5; and block 2 was different from block 5. In the offline-0.75 mA condition, block baseline was different from block 4. In the sham condition, block baseline was different from blocks 1 and 5 and block 1 was different from block 2.

A One-Way ANOVA on block baseline showed that in this block, d′ was not different between the stimulation conditions [$F_{(2, 27)} = 0.064$; $p = 0.938$].

In Experiment 3, the presence of a block of baseline allowed us to show a different rate of learning between the stimulation conditions. For this purpose, we executed two different analyses. A One-Way ANOVA on slope [$F_{(2, 27)} = 4.630$; $p = 0.019$; $\eta_p^2 =$

0.255] demonstrated that offline was different from sham ($p = 0.008$) and 0.75 mA ($p = 0.027$). A One-Way ANOVA on the learning index [$F_{(2, 27)} = 3.658$; $p = 0.039$; $\eta_p^2 = 0.213$] showed that offline was different from sham ($p = 0.034$) and 0.75 mA ($p = 0.022$) (see **Figure 5**).

Sensations induced by different conditions

In the tDCS sensation questionnaire (Fertonani et al., 2010), each participant reported having tolerated the stimulation without discomfort. The results of the questionnaire are reported in **Table 1** (Experiments 1 and 2) and **Table 2** (Experiment 3). In Experiments 1 and 2, the analysis did not reveal any differences between the stimulations for pain, burning, heat, iron taste, and fatigue sensations. The analysis demonstrated a statistically significant difference between stimulations with respect to itchiness [$H_{(6, N=92)} = 17.382$, $p = 0.008$] and pinching [$H_{(6, N=92)} = 18.974$, $p = 0.004$]. Subsequently, multiple comparisons were performed for these two sensations. For itchiness, offline continuous was significantly different ($p = 0.03$) from sham, whereas for pinching, online paused and offline paused were significantly different from sham (respectively $p = 0.03$ and $p = 0.01$). The subjective influence on performance was equal for all the stimulations. In Experiment 3, the analysis did not reveal any difference between the stimulation conditions in the perceived sensations.

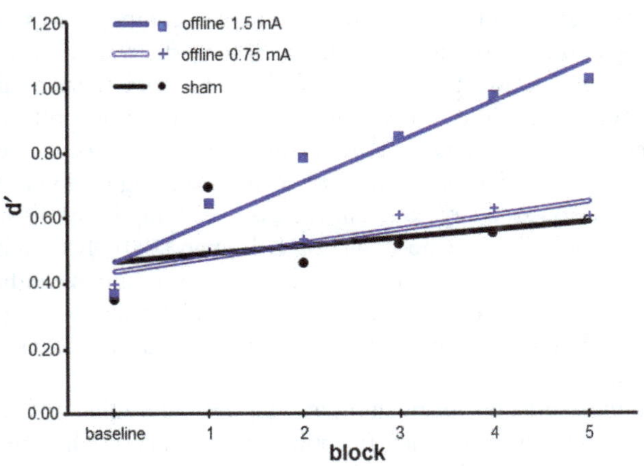

FIGURE 5 | Results of Experiment 3. Data are represented as the mean d' values. The lines represent the fit of each condition. The blue line represents the offline 1.5 mA for the 22 min condition. The double blue line represents the offline 0.75 mA for the 22 min condition. The sham condition is shown in black.

DISCUSSION

In this work, we demonstrated that c-tDCS, which is often considered to be inhibitory at the behavioral level, can actually induce facilitatory effects, enhancing subjects' performance. In the Experiment 1, we showed that the effects of c-tDCS are dependent on the timing of stimulation. Only c-tDCS before the task induced an improvement of performance. Moreover, in this experiment, we applied 22 min of stimulation interspersed by pauses of 2 min and compared this protocol to a continuous protocol. We found that short pauses do not play any role in shaping the final outcome. In Experiment 2, we applied offline stimulation and found that 9 min of c-tDCS facilitated the performance only slightly less. Instead, current density induced a facilitatory effect in our protocol. Finally, Experiment 3 confirmed the importance of current density and showed that the facilitatory effect is not due to skill differences between subjects (i.e., differences in accuracy) because all the groups had the same performance at baseline.

The presence of short pauses (2 min) during c-tDCS, both in the online and in the offline conditions, did not influence the results. In previous works, it has been shown that inter-stimulation intervals determine the effects of c-tDCS on the

Table 1 | Transcranial direct current stimulation (tDCS)-induced sensations—Experiments 1 and 2: mean intensity of the sensations reported by subjects after tDCS and the percentage of subjects who reported each sensation.

Stimulation condition		Itchiness	Pain	Burning	Heat	Pinching	Iron taste	Fatigue	Effect on performance
Sham	Intensity	0.3	0.0	0.2	0.2	0.5	0.0	0.3	–
	Subjects (%)	25	0	17	17	38	4	25	–
Online paused	Intensity	0.6	0.1	0.3	0.1	1.4	0.1	0.2	0.1
	Subjects (%)	50	7	21	7	93	7	14	14
Online continuous	Intensity	0.9	0.2	0.3	0.3	1.0	0.0	0.2	0.2
	Subjects (%)	50	20	30	30	70	0	20	20
Offline paused	Intensity	0.6	0.3	0.6	0.1	1.5	0.1	0.4	–
	Subjects (%)	50	14	43	7	93	7	21	–
Offline continuous	Intensity	1.1	0.2	0.7	0.2	1.2	0.0	0.1	–
	Subjects (%)	90	20	60	20	80	0	10	–
Offline 9 min	Intensity	1.2	0.1	0.2	0.1	1.1	0.0	0.1	–
	Subjects (%)	80	10	20	10	80	0	10	–
Offline 0.75 mA	Intensity	0.7	0.1	0.3	0.3	1.0	0.0	0.0	–
	Subjects (%)	70	10	30	30	100	0	0	–

Sensation intensity was evaluated on a 5-point scale: 0 none, 1 mild, 2 moderate, 3 considerable, and 4 strong. The column "Effect on performance" indicates the subjective feelings of the participants relative to the effect of the tDCS-induced sensation on performance (valid only for the online condition).

Table 2 | Transcranial direct current stimulation (tDCS)-induced sensations—Experiment 3 (See Table 1 description).

Stimulation condition		Itchiness	Pain	Burning	Heat	Pinching	Iron taste	Fatigue
Sham	Intensity	0.4	0.0	0.3	0.1	0.6	0.0	0.0
	Subjects (%)	40	0	30	10	60	0	0
1.5 mA	Intensity	0.6	0.0	0.4	0.3	1.1	0.1	0.0
	Subjects (%)	50	0	30	30	90	10	0
0.75 mA	Intensity	1.3	0.1	0.1	0.2	0.9	0.0	0.3
	Subjects (%)	70	10	10	10	70	0	30

motor cortex (Monte-Silva et al., 2010; Fricke et al., 2011). These previous studies found that varying the length of the pause between two stimulations modified the effects on cortex excitability. Fricke et al. (2011) demonstrated that short inter-stimulation intervals (3 min) induced an inversion of the inhibitory effect of c-tDCS, resulting in MEP amplitude enhancement. Monte-Silva et al. (2010) showed that the inhibitory effects of c-tDCS were more efficacious if a second period of stimulation was applied during the after-effects of the first stimulation with an interval of 3 or 20 min. However, with long inter-stimulation intervals, the c-tDCS-induced inhibitory after-effects were diminished. In Experiment 2 of our study, we confirmed that c-tDCS applied before the task induces a significant improvement in performance, regardless of the presence of pauses during stimulation. A possible explanation for these partially contrasting data could be the differences in stimulation parameters (i.e., the intensity and number of pauses\blocks of stimulation). A higher intensity of stimulation (1.5 mA) may induce a stable excitability shifts in relation to the execution of the task, and therefore, the additional presence of pauses might not further affect the cortical state (see Batsikadze et al., 2013). Similarly the presence of successive multiple pauses\blocks of stimulation might decrease further changes of the cortical state through adaptation.

During the online application of c-tDCS, while the subjects were performing the ODT, we expected a worsening of performance. However, it was difficult to observe a decline in subject accuracy in our learning task because subjects could not have a performance level lower than chance ("floor effect"). This result suggests that the behavioral level of task performance at baseline is a key factor in determining a null effect of c-tDCS. Additionally, compensatory networks can be activated during stimulation (Sack et al., 2005), and therefore, a functional compensation might intervene, maintaining behavior after neuronal challenge (O'Shea et al., 2007). Nevertheless, the absence of inhibition by online c-tDCS is in line with previous data (Jacobson et al., 2012).

Our most important result involves the fact that c-tDCS applied before the task at 1.5 mA induced a facilitatory effect on subjects' accuracy during the ODT (see also Dockery et al., 2009; Moos et al., 2012; Weiss and Lavidor, 2012; Filmer et al., 2013). Most studies that have applied 1 mA c-tDCS in the motor system found decreased cortical excitability; this has also been shown with a decrease in MEP amplitude (see Nitsche and Paulus, 2011; Medeiros et al., 2012). However, these physiological effects are not linear, but they seem to depend on several parameters. In a recently published work, Batsikadze et al. (2013) showed that 20 min of c-tDCS at 2 mA applied to the motor cortex significantly increased MEP amplitudes, while 1 mA of the same stimulation decreased cortico-spinal excitability. This result highlights that an increase in intensity (2 mA) and duration (20 min) of stimulation induces an opposite outcome compared to standard parameters. Batsikadze et al. (2013) suggested that this result might be due to the direction of plasticity from the amount of neuronal calcium influx caused by the stimulation protocol: whereas low postsynaptic calcium enhancement induced by low-intensity c-tDCS causes long-term depression, higher intensity c-tDCS induces a large calcium increase, resulting in long-term potentiation (LTP) (Cho et al., 2001; Lisman, 2001; Batsikadze et al., 2013). Our data are in line with this result; nevertheless, at a systems level, different intensities of stimulation might induce different adaptive responses by the brain, as discussed below.

Importantly, our stimulation was applied before the task execution. The time at which the stimulation is applied has been investigated at the behavioral level in the motor (Stagg et al., 2011) and visual domains (Pirulli et al., 2013). Stagg et al. (2011) showed that a-tDCS on the motor cortex has opposite effects if applied during or before a sequence—a motor learning task. However, the effects of c-tDCS do not seem to be timing dependent. c-tDCS application during or before an explicit motor learning task induces a slowing in reaction time (Stagg et al., 2011). Nevertheless, in a previous work (Pirulli et al., 2013), we demonstrated that the same type of current can induce different effects on visual performance depending on the state of activation of the cortex.

Here, we demonstrated that the application of c-tDCS before the VPL induces an improvement in performance that is not present if c-tDCS is applied during the execution of the task. Therefore, c-tDCS causes different effects depending on the state level of the neurons at the moment of stimulation (Dockery et al., 2009; Tseng et al., 2012; Weiss and Lavidor, 2012; Filmer et al., 2013; Hsu et al., 2014; Nozari et al., 2014). While an online effect would rely mainly on the depolarization or hyperpolarization induced by tDCS interacting with task execution (see Miniussi et al., 2013), an offline protocol would rely more on a change in the state of the stimulated area induced by the stimulation i.e., a shift in the input strength needed for the final response (see Figure 5 in Miniussi et al., 2013). Thus, all these aspects, which can be defined as "relatively simple" technical parameters, influence brain activity in response to exogenous stimulation.

Artificially altering neuronal function can trigger homeostatic changes at the synaptic level (Turrigiano and Nelson, 2004). For example, if a synapse is constantly over-inhibited, there can be a compensatory increase in receptor activity at the postsynaptic membrane, termed up-regulation. Homeostatic plasticity is a fundamental physiological mechanism that maintains neural functions within predefined optimal ranges (Bienenstock et al., 1982; Turrigiano and Nelson, 2004; Abraham, 2008). The basis of homeostatic plasticity is that the threshold for LTP induction is not stable but varies depending on previous neuronal activity induced by non-invasive stimulation (Ziemann and Siebner, 2008; Siebner, 2010). Therefore, the application of tDCS before and during the task of interest may result in different functional states. The application of c-tDCS before the execution of the task would lower the level of postsynaptic neural activity, causing a decrease in the threshold for the induction of successive facilitatory mechanisms. The induced neural modification could then facilitate LTP-like mechanisms and consequently induce an improvement in behavioral performance (Bienenstock et al., 1982; Abraham, 2008). Homeostatic mechanisms can stabilize cortical excitability within a range (Siebner et al., 2004). Thus, an initial down-regulation induced by c-tDCS can be reverted. Applying this theory to our data, pre-conditioning the V1 cortex with 22 min of inhibitory stimulation could render neurons that are involved in task execution more easily excitable. In classical studies, a release phenomenon (rebound) has been found at the end of the cathodal DC (Creutzfeldt et al., 1962). However, the timing of this inversion might depend, at least in part, on stimulation parameters like intensity and duration. Indeed, stimulating offline with a different duration or intensity changes the behavioral effects. Our data highlighted the fact that the final behavioral response, obtained by applying tDCS, depends on the history of the stimulated area (i.e., metaplasticity). This has been previously demonstrated in animal studies in which the direction and magnitude of synaptic plasticity depends on the previous history of postsynaptic activity (Huang et al., 1992; Wang and Wagner, 1999).

From a physiological perspective, c-tDCS over the scalp can induce a hyperpolarization at the soma of perpendicularly oriented neurons (Jefferys, 1981; Bikson et al., 2004). However, we are measuring behavior and therefore should consider a network level of reasoning rather than just a cellular one and present data testify the complexity of a neural network response. Indeed, changes in hyperpolarization alter the sensitivity of the entire system and therefore its response threshold, but these changes are ultimately expressed on subject performance. The final response to the task depends on the strength of the signal and on the signal-to-noise ratio, where the signal is the neural activity operational to the task and the noise is random neural activity. Clearly, in this case, the signal-to-noise ratio relies on a system that has changed its state after c-tDCS, a system that has adapted to exogenous stimulation. Adaptation occurs when receptors\neurons change their sensitivity to a stimulus. In the visual system, adaptation to reduced light intensity increases the visual system's ability to detect a stimulus. In the same way, the reduced cortical activity induced by c-tDCS causes an improved threshold for orientation sensitivity (d′) by reducing background noise. Therefore, an inhibitory stimulation may increase the signal-to-noise ratio in the system and facilitate perceptual learning (Miniussi et al., 2013).

In conclusion, the present data show that an inhibitory stimulation does not always induce a deterioration in performance. The effects of c-tDCS should be considered in relation to the timing and the application parameters that will alter the state of the cortical network carrying out a task. We suggest that when applying c-tDCS before a task, it is necessary to consider the involvement of cognitive and non-cognitive adaptation mechanisms. The application of a tDCS protocol that induces a depression in cortical activity over a specific stimulated area might result in increased sensitivity in visual performance. This is a further example of how the nervous system maintains a dynamic state to maintain performance in different environments.

REFERENCES

Abraham, W. C. (2008). Metaplasticity: tuning synapses and networks for plasticity. *Nat. Rev. Neurosci.* 9, 387. doi: 10.1038/nrn2356

Accornero, N., Li, P., Maurizio, V., and Riccia, L. (2007). Visual evoked potentials modulation during direct current cortical polarization. *Exp. Brain Res.* 178, 261–266. doi: 10.1007/s00221-006-0733-y

Antal, A., Kincses, Z. T., Nitsche, M. A, Bartfai, O., and Paulus, W. (2004a). Excitability changes induced in the human primary visual cortex by transcranial direct current stimulation: direct electrophysiological evidence. *Invest. Ophthalmol. Vis. Sci.* 45, 702–707. doi: 10.1167/iovs.03-0688

Antal, A., Nitsche, M. A., Kruse, W., Kincses, T. Z., Hoffmann, K.-P., and Paulus, W. (2004b). Direct current stimulation over V5 enhances visuomotor coordination by improving motion perception in humans. *J. Cogn. Neurosci.* 16, 521–527. doi: 10.1162/089892904323057263.

Antal, A., Nitsche, M. A., and Paulus, W. (2001). External modulation of visual perception in humans. *Neuroreport* 12, 3553–3555. doi: 10.1097/00001756-200111160-00036

Batsikadze, G., Moliadze, V., Paulus, W., Kuo, M.-F., and Nitsche, M. A. (2013). Partially non-linear stimulation intensity-dependent effects of direct current stimulation on motor cortex excitability in humans. *J. Physiol.* 591, 1987–2000. doi: 10.1113/jphysiol.2012.249730

Berryhill, M. E., and Jones, K. T. (2012). tDCS selectively improves working memory in older adults with more education. *Neurosci. Lett.* 521, 148–151. doi: 10.1016/j.neulet.2012.05.074

Bienenstock, E. L., Cooper, L. N., and Munro, P. W. (1982). Theory for the development of neuron selectivity: orientation specificity and binocular interaction in visual cortex. *J. Neurosci.* 2, 32–48.

Bikson, M., Inoue, M., Akiyama, H., Deans, J. K., Fox, J. E., Miyakawa, H., et al. (2004). Effects of uniform extracellular DC electric fields on excitability in rat hippocampal slices *in vitro*. *J. Physiol.* 557, 175–190. doi: 10.1113/jphysiol.2003.055772

Bindman, L. J., Lippold, O. C., and Redfearn, J. W. (1964). The action of brief polarizing currents on the cerebral cortex of the rat (1) during current flow and (2) in the production of long-lasting after-effects. *J Physiol* 172, 369–382.

Brunoni, A. R., Nitsche, M. A., Bolognini, N., Bikson, M., Wagner, T., Merabet, L., et al. (2012). Clinical research with transcranial direct current stimulation (tDCS): challenges and future directions. *Brain Stimul.* 5, 175–195. doi: 10.1016/j.brs.2011.03.002

Cerruti, C., and Schlaug, G. (2009). Anodal transcranial direct current stimulation of the prefrontal cortex enhances complex verbal associative thought. *J. Cogn. Neurosci.* 21, 1980–1987. doi: 10.1162/jocn.2008.21143

Cho, K., Aggleton, J. P., Brown, M. W., and Bashir, Z. I. (2001). An experimental test of the role of postsynaptic calcium levels in determining synaptic strength using perirhinal cortex of rat. *J. Physiol.* 532, 459–466. doi: 10.1111/j.1469-7793.2001.0459f.x

Cooper, S. J. (2008). From claude bernard to walter cannon. Emergence of the concept of homeostasis. *Appetite* 51, 419–427. doi: 10.1016/j.appet.2008.06.005

Creutzfeldt, O. D., Fromm, G. H., and Kapp, H. (1962). Influence of transcortical d-c currents on cortical neuronal activity. *Exp. Neurol.* 5, 436–452.

Dockery, C. A, Hueckel-Weng, R., Birbaumer, N., and Plewnia, C. (2009). Enhancement of planning ability by transcranial direct current stimulation. *J. Neurosci.* 29, 7271–7277. doi: 10.1523/JNEUROSCI.0065-09.2009

Fertonani, A., Brambilla, M., Cotelli, M., and Miniussi, C. (2014). The timing of cognitive plasticity in physiological aging: a tDCS study of naming. *Front. Aging Neurosci.* doi: 10.3389/fnagi.2014.00131

Fertonani, A., Pirulli, C., and Miniussi, C. (2011). Random noise stimulation improves neuroplasticity in perceptual learning. *J. Neurosci.* 31, 15416–15423. doi: 10.1523/JNEUROSCI.2002-11.2011

Fertonani, A., Rosini, S., Cotelli, M., Rossini, P. M., and Miniussi, C. (2010). Naming facilitation induced by transcranial direct current stimulation. *Behav. Brain Res.* 208, 311–318. doi: 10.1016/j.bbr.2009.10.030

Filmer, H. L., Mattingley, J. B., and Dux, P. E. (2013). Improved multitasking following prefrontal tDCS. *Cortex* 49, 2845–2852. doi: 10.1016/j.cortex.2013.08.015

Fricke, K., Seeber, A. A., Thirugnanasambandam, N., Paulus, W., Nitsche, M. A., and Rothwell, J. C. (2011). Time course of the induction of homeostatic plasticity generated by repeated transcranial direct current stimulation of the human motor cortex. *J. Neurophysiol.* 105, 1141–1149. doi: 10.1152/jn.00608.2009

Hoy, K. E., Emonson, M. R. L., Arnold, S. L., Thomson, R. H., Daskalakis, Z. J., and Fitzgerald, P. B. (2013). Testing the limits: Investigating the effect of tDCS dose on working memory enhancement in healthy controls. *Neuropsychologia* 51, 1777–1784. doi: 10.1016/j.neuropsychologia.2013.05.018

Hsu, T.-Y., Tseng, P., Liang, W.-K., Cheng, S.-K., and Juan, C.-H. (2014). Transcranial direct current stimulation over right posterior parietal cortex changes prestimulus alpha oscillation in visual short-term memory task. *Neuroimage.* doi: 10.1016/j.neuroimage.2014.04.069. [Epub ahead of print].

Huang, Y. Y., Colino, A., Selig, D. K., and Malenka, R. C. (1992). The influence of prior synaptic activity on the induction of long-term potentiation. *Science* 255, 730–733.

Iyer, M. B., Mattu, U., Grafman, J., Lomarev, M., Sato, S., and Wassermann, E. M. (2005). Safety and cognitive effect of frontal DC brain polarization in healthy individuals. *Neurology* 64, 872–875. doi: 10.1212/01.WNL.0000152986.07469.E9

Jacobson, L., Koslowsky, M., and Lavidor, M. (2012). tDCS polarity effects in motor and cognitive domains: a meta-analytical review. *Exp. brain Res.* 216, 1–10. doi: 10.1007/s00221-011-2891-9

Jefferys, J. G. (1981). Influence of electric fields on the excitability of granule cells in guinea-pig hippocampal slices. *J. Physiol.* 319, 143–152.

Kincses, T. Z., Antal, A., Nitsche, M. A., Bartfai, O., and Paulus, W. (2004). Facilitation of probabilistic classification learning by transcranial direct current stimulation of the prefrontal cortex in the human. *Neuropsychologia* 42, 113–117. doi: 10.1016/S0028-3932(03)00124-6

Kraft, A., Roehmel, J., Olma, M. C., Schmidt, S., Irlbacher, K., and Brandt, S. A. (2010). Transcranial direct current stimulation affects visual perception measured by threshold perimetry. *Exp. Brain Res.* 207, 283–290. doi: 10.1007/s00221-010-2453-6

Li, W., Piëch, V., and Gilbert, C. D. (2004). Perceptual learning and top-down influences in primary visual cortex. *Nat. Neurosci.* 7, 651–657. doi: 10.1038/nn1255

Liebetanz, D., Nitsche, M. A., Tergau, F., and Paulus, W. (2002). Pharmacological approach to the mechanisms of transcranial DC-stimulation-induced after-effects of human motor cortex excitability. *Brain* 125, 2238–2247. doi: 10.1093/brain/awf238

Lisman, J. E. (2001). Three Ca2+ levels affect plasticity differently: the LTP zone, the LTD zone and no man's land. *J. Physiol.* 532, 285. doi: 10.1111/j.1469-7793.2001.0285f.x

Matsunaga, K. (2004). Effect of transcranial DC sensorimotor cortex stimulation on somatosensory evoked potentials in humans. *Clin. Neurophysiol.* 115, 456–460. doi: 10.1016/S1388-2457(03)00362-6

Medeiros, L. F., de Souza, I. C. C., Vidor, L. P., de Souza, A., Deitos, A., Volz, M. S., et al. (2012). Neurobiological effects of transcranial direct current stimulation: a review. *Front. Psychiatry* 3:110. doi: 10.3389/fpsyt.2012.00110

Miniussi, C., Harris, J. A., and Ruzzoli, M. (2013). Modelling non-invasive brain stimulation in cognitive neuroscience. *Neurosci. Biobehav. Rev.* 37, 1702–1712. doi: 10.1016/j.neubiorev.2013.06.014

Miranda, P. C., Lomarev, M., and Hallett, M. (2006). Modeling the current distribution during transcranial direct current stimulation. *Clin. Neurophysiol.* 117, 1623–1629. doi: 10.1016/j.clinph.2006.04.009

Monte-Silva, K., Kuo, M. F., Liebetanz, D., Paulus, W., and Nitsche, M. A. (2010). Shaping the optimal repetition interval for cathodal transcranial direct current stimulation (tDCS). *J Neurophysiol* 103, 1735–1740. doi: 10.1152/jn.00924.2009

Monti, A., Cogiamanian, F., Marceglia, S., Ferrucci, R., Mameli, F., Mrakic-Sposta, S., et al. (2008). Improved naming after transcranial direct current stimulation in aphasia. *J. Neurol. Neurosurg. Psychiatry* 79, 451–453. doi: 10.1136/jnnp.2007.135277

Moos, K., Vossel, S., Weidner, R., Sparing, R., and Fink, G. R. (2012). Modulation of top-down control of visual attention by cathodal tDCS over right IPS. *J. Neurosci.* 32, 16360–16368. doi: 10.1523/JNEUROSCI.6233-11.2012

Nitsche, M. A., Cohen, L. G., Wassermann, E. M., Priori, A., Lang, N., Antal, A., et al. (2008). Transcranial direct current stimulation: State of the art 2008. *Brain Stimul.* 1, 206–223. doi: 10.1016/j.brs.2008.06.004

Nitsche, M. A., Fricke, K., Henschke, U., Schlitterlau, A., Liebetanz, D., Lang, N., et al. (2003a). Pharmacological modulation of cortical excitability shifts induced by transcranial direct current stimulation in humans. *J. Physiol.* 553, 293–301. doi: 10.1113/jphysiol.2003.049916

Nitsche, M. A., Grundey, J., Liebetanz, D., Lang, N., Tergau, F., and Paulus, W. (2004a). Catecholaminergic consolidation of motor cortical neuroplasticity in humans. *Cereb. Cortex* 14, 1240–1245. doi: 10.1093/cercor/bhh085

Nitsche, M. A., Jaussi, W., Liebetanz, D., Lang, N., Tergau, F., and Paulus, W. (2004b). Consolidation of human motor cortical neuroplasticity by D-cycloserine. *Neuropsychopharmacology* 29, 1573–1578. doi: 10.1038/sj.npp.1300517

Nitsche, M. A., Nitsche, M. S., Klein, C. C., Tergau, F., Rothwell, J. C., and Paulus, W. (2003b). Level of action of cathodal DC polarisation induced inhibition of the human motor cortex. *Clin. Neurophysiol.* 114, 600–604. doi: 10.1016/S1388-2457(02)00412-1

Nitsche, M. A., and Paulus, W. (2000). Excitability changes induced in the human motor cortex by weak transcranial direct current stimulation. *J. Physiol.* 527(Pt 3), 633–639. doi: 10.1111/j.1469-7793.2000.t01-1-00633.x

Nitsche, M. A., and Paulus, W. (2001). Sustained excitability elevations induced by transcranial DC motor cortex stimulation in humans. *Neurology* 57, 1899–1901. doi: 10.1212/WNL.57.10.1899

Nitsche, M. A., and Paulus, W. (2011). Transcranial direct current stimulation - update 2011. *Restor. Neurol. Neurosci.* 29, 463–492. doi: 10.3233/RNN-2011-0618

Nozari, N., Woodard, K., and Thompson-Schill, S. L. (2014). Consequences of cathodal stimulation for behavior: when does it help and when does it hurt performance? *PLoS ONE* 9:e84338. doi: 10.1371/journal.pone.0084338

O'Shea, J., Johansen-Berg, H., Trief, D., Göbel, S., and Rushworth, M. F. S. (2007). Functionally specific reorganization in human premotor cortex. *Neuron* 54, 479–490. doi: 10.1016/j.neuron.2007.04.021

Pellicciari, M. C., Brignani, D., and Miniussi, C. (2013). Excitability modulation of the motor system induced by transcranial direct current stimulation: a multimodal approach. *Neuroimage* 83, 569–580. doi: 10.1016/j.neuroimage.2013.06.076

Pirulli, C., Fertonani, A., and Miniussi, C. (2013). The role of timing in the induction of neuromodulation in perceptual learning by transcranial electric stimulation. *Brain Stimul.* 6, 683–689. doi: 10.1016/j.brs.2012.12.005

Poreisz, C., Boros, K., Antal, A., and Paulus, W. (2007). Safety aspects of transcranial direct current stimulation concerning healthy subjects and patients. *Brain Res. Bull.* 72, 208–214. doi: 10.1016/j.brainresbull.2007.01.004

Rossi, S., Hallett, M., Rossini, P. M., Pascual-Leone, A., and Safety of TMS Consensus Group. (2009). Safety, ethical considerations, and application guidelines for the use of transcranial magnetic stimulation in clinical practice and research. *Clin. Neurophysiol.* 120, 2008–2039. doi: 10.1016/j.clinph.2009.08.016

Sack, A. T., Camprodon, J. A., Pascual-Leone, A., and Goebel, R. (2005). The dynamics of interhemispheric compensatory processes in mental imagery. *Science* 308, 702–704. doi: 10.1126/science.1107784

Schoups, A., Vogels, R., Qian, N., and Orban, G. (2001). Practising orientation identification improves orientation coding in V1 neurons. *Nature* 412, 549–553. doi: 10.1038/35087601

Shiu, L. P., and Pashler, H. (1992). Improvement in line orientation discrimination is retinally local but dependent on cognitive set. *Percept. Psychophys.* 52, 582–588.

Siebner, H. R. (2010). A primer on priming the human motor cortex. *Clin. Neurophysiol.* 121, 461–463. doi: 10.1016/j.clinph.2009.12.009

Siebner, H. R., Lang, N., Rizzo, V., Nitsche, M. A., Paulus, W., Lemon, R. N., et al. (2004). Preconditioning of low-frequency repetitive transcranial magnetic stimulation with transcranial direct current stimulation: evidence for homeostatic plasticity in the human motor cortex. *J Neurosci* 24, 3379–3385. doi: 10.1523/JNEUROSCI.5316-03.2004

Sparing, R., Dafotakis, M., Meister, I. G., Thirugnanasambandam, N., and Fink, G. R. (2008). Enhancing language performance with non-invasive brain stimulation–a transcranial direct current stimulation study in healthy humans. *Neuropsychologia* 46, 261–268. doi: 10.1016/j.neuropsychologia.2007.07.009

Stagg, C. J., Jayaram, G., Pastor, D., Kincses, Z. T., Matthews, P. M., and Johansen-Berg, H. (2011). Polarity and timing-dependent effects of transcranial direct current stimulation in explicit motor learning. *Neuropsychologia* 49, 800–804. doi: 10.1016/j.neuropsychologia.2011.02.009

Stagg, C. J., and Nitsche, M. A. (2011). Physiological basis of transcranial direct current stimulation. *Neuroscientist* 17, 37–53. doi:10.1177/1073858410386614

Teo, F., Hoy, K. E., Daskalakis, Z. J., and Fitzgerald, P. B. (2011). Investigating the role of current strength in tDCS modulation of working memory performance in healthy controls. *Front. psychiatry* 2:45. doi: 10.3389/fpsyt.2011.00045

Tseng, P., Hsu, T.-Y., Chang, C.-F., Tzeng, O. J. L., Hung, D. L., Muggleton, N. G., et al. (2012). Unleashing potential: transcranial direct current stimulation over the right posterior parietal cortex improves change detection in low-performing individuals. *J. Neurosci.* 32, 10554–10561. doi: 10.1523/JNEUROSCI.0362-12.2012

Turrigiano, G. G., and Nelson, S. B. (2004). Homeostatic plasticity in the developing nervous system. *Nat. Rev. Neurosci.* 5, 97–107. doi: 10.1038/nrn1327

Vallar, G., and Bolognini, N. (2011). Behavioral facilitation following brain stimulation: implications for neurorehabilitation. *Neuropsychol. Rehabil.* 21, 618–649. doi: 10.1080/09602011.2011.574050

Venkatakrishnan, A., Contreras-Vidal, J. L., Sandrini, M., and Cohen, L. G. (2011). Independent component analysis of resting brain activity reveals transient modulation of local cortical processing by transcranial direct current stimulation. *Conf. Proc. IEEE Eng. Med. Biol. Soc.* 2011, 8102–8105. doi: 10.1109/IEMBS.2011.6091998

Vicario, C. M., Martino, D., and Koch, G. (2013). Temporal accuracy and variability in the left and right posterior parietal cortex. *Neuroscience* 245, 121–128. doi: 10.1016/j.neuroscience.2013.04.041

Vogels, R., and Orban, G. A. (1985). The effect of practice on the oblique effect in line orientation judgments. *Vision Res.* 25, 1679–1687.

Wagner, T., Fregni, F., Fecteau, S., Grodzinsky, A., Zahn, M., and Pascual-Leone, A. (2007). Transcranial direct current stimulation: a computer-based human model study. *Neuroimage* 35, 1113–1124. doi: 10.1016/j.neuroimage.2007.01.027

Wang, H., and Wagner, J. J. (1999). Priming-induced shift in synaptic plasticity in the rat hippocampus. *J Neurophysiol* 82, 2024–2028.

Weiss, M., and Lavidor, M. (2012). When less is more: evidence for a facilitative cathodal tDCS effect in attentional abilities. *J. Cogn. Neurosci.* 24, 1826–1833. doi: 10.1162/jocn_a_00248

Wiethoff, S., Hamada, M., and Rothwell, J. C. (2014). Variability in response to transcranial direct current stimulation of the motor cortex. *Brain Stimul.* 7, 468–475. doi: 10.1016/j.brs.2014.02.003

Ziemann, U., and Siebner, H. R. (2008). Modifying motor learning through gating and homeostatic metaplasticity. *Brain Stimul.* 1, 60–66. doi: 10.1016/j.brs.2007.08.003

17

Winning the game: brain processes in expert, young elite and amateur table tennis players

Sebastian Wolf[1]*[†], Ellen Brölz[2], David Scholz[3], Ander Ramos-Murguialday[3,4], Philipp M. Keune[5,6], Martin Hautzinger[1], Niels Birbaumer[3,7,8] and Ute Strehl[3]

[1] Faculty of Science, Institute of Clinical Psychology and Psychotherapy, University of Tuebingen, Tuebingen, Germany
[2] Department of Internal Medicine VI: Psychosomatic Medicine, University Hospital Tuebingen, Tuebingen, Germany
[3] Institute of Medical Psychology and Behavioral Neurobiology, University of Tuebingen, Tuebingen, Germany
[4] TECNALIA, Health-Technologies, San Sebastian, Spain
[5] Department of Neurology, Klinikum Bayreuth, Bayreuth, Germany
[6] Department of Physiological Psychology, Otto-Friedrich-University, Bamberg, Germany
[7] Ospedale San Camillo, Istituto di Ricovero e Cura a Carattere Scientifico (IRCCS), Venice, Italy
[8] German Center for Diabetes Research, Tuebingen, Germany

Correspondence:
Sebastian Wolf, Faculty of Science, Institute of Clinical Psychology and Psychotherapy, University of Tuebingen, Schleichstr. 4, Tuebingen, 72076, Germany
e-mail: sebastian.wolf@uni-tuebingen.de

This study tested two hypotheses: (1) compared with amateurs and young elite, expert table tennis players are characterized by enhanced cortical activation in the motor and fronto-parietal cortex during motor imagery in response to table tennis videos; (2) in elite athletes, world rank points are associated with stronger cortical activation. To this aim, electroencephalographic data were recorded in 14 expert, 15 amateur and 15 young elite right-handed table tennis players. All subjects watched videos of a serve and imagined themselves responding with a specific table tennis stroke. With reference to a baseline period, power decrease/increase of the sensorimotor rhythm (SMR) during the pretask- and task period indexed the cortical activation/deactivation (event-related desynchronization/synchronization, ERD/ERS). Regarding hypothesis (1), 8–10 Hz SMR ERD was stronger in elite athletes than in amateurs with an intermediate ERD in young elite athletes in the motor cortex. Regarding hypothesis (2), there was no correlation between ERD/ERS in the motor cortex and world rank points in elite experts, but a weaker ERD in the fronto-parietal cortex was associated with higher world rank points. These results suggest that motor skill in table tennis is associated with focused excitability of the motor cortex during reaction, movement planning and execution with high attentional demands. Among elite experts, less activation of the fronto-parietal attention network may be necessary to become a world champion.

Keywords: ERD/ERS, EEG, sensorimotor rhythm, elite athletes, table tennis, motor efficiency, motor skill

INTRODUCTION

Motor efficiency plays a crucial role in determining athletic skill, characterized by automaticity, speed and accuracy. Experts in a highly reactive sport, such as table tennis, move rapidly, effortlessly and smoothly. Motor efficiency can be achieved through intensive training, which leads to improved perception, focus, anticipation, planning and fast responses (Yarrow et al., 2009). These skills are especially important in a fast pace sport like table tennis, where athletes have to process many cues simultaneously in order to react appropriately. Studies of self-paced movements using electroencephalography (EEG) found a frequency increase and a desynchronization with a reduction in amplitude in the 8–15 Hz frequency band recorded from sensorimotor areas (sensorimotor rhythm, SMR). A desynchronization of the SMR prior to and during a self-paced movement is called movement event-related desynchronization (ERD) and is linked to activation of the central motor system. An increase in SMR is referred to as event-related synchronization (ERS) and is associated with inhibition of the motor cortex (Pfurtscheller et al., 1996; Pfurtscheller and Lopes Da Silva, 1999; Klimesch et al., 2007, 2011). Synchronization in the SMR rhythm (ERS) is often observed at electrodes recording from task irrelevant brain areas during cognitive (Worden et al., 2000; Sauseng et al., 2005) or motor tasks (Alegre et al., 2004): For example, after movement onset, the contralateral motor cortex desynchronizes while the ipsilateral cortex and the surrounding areas synchronize. This pattern has been named focal ERD surrounded by ERS (Pfurtscheller and Neuper, 1994, 2006). However, recent findings in healthy participants (Ramos-Murguialday and Birbaumer, under review) and in stroke patients (Antelis et al., 2012) observed ERD in contralateral and ipsilateral electrodes. ERD can be divided into two functionally and topographically different components: 8–10 Hz ERD and 10–12 Hz ERD. The low-frequency ERD occurs especially when movements become more complex and is widespread over the entire scalp in all cortical areas involved in a motor task including primary sensorimotor, premotor and parietal areas. 8–10 Hz ERD seems to be further related to attentional processes during motor tasks (Klimesch, 1999;

Pfurtscheller and Lopes Da Silva, 1999; Pfurtscheller et al., 2000; Klimesch et al., 2007). The high-frequency ERD is restricted to sensorimotor areas and seems to reflect processing specific to simple motor-tasks (Klimesch, 1999; Pfurtscheller and Lopes Da Silva, 1999; Pfurtscheller et al., 2000; Klimesch et al., 2007).

In the context of athletic performance several authors stated that elite athletes require less brain activation (weaker ERD) in task relevant brain areas compared to novices, which had led to the formulation of the "neural efficiency" hypothesis in the athletic context (Babiloni et al., 2010). In line with these assumptions, the EEG literature emphasizes that low-frequency and high-frequency ERD is weaker in elite athletes. Babiloni et al. (2009) for example found that elite rhythmic gymnasts showed weaker low- and high frequency alpha ERD compared to non-gymnasts in occipital and temporal areas and in the dorsal pathway while observing rhythmic gymnastics videos. A similar study found, that low- and high-frequency alpha ERD was weaker in dorsal and fronto-parietal pathways in elite karate athletes compared to amateurs and non-athletes while watching and judging karate videos (Babiloni et al., 2010). Karate and fencing athletes showed weaker low-frequency alpha ERD at left central, right central, mid-parietal, and right parietal areas and weaker high-frequency alpha ERD at right frontal, left central, right central, and mid-parietal areas during a monopodalic upright standing task compared to non-athletes (Del Percio et al., 2009b). Elite pistol shooters showed weaker low- and high-frequency alpha ERD than non-athletes over the whole scalp in a shooting task and best shots were correlated with right parietal and left central high-frequency ERS (Del Percio et al., 2009a). Furthermore, compared to amateur rifle shooters, elite shooters showed stronger occipital alpha ERS during a pre-shot period and stronger high-frequency alpha ERS over left central electrodes (Haufler et al., 2000). In sum, these EEG studies indicate that skilled athletes show less cortical activation (weaker low- and high frequency ERD) when performing tasks specific to their discipline.

However, some EEG literature emphasizes, that athletic expertise is associated with increased brain activation in task relevant brain areas (stronger ERD). High-frequency alpha ERD was stronger in successful compared to unsuccessful putts over the frontal midline and the arm and hand region of the right primary sensorimotor area in expert golfers (Babiloni et al., 2008). Research on motor related ERD in the athletes has mainly focused on self-paced sports like shooting, golf or gymnastics. However, highly reactive sports are different from self-paced sports: They require the perception and integration of quickly changing visual, auditory and tactile cues. Thus highly reactive sports are similar to complex procedural multisensory integration motor tasks. There is evidence indicating that these tasks produce increased brain activation in premotor, motor and visual areas with the development of expertise or automaticity (Weisberg et al., 2007; Waldschmidt and Ashby, 2011). Karni et al. (1995) used fMRI to show stronger activity in the primary motor cortex after learning a complex motor task. An EEG study with karate and fencing athletes during an upright standing task, which required the integration of visual cues for body sway indicated stronger high-frequency ERD at right ventral centro-parietal electrodes in elite compared to novice athletes (Del Percio et al., 2007). Overall, evidence whether expertise in sports is correlated with reduced or increased cortical activation in task relevant brain areas is still ambiguous, indicating a need for larger and controlled studies to clarify this issue.

We are not aware of any published study examining athlete's cortical activation patterns in table tennis athletes and suggest, that demands of table tennis and complex motor learning tasks are highly similar. Therefore we expect stronger activation in motor and fronto-parietal areas in expert table tennis players. We further assume, that attentional processes play a more important role in highly reactive sports than in self-paced sports and that movements in table tennis are much more complex. We hypothesize that table tennis athletes show predominantly ERD in the low-frequency alpha band (8–10 Hz), that seem to reflect general motor attentional processes and occurs predominantly in complex motor tasks (Klimesch, 1999; Pfurtscheller et al., 2000; Klimesch et al., 2007).

Most EEG studies looking at athletes have focused on differences between experts and novices, who are entirely unfamiliar with the specific athletic discipline. Thus, it is still unclear if the observed differences in cortical activation represent a psychophysiological mechanism induced by the amount of training that underlies superior performance in sports. To assure that the activation differences are dependent on expertise, we added young elite athletes as a group with an intermediate skill level and assumed that the cortical activation lies in between experts and amateurs. We developed a research design to compare different skill level groups from the same discipline and attempted to answer the following questions:

1. Do table tennis experts show higher activation of the motor and fronto-parietal cortex, reflected by more pronounced 8–10 Hz ERD, compared to amateurs in the end of a sport specific motor task in a competitive situation?
2. Does 8–10 Hz ERD in the motor cortex correlate positively with world rank points in expert table tennis players?

MATERIAL AND METHODS

PARTICIPANTS

A total of 60 table tennis players were recruited from the German Table Tennis Association (DTTB, experts: $N = 16$), clubs from regional district leagues around Tuebingen, Germany (amateurs: $N = 19$) and from the squad of the Table Tennis Association of Baden-Wuerttemberg (TTBW), Germany (young elite athletes: $N = 25$). All young elite athletes were the best upcoming teen table tennis players in Baden-Württemberg with a realistic chance to become an elite expert in their career. Inclusion criteria were: right-handedness, 14–36 years of age, no medical disorders, no use of medication or drugs and no pregnancy. Of the recruited participants, 14 experts (5 female), 15 amateurs (4 female) and 15 young elites (6 female) met all criteria and were included in the analysis. There were no differences in the distribution of gender between groups ($c^2_{(2,44)} = 0.62$, $p = 0.73$) and no difference in age between experts ($M = 23.8$, $sd = 4.86$) and amateurs ($M = 22.8$, $sd = 4.16$). Naturally, young elite athletes ($M = 14.9$, $sd = 0.96$) were younger than experts ($p < 0.001$) and amateurs ($p < 0.001$). Subjects signed an informed written consent and received monetary compensation for participation. All experiments reported here were approved by the local ethics committee and are in accordance with the Declaration of Helsinki.

EXPERIMENTAL PARADIGM

We chose a motor imagery paradigm to minimize electromyographic (EMG) artifacts in the EEG data. Cortical activation patterns of real motor action and kinesthetic motor imagery, are similar (Porro et al., 1996; Roth et al., 1996; Jeannerod, 2001; Naito et al., 2002; Ehrsson et al., 2003; Neuper et al., 2005), although activation is stronger during active movements (Pfurtscheller and Neuper, 1997; Jeannerod and Frak, 1999). There is also evidence, that cortical activation during the preparatory period of motor imagery is similar to the activation preceding real movements (Kranczioch et al., 2009) although the preparation for real movements induces larger activations (Ramos-Murguialday and Birbaumer, under review). The mere observation of movements appears to activate the same sensorimotor areas that are involved in motor preparation and motor programming (Grezes and Costes, 1998; Babiloni et al., 2009, 2010; Halder et al., 2011). Based on these findings, we assume motor imagery to be a reliable and valid experimental paradigm to test our hypothesis. Participants were instructed to imagine themselves (kinesthetic motor imagery) playing table tennis, i.e., reacting to an opponent serving a ball presented in different video formats (for detailed information about the task please refer to paragraph 2.4 "task" and **Figure 2**).

PROCEDURE

For an overview of the general procedure, please refer to **Figure 1**. Data was collected at a training center in Faak, Austria (male experts), at a training center in Oberhof, Germany (female experts), at the Institute of Medical Psychology, University in Tuebingen, Germany (amateurs) and at the Landessportschule in Tailfingen, Germany (young elite athletes).

EEG was recorded continuously while subjects sat on a chair facing the wall, on which all instructions and the table tennis videos were projected. At the beginning of the experiment subjects watched a video of Prof. Birbaumer, explaining the importance of the study in order to standardize the introduction and to induce motivation. Following the introduction, the player's level of arousal was self-rated using the Self Assessment Mannequin (SAM; Bradley and Lang, 1994). Participants received detailed instructions projected onto the wall. They were then presented with a total of 40 video-clips of a table tennis player serving a ball. In each of the clips, they had to imagine the score to be 10:10 in the last set of an important match and react to the serve with a specific table tennis stroke: a forehand top spin. In order to further enhance ecological validity and to meet the degree of mental pressure experienced in a real competition situation, the athletes were told the imagined forehand topspins of all participants will be ranked in order of intensity and quality based on the EEG recording. Immediately after this pressure induction the level of arousal was self-rated again using the SAM questionnaire. There was a break (duration was chosen by the participant) after the first 20 videos and a 5 s break after each video. During the 5 s break the sentence "10:10 last set" was displayed and subjects were instructed to look at this sentence in order to prevent distraction and to ensure a competitive mindset. After the task, subjects were given questionnaires to assess demographic and control variables.

All experiments were carried out in a quiet room using the same EEG equipment, software and set up (beamer, notebooks, screen, distance from the participant to the screen). All instructions for the task were presented with E-Prime (Science Plus Group BV, Groningen, Netherlands). Start and end triggers of the videos were sent from E-Prime via a trigger interface (NeXus Trigger Interface, Mind Media, Herten, Holland) to a Lenovo Thinkpad T500 Notebook on which all EEG data were recorded.

TASK

Each video trial lasted 7 s (see **Figure 2**). Between the 3rd and the 4th second the player in the video throws up the ball (the ball leaves the passive hand of the opponent), to perform the serve. We termed the first 3 s of the video to comprise the "preparatory phase" in which the return movement is planned, because height, speed, rotation and direction of the arriving ball can only be anticipated when the opponent's specific wrist-, arm- and shoulder movements, racket angle and body orientation can be perceived (Singer et al., 1996).

Seconds 4, 5 and 6 of each trial comprise the "movement phase", during which we assume the subject imagines the execution of the forehand topspin. Four videos with different serves were presented 10 times in random order. Each serve was either directed more to the middle or to the right side of the table and was served with back- or sidespin. The player in the video served the ball in a way (length, height, rotation) to make a forehand top spin the most appropriate return option. This was confirmed by several expert trainers, who evaluated all videos and consistently regarded a forehand top spin as a suitable return. The forehand topspin was chosen, because it is one of the most important and profitable table tennis strokes.

To ensure ecological task validity and motivation of the participants, skill level and gender of the player in the video were adapted for each group. The videos of the young elite table tennis players were further adapted for younger (under 15 years of age) and older (under 18 years of age) participants. This resulted in 8 different video sets comprising each of four different videos in which the ball was presented to two directions (forehand side or middle side of the table) and with two different rotations (sidespin or underspin).

All videos were recorded in a coliseum, standardized in length, height of table, direction, rotation and sequence of the serve, the table set-up and were presented without sound. The only differences between videos were the table tennis player's clothes, age, gender and handedness: only male experts watched a left-handed opponents. Female experts, all amateurs and all young elite athletes watched right-handed table tennis players.

EEG

EEG was recorded from 21 electrodes using a 32-channel system with sintered ring-electrodes with carbon coating and active shielding (Nexus 32, Mind Media B.V., Herten, Holland) according to the 10–20 system (Jasper, 1958). A common average reference was used to minimize biases introduced by single

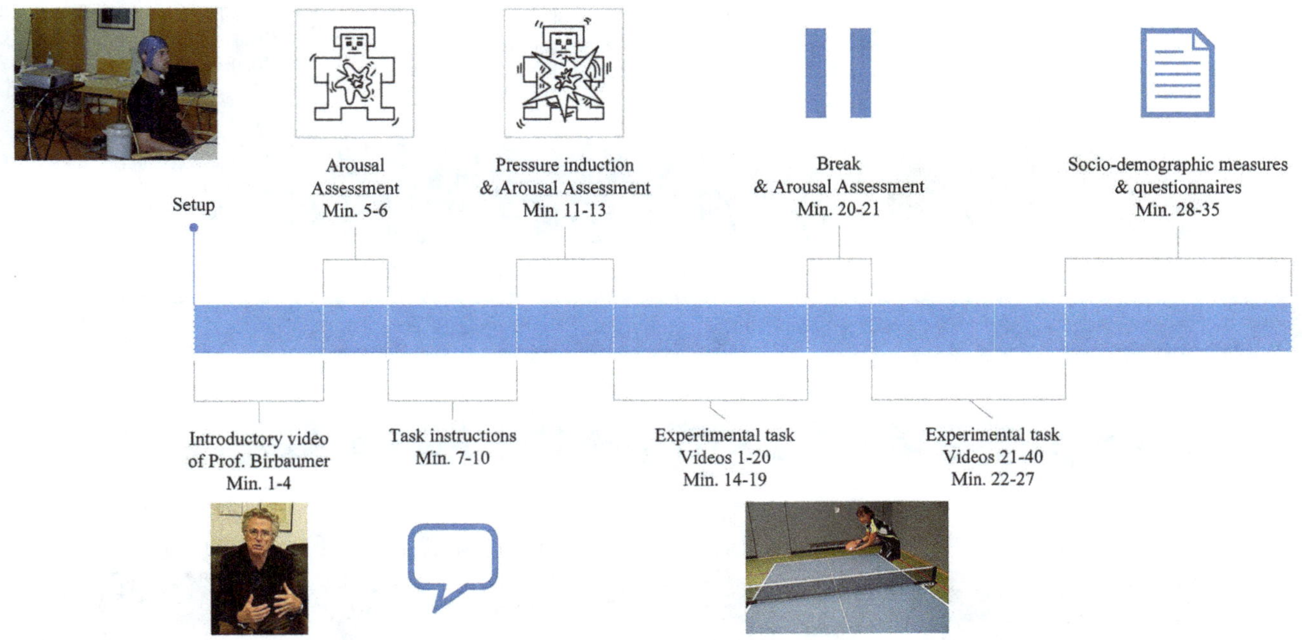

FIGURE 1 | Illustration of the general procedure as described in the Materials and Methods section.

electrode referencing (Qin et al., 2010). DC offset was kept below 25 μV during the whole recording. The signal was amplified with a NeXus 32 amplifier (Mind Media B.V., Herten, Holland) using a 24 bit A/D conversion, and was digitized at a rate of 2048 Hz. Data was exported in EDF+ format and imported to Brain Vision Analyzer (Brain Products, Gilching, Germany). A band pass filter (0.1 and 50 Hz) was applied and the data was down-sampled to 512 Hz. Additionally a 50 Hz notch filter was used to remove 50 Hz noise. For ocular artifact control, we used the independent component analysis (ICA) algorithm infomax (Bell and Sejnowski, 1995; Delorme et al., 2007). By using this algorithm we avoid rejecting large portions of EEG signal due to eye blinks, thus reducing the amount of brain activity subtracted from the measurements (Vigário, 1997; Iriarte et al., 2003). EEG data were then semi-automatically screened for artifacts by the following criteria: maximal voltage step of 50 μV/ms, maximal amplitude of ± 100 μV, values greater than 200 μV per 200 ms interval, activity below 0.5 μV in a 100 ms period. This semiautomatic mode allowed for additional visual inspection and the possibility to reject additional artifacts missed by the software. Artifact free, 15- s long segmented EEG data (see **Figure 2**) were then exported into MATLAB for further analysis. There were no significant differences between groups in the amount of artifact-free segments included for further analysis ($F_{(2,41)} = 2.46$, $p = 0.10$).

EEG AND STATISTICAL ANALYSIS: ERS/ERD

Event related spectral perturbation (ERSP) is a measure of a signal's time-frequency composition changes in a particular frequency range in reference to a baseline time interval. ERSP was computed using the MATLAB toolbox EEGlab (Delorme and Makeig, 2004) using Morlet Wavelets for spectral wavelet transformation. $ERSP_{\%}$ values were transformed in log-units and converted to decibel unit (dB), by multiplying the log ratio with the factor 10 (Grandchamp and Delorme, 2011). Negative $ERSP_{log}$ values which are shown green and red in the plots indicate a decrease in power from baseline which is further called ERD. Positive values plotted in blue indicate increase in power which implies ERS. The Morlet transforms used 3 cycles at the lowest frequencies, 30 at the highest, a time window of 2229 ms and overlap of 27 ms. 300 linear-spaced frequencies from 1.5 Hz to 30 Hz and 400 time points were generated.

The "video-end" trigger marked the end of each video in the EEG recording and was used to extract relevant epochs from the signal. Since each video lasted 7 s, time 0 ms depicts exactly the start of a video. As a baseline interval for the calculation of the ERSP values, a 1-s time window from −2500 ms to −1500 ms before the start of the video was used. The result of these calculations were one ERSP matrix per electrode per participant. Statistical analysis was performed on time-frequency-averaged ERSP values representing larger areas of interest in the frequency range 8–10 Hz from −1000 ms to 7000 in time-intervals of 1000 ms. This was done for all electrodes separately. The 1000 ms before the start of the video marked a baseline period, whereas the first 3 s of the task marked the preparatory phase and seconds four to six marked the motor execution phase (see **Figure 2**). The 1-s segments were further included in statistical ANOVA analysis as variables. For correlation analysis the mean ERD/ERS values for each phase (baseline vs. preparatory vs. execution) were computed. In order to find outliers within

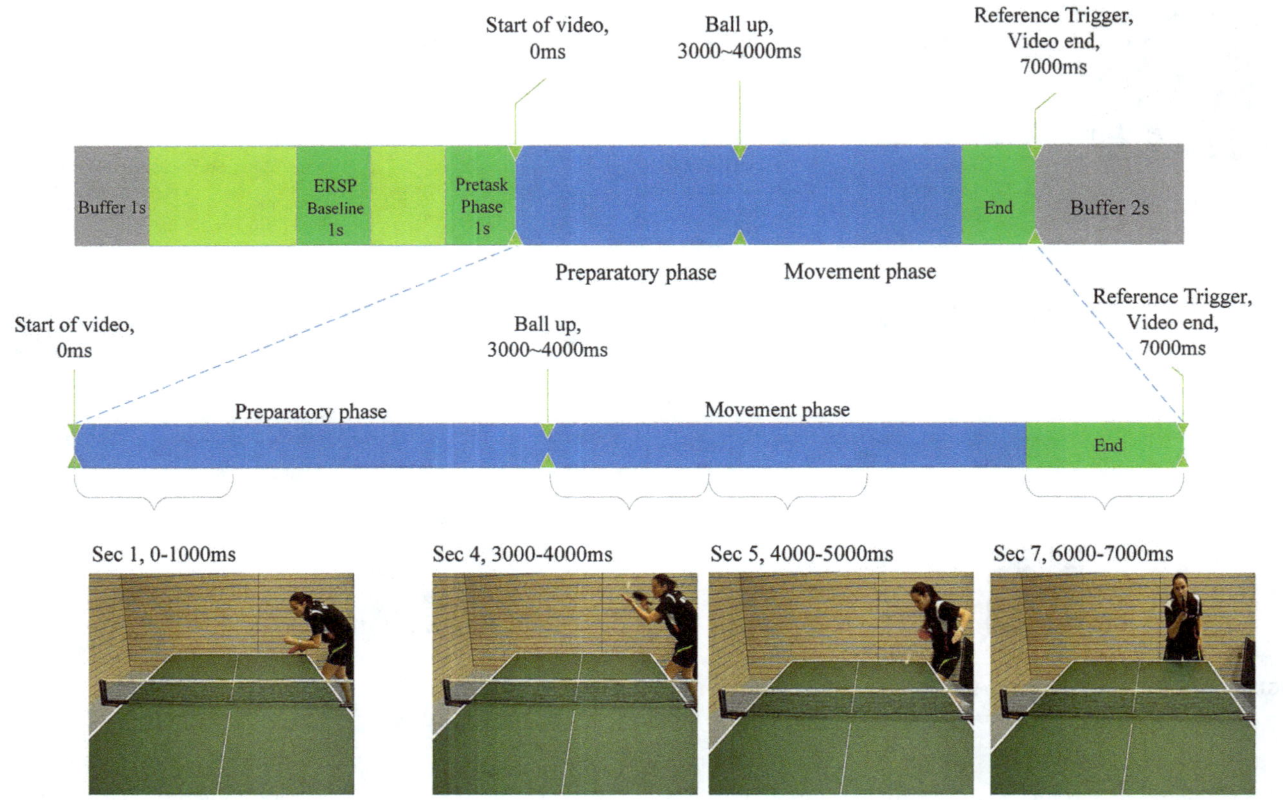

FIGURE 2 | Illustration of the experimental task as described in the Materials and Methods section. Indicated are baseline period for the calculation of ERD/ERS, the start and end of the video clips and the differentiation between preparatory and movement phase. Screenshots of each phase are presented.

the groups (amateurs, young elite and experts) ERD/ERS values were pooled by group and second in the preparatory phase (second 1 until second 3). ERD/ERS values in three electrode groups (P3, PZ, P4; F3, FZ, F4; C3, CZ, C4) were averaged for each of the three participant group over the preparatory phase resulting in 27 samples. Mean and standard deviation were calculated for each of these samples. Participants who differed more than three standard deviations from the mean were considered to be outliers and excluded from statistical analysis of EEG data. One outlier was found and excluded from the amateurs group.

QUESTIONNAIRES

To assess subjective arousal, the SAM questionnaire was used (Bradley and Lang, 1994) as a non-verbal pictorial assessment technique that directly measures arousal along a 9-point scale. Participants rated the videos based on perceived quality of the serve (complexity, rotation, variability and realism) of the opponent. Additionally participants rated the quality and intensity of their own motor imagination. To assess general commitment to the study, the subjects rated motivation, interest in the study, professionalism of the researchers and perceived relevance of the research project. Participants were also asked about the relevance of the forehand top spin within their own playing system and the perceived ability of their own forehand topspin. Rankings by the International Table Tennis Federation served as an objective performance measure for experts[1].

RESULTS

ERD/ERS AT THE MOTOR CORTEX

To test hypothesis (1), that table tennis experts show stronger 8–10 Hz ERD in the motor cortex at the end of the movement period, we analyzed differences in ERD in the motor cortex (C3, CZ, C4) over time between amateurs, young elite athletes and experts. Visual inspection and frequency analysis indicate ERD predominantly in the 8–10 Hz frequency band as expected (see **Figure 3**). An ANOVA of 8–10 Hz ERD/ERS (dB values) with time (−1000 ms to 6000 ms in 1-s bins), electrode position (C3 vs. Cz vs. C4) and group (experts vs. amateurs vs. young elite athletes) as independent factors showed a significant main effect of time ($F_{(2.89,115.63)} = 17.50$, $p < 0.001$, *partial* $\eta^2 = 0.30$), a significant main effect of group ($F_{(2,40)} = 4.309$, $p < 0.05$, *partial* $\eta^2 = 0.177$) and a significant interaction of time and group ($F_{(5.78,115.63)} = 2.781$, $p < 0.05$, *partial* $\eta^2 = 0.012$)[2]. Bonferroni corrected *post hoc* tests of the main effect of time with aggregated

[1]Reliable and valid performance indices for young elite and amateur players cannot be provided because there are no consistent ranking systems for these athletes.

[2]All results have been corrected for violations of sphericity (Greenhouse-Geisser).

db values over groups and electrode positions showed significant decreases in db values from second -1 (baseline) to second 2 ($p < 0.001$) and second 3 ($p < 0.01$) of preparatory and all other time points of the movement phase ($p < 0.001$). From second 1 of the preparatory phase there were significant decreases to second 2 ($p < 0.001$) of preparation and second 4 ($p < 0.005$), 5 ($p < 0.001$) and 6 ($p < 0.001$) of the movement phase. Further decreases have been shown from the last second of preparation (second 3) to the last second of the movement (second 6, $p < 0.05$) and from first (second 4) to the last second of movement (second 6, $p < 0.05$). The *post hoc* tests of the main effect of group should be regarded with caution because of the significant interaction between time and group. Bonferroni corrected *post hoc* tests with mean db values over all positions and time segments showed significant stronger ERD in experts compared to amateurs ($p < 0.05$) and no differences between experts and young elite athletes ($p <= 0.69$) and between young elite and amateur athletes ($p = 0.26$). We conducted ANOVAs of aggregated db values (mean of db values at C3, Cz, C4) at each time segment to explain the significant interaction of time and group and to assess differences in ERD between groups in the end of the motor execution phase (main hypothesis). When adjusting for multiple comparisons (Bonferroni), only the differences between groups at second 5 of the motor execution phase were significant ($F_{(2,40)} = 5.94$, $p < 0.01$, *partial* $\eta^2 = 0.23$). Further Bonferroni corrected t-tests showed significant stronger ERD in experts compared to amateurs ($p < 0.01$) with a strong effect size ($d = 1.13$), but no differences between experts and young elite athletes ($p = 0.55$) and no differences between young elite athletes and amateurs ($p = 0.12$). Since we a priori stated the strongest differences at the last second of the movement phase (second 6), we also present ANOVA results for this time segment without Bonferroni correction. There was a significant main effect of group ($F_{(2,40)} = 4.16$, $p < 0.05$, *partial* $\eta^2 = 0.17$). Experts showed significantly stronger ERD than amateurs ($p < 0.05$) with a slightly stronger effect size ($d = 1.17$) compared to second 5. There were marginal significant differences between young elite athletes and amateurs ($p = 0.08$) and no differences between experts and young elite athletes ($p = 0.1$).

ERD/ERS AT THE FRONTO-PARIETAL CORTEX

To test the second part of hypothesis (1) of increased fronto-parietal activation in experts, we conducted an ANOVA of 8–10 Hz ERD/ERS with time (−1000 ms to 6000 ms in 1-s bins), region (frontal vs. parietal), position (F3/P3 vs. Fz/Pz vs. F4/P4) and group (experts vs. amateurs vs. young elite athletes) as independent factors. As at the motor cortex, there was a significant main effect of time ($F_{(2.06,82.72)} = 23.14$, $p < 0.001$, *partial* $\eta^2 = 0.37$), but no significant effects of group ($F_{(1,40)} = 2.87$, $p = 0.07$, *partial* $\eta^2 = 0.13$) and no significant interaction between time and group ($F_{(4.14,82.72)} = 2.18$, $p = 0.08$, *partial* $\eta^2 = 0.01$). But there was a significant interaction between time, region and group ($F_{(8.29,165.88)} = 3.01$, $p < 0.01$, *partial* $\eta^2 = 0.13$). There were no significant interactions between group, time, region and electrode position (left, central, right). Bonferroni corrected *post hoc* tests of the main effect of time with aggregated db values over groups and electrode positions showed significant decreases in db values from second -1 (baseline) to second 1 ($p < 0.05$), second 2 ($p < 0.001$), second 3 ($p < 0.005$) of preparatory and all other time points of the movement phase ($p < 0.001$). From second 1 of the preparatory phase there were significant decreases to second 2 ($p < 0.001$) of preparation and second 4 ($p < 0.005$), 5 ($p < 0.001$) and 6 ($p < 0.001$) of the movement phase. Further decreases have been shown from the last second of preparation (second 3) to seconds 5 ($p < 0.01$) and 6 ($p < 0.01$) of motor execution and from first (second 4) to the last second of movement (second 6, $p < 0.05$). To test the hypothesis of increased fronto-parietal activation in experts in the end of the motor execution phase, we report the *post hoc* tests of the three-way interaction time x region x group and focus on differences between groups in the last second of the movement phase (second 6). ANOVA at this time point with group (expert vs. amateur vs. young elite) and region (frontal vs. parietal) as independent factors showed no significant main effect of group ($F_{(2,40)} = 2.90$, $p = 0.07$, *partial* $\eta^2 = 0.13$), a significant main effect of region ($F_{(1,40)} = 30.71$, $p < 0.001$, *partial* $\eta^2 = 0.43$) and a significant interaction between region and group ($F_{(2,40)} = 3.49$, $p < 0.05$, *partial* $\eta^2 = 0.15$). The main effect of region indicates significant stronger ERD at the parietal ($M = -3.43$, SD = 3.77) than at the frontal cortex ($M = -1.65$, SD = 2.06). There were no significant differences between groups at the frontal cortex ($F_{(2,40)} = 2.69$, $p = 0.08$, *partial* $\eta^2 = 0.12$) nor at the parietal cortex ($F_{(2,40)} = 3.07$, $p = 0.06$, *partial* $\eta^2 = 0.13$), but there was a significant main effect of group ($F_{(2,40)} = 3.49$, $p < 0.05$, *partial* $\eta^2 = 0.15$) when comparing the contrasts of frontal and parietal ERD (frontal ERD/ERS minus parietal ERD/ERS). Young elite athletes showed significant stronger parietal ERD (relative to frontal) compared to amateurs ($p < 0.05$). There were no significant differences in the parietal ERD (relative to frontal ERD) between experts and amateurs nor between experts and young elite athletes. The results indicate that there is ERD also in the fronto-parietal cortex in experts, amateurs and young elite athletes, but experts did not show significant stronger ERD at frontal or parietal electrodes.

ACTIVATION OF THE MOTOR CORTEX AND PREDICTION OF WORLD RANK

There were no correlations between 8–10 Hz ERD at the motor cortex and world rank in experts. However there were significant correlations between 8–10 Hz ERD within the task in frontal and parietal electrodes and world rank points: The weaker the ERD (the stronger the ERS) the more world rank points. The correlations were not different for left, central or right electrode positions. However, they were higher in the preparatory phase at parietal electrodes and higher in the movement phase at frontal electrodes (see **Table 1** and **Figure 4**). There were no correlations in the baseline period.

CONTROL ANALYSIS: OCCIPITAL CORTEX

To demonstrate, that the stronger ERD in experts compared to amateurs at the motor cortex (hypothesis 1) relies on differences in cerebral motor cortical processes and not on differences in visual attention processes, we conducted an ANOVA of 8–10 Hz ERD/ERS at the occipital cortex at the last second of the movement phase (second 6) with electrode position (O1, O2)

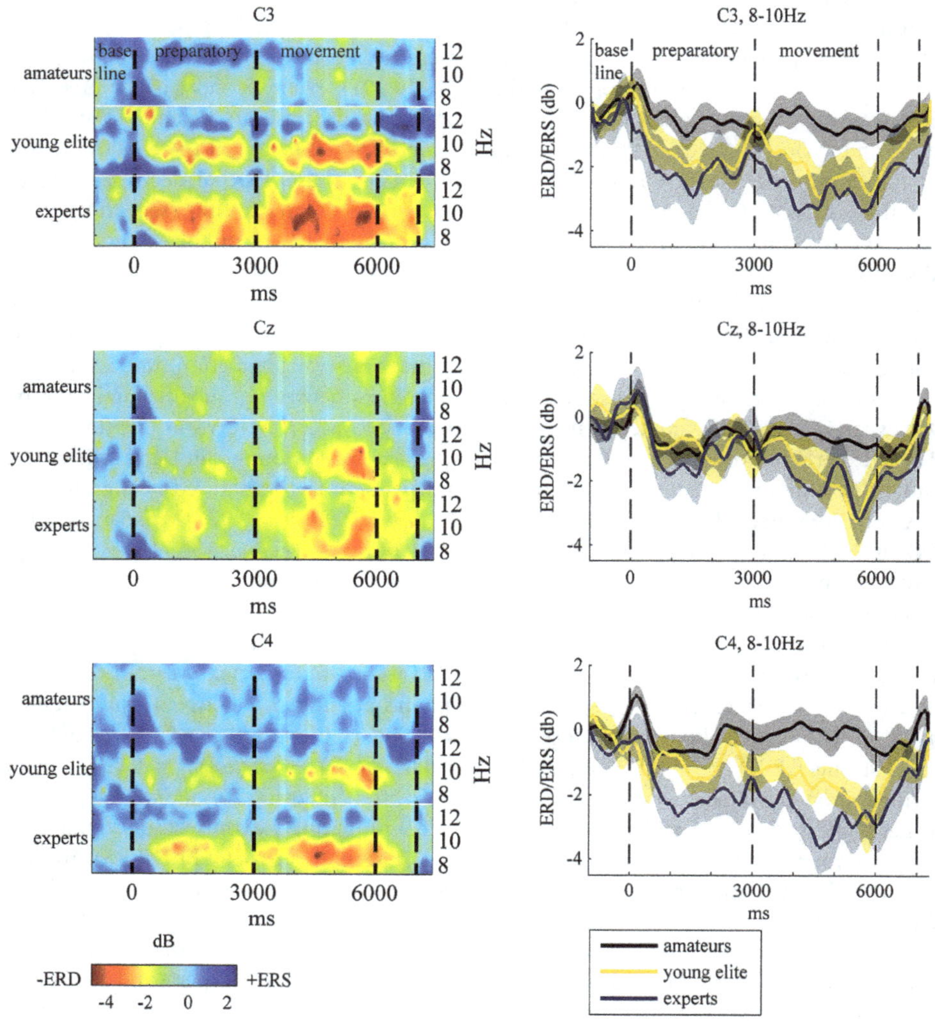

FIGURE 3 | Left: Event-Related-Spectral-Pertubation (ERSP) plots at central electrodes at 8–12 Hz for each group during the task. Subjects watched 40 table tennis videos and imagined a specific table tennis stroke. Seconds 1 to 3 comprise the preparatory period and seconds 4 to 6 comprise the movement period. Event-Related-Desynchronization (ERD) and Synchronization (ERS) are indexed by power decrease in red and green (ERD) and power increase in blue (ERS). Right: ERD/ERS in the 8–10 Hz frequency band with standard error of mean (transparent shadow) are displayed over time at the motor cortex for experts (blue line), amateurs (black line) and young elite athletes (yellow line). ERD/ERS is indexed by ERSP values that were transformed to log-units and converted to decibel unit (db). See EEG and statistical analysis: ERS/ERD in Method and Material section for a detailed description.

Table 1 | Correlation coefficients between mean frontal (F3, Fz, F4), central (C3, Cz, C4) and parietal (P3, Pz, P4) ERD/ERS and world rank points in experts for baseline (second -1), preparatory (mean second 1 to second 3) and movement (mean second 4 to second 6) period.

Baseline: $r(12)$			Preparatory: $r(12)$			Movement: $r(12)$		
Frontal	Central	Parietal	Frontal	Central	Parietal	Frontal	Central	Parietal
0.06	−0.10	−0.03	0.60*	0.24	0.53^{+}	0.63*	0.40	0.51^{++}

Positive correlation coefficients imply that weaker ERD (or stronger ERS) is correlated with more world rank points in experts.

$^{*}p < 0.05$; $^{+}p = 0.05$; $^{++}p < 0.07$

and groups (experts, amateurs, young elite athletes) as independent factors. As expected, there were no significant differences between groups ($F_{(2,40)} = 2.23$, $p = 0.12$, *partial* $\eta^2 = 0.10$) and no significant interaction between group and electrode site ($F_{(2,40)} = 2.06$, $p = 0.14$, *partial* $\eta^2 = 0.09$).

CONTROL ANALYSIS: QUESTIONNAIRES

To investigate whether the pressure induction was successful, we conducted an ANOVA to assess differences in subjective arousal (SAM) between groups at the different measurement times. ANOVA indicate a strong main effect of time ($F_{(2,80)} = 14.747$,

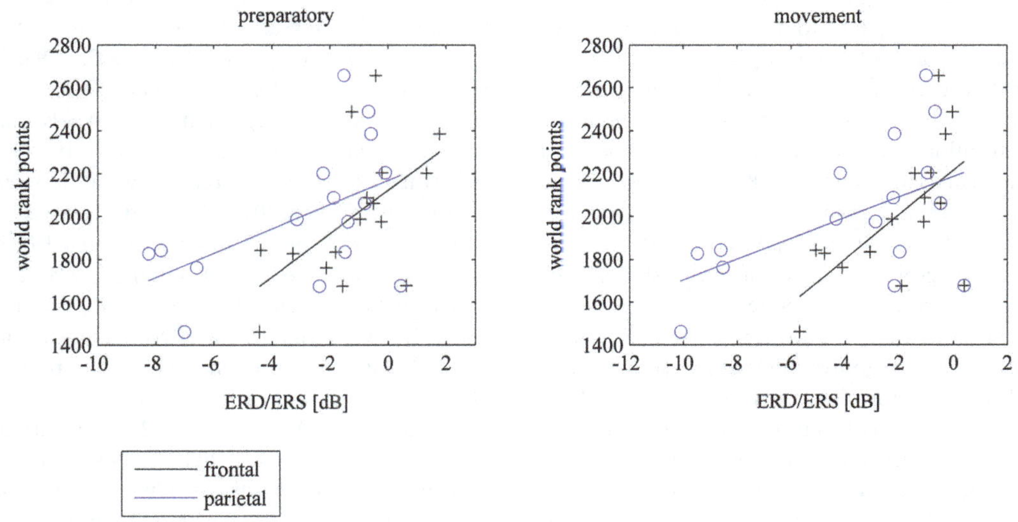

FIGURE 4 | Scatterplots of mean frontal (F3, Fz, F4) and parietal (P3, Pz, P4) ERD/ERS and world rank points for the preparatory und movement period during the task, where subjects watched 40 table tennis videos and imagined a specific table tennis stroke. Seconds 1 to 3 comprise the preparatory period and seconds 4 to 6 comprise the movement period. ERD implies power decrease (negative values) and ERS imply power increase (positive values). ERD/ERS is indexed by ERSP values that were transformed to log-units and then converted to decibel unit (db). See EEG and statistical analysis: ERS/ERD in Method and Material section for a detailed description).

$p < 0.001$, *partial* $\eta^2 = 0.27$). However neither significant differences between groups nor an interaction of time and skill level emerged, indicating that there were no differences in total arousal between groups nor between groups at the different measurement points. *Post hoc* analyzes indicate a strong increase of arousal after the pressure induction ($p < 0.005$) but no significant increase in arousal after the first 20 video trials ($p = 0.12$), verifying, that all participants experienced an increase in performance pressure. There were no significant differences between groups in the perception of the expertise of the player in the videos ($F_{(2,40)} = 1.83$, $p = 0.17$, *partial* $\eta^2 = 0.08$). There were no differences between groups in the perceived quality of the serve ($F_{(2,40)} = 0.464$, $p = 0.63$, *partial* $\eta^2 = 0.02$). Overall, amateurs ($M = 2.79$, SD = 0.82) rated their imagination quality slightly more vivid than experts ($M = 2.45$, SD = 0.81) and young elite athletes ($M = 2.2$, SD = 0.79), but these differences were not statistically significant ($F_{(2,40)} = 0.13$, $p = 0.18$, *partial* $\eta^2 = 0.08$). Young elite athletes showed the highest commitment ($M = 3.3$, SD = 0.51), similar to amateurs ($M = 3.29$, SD = 0.31) and higher than experts ($M = 2.87$, SD = 0.58). These differences between groups were significant ($F_{(2,40)} = 3.72$, $p < 0.05$, *partial* $\eta^2 = 0.16$), however bonferroni corrected *post hoc* tests showed no significant differences between experts and amateurs ($p = 0.08$), between amateurs and young elite athletes ($p = 0.1$) and only marginal significant differences between experts and young elite athletes ($p = 0.06$). Neither the relevance of the forehand topspin ($F_{(2,40)} = 1.32$, $p = 0.29$, *partial* $\eta^2 = 0.06$) nor the perceived expertise of the forehand topspin differed significantly between groups ($F_{(2,40)} = 0.45$, $p = 0.64$, *partial* $\eta^2 = 0.02$). We further assessed, if the commitment to the study, arousal during the task and the imagination quality is correlated with ERD in the motor and fronto-parietal cortex. We correlated mean motor and mean fronto-parietal ERD during the preparatory phase and the movement phase with these three control variables. Only the commitment to the study showed small positive correlation coefficients with motor ERD, indicating a slight association between higher commitment to the study and weaker ERD at the motor cortex. However, after controlling for multiple comparisons (Bonferroni), these correlations did not reach significance and were thus not included as a covariates into the main analysis.

DISCUSSION

We tested the hypothesis that expert compared to amateur table tennis athletes exhibit stronger activation (indexed by stronger 8–10 Hz alpha ERD) in the motor and fronto-parietal cortex during a motor imagery task, in which athletes had to react to a table tennis stroke presented in different video clips. We expected an intermediate activation level in a third group with an intermediate skill level (young elite athletes). To our knowledge to this date there is no study assessing differences in ERD between groups of different skill levels in high reactive sports like table tennis. Since elaborated attentional skills and multisensory integration are important features of motor skills in table tennis, we argued that there are differences in motor and fronto-parietal cortex activation. We further assumed ERD in the low-frequency 8–10 Hz band reflecting motor and motor attentional processes during complex motor tasks. To demonstrate that ERD in the motor cortex predicts performance in elite athletes, we assumed a positive correlation between the activation of the motor cortex (stronger ERD) and world rank points.

The results demonstrate a significantly stronger 8–10 Hz ERD in experts compared to amateurs in the motor cortex (C3, Cz, C4) at the end of the motor execution phase with an intermediate 8–10 Hz ERD in young elite athletes. There was a trend towards stronger 8–10 Hz ERD in the frontal and parietal cortex in experts and young elite athletes compared to amateurs, however these differences were not significant. Contrary to our expectation, less activation or even cortical inhibition in the fronto-parietal cortex was correlated with more world rank points during motor preparation and execution. This association was task-dependent, since there was no correlation between 8–10 Hz ERD in the baseline period and world rank points.

The data suggests that 8–10 Hz ERD in the motor cortex might reflect a physiological mechanism of motor skill in table tennis. SMR and alpha rhythms are generated by thalamo-cortical and cortico-cortical loops that control the access and retrieval of stored sensorimotor and cognitive information (Pfurtscheller and Lopes Da Silva, 1999) and the functional meaning of low frequency 8–10 Hz ERD seems to be related to general motor attention and readiness during motor tasks (Klimesch, 1999; Pfurtscheller and Lopes Da Silva, 1999; Pfurtscheller et al., 2000; Klimesch et al., 2007). The present results indicate that high motor skills in table tennis imply selective engagement of thalamocortical and cortico-cortical loops for motor-attentional performance: excitability of the motor cortex during motor reaction, planning and execution with high attentional demands and, once elite expertise is reached, less activation of the fronto-parietal attention network. Motor cortical excitability indicates higher focal neuronal firing, which is often observed after motor learning (Koeneke et al., 2006b; Cirillo et al., 2011).

Our finding of a stronger activation of the motor cortex contradicts several studies showing that elite athletes (shooters, karateka, gymnasts, kendoists) require "less" brain activation (weaker ERD) in task relevant brain areas compared to novices during sport specific tasks (Kita et al., 2001; Di Russo et al., 2005; Del Percio et al., 2008, 2009a; Babiloni et al., 2009). These authors state a more efficient cortical function in more skilled individuals by means of less cortical activation (weaker ERD) when skills are highly elaborated and become automatic ("neural efficiency hypothesis"). These assumptions are also based on studies showing a reduction of brain activity during cognitive tasks with the development of expertise (Grabner et al., 2006; Dunst et al., 2014) and on motor skill learning tasks showing a reduction in brain activity in the motor cortex from pre- to posttraining measurements indicating an optimization of cortical resources (Haufler et al., 2000; Jäncke et al., 2006; Koeneke et al., 2006a). The association of less fronto-parietal activation (weaker ERD) with higher world rank points in elite experts in our study can be interpreted in terms of the "neural efficiency hypothesis": the better the performance of elite table tennis players the fewer attentional resources they require for motor tasks with high attentional demands. Less attentional resources and executive control processes are often observed also in slow motor learning tasks (for a review see Dayan and Cohen, 2011).

The stronger activation of the motor cortex in elite experts compared to amateurs in our study resembles an EEG study with karate and fencing athletes that found stronger ERD in elite compared to novice athletes during a sport specific visual integration task (Del Percio et al., 2007) and functional imaging studies with musicians that showed stronger activations in the contralateral primary sensory cortex in expert violinists compared to amateurs (Lotze et al., 2003). Further, our results are in line with studies looking at cortical activation patterns of complex motor learning tasks (Karni et al., 1995, 1998; Hazeltine et al., 1997; Rauch et al., 1997; Seidler et al., 2005) and complex motor visual multisensory integration tasks (Waldschmidt and Ashby, 2011), that showed increased cortical activity in task-relevant areas, when expertise or automaticity was developed (for reviews see Dayan and Cohen, 2011; Chang, 2014). Several motor learning studies using fMRI or PET showed an initial decrease of activity at the primary motor region (M1) in the first motor learning stage, further an increase in activation of M1, supplementary motor area (SMA), whole motor cortex and other subcortical areas after 3–5 weeks of training when motor skills become implicit and automatic (Karni et al., 1995; Inoue et al., 2000; Floyer-Lea and Matthews, 2004, 2005; Xiong et al., 2009). Contradictory evidence also exists (Hlustík et al., 2004; Pollok et al., 2014). A recent experimental motor learning study in monkeys showed reduced metabolic activity at M1 after training only when the motor task was fully self-generated and not visually guided (Picard et al., 2013). We argue, that table tennis is highly similar to complex motor tasks that require perception, visual attention and multisensory integration. Therefore it differs from the sport disciplines such as rifle shooting, golf and gymnastics, which have been the focus of investigations using EEG and analyzing ERD/ERS during motor actions in elite experts. These sport disciplines are rather characterized by simple, self-generated movements with low attentional demands. We argue, that the stronger and focused activation of the motor cortex in table tennis athletes found in our study is a physiological mechanism in highly developed motor skills in complex motor tasks with high attentional demands that require anticipation, multi-sensory integration and fast reactions.

Further, our study extends recent neuroimaging findings on motor expertise in action observation (for a review see Turella et al., 2013). There is strong evidence that elite experts of several disciplines like archery (Kim et al., 2011), badminton (Wright et al., 2010) or basketball (Abreu et al., 2012) showed stronger activation in brain regions typically involved in action observation during observation of sport specific movements. In two FMRI studies (Calvo-Merino et al., 2005, 2006), Calvo-Merino et al. (2005) could demonstrate that ballet dancers and capoeira fighters showed stronger activation for the observation of trained in comparison to untrained dance styles in brain regions (bilateral premotor cortex, bilateral superior parietal lobule, and anterior intraparietal sulcus, left ventral premotor cortex and left superior temporal sulcus) typically involved in action observation (Rizzolatti and Craighero, 2004; Caspers et al., 2010; Rizzolatti and Sinigaglia, 2010). There were no such differences in non-dancers. Calvo-Merino et al. (2006) further showed, that activity within the left premotor cortex and the bilateral anterior intraparietal sulcus was higher when observing actions within the observer's motor repertoire emphasizing an effect of motor expertise rather than visual familiarity with the dance styles presented. The result of a stronger engagement of the motor cortex during action observation and motor imagery in our study is thus in line with the results of a stronger engagement of task relevant brain areas in highly-skilled athletes or dancers during action observation of skilled and familiar motor actions in their discipline.

LIMITATIONS

It should be noted, that due to the constraints of EEG (spatial resolution) and the small number of electrodes, we cannot exactly conclude that the source of the 8–10 Hz ERD is the motor cortex (SMR). Nevertheless, the differences between experts and amateurs were only significant in the motor cortex with no differences between groups at the occipital cortex. Consequently, we argue that the source of the ERD is the cerebral motor system. Also, the EEG data does not allow us to analyze localized functional topographical details in motor or parietal cortex compared. However, we decided to use EEG in order to get exquisite temporal resolution needed for the specific task demands of table tennis which comprises short reaction times and fast movements. We also aimed to extend the existing literature of ERD/ERS in elite athletes to indicate that ERD serves as a physiological mechanism of elaborated motor skills in table tennis. Another apparent limitation is the difference in age between young elite athletes, experts and amateurs. There is some evidence that movement related ERD in young children (around 7 years of age) is weaker compared to adults during motor tasks (Pangelinan et al., 2011). Thus we included only children that most probably already reached puberty (14 years of age and older). However, we still cannot rule out the possibility, that the age of the young elite athletes might influenced our results. Another limitation is the small sample size ($N = 14$) especially for the correlation analysis. Thus also these analysis should be regarded as preliminary which needs replication. These results should therefore be interpreted with caution. However, the strong effect sizes of the differences between experts and amateurs at the motor cortex and the high correlation coefficients underpin the quality of the results.

CONCLUSIONS

In conclusion, the present study shows that 8–10 Hz ERD is stronger in elite table tennis players compared to amateurs at the motor cortex and a weaker 8–10 Hz ERD in the fronto-parietal cortex is associated with more world rank points in experts. These results suggest that high motor skills in table tennis are associated with focused excitability of the motor cortex during reaction, movements planning and execution with high attentional demands. Among elite experts however, less activation of the fronto-parietal attention network may be necessary to become a world champion.

AUTHOR AND CONTRIBUTORS

We declare that all authors substantially contributed to the conception or design of the work, or the acquisition, analysis, or interpretation of data for the work and drafting the work or revising it critically for important intellectual content. All authors further approved the version to be published and agreed to be accountable for all aspects of the work in ensuring that questions related to the accuracy or integrity of any part of the work are appropriately investigated and resolved. More specifically, authors contributed with the following focuses:

Sebastian Wolf: Design of the work, application for funding, data acquisition, data processing, data analysis, drafting the work, revision.

Ellen Broelz: data acquisition (amateurs, young elite athletes), interpretation of the work, drafting.

David Scholz: data acquisition, data processing, data analysis, drafting (figures) and ERD/ERS.

Ander Ramos Murguialday: conceptualizaion, data processing (MATLAB Code), data analysis, drafting, revision.

Philipp M. Keune: conceptualization, data analysis, drafting.

Martin Hautzinger: design of the work, data interpretation, drafting, revision.

Niels Birbaumer: design of the work, data interpretation, drafting, revision.

Ute Strehl: design of the work, data interpretation, drafting, revision.

ACKNOWLEDGMENTS

We thank the German Table Tennis Association (DTTB) and the Table Tennis Association of Baden-Württemberg (TTBW) for their participation. Especially we thank the chief trainers Dirk Schimmelpfennig (DTTB), Soenke Geil (TTBW) and Frank Fuerste (TTBW) for their support to contact the table tennis athletes. Moreover, we would particularly like to thank Benjamin Wesa for his perseveringly support during the data acquisition phase. We are deeply saddened that he died in an accident in the end of the data acquisition phase. Helena Schütze and Benedikt Joost contributed significantly with their patient and flexible support during data acquisition. We further thank all table tennis players that served as a video model: Qianhong Gotsch, Peter Franz, Silke Fürste, Harald Maier, Katharina Sabo, Carolin Reisig and Michael Klyeisen. The project was funded by the German research association (DFG, BI 195/67-1). The authors also acknowledge the support by the DFG and the Open Access Publishing Fund of Tuebingen University. The DFG had no involvement in study design, the collection, analysis and interpretation of data, in the writing of the report nor in the decision to submit the article for publication.

REFERENCES

Abreu, A. M., Macaluso, E., Azevedo, R. T., Cesari, P., Urgesi, C., and Aglioti, S. M. (2012). Action anticipation beyond the action observation network: a functional magnetic resonance imaging study in expert basketball players. *Eur. J. Neurosci.* 35, 1646–1654. doi: 10.1111/j.1460-9568.2012.08104.x

Alegre, M., De Gurtubay, I. G., Labarga, A., Iriarte, J., Malanda, A., and Artieda, J. (2004). Alpha and beta oscillatory activity during a sequence of two movements. *Clin. Neurophysiol.* 115, 124–130. doi: 10.1016/s1388-2457(03)00311-0

Antelis, J. M., Montesano, L., Ramos-Murguialday, A., Birbaumer, N., and Minguez, J. (2012). Continuous decoding of intention to move from contralesional hemisphere brain oscillations in severely affected chronic stroke patients. *Conf. Proc. IEEE Eng. Med. Biol. Soc.* 2012, 4099–4103. doi: 10.1109/embc.2012.6346868

Babiloni, C., Del Percio, C., Iacoboni, M., Infarinato, F., Lizio, R., Marzano, N., et al. (2008). Golf putt outcomes are predicted by sensorimotor cerebral EEG rhythms. *J. Physiol.* 586, 131–139. doi: 10.1113/jphysiol.2007.141630

Babiloni, C., Del Percio, C., Rossini, P. M., Marzano, N., Iacoboni, M., Infarinato, F., et al. (2009). Judgment of actions in experts: a high-resolution EEG study in elite athletes. *Neuroimage* 45, 512–521. doi: 10.1016/j.neuroimage.2008.11.035

Babiloni, C., Marzano, N., Infarinato, F., Iacoboni, M., Rizza, G., Aschieri, P., et al. (2010). "Neural efficiency" of experts' brain during judgment of actions: a high-resolution EEG study in elite and amateur karate athletes. *Behav. Brain Res.* 207, 466–475. doi: 10.1016/j.bbr.2009.10.034

Bell, A. J., and Sejnowski, T. J. (1995). An information-maximization approach to blind separation and blind deconvolution. *Neural Comput.* 7, 1129–1159. doi: 10.1162/neco.1995.7.6.1129

Bradley, M. M., and Lang, P. J. (1994). Measuring emotion: the self-assessment manikin and the semantic differential. *J. Behav. Ther. Exp. Psychiatry* 25, 49–59. doi: 10.1016/0005-7916(94)90063-9

Calvo-Merino, B., Glaser, D. E., Grèzes, J., Passingham, R. E., and Haggard, P. (2005). Action observation and acquired motor skills: an FMRI study with expert dancers. *Cereb. Cortex* 15, 1243–1249. doi: 10.1093/cercor/bhi007

Calvo-Merino, B., Grèzes, J., Glaser, D. E., Passingham, R. E., and Haggard, P. (2006). Seeing or doing? Influence of visual and motor familiarity in action observation. *Curr. Biol.* 16, 1905–1910. doi: 10.1016/j.cub.2006.07.065

Caspers, S., Zilles, K., Laird, A. R., and Eickhoff, S. B. (2010). ALE meta-analysis of action observation and imitation in the human brain. *Neuroimage* 50, 1148–1167. doi: 10.1016/j.neuroimage.2009.12.112

Chang, Y. (2014). Reorganization and plastic changes of the human brain associated with skill learning and expertise. *Front. Hum. Neurosci.* 8:35. doi: 10.3389/fnhum.2014.00035

Cirillo, J., Todd, G., and Semmler, J. G. (2011). Corticomotor excitability and plasticity following complex visuomotor training in young and old adults. *Eur. J. Neurosci.* 34, 1847–1856. doi: 10.1111/j.1460-9568.2011.07870.x

Dayan, E., and Cohen, L. G. (2011). Neuroplasticity subserving motor skill learning. *Neuron* 72, 443–454. doi: 10.1016/j.neuron.2011.10.008

Delorme, A., Sejnowski, T., and Makeig, S. (2007). Enhanced detection of artifacts in EEG data using higher-order statistics and independent component analysis. *Neuroimage* 34, 1443–1449. doi: 10.1016/j.neuroimage.2006.11.004

Del Percio, C., Babiloni, C., Bertollo, M., Marzano, N., Iacoboni, M., Infarinato, F., et al. (2009a). Visuo-attentional and sensorimotor alpha rhythms are related to visuo-motor performance in athletes. *Hum. Brain Mapp.* 30, 3527–3540. doi: 10.1002/hbm.20776

Del Percio, C., Babiloni, C., Marzano, N., Iacoboni, M., Infarinato, F., Vecchio, F., et al. (2009b). "Neural efficiency" of athletes' brain for upright standing: a high-resolution EEG study. *Brain Res. Bull.* 79, 193–200. doi: 10.1016/j.brainresbull.2009.02.001

Del Percio, C., Brancucci, A., Bergami, F., Marzano, N., Fiore, A., Di Ciolo, E., et al. (2007). Cortical alpha rhythms are correlated with body sway during quiet open-eyes standing in athletes: a high-resolution EEG study. *Neuroimage* 36, 822–829. doi: 10.1016/j.neuroimage.2007.02.054

Del Percio, C., Rossini, P. M., Marzano, N., Iacoboni, M., Infarinato, F., Aschieri, P., et al. (2008). Is there a "neural efficiency" in athletes? A high-resolution EEG study. *Neuroimage* 42, 1544–1553. doi: 10.1016/j.neuroimage.2008.05.061

Di Russo, F., Pitzalis, S., Aprile, T., and Spinelli, D. (2005). Effect of practice on brain activity: an investigation in top-level rifle shooters. *Med. Sci. Sports Exerc.* 37, 1586–1593. doi: 10.1249/01.mss.0000177458.71676.0d

Dunst, B., Benedek, M., Jauk, E., Bergner, S., Koschutnig, K., Sommer, M., et al. (2014). Neural efficiency as a function of task demands. *Intelligence* 42, 22–30. doi: 10.1016/j.intell.2013.09.005

Ehrsson, H. H., Geyer, S., and Naito, E. (2003). Imagery of voluntary movement of fingers, toes and tongue activates corresponding body-part-specific motor representations. *J. Neurophysiol.* 90, 3304–3316. doi: 10.1152/jn.01113.2002

Floyer-Lea, A., and Matthews, P. M. (2004). Changing brain networks for visuomotor control with increased movement automaticity. *J. Neurophysiol.* 92, 2405–2412. doi: 10.1152/jn.01092.2003

Floyer-Lea, A., and Matthews, P. M. (2005). Distinguishable brain activation networks for short- and long-term motor skill learning. *J. Neurophysiol.* 94, 512–518. doi: 10.1152/jn.00717.2004

Grabner, R. H., Neubauer, A. C., and Stern, E. (2006). Superior performance and neural efficiency: the impact of intelligence and expertise. *Brain Res. Bull.* 69, 422–439. doi: 10.1016/j.brainresbull.2006.02.009

Grandchamp, R., and Delorme, A. (2011). Single-trial normalization for event-related spectral decomposition reduces sensitivity to noisy trials. *Front. Psychol.* 2:236. doi: 10.1016/j.neuroimage.2008.05.061

Grezes, J., and Costes, N. (1998). Top-down effect of strategy on the perception of human biological motion: a PET investigation. *Cogn. Neuropsychol.* 15, 553–582. doi: 10.1080/026432998381023

Halder, S., Agorastos, D., Veit, R., Hammer, E. M., Lee, S., Varkuti, B., et al. (2011). Neural mechanisms of brain-computer interface control. *Neuroimage* 55, 1779–1790. doi: 10.1016/j.neuroimage.2011.01.021

Haufler, A. J., Spalding, T. W., Maria, D. L. S., and Hatfield, B. D. (2000). Neuro-cognitive activity during a self-paced visuospatial task: comparative EEG profiles in marksmen and novice shooters. *Biol. Psychol.* 53, 131–160. doi: 10.1016/s0301-0511(00)00047-8

Hazeltine, E., Grafton, S. T., and Ivry, R. (1997). Attention and stimulus characteristics determine the locus of motor-sequence encoding. A PET study. *Brain* 120(Pt. 1), 123–140. doi: 10.1093/brain/120.1.123

Hlustík, P., Solodkin, A., Noll, D. C., and Small, S. L. (2004). Cortical plasticity during three-week motor skill learning. *J. Clin. Neurophysiol.* 21, 180–191. doi: 10.1097/00004691-200405000-00006

Inoue, K., Kawashima, R., Satoh, K., Kinomura, S., Sugiura, M., Goto, R., et al. (2000). A PET study of visuomotor learning under optical rotation. *Neuroimage* 11, 505–516. doi: 10.1006/nimg.2000.0554

Iriarte, J., Urrestarazu, E., Valencia, M., Alegre, M., Malanda, A., Viteri, C., et al. (2003). Independent component analysis as a tool to eliminate artifacts in EEG: a quantitative study. *J. Clin. Neurophysiol.* 20, 249–257. doi: 10.1097/00004691-200307000-00004

Jäncke, L., Lutz, K., and Koeneke, S. (2006). Converging evidence of ERD/ERS and BOLD responses in motor control research. *Prog. Brain Res.* 159, 261–271. doi: 10.1016/s0079-6123(06)59018-1

Jasper, H. H. (1958). Report of the committee on methods of clinical examination in electroencephalography: 1957. *Electroencephalogr. Clin. Neurophysiol.* 10, 370–375. doi: 10.1016/0013-4694(58)90053-1

Jeannerod, M. (2001). Neural simulation of action: a unifying mechanism for motor cognition. *Neuroimage* 14, S103–109. doi: 10.1006/nimg.2001.0832

Jeannerod, M., and Frak, V. (1999). Mental imaging of motor activity in humans. *Curr. Opin. Neurobiol.* 9, 735–739. doi: 10.1016/s0959-4388(99)00038-0

Karni, A., Meyer, G., Jezzard, P., Adams, M. M., Turner, R., and Ungerleider, L. G. (1995). Functional MRI evidence for adult motor cortex plasticity during motor skill learning. *Nature* 377, 155–158. doi: 10.1038/377155a0

Karni, A., Meyer, G., Rey-Hipolito, C., Jezzard, P., Adams, M. M., Turner, R., et al. (1998). The acquisition of skilled motor performance: fast and slow experience-driven changes in primary motor cortex. *Proc. Natl. Acad. Sci. U S A* 95, 861–868. doi: 10.1073/pnas.95.3.861

Kim, Y. T., Seo, J. H., Song, H. J., Yoo, D. S., Lee, H. J., Lee, J., et al. (2011). Neural correlates related to action observation in expert archers. *Behav. Brain Res.* 223, 342–347. doi: 10.1016/j.bbr.2011.04.053

Kita, Y., Mori, A., and Nara, M. (2001). Two types of movement-related cortical potentials preceding wrist extension in humans. *Neuroreport* 12, 2221–2225. doi: 10.1097/00001756-200107200-00035

Klimesch, W. (1999). EEG alpha and theta oscillations reflect cognitive and memory performance: a review and analysis. *Brain Res. Brain Res. Rev.* 29, 169–195. doi: 10.1016/s0165-0173(98)00056-3

Klimesch, W., Fellinger, R., and Freunberger, R. (2011). Alpha oscillations and early stages of visual encoding. *Front. Psychol.* 2:118. doi: 10.3389/fpsyg.2011.00118

Klimesch, W., Sauseng, P., and Hanslmayr, S. (2007). EEG alpha oscillations: the inhibition-timing hypothesis. *Brain Res. Rev.* 53, 63–88. doi: 10.1016/j.brainresrev.2006.06.003

Koeneke, S., Lutz, K., Esslen, M., and Jäncke, L. (2006a). How finger tapping practice enhances efficiency of motor control. *Neuroreport* 17, 1565–1569. doi: 10.1097/01.wnr.0000234748.80936.1d

Koeneke, S., Lutz, K., Herwig, U., Ziemann, U., and Jäncke, L. (2006b). Extensive training of elementary finger tapping movements changes the pattern of motor cortex excitability. *Exp. Brain Res.* 174, 199–209. doi: 10.1007/s00221-006-0440-8

Kranczioch, C., Mathews, S., Dean, P. J., and Sterr, A. (2009). On the equivalence of executed and imagined movements: evidence from lateralized motor and nonmotor potentials. *Hum. Brain Mapp.* 30, 3275–3286. doi: 10.1002/hbm.20748

Lotze, M., Scheler, G., Tan, H. R., Braun, C., and Birbaumer, N. (2003). The musician's brain: functional imaging of amateurs and professionals during performance and imagery. *Neuroimage* 20, 1817–1829. doi: 10.1016/j.neuroimage.2003.07.018

Naito, E., Kochiyama, T., Kitada, R., Nakamura, S., Matsumura, M., Yonekura, Y., et al. (2002). Internally simulated movement sensations during motor imagery activate cortical motor areas and the cerebellum. *J. Neurosci.* 22, 3683–3691.

Neuper, C., Scherer, R., Reiner, M., and Pfurtscheller, G. (2005). Imagery of motor actions: differential effects of kinesthetic and visual-motor mode of imagery in single-trial EEG. *Brain Res. Cogn. Brain Res.* 25, 668–677. doi: 10.1016/j.cogbrainres.2005.08.014

Pangelinan, M. M., Kagerer, F. A., Momen, B., Hatfield, B. D., and Clark, J. E. (2011). Electrocortical dynamics reflect age-related differences in movement kinematics among children and adults. *Cereb. Cortex* 21, 737–747. doi: 10.1093/cercor/bhq162

Pfurtscheller, G., and Lopes Da Silva, F. H. (1999). Event-related EEG/MEG synchronization and desynchronization: basic principles. *Clin. Neurophysiol.* 110, 1842–1857. doi: 10.1016/s1388-2457(99)00141-8

Pfurtscheller, G., and Neuper, C. (1994). Event-related synchronization of mu rhythm in the EEG over the cortical hand area in man. *Neurosci. Lett.* 174, 93–96. doi: 10.1016/0304-3940(94)90127-9

Pfurtscheller, G., and Neuper, C. (1997). Motor imagery activates primary sensorimotor area in humans. *Neurosci. Lett.* 239, 65–68. doi: 10.1016/s0304-3940(97)00889-6

Pfurtscheller, G., and Neuper, C. (2006). Future prospects of ERD/ERS in the context of brain-computer interface (BCI) developments. *Prog. Brain Res.* 159, 433–437. doi: 10.1016/s0079-6123(06)59028-4

Pfurtscheller, G., Neuper, C., and Krausz, G. (2000). Functional dissociation of lower and upper frequency mu rhythms in relation to voluntary limb movement. *Clin. Neurophysiol.* 111, 1873–1879. doi: 10.1016/s1388-2457(00)00428-4

Pfurtscheller, G., Stancák, A., and Neuper, C. (1996). Event-related synchronization (ERS) in the alpha band—an electrophysiological correlate of cortical idling: a review. *Int. J. Psychophysiol.* 24, 39–46. doi: 10.1016/s0167-8760(96)00066-9

Picard, N., Matsuzaka, Y., and Strick, P. L. (2013). Extended practice of a motor skill is associated with reduced metabolic activity in M1. *Nat. Neurosci.* 16, 1340–1347. doi: 10.1038/nn.3477

Pollok, B., Latz, D., Krause, V., Butz, M., and Schnitzler, A. (2014). Changes of motor-cortical oscillations associated with motor learning. *Neuroscience* 275C, 47–53. doi: 10.1016/j.neuroscience.2014.06.008

Porro, C. A., Francescato, M. P., Cettolo, V., Diamond, M. E., Baraldi, P., Zuiani, C., et al. (1996). Primary motor and sensory cortex activation during motor performance and motor imagery: a functional magnetic resonance imaging study. *J. Neurosci.* 16, 7688–7698.

Qin, Y., Xu, P., and Yao, D. (2010). A comparative study of different references for EEG default mode network: the use of the infinity reference. *Clin. Neurophysiol.* 121, 1981–1991. doi: 10.1016/j.clinph.2010.03.056

Rauch, S. L., Whalen, P. J., Savage, C. R., Curran, T., Kendrick, A., Brown, H. D., et al. (1997). Striatal recruitment during an implicit sequence learning task as measured by functional magnetic resonance imaging. *Hum. Brain Mapp.* 5, 124–132. doi: 10.1002/(sici)1097-0193(1997)5:2<124::aid-hbm6>3.3.co;2-p

Rizzolatti, G., and Craighero, L. (2004). The mirror-neuron system. *Annu. Rev. Neurosci.* 27, 169–192. doi: 10.1146/annurev.neuro.27.070203.144230

Rizzolatti, G., and Sinigaglia, C. (2010). The functional role of the parieto-frontal mirror circuit: interpretations and misinterpretations. *Nat. Rev. Neurosci.* 11, 264–274. doi: 10.1038/nrn2805

Roth, R., Decety, J., Raybaudi, M., Massarelli, R., Delonmartin, C., Segebarth, C., et al. (1996). Possible involvement of primary motor cortex in mentally simulated movement: a functional magnetic resonance imaging study. *Neuroreport* 7, 1280–1284. doi: 10.1097/00001756-199605170-00012

Sauseng, P., Klimesch, W., Stadler, W., Schabus, M., Doppelmayr, M., Hanslmayr, S., et al. (2005). A shift of visual spatial attention is selectively associated with human EEG alpha activity. *Eur.J. Neurosci.* 22, 2917–2926. doi: 10.1111/j.1460-9568.2005.04482.x

Seidler, R. D., Purushotham, A., Kim, S. G., Ugurbil, K., Willingham, D., and Ashe, J. (2005). Neural correlates of encoding and expression in implicit sequence learning. *Exp. Brain Res.* 165, 114–124. doi: 10.1007/s00221-005-2284-z

Singer, R. N., Cauraugh, J. H., Chen, D. P., Steinberg, G. M., and Frehlich, S. G. (1996). Visual search, anticipation and reactive comparisons between highly-skilled and beginning tennis players. *J. Appl. Sport Psychol.* 8, 9–26. doi: 10.1080/10413209608406305

Turella, L., Wurm, M. F., Tucciarelli, R., and Lingnau, A. (2013). Expertise in action observation: recent neuroimaging findings and future perspectives. *Front. Hum. Neurosci.* 7:637. doi: 10.3389/fnhum.2013.00637

Vigário, R. N. (1997). Extraction of ocular artefacts from EEG using independent component analysis. *Electroencephalogr. Clin. Neurophysiol.* 103, 395–404. doi: 10.1016/s0013-4694(97)00042-8

Waldschmidt, J. G., and Ashby, F. G. (2011). Cortical and striatal contributions to automaticity in information-integration categorization. *Neuroimage* 56, 1791–1802. doi: 10.1016/j.neuroimage.2011.02.011

Weisberg, J., Van Turennout, M., and Martin, A. (2007). A neural system for learning about object function. *Cereb. Cortex* 17, 513–521. doi: 10.1093/cercor/bhj176

Worden, M. S., Foxe, J. J., Wang, N., and Simpson, G. V. (2000). Anticipatory biasing of visuospatial attention indexed by retinotopically specific alpha-band electroencephalography increases over occipital cortex. *J. Neurosci.* 20, RC63–RC66.

Wright, M. J., Bishop, D. T., Jackson, R. C., and Abernethy, B. (2010). Functional MRI reveals expert-novice differences during sport-related anticipation. *Neuroreport* 21, 94–98. doi: 10.1097/wnr.0b013e328333dff2

Xiong, J., Ma, L., Wang, B., Narayana, S., Duff, E. P., Egan, G. F., et al. (2009). Long-term motor training induced changes in regional cerebral blood flow in both task and resting states. *Neuroimage* 45, 75–82. doi: 10.1016/j.neuroimage.2008.11.016

Yarrow, K., Brown, P., and Krakauer, J. W. (2009). Inside the brain of an elite athlete: the neural processes that support high achievement in sports. *Nat. Rev. Neurosci.* 10, 585–596. doi: 10.1038/nrn2700

18

Lateralization of music processing with noises in the auditory cortex: an fNIRS study

Hendrik Santosa[1], Melissa Jiyoun Hong[2†] and Keum-Shik Hong[1,3]*

[1] Department of Cogno-Mechatronics Engineering, Pusan National University, Busan, South Korea
[2] Department of Education Policy and Social Analysis, Columbia University, New York, NY, USA
[3] School of Mechanical Engineering, Pusan National University, Busan, South Korea

***Correspondence:**
Keum-Shik Hong, School of Mechanical Engineering, Pusan National University, 2 Busandaehak-ro, Geumjeong-gu, Busan 609-735, South Korea
e-mail: kshong@pusan.ac.kr

The present study is to determine the effects of background noise on the hemispheric lateralization in music processing by exposing 14 subjects to four different auditory environments: music segments only, noise segments only, music + noise segments, and the entire music interfered by noise segments. The hemodynamic responses in both hemispheres caused by the perception of music in 10 different conditions were measured using functional near-infrared spectroscopy. As a feature to distinguish stimulus-evoked hemodynamics, the difference between the mean and the minimum value of the hemodynamic response for a given stimulus was used. The right-hemispheric lateralization in music processing was about 75% (instead of continuous music, only music segments were heard). If the stimuli were only noises, the lateralization was about 65%. But, if the music was mixed with noises, the right-hemispheric lateralization has increased. Particularly, if the noise was a little bit lower than the music (i.e., music level 10~15%, noise level 10%), the entire subjects showed the right-hemispheric lateralization: This is due to the subjects' effort to hear the music in the presence of noises. However, too much noise has reduced the subjects' discerning efforts.

Keywords: functional near-infrared spectroscopy (fNIRS), auditory cortex, lateralization, background noise, music processing

INTRODUCTION

Asymmetry in functional responses in the right and left hemispheres of a human brain has been observed (Toga and Thompson, 2003). Notable brain asymmetries include the dominance of the auditory cortex in the left hemisphere for speech processing (particularly, the left-side planum temporale region for consonant-vowel syllables, see Jancke et al. (2002), the theory of asymmetric sampling in time (Giraud et al., 2007), and that in the right hemisphere for music processing (Bever and Chiarello, 1974; Tervaniemi and Hugdahl, 2003). This asymmetric response is observed even in infants: speech (Dehaene-Lambertz et al., 2002) and music (Perani et al., 2010). However, Shtyrov et al. (1998) showed that, in a noisy environment, the involvement of the left auditory cortex in discerning speeches considerably decreases, while that of the right hemisphere increases. This reveals that the existence of background noise in spoken words diminishes the dominant role of the left hemisphere in the speech processing (i.e., non-lateralization) (Wong et al., 2008).

Music processing is one of the most complex cognitive activities that the human brain performs. The detailed mechanism of music processing is not well understood yet. Even Bever and Chiarello (1974) had shown that the right lateralization in music processing is even higher among musicians than non-musicians, but still there are contradicting results among different genders, musicians, and non-musicians (Schuppert et al., 2000; Ono et al., 2011). To the best of our knowledge, the influence of background noise in music processing has not been fully investigated yet. The objectives of this study are first to investigate whether, in the presence of noise, the right-lateralization of music processing (in contrast to the speech processing) is destructed or not and second to characterize the noise levels in the music to any differences in the hemodynamic responses between the right and left auditory cortices.

In a live music environment, it will be interesting to categorize the level of noise that would not disturb the music. Under the assumption that the right-hemispheric laterization exists (for some people), it will become the case that the introduced noise does not destroy the right laterization in enjoying the music. Three distinguishing features of a sound are its intensity, frequency, and perception duration, which may elicit different responses to different humans. The study of audition (i.e., hearing a sound transmitted as acoustic waves) involves the examination of the sensory responses to the surrounding environment. To measure sensory responses, various modalities have been pursued in the past: For instance, electroencephalography (EEG) for detecting the language processing (Sinai and Pratt, 2003; Zaehle et al., 2007; Kuhnis et al., 2013b) and the music processing (Meyer et al., 2006; Headley and Pare, 2013) in the auditory cortex, and for detecting the P300 signals in the motor cortex (Turnip et al., 2011; Turnip and Hong, 2012; Khan et al., 2014; Soekadar et al., 2014) magnetoencephalography (MEG) for the auditory cortex (Shtyrov et al., 2012) and the motor cortex (Boulenger et al., 2012), functional magnetic resonance imaging (fMRI) for the auditory cortex (Warrier et al., 2009; Wong et al., 2010) and the frontal cortex (May et al., 2014; Zhou et al., 2014), the positron emission tomography (Tervaniemi et al., 2000), and functional near-infrared spectroscopy (fNIRS) for the motor cortex (Hu et al., 2013) and for the prefrontal cortex (Guhn et al., 2014).

fNIRS is a non-invasive method that measures the absorbed quantity of near-infrared light in the 650~950 nm wavelength range. fNIRS can detect the hemoglobin concentration changes in response to neural activities. For brain imaging, fNIRS offers higher temporal resolution than fMRI and higher spatial resolution than EEG. Particularly, while fNIRS can be used in a natural environment (particularly important in music processing), fMRI should be used in its designated place (or at least a simultaneous hearing and measurement cannot be done without an earphone). Recent fNIRS studies include the hemodynamics analyses in the prefrontal cortex (Hu et al., 2012; Naseer et al., 2013; Santosa et al., 2013; Bhutta et al., 2014), the motor cortex (Aqil et al., 2012a; Kamran and Hong, 2013, 2014), the visual cortex (Hong and Nguyen, 2014), the motor imagery (Naseer and Hong, 2013), and the somatosensory cortex (Hu et al., 2011). Particularly, fNIRS is suitable for studying the auditory cortex because of its non-invasiveness, mobility, cost, and most importantly silence of the equipment. On the other hand, fMRI is relatively problematic in studying the auditory cortex because its measurements are accompanied by acoustic noise resulting from slice selection pulses, cryogen pumping, and magnetic resonance gradient interference (Gaab et al., 2007). To solve the noise problem in fMRI, many schemes have been employed to shield the subject from the machine's acoustic noise, although none of these methods have been proven effective: A few examples are sealing the gradient coil in a vacuum chamber (Katsunuma et al., 2002), using an active noise cancelation (McJury et al., 1997), and utilizing a low-noise gradient-coil design (Mansfield et al., 2001). The noise from an fMRI machine can even interfere with the stimuli designed to evoke neuronal activation: Fuchino et al. (2006) have shown that the level of oxy-hemoglobin in the sensorimotor cortex decreased with the increase of fMRI acoustic noise.

Conducting experiments using fNIRS, on the other hand, is much quieter than using an fMRI system, which makes fNIRS a much more suitable device for experiments related to audio stimulation. Another advantage of fNIRS is that it can detect two main chromophores: oxy-hemoglobin (HbO) and deoxy-hemoglobin (HbR), while fMRI can detect only the BOLD (blood oxygenation level dependent) signal (Plichta et al., 2006). When neuron fires, HbO decreases while HbR increases instantaneously (but it will bring more blood to the area, which will cause the increase of HbO). A drawback of fNIRS is the penetration depth of the light, which is limited to the cortical surface. However, even the relatively poor spatial resolution of fNIRS compared to fMRI (Kovelman et al., 2009) can be ignored due to its other strengths, the relatively faster time resolution than fMRI, low cost, portability, and quietness. While fNIRS enables testing under more relaxed conditions for the subjects, its results on the auditory cortex are relatively rare. The present study is to determine the effects of background noise in music processing: Fourteen healthy subjects participate, and the activations in the auditory cortices are recorded with fNIRS. Specifically, four different sound environments involving ten different conditions are designed for this experiment: music segments only, noise segments only, music segments including noise, and the entire music with noise segments. To investigate this, we examined the hemodynamic responses from 44 channels for three noise categories in both hemispheres.

Our interest exists in finding the (subjective) level of noise that does not disturb listening to music as well as hemispheric lateralization. The following questions will be pursued: (i) Are there more hemodynamic changes in the right auditory cortex than the left auditory cortex, when people hear music. Instead of listening to continuous music, music segments will be exposed to the subjects so that they can focus on. (ii) Can noise alone cause a similar behavior like music segments, or will it bring any difference? (iii) What would be the level of noise that distort the hearing status? (iv) What would be the noise enterance effects when listening to the entire music. As a feature to tell any difference, the gap between the mean value and the minimum value of the hemodynamic responses caused by various conditions will be used.

MATERIALS AND METHODS

SUBJECTS

Fourteen subjects (age: 28 ± 5 years; 7 males and 7 females, 12 right-handed and 2 left-handed) participated in the experiment, see **Table 1**. In this study, the handedness was obtained by asking the subjects about a better performance for use of a hand. Thirteen subjects knew (understood) the music and three subjects were musicians. The definition of musician in this work is whether they are able to play the music with piano or not. The response between musicians and non-musicians is known distinctly different (Kraus and Chandrasekaran, 2010; Kuhnis et al., 2013a, 2014). All musicians (1 male and 2 females; primary musical instrument: piano; mean age 25 ± 2 years) started their musical training between 6 and 12 years. They had more than 16 ± 2 years of musical training and practiced their musical instrument for 1.5 h/day when they started to learn piano. We selected the same number of subjects between male and female to examine a possible gender difference in the hemispheric lateralization (Shirao et al., 2005). All of them had normal hearing and none had a history of any neurological disorder. To reduce noise and artifacts, the subjects were asked to remain relaxed with closed eyes by enjoying the music and to avoid motions during the experiment (i.e., head movement, eye blinking, etc.). During the experiment, the subjects were asked to listen the auditory stimuli attentively (not passively), since selective attention is important to the activation pattern in the auditory cortex (Jancke et al., 1999). Moreover, musicians were asked to imagine playing the music with a piano. The work was approved by the Institutional Review Board of Pusan National University. The subjects were informed about the experimentation and written consents were obtained, which was conducted in accordance with the ethical standards encoded in the latest Declaration of Helsinki.

AUDIO STIMULI

Figure 1 shows the experimental paradigm used in this work. The audio stimuli (music) was *Für Elise* composed by Ludwig van Beethoven. The entire length of the music was 165 s. One

Table 1 | 14 Subjects in experiment.

Subject	Gender	Age	-handed	(Pre-knowledge on the music)
1	Male	29	Left	Yes
2	Male	27	Left	Yes
3	Male	34	Right	No
4	Male	29	Right	Yes
5*	Male	26	Right	Yes
6	Male	31	Right	Yes
7	Male	30	Right	Yes
8	Female	26	Right	Yes
9	Female	25	Right	Yes
10	Female	23	Right	Yes
11	Female	28	Right	Yes
12*	Female	25	Right	Yes
13*	Female	23	Right	Yes
14	Female	26	Right	Yes

They can play the music.

experiment consists of four stages involving ten conditions. The first 200 s after the pre-initiation trial constitutes Stage 1 (S1), which examines the basic condition (that is, a music hearing). In S1, the subjects are exposed to 25 s rest and 15 s music for 5 times (it is noted that the pre-initiation trial is not included in the analysis). The objective of S1 is to examine which side (right or left) in the brain is more active upon a musical stimulus. Stage 2 (S2) is the next 200 s after S1 that involves two different noise levels. Therefore, S2 constitutes three conditions: no noise (NN), mid-level noise (MN), and high-level noise (HN). The objective of S2 is to examine whether the noise alone can cause a similar response like the music in S1. Then, the subsequent 200 s after S2 becomes Stage 3 (S3), in which mixed music and noise segments are repeated 5 times. The objective of S3 is to find out whether a music + noise segment will induce more efforts in the brain than the cases of music or noise segments alone. Distinguishing NN, MN, and HN, 3 conditions are examined in S3. Finally, the interruption of noise when hearing the music has been mimicked in Stage 4 (S4). For comparison purposes, similar noise conditions like S2 and S3 are made in S4, yielding another 3 conditions. The noises introduced to the music appear in a pseudo random order. The durations of music and noise segments in S1~S4 are the same. The shaded boxes in S3 and S4 indicate the time periods where noises enter the music. The total experimental time was 14 min and 50 s. The music and noises were digitally mixed using the Adobe Audition software (a WAV-format file: 16 bit, 44,100 Hz, stereo). The same earphone (Sony MDR-NC100D; digital noise canceling earbuds) with the same sound level setting was used across the subjects.

NOISE LEVELS

The y-axis in **Figure 1** denotes the relative amplitude of the audio signal (its max. scale has 30,000 sample values, which corresponds to 100%) in the Adobe Audition software. In this work, the high-level noise is defined to be the white noise whose amplitude reaches 20% of the full scale. The mid-level noise means 10% in the full scale. To provide variability, the noises were introduced in a pseudo-random order (15 s for each stimulus). The average amplitude of the music was about 10–15% in the y-axis.

fNIRS DATA AND PROCESSING

Figure 2 shows the optodes configuration of the fNIRS system (DYNOT: DYnamic Near-infrared Optical Tomography; NIRx Medical Technologies, Brooklyn, NY) for imaging the auditory cortices in the left and right hemispheres. The distance between an emitter and a detector is 23 mm. The data were acquired at a sampling rate of 1.81 Hz and for two wavelengths (760 and 830 nm). A total of 22 channels were measured from 8 emitters (black circles) and 7 detectors (white circles) in both hemispheres. All the lights in the room were turned off during the experiment to minimize signal contamination from the ambient light sources. The optodes were placed on the scalp above the left and right auditory cortices. Ch. 16 in both left/right hemispheres was set to coincide with the T3/T4 locations, respectively, in the International 10–20 system. Since the optodes configuration in **Figure 2** covers the entire auditory cortex, the averaged value from the 22 channels is used in the analysis.

Relative changes of the concentrations of HbO and HbR were computed using the modified Beer-Lambert Law as follows,

$$\Delta A_i(\lambda, k) = \left[a^{HbO}(\lambda)\Delta c_i^{HbO}(k) + a^{HbR}(\lambda)\Delta c_i^{HbR}(k)\right] d_i l_i, \quad (1)$$

where $\Delta A\,(\cdot, k)$ is the absorbance variation at time k; the subscript i denotes the channel number; λ is the wavelength of the laser source; a^{HbO} and a^{HbR} are the absorption coefficients of HbO and HbR, respectively; Δc^{HbO} and Δc^{HbR} are the concentration changes of HbO and HbR, respectively; d is the differential path length factor (in this study, constant values $d = 7.15$ for $\lambda = 760$ nm and $d = 5.98$ for $\lambda = 830$ nm were used for all the channels), and l is the distance between a source and a detector.

To analyse the fNIRS data, the open-source software NIRS-SPM (Ye et al., 2009) was utilized in our own Matlab® (Mathworks, Natick, MA) code. The respiration and cardiac noises contained in the hemodynamic responses were removed by a low-pass filter of a cut-off frequency 0.15 Hz.

CLASSIFICATION FEATURE

The difference between the mean and the minimum value of a given hemodynamic response has been used as a feature to classify whether the hemispheric lateralization occurred or not. **Figure 3** depicts a typical activated hemodynamic response obtained by convolving a stimulus pattern and the impulse hemodynamic response function as

$$h_M(k) = \sum_{n=-\infty}^{\infty} Box(k)\, h(k-n), \quad (2)$$

where $h_M\,(k)$ denotes the "modeled" hemodynamic response to be used as a reference signal, $Box(k)$ is the box-type stimulus pattern (in this paper, the 15 s activation period) and $h(k)$ is the impulse hemodynamic response function adopted from the SPM8 (Wellcome Trust Centre for Neuroimaging, London, UK)

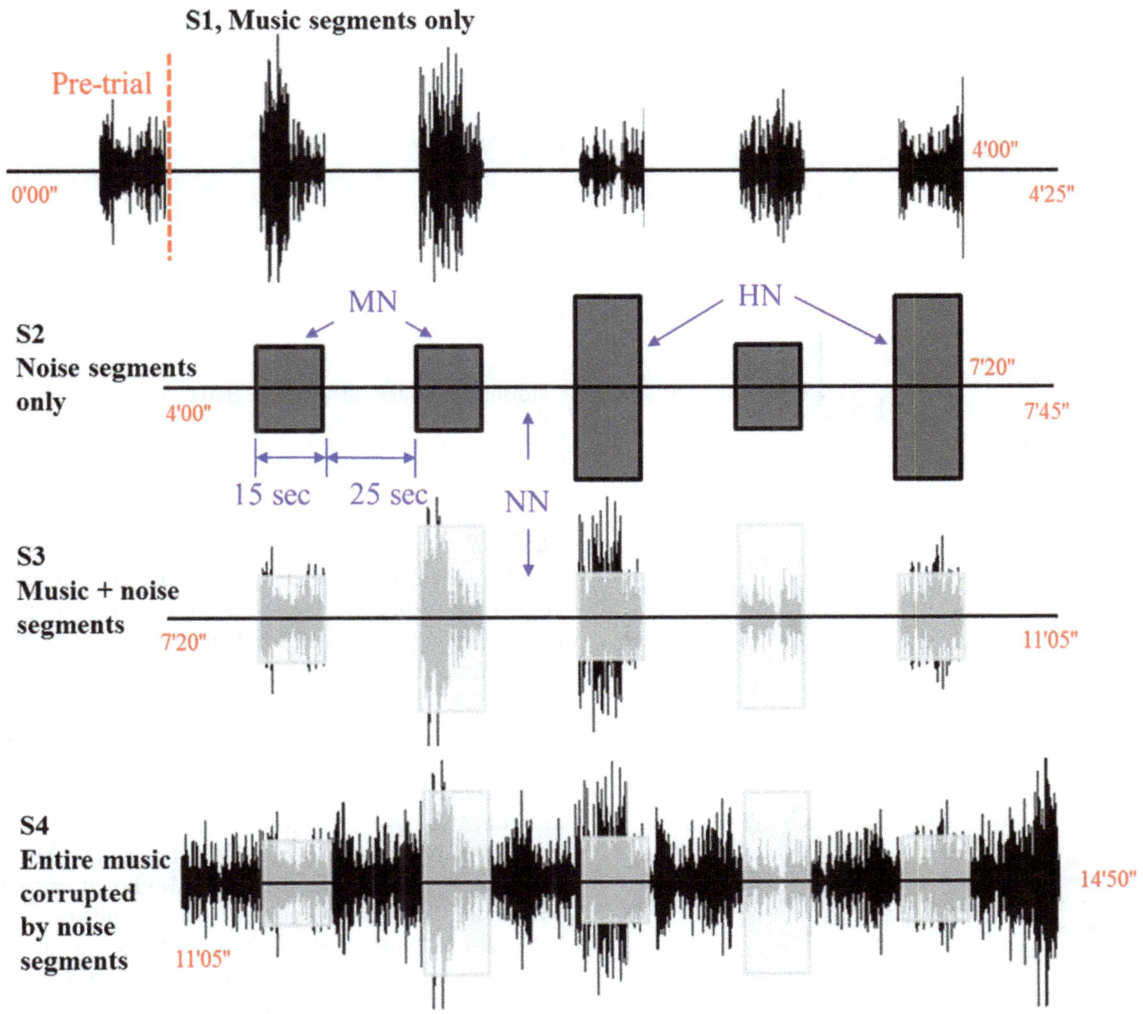

FIGURE 1 | Experimental paradigm. Four different sound conditions. The level of noise (i.e., NN, no noise; MN, mid-level noise; HN, high-level noise) changes in a pseudo-random order.

(Friston et al., 2008). For example, the curve in **Figure 3** shows that the mean value is 0.36 μM, the minimum value is -0.12 μM, and therefore the difference is 0.48 μM. The reason for using the gap between the mean and the minimum value of the hemodynamic response as a classification index in this work is that, with the current experimental paradigm in **Figure 1**, the hemodynamic response may not come back to the baseline value in a short time interval after each stimulus. Actually, it was so and the baseline drifting has been compensated by the mean-min difference.

STATISTICAL ANALYSIS

The estimation of the cortical activation is the most important factor in the analysis of fNIRS data. Previous studies showed that the activation could be statistically estimated by fitting the measured response to a regression model (Hu et al., 2010; Aqil et al., 2012b). Let $\mathbf{h}_i^j \in R^{N\times 1}$ be the measured fNIRS data at the i-th channel, the superscript j denote the j-th stimulus (i.e., the total 20 stimuli obtained by 5 stimuli/condition × 4 conditions), and N be the size of fNIRS data for each stimulus (in this study, $N = 72$ for the period of 15 s stimulus and 25 s rest using the sampling frequency of 1.81 Hz). Then, the general linear regression model is formulated as follows,

$$\mathbf{h}_i^j = \phi_i^j \mathbf{h}_\mathrm{M} + \psi_i^j \cdot \mathbf{1} + \boldsymbol{\varepsilon}_i^j, \tag{3}$$

where $\mathbf{h}_\mathrm{M} \in R^{N\times 1}$ is the modeled hemodynamic response obtained by (2), $\mathbf{1} \in R^{N\times 1}$ is a column vector of ones for correcting the baseline, ϕ is the unknown coefficient that indicates the activity strength of the modeled hemodynamic response, ψ is the coefficient to compensate the baseline drift of the signal, and $\boldsymbol{\varepsilon} \in R^{N\times 1}$ is the error term in the regression model. In this paper, the coefficient ϕ is estimated by using the *robustfit* function available in Matlab™ as follows,

$$\left(\begin{bmatrix} \hat{\phi}_i^j \\ \hat{\psi}_i^j \end{bmatrix}, stats \right) = robustfit([\mathbf{1}\ \mathbf{h}_\mathrm{M}], \mathbf{h}_i^j), \tag{4}$$

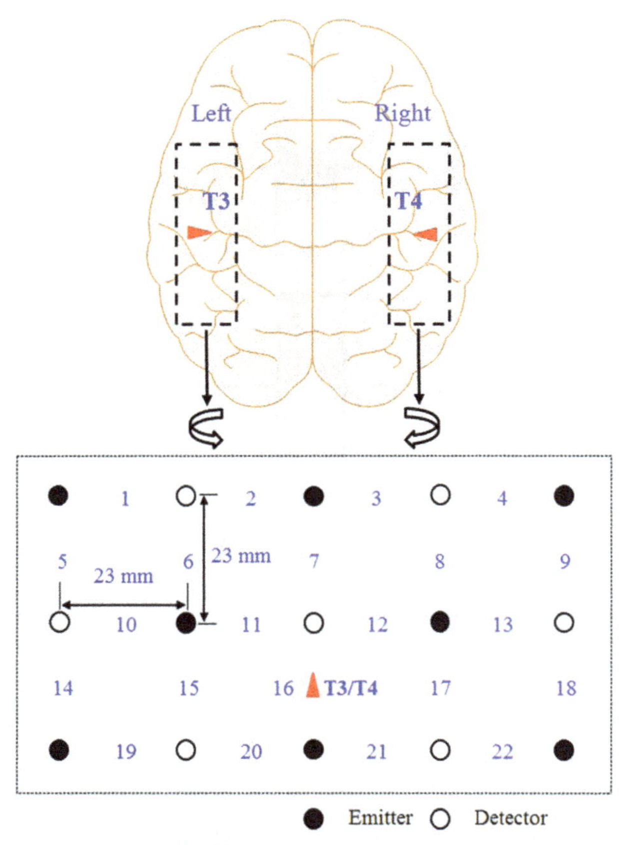

FIGURE 2 | Optodes configuration. Numbers represent the measurement channels: The channel number 16 coincides with the T3/T4 locations in the International 10–20 System.

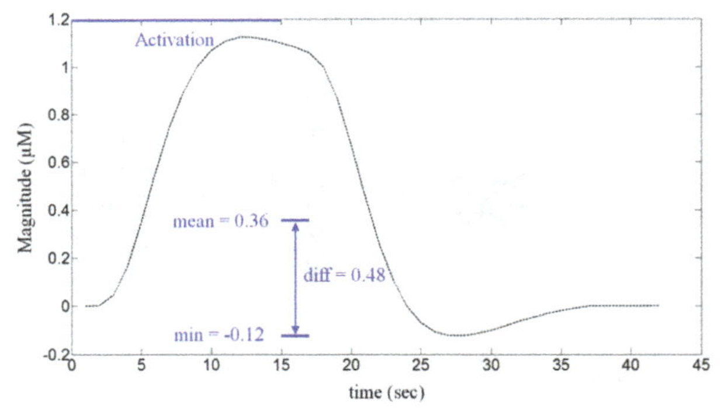

FIGURE 3 | The defined feature for classification. The difference between the mean and the minimum value of the HbO obtained from a 15 s stimulus (in μM).

where $\hat{\phi}_i^j$ and $\hat{\psi}_i^j$ denotes the estimate of ϕ_i^j and ψ_i^j, respectively, and *stats* denotes the statistical data including the *t*-value, *p*-value, standard errors, etc.

The idea is to test the null hypothesis that the estimated parameter $\hat{\phi}_i^j$ is equal to zero or not. Furthermore, if $\hat{\phi}_i^j$ is positive, the particular activation is assumed to be active, and if it is negative, the particular activation is not active for the *j*-the stimulus at the *i*-th channel, in which the *t*-value test has been used. In this paper, the *t*-value was computed using the following equation,

$$t_i^j = \frac{\hat{\phi}_i^j}{SE(\hat{\phi}_i^j)}, \tag{5}$$

where *SE* is the standard error of the estimated coefficient. We used two criteria to assess the selection reliability of a particular activation for further analysis. They were $t_i^j > 0$ and $p_i^j < \alpha$, where *p* denotes the *p*-value (in this work, $\alpha = 0.05$ was set). Alternatively, it could be done by checking $t_i^j > t_{crt}$, where t_{crt} denotes the critical *t*-value that depends on the degree of freedom (i.e., 71, which is *N* -1). In this case, $t_{crt} = 1.994$.

RESULTS

The hemodynamics changes in the auditory cortex upon the occurrence of noises in music processing have been examined. Using the paradigm in **Figure 1**, four different stages involving ten conditions in combination with three different noise levels were tested. The three-digit numbers in **Table 2** indicate the differences between the mean and the minimum value of the HbO concentration change in both left and right auditory cortices for 14 subjects (Subject 1~14). S1~S4 represent four different experimental stages in **Figure 1**. It is reminded that only those hemodynamic responses whose $p < 0.05$ and $t > 0$ were counted for averaging over 22 channels. It is also noted that (i) the data outside the 3 standard deviations were excluded (i.e., 9 cases in bold-italic in **Table 2** were outliers, see Subject 5 and Subject 12) and (ii) if a right-left difference is not significant (i.e., difference < 0.1σ), it was considered to be the same (they were marked in italic font). **Table 3** summarizes **Table 2**. The following observations are made:

i) Music segments stage (S1): This stage was to determine which brain side was dominant in music processing. Nine subjects showed the higher activation in the right auditory cortex, whereas three subjects showed it in the left auditory cortex (out of 14 subjects, Subject 12 was an outlier and the data of Subject 10 was undistinguishable). Therefore, the right-hemispheric lateralization in music processing is about 75% (i.e., 9/12).
ii) Noise segments stage (S2): This stage intended to characterize the auditory reponses to various noises. When there was no noise (see the first row in S2), a significant difference was not seen between the right and left auditory cortices, considering that two data (Subject 10, Subject 14) were un-distinguishable and one data (Subject 12) was an outlier. But, in the mid- and high-noise conditions, there was a slight increase in the number of subjects who showed the higher hemodynamics response in the right auditory cortex (i.e., 15/23, which is about 65%).
iii) Mixed music and noise stage (S3): Contrary to S1 (music only) and S2 (noise only), mixed signals of noise and music

were exposed to the subjects. Considering that the sound level of the music was about 10~15%, the mid-level noise and music segments showed the highest level of right-lateralization over the subjects (see the second row in S3). Actually, removing two undistinguishable subjects (Subject 11, Subject 14), all twelve subjects out of 14 subjects showed the higher activation in the right auditory cortex. This is due to that the subjects tried to hear the music in the presence of noise (recall that the noise level was 10%). But, if the noise level became higher than the sound level of music (i.e., the high-noise condition, 20%), the number of subjects who showed the higher activation in the right auditory cortex had reduced to 10. Another interesting observation was found from the first row in S3, which provided no sound in the middle of music + noise segments. No sound itself had shown almost the same level of right-lateralization in terms of number of subjects as the case of music + high-noise condition.

iv) The entire music with noise segments (S4): The final stage was to investigate the effect of noise interruptions in hearing music. When there was no noise (see the first row in S4), the tendency of the right-hemispheric lateralization was exactly the same as the case of S1 (i.e., 75%). Also, even upon the interruptions of noise, the tendency was similar.

For the 140 cases (i.e., 14 subjects × 10 conditions), 9 cases were outliers, 11 cases showed no significant difference, 32 cases showed the higher left auditory cortex, and finally 88 cases showed the higher right auditory cortex. Therefore, the overall lateralization across all the experimental conditions was about 73.3% (i.e., 88/120); specifically, for female 81.1% (i.e., 43/53) and for male 67.2% (i.e., 45/67). It is also noted that 20 cases were excluded.

Now, for analyzing the tendency/strength of lateralization, only the cases showing that the right hemisphere is more active than the left hemisphere were further considered (bold font). **Table 4** shows the average and its standard deviation of such cases. That is, the value 2.080 in S1 is the average of 1.453, 2.596, 2.458, 1.704, 2.494, 2.394, 2.357, 2.013, and 1.253 from **Table 2**. The following observations are made. (i) Comparing S1 and S4 in **Table 4**, the background noise intensifies the hemispheric lateralization (i.e., the Right Avg—Left Avg value has increased from 0.311 for music only condition to 0.533 for the mid-noise condition and 0.743 for the high-noise condition, respectively). (ii) As seen in the last column of S2, the difference in the mid-noise condition (i.e., 0.536) is larger than the other two cases (i.e., 0.315 and 0.403). This may reveal the fact that too much noise does destroy the subject's discerning efforts for music in the presence of noise. (iii) In S3, even if there is no sound, the difference in the right auditory cortex was higher than that of the left (i.e., 0.566). This reflects that, in the presence of noise, the subjects tried to listen to the music and this effort was continued even if there is no sound. A similar effort from the subjects was also shown in the mid- and high-noise conditions. Overall, the discerning efforts for music from noises has been seen, which is consistent throughout all three conditions.

Table 2 | Differences between the mean and the minimum value of the HbO concentration (unit: μM, scale-up by 10^{-4}).

Subject \ Condition		Subject 1		Subject 2		Subject 3		Subject 4		Subject 5*		Subject 6		Subject 7		Subject 8		Subject 9		Subject 10		Subject 11		Subject 12*		Subject 13*		Subject 14		Avg	Std
		Left	Right	Left	Right	Left	Right	Left	Right	Left	Right	Left	Right	Left	Right	Left	Right	Left	Right	Left	Right	Left	Right	Left	Right	Left	Right	Left	Right		
S1	Music only	2.814	2.749	**1.453**	**1.626**	**2.596**	**3.024**	**2.458**	**2.569**	1.897	1.672	1.709	1.620	**1.704**	**1.886**	**2.494**	**3.017**	**2.394**	**2.487**	*1.190*	*1.191*	**2.357**	**2.762**	4.012	***5.963***	**2.013**	**2.840**	**1.253**	**1.313**	2.324	0.969
S2	No sound	3.015	2.933	1.717	1.613	**2.696**	**2.940**	**2.614**	**3.059**	**2.709**	**2.799**	2.589	2.166	3.154	2.975	**2.903**	**3.234**	**2.297**	**2.729**	*1.120*	*1.127*	2.749	2.746	4.152	***6.708***	**2.537**	**2.888**	*1.644*	*1.679*	2.696	1.017
	Mid noise	**2.069**	**3.086**	1.618	1.466	**2.361**	**2.644**	*2.433*	*2.474*	2.411	2.140	**1.298**	**1.639**	**2.559**	**3.466**	**2.551**	**3.158**	**2.244**	**2.531**	1.065	0.983	*2.730*	*2.763*	3.081	***5.886***	*2.171*	*2.173*	**1.088**	**1.397**	2.339	0.948
	High noise	**2.540**	**2.824**	2.954	2.053	**2.890**	**3.015**	2.580	2.174	3.478	2.518	3.787	3.492	**1.640**	**1.940**	3.131	2.654	**1.894**	**2.613**	**0.948**	**1.257**	**2.158**	**2.417**	**1.886**	**2.387**	**2.131**	**2.861**	*1.131*	*1.135*	2.375	0.720
S3	No sound	**2.948**	**3.083**	**2.210**	**2.380**	**3.034**	**3.325**	2.385	2.193	**2.407**	**3.076**	**2.359**	**2.758**	**4.103**	**4.862**	**2.644**	**3.316**	**1.510**	**3.412**	**0.878**	**1.239**	**2.814**	**3.117**	2.352	***8.061***	2.840	2.792	1.951	1.464	2.840	1.293
	Mid noise	**2.587**	**2.851**	**0.606**	**0.824**	**1.942**	**2.438**	**2.256**	**2.845**	**2.455**	**3.409**	**2.553**	**3.078**	**2.615**	**2.732**	**2.178**	**2.474**	**2.258**	**2.488**	**0.921**	**1.120**	*2.261*	*2.294*	**2.125**	**3.095**	**2.348**	**2.699**	*1.144*	*1.196*	2.207	0.722
	High noise	3.256	2.304	**1.658**	**2.027**	2.721	2.713	**2.340**	**2.653**	**2.074**	**2.271**	**1.720**	**2.266**	**2.451**	**3.452**	**2.180**	**2.946**	**1.798**	**2.317**	**0.828**	**1.045**	**2.578**	**2.832**	4.766	***8.638***	**2.094**	**2.791**	1.256	1.134	2.540	1.411
S4	Music only	**3.147**	**3.363**	1.878	1.646	**2.691**	**3.217**	**3.060**	**3.233**	**2.927**	**4.379**	**2.300**	**2.695**	**2.093**	**2.199**	3.099	2.994	**2.505**	**3.029**	*1.131*	*1.152*	**2.659**	**3.041**	6.098	***7353***	2.729	2.692	**2.659**	**3.087**	2.966	1.246
	Mid noise	**2.607**	**2.858**	**1.971**	**2.239**	**1.906**	**2.675**	**2.132**	**3.331**	2.880	***6.206***	3.380	2.283	2.848	1.767	2.342	2.332	**1.553**	**2.683**	**0.961**	**1.061**	*2.396*	*2.399*	3.236	***6.470***	**1.918**	**2.132**	**1.923**	**2.252**	2.598	1.186
	High noise	**2.419**	**2.765**	2.676	1.806	2.536	2.258	3.022	2.076	2.675	***4.914***	**1.823**	**3.133**	**1.526**	**2.773**	**1.874**	**2.659**	3.041	2.710	**0.905**	**1.186**	**2.358**	**3.293**	**1.661**	**2.044**	**2.027**	**2.604**	**2.193**	**3.019**	2.428	0.753

Subs. 1~7 are males and 8~14 are females. Bold-face numbers indicate that the mean-min difference in the right hemisphere is larger than that in the left hemisphere.
**indicates the subjects who can play the music.*

Table 3 | Statisics of hemispheric lateralization (from Table 2).

		Left is higher	Undistinguishable (diff. < 0.1 Std)	Right is higher	Outliers
S1	Music only	3(0)	1(1)	9(5)	1(1)
S2	No sound	5(1)	2(2)	6(3)	1(1)
	Mid noise	3(1)	3(2)	7(3)	1(1)
	High noise	5(1)	1(1)	8(5)	0(0)
S3	No sound	3(2)	0(0)	10(4)	1(1)
	Mid noise	0(0)	2(2)	12(5)	0(0)
	High noise	3(1)	0(0)	10(5)	1(1)
S4	Music only	3(2)	1(1)	9(3)	1(1)
	Mid noise	3(1)	1(1)	8(4)	2(1)
	High noise	4(1)	0(0)	9(6)	1(0)
	Grand total	32(10)	11(10)	88(43)	9(7)

The numbers in the parenthesis indicate the number of females (overall: 73.3%, female: 81.1%, male: 67.2%).

Table 4 | Average of only those cases where Right > Left from Table 2.

Condition \ Subject		Left Avg	Left Std	Right Avg	Right Std	Right Avg−Left Avg
S1	Music only	2.080	0.469	2.391	0.594	0.311
S2	No sound	2.626	0.185	2.941	0.167	0.315
	Mid noise	2.024	0.552	2.560	0.724	0.536
	High noise	2.011	0.546	2.414	0.540	0.403
S3	No sound	2.490	0.831	3.057	0.859	0.566
	Mid noise	2.070	0.618	2.504	0.740	0.434
	High noise	1.972	0.480	2.460	0.616	0.488
S4	Music only	2.671	0.324	3.138	0.548	0.467
	Mid noise	1.871	0.441	2.404	0.627	0.533
	High noise	1.865	0.443	2.608	0.606	0.743

Avg and Std denote average and standard deviation, respectively.

DISCUSSION

This was the first fNIRS study to examine whether auditory-cortex activation by background-noise and music stimuli could change the hemispheric lateralization in both hemispheres. To investigate the effects of noise on music processing, the participants were subjected to various levels of noises in different conditions in the experiment. It was found that exposure to any noise compared to no noise led to higher auditory-cortex activation in the right hemisphere. This result, in fact, is in line with the previous MEG data on speech stimuli (Shtyrov et al., 1998), wherein instead the left hemisphere was dominant in the perception and production of speech. However, when high-level noise was introduced, activation was observed in both hemispheres resulting in a lack of lateralization in auditory-cortex activation. This clearly demonstrates that auditory-cortex activation by music stimuli with noise changes the hemispheric lateralization when a sufficiently loud distraction is introduced to reduce the specialized function of the brain. Similar results from the previous studies on speech stimuli show that lateralization occurs in different responses for noisy condition.

fNIRS have its advantages over fMRI. Previous studies have employed fMRI to determine the effects of various stimuli on neuronal activation in the auditory cortex (Scarff et al., 2004). The drawback of this modality is the problematic effect of acoustic noise from baseline activity in the auditory cortex. Whereas fMRI can measure the changes in magnetic susceptibility in the blood, fNIRS can directly measure hemodynamic changes, HbO and HbR. fMRI signals are physiologically ambiguous, because they reflect changes in cerebral blood flow, cerebral blood volume, and oxidative metabolism. Many studies have investigated the correlation between fMRI and fNIRS signals (Yuan and Ye, 2013). By contrast, the present study focused on the HbO values, as they offer results that are more direct than HbR (Plichta et al., 2006).

We employed the fNIRS technique directly because of its inherent advantages in the analyses of sound-evoked activation: indeed, as a brain-imaging tool, it works non-invasive and silent. Lateralization means a more blood flow in one hemisphere in fNIRS. With this, we assume that more neuronal activity has been made in that region (but, this might be caused by different capillaries in that region or from other aspect, which deserves further neurophysiological inverstigation). We obtained all of the music stimuli results by examining the gap between the mean value and the minimum value of the HbO taken from individual channels covering the auditory cortex. This study observed a pattern of HbO activation that supports the view of functional lateralization in the auditory cortex. Since a variety of light penetrates through the scalp, we can get reliable experimental results by using the difference between the mean and the minimum value of the HbO with two criteria (t and p values) for statistical analyses. A possible explanation for the difference between S3 and S4 could be due to the influence of emotional behavior on the classical music. Music may contain features that evoke positive (or negative) emotional responses. Hemispheric lateralization increases when noise appeared in S4, which was different from S3.

Another possible explanation for the differences between the results of S3 and S4 could be the full-length music played in the background while introducing the different level of noise. *Für Elise* composed by Ludwig van Beethoven is a commonly known music that everyone can recognize and possibly imagine. Prior research has shown that music perception and music imagination has similarities in brain activation and neural mechanism (Zatorre et al., 1996). If a continuous music was cut off due to noise for a short period of time, the noise level should not make a difference if the subject can imagine the missing portion of the music. These findings further support the idea of the specialization in the auditory cortex evoked by audio stimuli.

CONCLUSIONS

The main finding of this study was that background noise affects the hemodynamic response in the activation of the auditory cortex in music processing. Under various noise levels throughout the four different stages involving ten conditions of the experiment, the involvement of the right hemisphere's auditory cortex was higher than that of the left hemisphere (overall 73.3%, specifically, 67.1% for male and 81.1% for female). Particularly, the subjects listened to the music segments, the lateralization was 75%. Also, if only noise segments were heard, the lateralization was about 65%. But if the music was mixed with noise, such lateralization tendency became intensified. Particularly, the music + noise segments condition revealed 100% right-lateralization when the music level was 10~15% and the noise level was 10%. However, the noise level became too big (i.e., noise 20%, music 10%), the lateralization had reduced. This is an indication that too much noise diminishes the human's efforts to discern the music from surrounding noises. The obtained results support the theory that the brain is divided into compartments specializing in specific functions.

AUTHOR CONTRIBUTIONS

Hendrik Santosa performed the experiment and carried out the data processing, Melissa Jiyoun Hong provided suggestions to improve the manuscript, and Keum-Shik Hong supervised the research and corrected the entire manuscript. All of the authors read and approved the final manuscript.

ACKNOWLEDGMENTS

This work was supported by the National Research Foundation of Korea (grant no. NRF-2012-R1A2A2A01046411 and NRF-2014-R1A2A1A10049727).

REFERENCES

Aqil, M., Hong, K.-S., Jeong, M.-Y., and Ge, S. S. (2012a). Cortical brain imaging by adaptive filtering of NIRS signal. *Neurosci. Lett.* 514, 35–41. doi: 10.1016/j.neulet.2012.02.048

Aqil, M., Hong, K.-S., Jeong, M.-Y., and Ge, S. S. (2012b). Detection of event-related hemodynamic response to neuroactivation by dynamic modeling of brain activity. *Neuroimage* 63, 553–568. doi: 10.1016/j.neuroimage.2012.07.006

Bever, T. G., and Chiarello, R. J. (1974). Cerebral dominance in musicians and nonmusicians. *Science* 185, 537–539. doi: 10.1126/science.185.4150.537

Bhutta, M. R., Hong, K.-S., Kim, B.-M., Hong, M. J., Kim, Y.-H., and Lee, S.-H. (2014). Note: three wavelengths near-infrared spectroscopy system for compensating the light absorbance by water. *Rev. Sci. Instrum.* 85, 026111. doi: 10.1063/1.4865124

Boulenger, V., Shtyrov, Y., and Pulvermuller, F. (2012). When do you grasp the idea? MEG evidence for instantaneous idiom understanding. *Neuroimage* 59, 3502–3513. doi: 10.1016/j.neuroimage.2011.11.011

Dehaene-Lambertz, G., Dehaene, S., and Hertz-Pannier, L. (2002). Functional neuroimaging of speech perception in infants. *Science* 298, 2013–2015. doi: 10.1126/science.1077066

Friston, K. J., Ashburner, J. T., Kiebel, S., Nichols, T., and Penny, W. (2008). *Statistical Parametric Mapping: The Analysis of Functional Brain Images.* San Diego: Academic Press.

Fuchino, Y., Sato, H., Maki, A., Yamamoto, Y., Katura, T., Obata, A., et al. (2006). Effect of fMRI acoustic noise on sensorimotor activation examined using optical topography. *Neuroimage* 32, 771–777. doi: 10.1016/j.neuroimaging.2006.04.197

Gaab, N., Gabrieli, J. D. E., and Glover, G. H. (2007). Assessing the influence of scanner background noise on auditory processing. II. an fMRI study comparing auditory processing in the absence and presence of recorded scanner noise using a sparse design. *Hum. Brain Mapp.* 28, 721–732. doi: 10.1002/hbm.20299

Giraud, A. L., Kleinschmidt, A., Poeppel, D., Lund, T. E., Frackowiak, R. S. J., and Laufs, H. (2007). Endogenous cortical rhythms determine cerebral specialization for speech perception and production. *Neuron* 56, 1127–1134. doi: 10.1016/j.neuron.2007.09.038

Guhn, A., Dresler, T., Andreatta, M., and Muller, L. D. (2014). Medial prefrontal cortex stimulation modulates the processing of conditioned fear. *Front. Behav. Neurosci.* 8:44. doi: 10.3389/fnbeh.2014.00044

Headley, D. B., and Pare, D. (2013). In sync: Gamma oscillations and emotional memory. *Front. Behav. Neurosci.* 7:170. doi: 10.3389/fnbeh.2013.00170

Hong, K.-S., and Nguyen, H.-D. (2014). State-space of impulse hemodynamic responses over motor, somatosensory, and visual cortices. *Biomed. Opt. Express* 5, 1778–1798. doi: 10.1364/BOE.5.001778

Hu, X.-S., Hong, K.-S., and Ge, S. S. (2011). Recognition of stimulus-evoked neuronal optical response by identifying chaos levels of near-infrared spectroscopy time series. *Neurosci. Lett.* 504, 115–120. doi: 10.1016/j.neulet.2011.09.011

Hu, X.-S., Hong, K.-S., and Ge, S. S. (2012). fNIRS-based online deception decoding. *J. Neural. Eng.* 9:026012. doi: 10.1088/1741-2560/9/2/026012

Hu, X.-S., Hong, K.-S., and Ge, S. S. (2013). Reduction of trial-to-trial variability in functional near-infrared spectroscopy signals by accounting for resting-state functional connectivity. *J. Biomed. Opt.* 18:017003. doi: 10.1117/1.JBO.18.1.017003

Hu, X.-S., Hong, K.-S., Ge, S. S., and Jeong, M.-Y. (2010). Kalman estimator- and general linear model-based on-line brain activation mapping by near-infrared spectroscopy. *Biomed. Eng. Online* 9:82. doi: 10.1186/1475-925X-9-82

Jancke, L., Mirzazade, S., and Shah, N. J. (1999). Attention modulates activity in the primary and the secondary auditory cortex: a functional magnetic resonance imaging study in human subjects. *Neurosci. Lett.* 266, 125–128. doi: 10.1016/S0304-3940(99)00288-8

Jancke, L., Wustenberg, T., Scheich, H., and Heinze, H. J. (2002). Phonetic perception and the temporal cortex. *Neuroimage* 15, 733–746. doi: 10.1006/nimg.2001.1027

Kamran, M. A., and Hong, K.-S. (2013). Linear parameter-varying model and adaptive filtering technique for detecting neuronal activities: an fNIRS study. *J. Neural. Eng.* 10:056002. doi: 10.1088/1741-2560/10/5/056002

Kamran, M. A., and Hong, K.-S. (2014). Reduction of physiological effects in fNRS waveforms for efficient brain-state decoding. *Neurosci. Lett.* 580, 130–136. doi: 10.1016/j.neulet.2014.07.058

Katsunuma, A., Takamori, H., Sakakura, Y., Hamamura, Y., Ogo,Y., and Katayama, R. (2002). Quiet MRI with novel acoustic noise reduction. *Magn. Reson. Mater. Phys.* 13, 139–144. doi: 10.1016/S1352-8661(01)00142-9

Khan, M. J., Hong, M. J., and Hong, K.-S. (2014). Decoding of four movement directions using hybrid NIRS-EEG brain-computer interface. *Front. Hum. Neurosci.* 8:244. doi: 10.3389/fnhum.2014.00244

Kovelman, I., Shalinsky, M. H., White, K. S., Schmitt, S. N., Berens, M. S., Paymer, N., et al. (2009). Dual language use in sign-speech bimodal bilinguals: fNIRS brain-imaging evidence. *Brain. Lang.* 109, 112–123. doi: 10.1016/j.bandl.2008.09.008

Kraus, N., and Chandrasekaran, B. (2010). Music training for the development of auditory skills. *Nat. Rev. Neurosci.* 11, 599–605. doi: 10.1038/nrn2882

Kuhnis, J., Elmer, S., and Jancke, L. (2014). Auditory evoked responses in musicians during passive vowel listening are modulated by functional connectivity between bilateral auditory-related brain regions. *J. Cogn. Neurosci.* 26, 2750–2761. doi: 10.1162/jocn_a_00674

Kuhnis, J., Elmer, S., Meyer, M., and Jancke, L. (2013a). Musicianship boosts perceptual learning of pseudoword-chimeras: an electrophysiological approach. *Brain Topogr.* 26, 110–125. doi: 10.1007/s10548-012-0237-y

Kuhnis, J., Elmer, S., Meyer, M., and Jancke, L. (2013b). The encoding of vowels and temporal speech cues in the auditory cortex of professional musicians: an EEG study. *Neuropsychologia* 51, 1608–1618. doi: 10.1016/j.neuropsychologia.2013.04.007

Mansfield, P., Haywood, B., and Coxon, R. (2001). Active acoustic control in gradient coils for MRI. *Magn. Reson. Med.* 46, 807–818. doi: 10.1002/mrm.1261

May, A. C., Stewart, J. L., Tapert, S. E., and Paulus, M. P. (2014). The effect of age on neural processing of pleasant soft touch stimuli. *Front. Behav. Neurosci.* 8:52. doi: 10.3389/fnbeh.2014.00052

McJury, M., Stewart, R. W., Crawford, D., and Toma, E. (1997). The use of active noise control (ANC) to reduce acoustic noise generated during MRI scanning: some initial results. *Magn. Reson. Med.* 15, 319–322. doi: 10.1016/S0730-725X(96)00337-2

Meyer, M., Baumann, S., and Jancke, L. (2006). Electrical brain imaging reveals spatio-temporal dynamics of timbre perception in humans. *Neuroimage* 32, 1510–1523. doi: 10.1016/j.neuroimage.2006.04.193

Naseer, N., and Hong, K.-S. (2013). Classification of functional near-infrared spectroscopy signals corresponding to the right- and left-wrist motor imagery for development of a brain-computer interface. *Neurosci. Lett.* 553, 84–89. doi: 10.1016/j.neulet.2013.08.021

Naseer, N., Hong, M. J., and Hong, K.-S. (2013). Online binary decision decoding using functional near-infrared spectroscopy for the development of brain-computer interface. *Exp. Brain Res.* 232, 555–564. doi: 10.1007/s00221-013-3764-1

Ono, K., Nakamura, A., Yoshiyama, K., Kinkori, T., Bundo, M., Kato, Y., et al. (2011). The effect of musical experience on hemispheric lateralization in musical feature processing. *Neurosci. Lett.* 496, 1414–1145. doi: 10.1016/j.neulet.2011.04.002

Perani, D., Saccuman, M. C., Scifo, P., Spada, D., Andreolli, G., Rovelli, R., et al. (2010). Functional specializations for music processing in the human newborn brain. *Proc. Natl. Acad. Sci.U.S.A.* 107, 4758–4763. doi: 10.1073/pnas.0909074107

Plichta, M. M., Herrmann, M. J., Baehne, C. G., Ehlis, A. C., Richter, M. M., Pauli, P., et al. (2006). Event-related functional near-infrared spectroscopy (fNIRS): are the measurements reliable? *Neuroimage* 31, 116–124. doi: 10.1016/j.neuroimage.2005.12.008

Santosa, H., Hong, M. J., Kim, S.-P., and Hong, K.-S. (2013). Noise reduction in functional near-infrared spectroscopy signals by independent component analysis. *Rev. Sci. Instrum.* 84, 073106. doi: 10.1063/1.4812785

Scarff, C. J., Dort, J. C., Eggermont, J. J., and Goodyear, B. G. (2004). The effect of MR scanner noise on auditory cortex activity using fMRI. *Hum. Brain Mapp.* 22, 341–349. doi: 10.1002/hbm.20043

Schuppert, M., Münte, T. F., Wieringa, B. M., and Altenmüller, E. (2000). Receptive amusia: evidence for cross-hemispheric neural networks underlying music processing strategies. *Brain* 123, 546–559. doi: 10.1093/brain/123.3.546

Shirao, N., Okamoto, Y., Mantani, T., Okamoto, Y., and Yamawaki, S. (2005). Gender differences in brain activity generated by unpleasant word stimuli concerning body image: an fMRI study. *Br. J. Psychiatry* 186, 48–53. doi: 10.1192/bjp.186.1.48

Shtyrov, Y., Kujala, T., Ahveninen, J., Tervaniemi, M., Alku, P., Ilmoniemi, R. J., et al. (1998). Background acoustic noise and the hemispheric lateralization of speech processing in the human brain: magnetic mismatch negativity study. *Neurosci. Lett.* 251, 141–144. doi: 10.1016/S0304-3940(98)00529-1

Shtyrov, Y., Smith, M. L., Horner, A. J., Henson, R., Nathan, P. J., Bullmore, E. T., et al. (2012). Attention to language: novel MEG paradigm for registering involuntary language processing in the brain. *Neuropsychologia* 50, 2605–2616. doi: 10.1016/j.neuropsychologia.2012.07.012

Sinai, A., and Pratt, H. (2003). High-resolution time course of hemispheric dominance revealed by low-resolution electromagnetic tomography. *Clin. Neurophysiol.* 114, 1181–1188. doi: 10.1016/S388-2457(03)000087-7

Soekadar, S. R., Witkowski, M., Cossio, E. G., Birbaumer, N., and Cohen, L. G. (2014). Learned EEG-based brain self-regulation of motor-related oscillations during application of transcranial electric brain stimulation: feasibility limitations. *Front. Behav. Neurosci.* 8:93. doi: 10.3389/fnbeh.2014.00093

Tervaniemi, M., and Hugdahl, K. (2003). Lateralization of auditory-cortex functions. *Brain Res. Rev.* 43, 231–246. doi: 10.1016/j.brainresrev.2003.08.004

Tervaniemi, M., Medvedev, S. V., Alho, K., Pakhomov, S. V., Roudas, M. S., van Zuijen, T. L., et al. (2000). Lateralized automatic auditory processing of phonetic versus musical information: a PET study. *Hum. Brain. Mapp.* 10, 74–79. doi: 10.1002/(SICI)1097-0193(200006)10:2<74::AID-HBM30>3.0.CO;2-2

Toga, A. W., and Thompson, P. M. (2003). Mapping brain asymmetry. *Nat. Rev. Neurosci.* 4, 37–48. doi: 10.1038/nrn1009

Turnip, A., and Hong, K.-S. (2012). Classifying mental activities from EEG-P300 signals using adaptive neural networks. *Int. J. Innov. Comput. Inform. Control* 8, 6429–6443.

Turnip, A., Hong, K.-S., and Jeong, M.-Y. (2011). Real-time feature extraction of P300 component using adaptive nonlinear principal component analysis. *Biomed. Eng. Online* 10:83. doi: 10.1186/1475-925X-10-83

Warrier, C., Wong, P. C. M., Penhune, V., Zatorre, R., Parrish, T., Abrams, D., et al. (2009). Relating structure to function: Heschl's gyrus and acoustic processing. *J. Neurosci.* 29, 61–69. doi: 10.1523/JNEUROSCI.3489-08.2009

Wong, P. C. M., Ettlinger, M., Sheppard, J. P., Gunasekera, G. M., and Dhar, S. (2010). Neuroanatomical characteristics and speech perception in noise in older adults. *Ear. Hear.* 31, 471–479. doi: 10.1097/AUD.0b013e3181d709c2

Wong, P. C. M., Uppunda, A. K., Parrish, T. B., and Dhar, S. (2008). Cortical mechanisms of speech perception in noise. *J. Speech Lang. Hear. R.* 51, 1026–1041. doi: 10.1044/1092-4388(2008/075)

Ye, J.-C., Tak, S., Jang, K.-E., Jung, J., and Jang, J. (2009). NIRS-SPM: statistical parametric mapping for near-infrared spectroscopy. *Neuroimage* 44, 428–447. doi: 10.1016/j.neuroimage.2008.08.036

Yuan, Z., and Ye, J.-C. (2013). Fusion of fNIRS and fMRI data: identifying when and where hemodynamic signals are changing in human brains. *Front. Hum. Neurosci.* 7:676. doi: 10.3389/fnhum.2013.00676

Zaehle, T., Jancke, L., and Meyer, M. (2007). Electrical brain imaging evidences left auditory cortex involvement in speech and non-speech discrimination based on temporal features. *Behav. Brain Funct.* 3:63. doi: 10.1186/1744-9081-3-63

Zatorre, R. J., Halpern, A. R., Perry, D. W., Meyer, E., and Evans, A. C. (1996). Hearing in the mind's ear: a PET investigation of musical imagery and perception. *J. Cogn. Neurosci.* 8, 29–46. doi: 10.1162/jocn.1996.8.1.29

Zhou, Y., Li, S., Dunn, J., Li, H. D., Qin, W., Zhu, M. H., et al. (2014). The neural correlates of risk propensity in males and females using resting-state fMRI. *Front. Behav. Neurosci.* 8:2. doi: 10.3389/fnbeh.2014.00002

19

Real-time fMRI brain-computer interface: development of a "motivational feedback" subsystem for the regulation of visual cue reactivity

Moses O. Sokunbi[1,2]*, David E. J. Linden[1,2], Isabelle Habes[1,2], Stephen Johnston[3] and Niklas Ihssen[1,2]

[1] MRC Centre for Neuropsychiatric Genetics and Genomics, Institute of Psychological Medicine and Clinical Neurosciences, Cardiff School of Medicine, Cardiff University, Cardiff, UK
[2] Cardiff University Brain Research Imaging Centre (CUBRIC), Cardiff University, Cardiff, UK
[3] Department of Psychology, Swansea University, Swansea, UK

***Correspondence:**
Moses O. Sokunbi, MRC Centre for Neuropsychiatric Genetics and Genomics, Institute of Psychological Medicine and Clinical Neurosciences, Cardiff School of Medicine, Cardiff University, Hadyn Ellis Building, Maindy Road, Cathays, Cardiff, CF24 4HQ, Wales, UK
e-mail: SokunbiMO@cardiff.ac.uk

Here we present a novel neurofeedback subsystem for the presentation of motivationally relevant visual feedback during the self-regulation of functional brain activation. Our "motivational neurofeedback" approach uses functional magnetic resonance imaging (fMRI) signals elicited by visual cues (pictures) and related to motivational processes such as craving or hunger. The visual feedback subsystem provides simultaneous feedback through these images as their size corresponds to the magnitude of fMRI signal change from a target brain area. During self-regulation of cue-evoked brain responses, decreases and increases in picture size thus provide real motivational consequences in terms of cue approach vs. cue avoidance, which increases face validity of the approach in applied settings. Further, the outlined approach comprises of neurofeedback (regulation) and "mirror" runs that allow to control for non-specific and task-unrelated effects, such as habituation or neural adaptation. The approach was implemented in the Python programming language. Pilot data from 10 volunteers showed that participants were able to successfully down-regulate individually defined target areas, demonstrating feasibility of the approach. The newly developed visual feedback subsystem can be integrated into protocols for imaging-based brain-computer interfaces (BCI) and may facilitate neurofeedback research and applications into healthy and dysfunctional motivational processes, such as food craving or addiction.

Keywords: brain-computer interface (BCI), hunger, visual cue reactivity, food craving, functional magnetic resonance imaging (fMRI), neurofeedback, self-regulation

INTRODUCTION

Recent advancements in real-time functional magnetic resonance imaging (fMRI) have been based on the increased availability of high-field (in excess of 1.5 tesla) MRI scanners, fast data acquisition sequences, improved real-time pre-processing, improved statistical analysis techniques and methods of data visualization and feedback. These developments have made the implementation of fMRI brain-computer interfaces (fMRI-BCI) and neurofeedback possible (Weiskopf, 2012). In fMRI-BCI, the self-regulation of brain activity in a target region can be achieved by providing real-time feedback of brain activation levels in that target region. While paradigms more commonly utilize feedback signals based on overall activity levels in a given region, more complex metrics of brain activation are being used based on multivariate statistical techniques (LaConte et al., 2007; Sitaram et al., 2008) or correlation of activity in several brain areas (Zilverstand et al., 2014).

NEUROFEEDBACK AND VISUAL CUE REACTIVITY

In recent years an emerging but technically challenging field in neurofeedback research has been the pairing of feedback signals (and regulation instructions) with simultaneous visual stimulus presentation. Such approaches are especially interesting for research into neural and behavioral responses that are passively triggered by salient emotional or motivational cues, such as fear responses evoked by emotional pictures or craving elicited by drug-related pictures. The degree of drug cue-elicited neural activation within circuits of the orbitofrontal cortex (Ernst et al., 2014), the nucleus accumbens and medial prefrontal cortex (PFC; Wiers et al., 2014) has been shown to determine the degree of cue approach vs. avoidance behavior in alcohol dependent patients. Moreover, alcohol cues automatically evoke cognitive processes that are biased towards approaching the cue and correlate with drinking behavior in adolescents (Peeters et al., 2012). Neurofeedback training to control these emotional/motivational responses should thus aim at the down-regulation of blood oxygen level dependent (BOLD) responses, especially when the targeted neurocognitive process is considered to be dysfunctional. To date, however, most fMRI neurofeedback studies have trained participants to up-regulate activation of a target area. Further, a direct comparison between up- and down-regulation training of the same brain region (anterior insula) showed that down-regulation was more difficult to learn (Veit et al., 2012). In light of its promising clinical applications, this underscores the need for methodological development and research into the area of neurofeedback related to visual cue reactivity. Here we present a novel neurofeedback subsystem for the presentation of motivationally relevant feedback during exposure to appetitive pictures.

THE CHOICE OF FEEDBACK TYPE

When setting up visual cue reactivity neurofeedback paradigms, researchers are confronted with several challenges. One relates to the choice of feedback type: With the simultaneous visual presentation of feedback information and task stimulus, there is a potential risk that monitoring the feedback stimulus distracts attention from the emotional/motivational cue which will confound any effortful down-regulation of the targeted neural response. Since the pioneering neurofeedback studies at the beginning of the last decade, various techniques have been employed to present visual feedback for the self-regulation of BOLD activation over time. Weiskopf et al. (2003, 2004) and deCharms et al. (2004) have used scrolling time series graphs and curves of BOLD activation in the region of interest (ROI) to provide immediate information to the participant. Sitaram et al. (2005) introduced the "thermometer" as a type of visual feedback for the display of brain activity. Positive BOLD activity, compared to a baseline period is shown as an increasing number of red "hot" bars, whereas negative BOLD activity is similarly shown in blue. The authors also introduced a virtual reality feedback system (Sitaram et al., 2005) where volunteers controlled a 3D animated character (a fish in water). Other visual feedback approaches include the presentation of functional maps of the brain (Yoo and Jolesz, 2002) or video-based feedback that has been used to train stroke patients to self-regulate ventromedial premotor cortex (Sitaram, 2007a).

Most studies using simultaneous visual stimulation during feedback-guided regulation have adopted the thermometer approach as described above but temporally separated the feedback presentation from the regulation/visual stimulation period (Posse et al., 2003; Li et al., 2013). In contrast to such delayed feedback, continuous/on-line feedback during regulation has the advantage that participants can adaptively test different mental strategies to optimize regulation. Only few studies have paired the presentation of pictorial cues with BOLD signal feedback in a simultaneous manner. Brühl et al. (2014) trained participants to down-regulate activity of the right amygdala while being exposed to negative emotional faces. During the 20-sec down-regulation blocks, a feedback stimulus reflecting activation levels of the amygdala was presented to the participants, showing two colored rectangles at the picture edges which color-coded activity levels in a similar way as the thermometer approach described above. Rather than using a peripheral feedback stimulus, Veit et al. (2012) embedded the thermometer inside the simultaneously presented emotional cues that consisted of blocks of aversive pictures. Also, Mathiak et al. (2010) provided a positive feedback through facial expression (smiling) when activity in the anterior cingulate cortex (ACC) increased and gradually returned to a neutral expression when the activity dropped.

Critically, such spatial or feature-based distinction between the feedback and the task stimulus can induce distraction or interference effects as seen in dual tasks. As a consequence, responses to the task stimulus (e.g., emotional picture) may be reduced, confounding the effects of effortful down-regulation. Here, we delineate a novel approach in which feedback-guided self-regulation is based on visual changes in the stimulus responsible for the targeted brain responses itself. Specifically, the present paradigm uses appetitive food pictures to evoke responses in brain circuits related to hunger and food craving. The success of regulating those responses during picture exposure in the neurofeedback session is represented as gradual changes in image size. Compared to the feedback stimuli used by Veit et al. and Brühl et al. our paradigm has the advantage that distracting/dual-task effects associated with monitoring the feedback stimulus during cue exposure are minimized. At the same time, by linking decreases in image size to successful down-regulation and image size increases to failure, respectively, the paradigm provides real motivational consequences of the participant's regulation effort, i.e., the stimuli mimic avoidance behavior during successful down-regulation and approach behavior during unsuccessful down-regulation. Such behavioral/motivational relevance of the task can increase face validity of the neurofeedback training and may thus facilitate its therapeutic use in pathologies of motivational systems, such as obesity or addiction.

THE ISSUE OF HABITUATION

Another challenge of visual cue reactivity neurofeedback is that repeated exposure to the same or similar visual stimulus will lead to a decrease of neural responses. Such effects have been well documented in brain imaging tasks using fMRI adaption or "repetition suppression" techniques, in which the reduction of BOLD responses associated with the repeated presentation of identical stimuli is used as a tool to characterize the neural representation of visual objects (Grill-Spector et al., 2006). Similar effects of neural adaptation can also occur in brain circuits involved in emotional processes. For instance, multiple presentations of threatening pictures will lead to a gradually weaker activation of the amygdala (Wright et al., 2001). In the present context of down-regulation of cue-induced BOLD activation patterns, it is thus crucial to control for such effects, as a gradual habituation effect over successive regulation blocks may be misinterpreted as reflecting successful regulation. In previous research such control measures have been implemented, for instance, by including a passive viewing condition (either within- or between-runs) where the same set of pictures and the feedback stimulus shown during regulation is repeated but participants are instructed not to regulate their brain responses (Brühl et al., 2014). Here, we took a similar approach by including "mirror" runs in the paradigm, in which participants were exposed to the same size sequence that was "produced" during a previous regulation block but instructed not to regulate target area activation.

COMPUTATIONAL TRANSLATION AND RESPONSE RANGE ADAPTATION OF THE BOLD SIGNAL

All BCIs include a series of steps for converting the measured brain signal, such as percentage signal change, into commands (Linden, 2014). First, the relevant feature is extracted from the wealth of information that the measurement device picks up, ideally in real time. Secondly, the extracted feature needs to be converted into an output signal for the participant to use through a translation algorithm. Finally, the translation from the extracted feature of the brain signal to the output needs to be adaptive. Peoples' individual neurophysiological responses vary widely yet all must ultimately appear in an identical summary form, for their use, projected onto a computer screen. Thus the conversion has to be adapted to an individual's response range. This adaptation to the original signal also has to take into account the fluctuation of the signal over time and the improvement with training as well as an individual's training capacity. For example the duration of the training has to be adjusted to psychological factors like motivation and fatigue, which again corresponds to well-known general principles from teaching and training.

A well designed feedback system is an important criterion in successfully training participants to self-regulate their BOLD response. Contingent feedback following the participant's response with minimum lag and with reliable information content pertaining to task success improves learning (Sitaram et al., 2008). As detailed below, in the current project we developed a solution for steps two (translation algorithm) and three (adaptation) of the motivational BCI approach outlined above.

MATERIALS AND METHODS

fMRI BRAIN-COMPUTER NEUROFEEDBACK ARCHITECTURE

Figure 1 describes the fMRI-BCI architecture for neurofeedback training at our center. Our architecture is a closed-loop system with the following major subsystems; signal acquisition, signal analysis and signal feedback. In **Figure 1**, the MRI image pool is the end point of the signal acquisition subsystem and is connected to the signal analysis and signal feedback subsystems through a local area network (LAN). The signal analysis subsystem communicates with the signal feedback subsystem and they both reside on the same computer. The signal feedback subsystem is connected to the projector screen, where the feedback signal is presented.

At the signal acquisition subsystem, localized brain activity of the participant while viewing images on the projector screen is measured by fMRI using a BOLD sequence; a contrast is then made between the signal elicited by the target stimuli (food pictures) and neutral control stimuli (household objects in localiser run, see below), or a fixation baseline (regulation runs). A 3 T whole body scanner (General Electric, Milwaukee, USA) with an 8-channel head coil is used. The parameterisation of the BOLD sensitive echo planar imaging (EPI) sequence is as follows: TR = 2 s, TE = 45 ms, flip angle = 80°, 30 slices, FOV = 192 mm, image matrix 64 × 64, in-plane voxel size = 3 mm × 3 mm, slice thickness = 4 mm and a gap of 1 mm. Image reconstruction, distortion correction and image averaging are performed on the MRI scanner computer and stored in the MRI image pool.

The signal analysis subsystem is performed using Turbo-Brainvoyager (TBV) version 3.0 (Brain Innovation, Maastricht, The Netherlands; (Goebel, 2001)). TBV retrieves reconstructed fMRI images from the MRI pool via the LAN and performs online 3D motion correction, temporal filtering, spatial smoothing, spatial normalization and online statistical analysis calculating beta parameters from an incremental general linear model (GLM) based on the predictors of interest (e.g., food vs. neutral pictures). A static ROI is selected by drawing an area on the functional map (3D BOLD signal) computed in TBV. All supra-threshold voxels (according to an investigator-chosen statistical threshold between 2 and 3) are included in the target area for signal extraction. Average BOLD signal values (betas) from the target area are extracted by TBV and stored in a continuously updated real-time protocol file (rtp file).

The signal feedback subsystem retrieves the rtp files, processes and analyses the BOLD signal values contained within. Feedback is presented to the participant in real-time as food image sizes corresponding to the percentage change in BOLD signal values of the ROI during food picture presentation relative to fixation baseline using a moving average across three consecutive TRs. Feedback is presented to the participant with a delay that depends on the time for signal acquisition, signal analysis and signal feedback processing. Minimizing the delay is critical for volitional control (Sitaram et al., 2007b). Applying the general experience from operant conditioning experiments, the maximum delay for successful learning of biological responses is 2 min (Yoo et al., 2004). The design and implementation of the visual feedback subsystem for the regulation of hunger or food craving is described in the following sub-sections.

DESIGN

The visual feedback subsystem involves two types of functional imaging run; the neurofeedback and mirror/control runs. The present paradigm involves four runs of each type presented in an alternating order. The neurofeedback runs are the experimental runs, where the participants learn to control their fMRI signal in a block design with periods of rest followed by periods of down-regulation. During the rest blocks, a fixation cross is displayed for 20 s. During the down-regulation block, also 20 s in duration, one food image is presented which varies in size dependent on the percent fMRI signal change, during the block, relative to the preceding fixation block. There are five rest blocks and four down-regulation blocks in the entire display sequence of the neurofeedback run totalling a run length of 180 s. During the down-regulation block, the size of the food image is updated every TR (2 s) leading to a consecutive display of 11 different image sizes in total. Image sizes can vary between 10% and 100% of the original image size (1013 by 760 pixels) that are distributed across the whole size range. The size of the food image displayed at the first TR of each down-regulation block is set to 50% of the maximum image size, which corresponds to the percent signal change (PSC) at the first TR (FPSC) relative to the preceding rest

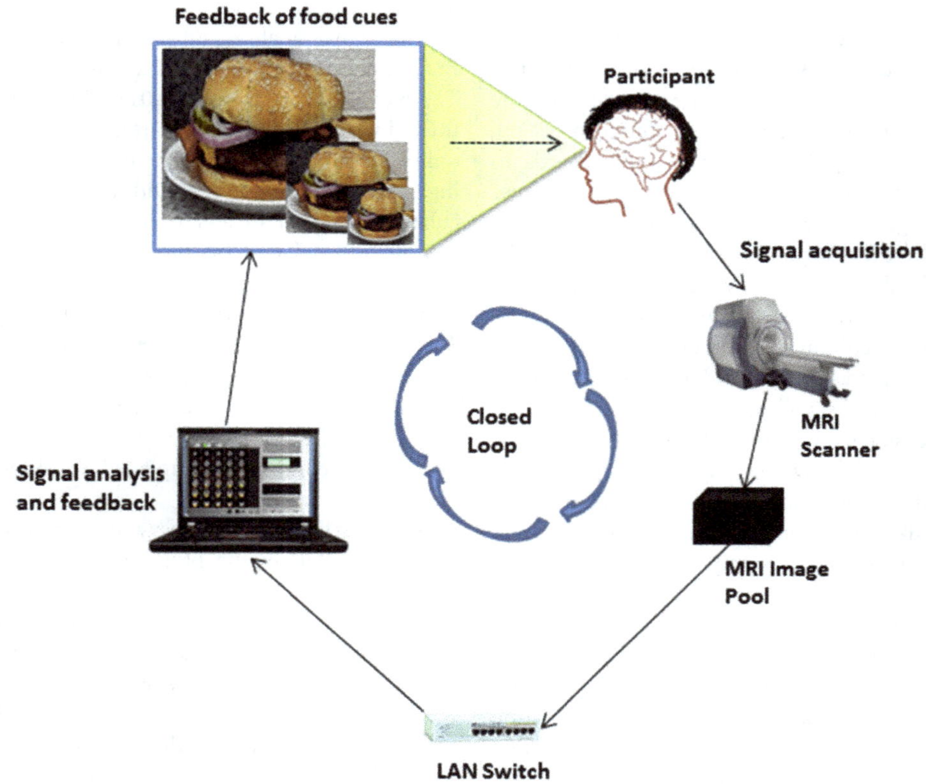

FIGURE 1 | fMRI BCI architecture.

block. Here, the FPSC is taken as the reference scaling point for the calibration of subsequent PSCs. The increase or decrease in image size calibration of the PSC is described using the following calibration algorithm:

```
def PSCDisplay(PSC):
  if PSC < FPSC - 100:
    Display 10% of the image size
  elif FPSC - 100 <= PSC < FPSC - 75:
    Display 15% of the image size
  elif FPSC - 75 <= PSC < FPSC - 50:
    Display 20% of the image size
  elif FPSC - 50 <= PSC < FPSC - 25:
    Display 30% of the image size
  elif FPSC - 25 <= PSC < FPSC:
    Display 40% of the image size
  elif PSC == FPSC:
    Display 50% of the image size
  elif FPSC + 25 >= PSC > FPSC:
    Display 60% of the image size
  elif FPSC + 50 >= PSC > FPSC + 25:
    Display 70% of the image size
  elif FPSC + 75 >= PSC > FPSC + 50:
    Display 80% of the image size
  elif FPSC + 100 >= PSC > FPSC + 75:
    Display 90% of the image size
  elif PSC > FPSC + 100:
    Display 100% of the image size
retun Display
```

This manner of calibrating the PSCs ensures that the effect of the FPSC is reflected in all the image sizes and adapts the feedback subsystem to peoples' individual neurophysiological response range. Each neurofeedback block uses as its feedback signal a different food image from a pool of 16 pictures selected at random. By default the range of the response is set to a 1% deviation from baseline (upwards or downwards), which implies that a 1% up-regulation will result in presentation of the full-size image and 1% down-regulation in presentation of the smallest image. Further up- or down-regulation will then not be reflected in further in- or decreases of the image size. However, the gain of the conversion from the extracted brain signal feature (% BOLD signal change) to image size can be set freely to reflect an individual's response range, and can be adjusted adaptively to reflect dynamic changes in self-regulation ability. The food images were taken from the International Affective Picture System (Lang et al., 2005) and the Internet.

After each neurofeedback run, an associated mirror/control run is presented to the participant. In the mirror run the exact same picture (size) sequence (using the same picture

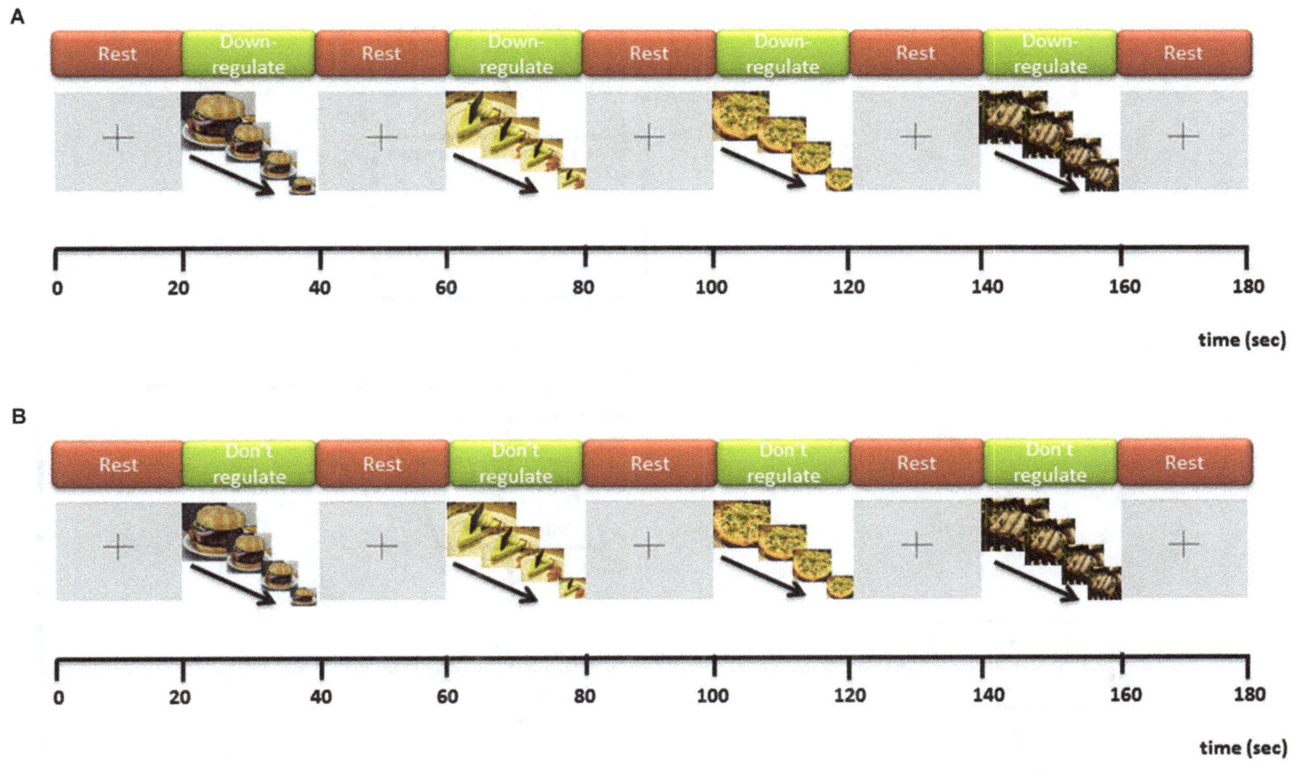

FIGURE 2 | Temporal structure of one neurofeedback run (A) and one mirror run (B).

exemplar) is repeated that was shown in the preceding neurofeedback run. The only difference is that during the mirror run participants are instructed NOT to regulate their brain responses during exposure to the food images but should passively watch the image (size) sequences instead. By this means, the mirror run can serve as a perceptual control: when BOLD responses from the mirror run are (offline) subtracted from BOLD responses in the neurofeedback run, any decrease in brain activation (in the target ROI or elsewhere in the brain) *cannot* be attributed to differences in physical stimulation—which may include diminishing brain activation to motivational cues as a result of habituation over time/successive runs—but will likely reflect the down-regulation effort. Importantly, each mirror run is always presented *after* its corresponding regulation run showing the same picture exemplar and size sequence. Any habituation-related reduction of brain responses caused by repeating the same stimulation in the mirror run thus *cannot* lead to an erroneous detection of down-regulation success (difference regulation—mirror) as it works in the opposite direction. **Figures 2A,B** depicts the temporal structure of the neurofeedback and mirror runs.

IMPLEMENTATION

Figures 3, 4 depict flow-charts of the execution path of the neurofeedback and mirror runs respectively. The flow-charts were implemented by writing the sequence of executed events in the Python programming language and executed using the PsychoPy graphical user interface (Peirce, 2007). During the neurofeedback run, the signal feedback subsystem accesses the average BOLD signal values of the ROI time courses (in the rtp files) computed by TBV and presents the feedback display in **Figure 2A**. The mirror run presents a visually identical feedback display (see **Figure 2B**) which uses the average BOLD signal values of the neurofeedback run stored in a separate directory (termed "mirror files"). The mirror files are processed and displayed in synchronization with the average BOLD signal values of the ROI time courses (rtp files) computed by TBV during the mirror run (scanner files).

PILOT STUDY TESTING THE FEASIBILITY OF "MOTIVATIONAL NEUROFEEDBACK"

Data from 10 female participants (mean age M = 21.40 years, Standard Deviation (SD) = 2.27) were acquired to test whether the newly developed motivational neurofeedback paradigm can be successfully used to down-regulate brain activation in response to appetitive food pictures. Participants were asked not to eat for 4 h before the scanning session to increase motivational brain responses related to hunger or food craving. Written informed consent was obtained in accordance with the local ethics committee prior to the start of the study.

The experiment began with the functional localizer run followed by an alternating sequence of four neurofeedback and four mirror runs. During the localizer run the participants passively viewed five blocks of food pictures and five blocks of

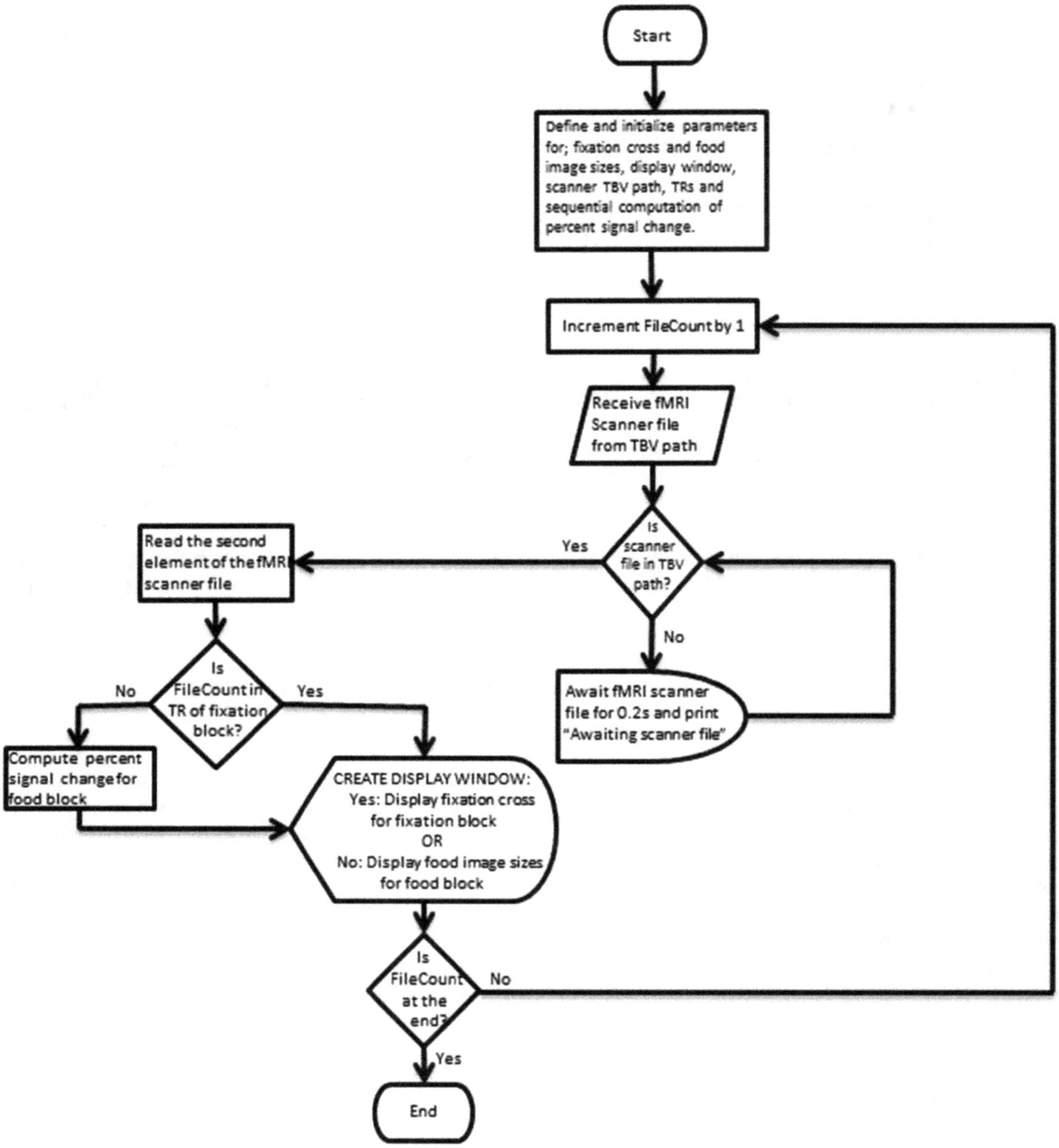

FIGURE 3 | Flow-chart depicting the execution path of the neurofeedback run.

pictures showing neutral household objects in alternating order. The picture blocks contained five pictures randomly selected from the relevant category, presented for 2 s each. Blocks were interleaved with a 10 s fixation period (with the exception of an initial fixation period at the start of the experiment which was 12 s in duration), resulting in a total run length of 222 s. The sequence of four neurofeedback and mirror runs were presented using the trial/run structure described above. Due to technical problems, for three participants only three neurofeedback/mirror runs could be acquired. For ROI analyses testing the feasibility of down-regulation of the target area in the neurofeedback runs, we used the pre-processed functional images created by the TBV software, which were co-registered to individual high-resolution T1-weighted anatomical images and spatially normalized to Talairach space. Individual volume time courses were spatially smoothed using a kernel with a full

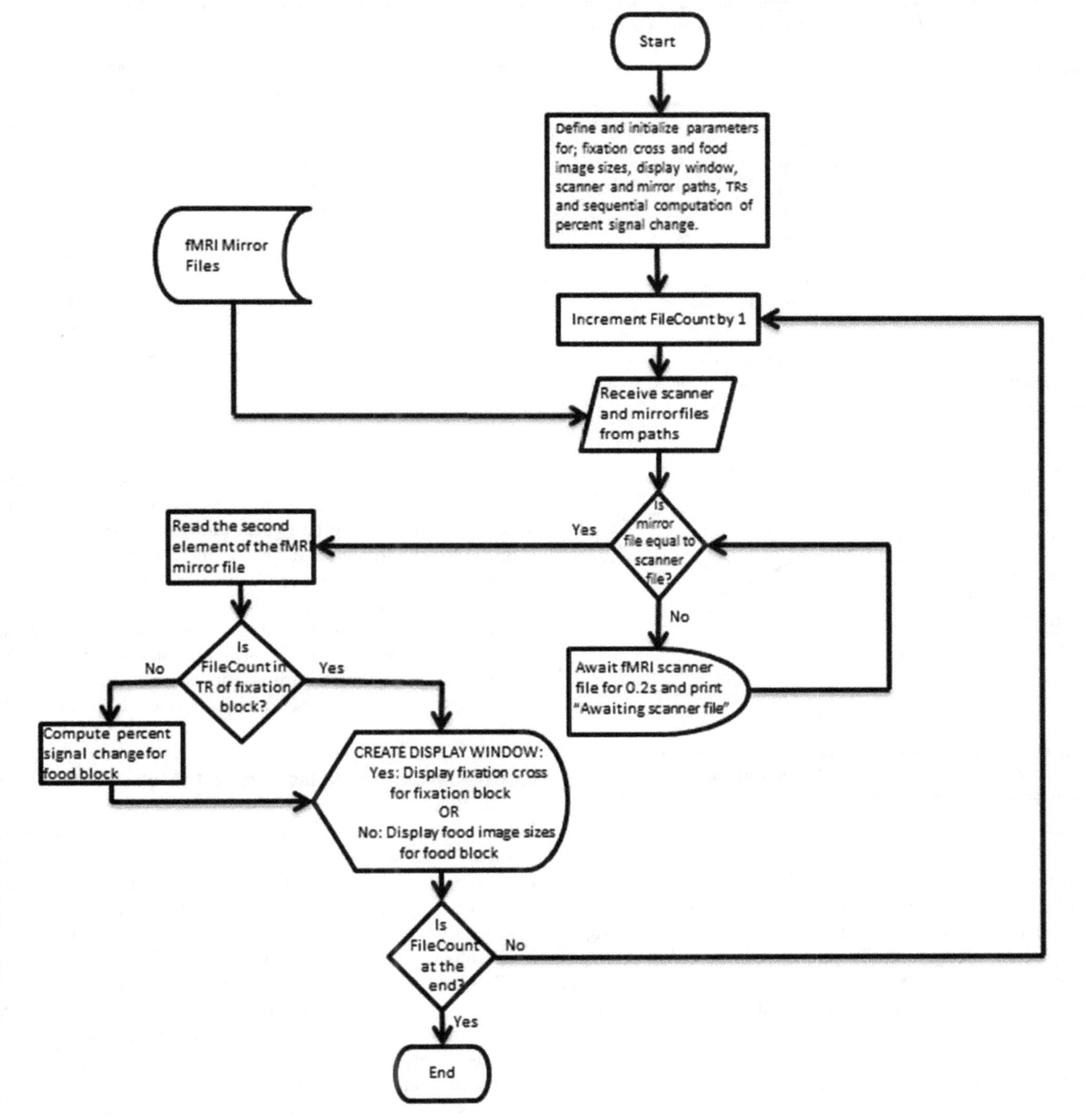

FIGURE 4 | Flow-chart depicting the execution path of the mirror run.

width at half maximum (FWHM) of 4 mm and temporally filtered with a high pass filter of 2 cycles/time course. For each run and participant separately, mean beta estimates in the target area were then extracted based on individual whole-brain GLMs and three different predictors for BOLD signal changes during (i) mirror, (ii) regulation (neurofeedback); and (iii) rest blocks. **Table 1** shows the associated brain regions, mean Talairach coordinates and size of activation clusters selected as target areas for neurofeedback-guided down-regulation in the pilot sample.

RESULTS AND DISCUSSION

Based on a whole brain GLM analysis for the contrast between food and neutral pictures during the localiser run we visually selected for each participant individually a target area (ROI) encompassing the cluster showing the strongest response in the

Table 1 | Associated brain region (Left/Right), mean Talairach coordinates and size (1 × 1 × 1 mm^3 voxels) of activation clusters selected as target areas for neurofeedback-guided down-regulation in the pilot sample.

Participant	Region	Mean coordinates (*x, y, z*)	Size (voxels)	Mean beta difference regulation-mirror
01	Amygdala (L & R)	−2, −4, −14	1853	−0.18
02	Amygdala (R)	16, 2, −16	3185	−0.51
03	Amygdala (R)	28, −4, −12	3488	−0.25
04	Amygdala (L)	−27, −6, −20	1530	0.06
05	Amygdala (L & R)	4, −5, −14	3887	−0.10
06	Putamen (R)	−22, 14, -5	1534	−0.28
07	Insula (L)	−32, −1, 6	3979	−0.16
08	Caudate (R)	11, 0, 17	4637	−0.11
09	Thalamus (R)	24, −24, 3	1128	−0.14
10	Parahippocampal Gyrus (L)	−19, −30, −4	878	0.02

Target areas were functionally selected using a localizer scan with food and neutral pictures. The table also includes mean beta differences for the regulation/neurofeedback vs. mirror/passive viewing condition across runs. Negative values indicate successful down-regulation of target area activation during neurofeedback runs.

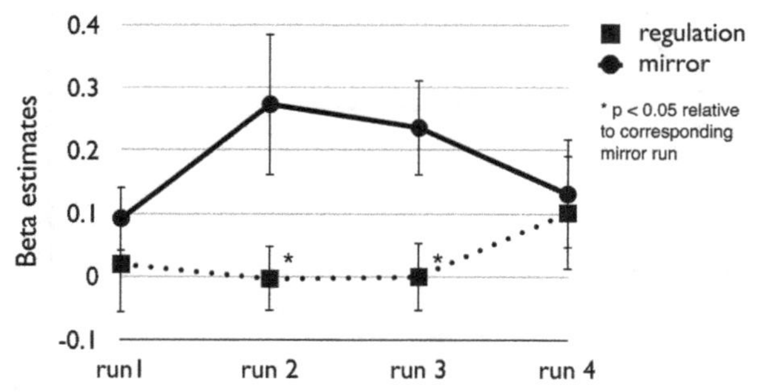

FIGURE 5 | Mean beta weights reflecting brain activation of individually selected target areas in 10 pilot participants during four consecutive neurofeedback (regulation) and mirror (passive viewing) runs. Error bars indicate standard errors of the mean.

statistical activation maps (see **Table 1**). The feedback signals (and its corresponding picture sizes) in the subsequent neurofeedback runs were computed as the average percent signal change from all significantly activated voxels within a rectangle drawn over the target region across three axial slices. We constrained the selection to regions with a known involvement in emotional-motivational processes and to non-visual brain areas.

During the neurofeedback run participants were asked to reduce the size of the food images displayed on the projector screen by reducing the average fMRI signal strength in the target ROI. During the mirror run the participants were instructed to passively view the food image sequence repeated from the previous neurofeedback run. **Figure 5** shows mean beta estimates for the pilot sample, separated for the four consecutive regulation and mirror runs. Paired *t*-tests showed that the regulation condition led to significantly lower target area activation in run 2, $t_{(9)} = 2.49$, $p = 0.034$, and in run 3, $t_{(9)} = 2.77$, $p = 0.022$. Activation levels were not significantly different between regulation and passive viewing in run 1 and run 4, $ts < 1.0$. However, as indicated in **Figure 5** this was caused by increased activation in the mirror condition in the first and fourth run while target area activation during regulation was low throughout the session, with beta estimates not exceeding 0.1. Across runs, 8 out of 10 participants successfully reduced target area activation during neurofeedback, showing lower mean beta values for the regulation vs. passive viewing condition (see **Table 1**). To summarize, pilot data suggests that our paradigm enables participants to successfully down-regulate brain areas involved in processing motivational cues, such as appetitive food pictures. These results may be relevant to the increasing interest in the combination of Pavlovian and instrumental techniques in neurofeedback research (Mendelsohn et al., 2014).

MOTIVATIONAL NEUROFEEDBACK—RELEVANCE FOR CLINICAL APPLICATIONS

Providing motivationally relevant neurofeedback through changes in stimulus size may also provide an avenue to help patients gain control over dysfunctional motivational processes, such as craving elicited by environmental cues in substance dependence. It is well known that visual cue reactivity, and specifically craving responses to drug-related cues (e.g., in the media or during social interactions) are a major determinant of relapse after treatment of addiction (Weiss, 2005). Moreover, maladaptive brain responses to visual drug cues can be identified in early stages of addictive disorders (Ihssen et al., 2011). Identifying a suitable neurofeedback approach that can help to alter these activation patterns directly would thus provide an important clinical tool complementing traditional psychological and pharmacological interventions. A few studies have begun to test the effects of neurofeedback in the context of addiction. For instance, Li et al. (2013) and Hanlon et al. (2013) trained treatment-seeking smokers to regulate brain responses in craving-related brain areas ACC and PFC during exposure to smoking-related pictures. Pictures were presented in blocks of 22 s during which participants were asked to regulate ACC/PFC activity, followed by a thermometer feedback shown for 4 s. However, these studies did not control for habituation effects as described above, presenting regulation runs always after passive viewing control runs. Moreover, feedback was implemented with a delay. The present approach overcomes these limitations. It may also be especially suitable in an applied setting as it has high face validity and presents to the participant visible, quasi-behavioral consequences of his/her mental regulation effort: Visual cues, such as picture showing high-calorie food or alcoholic beverages, can be directly manipulated through the regulation, i.e., "pushed away" through successful down-regulation or "dragged towards oneself" through up-regulation (or non-regulation). Providing such approach and avoidance consequences of neural self-regulation may increase the likelihood that learned strategies are transferred to a natural environment. The importance of such motivational factors for drug addiction is demonstrated by behavioral interventions showing that making avoidance movements (pushing a joystick) in response to alcohol pictures can change the automatic approach bias and improve treatment outcomes of alcohol-dependent patients (Wiers et al., 2011; Eberl et al., 2013).

On the other hand, the present paradigm allows participants to directly manipulate and control the visual cue which can be predicted to increase the participant's sense of agency and perception of self-efficacy (Bandura, 1977)—factors that are central for the maintenance of drug-abstinent behavior (Greenfield et al., 2000). One limitation of our paradigm relates to the effects that visual changes in picture size may themselves have on motivational brain responses. However, changes in picture size have been shown to affect neural responses of emotional brain networks only marginally (De Cesarei and Codispoti, 2006). More importantly, in the present paradigm such effects are also controlled for by the mirror runs, which repeat the size changes of the regulation run. Nonetheless, care should be taken when defining maximal and minimum picture sizes for a specific scanner-projector set-up in order to remain within a visible range.

SUMMARY AND CONCLUSIONS

The visual feedback subsystem we have developed has been tailored to specifically allow (i) feedback-guided regulation of visual cue reactivity, i.e., to control brain responses to pictorial cues *during* exposure to those cues; and (ii) to increase motivational relevance of visual feedback by using decreases (avoidance) or increases (approach) of stimulus size as an indication of successful or unsuccessful down-regulation. Further, the feedback subsystem is able to adapt to peoples' individual neurophysiological response range. These individual ranges are scaled to fall within a standard range before being mapped to the corresponding image sizes for display. Importantly, the introduction of the mirror run controls for physical/perceptual confounds, allowing separation of BOLD response changes resulting from successful regulation from those related to variations of visual stimulus properties or visual responses, such as habituation. Finally, the present feedback subsystem displays a new food image size every 2 s allowing good performance and providing a minimum delay in line with existing visual feedback subsystems (Weiskopf et al., 2003, 2004; Sitaram et al., 2007b, 2008). To conclude, our approach may facilitate the control of brain activation during neurofeedback training involving simultaneous presentation of visual cues and may thus help the translation of neurofeedback into clinical applications, such as the regulation of craving responses to substance-related visual cues in addictive disorders.

ACKNOWLEDGMENTS

This study was supported by the BRAINTRAIN grant, funded by the European Union's Seventh Framework Programme for research, technological development and demonstration under grant agreement no. 602186, a seed corn grant of the MRC Centre for Neuropsychiatric Genetics and Genomics, Cardiff University and MRC grant G1100629.

REFERENCES

Bandura, A. (1977). Self-efficacy: toward a unifying theory of behavioral change. *Psychol. Rev.* 84, 191–215. doi: 10.1037//0033-295x.84.2.191

Brühl, A. B., Scherpiet, S., Sulzer, J., Stämpfli, P., Seifritz, E., and Herwig, U. (2014). Real-time neurofeedback using functional MRI could improve down-regulation of amygdala activity during emotional stimulation: a proof-of-concept study. *Brain Topogr.* 27, 138–148. doi: 10.1007/s10548-013-0331-9

De Cesarei, A., and Codispoti, M. (2006). When does size not matter? Effects of stimulus size on affective modulation. *Psychophysiology* 43, 207–215. doi: 10.1111/j.1469-8986.2006.00392.x

deCharms, R. C., Christoff, K., Glover, G. H., Pauly, J. M., Whitfield, S., and Gabrieli, J. D. E. (2004). Learned regulation of spatially localized brain activation using real-time fMRI. *Neuroimage* 21, 436–443. doi: 10.1016/j.neuroimage.2003.08.041

Eberl, C., Wiers, R. W., Pawelczack, S., Rinck, M., Becker, E. S., and Lindenmeyer, J. (2013). Approach bias modification in alcohol dependence: do clinical effects replicate and for whom does it work best? *Dev. Cogn. Neurosci.* 4, 38–51. doi: 10.1016/j.dcn.2012.11.002

Ernst, L. H., Plichta, M. M., Dresler, T., Zesewitz, A. K., Tupak, S. V., Haeussinger, F. B., et al. (2014). Prefrontal correlates of approach preferences for alcohol stimuli in alcohol dependence. *Addict. Biol.* 19, 497–508. doi: 10.1111/adb.12005

Goebel, R. (2001). Cortex-based real-time fMRI. *Neuroimage* 13:S129. doi: 10.1016/s1053-8119(01)91472-7

Greenfield, S. F., Hufford, M. R., Vagge, L. M., Muenz, L. R., Costello, M. E., and Weiss, R. D. (2000). The relationship of self-efficacy expectancies to relapse among alcohol dependent men and women: a prospective study. *J. Stud. Alcohol* 61, 345–351.

Grill-Spector, K., Henson, R., and Martin, A. (2006). Repetition and the brain: neural models of stimulus-specific effects. *Trends Cogn. Sci.* 10, 14–23. doi: 10.1016/j.tics.2005.11.006

Hanlon, C. A., Hartwell, K. J., Canterberry, M., Li, X., Owens, M., Lematty, T., et al. (2013). Reduction of cue-induced craving through realtime neurofeedback in nicotine users: the role of region of interest selection and multiple visits. *Psychiatry Res.* 213, 79–81. doi: 10.1016/j.pscychresns.2013.03.003

Ihssen, N., Cox, W. M., Wiggett, A., Fadardi, J. S., and Linden, D. E. (2011). Differentiating heavy from light drinkers by neural responses to visual alcohol cues and other motivational stimuli. *Cereb. Cortex* 21, 1408–1415. doi: 10.1093/cercor/bhq220

LaConte, S. M., Peltier, S. J., and Hu, X. P. (2007). Real-time fMRI using brain-state classification. *Hum. Brain Mapp.* 28, 1033–1044. doi: 10.1002/hbm.20326

Lang, P. J., Bradley, M. M., and Cuthbert, B. N. (2005). *International Affective Picture System (IAPS): Affective Ratings of Pictures and Instruction Manual.* Gainesville, FL: University of Florida.

Li, X., Hartwell, K. J., Borckardt, J., Prisciandaro, J. J., Saladin, M. E., Morgan, P. S., et al. (2013). Volitional reduction of anterior cingulate cortex activity produces decreased cue craving in smoking cessation: a preliminary real-time fMRI study. *Addict. Biol.* 18, 739–748. doi: 10.1111/j.1369-1600.2012.00449.x

Linden, D. E. J. (2014). *Brain Control—Developments in Therapy and Implications for Society.* Houndmills: Palgrave Macmillan.

Mathiak, K. A., Koush, Y., Dyck, M., Gaber, T. J., Alawi, E., Zepf, F. D., et al. (2010). Social reinforcement can regulate localized brain activity. *Eur. Arch. Psychiatry Clin. Neurosci.* 260(Suppl. 2), S132–S136. doi: 10.1007/s00406-010-0135-9

Mendelsohn, A., Pine, A., and Schiller, D. (2014). Between thoughts and actions: motivationally salient cues invigorate mental action in the human brain. *Neuron* 81, 207–217. doi: 10.1016/j.neuron.2013.10.019

Peeters, M., Wiers, R. W., Monshouwer, K., Van de Schoot, R., Janssen, T., and Vollebergh, W. A. (2012). Automatic processes in at-risk adolescents: the role of alcohol-approach tendencies and response inhibition in drinking behavior. *Addiction* 107, 1939–1946. doi: 10.1111/j.1360-0443.2012.03948.x

Peirce, J. W. (2007). PsychoPy—Psychophysics software in Python. *J. Neurosci. Methods* 162, 8–13. doi: 10.1016/j.jneumeth.2006.11.017

Posse, S., Fitzgerald, D., Gao, K. X., Habel, U., Rosenberg, D., Moore, G. J., et al. (2003). Real-time fMRI of temporolimbic regions detects amygdala activation during single-trial self-induced sadness. *Neuroimage* 18, 760–768. doi: 10.1016/s1053-8119(03)00004-1

Sitaram, R. (2007a). "fMRI brain-computer interfaces," in *15th Annual Conference of the International Society for Neurofeedback and Research*, Current Perspectives in Neuroscience: Neuroplasticity and Neurofeedback (San Diego, CA).

Sitaram, R., Caria, A., Veit, R., Gaber, T., Kuebler, A., and Birbaumer, N. (2005). "Real-time fMRI based brain-computer interface enhanced by interactive virtual worlds," in *45th Annual Meeting Society for Psychophysiological Research* (Lisbon, Portugal).

Sitaram, R., Caria, A., Veit, R., Gaber, T., Rota, G., Kuebler, A., et al. (2007b). FMRI brain-computer interface: a tool for neuroscientific research and treatment. *Comput. Intell. Neurosci.* 2007:25487. doi: 10.1155/2007/25487

Sitaram, R., Weiskopf, N., Caria, A., Veit, R., Erb, M., and Birbaumer, N. (2008). fMRI brain-computer interfaces. *IEEE Signal Process. Mag.* 25, 95–106. doi: 10.1109/msp.2008.4408446

Veit, R., Singh, V., Sitaram, R., Caria, A., Rauss, K., and Birbaumer, N. (2012). Using real-time fMRI to learn voluntary regulation of the anterior insula in the presence of threat-related stimuli. *Soc. Cogn. Affect. Neurosci.* 7, 623–634. doi: 10.1093/scan/nsr061

Weiskopf, N. (2012). Real-time fMRI and its application to neurofeedback. *Neuroimage* 62, 682–692. doi: 10.1016/j.neuroimage.2011.10.009

Weiskopf, N., Scharnowski, F., Veit, R., Goebel, R., Birbaumer, N., and Mathiak, K. (2004). Self-regulation of local brain activity using real-time functional magnetic resonance imaging (fMRI). *J. Physiol. Paris* 98, 357–373. doi: 10.1016/j.jphysparis.2005.09.019

Weiskopf, N., Veit, R., Erb, M., Mathiak, K., Grodd, W., Goebel, R., et al. (2003). Physiological self-regulation of regional brain activity using real-time functional magnetic resonance imaging (fMRI): methodology and exemplary data. *Neuroimage* 19, 577–586. doi: 10.1016/s1053-8119(03)00145-9

Weiss, F. (2005). Neurobiology of craving, conditioned reward and relapse. *Curr. Opin. Pharmacol.* 5, 9–19. doi: 10.1016/j.coph.2004.11.001

Wiers, R. W., Eberl, C., Rinck, M., Becker, E. S., and Lindenmeyer, J. (2011). Retraining automatic action tendencies changes alcoholic patients' approach bias for alcohol and improves treatment outcome. *Psychol. Sci.* 22, 490–497. doi: 10.1177/0956797611400615

Wiers, C. E., Stelzel, C., Park, S. Q., Gawron, C. K., Ludwig, V. U., Gutwinski, S., et al. (2014). Neural correlates of alcohol-approach bias in alcohol addiction: the spirit is willing but the flesh is weak for spirits. *Neuropsychopharmacology* 39, 688–697. doi: 10.1038/npp.2013.252

Wright, C. I., Fischer, H., Whalen, P. J., McInerney, S. C., Shin, L. M., and Rauch, S. L. (2001). Differential prefrontal cortex and amygdala habituation to repeatedly presented emotional stimuli. *Neuroreport* 12, 379–383. doi: 10.1097/00001756-200102120-00039

Yoo, S. S., Fairneny, T., Chen, N. K., Choo, S. E., Panych, L. P., Park, H., et al. (2004). Brain-computer interface using fMRI: spatial navigation by thoughts. *Neuroreport* 15, 1591–1595. doi: 10.1097/01.wnr.0000133296.39160.fe

Yoo, S. S., and Jolesz, F. A. (2002). Functional MRI for neurofeedback: feasibility study on a hand motor task. *Neuroreport* 13, 1377–1381. doi: 10.1097/00001756-200208070-00005

Zilverstand, A., Sorger, B., Zimmermann, J., Kaas, A., and Goebel, R. (2014). Windowed correlation: a suitable tool for providing dynamic fMRI-based functional connectivity neurofeedback on task difficulty. *PLoS One* 9:e85929. doi: 10.1371/journal.pone.0085929

20

Detaching from the negative by reappraisal: the role of right superior frontal gyrus (BA9/32)

Rosalux Falquez[1]*, Blas Couto[2,3], Agustin Ibanez[2,3,4], Martin T. Freitag[5], Moritz Berger[5], Elisabeth A. Arens[1], Simone Lang[1] and Sven Barnow[1]

[1] *Department of Clinical Psychology and Psychotherapy, Institute of Psychology, University of Heidelberg, Heidelberg, Germany*
[2] *Laboratory of Experimental Psychology and Neuroscience, Institute of Cognitive Neurology, Favaloro University, Buenos Aires, Argentina*
[3] *UDP-INECO Foundation Core on Neuroscience, Diego Portales University, Santiago, Chile*
[4] *Departamento de Psicología, Universidad Autónoma del Caribe, Barranquilla, Colombia*
[5] *Department of Radiology, German Cancer Research Center, Heidelberg, Germany*

Correspondence:
Rosalux Falquez, Department of Clinical Psychology and Psychotherapy, Institute of Psychology, University of Heidelberg, Hauptstrasse 47-51, 69117 Heidelberg, Germany
e-mail: rosalux.falquez@psychologie.uni-heidelberg.de

The ability to reappraise the emotional impact of events is related to long-term mental health. Self-focused reappraisal (REAPPself), i.e., reducing the personal relevance of the negative events, has been previously associated with neural activity in regions near right medial prefrontal cortex, but rarely investigated among brain-damaged individuals. Thus, we aimed to examine the REAPPself ability of brain-damaged patients and healthy controls considering structural atrophies and gray matter intensities, respectively. Twenty patients with well-defined cortex lesions due to an acquired circumscribed tumor or cyst and 23 healthy controls performed a REAPPself task, in which they had to either observe negative stimuli or decrease emotional responding by REAPPself. Next, they rated the impact of negative arousal and valence. REAPPself ability scores were calculated by subtracting the negative picture ratings after applying REAPPself from the ratings of the observing condition. The scores of the patients were included in a voxel-based lesion-symptom mapping (VLSM) analysis to identify deficit related areas (ROI). Then, a ROI group-wise comparison was performed. Additionally, a whole-brain voxel-based-morphometry (VBM) analysis was run, in which healthy participant's REAPPself ability scores were correlated with gray matter intensities. Results showed that (1) regions in the right superior frontal gyrus (SFG), comprising the right dorsolateral prefrontal cortex (BA9) and the right dorsal anterior cingulate cortex (BA32), were associated with patient's impaired down-regulation of arousal, (2) a lesion in the depicted ROI occasioned significant REAPPself impairments, (3) REAPPself ability of controls was linked with increased gray matter intensities in the ROI regions. Our findings show for the first time that the neural integrity and the structural volume of right SFG regions (BA9/32) might be indispensable for REAPPself. Implications for neurofeedback research are discussed.

Keywords: emotion regulation, self-focused reappraisal, VLSM, VBM, right SFG

INTRODUCTION

Cognitive emotion regulation (ER) is conceptualized as the ability to modulate the spontaneous flow of emotional states by means of cognitive control. That means, the ability to manage not only which emotion we feel, but when and how this emotion is experienced and expressed (Gross, 1999). Thus, people can effectively take control over their own emotional responses by adjusting them to everyday events and context demands. Conversely, disturbances in ER abilities might disrupt human adaptation and therefore compromise well-being as well as lead to unhealthy social functioning (Aldao and Dixon-Gordon, 2013). For instance, previous studies have emphasized that an impaired ER constitutes a core feature of affective (Goldin et al., 2009; Hermann et al., 2009; New et al., 2009; Abler et al., 2010) and personality disorders (Slee et al., 2008; Lang et al., 2012). According to Gross's *process model of ER*, some regulation strategies might be more protective than others, particularly when they act early in the emotion-generative process (Gross, 1999, 2002). The early change of the way an emotional stimulus is appraised in order to decrease its emotional impact (i.e., reappraisal) is associated with long-term psychological health outcomes (Gross and John, 2003; Goldin et al., 2008; Barnow, 2012). Reappraisal is held to be very effective for the down-regulation of negative emotions, as it has been shown to decrease peripheral psychophysiology (Ray et al., 2010; Kim and Hamann, 2012) and self-reported negative affect (Gross, 1998; Ochsner et al., 2002). Moreover, previous studies investigating neural activation pattern during reappraisal show decreased activation of emotional limbic regions such as the amygdala (Ochsner et al., 2002; Banks et al., 2007; Wager et al., 2008).

Importantly, the down-regulation of emotional limbic regions through reappraisal has been shown to occur by means of top-down influences of cognitive control regions in the prefrontal cortex (PFC; Buhle et al., 2013). Reappraisal is one of the most complex strategies; it involves a variety of cognitive control abilities which serve to generate alternative explanations about an emotionally arousing cue. For example, participants need to rely on working memory (WM) so as to keep or update alternative reinterpretations in mind (Hofmann et al., 2012; Schweizer et al., 2013). Furthermore, flexibility skills are crucial in order to choose between new reinterpretations (Joormann and Gotlib, 2008; Malooly et al., 2013). Also, cognitive inhibition skills are similarly important, especially for the decrease of automatic emotional appraisals (Joormann, 2010; Pe et al., 2013). Following, all of these processes need to be monitored in order to keep track of the regulation success according to internal and external demands (Paret et al., 2011). In line with these assumptions, neural structures commonly shown in functional magnetic resonance imaging (fMRI) investigations examining reappraisal of negative stimuli include mainly regions in the superior frontal gyrus (SFG), like the dorsolateral PFC (dlPFC; BA9/46) and the anterior cingulate cortex (ACC, BA32; Harenski and Hamann, 2006; Banks et al., 2007; Erk et al., 2010; Leiberg et al., 2012; Ochsner et al., 2012). These regions are found to be highly involved in WM and inhibition performance (Lutcke and Frahm, 2008; Shackman et al., 2009; Balconi, 2013). Similarly, an increased blood-oxygen-level-dependent (BOLD) contrast of the dorsal ACC (dACC;BA32) has been observed during reappraisal of negative social situations (Koenigsberg et al., 2010), as well as during situations where error monitoring (van Veen et al., 2001; Ichikawa et al., 2011) and cognitive flexibility are required (Zastrow et al., 2009; Vriend et al., 2013). Therefore, reappraisal function relies to a great extent on the same regions involved in several complex cognitive control tasks (Schweizer et al., 2013).

Besides its functional complexity, there are several types of reappraisal (McRae et al., 2012a). To date, two main variants of strategies have been investigated with fMRI. The most investigated is the situation-focused strategy (REAPPsit), which involves reinterpreting the meaning of the emotional actions or events presented, in order to reduce the emotional response (e.g., seeing a diseased person and thinking the person will get better). The other type is the self-focused reappraisal strategy (REAPPself), which is also known as distancing (e.g., Ochsner et al., 2004), i.e., adopting the role of a detached third-person observer during the presentation of the emotional stimuli (e.g., thinking that the presented stimuli are randomly seen in a newspaper). Ochsner et al. (2004) compared the neural response of both reappraisal strategies, linking regions of the medial prefrontal cortex (mPFC) to REAPPself and more lateral prefrontal cortex regions (lPFC) to REAPPsit (Ochsner et al., 2004). Furthermore, it has been discussed that the ability to assume a subjective distance to emotional cues implies a change in the perceived self-relevance of emotion-inducing objects, which is associated with a right-lateralized, mPFC activity (Kalisch et al., 2005; Ochsner et al., 2005; Ochsner and Gross, 2008; Leiberg et al., 2012). On the other hand, the act of reinterpret negative events might require a more left-lateralized, lPFC involvement because of a highly verbal, externally focused control processing during REAPPsit (see also Ochsner et al., 2012).

In order to examine whether specific regions in the PFC are crucial for effective reappraisal of negative stimuli, brain lesion studies might be an excellent extension to fMRI data, as they do not only reflect which areas are associated with a given ability, but also show which regions are critical for function integrity (Rorden and Karnath, 2004). Furthermore, the need for this type of studies on ER has been highlighted in the past (firstly addressed by Beer and Lombardo, 2007). However, to date there have been only two studies investigating reappraisal performance after acquired brain damage. One recent case-study showed that emotional reappraisal is impaired after a left PFC stroke lesion (Salas et al., 2013). Another recently published study of the same author investigated behavioral data of reappraisal difficulty and productivity in brain injured patients. Results showed that cognitive skills, such as inhibition and verbal fluency might be strongly associated with the generation of reappraisals. Still, the reappraisal ability was not addressed (Salas et al., 2014). Therefore, the goal of the current study was to explore the reappraisal ability in brain-injured patients, and to infer which area of the PFC impairs this ability the most. For this purpose, considering that the effects of a brain lesion might impair the manipulation of thoughts (as held by Salas et al., 2014), we chose to hold the reappraisal strategy constant and instruct the REAPPself strategy. First, this strategy has been shown to be more effective than REAPPsit at overall reduction of affective responding (Shiota and Levenson, 2012). Second, REAPPself might be less difficult than REAPPsit for the brain-damaged patients, as REAPPsit might require more cognitive abilities for the spontaneous generation of alternative reinterpretations and involves more contextual encoding of stimuli than REAPPself (Ochsner et al., 2004, 2012; Ochsner and Gross, 2008). Furthermore, REAPPself might be a relevant strategy for brain-damaged patients, given the widely recognized importance of self-distancing for adaptive coping with autobiographical negative events (Ayduk and Kross, 2008, 2010).

To explore which lesion location is most likely to impair REAPPself, we first ran an exploratory voxel-based lesion-symptom mapping analysis (VLSM; for further explanation of this method see Bates et al., 2003; Rorden et al., 2007) in 20 patients with single brain lesions. We hypothesized that SFG regions, particularly regions near the mPFC, would be indispensable for REAPPself ability (Ochsner et al., 2004), as this region has anatomically been defined as a mediator between the lateral PFC and amygdala regions (Johnstone et al., 2007; Ray and Zald, 2012). Second, we predicted that subjects with a lesion in the areas highlighted by the VLSM analysis, defined as region-of-interest (ROI), would have deficits on REAPPself, whereas patients with a lesion sparing these ROI would show a better REAPPself ability. Third, we ran a regional voxel-based-morphometry (VBM; Ashburner and Friston, 2000) analysis with structural data of healthy participants expecting to find significant associations between ROI gray matter intensities and REAPPself function. All participants completed cognitive and affective screening tasks in order to characterize potential deficits of the patients. Here, we also aimed to explore which cognitive functions are more impaired in the group with a lesion in the ROI compared to the other groups.

METHODS AND MATERIALS

PARTICIPANTS

A total of 27 patients with lesions in different parts of the cortex, but predominantly affecting the frontal lobes, and 23 healthy volunteers were assessed. The patients were recruited either from the department of Neuro-Oncology of the University Hospital of Heidelberg, Germany, or from self-help groups in the community. The inclusion criterion was the presence of a lesion involving well-defined parts of the cortex with definable and segmentable margins in the T_2 weighted FLAIR (fluid-attenuated inversion recovery) sequence, assessed by an experienced radiologist. For all analyses, a potential edema zone was, if present, taken into account. Patients with multifocal brain lesions, previous history of head trauma or neurological disorders independent of brain injury, clinically detectable aphasia symptoms as well as presence of serious functional impairments (i.e., patients with a Karnofsky index below 80%; Clark and Fallowfield, 1986) were excluded. Healthy control participants (15 women; M age $= 39.65 \pm 11.23$) had no history of neurological or psychiatric disorders. No control participant was taking psychoactive drugs. They were recruited through advertisements posted in newspapers, and were matched as closely as possible to the patients for sex and age.

Nineteen patients with an acquired brain tumor and one patient with a cyst met the inclusion criterion. The diagnosis of patients with brain tumors has been histopathologically confirmed either by operation ($n = 17$) or by biopsy ($n = 2$) in agreement with the WHO staging system (Kleihues and Sobin, 2000). Seven patients had to be excluded, due to non-corrected vision problems ($n = 1$), multifocal lesions ($n = 5$) and severe microangiopathy ($n = 1$). The remaining 20 patients took part in the analysis (11 women, M age $= 45 \pm 10.04$ years; M lesion volume $= 35.27 \pm 32.19\,cm^3$). Of 19 brain tumor patients, 10 had single low-grade tumors (WHO°II) and 9 had single high-grade tumors (WHO°III-IV). Patients with brain tumors received radio- and/or chemotherapy. Brain tumor patients were tested at least 1 year after biopsy or maximum safe resection (M biopsy/resection $= 3.95 \pm 4.20$ years, range = 1–16 years), and the whole group was tested at least 2 years since lesion onset (M onset $= 5.00 \pm 3.96$ years, range = 2–15 years). Sixty-five percent of the 19 patients with brain tumors had no evidence for tumor recurrence and 35% had tumor recurrence in the same lesion site. Taking perifocal edemas into account, no lesion was bigger than $110\,cm^3$ (see **Table 1** for more detailed information about etiology, lesion laterality and tumor location).

All participants were informed about the risks of the study and signed a written informed consent prior to participation. This research was conducted with the approval of the ethical board of the University of Heidelberg according to the declaration of Helsinki. All participants were paid after finished assessment.

NEUROPSYCHOLOGICAL AND AFFECTIVE ASSESSMENT

All participants completed a brief screening of cognitive abilities, which included measures of cognitive flexibility (Trail Making Task A,B; Tombaugh, 2004); fluid intelligence using the *Culture-Fair-Intelligence-Test* (CFT-20; Cattell, 1960; Weiss, 1998); memory performance and processing speed (measured by the cognitive screening of the German Aphasia-Check-List ACL; Kalbe et al., 2002, 2005) and behavioral inhibition (Go/Nogo task from the German Attention Test Battery TAP; Zimmermann and Fimm, 2002). The Beck Depression Inventory (BDI-II; Kuhner et al., 2007) was included for the assessment of depressive symptoms (for more information see the Supplementary Material).

STIMULUS MATERIAL

A set of 20 negative and 20 neutral pictures was selected from the *International Affective Picture System* (IAPS; Lang et al., 2005). The selected negative pictures mainly contained unpleasant images of injured or mutilated persons, violent situations and diseases (M arousal $= 6.91 \pm 0.30$; M valence $= 2.01 \pm 0.53$), while the neutral pictures showed mainly ordinary home objects (M arousal $= 2.69 \pm 0.52$; M valence $= 4.98 \pm 0.23$). Neutral and negative pictures differed significantly in arousal [$t_{(26)} = -22.96$; $p < 0.001$] and valence ratings [$t_{(30.58)} = 31.59$; $p < 0.001$)].

REAPPself TASK

The task consisted of three conditions: the neutral condition, in which participants had to watch neutral pictures (LNeu); the negative condition, in which participants had to watch negative affective pictures (LNeg); and the REAPPself condition, in which participants had to decrease the triggered negative emotions by means of REAPPself during negative picture presentation (Dec). Sixty pseudo-randomized trials were presented using the *Presentation experiment driver* (www.neurobs.com). A typical trial started with a white fixation cross on a black background, which was presented for 2 s. Afterwards, the instruction was presented for 4 s: either "LOOK" (solely look at the picture without trying to manipulate the induced emotion) or "DISTANCING" (e. g. "It is a newspaper picture, and I am not involved"). Then, a brief fixation cross was presented again, followed by the negative emotional picture, presented for 6 s. Participants had to process the pictures according to the instructions. Self-assessment manikin (SAM Ratings; Bradley and Lang, 1994) were presented directly afterwards. Here, participants had to spontaneously rate the amount of emotional arousal as well as how displeasing the emotion induced by the previously presented picture was (valence); patients rated on a 1–9 scale. As the task was originally design for fMRI, a random jitter (6–9 s) relax trial appeared on the screen afterwards (Amaro and Barker, 2006). For a graphical description of the experimental order see **Figure 1**.

PROCEDURE

The assessment was separated into two sessions, with less than a week between assessments. The first session comprised cognitive and affective assessment, whereas the second session involved the magnetic resonance imaging (MRI) scan and the REAPPself fMRI-task. In the current article, only behavioral results are reported.

First, the examiner provided the reappraisal task instructions in a written form. Then, participants were confronted with negative pictures of the IAPS while becoming clear instructions of REAPPself: to decrease the induced negative emotion by perceiving the content of the stimuli in a detached, third-person perspective (as viewing the picture in a newspaper; e.g., Ochsner et al., 2004; Lang et al., 2012). Thus, participants had to think, for example, that the event showed in the picture occurs in a

Table 1 | Brain-damaged patient sample.

Nr.	Gender (m/f)	Age	Education level (1–8)	Etiology	Years post onset	Lesion side	Lesion location	Severity	Lesion volume (cm^3)
1	f	59	4	Resected Oligodendroglioma	10	Right	Frontobasal	WHO°III	1.19
2	f	42	4	Resected Meningioma	15	Left	Frontotemporal	WHO°II	3.74
3	f	65	8	Resected Glioblastoma	1	Right	Frontoparietal	WHO°IV	33.02
4	f	30	8	Resected Astrozytoma	2	Left	Parietal	WHO°II	43.92
5	f	38	8	Resected Oligodendroglioma	5	Left	Frontal	WHO°III	76.82
6	m	46	8	Resected Oligoastrozytoma	7	Right	Frontotemporo-parietal	WHO°III	70.02
7	m	46	8	Resected Oligoastrozytoma	6	Left	Frontal	WHO°III	39.98
8	f	40	3	Astrozytoma	2	Right	Frontal	WHO°II	5.67
9	m	55	8	Resected Oligodendroglioma	3	Bilateral	Frontal	WHO°III	90.09
10	f	52	6	Resected Glioblastoma	2	Right	Frontal	WHO°IV	46.53
11	f	61	2	Resected Glioblastoma	2	Left	Frontal	WHO°IV	14.56
12	m	32	2	Astrozytoma	2	Left	Frontal	WHO°II	9.58
13	m	32	8	Resected Astrozytoma	3	Left	Frontoparietal	WHO°II	11.61
14	f	45	8	Resected Oligodendroglioma	2	Right	Frontal	WHO°III	49.32
15	f	51	7	Resected Astrozytoma	4	Right	Frontal	WHO°II	15.74
16	m	40	2	Astrozytoma	4	Right	Insular	WHO°II	4.44
17	m	43	2	Astrozytoma	2	Right	Frontal	WHO°II	20.47
18	m	36	2	Resected Astrozytoma	12	Left	Temporal	WHO°II	55.20
19	m	49	2	Resected Astrozytoma	11	Bilateral	Frontotemporo-parietal	WHO°III	110.45
20	f	37	8	Cyst involving cortex	4	Right	Frontal	–	3.08

f, female; m, male.

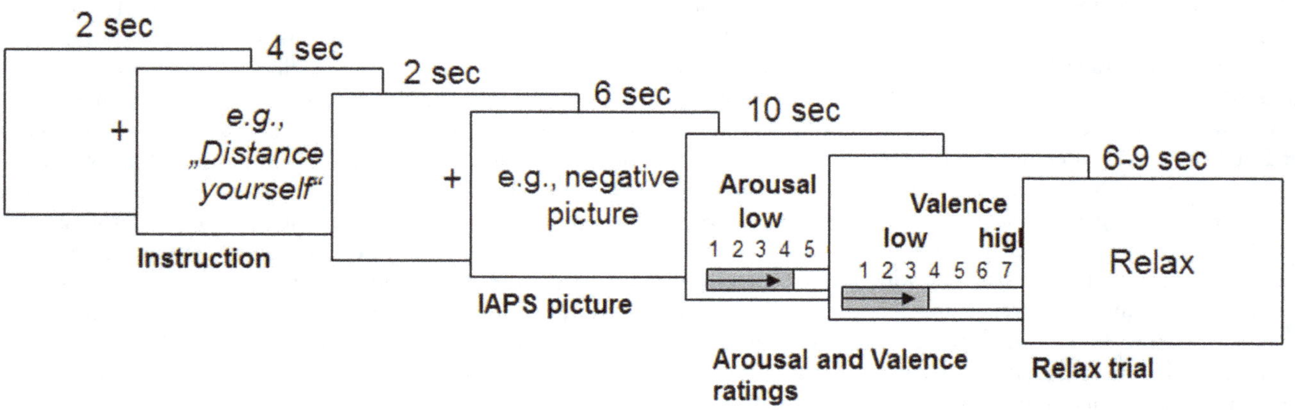

FIGURE 1 | Graphical description of the reappraisal task used with the durations of each trial (modified from Ochsner et al., 2004). Emotions were triggered by IAPS pictures after the instruction was presented for 4 s. From this point on, participants had to either only look at the picture or down-regulate the triggered emotions for 6 s. Then they had to rate their emotional arousal and valence for 5 s each. Afterwards, participants relaxed for 6–9 s.

place far away or is randomly seen in the newspaper. Further, they informed the examiner by saying out loud how they detached. Subsequently, participants were trained in REAPPself by performing three practice trials. The session ended after ensuring that the participant understood the task procedure and applied REAPPself properly. In the second session, four more practice trials were conducted in the MRI scanner, in order to ensure that the participants felt comfortable. After the investigator was sure that the task was understood, participants began with the task assessment, which was separated into two runs of 30 trials each.

STRUCTURAL IMAGING RECORDINGS AND LESION ANALYSIS

Structural images were obtained on a 3 Tesla MRI scanner system (MAGNETOM Trio, Siemens Medical Systems, Erlangen, Germany) equipped with a 32-channel head coil. All brains were visualized with high resolution scans, which were acquired using a T1-weighted flash 3D sequence ($TR = 1680$ ms; $TE = 2.6$ ms; voxel size $= 1.1 \times 1.1 \times 1.1$ mm). Individual edema and tumor tissue were traced from T2-weighted FLAIR anatomical scans ($TR = 9000$ ms; $TE = 95.0$ ms; voxel size $= 0.9 \times 0.9 \times 4.0$ mm) by a radiologist blind to task performances using MRIcron software (Rorden et al., 2007). Using a procedure endorsed by Crinion et al. (2007), the T2 scans with the identified lesions were co-registered to the T1-weighted scans. Finally, the T1 scans were normalized to standardized MNI-space via *Unified segmentation and normalization* of the MATLAB toolbox *Statistical Parametrical Mapping* (SPM8; Crinion et al., 2007; Seghier et al., 2008). The Montreal Neurological Institute (MNI) brain standardized lesions were used to estimate lesion sites on aal templates of the MRIcron software (www.mricro.com/mricron) and to create lesion overlap images.

VLSM ANALYSIS

The first analysis was run in VLSM (Bates et al., 2003) in order to explore which regions are associated with impairments of REAPPself ability. The input variables were the operationalization of the REAPPself ability (i.e., the amount of down-regulation), which comprised the subtractions in arousal and valence ratings from "LOOK" and "DISTANCING" conditions (LNeg-Dec). Then, a series of Brunner-Munzel (BM) t-tests at every voxel were run in order to compare the input variables in patients with and without a lesion in the voxel. Based on the results ($p < 0.05$), a colorized map was generated, showing which lesioned region/s is/are associated with poorer performance. For instance, if patients with a lesion in specific voxels show significantly poorer REAPPself ability, then the region in which these specific voxels are located would be visualized in the statistical map. We also generated a map to determine the distribution of statistical power for our sample, based on an effect size of 0.8 (Kimberg et al., 2007) and an alpha level of 0.05, which shows voxels with enough power to detect significant differences. As shown in **Figure 2**, mostly right PFC and left superior PFC areas had adequate power. For instance, predictions for the VLSM analysis were restricted to these regions. In order to prevent spurious results, solely voxels in which a minimum of three patients was affected were included (analogously to Tsuchida et al., 2010; Tsuchida and Fellows, 2012). Significant results were overlaid to an MRIcron template (http://www.mccauslandcenter.sc.edu/mricro/mricron/) in order to identify involved Brodmann areas (BA).

VLSM REGION-OF-INTEREST (ROI) GROUPWISE COMPARISON

The second analysis depicts group comparisons between patients presenting a lesion in the overlap area calculated by VLSM (ROI), patients with a lesion sparing the ROI (IntactROI), and the healthy control (HC) group. Mean arousal and valence ratings were included as dependent variables in 3 *groups* (ROI, IntactROI, HC) × 2 *tasks* (LNeg, Dec) repeated measures ANOVA, followed by *post-hoc* Tukey HSD pair-wise comparisons. For relevant control variables, we used the Kruskal-Wallis-Test. Variables differing significantly between groups were included as covariate in the ANOVA.

VBM ANALYSIS

Images for control subjects were preprocessed for VBM analysis using DARTEL Toolbox and followed procedures previously described (Ashburner and Friston, 2000). Following, the modulated images were smoothed with a Gaussian 12 mm full-width half-maximum kernel as suggested in other reports (Good et al., 2001) and normalized to the MNI standard space. Finally, these images were analyzed within different general linear models in SPM-8 2nd level analyses (http://www.fil.ion.ucl.ac.uk/spm/software/spm8). These consisted of multiple linear regressions accounting for total intracranial volume, age and gender as non-interest or nuisance covariates. First, two whole brain analyses were performed: (1) for arousal differences (LNeg-Dec) and (2) for valence difference scores (LNeg-Dec) of REAPPself ability. The analyses were performed and examined at $p < 0.001$, two-tailed uncorrected threshold. Second, in order to assess the specific regional pattern of gray matter involved in each domain, two linear regressions were performed within the VLSM depicted ROI of the patients group as a small volume correction.

RESULTS

SOCIODEMOGRAPHIC, NEUROPSYCHOLOGICAL, AND AFFECTIVE ASSESSMENT

The independent t-test revealed no significant differences between healthy controls ($n = 23$) and patients ($n = 20$) in age

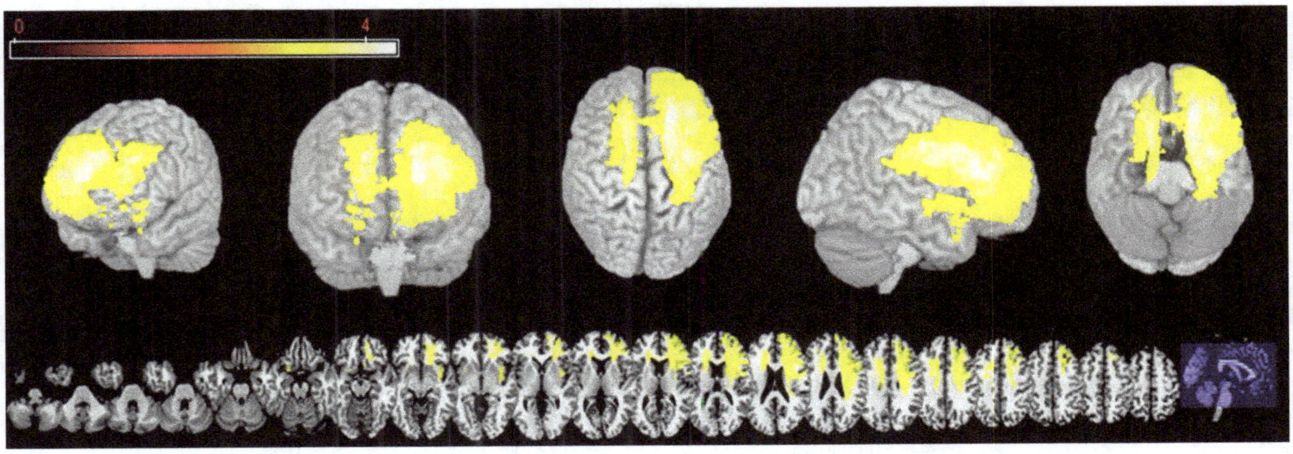

FIGURE 2 | Three-dimensional and multislice views of voxels (yellow), where there is sufficient statistical power to detect an effect of lesion on behavior.

[$t_{(41)} = -1.64$, $p = 0.11$], but significant differences in educational level [$t_{(26.81)} = 2.37$, $p = 0.03$], depression [$t_{(20.13)} = -5.05$, $p < 0.001$] and fluid intelligence scores [$t_{(37)} = 2.77$, $p = 0.01$] (see **Table 2**). Regarding the neuropsychological screening, patients differed significantly from the healthy control performance in processing speed assessed by phonemic verbal fluency [$t_{(41)} = 3.49$, $p = 0.001$], short-term memory [$t_{(29.97)} = 2.92$, $p = 0.007$], behavioral inhibition assessed by the number of Go/NoGo errors [$t_{(19.87)} = -2.70$, $p = 0.01$] and cognitive flexibility [$t_{(31.51)} = -2.49$, $p = 0.02$]. The cognitive profile of the patient group is consistent with several descriptions of performance on individuals with frontal lobe lesions (see **Table 3**; Dimitrov et al., 2003; Niki et al., 2009; Rodriguez-Bailon et al., 2012).

GROUP COMPARISONS IN EMOTIONAL REACTIVITY AND REGULATION

In order to examine the differences on emotional reactivity, we subtracted the arousal and valence ratings of LNeu conditions from LNeg. The independent t-test with both groups showed that on average, patient and control groups did not significantly differ in emotional reactivity, neither for arousal [$t_{(29.98)} = 0.72$, $p = 0.48$], nor for valence [$t_{(41)} = -0.52$, $p = 0.61$].

Following, to investigate whether patients and HC differed significantly in REAPPself ability, we ran two repeated-measures ANOVAs with arousal and valence ratings of LNeg and Dec *tasks* as within-subject factors, and *group* (patients vs. HC) as between factors. Given that depressive symptoms (arousal: $r = 0.43$; $p = 0.006$, valence: $r = 0.47$; $p = 0.002$), fluid intelligence (arousal: $r = -0.34$; $p = 0.04$), short-term/immediate memory (arousal: $r = -0.35$; $p = 0.02$, valence: $r = -0.36$; $p = 0.02$) and inhibition deficits (arousal: $r = 0.31$; $p = 0.05$) significantly correlated with arousal and valence ratings in the Dec condition, we included each of these variables as covariates in an ANOVA design of arousal and valence ratings, and tested their significance regarding interaction effects with the dependent variables. It is important to mention that the variables did not correlate with the ratings in the LNeg condition. No significant interaction effects with the dependent variables were found. Only the depression (BDI) scores reached significant main effects as a covariate for the arousal [$F_{(1, 38)} = 5.57$; $p = 0.02$] and valence [$F_{(1, 38)} = 7.27$; $p = 0.01$] ratings. So, controlling for depression, there was no main effect for group [arousal: $F_{(1, 38)} = 0.54$, $p = 0.47$; valence: $F_{(1, 38)} = 0.70$, $p = 0.41$] or interaction effects *group* x *task* [arousal: $F_{(1, 38)} = 0.23$, $p = 0.63$; valence: $F_{(1, 38)} = 1.41$, $p = 0.24$], whereas effects of task were highly significant [arousal: $F_{(1, 38)} = 63.18$, $p < 0.001$; valence: $F_{(1, 38)} = 58.23$, $p < 0.001$]. Thus, all participants were able to down-regulate the emotional valence of the pictures (see **Figure 3**). Interestingly, by excluding the depression covariate from the analysis, the valence ratings showed significant interaction effects *group* x *task* [$F_{(1, 41)} = 4.38$,

Table 2 | Demographic variables of brain-damaged patients and healthy controls.

Variables	Patients ($n = 20$, 11 f)	Controls ($n = 23$, 15 f)	p	Effect size (d)
Age	45 (10.04)	39.65 (11.23)	0.11	0.50
Educational level (1–8)	5.4 (2.74)	7 (1.35)	0.03	0.74
Depressive symptoms (BDI)	12.67 (8.44)	2.17 (2.88)	<0.001	1.67
Fluid IQ (CFT-20)	109 (12)	118.47 (9.12)	0.01	0.89

BDI, Becks Depression Inventory; CFT, Culture Fair Intelligence Test; f, female.

Table 3 | Summarized performance results on selected neuropsychological screening tests for brain-damaged patients and healthy controls.

	Mean (SD)			
Variables	**Patients ($n = 20$)**	**Controls ($n = 23$)**	p^a	**Effect size (d)**
PROCESSING SPEED (ACL)[b]				
Phonemic verbal fluency	12.05 (3.07)	15.74 (3.76)	0.001	1.13
Semantic verbal fluency	17.95 (5.21)	21 (4.99)	0.06	0.60
Cognitive Flexibility (TMT B-A)	35.39 (16.76)	24.48 (10.74)	0.02	0.78
MEMORY RECALL (ACL)[b]				
Inmediate recall	4.7 (1.22)	5.61 (0.72)	0.01	0.91
Delayed recall	4.9 (1.33)	5.52 (0.85)	0.08	0.56
BEHAVIORAL INHIBITION (GoNoGo)				
Median reaction time	401.06 (75.86)	420.09 (53.12)	0.36	0.29
Comission errors	1.72 (2.05)	0.36 (0.66)	0.01	0.89
Omissions	0.67 (1.85)	0.46 (0.21)	0.17	0.16
Outliers	0.28 (0.46)	0.27 (0.55)	0.98	0.02

[a] Independent t-test results, [b] Cognitive assessment section of the Aphasia Check List test battery; SD, standard deviation; ACL, Aphasia Check-List; TMT, Trail Making Task.

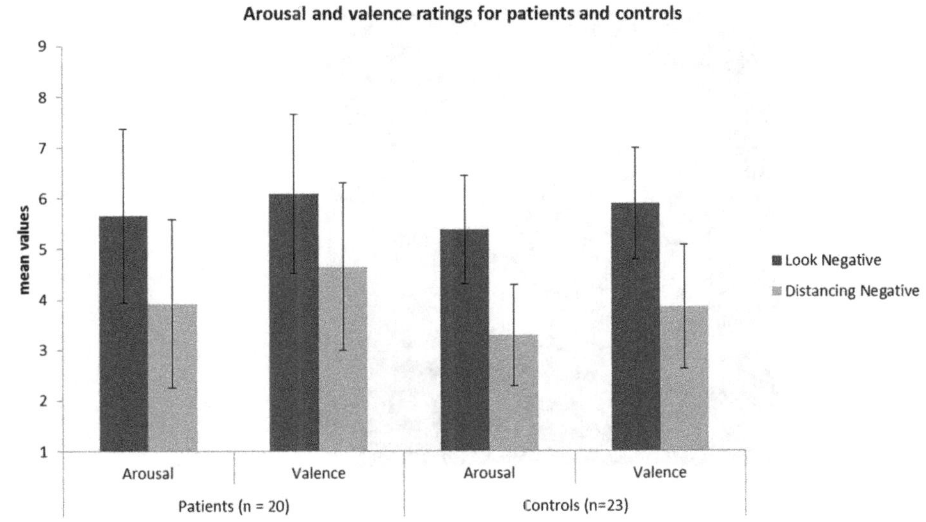

FIGURE 3 | Mean values of the arousal and valence ratings for the patient ($N = 20$) and HC ($N = 23$) sample in each condition.

$p = 0.04$], reflecting that the valence-related down-regulation was influenced by depressive symptoms.

BRAIN-DAMAGED PATIENTS' GRAY MATTER RESULTS

The VLSM analysis of the arousal-related REAPPself ability scores showed the involvement of a region in SFG overlapping the right dlPFC (BA9) and the right dACC (BA32). The valence-related REAPPself ability did not show any cortex involvement. The statistical map generated by the BM-test on each voxel is shown in **Figure 4A**. The color scale indicates BM-test Z-scores. It is important to mention that no voxel survived correction for multiple comparisons using conventional false discovery rate (FDR) thresholds (e.g., Tsuchida et al., 2010). However, the power map in **Figure 2** shows that this region in the right SFG had adequate power to detect effects at the uncorrected threshold depicted in **Figure 4A**. Nevertheless, the statistical map of the BM-test should be interpreted with caution, because of the risk of false-positive findings. We conducted a ROI-based analysis to further analyze the functional effects of lesions in the depicted voxels (Kimberg et al., 2007). For this purpose, we focused on the brighter regions showing results thresholded with a cut-off value of $Z > 2.5$.

ROI GROUPWISE COMPARISON

The patient sample was subsequently divided into two groups. The ROI group consisted of five patients presenting a lesion overlapping the region of the computed VLSM analysis ($N = 5$; see **Figure 4B**). The IntactROI group consisted of patients presenting a lesion sparing this region ($N = 15$; see **Figure 4C**). Compared with the HC in a Kruksall-Wallis-test, groups showed no significant differences in age ($p = 0.22$), education level ($p = 0.21$), or lesion volume ($p = 0.13$). However, groups differed significantly in depressive symptoms ($p < 0.001$; ROI>IntactROI>HC), fluid intelligence ($p = 0.01$; ROI<IntactROI<HC), phonemic verbal fluency ($p = 0.01$; ROI<IntactROI<HC), short-term memory ($p = 0.02$; ROI<IntactROI<HC), and inhibition deficits, as assessed by the number of Go/Nogo errors ($p = 0.002$; ROI>IntactROI>HC). Interestingly, the covariance main effect of depressive symptoms was significant for valence rating scores [$F_{(1, 37)} = 4.27$; $p = 0.05$], but not for arousal scores [$F_{(1, 37)} = 2.71$; $p = 0.11$]. However, no significant interaction effects BDI x *task* [arousal: $F_{(1, 38)} = 0.001$, $p = 0.98$; valence: $F_{(1, 37)} = 0.15$, $p = 0.71$] and no significant correlations with REAPPself ability scores were found (arousal: $r = -0.20, p = 0.21$; valence: $r = -0.30$, $p = 0.06$), so that they were not included in the analysis. In addition, the Kruksal-Wallis test showed that the groups did not significantly differ in emotional reactivity scores (LNeg-LNeu; arousal: $p = 0.54$; valence: $p = 0.87$).

Rating values demonstrated significant overall main effects of *group* [arousal: $F_{(2,40)} = 6.07$, $p = 0.005$; valence: $F_{(2,40)} = 4.93$, $p = 0.01$] and *task* [arousal: $F_{(1, 40)} = 94.35$, $p < 0.001$; valence: $F_{(1, 40)} = 80.65$, $p < 0.001$]. A significant interaction effect *group* × *task* of arousal ratings [$F_{(2, 40)} = 3.28$, $p = 0.05$] demonstrated that patients with a lesion in the ROI could not down-regulate arousal induced by negative emotions in the same manner as the two other control groups, as shown in **Figure 5** (see also Tukey comparisons in **Table 4**). In other words, negative arousal in the Dec condition was significantly higher for the ROI group compared to the other control groups. In addition, valence *group* × *task* interactions were marginally significant [$F_{(2, 40)} = 3.07$, $p = 0.06$]. Results of Tukey's test for multiple comparisons revealed that arousal and valence rating scores were significantly higher for the ROI group than the two other groups, which did not differ significantly in arousal and valence scores ($p = 0.99$; see **Table 5**). These results indicate a more successful down-regulation of negative emotions for the two control groups (REAPPself ability), but less successful for the ROI group. Regarding the valence ratings, this difference might be significantly influenced by the amount of depressive symptoms of the ROI group.

HEALTHY CONTROLS' GRAY MATTER RESULTS

Whole brain analyses

In the whole brain analyses, it was found that REAPPself ability scores (LNeg-Dec) had a positive correlation with gray matter

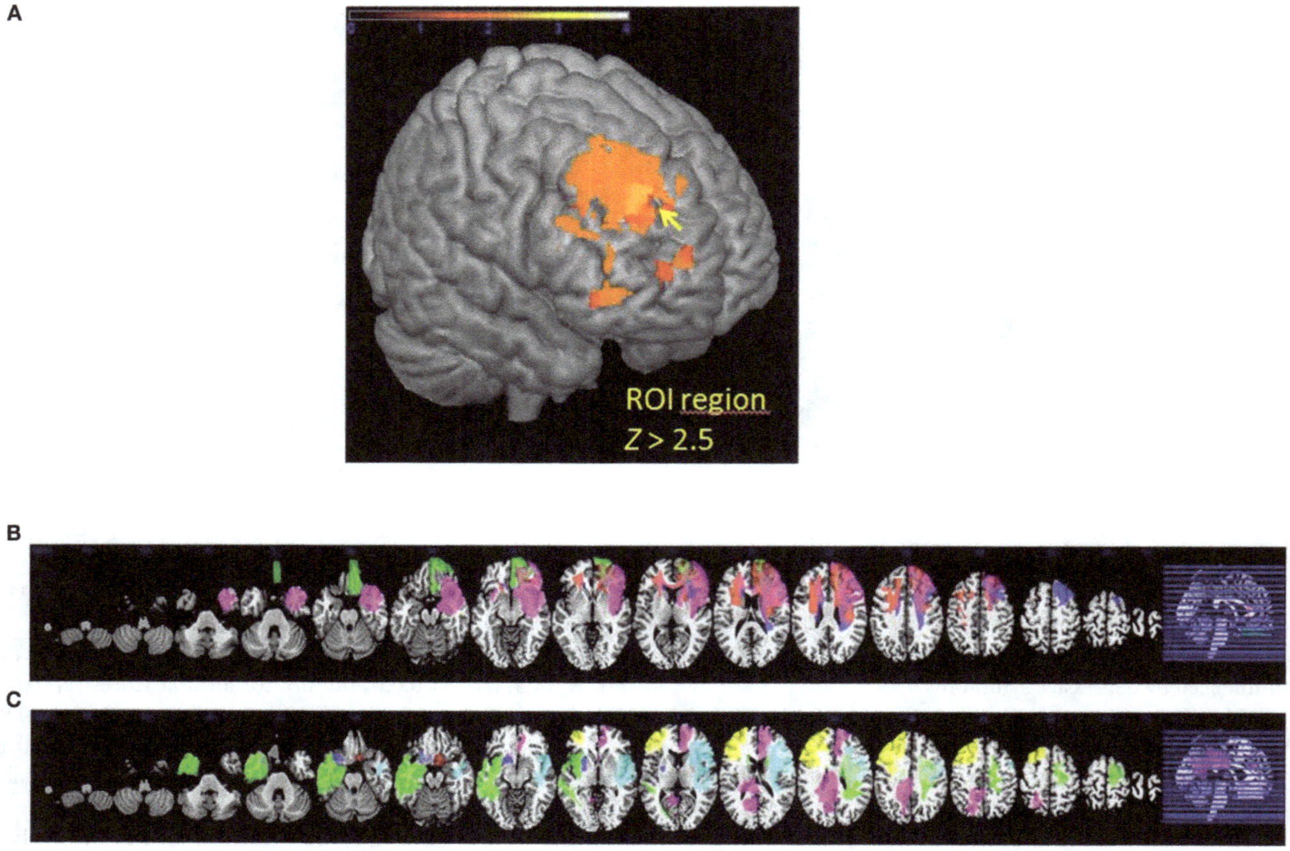

FIGURE 4 | (A) VLSM results: brighter regions showing more significant effects in dorsal regions of the PFC (cutoff $Z > 2.5$) **(B)** multislice view of lesion overlays of ROI group including edema zone ($N = 5$) **(C)** multislice view of the IntactROI group ($N = 15$).

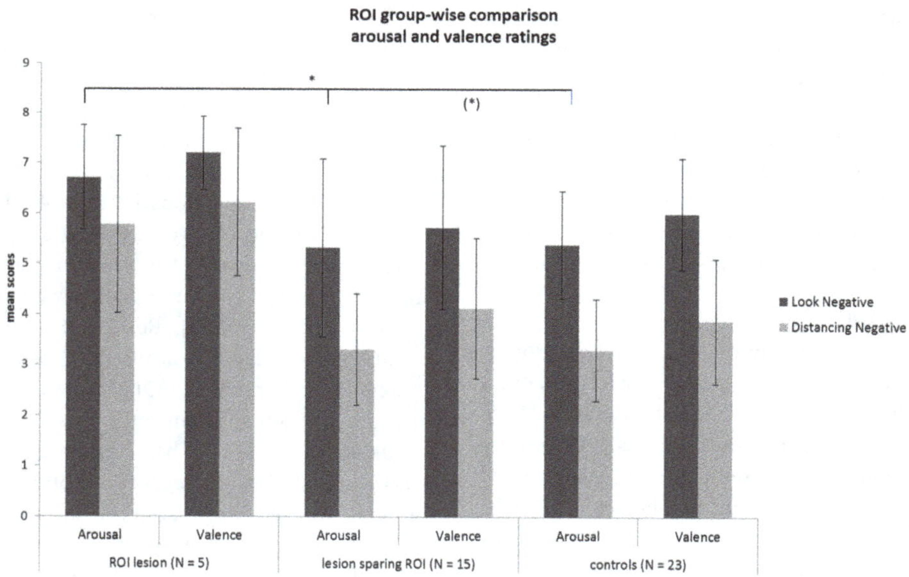

FIGURE 5 | Subjective ratings of arousal and valence after look and decrease conditions for each group. There was a significant group difference of decrease scores showing that the ROI-group was the less successful in down-regulating negative emotions. $*p < 0.05$.

Table 4 | Multiple comparisons (Tukey HD *post-hoc* tests) of arousal and valence ratings of ROI injured, ROI intact patients, and healthy controls.

		Arousal ratings			Valence ratings		
I Group	**II Group**	**Mean difference I-II**	**St. error**	***p***	**Mean difference I-II**	**St. error**	***p***
ROI group	Intact ROI	1.94	0.59	0.007	1.79	0.63	0.02
	HC	1.91	0.58	0.005	1.83	0.59	0.01
Intact ROI	ROI group	−1.94	0.59	0.007	−1.79	0.63	0.02
	HC	−0.032	0.38	0.99	0.04	0.40	0.99
HC	ROI group	−1.91	0.57	0.005	−1.83	0.59	0.001
	Intact ROI	0.032	0.38	0.99	−0.04	0.40	0.99

Table 5 | Whole brain Patterns of GM intensity correlated with task performance in controls.

		Coordinates				
Region	**BA**	***x***	***y***	***z***	***F* peak**	***p* (unc)**
A. AROUSAL						
Superior frontal gyrus R	9	18	34.5	40.5	20.97	<0.001
Cerebellum Crus 2 R		7.5	−90	−36	20.39	<0.001
Pallidum L		−13.5	6	0	16.79	<0.001
Mid temporal gyrus L	22	−52.5	−49.5	0	12.54	<0.001
Posterior Insula L	13	−34.5	−28.5	16.5	12.19	<0.001
Superior frontal gyrus L	9	−16.5	43.5	24	12.19	<0.001
Rolandic Operculum R	13	43.5	−9	22.5	11.84	<0.001
Insula L	13	−36	−9	19.5	11.83	<0.001
Cerebellum Crus 1 L		−36	−58.5	−37.5	11.80	<0.001
B. VALENCE						
Cerebellum 8 L		−27	−43.5	−54	15.82	<0.001
Mid frontal gyrus L	10	−34.5	49.5	16.5	15.80	<0.001
Cerebellum Crus 2 R		7.5	−88.5	−34.5	15.43	<0.001
Mid temporal gyrus R	21	42	−64.5	6	14.74	<0.001
Cerebellum Crus 10 R		22.5	−40.5	−46.5	14.04	<0.001
Putamen L		−16.5	3	−7.5	14	<0.001
Inferior parietal lobule R	7	30	−54	39	12.38	<0.001
Inferior frontal gyrus *Pars Triangularis* L	46	−48	19.5	9	12.08	<0.001
Superior temporal gyrus R	22	60	−31.5	10.5	11.97	<0.001
Superior frontal gyrus R	9	22.5	−22.5	58.5	11.73	<0.001

of a series of cortical and subcortical structures in the right and left hemispheres: at the frontal lobe, more specifically the right SFG (BA 9-32; see **Figure 6A**), left insula, basal ganglia and mid temporal gyrus, and bilateral cerebellum (See **Table 5A** for MNI coordinates). For the valence (LNeg-Dec) domain, this relation appeared at the left SFG (BA 9-32; see **Figure 6B**), right SFG, left mid and inferior frontal gyri, temporal cortex, parietal cortex, basal ganglia and cerebellum (See **Table 6B** for MNI coordinates). No significant negative correlations were found.

Regional brain analyses

Similar results were found in the regressions done at the patient's lesion ROI. HC showed greater gray matter amount in the right SFG (BA 9-32) for higher arousal-related REAPPself ability scores (LNeg-Dec; see **Figure 7A**), as well as for the valence domain (see **Figure 7B**). The MNI coordinates are presented in **Table 6**.

In summary, following results were obtained: First, we found an association between deficits in REAPPself ability performance and a dlSFG area overlapping the right SFG (BA9/32) using exploratory VLSM analysis. Second, repeated-measures ANOVA confirmed that the ROI group was less successful in regulating negative emotional responding (i.e., poorer REAPPself ability) compared to IntactROI and HC groups. Third, regional VBM analyses of the mentioned areas in the HC revealed that REAPPself ability was positively related to BA9/32 gray matter intensities.

DISCUSSION

The cognitive regulation of negative emotions is crucial for mental health, yet there is a lack of lesion studies investigating reappraisal. Therefore, the goal of this study was to identify critical PFC regions for reappraisal ability by analyzing the performance

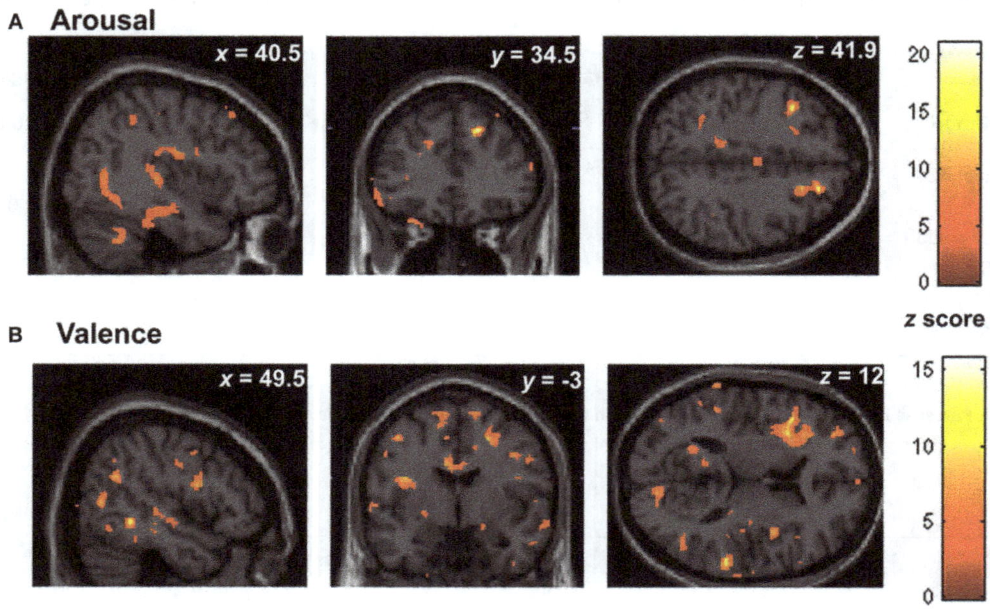

FIGURE 6 | Whole brain patterns of gray matter intensities correlated with task performance in controls. (A) Arousal rating differences **(B)** Valence rating differences.

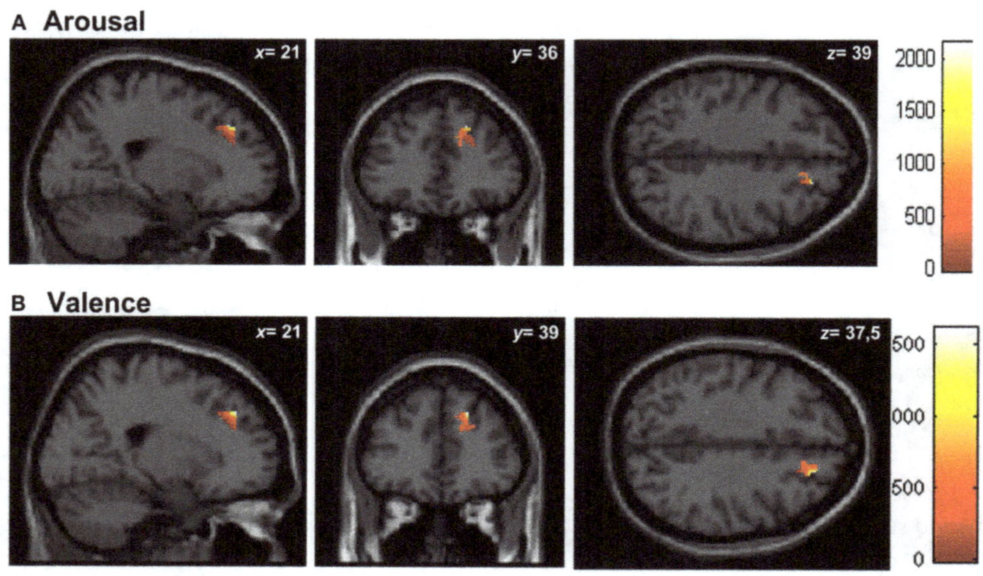

FIGURE 7 | Graphic display of regional gray matter patterns of intensity using the lesion overlap results of the VLSM analysis (BA9/32) correlated with task performance in controls. (A) Arousal and **(B)** Valence rating differences.

of brain-damaged patients and healthy participants. Taking in consideration the cognitive difficulties of the patients, we thoroughly trained REAPPself assuring that the participants apply the proper strategy. VLSM analysis among the patients and VBM analysis of the healthy control's gray matter showed that specific regions of the right SFG including the dlPFC (BA9) and the dACC (BA32) might be indispensable for REAPPself. Furthermore, ROI-based group comparisons supported the results, demonstrating that a lesion located in the mentioned areas significantly impaired down-regulation of negative arousal. To the best of our knowledge, the current study is the first lesion study using neuroimaging methods for the identification of circumscribed brain regions indispensable for the REAPPself ability.

THE SFG AND REAPPRAISAL OF NEGATIVE STIMULI

In line with previous investigations, the current study linked down-regulation of negative emotions by REAPPself to regions near the mPFC (Ochsner et al., 2004). Our results were also in

Table 6 | Patterns of regional GM intensity correlated with task performance in controls.

Region	BA	Coordinates x	y	z	F peak	P (FDR-cor)
A. AROUSAL						
Superior frontal gyrus R	9	21	36	39	2148	<0.001
		15	28.5	37.5	1135	<0.001
Anterior cingulate R	32	13.5	28.5	27	1063	<0.001
B. VALENCE						
Superior frontal gyrus R	9	21	39	37.5	1617	<0.001
		15	28.5	37.5	856	<0.001
Anterior cingulate R	32	13.5	28.5	27	996	<0.001

VBM, voxel-based morphometry; BA, Brodmann area; R, right; L, left; GM, gray matter; FDR, false-discovery rate correction.

accordance with latest fMRI data, as six from the 7 fMRI studies investigating down-regulation of negative emotions by REAPPself (as classified by Ochsner et al., 2012) have consistently demonstrated the involvement of areas in the depicted SFG, including the dlPFC (Erk et al., 2010), dorsomedial PFC (Schardt et al., 2010), and dACC (Koenigsberg et al., 2010; Lang et al., 2012). Given that the first descriptive comparison between HC and the whole patient group showed no significant differences, the current ROI groupwise comparisons demonstrate that a lesion in the target region was indeed crucial for REAPPself, especially for the down-regulation of arousal. Interestingly, a previous study has discussed that REAPPself might be particulary effective in the down-regulation of physiological responding (Shiota and Levenson, 2012).

Current results can be interpreted in the frame of a cognitive control of emotions based on anatomical connections between (1) ACC, insula and basal ganglia (Ongur and Price, 2000; Ibanez et al., 2010; Ibanez and Manes, 2012), (2) amygdala-OFC-ACC (Carmichael and Price, 1995; Cavada et al., 2000) as well as (3) dlPFC and basal ganglia (Heekeren et al., 2008). The SFG (BA6/BA8/BA9/BA32) can be divided in an anteromedial (amSFG), a dorsolateral (dlPFC) and a posterior region (pSFG), and is also supposed to be involved in several cognitive control tasks (du Boisgueheneuc et al., 2006; Moreno-Lopez et al., 2012; Li et al., 2013). Moreover, the SFG is highly interconnected, with pathways extending to the ACC, middle frontal gyrus, inferior frontal gyrus (IFG) as well as thalamus and caudate nucleus in the basal ganglia. This important PFC region lies in a unique position between emotional limbic regions and highly cognitive and executive process networks in the dorsal and medial areas of the PFC (Li et al., 2013). The dACC is also one of the few PFC areas that presents strong projections to amygdala nuclei, and might be the cue connection between prefrontal executive and limbic emotional areas during ER (Ray and Zald, 2012). Furthermore, our findings support previous studies in showing that the activation of dACC regions predicts cognitive reappraisal success (Ochsner et al., 2002). This assumption has been supported by *neurofeedback* techniques, in which the down-regulation of emotion-related insula activity was accompanied by the right SFG including ACC (BA32) involvement during reappraisal of threat-related stimuli (Veit et al., 2012). Moreover, conscious self-regulation of brain activity (e.g., right SFG top down control) may depend on an interaction with unconscious subcortical processes, involving not only emotional (amygdala) but also motor skill learning (basal ganglia) as shown in recent models of neurofeedback (Birbaumer et al., 2013).

RIGHT SFG LESION AND REAPPself IMPAIRMENTS

Several studies have demonstrated that the ROI depicted by our VLSM results (including the right dACC) is relevant not only for REAPPself, but also for inhibitory control, an executive function that excludes irrelevant information from WM in order to prevent undesirable behavioral responses (Garavan et al., 1999; Vanderhasselt et al., 2012). Thus, REAPPself of negative stimuli may imply the inhibition of dominant negative thoughts, permitting a detached third-person perspective. For instance, a recent study showed that a habitual reappraisal use is positively associated with the ability to inhibit dominant thoughts to negative cues (Vanderhasselt et al., 2013). Similarly, Salas et al. (2014) present a reappraisal model, in which behavioral inhibition is presented as an essential skill for reappraisal generation (Salas et al., 2014). Accordingly, our results showed that inhibition failures during the Go/NoGo task, assessed by the number of errors, were positively correlated with the raw scores of arousal in the Dec condition. Moreover, the ROI group not only showed deficits in REAPPself, but was also the group with most inhibition failures (number of errors) during Go/NoGo tasks. This is of particular interest, as one case study reported that inhibition impairments after a left frontoparietal lesion generated difficulties to spontaneously generate reappraisals (Salas et al., 2013). As previously shown in lesion studies, patients with right PFC lesions typically show inhibition difficulties, reflected by increased error rates in the interference condition of the Stroop task (Vendrell et al., 1995). Furthermore, studies investigating lesions of the right ACC and dlPFC regions report inhibition deficits (Turken and Swick, 1999; Swick and Turken, 2002), rule breaking and difficulties in strategy planning (Burgess et al., 2000). Considering this findings, it would be expectable to spot more right lateralized regions comprising overlapping areas for cognitive inhibition as being crucial for REAPPself (i.e., detaching) of negative events, which in turn, implies the inhibition of negative meanings. However, as inhibition failures (number of Go/NoGo errors) did not significantly correlate with the REAPPself ability scores (LNeg-Dec), our findings support the reappraisal model of Salas et al. (2014). That is, inhibition failures might have influenced reappraisal generation (Salas et al., 2014). As Go/NoGo errors were positively associated with the amount of negative arousal in the Dec condition (i.e., the more errors, the more arousal), it might be interpreted that automatic negative meaning of the stimuli could not be inhibited appropriately. For instance, our results support the findings of McRae et al. (2012a,b), who did not find significant associations of general reappraisal ability with response inhibition, but with WM capacity (McRae et al., 2012b). Therefore, our results revealed that REAPPself might not be dependent only on dACC and inhibition, but also on WM process and strategy planning functions that rely on dlPFC areas (Heyder et al., 2004; Kaller et al., 2011, 2013).

A previous fMRI study examining the contribution of PFC areas in ER shows that the right dlPFC is strongly involved in reappraisal function, regardless of the kind of stimuli that are reappraised (Golkar et al., 2012). This is not surprising, as reappraisal relies on executive functions that update emotional to new non-emotional "reappraised" thoughts and maintain these reinterpretations in mind (Malooly et al., 2013). The displayed areas in the dlSFG region enclose the dlPFC areas in BA9, which have not only been linked to WM and executive processes, but also with metacognitive evaluations of oneself and others, particularly the right dlPFC (Schmitz et al., 2004). That is, the right PFC might be recruited when self-evaluations are produced. For REAPPself, a self-focused strategy, evaluations about the self might be essential. Moreover, since a part of the identified ROI is placed in the white matter of the PFC (between BA9 and BA32), REAPPself ability might also be dependent on the interaction and connectivity of the mentioned areas. Further analysis of SFG connectivity and the influence on REAPPself might clarify these issues.

Interestingly, the ROI group showed not only more inhibition deficits, but also more immediate memory recall and processing speed deficits, as well as lower fluid intelligence scores as the IntactROI and HC group. Therefore, a lesion in the depicted region might lead to other cognitive impairments, besides of those of REAPPself and inhibition. These variables showed no significant correlations with REAPPself ability scores, but with the raw arousal and valence scores of the Dec condition. In other words, these cognitive variables had a significant influence on the amount of negative emotion during reappraisal. Here, results showed that cognitive abilities such as fluid intelligence and immediate memory, correlated negatively with arousal and valence scores during the Dec condition. This result might support the assumption of less negative affect through heightened cognitive control abilities (Williams et al., 2009).

ROI LESION AND DEPRESSION SYMPTOMS

The current findings show that the ROI group suffered more from depression than the two other groups. These results are in agreement with previous studies investigating lesions in the right hemisphere, which also show associations with impaired affective processing, reflected by the presence of anxiety and depression (Berg et al., 2000; Zorzon et al., 2001, 2002). In addition, our results support the findings of Königs and colleagues, which demonstrated increased vulnerability for depression after a bilateral dlPFC lesion (Koenigs et al., 2008). Apart from this, depression was also positively associated with the amount of negative emotionality during the Dec condition. Depression and other affective disorders have been related to inhibition failures of negative stimuli (Joormann and Gotlib, 2008; Joormann, 2010) and to impaired reappraisal (Johnstone et al., 2007; Moore et al., 2008; Ehring et al., 2010). For these reasons, depression might reflect a confounder; particularly for the analysis of valence rating scores (were depression was a significant influence). This finding might lead to the assumption that the depicted right SFG region might be important for a valence-related REAPPself ability, but probably not indispensable, as it might be with an arousal-related REAPPself ability. In addition to the lesion, depression might have influenced the subjective down-regulation of negative valence.

VBM RESULTS OF GRAY MATTER IN HEALTHY CONTROLS

Our whole-brain VBM findings showed that partially different neural structures were correlated with arousal- and valence-related REAPPself ability. For arousal REAPPself, we found positive associations with more subcortical regions as the insula, whereas valence was associated with highly cognitive areas as the middle and inferior frontal gyrus, as well as with the inferior parietal lobule. Although both of the constructs are assumed to be difficult to separate in the subjective experience (Kuppens et al., 2013), the obtained results lead to the assumption that arousal down-regulation comprise the involvement of limbic regions mainly related to emotional awareness and physiological responding, whereas valence down-regulation is a more elaborated process, in which highly cognitive regions are involved (Citron et al., 2014). Accordingly, insula activity has been consistently observed during changes in autonomic arousal (Critchley et al., 2002, 2003). However, in studies examining the evaluation of valence, more cortical, attentional structures are observed (Kensinger, 2004; Kensinger and Corkin, 2004). In addition, the SFG was significantly associated with the down-regulation of both, arousal, and valence self-reports. This was confirmed by the regional VBM analysis, were right SFG regions showed significant positive correlations with REAPPself ability. These findings support previous evidence showing that the anatomical volume of ACC (BA32) is positively associated with a cognitive reappraisal ability (Giuliani et al., 2011).

IMPLICATIONS FOR FURTHER RESEARCH

Summarizing, the involvement of SFG regions during reappraisal of negative stimuli has been strongly underlined in the majority of fMRI studies, and included in several reappraisal models (Ochsner et al., 2002, 2004, 2012; Wager et al., 2008; Koenigsberg et al., 2010; Buhle et al., 2013). Inhibition performance, which is supposed to be a right lateralized function (Garavan et al., 1999), might influence the ability of decreasing automatic negative appraisals, thus constituting a corner pillar for the architecture of reappraisal and especially, REAPPself (Salas et al., 2013, 2014). However, we cannot rule out the influences of depression symptoms, particularly on the down-regulation of valence. Although inhibition, depression and impaired REAPPself ability are strongly associated (Joormann and Gotlib, 2008; Joormann, 2010; Aldao and Nolen-Hoeksema, 2012; Barnow et al., 2013), additional research is needed to explain the direction of these associations with a bigger sample. Analyses about these associations are, unfortunately, outside the scope of this work. Nevertheless, to gain further insight into the effects of a trained modulation of the right SFG (specifically dACC and dlPFC areas) on REAPPself performance and their related limbic responses might be useful in the treatment of various psychiatric disorders involving emotional dysregulation. Furthermore, it would be of great interest to examine whether teaching patients to gain control over the neural activity (right SFG and related subcortical networks) via neurofeedback would yield positive therapeutic effects.

LIMITATIONS

No study is free of limitations or possible improvements. In the present study, the sample size was not large enough to reach significance with conventional multiple-measure corrections (see for example Medina et al., 2010). Therefore, our VLSM results have to be interpreted with caution due to the risk of false-positive findings. Additional research should replicate these findings with a larger sample of patients. However, the ROI based group comparison supported the VLSM results. Furthermore, although we were very conservative in lesion reconstruction, we cannot rule out the possibility of etiology and treatment confounders. We therefore controlled for the lesion volume in the statistical analysis, and it was not significantly different between groups. However, we have to take the influence of cortical reorganization of functions by slow-growing tumors into consideration (Desmurget et al., 2007). It is also important to mention that the infiltration pattern of brain tumors is diffuse *per se* and generally difficult to assess. The growth of such a tumor results in T2-weighted hyperintense signal alteration; the current methods in MRI make it impossible to differentiate between tumor and perifocal edema, as both features may lead to the MRI pattern (Essig et al., 1998). However, the employed T2-FLAIR sequence is regarded to be one of the most sensitive MRI sequences to detect the extensiveness of damaged brain tissue. Thus, by considering the whole T2 hyperintensity, the analysis was performed conservatively, as this type of segmentation includes the maximum area of damaged brain tissue, detectable with current methods. The highly educated control group might also represent a source of bias, although this variable did not significantly correlate with any of the outcome variables and no significant differences in demographic variables were found in the ROI group-wise comparison. Finally, although previous investigations studying reappraisal function in brain-damaged patients argue that reappraisal ability might be a problematic variable to measure due to the potential cognitive impairments of brain-damaged patients (Salas et al., 2014), our results show that these reappraisal difficulties might be dependent of the localization of the lesion (right SFG), as the descriptive patients-HC group comparison did not show any significant results in reappraisal ability (except for the significant influence of depression).

CONCLUSIONS

Considering our limitations, it is safe to conclude that the integrity of the right dACC and dlPFC might be of crucial importance not only for REAPPself ability, but also for affective and cognitive health. To the best of our knowledge, the current work is the first lesion study on cognitive reappraisal that targets circumscribed brain regions using imaging methods. It brings useful insights in the importance of specific right SFG areas for REAPPself. These findings might have important implications for studies using real-time fMRI techniques (Decharms et al., 2004). It would be of great interest to investigate whether the conscious modulation of right SFG BOLD activity could influence limbic responses using neurofeedback methods. The development of evidence-based neurofeedback trainings would be of prime importance in patients suffering from emotional dysregulation, depression, and other types of psychopathology.

ACKNOWLEDGMENTS

This project was supported by the Neuro-oncology section of the University Hospital and the German Cancer Research Center in Heidelberg, Germany. Agustin Ibanez is supported by grants CONICYT/FONDECYT Regular 1130920 and 1140114, FONCyT-PICT 2012-0412, FONCyT-PICT 2012-1309, CONICET and the INECO Foundation. The authors are very thankful for the professional collaboration of Dr. Benedikt Wiestler. We would also like to thank Adelheid Fuxa and Moritz Riese for their friendly assistance.

REFERENCES

Abler, B., Hofer, C., Walter, H., Erk, S., Hoffmann, H., Traue, H. C., et al. (2010). Habitual emotion regulation strategies and depressive symptoms in healthy subjects predict fMRI brain activation patterns related to major depression. *Psychiatry Res.* 183, 105–113. doi: 10.1016/j.pscychresns.2010.05.010

Aldao, A., and Dixon-Gordon, K. L. (2013). Broadening the scope of research on emotion regulation strategies and psychopathology. *Cogn. Behav. Ther.* 43, 22–33. doi: 10.1080/16506073.2013.816769

Aldao, A., and Nolen-Hoeksema, S. (2012). When are adaptive strategies most predictive of psychopathology? *J. Abnorm. Psychol.* 121, 276–281. doi: 10.1037/a0023598

Amaro, E. Jr., and Barker, G. J. (2006). Study design in fMRI: basic principles. *Brain Cogn.* 60, 220–232. doi: 10.1016/j.bandc.2005.11.009

Ashburner, J., and Friston, K. J. (2000). Voxel-based morphometry–the methods. *Neuroimage* 11, 805–821. doi: 10.1006/nimg.2000.0582

Ayduk, O., and Kross, E. (2008). Enhancing the pace of recovery: self-distanced analysis of negative experiences reduces blood pressure reactivity. *Psychol. Sci.* 19, 229–231. doi: 10.1111/j.1467-9280.2008.02073.x

Ayduk, O., and Kross, E. (2010). From a distance: implications of spontaneous self-distancing for adaptive self-reflection. *J. Pers. Soc. Psychol.* 98, 809–829. doi: 10.1037/a0019205

Balconi, M. (2013). Dorsolateral prefrontal cortex, working memory and episodic memory processes: insight through transcranial magnetic stimulation techniques. *Neurosci. Bull.* 29, 381–389. doi: 10.1007/s12264-013-1309-z

Banks, S. J., Eddy, K. T., Angstadt, M., Nathan, P. J., and Phan, K. L. (2007). Amygdala-frontal connectivity during emotion regulation. *Soc. Cogn. Affect. Neurosci.* 2, 303–312. doi: 10.1093/scan/nsm029

Barnow, S. (2012). Emotion regulation and psychopathology. An overview. *Psychol. Rundsch.* 63, 111–124. doi: 10.1026/0033-3042/a000119

Barnow, S., Aldinger, M., Ulrich, I., and Stopsack, M. (2013). Emotion regulation in depression: an overview of results using various methods. *Psychol. Rundsch.* 64, 235–243. doi: 10.1026/0033-3042/a000172

Bates, E., Wilson, S. M., Saygin, A. P., Dick, F., Sereno, M. I., Knight, R. T., et al. (2003). Voxel-based lesion-symptom mapping. *Nat. Neurosci.* 6, 448–450. doi: 10.1038/nn1050

Beer, J., and Lombardo, M. V. (2007). "Insights into emotion regulation from neuropsychology," in *Handbook of Emotion Regulation*, ed J. J. Gross (New York, NY: The Guilford Press), 69–83.

Berg, D., Supprian, T., Thomae, J., Warmuth-Metz, M., Horowski, A., Zeiler, B., et al. (2000). Lesion pattern in patients with multiple sclerosis and depression. *Mult. Scler.* 6, 156–162. doi: 10.1177/135245850000600304

Birbaumer, N., Ruiz, S., and Sitaram, R. (2013). Learned regulation of brain metabolism. *Trends Cogn. Sci.* 17, 295–302. doi: 10.1016/j.tics.2013.04.009

Bradley, M. M., and Lang, P. J. (1994). Measuring emotion: the self-assessment manikin and the semantic differential. *J. Behav. Ther. Exp. Psychiatry* 25, 49–59. doi: 10.1016/0005-7916(94)90063-9

Buhle, J. T., Silvers, J. A., Wager, T. D., Lopez, R., Onyemekwu, C., Kober, H., et al. (2013). Cognitive reappraisal of emotion: a meta-analysis of human neuroimaging studies. *Cereb. Cortex.* doi: 10.1093/cercor/bht154. [Epub ahead of print].

Burgess, P. W., Veitch, E., De Lacy Costello, A., and Shallice, T. (2000). The cognitive and neuroanatomical correlates of multitasking. *Neuropsychologia* 38, 848–863. doi: 10.1016/S0028-3932(99)00134-7

Carmichael, S. T., and Price, J. L. (1995). Limbic connections of the orbital and medial prefrontal cortex in macaque monkeys. *J. Comp. Neurol.* 363, 615–641. doi: 10.1002/cne.903630408

Cattell, R. B. (1960). *Culture Fair Intelligence Test: Scale 2.* Champaign, IL: Institute for Personality and Ability Testing.

Cavada, C., Company, T., Tejedor, J., Cruz-Rizzolo, R. J., and Reinoso-Suarez, F. (2000). The anatomical connections of the macaque monkey orbitofrontal cortex. A review. *Cereb. Cortex* 10, 220–242. doi: 10.1093/cercor/10.3.220

Citron, F. M., Gray, M. A., Critchley, H. D., Weekes, B. S., and Ferstl, E. C. (2014). Emotional valence and arousal affect reading in an interactive way: neuroimaging evidence for an approach-withdrawal framework. *Neuropsychologia* 56, 79–89. doi: 10.1016/j.neuropsychologia.2014.01.002

Clark, A., and Fallowfield, L. J. (1986). Quality of life measurements in patients with malignant disease: a review. *J. R. Soc. Med.* 79, 165–169.

Crinion, J., Ashburner, J., Leff, A., Brett, M., Price, C., and Friston, K. (2007). Spatial normalization of lesioned brains: performance evaluation and impact on fMRI analyses. *Neuroimage* 37, 866–875. doi: 10.1016/j.neuroimage.2007.04.065

Critchley, H. D., Mathias, C. J., and Dolan, R. J. (2002). Fear conditioning in humans: the influence of awareness and autonomic arousal on functional neuroanatomy. *Neuron* 33, 653–663. doi: 10.1016/S0896-6273(02)00588-3

Critchley, H. D., Mathias, C. J., Josephs, O., O'Doherty, J., Zanini, S., Dewar, B. K., et al. (2003). Human cingulate cortex and autonomic control: converging neuroimaging and clinical evidence. *Brain* 126, 2139–2152. doi: 10.1093/brain/awg216

Decharms, R. C., Christoff, K., Glover, G. H., Pauly, J. M., Whitfield, S., and Gabrieli, J. D. (2004). Learned regulation of spatially localized brain activation using real-time fMRI. *Neuroimage* 21, 436–443. doi: 10.1016/j.neuroimage.2003.08.041

Desmurget, M., Bonnetblanc, F., and Duffau, H. (2007). Contrasting acute and slow-growing lesions: a new door to brain plasticity. *Brain* 130, 898–914. doi: 10.1093/brain/awl300

Dimitrov, M., Nakic, M., Elpern-Waxman, J., Granetz, J., O'Grady, J., Phipps, M., et al. (2003). Inhibitory attentional control in patients with frontal lobe damage. *Brain Cogn.* 52, 258–270. doi: 10.1016/S0278-2626(03)00080-0

du Boisgueheneuc, F., Levy, R., Volle, E., Seassau, M., Duffau, H., Kinkingnehun, S., et al. (2006). Functions of the left superior frontal gyrus in humans: a lesion study. *Brain* 129, 3315–3328. doi: 10.1093/brain/awl244

Ehring, T., Tuschen-Caffier, B., Schnulle, J., Fischer, S., and Gross, J. J. (2010). Emotion regulation and vulnerability to depression: spontaneous versus instructed use of emotion suppression and reappraisal. *Emotion* 10, 563–572. doi: 10.1037/a0019010

Erk, S., Mikschl, A., Stier, S., Ciaramidaro, A., Gapp, V., Weber, B., et al. (2010). Acute and sustained effects of cognitive emotion regulation in major depression. *J. Neurosci.* 30, 15726–15734. doi: 10.1523/JNEUROSCI.1856-10.2010

Essig, M., Hawighorst, H., Schoenberg, S. O., Engenhart-Cabillic, R., Fuss, M., Debus, J., et al. (1998). Fast fluid-attenuated inversion-recovery (FLAIR) MRI in the assessment of intraaxial brain tumors. *J. Magn. Reson. Imaging* 8, 789–798. doi: 10.1002/jmri.1880080407

Garavan, H., Ross, T. J., and Stein, E. A. (1999). Right hemispheric dominance of inhibitory control: an event-related functional MRI study. *Proc. Natl. Acad. Sci. U.S.A.* 96, 8301–8306. doi: 10.1073/pnas.96.14.8301

Giuliani, N. R., Drabant, E. M., and Gross, J. J. (2011). Anterior cingulate cortex volume and emotion regulation: is bigger better? *Biol. Psychol.* 86, 379–382. doi: 10.1016/j.biopsycho.2010.11.010

Goldin, P. R., Manber-Ball, T., Werner, K., Heimberg, R., and Gross, J. J. (2009). Neural mechanisms of cognitive reappraisal of negative self-beliefs in social anxiety disorder. *Biol. Psychiatry* 66, 1091–1099. doi: 10.1016/j.biopsych.2009.07.014

Goldin, P. R., McRae, K., Ramel, W., and Gross, J. J. (2008). The neural bases of emotion regulation: reappraisal and suppression of negative emotion. *Biol. Psychiatry* 63, 577–586. doi: 10.1016/j.biopsych.2007.05.031

Golkar, A., Lonsdorf, T. B., Olsson, A., Lindstrom, K. M., Berrebi, J., Fransson, P., et al. (2012). Distinct contributions of the dorsolateral prefrontal and orbitofrontal cortex during emotion regulation. *PLoS ONE* 7:e48107. doi: 10.1371/journal.pone.0048107

Good, C. D., Johnsrude, I. S., Ashburner, J., Henson, R. N., Friston, K. J., and Frackowiak, R. S. (2001). A voxel-based morphometric study of ageing in 465 normal adult human brains. *Neuroimage* 14, 21–36. doi: 10.1006/nimg.2001.0786

Gross, J. J. (1998). Antecedent- and response-focused emotion regulation: divergent consequences for experience, expression, and physiology. *J. Pers. Soc. Psychol.* 74, 224–237. doi: 10.1037/0022-3514.74.1.224

Gross, J. J. (1999). Emotion regulation: past, present, future. *Cogn. Emot.* 13, 551–573. doi: 10.1080/026999399379186

Gross, J. J. (2002). Emotion regulation: affective, cognitive, and social consequences. *Psychophysiology* 39, 281–291. doi: 10.1017/S0048577201393198

Gross, J. J., and John, O. P. (2003). Individual differences in two emotion regulation processes: implications for affect, relationships, and well-being. *J. Pers. Soc. Psychol.* 85, 348–362. doi: 10.1037/0022-3514.85.2.348

Harenski, C. L., and Hamann, S. (2006). Neural correlates of regulating negative emotions related to moral violations. *Neuroimage* 30, 313–324. doi: 10.1016/j.neuroimage.2005.09.034

Heekeren, H. R., Marrett, S., and Ungerleider, L. G. (2008). The neural systems that mediate human perceptual decision making. *Nat. Rev. Neurosci.* 9, 467–479. doi: 10.1038/nrn2374

Hermann, A., Schafer, A., Walter, B., Stark, R., Vaitl, D., and Schienle, A. (2009). Emotion regulation in spider phobia: role of the medial prefrontal cortex. *Soc. Cogn. Affect. Neurosci.* 4, 257–267. doi: 10.1093/scan/nsp013

Heyder, K., Suchan, B., and Daum, I. (2004). Cortico-subcortical contributions to executive control. *Acta Psychol.* 115, 271–289. doi: 10.1016/j.actpsy.2003.12.010

Hofmann, W., Schmeichel, B. J., and Baddeley, A. D. (2012). Executive functions and self-regulation. *Trends Cogn. Sci.* 16, 174–180. doi: 10.1016/j.tics.2012.01.006

Ibanez, A., Gleichgerrcht, E., and Manes, F. (2010). Clinical effects of insular damage in humans. *Brain Struct. Funct.* 214, 397–410. doi: 10.1007/s00429-010-0256-y

Ibanez, A., and Manes, F. (2012). Contextual social cognition and the behavioral variant of frontotemporal dementia. *Neurology* 78, 1354–1362. doi: 10.1212/WNL.0b013e3182518375

Ichikawa, N., Siegle, G. J., Jones, N. P., Kamishima, K., Thompson, W. K., Gross, J. J., et al. (2011). Feeling bad about screwing up: emotion regulation and action monitoring in the anterior cingulate cortex. *Cogn. Affect. Behav. Neurosci.* 11, 354–371. doi: 10.3758/s13415-011-0028-z

Johnstone, T., van Reekum, C. M., Urry, H. L., Kalin, N. H., and Davidson, R. J. (2007). Failure to regulate: counterproductive recruitment of top-down prefrontal-subcortical circuitry in major depression. *J. Neurosci.* 27, 8877–8884. doi: 10.1523/JNEUROSCI.2063-07.2007

Joormann, J. (2010). Cognitive inhibition and emotion regulation in depression. *Curr. Direct. Psychol. Sci.* 19, 161–166. doi: 10.1177/0963721410370293

Joormann, J., and Gotlib, I. H. (2008). Updating the contents of working memory in depression: interference from irrelevant negative material. *J. Abnorm. Psychol.* 117, 182–192. doi: 10.1037/0021-843X.117.1.182

Kalbe, E., Reinhold, N., Brand, M., Markowitsch, H. J., and Kessler, J. (2005). A new test battery to assess aphasic disturbances and associated cognitive dysfunctions – German normative data on the aphasia check list. *J. Clin. Exp. Neuropsychol.* 27, 779–794. doi: 10.1080/13803390490918273

Kalbe, E., Reinhold, N., Ender, U., and Kessler, J. (2002). *Aphasie-Check-Liste (ACL)*. Köln: Prolog.

Kalisch, R., Wiech, K., Critchley, H. D., Seymour, B., O'Doherty, J. P., Oakley, D. A., et al. (2005). Anxiety reduction through detachment: subjective, physiological, and neural effects. *J. Cogn. Neurosci.* 17, 874–883. doi: 10.1162/0898929054021184

Kaller, C. P., Rahm, B., Spreer, J., Weiller, C., and Unterrainer, J. M. (2011). Dissociable contributions of left and right dorsolateral prefrontal cortex in planning. *Cereb. Cortex* 21, 307–317. doi: 10.1093/cercor/bhq096

Kaller, C. P., Reisert, M., Katzev, M., Umarova, R., Mader, I., Hennig, J., et al. (2013). Predicting planning performance from structural connectivity between left and right mid-dorsolateral prefrontal cortex: moderating effects of age during postadolescence and midadulthood. *Cereb. Cortex.* doi: 10.1093/cercor/bht276. [Epub ahead of print].

Kensinger, E. A. (2004). Remembering emotional experiences: the contribution of valence and arousal. *Rev. Neurosci.* 15, 241–251. doi: 10.1515/REVNEURO.2004.15.4.241

Kensinger, E. A., and Corkin, S. (2004). Two routes to emotional memory: distinct neural processes for valence and arousal. *Proc. Natl. Acad. Sci. U.S.A.* 101, 3310–3315. doi: 10.1073/pnas.0306408101

Kim, S. H., and Hamann, S. (2012). The effect of cognitive reappraisal on physiological reactivity and emotional memory. *Int. J. Psychophysiol.* 83, 348–356. doi: 10.1016/j.ijpsycho.2011.12.001

Kimberg, D. Y., Coslett, H. B., and Schwartz, M. F. (2007). Power in voxel-based lesion-symptom mapping. *J. Cogn. Neurosci.* 19, 1067–1080. doi: 10.1162/jocn.2007.19.7.1067

Kleihues, P., and Sobin, L. H. (2000). World health organization classification of tumors. *Cancer* 88:2887. doi: 10.1002/1097-0142(20000615)88:12%3C2887::AID-CNCR32%3E3.0.CO;2-F

Koenigs, M., Huey, E. D., Calamia, M., Raymont, V., Tranel, D., and Grafman, J. (2008). Distinct regions of prefrontal cortex mediate resistance and vulnerability to depression. *J. Neurosci.* 28, 12341–12348. doi: 10.1523/JNEUROSCI.2324-08.2008

Koenigsberg, H. W., Fan, J., Ochsner, K. N., Liu, X., Guise, K., Pizzarello, S., et al. (2010). Neural correlates of using distancing to regulate emotional responses to social situations. *Neuropsychologia* 48, 1813–1822. doi: 10.1016/j.neuropsychologia.2010.03.002

Kuhner, C., Burger, C., Keller, F., and Hautzinger, M. (2007). [Reliability and validity of the Revised Beck Depression Inventory (BDI-II). Results from German samples]. *Nervenarzt* 78, 651–656. doi: 10.1007/s00115-006-2098-7

Kuppens, P., Tuerlinckx, F., Russell, J. A., and Barrett, L. F. (2013). The relation between valence and arousal in subjective experience. *Psychol. Bull.* 139, 917–940. doi: 10.1037/a0030811

Lang, P. J., Bradley, M. M., and Cuthbert, B. N. (2005). "International affective picture system (IAPS): affective ratings of pictures and instruction manual. NIMH, Center for the Study of Emotion and Attention," in *Technical Report A-6* (Gainesville, FL: University of Florida).

Lang, S., Kotchoubey, B., Frick, C., Spitzer, C., Grabe, H. J., and Barnow, S. (2012). Cognitive reappraisal in trauma-exposed women with borderline personality disorder. *Neuroimage* 59, 1727–1734. doi: 10.1016/j.neuroimage.2011.08.061

Leiberg, S., Eippert, F., Veit, R., and Anders, S. (2012). Intentional social distance regulation alters affective responses towards victims of violence: an FMRI study. *Hum. Brain Mapp.* 33, 2464–2476. doi: 10.1002/hbm.21376

Li, W., Qin, W., Liu, H., Fan, L., Wang, J., Jiang, T., et al. (2013). Subregions of the human superior frontal gyrus and their connections. *Neuroimage* 78, 46–58. doi: 10.1016/j.neuroimage.2013.04.011

Lutcke, H., and Frahm, J. (2008). Lateralized anterior cingulate function during error processing and conflict monitoring as revealed by high-resolution fMRI. *Cereb. Cortex* 18, 508–515. doi: 10.1093/cercor/bhm090

Malooly, A. M., Genet, J. J., and Siemer, M. (2013). Individual differences in reappraisal effectiveness: the role of affective flexibility. *Emotion* 13, 302–313. doi: 10.1037/a0029980

McRae, K., Ciesielski, B., and Gross, J. J. (2012a). Unpacking cognitive reappraisal: goals, tactics, and outcomes. *Emotion* 12, 250–255. doi: 10.1037/a0026351

McRae, K., Jacobs, S. E., Ray, R. D., John, O. P., and Gross, J. J. (2012b). Individual differences in reappraisal ability: links to reappraisal frequency, well-being, and cognitive control. *J. Res. Pers.* 46, 2–7. doi: 10.1016/j.jrp.2011.10.003

Medina, J., Kimberg, D. Y., Chatterjee, A., and Coslett, H. B. (2010). Inappropriate usage of the Brunner-Munzel test in recent voxel-based lesion-symptom mapping studies. *Neuropsychologia* 48, 341–343. doi: 10.1016/j.neuropsychologia.2009.09.016

Moore, S. A., Zoellner, L. A., and Mollenholt, N. (2008). Are expressive suppression and cognitive reappraisal associated with stress-related symptoms? *Behav. Res. Ther.* 46, 993–1000. doi: 10.1016/j.brat.2008.05.001

Moreno-Lopez, L., Stamatakis, E. A., Fernandez-Serrano, M. J., Gomez-Rio, M., Rodriguez-Fernandez, A., Perez-Garcia, M., et al. (2012). Neural correlates of hot and cold executive functions in polysubstance addiction: association between neuropsychological performance and resting brain metabolism as measured by positron emission tomography. *Psychiatry Res. Neuroimaging* 203, 214–221. doi: 10.1016/j.pscychresns.2012.01.006

New, A. S., Fan, J., Murrough, J. W., Liu, X., Liebman, R. E., Guise, K. G., et al. (2009). A functional magnetic resonance imaging study of deliberate emotion regulation in resilience and posttraumatic stress disorder. *Biol. Psychiatry* 66, 656–664. doi: 10.1016/j.biopsych.2009.05.020

Niki, C., Maruyama, T., Muragaki, Y., and Kumada, T. (2009). Disinhibition of sequential actions following right frontal lobe damage. *Cogn. Neuropsychol.* 26, 266–285. doi: 10.1080/02643290903028484

Ochsner, K. N., Beer, J. S., Robertson, E. R., Cooper, J. C., Gabrieli, J. D., Kihsltrom, J. F., et al. (2005). The neural correlates of direct and reflected self-knowledge. *Neuroimage* 28, 797–814. doi: 10.1016/j.neuroimage.2005.06.069

Ochsner, K. N., Bunge, S. A., Gross, J. J., and Gabrieli, J. D. (2002). Rethinking feelings: an FMRI study of the cognitive regulation of emotion. *J. Cogn. Neurosci.* 14, 1215–1229. doi: 10.1162/089892902760807212

Ochsner, K. N., and Gross, J. J. (2008). Cognitive emotion regulation: insights from social cognitive and affective neuroscience. *Curr. Dir. Psychol. Sci.* 17, 153–158. doi: 10.1111/j.1467-8721.2008.00566.x

Ochsner, K. N., Ray, R. D., Cooper, J. C., Robertson, E. R., Chopra, S., Gabrieli, J. D., et al. (2004). For better or for worse: neural systems supporting the cognitive down- and up-regulation of negative emotion. *Neuroimage* 23, 483–499. doi: 10.1016/j.neuroimage.2004.06.030

Ochsner, K. N., Silvers, J. A., and Buhle, J. T. (2012). Functional imaging studies of emotion regulation: a synthetic review and evolving model of the cognitive control of emotion. *Ann. N.Y. Acad. Sci.* 1251, E1–E24. doi: 10.1111/j.1749-6632.2012.06751.x

Ongur, D., and Price, J. L. (2000). The organization of networks within the orbital and medial prefrontal cortex of rats, monkeys and humans. *Cereb. Cortex* 10, 206–219. doi: 10.1093/cercor/10.3.206

Paret, C., Brenninkmeyer, J., Meyer, B., Yuen, K. S., Gartmann, N., Mechias, M. L., et al. (2011). A test for the implementation-maintenance model of reappraisal. *Front. Psychol.* 2:216. doi: 10.3389/fpsyg.2011.00216

Pe, M. L., Raes, F., Koval, P., Brans, K., Verduyn, P., and Kuppens, P. (2013). Interference resolution moderates the impact of rumination and reappraisal on affective experiences in daily life. *Cogn. Emot.* 27, 492–501. doi: 10.1080/02699931.2012.719489

Ray, R. D., McRae, K., Ochsner, K. N., and Gross, J. J. (2010). Cognitive reappraisal of negative affect: converging evidence from EMG and self-report. *Emotion* 10, 587–592. doi: 10.1037/a0019015

Ray, R. D., and Zald, D. H. (2012). Anatomical insights into the interaction of emotion and cognition in the prefrontal cortex. *Neurosci. Biobehav. Rev.* 36, 479–501. doi: 10.1016/j.neubiorev.2011.08.005

Rodriguez-Bailon, M., Trivino, M., and Lupianez, J. (2012). Executive attention and personality variables in patients with frontal lobe damage. *Span. J. Psychol.* 15, 967–977. doi: 10.5209/rev_SJOP.2012.v15.n3.39388

Rorden, C., and Karnath, H. O. (2004). Using human brain lesions to infer function: a relic from a past era in the fMRI age? *Nat. Rev. Neurosci.* 5, 813–819. doi: 10.1038/nrn1521

Rorden, C., Karnath, H. O., and Bonilha, L. (2007). Improving lesion-symptom mapping. *J. Cogn. Neurosci.* 19, 1081–1088. doi: 10.1162/jocn.2007.19.7.1081

Salas, C. E., Gross, J. J., Rafal, R. D., Vinas-Guasch, N., and Turnbull, O. H. (2013). Concrete behaviour and reappraisal deficits after a left frontal stroke: a case study. *Neuropsychol. Rehabil.* 23, 467–500. doi: 10.1080/09602011.2013.784709

Salas, C. E., Gross, J. J., and Turnbull, O. H. (2014). Reappraisal generation after acquired brain damage: the role of laterality and cognitive control. *Front. Psychol.* 5:242. doi: 10.3389/fpsyg.2014.00242

Schardt, D. M., Erk, S., Nusser, C., Nothen, M. M., Cichon, S., Rietschel, M., et al. (2010). Volition diminishes genetically mediated amygdala hyperreactivity. *Neuroimage* 53, 943–951. doi: 10.1016/j.neuroimage.2009.11.078

Schmitz, T. W., Kawahara-Baccus, T. N., and Johnson, S. C. (2004). Metacognitive evaluation, self-relevance, and the right prefrontal cortex. *Neuroimage* 22, 941–947. doi: 10.1016/j.neuroimage.2004.02.018

Schweizer, S., Grahn, J., Hampshire, A., Mobbs, D., and Dalgleish, T. (2013). Training the emotional brain: improving affective control through emotional working memory training. *J. Neurosci.* 33, 5301–5311. doi: 10.1523/JNEUROSCI.2593-12.2013

Seghier, M. L., Ramlackhansingh, A., Crinion, J., Leff, A. P., and Price, C. J. (2008). Lesion identification using unified segmentation-normalisation models and fuzzy clustering. *Neuroimage* 41, 1253–1266. doi: 10.1016/j.neuroimage.2008.03.028

Shackman, A. J., McMenamin, B. W., Maxwell, J. S., Greischar, L. L., and Davidson, R. J. (2009). Right dorsolateral prefrontal cortical activity and behavioral inhibition. *Psychol. Sci.* 20, 1500–1506. doi: 10.1111/j.1467-9280.2009.02476.x

Shiota, M. N., and Levenson, R. W. (2012). Turn down the volume or change the channel? Emotional effects of detached versus positive reappraisal. *J. Pers. Soc. Psychol.* 103, 416–429. doi: 10.1037/a0029208

Slee, N., Garnefski, N., Spinhoven, P., and Arensman, E. (2008). The influence of cognitive emotion regulation strategies and depression severity on deliberate self-harm. *Suicide Life Threat. Behav.* 38, 274–286. doi: 10.1521/suli.2008.38.3.274

Swick, D., and Turken, A. U. (2002). Dissociation between conflict detection and error monitoring in the human anterior cingulate cortex. *Proc. Natl. Acad. Sci. U.S.A.* 99, 16354–16359. doi: 10.1073/pnas.252521499

Tombaugh, T. N. (2004). Trail making Test A and B: normative data stratified by age and education. *Arch. Clin. Neuropsychol.* 19, 203–214. doi: 10.1016/S0887-6177(03)00039-8

Tsuchida, A., Doll, B. B., and Fellows, L. K. (2010). Beyond reversal: a critical role for human orbitofrontal cortex in flexible learning from probabilistic feedback. *J. Neurosci.* 30, 16868–16875. doi: 10.1523/JNEUROSCI.1958-10.2010

Tsuchida, A., and Fellows, L. K. (2012). Are core component processes of executive function dissociable within the frontal lobes? Evidence from humans with focal prefrontal damage. *Cortex* 49, 1790–1800. doi: 10.1016/j.cortex.2012.10.014

Turken, A. U., and Swick, D. (1999). Response selection in the human anterior cingulate cortex. *Nat. Neurosci.* 2, 920–924. doi: 10.1038/13224

Vanderhasselt, M. A., Baeken, C., van Schuerbeek, P., Luypaert, R., and de Raedt, R. (2013). Inter-individual differences in the habitual use of cognitive reappraisal and expressive suppression are associated with variations in prefrontal cognitive control for emotional information: an event related fMRI study. *Biol. Psychol.* 92, 433–439. doi: 10.1016/j.biopsycho.2012.03.005

Vanderhasselt, M. A., Kuhn, S., and de Raedt, R. (2012). Put on your poker face: neural systems supporting the anticipation for expressive suppression and cognitive reappraisal. *Soc. Cogn. Affect. Neurosci.* 8, 903–910. doi: 10.1093/scan/nss090

van Veen, V., Cohen, J. D., Botvinick, M. M., Stenger, V. A., and Carter, C. S. (2001). Anterior cingulate cortex, conflict monitoring, and levels of processing. *Neuroimage* 14, 1302–1308. doi: 10.1006/nimg.2001.0923

Veit, R., Singh, V., Sitaram, R., Caria, A., Rauss, K., and Birbaumer, N. (2012). Using real-time fMRI to learn voluntary regulation of the anterior insula in the presence of threat-related stimuli. *Soc. Cogn. Affect. Neurosci.* 7, 623–634. doi: 10.1093/scan/nsr061

Vendrell, P., Junque, C., Pujol, J., Jurado, M. A., Molet, J., and Grafman, J. (1995). The role of prefrontal regions in the Stroop task. *Neuropsychologia* 33, 341–352. doi: 10.1016/0028-3932(94)00116-7

Vriend, C., de Wit, S. J., Remijnse, P. L., van Balkom, A. J., Veltman, D. J., and van den Heuvel, O. A. (2013). Switch the itch: a naturalistic follow-up study on the neural correlates of cognitive flexibility in obsessive-compulsive disorder. *Psychiatry Res.* 213, 31–38. doi: 10.1016/j.pscychresns.2012.12.006

Wager, T. D., Davidson, M. L., Hughes, B. L., Lindquist, M. A., and Ochsner, K. N. (2008). Prefrontal-subcortical pathways mediating successful emotion regulation. *Neuron* 59, 1037–1050. doi: 10.1016/j.neuron.2008.09.006

Weiss, R. H. (1998). *Cft-20 Culture Fair Intelligence Test With Additional Tests Vocabulary And Number Series.* Göttingen: Hogrefe.

Williams, P. G., Suchy, Y., and Rau, H. K. (2009). Individual differences in executive functioning: implications for stress regulation. *Ann. Behav. Med.* 37, 126–140. doi: 10.1007/s12160-009-9100-0

Zastrow, A., Kaiser, S., Stippich, C., Walther, S., Herzog, W., Tchanturia, K., et al. (2009). Neural correlates of impaired cognitive-behavioral flexibility in anorexia nervosa. *Am. J. Psychiatry* 166, 608–616. doi: 10.1176/appi.ajp.2008.080 50775

Zimmermann, P., and Fimm, B. (2002). *TAP - Testbatterie zur Aufmerksamkeitsprüfung.* Herzogenrath: Psytest.

Zorzon, M., de Masi, R., Nasuelli, D., Ukmar, M., Mucelli, R. P., Cazzato, G., et al. (2001). Depression and anxiety in multiple sclerosis. A clinical and MRI study in 95 subjects. *J. Neurol.* 248, 416–421. doi: 10.1007/s004150170184

Zorzon, M., Zivadinov, R., Nasuelli, D., Ukmar, M., Bratina, A., Tommasi, M. A., et al. (2002). Depressive symptoms and MRI changes in multiple sclerosis. *Eur. J. Neurol.* 9, 491–496. doi: 10.1046/j.1468-1331.2002.00442.x

21

Audiovisual emotional processing and neurocognitive functioning in patients with depression

Sophie Doose-Grünefeld[1], Simon B. Eickhoff[1,2] and Veronika I. Müller[1,2] *

[1] Department of Clinical Neuroscience and Medical Psychology, Medical Faculty, Heinrich Heine University Düsseldorf, Düsseldorf, Germany
[2] Institute of Neuroscience and Medicine, Research Centre Jülich, Jülich, Germany

Correspondence:
Veronika I. Müller, Institute of Neuroscience and Medicine, Research Centre Jülich, Wilhelm-Johnen-Straße, D-52428 Jülich, Germany
e-mail: v.mueller@fz-juelich.de

Alterations in the processing of emotional stimuli (e.g., facial expressions, prosody, music) have repeatedly been reported in patients with major depression. Such impairments may result from the likewise prevalent executive deficits in these patients. However, studies investigating this relationship are rare. Moreover, most studies to date have only assessed impairments in unimodal emotional processing, whereas in real life, emotions are primarily conveyed through more than just one sensory channel. The current study therefore aimed at investigating multi-modal emotional processing in patients with depression and to assess the relationship between emotional and neurocognitive impairments. Fourty one patients suffering from major depression and 41 never-depressed healthy controls participated in an audiovisual (faces-sounds) emotional integration paradigm as well as a neurocognitive test battery. Our results showed that depressed patients were specifically impaired in the processing of positive auditory stimuli as they rated faces significantly more fearful when presented with happy than with neutral sounds. Such an effect was absent in controls. Findings in emotional processing in patients did not correlate with Beck's depression inventory score. Furthermore, neurocognitive findings revealed significant group differences for two of the tests. The effects found in audiovisual emotional processing, however, did not correlate with performance in the neurocognitive tests. In summary, our results underline the diversity of impairments going along with depression and indicate that deficits found for unimodal emotional processing cannot trivially be generalized to deficits in a multi-modal setting. The mechanisms of impairments therefore might be far more complex than previously thought. Our findings furthermore contradict the assumption that emotional processing deficits in major depression are associated with impaired attention or inhibitory functioning.

Keywords: depression, emotional processing, neurocognitive functioning, audiovisual, executive deficits, congruent, symptom severity

INTRODUCTION

Major depression is a psychiatric disorder that is thought to represent one of the leading causes of disability worldwide (Ferrari et al., 2013). The disorder goes along with a range of symptoms including on the one hand emotional and social problems like low mood and loss of self-esteem as well as on the other hand cognitive impairments like poor concentration and indecisiveness (WHO, 2010). With regard to the former symptoms several theories have been postulated in order to gain a better understanding of the origins of these social and emotional problems in depression. The most influential theory suggests a negative bias for emotional but also neutral material, manifesting, for example, as more negative ratings of facial expressions or selective attention on negative stimuli. This has been supported by numerous studies (Gur et al., 1992; Bouhuys et al., 1999; Leppänen et al., 2004) reporting either a general negative bias or a bias specifically for neutral or ambiguous stimuli. However, most of these studies primarily investigated photographs or even schematic paintings of faces depicting emotions or neutrality (for a review, see Bourke et al., 2010). More recent studies now included on the one hand facial stimuli with varying intensity levels (Schaefer et al., 2010), and on the other hand other kinds of stimuli addressing different emotional channels such as voices (Schlipf et al., 2013) or music (Naranjo et al., 2011). Among these, fewer study outcomes indicated a clear negative bias in depression, but also an absence of a "healthy" positive bias. That is, while healthy non-depressed controls tend to interpret stimuli as positive, patients with depression do not. Joormann and Gotlib (2006) for example showed that when identifying emotions from faces, depressed individuals compared to controls needed significantly higher emotional intensity in order to correctly identify happy but not sad facial expressions. In addition, Loi et al. (2013) also only found labeling problems for happy body language depicted by photographs of body postures as well as frozen movie scenes and short clips of "Point-Light Walkers." Although Schlipf et al. (2013) report a negative bias in reference to judgments of neutral semantics, patients also rated positive semantics and positive prosody as less positive than healthy controls, thus also indicating an absence of a positive bias in the patient group.

To date, most previous studies have investigated emotional processing using only unimodal stimuli. In daily life, though, emotions are hardly ever conveyed through just one sensory modality but rather in a multimodal fashion, i.e., seeing a happy facial expression and concurrently hearing the sound of laughter. Thus, it is in question if findings from unimodal emotional processing reflect deficits in real life. However, there are very few studies, which used stimuli from more than just one modality. Schneider et al. (2012) for example presented short video clips of actors conveying emotions via facial expressions, semantics and prosody and found patients to be impaired in recognizing emotions, but did not find an overall negative bias. In addition, in an earlier study (Müller et al., 2014), we investigated audiovisual emotional integration in major depression using functional magnetic resonance imaging. There we demonstrated that impairments in emotional processing in patients with depression seem to be far more complex than a simple bias as we found patients to be impaired in the inhibition of auditory stimuli presented with emotionally congruent facial expressions. However, owing to the relatively low sample size in that imaging study, there were only tendencies toward a behavioral effect. Therefore the current study aims at complementing the previous study by investigating multi-modal emotional processing (on the behavioral level) in an extended sample of patients with depression.

Furthermore, besides the postulation of emotional biases, there is also an ongoing discussion if alterations in emotional processing result from the likewise prevalent executive deficits in these patients. Executive functions, however, rather ill defined, include amongst others inhibition, working memory as well as cognitive flexibility (Diamond, 2013). Furthermore executive skills as the basis for everyday life functioning also include cognitive domains like attention (as a precondition for inhibitory functions; DeBattista, 2005). Impairments in the mentioned cognitive functions have been shown to be present in depression. Airaksinen et al. (2004), for example, reported deficits in cognitive flexibility in individuals with depression, and Rose and Ebmeier (2006) described impairments in working memory. Furthermore, attentional deficits have been found to be present even in remitted states of depression (Paelecke-Habermann et al., 2005). Interestingly, Hoffstaedter et al. (2012) reported significantly worse performance on verbal vocabulary testing in patients with depression compared to controls, and they related these impairments to memory deficits. In addition, they found group differences in attention, cognitive flexibility, (visuo-) motor coordination, short-term and working memory, but not for basic motor speed. Overall, psychomotor retardation, however, has been described as a core feature of depression (Sobin and Sackeim, 1997) and Hoffstaedter et al. (2012) were able to show that patients were impaired in specific cognitive aspects of psychomotor functioning.

Regarding the treatment of cognitive aspects of depression, Owens et al. (2013) were able to show that working memory training in dysphoric individuals can improve inhibition of irrelevant information and thus lead to increased working memory capacity. Since poor inhibitory control has been shown to be related to problems in the interpretation of emotional information in depression (Joormann, 2004; Goeleven et al., 2006), cognitive functioning seems to be a valuable starting point in the therapy of depressive symptoms. In line with this view, Marazziti et al. (2010) hypothesized that decreased cognitive flexibility in patients with depression possibly prevents those individuals from being able to cope with life events which then leads to constant low mood due to increased stress exposition. All in all, there is much evidence that depression goes along with impaired cognitive performance, and symptom severity seems to be related especially to decreased episodic memory, executive functions, and processing speed (McDermott and Ebmeier, 2009). Thus, it seems reasonable that deficits in emotional and cognitive processing might be closely interrelated. However, studies in depression investigating the relationship between deficits in emotional perception of faces and sounds and impairments in cognitive functions, measured independently from emotional processing, are rather rare. Taken together, even though findings clearly indicate an impairment in emotional processing in major depression, authors do not agree on whether depression is associated with a general bias (present negative or absent positive bias), if it is possibly a result of cognitive deficits, or both.

The aims of the current study were therefore to first assess uni- and multi-modal emotional processing in patients with depression. Second, we explored executive functioning and related cognitive domains to be able to investigate the potential relationship of emotional and cognitive deficits. We chose a selection of different neurocognitive tests where patients with depression have been reported to be impaired (Hoffstaedter et al., 2012), i.e., that challenged the participants' attention, cognitive flexibility, (visuo-) motor speed and coordination, short-term as well as working memory, and verbal vocabulary.

Based on the previous literature regarding emotional processing in patients with depression, we hypothesized that for unimodal conditions, we would find a mood-congruent emotional bias in patients with depression (negative or absent positive), whereas in the multi-modal setting, impairments would probably appear in a manner different from a generalized bias as already described by Müller et al. (2014). Additionally we expected patients to perform worse than healthy controls on neurocognitive tests, especially those regarding cognitive flexibility and attention, and that these deficits would be associated with impairments in emotional processing, thus pointing in the direction that emotional problems in depression are related to likewise prevalent cognitive deficits.

MATERIALS AND METHODS

SUBJECTS

The current study is based on a previous study, which tested audio-visual emotional processing in depression by using fMRI (Müller et al., 2014). We now focus on the behavioral effects in an expanded sample of patients and healthy controls.

In total, 41 patients diagnosed with major depression (19 females, 22 males) and 41 healthy controls (19 females, 22 males) were now included. Data from 44 of these 82 subjects originated from the previous fMRI study, while the remaining 38 subjects conducted the paradigm outside the scanner. Both patients and controls gave informed consent into the study, which was approved by the ethics committee of the School of Medicine of the RWTH Aachen University. In addition to gender matching, the two groups did not differ in their age or years of education (age: $T_{80} = -0.47$, $p = 0.64$; EDU: $T_{80} = 0.08$, $p = 0.80$; see **Table 1** for means). All subjects were right-handed according to the Edinburgh Handedness Questionnaire (Oldfield, 1971) and had normal or corrected-to-normal vision. Patients were recruited from the inpatient and outpatient units of the Department of Psychiatry, Psychotherapy and Psychosomatics, RWTH University Hospital. They were diagnosed by their treating psychiatrist with a depressive episode or a recurrent depressive disorder according to the criteria of the ICD-10 (WHO, 2010; see **Table 2** for the patients' clinical profiles). To confirm their diagnosis and to screen for possible psychiatric co-morbidities, the structured clinical interview for DSM-IV (SCID; Wittchen et al., 1997) was conducted. Furthermore, the Beck Depression Inventory (BDI-II; Hautzinger et al., 2006) as well as the Hamilton depression scale (Hamilton, 1960) were used to quantify depression-related symptoms and thus the illness severity. We only included patients without co-morbidities, i.e., without an indication of any psychiatric or neurological disease other than major depression, and without any kind of addiction or substance abuse in at least 6 months. Control subjects did not report any history of psychiatric or neurological disorders as well as any addiction in their past. Sub-clinical depressive symptoms in the control group were also assessed with the BDI-II (Hautzinger et al., 2006).

STIMULI

For a detailed description of stimulus material and procedure see Müller et al. (2011). In brief, the visual stimuli were color pictures obtained from the FEBA inventory (Gur et al., 2002) showing either a happy, neutral, or fearful facial expression. In total, 30 different faces were used, with five different female and five different male actors, each showing all three (happy/neutral/fearful) expressions. As pre-tests revealed that happy and fearful facial expressions were too clear in their emotionality to allow any contextual framing effects (Müller et al., 2011), they were made more ambiguous by merging them with the neutral mouths of the same actors. As auditory stimuli 10 laughs, 10 yawns, and 10 screams, each produced by five females and five males and lasting for 1500 ms, were used. Blurred versions of the neutral faces served as masks during the initial 1000 ms of sound presentation before the target faces were shown.

Table 1 | Demographic and clinical profile of patients and controls.

	Patients	Controls
Gender (female/male)	19/22	19/22
Age (SD)	36,49 (10,87)	37,61 (10,79)
EDU (SD)	12,41 (3,32)	12,59 (2,65)
BDI (SD)	23,07 (11,89)	1,90 (3,07)
HAMD (SD)	11,54 (5,98)	–

SD, standard deviation; EDU, years of education; BDI, Beck's depression inventory score; HAMD, Hamilton depression scale score.

AUDIOVISUAL PARADIGM

In total, 180 stimulus pairs, each consisting of a visual and an auditory stimulus, were used. Every face condition (happy/neutral/fearful) was paired with every sound condition (happy/neutral/fearful) resulting in a 3 × 3 design with nine different audiovisual conditions (fearful/scream, fearful/yawn, fearful/laugh, neutral/scream, neutral/yawn, neutral/laugh, happy/scream, happy/yawn, happy/laugh) and 20 individual audiovisual stimulus pairs per condition. The pairs were matched pseudo-randomly with regard to gender so that a female (male) face was always paired with a female (male) sound.

Figure 1 illustrates the experimental procedure. Every trial started with the presentation of a sound in combination with a blurred neutral face. After 1000 ms, the screen switched to a non-blurred picture of an emotional or neutral face (the target face), which was presented for another 500 ms with the ongoing sound. Participants had the task to ignore the sound and rate the facial expression on an eight-point rating scale (not including a neutral option and ranging from extremely fearful to extremely happy) as fast and as accurate as possible by pressing one of eight buttons on a response pad. To avoid expectation-led effects on the outcome of the experiment, the participants were told that the study focuses on attention processes. Stimuli were presented with the software Presentation 14.2 (http://www.neurobs.com/).

UNIMODAL VALENCE AND AROUSAL RATINGS OF FACES AND SOUNDS

After the audiovisual paradigm, patients and controls rated emotional valence and arousal of all faces and sounds used in the audiovisual paradigm individually. For that, two separate runs were conducted, one for the unimodal facial expression rating and one for the unimodal sound rating. Both valence and arousal of the stimuli had to be rated on a 9-point rating scale, i.e., including a neutral option and ranging from very fearful to very happy/not at all arousing to very arousing.

NEUROPSYCHOLOGICAL TESTING

To measure neurocognitive and psychomotor skills of patients and controls, diverse neurocognitive tests were conducted.

Visual attention/visuomotor speed

Trail making tests (versions A and B). The two trail making tests [TMT-A and TMT-B; Army Individual Test Battery (AITB), 1944] were used to assess attention and visuomotor speed. Participants had the task to accurately connect as fast as possible (a) a consecutive sequence of numbers from 1 to 25 (TMT-A) and (b) a sequence of numbers from 1 to 13 mixed with the first 12 letters of the alphabet (TMT-B), respectively. The TMT-B, where numbers and letters had to be connected alternately, also assessed cognitive flexibility. Measurement for the test results was the time it took the participants to accomplish the task. Additionally we calculated difference scores between performance in TMT-A and TMT-B (TMT-Diff).

Motor speed/coordination

Finger tapping test. The finger tapping test was used to determine basic motor speed. Participants were asked to tap on the table as fast as possible for 10 s with their left or right index finger. This procedure was conducted three times for both (left and right)

Table 2 | Patients' demographic data and clinical profile.

Gender	Age	Diagnosis	Medication	Age of onset	Duration of illness
Female	57	F 32.1	Reboxetine, Citalopram	33	24
Female	54	F 33.1	Venlafaxine	50	5
Female	33	F 33.2	Venlafaxine	30	3
Female	34	F 32.1	Citalopram	24	10
Female	49	F 33.2	Venlafaxine, Quetiapine, Lithium carbonate	25	24
Female	33	F 33.3	Venlafaxine, Quetiapine	12	21
Female	33	F 32.1	Fluoxetine	33	1
Female	51	F 33.1	Agomelatine, Duloxetine	46	5
Female	27	F 32.2	Venlafaxine, Mirtazapine	21	6
Female	22	F 32.1	Venlafaxine	13	9
Female	26	F 32.1	Duloxetine	23	3
Female	31	F 33.1	Citalopram	11	20
Female	50	F 33.2	Duloxetine, Quetiapine	47	3
Female	38	F 33.1	Reboxetine	34	4
Female	30	F 32.1	"none"	30	1
Female	51	F 33.1	Escitalopram	31	20
Female	41	F 32.1	Venlafaxine	33	8
Female	29	F 32.2	Citalopram	29	1
Female	42	F 33.1	Mirtazapine	26	16
Male	45	F 32.1	Venlafaxine, Trimipramine	43	2
Male	55	F 33.2	Mirtazapine, Quetiapine, Duloxetine, Pipamperone	49	6
Male	37	F 33.1	Venlafaxine	35	2
Male	46	F 32.1	Venlafaxine, Opipramol	40	6
Male	52	F 32.1	Venlafaxine	44	8
Male	43	F 32.1	Mirtazapine	19	24
Male	27	F 32.1	Reboxetine	24	3
Male	25	F 32.1	Sertraline	21	4
Male	40	F 32.1	Venlafaxine	38	2
Male	30	F 33.1	Citalopram, Lithium	21	9
Male	38	F 32.1	Venlafaxine	35	3
Male	29	F 32.1	Lithium carbonate	24	5
Male	19	F 32.1	Citalopram	16	3
Male	28	F 33.2	Venlafaxine	27	1
Male	30	F 33.1	Opipramol, Sertraline, Mirtazapine	29	1
Male	53	F 33.2	Venlafaxine, Mirtazapine	44	9
Male	34	F 33.2	Venlafaxine, Quetiapine	25	9
Male	22	F 32.1	Venlafaxine	18	4
Male	41	F 33.1	Venlafaxine	36	5
Male	29	F 33.1	Bupropion, Quetiapine	20	9
Male	18	F 32.2	Remergil, Venlafaxine	17	1
Male	24	F 33.1	Citalopram	16	8

Data for age of onset of depression and duration of illness is taken from self-reported information by the patients. Age, age of onset, and duration of illness are specified in years.

FIGURE 1 | Experimental procedure of the audiovisual paradigm. Every trial started with a sound in combination with a blurred neutral face, after 1000 ms the screen switched to the target face, which was presented with the ongoing sound for another 500 ms.

index fingers with short pauses in between to increase reliability but avoid muscular fatigue. For all six tapping runs, the number of taps was counted and the mean of all runs from both hands calculated (Halstead, 1947; Behrwind et al., 2011).

Pointing movements. To assess basic motor coordination, the participants were asked to perform pointing movements with their left or right index finger (Defer et al., 1999). On the table in front of the subject, a 30 cm long horizontal line was marked and the task was to point on the two ends 10 times alternately as fast and as precise as possible. The time the participants needed to accomplish the task was measured. Again, this test was conducted three times for left and right index finger and the mean time of all six runs from both hands was calculated.

Crystalline intelligence

Multiple choice vocabulary intelligence test (MWT). The multiple choice vocabulary intelligence test, version B (Lehrl, 1989), measured the participants' crystalline intelligence. There were 37 rows of five words from which the participant had to choose the only actual word by ruling out four pseudo-words. The number of correctly detected words provided the test result.

Short-term and working memory

Digit span subtest of the Wechsler Adult Intelligence Scale (Tewes, 1991). This test, in which verbally presented digit spans had to be repeated by the participant, consisted of two parts. In the first, used to measure short-term verbal memory and attention, the participant had to repeat the digit span in the same order as it was read to him (DS-F). For part two which assessed manipulation within working memory, the participant had to repeat the numbers backward (DS-B). For both test parts the number of correctly reproduced digit sequences was used as the test result.

Due to technical problems, the neuropsychological test results of one control subject could not be used and one patient did not take part in the TMT-A and TMT-B, while another one did not take part in the TAP10s and TAP10x30. The MWT was only conducted with native German speaking participants, and thus results from one of the patients and two control subjects are not available.

STATISTICAL ANALYSIS

We analyzed our data using SPSS Statistics 21 (IBM). Most data except for those of the multimodal emotional processing task were not normally distributed and tests were individually chosen, adapted to the particular conditions. The threshold for significance was set at $p < 0.05$, Bonferroni-corrected for multiple comparisons if appropriate. Data from unimodal valence and arousal ratings of sounds and faces were analyzed with Mann–Whitney-U tests for group comparison and Wilcoxon-tests for comparisons between conditions (corrected for multiple comparisons). Data from the audiovisual paradigm were analyzed calculating a MANOVA (due to violation of sphericity) with the factors face, sound and group and the dependent variable emotional valence rating of faces. Significant main effects and interactions were furthermore analyzed with *post hoc* t-tests (corrected for multiple comparisons). To test for possible incongruence effects, two additional ANOVAS (for happy and fearful faces) with the factors congruence and group and the dependent variable emotional valence rating of faces were calculated. Significant findings were again further analyzed with *post hoc* t-tests (corrected for multiple comparisons). Furthermore, we calculated Spearman-rank-correlations between findings in emotional processing and Beck's depression inventory score (BDI-scores) for the patient group.

Group differences in neurocognitive performance were tested with Mann–Whitney-U tests. Within the domains visual attention/visuomotor speed, motor speed/coordination and short-term/working memory, results were corrected for multiple comparisons (Bonferroni).

To investigate the relationship of emotional processing and neurocognitive functioning, we again calculated Spearman-rank-correlations.

RESULTS

UNIMODAL VALENCE AND AROUSAL RATING OF SOUNDS AND FACES

In total 12 Mann–Whitney-U tests were calculated (all results are Bonferroni-corrected for multiple comparisons). No significant group differences were found in the unimodal ratings of valence and arousal of faces and sounds (see **Table 3**).

Comparisons between conditions across groups demonstrated that happy and fearful faces were rated as more arousing than neutral ones and that all types of faces as well as all types of sounds

Table 3 | Group comparisons of unimodal valence and arousal ratings of sounds and faces – findings of Mann–Whitney-*U* tests.

		Arousal		Valence	
		U	*p*	*U*	*p*
Sounds	Positive	−2.018	0.044	−0.046	0.963
	Neutral	−0.191	0.848	−0.254	0.799
	Negative	−1.049	0.294	−0.599	0.549
Faces	Positive	−1.499	0.134	−0.803	0.422
	Neutral	−0.772	0.440	−1.545	0.122
	Negative	−0.603	0.546	−0.390	0.697

No significant group differences were found (Bonferroni-corrected cut-off $p < 0.017$).

Table 4 | Mean values and SD for emotional valence and arousal ratings of faces and sounds.

	Happy (SD)	Neutral (SD)	Fearful (SD)
Patients			
Emotional valence rating of faces	**7.049** (0.672)	**4.661** (0.536)	**3.437** (0.830)
Emotional valence rating of sounds	**7.742** (0.764)	**5.117** (0.483)	**1.649** (0.793)
Arousal rating of faces	**4.027** (1.521)	**3.698** (1.513)	**4.789** (1.635)
Arousal rating of sounds	**3.815** (1.640)	**3.129** (1.597)	**6.366** (2.095)
Controls			
Emotional valence rating of faces	**6.917** (0.816)	**4.481** (0.583)	**3.527** (0.658)
Emotional valence rating of sounds	**7.707** (0.847)	**5.117** (0.785)	**1.576** (0.806)
Arousal rating of faces	**4.539** (1.865)	**3.963** (1.507)	**5.034** (1.417)
Arousal rating of sounds	**4.642** (2.022)	**3.061** (1.646)	**6.868** (1.837)

There are no significant differences between patients and controls (Bonferroni-corrected cut-off $p < 0.017$).

differed from each other in their emotional valence rating (for mean values and SD see **Table 4**, all $p < 0.017$). In particular, fearful stimuli got the lowest ratings, followed by neutral faces and sounds, while the most positive ratings were given for happy stimuli.

AUDIOVISUAL PARADIGM

Valence ratings of faces in audiovisual setting

A MANOVA with the factors face (happy/neutral/fearful), sound (happy/neutral/fearful) and group (controls/patients), and the dependent variable emotional valence rating was calculated. Multivariate testing was chosen due to violation of sphericity of sounds [$\chi^2(2) = 6.267$, $p = 0.044$] and faces [$\chi^2(2) = 57.726$, $p < 0.001$]. Assumptions of equality of error variances and equality of covariance matrices were met, indicated by non-significant Box's M test and Levene's tests. Results revealed significant main effects of sound ($F_{2,79} = 12.89$, $p < 0.001$, effect size: partial $\eta^2 = 0.25$) and face ($F_{2,79} = 401.81$, $p < 0.001$, effect size: partial $\eta^2 = 0.91$), but no main effect of group ($F_{1,80} = 0.23$, $p = 0.63$). Furthermore an interaction between sound × group could be found ($F_{2,79} = 4.20$, $p = 0.018$, effect size: partial $\eta^2 = 0.10$), but no interactions of face × group ($F_{2,79} = 1.91$, $p = 0.155$), sound × face ($F_{4,77} = 2.40$, $p = 0.058$) or sound × face × group ($F_{4,77} = 0.96$, $p = 0.437$). To further analyze the significant interaction between sound × group *post hoc* t-tests were calculated (all results are Bonferroni-corrected for multiple comparisons). We found no significant global differences (across all types of concurrently presented faces) between groups, neither in the happy, nor neutral, nor fearful sound condition (faces paired with happy sounds: $T_{80} = -0.065$, $p = 0.948$; faces paired with neutral sounds: $T_{80} = 0.861$, $p = 0.392$; faces paired with fearful sounds: $T_{80} = 0.602$, $p = 0.549$). However, the *post hoc* tests demonstrated that while in healthy controls there was no difference in the rating of faces when concurrently hearing happy compared to neutral sounds ($T_{40} = -0.08$, $p = 0.939$), patients with depression rated faces as more fearful when presented with happy compared to neutral sounds ($T_{40} = 4.61$, $p < 0.001$). Furthermore, in controls the ratings of faces differed between the happy and fearful sound condition ($T_{40} = -3.36$, $p = 0.002$), whereas there was no difference between these two conditions in the patient group ($T_{40} = -1.28$, $p = 0.209$). Additionally, in both groups presentation of fearful compared to neutral sounds led to more fearful ratings of faces (controls: $T_{40} = -3.09$, $p = 0.004$; patients: $T_{40} = -4.22$, $p < 0.001$). These differences in the impact of sounds on the emotional valence ratings of faces between patients and controls are illustrated in **Figure 2**. For a more detailed analysis of the interaction, we further calculated difference scores in emotional valence ratings of faces between sound conditions, i.e., happy–neutral, happy–fearful, fearful–neutral. These difference scores were then compared between patients and controls using independent samples t-tests. The t-tests revealed a significant difference between patients and controls in the difference scores between the happy and neutral sound condition ($T_{80} = -2.723$, $p = 0.008$, effect size: Cohen's $d = 0.60$). For patients, the mean value of the difference scores happy minus neutral was −0.068, indicating more fearful ratings of faces when presented with happy compared to neutral sounds. In contrast, the mean value of the respective difference scores in controls was 0.002, indicating only slightly happier ratings of faces when presented with happy sounds compared to neutral sounds. In contrast, neither the difference score of the happy minus fearful (mean values: patients 0.024; controls 0.077) nor the one of the fearful minus neutral sound condition (mean values: patients −0.092; controls −0.076) revealed any significant group differences (happy–fearful: $T_{80} = -1.818$, $p = 0.073$; fearful–neutral: $T_{80} = -0.496$, $p = 0.621$).

In summary, the main difference in face ratings between patients and controls was that patients rated faces in combination with happy sounds as more fearful than in combination with neutral sounds while controls did not.

Spearman-rank-correlations of difference scores between the happy and neutral sound conditions with BDI-scores were calculated for the patient group. Results did not reveal any significant associations ($r = -0.087$, $p = 0.590$).

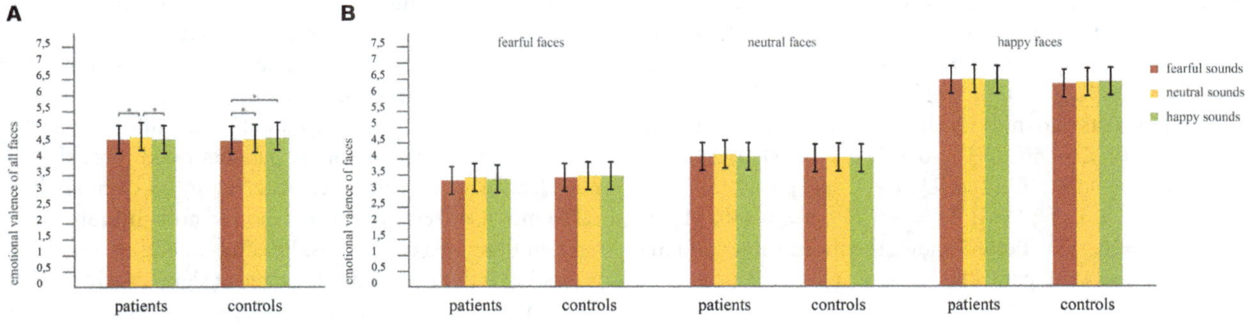

FIGURE 2 | Mean ratings of faces in the audiovisual setting. Error bars indicate the SD of mean. Significant interaction group × sound. **(A)** Mean ratings for each sound condition across all face conditions. Asterisks indicate significant differences revealed by *post hoc* tests at $p < 0.05$, Bonferroni-corrected for multiple comparisons. Patients rated faces significantly more fearful when presented with fearful or happy sounds than when presented with neutral sounds, while controls rated faces significantly more fearful when presented with fearful sounds than when presented with neutral sounds, but ratings did not differ between the neutral and the happy sound conditions. **(B)** Mean values of the ratings of fearful, neutral, and happy faces separately. No interaction sound × face × group was found in the MANOVA, therefore no further *post hoc* tests were calculated.

Incongruence effect

To investigate the interaction sound × group described above, we analyzed the audiovisual data more in detail. That is, we focused on the impact of emotional congruence/incongruence between concurrently presented sounds and faces on the valence ratings separately for happy and fearful faces. Therefore, we calculated two ANOVAs, one for happy faces and one for fearful faces. Both contained the factors congruence (congruent sound/incongruent sound) and group (controls/patients). In **Figure 3** the results are illustrated. For happy faces, we found a significant main effect of congruence ($F_{1,80} = 5.40$, $p = 0.023$, effect size: partial $\eta^2 = 0.06$) and an interaction congruence × group ($F_{1,80} = 6.15$, $p = 0.015$, effect size: partial $\eta^2 = 0.07$), but no main effect of group ($F_{1,80} = 1.59$, $p = 0.211$). In contrast, the ANOVA of fearful faces only revealed a significant main effect of congruence ($F_{1,80} = 11.81$, $p = 0.001$, effect size: partial $\eta^2 = 0.13$) but neither a significant interaction congruence × group ($F_{1,80} = 0.04$, $p = 0.834$) nor a main effect of group ($F_{1,80} = 1.23$, $p = 0.271$). To further analyze the significant interaction between congruence × group for happy faces, we calculated *post hoc* t-tests (all results are Bonferroni-corrected for multiple comparisons). Those did not reveal any significant differences in emotional valence rating of faces between patients and controls, neither for the congruent nor for the incongruent condition (congruent: $T_{80} = 0.76$, $p = 0.452$; incongruent: $T_{80} = 1.76$, $p = 0.083$; see **Figure 3**). However, patients did not rate happy faces significantly different when paired with happy sounds (congruent condition) compared to fearful sounds (incongruent condition, $T_{40} = -0.11$, $p = 0.910$). In contrast, controls rated happy faces significantly happier when paired with happy sounds compared to fearful sounds ($T_{40} = 3.29$, $p = 0.002$; mean value happy sound: 6.35/mean value fearful sound: 6.24; see **Figure 3**).

NEUROCOGNITIVE TESTS

Group comparisons

Mann–Whitney-U tests were calculated to compare the scores of the neurocognitive tests between the two groups (controls/patients). All results are Bonferroni-corrected for the

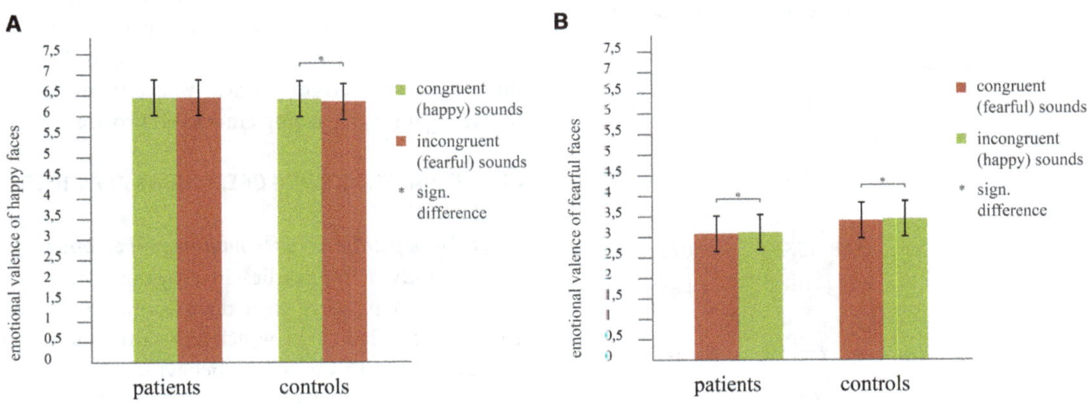

FIGURE 3 | Incongruence effect for (A) happy faces, revealing a significant interaction congruence × group and (B) fearful faces showing no group differences. Error bars indicate the SD of mean. Asterisks indicate significant differences revealed by *post hoc* tests at $p < 0.05$, Bonferroni-corrected for multiple comparisons.

number of tests within each test category. Significant differences between controls and patients were found for the TMT-A and TMT-B (TMT-A: $U = -2.723$, $p = 0.006$, effect size: $r = 0.30$; TMT-B: $U = -2.492$, $p = 0.013$, effect size: $r = 0.29$). In contrast, the other tests did not reveal any significant differences between groups (TMT-Diff: $U = -0.385$, $p = 0.700$; TAP10x30: $U = -1.304$, $p = 0.192$; TAP10s: $U = -1.411$, $p = 0.158$; DS-F:$U = -1.215$, $p = 0.224$; DS-B: $U = -0.739$, $p = 0.460$; MWT: $U = -1.542$, $p = 0.123$). **Table 5** shows the mean values and SD of all tests in patients and controls.

Correlations of findings in audiovisual emotional processing and neurocognitive functioning

To investigate the relationship between findings in audiovisual emotional processing and neurocognitive functioning in the patient group, Spearman-rank-correlations were calculated between neurocognitive test scores and the difference scores of the happy and neutral sound condition. All results are Bonferroni-corrected for the number of tests within each test category. No significant correlations between the difference scores and neurocognitive test scores were found (difference score between happy-neutral with: TMT-A: $r = 0.326$, $p = 0.040$; TMT-B: $r = 0.235$, $p = 0.145$; TMT-Diff: $r = -0.096$, $p = 0.554$; TAP10s: $r = -0.30$, $p = 0.856$; TAP10x30: $r = -0.263$, $p = 0.101$; DS-F: $r = 0.076$, $p = 0.637$; DS-B: $r = -0.015$, $p = 0.928$; MWT: $r = 0.044$, $p = 0.787$).

DISCUSSION

The aim of the current study was to investigate emotional processing in a more naturalistic setting by adding an auditory context to visual stimuli, and furthermore the relationship between emotional and neurocognitive deficits in patients with depression. For that purpose, an audiovisual paradigm was conducted, where happy, fearful, and neutral faces had to be rated whilst ignoring concurrently presented emotional or neutral sounds. In addition, patients and controls completed diverse neurocognitive tests challenging attention, working memory, (visuo-)motor speed, coordination, and crystalline intelligence. Results in audiovisual emotional processing revealed an aberrant integration of happy sounds in major depression as patients rated faces significantly more fearful when combined with happy as compared to neutral sounds. Conversely, controls showed no significant differences between these two conditions. Findings in audiovisual emotional processing in patients did not correlate significantly with depressive symptom severity as indicated by BDI-scores. We only found significant group differences for two of the neurocognitive tests. Despite the fact that patients with depression were impaired both in audiovisual emotional processing and neurocognitive performance, we found no significant correlations between these two fields.

Table 5 | Mean values and SD of the neuropsychological tests of all participants.

	Patients: **mean value (SD)**	***Controls:*** **mean value (SD)**
Visual attention/visuomotor speed		
TMT-A**	26.38 (15.61)	19.55 (5.68)
TMT-B**	47.32 (19.94)	37.54 (11.48)
TMT-Diff	20.94 (14.47)	18.00 (9.43)
Motor speed/coordination		
TAP10s	101.66 (15.97)	107.01 (11.65)
TAP10x30	16.76 (4.01)	15.63 (4.66)
Short-term and working memory		
DS-F	7.68 (1.93)	8.35 (1.98)
DS-B	6.80 (1.79)	7.18 (1.82)
Crystalline intelligence		
MWT	27.68 (4.45)	29.50 (3.80)

***significant ($p < 0.05$, Bonferroni-corrected).*

UNIMODAL VALENCE AND AROUSAL RATINGS OF FACES AND SOUNDS

Several studies investigating unimodal emotional processing in patients with depression reported that patients showed a general bias toward more negative ratings of emotional and neutral stimuli such as faces, prosody, and music (Leppänen et al., 2004; Douglas and Porter, 2010; Naranjo et al., 2011) as well as an attentional bias toward negative emotional material (Leung et al., 2009; Milders et al., 2010). In the current study, however, we found no group differences with regard to valence and arousal ratings, neither for faces, nor for sounds. Apart from a general negative bias, these findings also contradict previous studies in depression, which reported respective group differences for unimodal stimuli (Csukly et al., 2009; Schlipf et al., 2013). They are rather in line with findings showing no group differences in unimodal emotional processing (Kan et al., 2004; Bourke et al., 2012; Müller et al., 2014). Müller et al. (2014) already suggested that such discrepancies might arise from differences in methodology like varying stimulus presentation times (Surguladze et al., 2004) or different emotions (fear vs. sadness) used as negative stimuli (Hu et al., 2012).

Thus, we would argue that the current findings suggest that, contradictory to our hypothesis, patients did neither show a general negative bias nor an emotional blunting with regard to unimodal ratings of emotional and neutral stimuli. This result, however, has to be taken with caution since differences in methodology (as mentioned above) clearly have an impact on the outcome of investigations regarding emotional processing.

AUDIOVISUAL PROCESSING OF EMOTIONS IN PATIENTS WITH DEPRESSION

General group differences in multi-modal emotional processing

To date, only a few studies investigated audiovisual emotional processing in patients with depression. In our previous study (Müller et al., 2014), in which the same audiovisual task as in the current study was used, behavioral results revealed significant main effects of sounds and faces, but no main effect of group nor interactions. However, the further analysis in that paper indicated a deficit in patients when congruent emotional sound information had to be ignored. Since that previous sample was rather small and some of the reported behavioral findings only showed a trend toward significance, we here aimed to further investigate these effects within an extended sample. Overall, our results across groups are similar to that in the previous smaller sample, but now we found a significant sound × group interaction. This indicates that the impact of sounds on the perception (and therefore ratings) of faces was different in patients compared to controls. In particular, *post hoc* calculations in the current study showed that while controls rated faces quite similar in combination with neutral and happy sounds, patients rated faces significantly more fearful when combined with happy rather than neutral sounds. Further *t*-tests support this result by showing that the difference scores between the happy and neutral sound conditions differed significantly between patients and controls. These results thus highlight the aberrant integration and inhibition of irrelevant and especially positive auditory information in patients with depression. Correlational analyses, however, indicate that this effect is not related to symptom severity.

With regard to existing theories of emotional processing in depression, the current findings can be explained in different ways.

On the one hand, the sound × group interaction could be interpreted as a missing influence of concurrently presented positive auditory stimuli on the ratings of facial expressions in patients with depression. In line with this view, Surguladze et al. (2004) reported that patients exhibited a decreased tendency to interpret happy (but also neutral) faces as happy. Likewise Douglas and Porter (2010) described patients with depression as being less likely to interpret neutral faces as happy, while Loi et al. (2013) reported a reduced ability of patients to appraise positive stimuli of emotional body language. Importantly, however, our *post hoc* tests did not reveal group differences for any stimulus combination and rather indicated that patients differed in the ratings of faces paired with a positive sound compared to a neutral one while controls did not. Furthermore we only found this effect for the audiovisual processing task but not in the unimodal setting. Thus, the current results cannot support the view of an absent positive bias in patients with depression.

On the other hand, our results could also be explained in terms of a negative bias. In particular, for patients with depression, the current results show that any emotional sound (positive or negative) led to more negative ratings of concurrently seen emotional or neutral faces. This suggests that in depressed patients increased emotional input and higher arousal (cf. see Unimodal Valence and Arousal Rating of Sounds and Faces, emotional stimuli were rated as more arousing than neutral stimuli) received from two different channels generally leads to a more negative perception. Nevertheless, although fitting into the view of a more negative perception of emotions going along with depression (Gur et al., 1992; Bouhuys et al., 1999; Leppänen et al., 2004; Naranjo et al., 2011; Kaletsch et al., 2014), it has to be noted that this negative bias is limited to processing of emotions in an audiovisual setting (not for unimodal ratings of faces and sounds). Furthermore it only appears when facial stimuli are paired with happy sounds as healthy individuals are likewise negatively influenced by fearful sounds as patients are. Therefore the negative bias theory also does not explain the results sufficiently.

Yet our results can also be related to another more recent bias theory: Everaert et al. (2014) investigated the combined cognitive bias theory that has been reported for individuals with social phobia (Hirsch et al., 2006) in depression. They found that emotional biases in attention, interpretation, and memory in subclinical depression are strongly interrelated which potentially influences how daily life events are perceived. In particular, participants with higher depression scores paid more attention to negative emotional stimuli, made more negative interpretations and remembered negative material more frequently. When relating these findings to our results, it can be argued that patients paid special attention to fearful sounds and therefore held them in memory during the whole paradigm. Subsequently, their ratings of faces during concurrent presentation of laughter were then influenced by negatively biased memory of previous stimuli which led to a more fearful interpretation of faces. Although fitting with the impaired integration of happy sounds, this interpretation can, however, also not completely explain our findings. If the more fearful rating of faces during laughter had been due to maintenance of screams in memory, neutral sound presentation should have been influenced by this effect as well. However, our patients rated faces in combination with laughter significantly more fearful than in combination with yawning, and this was the only difference compared to controls.

In summary, none of the three presented bias theories can fully explain the current findings in patients with depression. Thus, our results suggest that in a multi-modal setting, impairments in emotional processing in depression cannot be reduced to a specific bias but are far more complex than previously thought.

Incongruence effects for happy and fearful faces

With reference to Müller et al. (2014) and in order to investigate the general effects found for audiovisual emotional processing in patients with depression more in detail, we specifically analyzed incongruence effects in emotional valence separately for happy and fearful faces. In particular, Müller et al. (2014) described a trend toward significance for the congruence × group interaction when analyzing the happy face condition, whereas they did not find any significant effect for the fearful face condition. Furthermore, their neuroimaging data revealed that for the congruent happy condition (happy face paired with happy sound), controls showed stronger deactivation in both left inferior parietal cortex (IPC) and left inferior frontal gyrus (IFG) compared to the patient group. Our current findings confirm the behavioral findings in a larger sample, thus providing increased power of results: patients with depression did not rate happy faces significantly different when paired with congruent (= happy) sounds in contrast to incongruent (= fearful) sounds, while controls rated happy faces significantly happier when paired with happy sounds than paired with fearful sounds. These behavioral findings fit well with the dysregulation of left IPC and IFG, which was found especially for the congruent happy condition (Müller et al., 2014). Thus, a failure to deactivate those two regions during processing of congruent positive audiovisual information in patients with depression might be associated with the missing behavioral incongruence effect found in the current study.

Our results regarding incongruence in emotional valence also shed further light on the effect found in the overall calculations described above (sound × group interaction) by showing that the effect of impaired integration of happy sounds is strongly connected to the happy face condition. Ratings of happy faces indeed became more negative in both patients and controls by incongruent (= fearful) sounds. However, when happy faces were paired with congruent (= happy) sounds, it seems that controls were able to inhibit or were positively influenced by these, while this was not the case in patients. Our findings hence suggest that patients are impaired in the inhibition of positive information in an additional sensory channel, especially when the target information is also positive. This additional presentation of positive information then has a negative impact on the ratings of the positive target emotion, what might reflect a tendency to perceive actually positive emotional input as threat.

Apart from the study by Müller et al. (2014), findings of multimodal emotional processing in patients with depression are rare, but some studies exist, which investigate the impact of irrelevant (congruent/incongruent) emotional information on the perception and processing of emotional stimuli. Uekermann et al. (2008), for example, conducted several tests on identification and matching skills in depressed and healthy individuals, e.g., matching emotional/neutral prosody to semantics and faces. They reported deficits for all of these tests, except for conditions where information was congruent or in which sad stimuli were presented. These findings at first glance contradict the effect of impaired integration of congruent happy sounds in depression as found in the current study. However, this discrepancy may arise from the fact that the task in the current study was to rate the emotion of the faces on an intensity scale, while Uekermann et al. (2008) did not directly measure the influence of distracting information on perception. Rather they investigated differences in accuracy when matching/labeling concurrently presented information. Obviously patients are able to identify information from different channels as congruent, even when positive, but this does not necessarily mean that they perceive stimuli as equally positive as controls do.

Findings in the emotional Stroop task in depression shed further light on how irrelevant emotional information is processed by these patients. However, existing findings are quite inconsistent (Mogg and Bradley, 2005). A recent meta-analysis (Epp et al., 2012) thus quantified findings from behavioral studies investigating the (emotional) Stroop task and showed that depressed individuals exhibited a general attentional bias for emotional content, i.e., negative but importantly also positive words. With regard to positive stimuli, these findings are in line with the current results. The fact that we did not find an effect for the negative sound condition might again be due to the use of fearful rather than sad sounds as negative distractors (cf. see Unimodal Valence and Arousal Ratings of Faces and Sounds).

In summary, our results indicate that when confronted with audiovisual emotional information, patients with depression show in particular impairments when distracted by positive auditory information, especially when the visual information is also positive. This may – in line with studies showing that depression goes along with decreased responsiveness to reward (Henriques and Davidson, 2000) – suggest that depressed individuals are less likely to accept positive feedback as a kind of social reward from their environment, resulting in a more negative view on life and low mood.

NEUROCOGNITIVE PERFORMANCE

Deficits in neurocognitive functioning in depression have been reported by numerous studies (e.g., Breslow et al., 1980; Fisher et al., 1986; Veiel, 1997; Zakzanis et al., 1998; Stordal et al., 2004). It is suggested that these deficits account for or at least substantially contribute to problems in everyday life like occupational functioning deficits, which are experienced by individuals with depression (Evans et al., 2013). However, findings on the pattern, extent and specificity of cognitive deficits in depression are quite heterogeneous (Ottowitz et al., 2002; Naismith et al., 2003; Marazziti et al., 2010; Lee et al., 2012; Quinn et al., 2012). For example, there is no agreement whether impairments are limited to executive functioning (Baune et al., 2012) or also relate to other domains like attention (Godard et al., 2012), psychomotor speed, visual learning/memory, and others (Lee et al., 2012). The current study revealed significant differences between patients and controls only in (both versions of) the trail making test. Conversely, there were no significant differences in any other neurocognitive test, contradicting the findings by Hoffstaedter et al. (2012) who conducted the same tests and reported group differences for most of them. Since motor speed was also assessed by TAP10s and Tap10x30, which both did not reveal group differences, our results indicate relatively specific deficits of visual attention and cognitive flexibility. Also, group differences in TMT-B in particular may point in the direction of a deficit in dealing with distracting information in patients with depression. These results highlight the importance of the specificity of assessment instruments for neurocognitive performance in depression (cf. Trivedi and Greer, 2014). Executive functioning, for example, may be operationalized and then measured by a large number of different tests and study designs. The ensuing results, however, would all be interpreted under the domain of executive functioning. This might explain heterogeneity in study findings. In addition, findings are also influenced by the patient sample investigated. The patient status (inpatient/outpatient) has, for example, an impact on the severity of impairments (Burt et al., 1995), possibly due to the fact that inpatients exhibit generally worse symptomatology (or rather, patients with worse symptoms are more likely to receive inpatient treatment). Furthermore, subtypes of depression also have to be considered when investigating neurocognitive performance (Naismith et al., 2003; Lee et al., 2012), as co-morbidities like anxiety disorder or bipolar disorder might have crucial impact on the outcome of neurocognitive test batteries. Thus, the fact that the patient group tested in the current study consisted exclusively of patients with unipolar depression who were free of co-morbidities may explain inconsistencies to some previous findings where patient groups were variably mixed. At last, antidepressant medication also plays a role, since medicated patients have been reported to perform better on neurocognitive tests than unmedicated ones (Gualtieri et al., 2006). Wagner et al. (2012) investigated changes in neurocognitive functioning during antidepressant treatment and found that performance of patients only improves in certain domains but not all. Especially test performance in TMT-B was excluded from improvement. This might provide an explanation for our results, as all but one patient of the current study were receiving antidepressant medication. However, subgroup analysis with regard to type of antidepressant medication was not possible due to the large variety in medication composition from patient to patient (see **Table 2**). Thus, future studies should deal with detailed analysis of the impact of certain antidepressant medication types on neurocognitive performance to be able to identify crucial factors on test results.

In summary, our findings show that when comparing patients with controls, differences are only found for attention and cognitive flexibility. This supports but also contradicts findings of other studies on neurocognitive functioning in depression and underlines the heterogeneity of depression.

RELATIONSHIP BETWEEN AUDIOVISUAL EMOTIONAL PROCESSING AND NEUROCOGNITIVE FUNCTIONING

Emotional and neurocognitive aberrations have already been reported for depressed patients in numerous studies. However, only few have yet investigated how deficits in these two domains are related to each other. We thus correlated the effects found in the emotional processing task and the performance in the different neurocognitive tests and found that the effects revealed for audiovisual emotional processing, i.e., the difference of valence ratings of faces paired with happy compared to neutral sounds, were not related to performance in the neurocognitive tests. However, when not correcting for multiple comparisons, correlational analysis of the TMT-A test findings with impairments in emotional processing would reach significance. This is interesting, because the only two tests that revealed group differences were the two trail making tests. One could hence argue that impairments in the processing of interpersonal stimuli are possibly related to general deficits in visual attention. This would expand the findings of studies reporting selective visual attention for negative emotional material in depressed individuals (Eizenman et al., 2003; Kellough et al., 2008), indicating that attentional biases toward negative emotions alone cannot sufficiently explain impairments in emotional processing in depression. Rather, general attentional deficits might also lead to problems in concentrating on visual emotional material. This would fit with our finding that patients with depression are distracted more easily than healthy controls by additional irrelevant (especially positive) auditory stimuli. All in all, however, as this result did not survive correction for multiple comparisons, our findings nevertheless argue against a (direct) relationship between emotional processing and neurocognitive functioning. This contradicts findings of one previous study (Uekermann et al., 2008) reporting correlations between perception of affective prosody with inhibition abilities, set shifting, and working memory. On the other hand, another study (Langenecker et al., 2005) reported no correlations between impairments in emotional perception and neurocognitive performance and is hence well in line with our findings. Discussing their results, the authors mentioned that executive impairments are a feature of several different disorders, indicating that cognitive disturbances may not necessarily account for emotional impairments in depression. Likewise, Bourke et al. (2012) found that patients with depression perform significantly worse on verbal memory and spatial working memory tasks, but they did not find differences to healthy controls on unimodal emotional face recognition tasks (going in line with our findings in unimodal emotional processing). Even though they did not directly correlate emotional with cognitive performance, their results indicate that neurocognitive impairments are largely independent from emotional deficits.

Other studies (Everaert et al., 2014), however, reported associations of emotion perception and cognition in the sense of cognitive biases for negative emotions. In particular, they could show that emotionally biased cognitive processes like attention, interpretation and memory are highly interrelated with each other. Under this aspect, it has to be pointed out that it seems to make a huge difference if, on the one hand, general cognitive functions in absence of emotional material are examined or if, on the other hand, cognitive processing of emotional material is assessed. Thus, with regard to our findings, we can only infer that there is no relationship between general cognitive performance and impairments in emotional processing.

In summary, our results thus indicate that deficits in audiovisual emotional processing in depression seem to be widely independent from general neurocognitive functioning. Thus they do not support the assumption that deficits in emotional processing in patients with major depression are the results of impaired general attention or inhibitory functioning. Nevertheless we cannot completely rule out a bias component especially toward emotional material.

SUMMARY

Our findings suggest that audiovisual integration of especially happy sounds is altered in patients with depression and that these alterations cannot be related directly to impairments in cognitive skills. Group differences in neurocognitive test performance were only revealed for measures of attention and cognitive flexibility. These results indicate that in real life, when emotions are processed in a multimodal fashion, deficits in depression cannot be reduced to an overall negative attitude toward emotional and neutral stimuli or a general absence of a positive bias. Rather, it is the influence of irrelevant positive stimuli, which plays a key role in emotion perception in depression. Though, impairments in audiovisual emotional processing do not change as a function of depressive symptom severity in patients. Furthermore there is no clear connection between emotional and neurocognitive impairments.

Although the current study did not directly investigate the role of attention in multisensory integration, our study adds further knowledge to this topic by investigating the relationship between both aspects in major depression and indicates that alterations in multi-modal emotional processing are not directly related to impaired attention.

AUTHOR CONTRIBUTIONS

Veronika I. Müller and Simon B. Eickhoff designed the study, Veronika I. Müller acquired the data, Sophie Doose-Grünefeld and Veronika I. Müller analyzed the data, Sophie

Doose-Grünefeld, Simon B. Eickhoff, and Veronika I. Müller wrote the paper.

ACKNOWLEDGMENTS

Simon B. Eickhoff is supported by the Deutsche Forschungsgemeinschaft (DFG, EI 816/4-1, EI 816/6-1, LA 3071/3-1) and the National Institute of Mental Health (R01-MH074457).

REFERENCES

Airaksinen, E., Larsson, M., Lundberg, I., and Forsell, Y. (2004). Cognitive functions in depressive disorders: evidence from a population-based study. *Psychol. Med.* 34, 83–91. doi: 10.1017/S0033291703008559

Army Individual Test Battery. (AITB). (1944). *Manual of Directions and Scoring.* Washington, DC: War Department, Adjutant General's Office.

Baune, B. T., Czira, M. E., Smith, A. L., Mitchell, D., and Sinnamon, G. (2012). Neuropsychological performance in a sample of 13-25 year olds with a history of non-psychotic major depressive disorder. *J. Affect. Disord.* 141, 441–448. doi: 10.1016/j.jad.2012.02.041

Behrwind, S. D., Dafotakis, M., Halfter, S., Hobusch, K., Berthold-Losleben, M., Cieslik, E. C., et al. (2011). Executive control in chronic schizophrenia: a perspective from manual stimulus-response compatibility task performance. *Behav. Brain Res.* 223, 24–29. doi: 10.1016/j.bbr.2011.04.009

Bouhuys, A. L., Geerts, E., and Gordijn, M. C. (1999). Depressed patients' perceptions of facial emotions in depressed and remitted states are associated with relapse: a longitudinal study. *J. Nerv. Ment. Dis.* 187, 595–602. doi: 10.1097/00005053-199910000-00002

Bourke, C., Douglas, K., and Porter, R. (2010). Processing of facial emotion expression in major depression: a review. *Aust. N. Z. J. Psychiatry* 44, 681–696. doi: 10.3109/00048674.2010.496359

Bourke, C., Porter, R. J., Carter, J. D., McIntosh, V. V., Jordan, J., Bell, C., et al. (2012). Comparison of neuropsychological functioning and emotional processing in major depression and social anxiety disorder subjects, and matched healthy controls. *Aust. N. Z. J. Psychiatry* 46, 972–981. doi: 10.1177/000486741 2451502

Breslow, R., Kocsis, J., and Belkin, B. (1980). Memory deficits in depression: evidence utilizing the Wechsler Memory Scale. *Percept. Mot. Skills* 51, 541–542. doi: 10.2466/pms.1980.51.2.541

Burt, D. B., Zembar, M. J., and Niederehe, G. (1995). Depression and memory impairment: a meta-analysis of the association, its pattern, and specificity. *Psychol. Bull.* 117, 285–305. doi: 10.1037/0033-2909.117.2.285

Csukly, G., Czobor, P., Szily, E., Takacs, B., and Simon, L. (2009). Facial expression recognition in depressed subjects: the impact of intensity level and arousal dimension. *J. Nerv. Ment. Dis.* 197, 98–103. doi: 10.1097/NMD.0b013e3181923f82

DeBattista, C. (2005). Executive dysfunction in major depressive disorder. *Expert Rev. Neurother.* 5, 79–83. doi: 10.1586/14737175.5.1.79

Defer, G. L., Widner, H., Marie, R. M., Remy, P., and Levivier, M. (1999). Core assessment program for surgical interventional therapies in Parkinson's disease (CAPSIT-PD). *Mov. Disord.* 14, 572–584. doi: 10.1002/1531-8257(199907)14:4<572::AID-MDS1005>3.0.CO;2-C

Diamond, A. (2013). Executive functions. *Annu. Rev. Psychol.* 64, 135–168. doi: 10.1146/annurev-psych-113011-143750

Douglas, K. M., and Porter, R. J. (2010). Recognition of disgusted facial expressions in severe depression. *Br. J. Psychiatry* 197, 156–157. doi: 10.1192/bjp.bp.110.078113

Eizenman, M., Yu, L. H., Grupp, L., Eizenman, E., Ellenbogen, M., Gemar, M., et al. (2003). A naturalistic visual scanning approach to assess selective attention in major depressive disorder. *Psychiatry Res.* 118, 117–128. doi: 10.1016/S0165-1781(03)00068-4

Epp, A. M., Dobson, K. S., Dozois, D. J., and Frewen, P. A. (2012). A systematic meta-analysis of the Stroop task in depression. *Clin. Psychol. Rev.* 32, 316–328. doi: 10.1016/j.cpr.2012.02.005

Evans, V., Chan, S., Iverson, G. L., Bond, D., Yatham, L., and Lam, R. (2013). Systematic review of neurocognition and occupational functioning in major depressive disorder. *Neuropsychiatry* 3, 97–105. doi: 10.2217/npy.13.3

Everaert, J., Duyck, W., and Koster, E. H. (2014). Attention, interpretation, and memory biases in subclinical depression: a proof-of-principle test of the combined cognitive biases hypothesis. *Emotion* 14, 331–340. doi: 10.1037/a0035250

Ferrari, A. J., Charlson, F. J., Norman, R. E., Patten, S. B., Freedman, G., Murray, C. J., et al. (2013). Burden of depressive disorders by country, sex, age, and year: findings from the global burden of disease study 2010. *PLoS Med.* 10:e1001547. doi: 10.1371/journal.pmed.1001547

Fisher, D. G., Sweet, J. J., and Pfaelzersmith, E. A. (1986). Influence of depression on repeated neuropsychological testing. *Int. J. Clin. Neuropsychol.* 8, 14–18.

Godard, J., Baruch, P., Grondin, S., and Lafleur, M. F. (2012). Psychosocial and neurocognitive functioning in unipolar and bipolar depression: a 12-month prospective study. *Psychiatry Res.* 196, 145–153. doi: 10.1016/j.psychres.2011.09.013

Goeleven, E., De Raedt, R., Baert, S., and Koster, E. H. (2006). Deficient inhibition of emotional information in depression. *J. Affect. Disord.* 93, 149–157. doi: 10.1016/j.jad.2006.03.007

Gualtieri, C. T., Johnson, L. G., and Benedict, K. B. (2006). Neurocognition in depression: patients on and off medication versus healthy comparison subjects. *J. Neuropsychiatry Clin. Neurosci.* 18, 217–225. doi: 10.1176/jnp.2006.18.2.217

Gur, R. C., Erwin, R. J., Gur, R. E., Zwil, A. S., Heimberg, C., and Kraemer, H. C. (1992). Facial emotion discrimination: II. Behavioral findings in depression. *Psychiatry Res.* 42, 241–251. doi: 10.1016/0165-1781(92)90116-K

Gur, R. C., Sara, R., Hagendoorn, M., Marom, O., Hughett, P., Macy, L., et al. (2002). A method for obtaining 3-dimensional facial expressions and its standardization for use in neurocognitive studies. *J. Neurosci. Methods* 115, 137–143. doi: 10.1016/S0165-0270(02)00006-7

Halstead, W. (1947). *Brain and Intelligence: A Quantitative Study of the Frontal Lobes.* Chicago: University of Chicago Press.

Hamilton, M. (1960). A rating scale for depression. *J. Neurol. Neurosurg. Psychiatry* 23, 56–62. doi: 10.1136/jnnp.23.1.56

Hautzinger, M., Keller, F., and Kühner, C. (2006). *Beck-Depressions-Inventar (BDI-II)*, Revision, 2nd Edn. Frankfurt: Harcourt Test Services.

Henriques, J. B., and Davidson, R. J. (2000). Decreased responsiveness to reward in depression. *Cogn. Emot.* 14, 711–724. doi: 10.1080/026999300501 17684

Hirsch, C. R., Clark, D. M., and Mathews, A. (2006). Imagery and interpretations in social phobia: support for the combined cognitive biases hypothesis. *Behav. Ther.* 37, 223–236. doi: 10.1016/j.beth.2006.02.001

Hoffstaedter, F., Sarlon, J., Grefkes, C., and Eickhoff, S. B. (2012). Internally vs. externally triggered movements in patients with major depression. *Behav. Brain Res.* 228, 125–132. doi: 10.1016/j.bbr.2011.11.024

Hu, Z., Liu, H., Weng, X., and Northoff, G. (2012). Is there a valence-specific pattern in emotional conflict in major depressive disorder? An exploratory psychological study. *PLoS ONE* 7:e31983. doi: 10.1371/journal.pone.0031983

Joormann, J. (2004). Attentional bias in dysphoria: the role of inhibitory processes. *Cogn. Emot.* 18, 125–147. doi: 10.1080/02699930244000480

Joormann, J., and Gotlib, I. H. (2006). Is this happiness I see? Biases in the identification of emotional facial expressions in depression and social phobia. *J. Abnorm. Psychol.* 115, 705–714. doi: 10.1037/0021-843X.115.4.705

Kaletsch, M., Pilgramm, S., Bischoff, M., Kindermann, S., Sauerbier, I., Stark, R., et al. (2014). Major depressive disorder alters perception of emotional body movements. *Front. Psychiatry* 5:4. doi: 10.3389/fpsyt.2014.00004

Kan, Y., Mimura, M., Kamijima, K., and Kawamura, M. (2004). Recognition of emotion from moving facial and prosodic stimuli in depressed patients. *J. Neurol. Neurosurg. Psychiatry* 75, 1667–1671. doi: 10.1136/jnnp.2004.036079

Kellough, J. L., Beevers, C. G., Ellis, A. J., and Wells, T. T. (2008). Time course of selective attention in clinically depressed young adults: an eye tracking study. *Behav. Res. Ther.* 46, 1238–1243. doi: 10.1016/j.brat.2008.07.004

Langenecker, S. A., Bieliauskas, L. A., Rapport, L. J., Zubieta, J. K., Wilde, E. A., and Berent, S. (2005). Face emotion perception and executive functioning deficits in depression. *J. Clin. Exp. Neuropsychol.* 27, 320–333. doi: 10.1080/13803390490490515720

Lee, R. S., Hermens, D. F., Porter, M. A., and Redoblado-Hodge, M. A. (2012). A meta-analysis of cognitive deficits in first-episode major depressive disorder. *J. Affect. Disord.* 140, 113–124. doi: 10.1016/j.jad.2011.10.023

Lehrl, S. (1989). *Mehrfach-Wortschatz-Intelligenztest MWT-B*, 2nd Edn. Erlangen: Perimed Fachbuch-Verlagsgesellschaft mbH.

Leppänen, J. M., Milders, M., Bell, J. S., Terriere, E., and Hietanen, J. K. (2004). Depression biases the recognition of emotionally neutral faces. *Psychiatry Res.* 128, 123–133. doi: 10.1016/j.psychres.2004.05.020

Leung, K. K., Lee, T. M., Yip, P., Li, L. S., and Wong, M. M. (2009). Selective attention biases of people with depression: positive and negative priming of depression-related information. *Psychiatry Res.* 165, 241–251. doi: 10.1016/j.psychres.2007.10.022

Loi, F., Vaidya, J. G., and Paradiso, S. (2013). Recognition of emotion from body language among patients with unipolar depression. *Psychiatry Res.* 209, 40–49. doi: 10.1016/j.psychres.2013.03.001

Marazziti, D., Consoli, G., Picchetti, M., Carlini, M., and Faravelli, L. (2010). Cognitive impairment in major depression. *Eur. J. Pharmacol.* 626, 83–86. doi: 10.1016/j.ejphar.2009.08.046

McDermott, L. M., and Ebmeier, K. P. (2009). A meta-analysis of depression severity and cognitive function. *J. Affect. Disord.* 119, 1–8. doi: 10.1016/j.jad.2009.04.022

Milders, M., Bell, S., Platt, J., Serrano, R., and Runcie, O. (2010). Stable expression recognition abnormalities in unipolar depression. *Psychiatry Res.* 179, 38–42. doi: 10.1016/j.psychres.2009.05.015

Mogg, K., and Bradley, B. P. (2005). Attentional bias in generalized anxiety disorder versus depressive disorder. *Cogn. Ther. Res.* 29, 29–45. doi: 10.1007/s10608-005-1646-y

Müller, V. I., Cieslik, E. C., Kellermann, T. S., and Eickhoff, S. B. (2014). Crossmodal emotional integration in major depression. *Soc. Cogn. Affect. Neurosci.* 9, 839–848. doi: 10.1093/scan/nst057

Müller, V. I., Habel, U., Derntl, B., Schneider, F., Zilles, K., Turetsky, B. I., et al. (2011). Incongruence effects in crossmodal emotional integration. *Neuroimage* 54, 2257–2266. doi: 10.1016/j.neuroimage.2010.10.047

Naismith, S. L., Hickie, I. B., Turner, K., Little, C. L., Winter, V., Ward, P. B., et al. (2003). Neuropsychological performance in patients with depression is associated with clinical, etiological and genetic risk factors. *J. Clin. Exp. Neuropsychol.* 25, 866–877. doi: 10.1076/jcen.25.6.866.16472

Naranjo, C., Kornreich, C., Campanella, S., Noel, X., Vandriette, Y., Gillain, B., et al. (2011). Major depression is associated with impaired processing of emotion in music as well as in facial and vocal stimuli. *J. Affect. Disord.* 128, 243–251. doi: 10.1016/j.jad.2010.06.039

Oldfield, R. C. (1971). The assessment and analysis of handedness: the Edinburgh inventory. *Neuropsychologia* 9, 97–113. doi: 10.1016/0028-3932(71)90067-4

Ottowitz, W. E., Dougherty, D. D., and Savage, C. R. (2002). The neural network basis for abnormalities of attention and executive function in major depressive disorder: implications for application of the medical disease model to psychiatric disorders. *Harv. Rev. Psychiatry* 10, 86–99. doi: 10.1080/10673220216210

Owens, M., Koster, E. H., and Derakshan, N. (2013). Improving attention control in dysphoria through cognitive training: transfer effects on working memory capacity and filtering efficiency. *Psychophysiology* 50, 297–307. doi: 10.1111/psyp.12010

Paelecke-Habermann, Y., Pohl, J., and Leplow, B. (2005). Attention and executive functions in remitted major depression patients. *J. Affect. Disord.* 89, 125–135. doi: 10.1016/j.jad.2005.09.006

Quinn, C. R., Harris, A., Felmingham, K., Boyce, P., and Kemp, A. (2012). The impact of depression heterogeneity on cognitive control in major depressive disorder. *Aust. N. Z. J. Psychiatry* 46, 1079–1088. doi: 10.1177/0004867412461383

Rose, E. J., and Ebmeier, K. P. (2006). Pattern of impaired working memory during major depression. *J. Affect. Disord.* 90, 149–161. doi: 10.1016/j.jad.2005.11.003

Schaefer, K. L., Baumann, J., Rich, B. A., Luckenbaugh, D. A., and Zarate, C. A. Jr. (2010). Perception of facial emotion in adults with bipolar or unipolar depression and controls. *J. Psychiatr. Res.* 44, 1229–1235. doi: 10.1016/j.jpsychires.2010.04.024

Schlipf, S., Batra, A., Walter, G., Zeep, C., Wildgruber, D., Fallgatter, A., et al. (2013). Judgment of emotional information expressed by prosody and semantics in patients with unipolar depression. *Front. Psychol.* 4:461. doi: 10.3389/fpsyg.2013.00461

Schneider, D., Regenbogen, C., Kellermann, T., Finkelmeyer, A., Kohn, N., Derntl, B., et al. (2012). Empathic behavioral and physiological responses to dynamic stimuli in depression. *Psychiatry Res.* 200, 294–305. doi: 10.1016/j.psychres.2012.03.054

Sobin, C., and Sackeim, H. A. (1997). Psychomotor symptoms of depression. *Am. J. Psychiatry* 154, 4–17. doi: 10.1176/ajp.154.1.4

Stordal, K. I., Lundervold, A. J., Egeland, J., Mykletun, A., Asbjornsen, A., Landro, N. I., et al. (2004). Impairment across executive functions in recurrent major depression. *Nord. J. Psychiatry* 58, 41–47. doi: 10.1080/08039480310000789

Surguladze, S. A., Young, A. W., Senior, C., Brebion, G., Travis, M. J., and Phillips, M. L. (2004). Recognition accuracy and response bias to happy and sad facial expressions in patients with major depression. *Neuropsychology* 18, 212–218. doi: 10.1037/0894-4105.18.2.212

Tewes, U. (1991). *HAWIE-R. Hamburg-Wechsler-Intelligenztest für Erwachsene. Revision 1991; Handbuch und Testanweisung.* Bern: Verlag Hans Huber.

Trivedi, M. H., and Greer, T. L. (2014). Cognitive dysfunction in unipolar depression: implications for treatment. *J. Affect. Disord.* 152–154, 19–27. doi: 10.1016/j.jad.2013.09.012

Uekermann, J., Abdel-Hamid, M., Lehmkamper, C., Vollmoeller, W., and Daum, I. (2008). Perception of affective prosody in major depression: a link to executive functions? *J. Int. Neuropsychol. Soc.* 14, 552–561. doi: 10.1017/S1355617708080740

Veiel, H. O. (1997). A preliminary profile of neuropsychological deficits associated with major depression. *J. Clin. Exp. Neuropsychol.* 19, 587–603. doi: 10.1080/01688639708403745

Wagner, S., Doering, B., Helmreich, I., Lieb, K., and Tadic, A. (2012). A meta-analysis of executive dysfunctions in unipolar major depressive disorder without psychotic symptoms and their changes during antidepressant treatment. *Acta Psychiatr. Scand.* 125, 281–292. doi: 10.1111/j.1600-0447.2011.01762.x

WHO. (2010). *International Statistical Classification of Diseases and Related Health Problems,* 10th Revision. Geneva: WHO.

Wittchen, H. U., Zaudig, M., and Fydrich, T. (1997). *Strukturiertes Klinisches Interview für DSM-IV.* Göttingen: Hogrefe.

Zakzanis, K. K., Leach, L., and Kaplan, E. (1998). On the nature and pattern of neurocognitive function in major depressive disorder. *Neuropsychiatry Neuropsychol. Behav. Neurol.* 11, 111–119.

Permissions

All chapters in this book were first published by Frontiers; hereby published with permission under the Creative Commons Attribution License or equivalent. Every chapter published in this book has been scrutinized by our experts. Their significance has been extensively debated. The topics covered herein carry significant findings which will fuel the growth of the discipline. They may even be implemented as practical applications or may be referred to as a beginning point for another development.

The contributors of this book come from diverse backgrounds, making this book a truly international effort. This book will bring forth new frontiers with its revolutionizing research information and detailed analysis of the nascent developments around the world.

We would like to thank all the contributing authors for lending their expertise to make the book truly unique. They have played a crucial role in the development of this book. Without their invaluable contributions this book wouldn't have been possible. They have made vital efforts to compile up to date information on the varied aspects of this subject to make this book a valuable addition to the collection of many professionals and students.

This book was conceptualized with the vision of imparting up-to-date information and advanced data in this field. To ensure the same, a matchless editorial board was set up. Every individual on the board went through rigorous rounds of assessment to prove their worth. After which they invested a large part of their time researching and compiling the most relevant data for our readers.

The editorial board has been involved in producing this book since its inception. They have spent rigorous hours researching and exploring the diverse topics which have resulted in the successful publishing of this book. They have passed on their knowledge of decades through this book. To expedite this challenging task, the publisher supported the team at every step. A small team of assistant editors was also appointed to further simplify the editing procedure and attain best results for the readers.

Apart from the editorial board, the designing team has also invested a significant amount of their time in understanding the subject and creating the most relevant covers. They scrutinized every image to scout for the most suitable representation of the subject and create an appropriate cover for the book.

The publishing team has been an ardent support to the editorial, designing and production team. Their endless efforts to recruit the best for this project, has resulted in the accomplishment of this book. They are a veteran in the field of academics and their pool of knowledge is as vast as their experience in printing. Their expertise and guidance has proved useful at every step. Their uncompromising quality standards have made this book an exceptional effort. Their encouragement from time to time has been an inspiration for everyone.

The publisher and the editorial board hope that this book will prove to be a valuable piece of knowledge for researchers, students, practitioners and scholars across the globe.

List of Contributors

David J. White
Centre for Human Psychopharmacology, School of Health Sciences, Swinburne University of Technology, Hawthorn, VIC, Australia

Marco Congedo
Grenoble Images Parole Signal Automatique (Gipsa-lab), CNRS and Grenoble University, Grenoble, France

Joseph Ciorciari
Brain and Psychological Sciences Research Centre, School of Health Sciences, Swinburne University of Technology, Hawthorn, VIC, Australia

Linda van der Heiden
Department of Cognitive Psychology, University of Finance and Management, Pawia, Warsaw, Poland
Institute of Medical Psychology and Behavioral Neurobiology, Eberhard Karls-University, Tübingen, Germany

Giulia Liberati
Institute of Medical Psychology and Behavioral Neurobiology, Eberhard Karls-University, Tübingen, Germany
Interuniversity Centre for Research on Cognitive Processing in Natural and Artificial Systems (ECONA), Rome, Italy
Institute of Neuroscience, Université Catholique de Louvain, Brussels, Louvain-la-Neuve, Belgium

Ranganatha Sitaram
Institute of Medical Psychology and Behavioral Neurobiology, Eberhard Karls-University, Tübingen, Germany
Department of Biomedical Engineering, University of Florida, Gainesville, FL, USA
Biomedical Engineering, Sri Chitra Tirunal Institute of Medical Sciences and Technology, Trivandrum, India

Sunjung Kim and Ralf Veit
Institute of Medical Psychology and Behavioral Neurobiology, Eberhard Karls-University, Tübingen, Germany

Piotr Jaśkowski
Department of Cognitive Psychology, University of Finance and Management, Pawia, Warsaw, Poland

Antonino Raffone and Marta Olivetti Belardinelli
Interuniversity Centre for Research on Cognitive Processing in Natural and Artificial Systems (ECONA), Rome, Italy
Department of Psychology, University "Sapienza" of Rome, Rome, Italy

Niels Birbaumer
Institute of Medical Psychology and Behavioral Neurobiology, Eberhard Karls-University, Tübingen, Germany
Ospedale San Camillo—IRCCS, Istituto di Ricovero e Cura a Carattere Scientifico, Venezia Lido, Italy

Rodrigo Basilio, Griselda J. Garrido, Sebastian Hoefle, Bruno R. P. Melo, Fabricio A. Pamplona and Jorge Moll
Cognitive and Behavioral Neuroscience Unit and Neuroinformatics Workgroup, D'Or Institute for Research and Education, Rio de Janeiro, Brazil

João R. Sato
Cognitive and Behavioral Neuroscience Unit and Neuroinformatics Workgroup, D'Or Institute for Research and Education, Rio de Janeiro, Brazil
Center of Mathematics, Computation and Cognition, Universidade Federal do ABC, Santo André, Brazil

Roland Zahn
Department of Psychological Medicine, Institute of Psychiatry, King's College, London, UK

Stefanie Enriquez-Geppert
Experimental Psychology Laboratory, Department of Psychology, European Medical School, Carl von Ossietzky University of Oldenburg, Oldenburg, Germany
Karl-Jaspers Clinic, European Medical School Oldenburg-Groningen, Oldenburg, Germany

René J. Huster
Experimental Psychology Laboratory, Department of Psychology, European Medical School, Carl von Ossietzky University of Oldenburg, Oldenburg, Germany
Research Center Neurosensory Science, Carl von Ossietzky University, Oldenburg, Germany

Christoph S. Herrmann
Experimental Psychology Laboratory, Department of Psychology, European Medical School, Carl von Ossietzky University of Oldenburg, Oldenburg, Germany
Research Center Neurosensory Science, Carl von Ossietzky University, Oldenburg, Germany
Center for Excellence 'Hearing4all', Carl von Ossietzky University of Oldenburg, Oldenburg, Germany

Christian Figge
Karl-Jaspers Clinic, European Medical School Oldenburg-Groningen, Oldenburg, Germany

Christian Paret
Department Neuroimaging, Central Institute of Mental Health Mannheim, Medical Faculty Mannheim/ Heidelberg University, Mannheim, Germany
Department of Psychosomatic Medicine and Psychotherapy, Central Institute of Mental Health Mannheim, Medical Faculty Mannheim/Heidelberg University, Mannheim, Germany

Rosemarie Kluetsch and Christian Schmahl
Department of Psychosomatic Medicine and Psychotherapy, Central Institute of Mental Health Mannheim, Medical Faculty Mannheim/Heidelberg University, Mannheim, Germany

Matthias Ruf, Traute Demirakca, Steffen Hoesterey and Gabriele Ende
Department Neuroimaging, Central Institute of Mental Health Mannheim, Medical Faculty Mannheim/ Heidelberg University, Mannheim, Germany

Robert Bauer and Alireza Gharabaghi
Division of Functional and Restorative Neurosurgery and Division of Translational Neurosurgery, Department of Neurosurgery, Eberhard Karls University Tuebingen, Tuebingen, Germany
Neuroprosthetics Research Group, Werner Reichardt Centre for Integrative Neuroscience, Eberhard Karls University Tuebingen, Tuebingen, Germany

Kirsten Emmert and Dimitri Van De Ville
Department of Radiology and Medical Informatics, University of Geneva, Geneva, Switzerland
Medical Image Processing Laboratory, Institute of Bioengineering, Ecole Polytechnique Fédérale de Lausanne, Lausanne, Switzerland

Markus Breimhorst and Frank Birklein
Department of Neurology, University Medical Center of the Johannes Gutenberg-University Mainz, Mainz, Germany

Thomas Bauermann
Institute of Neuroradiology, University Medical Center of the Johannes Gutenberg-University Mainz, Mainz, Germany

Mariela Rance, Frauke Nees and Herta Flor
Department of Cognitive and Clinical Neuroscience, Medical Faculty Mannheim, Central Institute of Mental Health, Heidelberg University, Mannheim, Germany

Sven Haller
Department of Radiology and Medical Informatics, University of Geneva, Geneva, Switzerland

Michaela Ruttorf and Lothar R. Schad
Computer Assisted Clinical Medicine, Medical Faculty Mannheim, Heidelberg University, Mannheim, Germany

Daniele De Massari, Niels Birbaumer and Andrea Caria
Institut für Medizinische Psychologie und Verhaltensneurobiologie, Universität Tübingen, Tübingen, Germany
Fondazione Ospedale San Camillo, Istituto di Ricovero e Cura a Carattere Scientifico, Venezia, Italy

Daniel Pacheco and Alberto Betella
SPECS - Laboratory of Synthetic Perceptive, Emotive and Cognitive Systems, Department of Technology, Center of Autonomous Systems and Neurorobotics, Universitat Pompeu Fabra, Barcelona, Spain

Rahim Malekshahi
Institut für Medizinische Psychologie und Verhaltensneurobiologie, Universität Tübingen, Tübingen, Germany
Graduate School of Neural & Behavioural Sciences, International Max Planck Research School, Tübingen, Germany

Paul F. M. J. Verschure
SPECS - Laboratory of Synthetic Perceptive, Emotive and Cognitive Systems, Department of Technology, Center of Autonomous Systems and Neurorobotics, Universitat Pompeu Fabra, Barcelona, Spain
Institució Catalana de Recerca i Estudis Avançats, Barcelona, Spain

Carlos Escolano
Department of Robotics, Perception and Real Time Group, Aragon Institute of Engineering Research (I3A), University of Zaragoza, Zaragoza, Spain
Department of Computer Science and Systems Engineering (DIIS), University of Zaragoza, Zaragoza, Spain

Mayte Navarro-Gil
BitBrain Technologies SL, Zaragoza, Spain

Javier Garcia-Campayo
Department of Mental Health in Primary Care, Aragon Health Sciences Institute (IACS), University of Zaragoza, Zaragoza, Spain
Psychiatric Service in the Miguel Servet University Hospital, University of Zaragoza, Zaragoza, Spain

Marco Congedo
GIPSA-Lab, Départment Images et Signal, CNRS, University of Grenoble, Grenoble, France

Dirk De Ridder
Department of Surgical Sciences, Dunedin School of Medicine, University of Otago, North Dunedin, New Zealand

Javier Minguez
Department of Robotics, Perception and Real Time Group, Aragon Institute of Engineering Research (I3A), University of Zaragoza, Zaragoza, Spain
BitBrain Technologies SL, Zaragoza, Spain

Ranganatha Sitaram
Institute of Medical Psychology and Behavioral Neurobiology, University of Tübingen, Tübingen, Germany
Department of Biomedical Engineering, University of Florida, Gainesville, FL, USA
Sri Chitra Tirunal Institute of Medical Sciences and Technology, Thiruvananthapuram, Kerala, India

Andrea Caria, Ralf Veit and Tilman Gaber
Institute of Medical Psychology and Behavioral Neurobiology, University of Tübingen, Tübingen, Germany

Sergio Ruiz
Institute of Medical Psychology and Behavioral Neurobiology, University of Tübingen, Tübingen, Germany
Departamento de Psiquiatría, Escuela de Medicina, Centro Interdisciplinario de Neurociencias, Pontificia Universidad Católica de Chile, Santiago, Chile

Niels Birbaumer
Institute of Medical Psychology and Behavioral Neurobiology, University of Tübingen, Tübingen, Germany
Ospedale San Camillo, Istituto di Ricovero e Cura a Carattere Scientifico (IRCCS), Venezia, Italy

Surjo R. Soekadar and Matthias Witkowski
Human Cortical Physiology and Neurorehabilitation Section, NINDS, NIH, Bethesda, MD, USA
Applied Neurotechnology Lab, Department of Psychiatry and Psychotherapy, University Hospital Tübingen, Tübingen, Germany

Eliana G. Cossio
Applied Neurotechnology Lab, Department of Psychiatry and Psychotherapy, University Hospital Tübingen, Tübingen, Germany
Institute of Medical Psychology and Behavioral Neurobiology, University of Tübingen, Tübingen, Germany

Leonardo G. Cohen
Human Cortical Physiology and Neurorehabilitation Section, NINDS, NIH, Bethesda, MD, USA

Alireza Gharabaghi, Georgios Naros, Fatemeh Khademi and Jessica Jesser
Division of Functional and Restorative Neurosurgery and Division of Translational Neurosurgery, Department of Neurosurgery, Eberhard Karls University Tuebingen, Tuebingen, Germany
Neuroprosthetics Research Group, Werner Reichardt Centre for Integrative Neuroscience, Eberhard Karls University Tuebingen, Tuebingen, Germany

Martin Spüler, Armin Walter and Wolfgang Rosenstiel
Department of Computer Engineering, Wilhelm-Schickard Institute for Computer Science, Eberhard Karls University Tuebingen, Tuebingen, Germany

Martin Bogdan
Department of Computer Engineering, Wilhelm-Schickard Institute for Computer Science, Eberhard Karls University Tuebingen, Tuebingen, Germany
Department of Computer Engineering, University of Leipzig, Leipzig, Germany

Niels Birbaumer
Institute for Medical Psychology and Behavioural Neurobiology, Eberhard Karls University Tuebingen, Tuebingen, Germany
Ospedale San Camillo, IRCCS, Venice, Italy
DZD, Eberhard Karls University Tuebingen, Tuebingen, Germany

Dustin Scheinost, Teodora Stoica and Michelle Hampson
Magnetic Resonance Research Center (MRRC), Department of Diagnostic Radiology, Yale School of Medicine, New Haven, CT, USA

Suzanne Wasylink, Patricia Gruner and John Saksa
Department of Psychiatry, Yale School of Medicine, New Haven, CT, USA

Christopher Pittenger
Department of Psychiatry, Yale School of Medicine, New Haven, CT, USA
Department of Psychology, Yale University, New Haven, CT, USA
Child Study Center, Yale School of Medicine, New Haven, CT, USA

Zhenhe Zhou, Hongmei Zhu, Cui Li and Jun Wang
Department of Psychiatry, Wuxi Mental Health Center, Wuxi, China

Cornelia Pirulli and Anna Fertonani
Cognitive Neuroscience Section, IRCCS Istituto Centro San Giovanni di Dio Fatebenefratelli, Brescia, Italy

Carlo Miniussi
Cognitive Neuroscience Section, IRCCS Istituto Centro San Giovanni di Dio Fatebenefratelli, Brescia, Italy
Neuroscience Section, Department of Clinical and Experimental Sciences, University of Brescia, Brescia, Italy

Sebastian Wolf and Martin Hautzinger
Faculty of Science, Institute of Clinical Psychology and Psychotherapy, University of Tuebingen, Tuebingen, Germany

Ellen Brölz
Department of Internal Medicine VI: Psychosomatic Medicine, University Hospital Tuebingen, Tuebingen, Germany

David Scholz and Ute Strehl
Institute of Medical Psychology and Behavioral Neurobiology, University of Tuebingen, Tuebingen, Germany

Ander Ramos-Murguialday
Institute of Medical Psychology and Behavioral Neurobiology, University of Tuebingen, Tuebingen, Germany
TECNALIA, Health-Technologies, San Sebastian, Spain

Philipp M. Keune
Department of Neurology, Klinikum Bayreuth, Bayreuth, Germany
Department of Physiological Psychology, Otto-Friedrich-University, Bamberg, Germany

Niels Birbaumer
Institute of Medical Psychology and Behavioral Neurobiology, University of Tuebingen, Tuebingen, Germany
Ospedale San Camillo, Istituto di Ricovero e Cura a Carattere Scientifico (IRCCS), Venice, Italy
German Center for Diabetes Research, Tuebingen, Germany

Hendrik Santosa
Department of Cogno-Mechatronics Engineering, Pusan National University, Busan, South Korea

Melissa Jiyoun Hong
Department of Education Policy and Social Analysis, Columbia University, New York, NY, USA

Keum-Shik Hong
Department of Cogno-Mechatronics Engineering, Pusan National University, Busan, South Korea
School of Mechanical Engineering, Pusan National University, Busan, South Korea

Moses O. Sokunbi, David E. J. Linden, Isabelle Habes and Niklas Ihssen
MRC Centre for Neuropsychiatric Genetics and Genomics, Institute of Psychological Medicine and Clinical Neurosciences, Cardiff School of Medicine, Cardiff University, Cardiff, UK
Cardiff University Brain Research Imaging Centre (CUBRIC), Cardiff University, Cardiff, UK

Stephen Johnston
Department of Psychology, Swansea University, Swansea, UK

Rosalux Falquez, Elisabeth A. Arens, Simone Lang and Sven Barnow
Department of Clinical Psychology and Psychotherapy, Institute of Psychology, University of Heidelberg, Heidelberg, Germany

Blas Couto
Laboratory of Experimental Psychology and Neuroscience, Institute of Cognitive Neurology, Favaloro University, Buenos Aires, Argentina
UDP-INECO Foundation Core on Neuroscience, Diego Portales University, Santiago, Chile

Agustin Ibanez
Laboratory of Experimental Psychology and Neuroscience, Institute of Cognitive Neurology, Favaloro University, Buenos Aires, Argentina
UDP-INECO Foundation Core on Neuroscience, Diego Portales University, Santiago, Chile
Departamento de Psicología, Universidad Autónoma del Caribe, Barranquilla, Colombia

Martin T. Freitag and Moritz Berger
Department of Radiology, German Cancer Research Center, Heidelberg, Germany

Sophie Doose-Grünefeld
Department of Clinical Neuroscience and Medical Psychology, Medical Faculty, Heinrich Heine University Düsseldorf, Düsseldorf, Germany

Simon B. Eickhoff and Veronika I. Müller
Department of Clinical Neuroscience and Medical Psychology, Medical Faculty, Heinrich Heine University Düsseldorf, Düsseldorf, Germany
Institute of Neuroscience and Medicine, Research Centre Jülich, Jülich, Germany

Index